Business Events

The dynamic and fast-expanding business events sector plays a vital role in the professional lives of hundreds of millions of people worldwide by providing settings in which they can meet for the purposes of negotiation, deliberation, motivation, the dissemination of knowledge, and the celebration of their greatest career-related achievements.

This book provides a sound practical and theoretical context for the study of this subject by covering, in depth, all categories of business-related events including corporate meetings, association conferences, political events, incentive travel, exhibitions, corporate hospitality, awards ceremonies and SMERF (social, military, educational, religious and fraternal) gatherings.

This new edition has been extensively revised and updated to reflect recent developments in business events, including:

- Five new chapters on business events destination marketing, knowledge, sustainability, ethics and technology
- New 'It's my job' voice boxes offering practical insights from people employed in the business events industry
- A wide range of new case studies illustrating business events throughout the world, including emerging business events destinations such as Russia and the Middle East

Written in an accessible yet analytical manner, *Business Events* is essential reading for all students of events, tourism and hospitality management.

Dr Rob Davidson is the Managing Director of MICE Knowledge, a consultancy specialising in research, education and training services for the business events industry. He is also a Visiting Professor in four European universities (Strasbourg, France; Karlsruhe, Germany; Lugano, Switzerland; and Krems, Austria) and he is a Visiting Fellow at the University of Greenwich in London, UK.

Business Events

Second Edition

Rob Davidson

Routledge
Taylor & Francis Group

LONDON AND NEW YORK

Second edition published 2019
by Routledge
2 Park Square, Milton Park, Abingdon, Oxon, OX14 4RN

and by Routledge
52 Vanderbilt Avenue, New York, NY 10017

Routledge is an imprint of the Taylor & Francis Group, an informa business

First edition published by Pearson 2002

British Library Cataloguing-in-Publication Data
A catalogue record for this book is available from the British Library

Library of Congress Cataloging-in-Publication Data
A catalog record for this book has been requested

ISBN: 978-1-138-73574-3 (hbk)
ISBN: 978-1-138-73576-7 (pbk)
ISBN: 978-1-315-18634-4 (ebk)

Typeset in ITC Stone Serif
by Apex CoVantage, LLC

Visit the eResources: www.routledge.com/9781138735767

This book is dedicated to Marion.
In loving memory.

Contents

Figures

Tables

Images

CASE STUDIES

'IT'S MY JOB' VOICE BOXES

Preface

At first sight, business events may understandably appear to lack much of the excitement, colour and glamour of their counterparts in the cultural, sports and social domains. After all, who doesn't enjoy a family wedding, a party, a rock concert, a football stadium packed with cheering fans? Events such as these are already familiar to and appreciated by most people even before they enter adulthood. By way of contrast, the words 'business events' – especially for those who have no direct experience of them – often conjure up uninspiring images of middle-aged men in suits sitting in windowless rooms struggling to keep their attention focused on protracted PowerPoint presentations of last month's sales figures.

My primary reason for writing this book is to fundamentally change that perception and to inspire readers by sharing with them my long-standing passion for business events and their power to bring people together to share their ideas, interests and enthusiasm with each other. Business events play a crucial role in the business, intellectual, and political lives of communities worldwide by providing settings in which people can congregate for the purposes of negotiation, education, deliberation, motivation and the celebration of their greatest professional achievements.

Events such as conferences, seminars and colloquia are important occasions for the creation and transfer of knowledge between participants which produce a wide range of outcomes, from innovative business practices and problem-solving to breakthroughs in scientific research that benefit society as a whole. Exhibitions play a vital role in providing companies and other organisations with an environment in which they can display their goods and services to potential buyers and network with others in the same industry. And incentive trips and award ceremonies are exciting, celebratory occasions designed to recognise and reward the successes and outstanding achievements of the participants.

The contents of this book are structured as follows. After an introductory chapter, eight chapters analyse the principal sectors of the business events industry: corporate meetings, association conferences, SMERF (social, military, educational, religious and fraternal) gatherings, awards ceremonies, political events, incentive travel, exhibitions and corporate hospitality. The topic of business events destination marketing is explored in Chapter 10. And this is followed by four thematic chapters focusing on knowledge, sustainability, ethics and technology for business events. The vast majority of chapters conclude with a number of real-life case studies illustrating some of the key points covered in the chapters. Many of these case studies are written in the words of young men and women from around the world who have chosen business events as their career paths.

Their obvious enthusiasm and their dedication to their work should reinforce my overall intent in writing this book: that it should become a source of inspiration for others who may be motivated to invest their talent, creativity and energy in the business events industry of tomorrow.

Rob Davidson
London 2018

Acknowledgements

This book could not have been written without the cooperation of the many people all over the world who kindly provided detailed information for the case studies. I am indebted to all of them for their valuable time and patience, as well as their very positive attitude towards this project.

Jane Ali-Knight, Edinburgh Napier University
Lluís Amat, Klass Representaciones Turísticas
Paul Barron, Edinburgh Napier University
Stella Bedeur, European Lift Association
Jörg Beier, Global Association of the Exhibition Industry
Marie-Dominique Bellamy-Clauzel, Office de tourisme & des congrès Montpellier
    Méditerranée Métropole
Paul Bergamini, Incite Group
Guy Bigwood, MCI
Jared Bodnar, Attendify
Helga Boss, Messe Dornbirn
Adem Braco Suljić, MEETEX
Simon Burton, Exposure Communications
Tatiana Canaval, BCD Meetings & Events
Lucie Čapková, Prague Convention Bureau
Michael Caplan, Sensix Communications & Events
Daniel Cooper, The Jockey Club
Aileen Crawford, Glasgow Convention Bureau
Jovan Dragić, Serbia Tourism Organisation
Amanda Evans, Primary
Ranko Filipović, Croatian Meeting Professionals Association
Isaline Grichting, Lucerne Convention Bureau
Michael Hawkins, Asia Pacific Screen Awards
Erman Hendem, Hilton Istanbul Bosphorus
Lisa Hurley, Special Events Magazine
Julian Jost, Spacebase
Tzveta Kambourova, Prague Convention Bureau
Peter Komornik, Slido
Shani Kupershmidt, Kenes
Ryan Lewis, National Association of Free Will Baptists
Chrystine Loriaux, Palais des congrès de Montréal

Judith Mair, University of Queensland
Vugar Mammadov, World Association for Medical Law
Johnny Martinez, Shocklogic
Omar Massoud, Events Middle East
Taubie Motlhabane, Tshwane Convention & Visitors Bureau
Robert Metzger, 24 Degrees
Louise Murray, ASOS
Michelle Muscat, DMS
Birgitte Nestande, Norway Convention Bureau
Daria Ostrovskaya, Russia Convention Bureau
Eda Ozden, Meptur
Olivier Ponti, Amsterdam Marketing
Mathias Posch, ICS
Thomas Reiser, International Society on Thrombosis and Haemostasis
Jan Rienermann, 24 Degrees
Matt Riley, The Conference Agency
Ognena Ristovska, Momentum
Sergio Roth, Lucerne Convention Bureau
Markéta Růtová, Prague Convention Bureau
Dan Stevens, Primary
Emanuela Stigliani, Federazione Italiana Rugby
Stéphanie Strika, Experience Scotland
Nellie Swart, University of South Africa
Stefanie Thiele, Mack Brooks Exhibitions Group
Mandy Torrens, Reed Travel Exhibitions
Laraine Wilkinson, Foundry 45
Jenny Yu-Mattson, Sands

1 An introduction to business events

Chapter objectives

On completion of this chapter the reader should be able to:

- Understand the role played by business events in society.
- Identify the principal distinguishing characteristics of business events.
- Understand the various terminologies used to describe business events.
- Appreciate the various benefits of business events and how they may be measured.
- Appreciate the environmental and economic costs of business events.

Introduction to business events: concepts and definitions

It is impossible to imagine how human society could have evolved into our highly inter-connected and globalised modern world if the type of events analysed in this book had not existed in various forms since the earliest days of mankind's use of language. The human drive to meet for the purposes of conferring and trading has been one of the principal factors in our remarkable evolution as a species. Whether the gathering was a tribal sharing of hunting knowledge or ancestral stories; or whether it was the more formal gatherings of ancient Greek or Roman patricians for the seeking of consensus on law and government; or whether it was a medieval fair at which artisans and farmers displayed their products for sale, such events have been an essential element in the development of civilisation and the advancement of human achievement.

In the 21st century, face-to-face business events continue to represent a vital channel for trade and for knowledge transfer and knowledge creation, playing a crucial role in the business, intellectual, and political lives of communities worldwide. They also constitute a major global economic activity, as an entire industry has emerged, comprising the specialist professionals who plan, design and host business events. The activities of many of these individual professions will be highlighted in the pages of this book.

Fundamental to all business events is the basic objective of facilitating *communication* between the participants. Accordingly, they may be defined as planned, time-bound events that bring together colleagues from similar industries, professions or interest groups to connect with each other in order to share ideas and information, to make decisions, or simply to enjoy and celebrate their work-related achievements. But while most business events have multiple purposes, the fundamental objective is almost always to change the behaviour of the participants in some way, through the facilitating of education, negotiation, inspiration, motivation, celebration and business connections between participants.

Individual chapters of this book analyse the specific characteristics and uses of the principal types of business events and the ways in which they may be designed and planned for maximum effectiveness: corporate meetings, association conferences, SMERF (social, military, educational, religious and fraternal) gatherings, awards ceremonies, governmental and political events, incentive travel, exhibitions, and corporate hospitality. It can be seen from this list of sectors of the business events industry that the definition of 'business' employed here goes beyond simple commerce and trade to encompass, for example, the business of government and the business of associations, whether they represent a particular profession or an interest or cause entirely unrelated to the members' employment.

The distinguishing characteristics of business events

While business events take a great number of different forms, they demonstrate several characteristics that are common to all types.

Location

The vast majority of business events take place in towns and cities. These are the most commonly used destinations as most of them offer the supporting infrastructure required for the hosting of conferences, exhibitions and political events – for example: venues, hospitality suppliers and multiple transport connections. They also tend to offer the type of prestigious sporting and cultural events that are the focus of most corporate hospitality experiences.

But there are exceptions to this rule, and business events are not exclusively confined to urban centres. Incentive trips, for example, may take place in resorts and spas or in wilderness areas offering nature-based activities for participants. And, for security reasons, high-profile political conferences such as the gatherings of the G20 group of nations have occasionally been held in remote communities such as mountain villages or on small islands, where the participants can be more easily protected from disturbances created by protestors. These examples are, however, fairly rare exceptions to the general rule that business events are predominantly urban-based.

Timing

In terms of days of the week, by far most business events are held between Monday and Friday, which tend to be the working days of the majority of participants in Western societies. For corporate meetings in those countries, Tuesdays, Wednesdays and Thursdays are usually the peak periods, as witnessed by the higher rates often charged by venues for meetings held on those days. Spring and autumn are the peak seasons for business events, which generally avoid the summer months, when potential participants' ability to attend can be limited by their personal holiday plans.

It can be seen from the above patterns that the timing of most business events is complementary to the seasonality of leisure travel, most of which takes place at weekends and during the traditional holiday period of the summer months. This complementarity with leisure travel adds to the appeal, for destinations and suppliers such as hotels, of hosting business events, which can offer them a means of levelling out the peaks and troughs of tourism's seasonality patterns.

Mobility

With very few exceptions, the organisers of business events are able to use a degree of discretion in their choice of destinations for the events they plan, because such events tend to be extremely flexible in terms of where they are held. For example, annual events such as association conferences and incentive trips almost always change their destination from year to year, as a means of making themselves more attractive to potential participants. Even exhibitions, which may be held in the same venue and destination for many years, are also capable of being moved by the organisers to a different location if there is a strong business case for doing so. This characteristic of business events makes them an important focus of the marketing and promotion strategies of destinations and suppliers aiming to influence the organisers' decisions as to where the events are held. The techniques used by destination marketing organisations to win business events for their countries and cities are explored in Chapter 10.

The mobile quality of business events is often contrasted with the non-discretionary nature of individual business travel, the destinations of which are generally determined by the location of the assignment to be carried out by the traveller. The objective of such trips could be, for example, to 'visit clients to close deals, pitch for business or provide product support; and visit sub-contractors and suppliers to monitor quality control or negotiate new business' (Beaverstock et al., 2010:1). Opportunities for destinations to attract individual business trips are extremely limited, as the locations of such trips are pre-determined and beyond the influence of the promotional activities of destination marketing organisations and individual venues.

Fusion

Although the different sectors of the business events industry – corporate meetings, association conferences, SMERF gatherings, awards ceremonies, governmental and political events, incentive travel, exhibitions, and corporate hospitality – are widely accepted to be discrete types of events, each with its own objectives and formats, in practice they are often combined into hybrid forms. For example, many large conferences include an exhibition of products and services of interest to the participants. Accordingly, a major conference for dentists may have, running in parallel in the same venue, an exhibition of dental tools, equipment and drugs that participants can visit during breaks in the conference programme. Similarly, most exhibitions are accompanied by an educational seminar programme, whereby visitors are able to attend presentations by experts and panel discussions related to the topic of the exhibition. And many incentive trips include a work element such as a half-day training session or a brainstorming meeting. This fusion between different types of business event is characteristic of this industry and it offers the potential to add considerable value to the events, from the participants' point of view.

In-person interaction

Even in the age of widespread electronic communication, the type of in-person interaction facilitated by business events represents a major aspect of their distinctive and enduring power. From a psychological perspective, there are a number of characteristics of face-to-face events that give them considerable advantages over other forms of communication. Arvey (2009) outlines these as follows:

- Face-to-face meetings allow members to engage in and observe verbal and non-verbal behavioural styles not captured in most computer-mediated communication.
- Face-to-face meetings occur in 'real time' as opposed to non-synchronised time. Computer-mediated communications can be delayed for a variety of reasons, not always received, and sometimes disrupted because of technical problems.
- Face-to-face business meetings provide human contact, which is a fundamental primitive need among human beings, as we are social creatures.
- Face-to-face business meetings afford participants opportunities to develop transparency and trust among each other in ways that are not always possible with other forms of communications.

- Face-to-face business meetings allow members to evaluate and judge the integrity, competencies and skills (for example, the verbal skills) of other participants and leaders in ways that are not easily evaluated in computer-mediated communications.

Nevertheless, it is undeniable that the extraordinary advances in technology-enabled communication formats in the 21st century have produced systems that, for the organisers of some types of event, provide an attractive alternative to in-person events at which all participants are physically present. This theme is explored in Chapter 14, which focuses on technology.

McEuen and Duffy (2010) contend that the decision as to whether to use technology-enabled formats for meetings or to bring the participants physically together is an extremely important one, because face-to-face meetings require the greatest investment of all meeting types, and thus carry the greatest expectations for a high return on investment. But these authors highlight three business situations in which they believe that a face-to-face format is most likely to be the best approach:

1 *To capture attention:* when participants' full attention is required, as the objective of the event is to initiate something new or different, such as a new or different relationship, culture, strategy or product
2 *To inspire a positive emotional climate:* when, in recognition of the power of inspiration and the importance of a positive emotional climate as a real currency of business, the event is designed to energise and inspire participants
3 *To build human networks and relationships:* when, in acknowledgement of the fact that information and resources are not the only things needed for work to get done effectively, the objective of the event is to build human networks and relationships.

Table 1.1 provides examples of business events in these three categories.

Table 1.1 The strategic purposes of face-to-face meetings	
Broad Business Need	**Examples of Specific Business Needs**
Capture Attention for Change	• Initiate a new strategic direction for the organization. • Launch a new product or suite of products. • Merge two cultures into a new culture. • Renew focus and attention on an existing strategy.
Inspire a Positive Emotional Climate	• Annual or semi-annual meetings to energize people around company goals, values, and priorities. • Inspirational events to build community and cohesion toward a shared interest or goal. • Recognition events to celebrate top performing individuals and teams. • Celebration events that mark important milestones.

(Continued)

Table 1.1 (Continued)

Broad Business Need	Examples of Specific Business Needs
Build Human Networks and Relationships	• Annual or semi-annual meetings to enable cultural cohesion and relationship-building. • For dispersed workforces, a regular rhythm of face-to-face meetings to build trust and effective working relationships. • Practitioner, user group, and professional community conferences. • Dynamic knowledge-sharing and innovation summits.

Source: McEuen, M. B., & Duffy, C. (2010).

Terminology

Davidson and Hyde (2014) observe that any analysis of the business events industry inevitably encounters problems of terminology. Despite the rapid growth of the industry – or perhaps, *because* of that rapid growth, there is still a lack of standardised, universally accepted terminology for discussion of the industry as a whole and its constituent sectors. Many terms are used interchangeably, and even within the English language terminology, there are marked differences between how certain concepts are labelled in North American English and in English as the language is used in Europe. For example, the designations 'conference', 'convention' and 'congress' are variously used in the UK, the US and the European continent, respectively, to define large-scale meetings (Marques and Santos, 2017). The nuances between the various uses of these three terms are demonstrated in Table 1.2, together with additional definitions as proposed by the Convention Industry Council.

Table 1.2 The categorisation of meetings

Conferences/ Conventions/ Congresses	A general term covering all non business-oriented gatherings of participants at a predetermined site and time to attend an organized meeting in which they have an interactive, debating, seminar, and/or competitive role, and of which the theme or purpose may be of any nature. These are hosted by professional, trade, or other non-corporate organisations. (See also specific definitions below).
Conference	1) Participatory meeting designed for discussion, fact-finding, problem-solving and consultation. 2) An event used by any organization to meet and exchange views, convey a message, open a debate or give publicity to some area of opinion on a specific issue. No tradition, continuity, or periodicity is required to convene a conference. Although not generally limited in time, conferences are usually of short duration with specific objectives. Conferences are generally on a smaller scale than congresses.

Convention	1) A general and formal meeting of a legislative body, social, or economic group in order to provide information, deliberate or establish consent or policies among participants. In the United States, the term is used to describe large, usually national meetings of business circles, for discussion and/or commercial exhibition. 2) An event where the primary activity is to attend educational sessions, participate in meetings/discussions, socialise, or attend other organised events. There is a secondary exhibition component.
Congress	1) The regular coming together of large groups of individuals, generally to discuss a particular subject. A congress will often last several days and have several simultaneous sessions. The length of time between congresses is usually established in advance of the implementation stage and may be pluri-annual or annual. Most international or world congresses are of the former type while national congresses are more frequently held annually. 2) Meeting of an association of delegates or representatives from constituent organizations. 3) European term for convention.
Seminar	1) Lecture and dialogue allowing participants to share experiences in a particular field under the guidance of an expert discussion leader. 2) A meeting or series of meetings from 10 to 50 specialists who have different specific skills but have a common interest and come together for learning purposes. The work schedule of a seminar has the specific objective of enriching the skills of the participants.
Trade show/business exhibition	1) An exhibition of products and/or services held for members of a common industry. The primary activity of attendees is visiting exhibits on the show floor. These events focus primarily on business-to-business relationships, but part of the event may be open to the general public. 2) Display of products or promotional material for the purpose of public relations, sales and/or marketing.
Incentive event	A reward event intended to showcase persons who meet or exceed sales or production goals.
Corporate/business meeting	1) Business-oriented meeting usually hosted by a corporation, in which participants represent the same company, corporate group or client/provider relationships. 2) Gathering of employees or representatives of a commercial organisation. Usually, attendance is required and most expenses are paid for by the organisation.

Source: Adapted from Convention Industry Council (2011).

The lack of standardised terminology presents a number of problems in communication both within the industry and with other stakeholders, not least the challenge of making international comparisons of meetings industry data for statistical analyses, as there is often no consistency in characterising the size and type of meetings, for example (UNWTO, 2006). In the ongoing absence of a standardised terminology, various acronyms have been used in recent times to define the set of different activities that comprise business events. Marques and Santos (2017) identify some of these as MECE (Meetings, Events, Conventions, Exhibitions), MCE (Meetings, Conventions, Exhibitions), CEMI (Conventions, Exhibitions, Meetings, Incentives), MC & IT (Meetings, Conventions & Incentive Travel) and MICE (Meetings, Incentives, Conventions, Exhibitions).

However, it is the last of these, MICE, that has entered furthest into common currency in academic and practitioner circles, joined by three others, business tourism, the meetings industry and business events. Each of these will now be considered in turn:

- *MICE* as an acronym holds considerable appeal as a memorable, shorthand expression, but its use is beset with problems. For example, there is no universally agreed definition of what MICE stands for. In addition to the version cited by Marques and Santos, MICE has been variously defined as Meetings, Incentives, Conferences and Exhibitions, and Meetings, Incentives, Conferences and Events, with the term 'Congresses' occasionally being substituted for 'Conferences'. However, the main problem with this term is that practically no-one outside this industry understands what it means, not least the politicians whose support is so vital to the industry's growth. It is criticised by many practitioners as being merely a convenient private joke, lacking wider recognition and even presenting an impediment to the industry being taken seriously, due to the term's association with rodents and vermin. Nevertheless, although rarely used in the US, the world's largest market for business events, the term MICE has been widely adopted elsewhere – in particular in those regions in which the industry is growing rapidly, such as the Middle East and South-East Asia. In China, for example, the title of the leading trade publication is *MICE China* and the annual event to celebrate this industry is named World MICE Day (www.worldmiceday.com).
- *Business tourism* is also well established, particularly in academic circles, where tourism educators and researchers have made a substantial contribution to our understanding of this industry, as will be explored in Chapter 11. However, there is growing recognition in academia as well as by practitioners that the link between certain types of business events and tourism is at best tenuous. While the behaviour of participants in some forms of business events somewhat resembles that of leisure tourists – travelling outside their normal places of work and residence and making use of facilities such as hotel accommodation in the same way that holidaymakers do – participation in other types of business events demonstrates a very different pattern of consumption. For example, those attending one-day corporate meetings in a local hotel, an evening awards ceremony in their own town or an afternoon at a nearby corporate hospitality event may travel a very short distance and make no use of accommodation facilities. Moreover, the term is hardly ever used in

North American English, where 'business' and 'tourism' are contrasting terms and to combine them would amount to an oxymoron.

- *The meetings industry* as a term was officially introduced in 2006 as an attempt by a number of organisations including the International Congress and Convention Association, Meeting Professionals International, Reed Travel Exhibitions and the United Nations World Tourism Organization, to create a stronger image for the industry by replacing alternative terms such as MICE. According to this definition, the meetings industry includes activities based on the organisation, promotion, sale and hosting of meetings and other events. It encompasses products and services related to corporate, associative and governmental meetings, corporate incentives, seminars, congresses, conferences, conventions, exhibitions and fairs, whose objectives are related to the motivation of the participants, conducting business, the exchange of ideas, learning, socialising and debates or discussions (UNWTO, 2006). The term is in widespread use, even though the organisers of certain types of more celebratory occasions, such as awards ceremonies, incentive travel and corporate hospitality may not readily classify their events as 'meetings'.

- *Business events* is an alternative term that has been adopted more recently in some major markets such as Australia and Canada, based on the premise that business events have much in common with other types of events (cultural, sports or community events, for example) in the sense that they are planned, temporary occasions taking place in venues and aimed at specific, invited, audiences, with a focus on creating a meaningful experience and a temporary community for those attending or participating.

The Business Events Council of Australia (BECA), an industry body in Australia, defines business events as

> any public or private activity consisting of a minimum of 15 persons with a common interest or vocation, held in a specific venue or venues, and hosted by an organisation (or organisations). This may include (but is not limited to) conferences, conventions, symposia, congresses, incentive group events, marketing events, special celebrations, seminar, courses, public or trade shows, product launches, exhibitions, company general meetings, corporate retreats, study tours or training programmes. The demand for a business event is driven mainly by organisations choosing it as a forum to communicate messages, to educate or train, to promote a product, to reward or celebrate, to collaborate on issues and solutions, or to generate resources.

The comprehensiveness of this definition and the fact that the expression is being rapidly adopted by practitioners and academics in the field of events management makes it the term of choice in this book.

The benefits of business events

Tourism-related benefits

Traditionally, the benefits of business events have been considered primarily in terms of their economic impacts on the destinations where they take place, generated by the spending of the organisers of such events as well as those who attend them. These tourism-related benefits generally accrue to the suppliers of travel, tourism and hospitality businesses based in the destination. As observed by Davidson and Hyde (2014), those attending business events fill hotel bedrooms, seats on aircraft and other forms of transport, and places at restaurant tables; and their spending can extend further, into local shops as well as entertainment and leisure facilities. Furthermore, there tends to be a high per-capita value associated with such visitors as they often represent the high-quality, high-yield end of the tourism spectrum, with corporate and political meetings in particular creating demand for premium seats on trains and planes, and for the higher categories of hotel accommodation. The higher spending levels of participants coming to a destination to attend a business event, compared with the spending of leisure tourists in the same destination, are often highlighted in tourism surveys. For example, data from Tourism Research Australia indicates that in 2017 the daily expenditure of international business visitors to that country was almost double that of holiday visitors in the same year (Tourism Research Australia, 2017).

To these economic benefits must be added the advantage to destinations that, as discussed above regarding seasonality, attendance at business events is an all-year-round activity; and even if demand tends to dip in the summer months and during weekends, most tourism businesses are able to rely on leisure visitors as an alternative source of demand in those periods. The tourism industry further benefits indirectly from business events whenever participants take one or more of these actions:

- Come accompanied by family members or friends who make use of the tourism attractions of the destination
- Extend their business trip for leisure-related purposes, by arriving some days before the business event and/or remaining a few days afterwards, in effect turning the business trip into a holiday
- Return subsequently to the business event destination, with friends or family, for leisure purposes, if they are satisfied with their initial visit
- Recommend the destination to their circles of influence (friends, family and professional network).

The potential for business events to generate additional leisure tourism for destinations has been widely acknowledged (for example, Davidson, 2002) as a major benefit of this industry. Indeed, Kerr et al. (2012) suggest that business travellers may even use business trips to a new destination to assess its potential for future leisure travel.

The economic benefits are undoubtedly the principal reason for the great expansion in the supply of destinations and facilities for business events in the 21st century. Campiranon and Arcodia (2008) and Monge and Brandimarte (2011) are among the commentators who have noted the rapidly increasing number of countries and cities that are building conference centres and bidding for events in order to capitalise on this market.

Non-tourism benefits

However, to focus exclusively on the tourism-related benefits of business events would be to ignore the other important advantages that they can offer to the destinations in which they take place. In the 21st century, commentators have increasingly highlighted how business events make a much broader contribution to the host destinations than simply tourism. A report commissioned by the World Tourism Organization on the topic of the global meetings industry summarises the potential benefits to the economic development of destinations as follows:

> As attractive as the financial returns are from the meetings business, these are often far outweighed by broader community and economic development benefits. Meetings and conventions essentially take place for the purposes of business, professional and scientific development as well as sharing knowledge and expertise, therefore both the delegates and the events themselves have a lot to offer to the host community. From an economic development perspective, meetings and conventions attract people who are much more likely to be business decision makers – and this can generate not only local business prospects but trade and investment potential as well.
>
> (UNWTO, 2014:21).

Davidson and Hyde also highlight the links between business events and the economic development of the destinations where they take place, noting that many cities have invested in meetings facilities, such as flagship conference centres, as an element of plans to regenerate urban areas in need of re-development:

> From Glasgow and Philadelphia to Cape Town and Dublin, large-scale meetings facilities have been built as a means of bringing prosperity and animation back into previously neglected parts of those cities. More intangibly, the fact of hosting a conference, in particular an international event, can be a source of pride and prestige for the city or country where the conference takes place, as well as a means of creating an image or brand for itself in the international community of nations.
>
> (Davidson and Hyde, 2014:3)

Rogers (2013:28) also emphasises the potential impact upon the destination's brand whenever it hosts a high-profile business event: 'There is undoubted prestige in being selected to host a major international conference, and some less developed countries would see this as a way of gaining credibility and acceptance on the international political stage'. An example of an event being used for this purpose is found in the former Yugoslavia's hosting of the 1979 International Monetary Fund conference, for which a new venue, the Sava Centar in Belgrade, was constructed specifically for the event.

There can be little doubt that national pride and image-building were factors behind that country offering to host this global event, which attracted the attention of the world's media.

But in recent years, attention has increasingly focused upon another non-tourism – or 'beyond-tourism' – impact of business events, notably the important benefits that they offer for knowledge transfer, knowledge creation and building the skills-base in host destinations. According to the World Tourism Organization,

> Events in any area of discipline – particularly major national or international events – often attract literally the very best expertise in the world, which means local access to a high level of knowledge transfer and international exposure for local professionals. In areas like medical practice, this can have huge implications for how local skills develop – which creates, in turn, big benefits for the quality of service in the community. All these factors combine to create a strong and diverse return on an investment in the business events sector.
>
> (UNWTO, 2014:21)

Other sources have focused upon the links between business events and the modern 'knowledge economy'. For example, Rogerson (2015:184) observes that business events are

> fundamental to constructing 'the network society' as well as for the functioning of knowledge-based economies. This leads to an increased need for updates and knowledge transfer, most effectively and efficiently undertaken through the organising of meetings or the hosting of conferences.

Deery and Jago (2010) also elaborate upon the role of meetings and events in the knowledge creation and dissemination processes, emphasising their valuable role in improving business performance and underpinning innovation. While acknowledging that such impacts are longer term and more difficult to quantify than tourism benefits, they nevertheless make a convincing case that meetings can bring many beneficial outcomes leading to the creation and dissemination of innovative practices and the enhancement of individual and organisational performance. Figure 1.1 suggests how the core motives and needs of the business world and society more generally can be achieved by people's participation in business events.

Figure 1.1 serves as a valuable reminder that, in addition to the considerable advantages that business events offer to destinations and to society as a whole, they ultimately bring a range of benefits to the end-users of events – those who attend them and the organisations that employ them. The Events Industry Council summarises these benefits thus:

> To the millions of attendees annually, these events provide an invaluable source of adult learning, continuing education for professional certifications and licensure, a forum for developing and maintaining professional contacts, an effective and

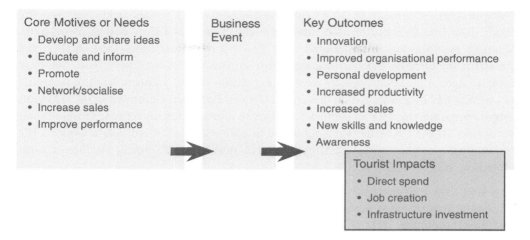

Figure 1.1
Key motives and outcomes for meetings and events
Source: Jago and Deery (2010).

efficient means of enhancing sales efforts, a medium for information exchange lead-ing to innovation, new medical treatments and research breakthroughs.

(EIC, 2018:2)

Measuring the benefits of business events

Measuring the economic benefits

While the multiple advantages to destinations of attracting business events are widely acknowledged, the challenge of measuring them with a reasonable degree of accuracy has proved to be a formidable one. One of the key long-term challenges for measuring eco-nomic impacts has been the lack of a consistent methodology for measuring the extent of the economic impact of business events on the host destinations and for comparing the volume of business events between different destinations and over a period of time. This challenge has been compounded by a number of the characteristics of the business events industry itself, including its fragmented and complex structure of organisers, venues and other suppliers; lack of clarity on definitions; and poor reporting systems (ICCA, 2015).

However, various methods for assessing the economic impacts have been tested, often with a view to justifying the very significant public expenditure required for investment in business events–related infrastructure such as conference facilities and exhibition centres (Dwyer and Forsyth, 1996, 1997; Kim et al., 2003; Lee, 2007). Lee (2007) and Jones and Li (2015) note that among those methods, the input-output (I-O) model has been used in economic impact assessments of business events and of tourism, despite the numerous limitations of this system of analysis (Li and Jago, 2013).

Some progress was made in 2006 when, as the result of a collaboration between the World Tourism Organization, the International Congress and Convention Association, Meeting Professionals International and Reed Travel Exhibitions, the first global standards for carrying out national economic impact studies were published: Meetings Satellite Accounts (MSAs), which were an expansion of the Tourism Satellite Accounts (TSAs) that had been adopted by the United Nations Statistical Commission in 2000 as an international standard for all countries wishing to measure the impact of tourism on their economies. These guidelines were published in a UNWTO report entitled 'Measuring the economic importance of the meetings industry – developing a Tourism Satellite Account extension' (UNWTO, 2006).

The MSA is a measurement framework that aims to estimate key national headline economic indicators for business events – most critically the gross value added (GVA) and the employment directly supported by such activities. The use of this framework to estimate these economic indicators is far from simple, however, as it requires researchers to populate the MSA structure with data from a broad range of stakeholders including participants, organisers, exhibitors and venues. In addition, commentators agree that the TSA system of analysis upon which MSAs are based has its own limitations, which were in turn shared by MSAs. Jones and Li (2015), for example, suggest that one of the principal limitations of the MSA systems is that it calculates direct expenditure spent by business events attendees, organisers and venues, but does not evaluate the indirect and induced impacts of their activity at the destination. In his evaluation of five national studies that had been carried out using the UNWTO guidelines, Jago (2012) focuses on two further limitations. He found that while the studies produced estimates of the economic contributions made by business events to the national economies in a consistent fashion, the methodology had two weaknesses:

- The fact that the studies require the collection of data from such a wide range of different meetings industry stakeholders makes the national estimates very costly to produce.
- Their outputs have little relevance at the regional destination level (states or provinces), let alone at the city level, where key decisions – about investment in infrastructure and marketing, for example – need to be made.

This latter weakness is perhaps the most significant. Given that management and investment decisions are generally made at the level of individual cities, there has long been considerable interest in calculating the economic contribution that business events make to the local, rather than national, economy. In particular, cities which are considering investing in infrastructure or marketing for business events usually have a pressing need for supporting evidence of the existing and potential economic impact of that industry in their locality. But as researchers such as Jones and Li (2015) have indicated, there is considerable difficulty in extending MSA approaches to regional and sub-regional analysis. As yet, the development of a fully reliable method for assessing the economic impacts at the level of individual cities has proved to be elusive.

Individual organisations seeking to calculate the return on investment (ROI) from their business events face similar challenges. Although exhibiting at a trade show, running an incentive programme or holding a corporate hospitality event, for example, absorbs valuable corporate resources in terms of time and money, there are insufficient empirical studies accurately demonstrating that the resulting ROI is financially justified in terms of, for instance, a higher volume of sales of the company's products, a reduction in staff turnover or improved customer loyalty. A major part of the difficulty in measuring this type of ROI from business events is due to what has been called 'the lag effect'. This effect occurs due to the period that can elapse between, for instance, guests being entertained at a corporate event or an employee attending a training course and the appearance of the desired attitudinal change or action resulting from their participation in those events. Similarly, a car manufacturer may find that incremental sales arising from their exhibiting at a trade show may take two or three years to materialise, making it difficult to attribute them with any certainty to the company's investment in the exhibition.

Anecdotally, it would appear that, due to the complexity of doing so, many companies make little attempt to measure the ROI from their use of business events. For example, in the context of corporate hospitality, Minnaert's (2008) research indicated that many companies simply define ROI by high attendance levels or by their gut instinct, instead of more rigorous measurements.

Nevertheless, in an era when companies are increasingly obliged to justify their expenditure on everything from staff costs to advertising, it is only natural that spending on business events will also have to be defended with reference to the advantages it brings to the firm. According to Ferdinand and Kitchin (2012), event managers are now under more pressure to prove the value of their events, bringing a new level of scrutiny to claims that events are effective in enhancing organisational performance.

Measuring the non-tourism benefits

As the attention of decision makers is increasingly focused on the non-tourism benefits that business events can bring to host destinations – such as an improvement in local business performance and growth in productivity and innovation – the issue of how such benefits might be measured has inevitably been raised. But, if the economic benefits of this industry have proven difficult to estimate with a convincing degree of accuracy, measuring the non-tourism or 'beyond tourism' benefits has so far confounded those who have attempted this task.

Among such researchers is Jago (2012:5), who concludes:

> Studies have demonstrated that a wide range of 'beyond tourism' benefits of business events exist but that these benefits are extremely difficult to quantify in any meaning-ful manner. There seems little value in continuing to try and replicate these studies. Instead, the fact that the benefits exist and are generally substantial should be accepted and all effort should be put into leveraging those benefits for maximum return.

He adds, however, that he believes that there is value in developing local case studies to highlight the range of 'beyond tourism' benefits that can be generated by business events in a way that helps the local government authority and other relevant parties understand in a tangible fashion the types of benefits that can be derived.

Jago and Deery offer a number of typical examples of non-tourism benefits that accrued to Australian destinations as a result of hosting business events. For instance, Darwin's hosting of the 2009 conference of the Australian Petroleum Production & Exploration Association was shown to have boosted the Northern Territory's profile within the international oil and gas community and the wider national and international media – a significant benefit as Darwin positions itself as an oil and gas hub in the region. During the event, the Northern Territory was able to promote its oil and gas capabilities to a relevant audience. The Northern Territory government took the opportunity to meet with the key industry stakeholders who were attracted to Darwin for the conference, and these meetings established new relationships and strengthened existing ones (Jago and Deery, 2010).

The costs of business events

This chapter would be incomplete if it ended without acknowledging that business events have the potential to bring costs as well as benefits to the destinations that host them, and that any balanced review of the impacts of this industry must take into account its externalities and costs as well as its advantages. The principal costs of business events are environmental and economic.

Environmental costs

It has been recognised that business events can have a significant and negative impact on the wider environment (Mair and Jago, 2010). In particular, the environmental costs associated with travel (and especially international air travel) for the purpose of attending business events have emerged as a dominant issue. For instance, Park and Boo's (2010) study of green attitudes associated with two US conventions found that the environmental impact of travel was a prime concern of the attendees, meeting planners and suppliers surveyed. Similarly, Hoyer and Naess (2001:467) expressed the view that

> the increase in travel to international meetings forms one of the environmentally most worrying changes in the mobility of post-industrial society. It is a paradox that the consequences for global environmental problems arising from the use of local transport have gradually been put higher on the environmental agenda, while there is virtually no focus on long, job-related, journeys. For the individual conference participant, one such trip usually represents an amount of transportation larger than the total mobility for all other purposes during a whole year.

While Hoyer and Naess focus on the travel of participants in international academic conferences, other authors have turned their attention to the impact of those travelling to attend international medical conferences – although an interesting debate on this issue in the pages of the *British Medical Journal* (Green, 2008; Drife, 2008) demonstrates that opinion is divided as to whether abandoning such conferences would make a material difference to the CO_2 emissions caused by air travel. Inevitably, ecology-related conferences have also been criticised for their impact on air quality (Bossdorf et al., 2010).

But the environmental footprint of business events extends beyond their impact on air quality. While CO_2 emissions are a serious issue, climate change constitutes only a part of the problem. Business events can also have a significant water and biodiversity footprint, in particular those held in large exhibition and conference centres. The vast scale of these venues means that they can have a significant toll on the natural environment, not only in terms of the land they occupy but also in the process of their construction. In his blog, McNally (2017) highlights the fact that construction activity can significantly change the surface of the land, due in large part to the clearing of vegetation and excavating which is common on many construction projects. He cites the research of the Environmental Protection Agency which demonstrates that surrounding environments – particularly water pools – can be heavily polluted as a result of large-scale construction projects. In addition, the author quotes research by Kleiwerks International which claims that building material, such as concrete, aluminium and steel, are directly responsible for large quantities of CO_2 emissions due to their high contents of 'embodied energy content', with, for example, 9.8 million tons of CO_2 generated from the production of 76 million tons of finished concrete in the US.

Furthermore, the vast interior spaces of many conference and exhibitions venues mean that they have an additional environmental cost in terms of the energy they consume and the emissions they produce as a result of their temperature control. According to Bossdorf et al. (2010), the CO_2 emissions due to the heating and air conditioning of conference venues are second in volume only to those produced as a result of the participants' travel to the destination.

Initiatives to moderate the impacts of business events on the environment are discussed in Chapter 12.

Economic costs

While the actual and potential economic rewards of business events help to explain the appeal of this industry for destination authorities, there are also economic costs which must be taken into account, but which are often overlooked. For example, the expense of establishing and running a convention bureau for the purposes of destination marketing can be significant and is usually funded at least partly from public finances. In addition, several authors have highlighted the 'opportunity costs' of developing an infrastructure for business events, using public funds that could have been invested in other projects such as education or healthcare. For example, Henderson (2007:544) explains that

> the construction and maintenance of specialised [conference] centres often require substantial public funding, and the space is not always fully utilised after opening,

provoking complaints that scarce resources would have been better allocated to schemes for the direct welfare of residents.

She continues by drawing attention to another potential cost – the impact of large-scale business events on the destination's tourism industry: 'Tourists travelling for other reasons could be deterred by worries about disruption or overcrowding when highly-publicised major gatherings are scheduled' (ibid.). Baade et al. (2009:4) express similar concerns, highlighting how local businesses may be negatively affected by large-scale business events:

> While hotels, bars and restaurants, may do well during the convention, other retailers and service providers may not benefit from the event and potentially could lose sales. This issue is of particular concern during a national political convention which necessitates a high degree of security and also may generate large crowds of protesters both of which will serve to dissuade casual shoppers and diners and result in major disruptions for local residents.

The theme of disruptive protests during political events is further explored in Chapter 6.

Chapter summary

This chapter began by defining business events, also known as business tourism, the meetings industry and the MICE industry, and emphasised the importance of their role in the business, intellectual, political and cultural life of communities worldwide. The business events industry was defined as comprising a number of individual sectors, each of which has a dedicated chapter in this book: corporate meetings, association conferences, SMERF gatherings, awards ceremonies, governmental and political events, incentive travel, exhibitions, and corporate hospitality. The defining characteristics of business events in general were identified with reference to what differentiates them from other types of events. This was followed by a discussion of the terminology used for business events. The tourism-related benefits of the business events industry were reviewed, as well as the non-tourism benefits such as knowledge transfer, destination branding and inward investment. Finally, the environmental and economic costs of business events were discussed.

References

Arvey, R. D. (2009) Why face-to-face business meetings matter. White Paper for the Hilton Group.

Baade, R. A., Baumann, R. and Matheson, V. A. (2009) Rejecting 'conventional' wisdom: Estimating the economic impact of national political conventions. *Eastern Economic Journal* 35(4): 520–530.

Beaverstock, J. V., Derudder, B., Faulconbridge, J. and Witlox, F. (2010) International business travel and the global economy: Setting the context, in *International Business Travel in the Global Economy*, Farnham: Ashgate Publishing, pp. 1–7.

Bossdorf, O., Parepa, M. and Fischer, M. (2010) Climate-neutral ecology conferences: Just do it! *Trends in Ecology and Evolution* 25(2): 61.

Campiranon, K. and Arcodia, C. (2008) Market segmentation in time of crisis: A case study of the MICE sector in Thailand. *Journal of Travel and Tourism Marketing* 23: 151–161.

CIC (2011) The economic significance of meetings to the US economy. Convention Industry Council.

Davidson, R. (2002) Leisure extensions to business trips. *Travel and Tourism Analyst,* October: 1–17.

Davidson, R. and Hyde, A. (2014) *Winning Meetings and Events for Your Venue,* Oxford: Goodfellow Publishers.

Drife, J. O. (2008) Are international medical conferences an outdated luxury the planet can't afford? No. *BMJ* 336(7659): 1467.

Dwyer, L. and Forsyth, P. (1996) MICE tourism to Australia: A framework to assess impacts. Proceedings of the Australian Tourism and Hospitality Research Conference, Coffs Harbour, NSW: 313–323.

Dwyer, L. and Forsyth, P. (1997) Impact and benefits of MICE tourism: A framework for analysis. *Tourism Economics* 3(1): 21–38.

Ferdinand, N. and Kitchin, P. (2012) *Events Management: An international approach,* London: Sage.

Green, M. (2008) Are international medical conferences an outdated luxury the planet can't afford? Yes. *BMJ* 336(7659): 1466.

Henderson, J. C. (2007) Hosting major meetings and accompanying protestors: Singapore 2006. *Current Issues in Tourism* 10(6): 543–557.

Hoyer, K. G. and Naess, P. (2001) Conference tourism: A problem for the environment, as well as for research? *Journal of Sustainable Tourism* 9: 451–470.

ICCA (2015) Measuring the economic impact of the meetings industry. Available at http://www.iccaworld.com/cdps/cditem.cfm?nid=5173.

Jago, L. (2012) *The Value of Business Events, Tourism & Business Events International,* Brussels: Joint Meetings Industry Council.

Jago, L.K. and Deery, M. (2010) Delivering innovation, knowledge and performance: The role of business events. Business Events Council of Australia.

Jones, C. and Li, S. (2015) The economic importance of meetings and conferences: A satellite account approach. *Annals of Tourism Research* 52: 117–133.

Kerr, G., Cliff, K. and Dolnicar, S. (2012) Harvesting the 'business test trip': Converting business travellers to holidaymakers. *Journal of Travel and Tourism Marketing* 29: 405–415.

Kim, S. S., Chon, K. and Chung, K. (2003) Convention industry in South Korea: An economic impact analysis. *Tourism Management* 24(5): 533–541.

Lee, M. J. (2007) Analytical reflections on the economic impact assessment of conventions and special events. *Journal of Convention & Event Tourism* 8(3): 71–85.

Li, S. and Jago, L. (2013) Evaluating economic impacts of major sports events – a meta analysis of the key trends. *Current Issues in Tourism* 16(6): 591–611.

Marques, J. and Santos, N. (2017) Tourism development strategies for business tourism destinations: Case study in the central region of Portugal. *Tourism* 65(4): 437–449.

McEuen, M. B. and Duffy, C. (2010) The future of meetings: The case for face-to-face. The Maritz Institute White Paper.

McKenzie, S. (1997) The trick of treats. *Marketing Week,* 17 January.

McNally, C. (2017) How does construction impact the environment. *Initiafy.* Available at: www.initiafy.com/blog/how-does-construction-impact-the-environment/.

Minnaert, L. (2008) Corporate hospitality in the economic downturn, in Celuch, K. and Davidson, R. (eds) *Advances in Business Tourism Research*, Arnhem: ATLAS Publications, pp. 41–52.

Monge, F. and Brandimarte, P. (2011) MICE tourism in Piedmont: Economic perspective and quantitative analysis of customer satisfaction. *Tourismos: An International Multidisciplinary Journal of Tourism* 6: 213–220.

Park, E. and Boo, S. (2010) An assessment of convention tourism's potential contribution to environmentally sustainable growth. *Journal of Sustainable Tourism* 18(1): 95–113.

Rogers, T. (2013) *Conferences and Conventions: A global industry*, 3rd edn, Oxford: Routledge.

Rogerson, C. M. (2015) The uneven geography of business tourism in South Africa. *South African Geographical Journal* 97(2): 183–202.

Tourism Research Australia (2017) International Visitors in Australia 2017.

UNWTO (2006) Measuring the economic importance of the meetings industry – developing a Tourism Satellite Account extension. World Tourism Organization.

UNWTO (2014) AM reports, volume 7 – global report on the meetings industry. World Tourism Organization.

2 Corporate meetings

Corporate meetings in the 21st century

- The new Range Rover Velar was launched at a spectacular world-premiere event at the Design Museum in London, attended by representatives from the car manufacturer, the automotive press, and by many British celebrities.
- Cisco Systems, the American multinational corporation, chose Cape Town as the destination for a meeting of 260 of the company's partners, with the objectives of informing them of recent developments in the company's products as well as encouraging networking and loyalty to the company.
- Standard Chartered Bank (SCB) hosted a launch event to show off its new global service centre in Bangalore. Over 300 senior financial and information technology leaders and influencers from Asia attended the 2-hour event and heard presentations about SCB's ambitions as a global digital bank.
- 90 managers from across all L'Oréal divisions around the world gathered at Fontainebleau in France for the company's Global Leadership for Growth series of training seminars, aiming to deepen the participants' understanding of core business elements such as strategy and innovation and develop a strong international network of employees.

Chapter objectives

On completion of this chapter the reader should be able to:

- Locate corporate meetings within companies' broader internal and external communications strategies.
- Understand the various uses of corporate meetings.
- Appreciate the key distinguishing characteristics of corporate meetings.
- Understand the principal stages in the corporate meeting planning process.
- Recognise the roles of strategic meetings management programmes.

Corporate communications

In today's world, the success of any company partly depends upon how it is perceived by key stakeholders such as its employees, investors, consumers and other members of the wider community in which the company operates. For that reason, effective communications between companies and their various stakeholder groups is now widely considered to be of considerable strategic importance to the health and growth of businesses and their ability to achieve their objectives.

The set of tools used by companies to manage their communications with their various stakeholder groups is known as corporate communications. One of the earliest definitions of corporate communications is that of Jackson (1987), who described it as the total communication activity generated by a company to achieve its planned objectives. However, Van Riel (1995:26) suggested a more nuanced definition of corporate communications as

> an instrument of management by means of which all consciously-used forms of internal and external communications are harmonised as effectively and efficiently as possible [with the overall objective of creating] a favourable basis for relationships with groups upon which the company is dependent.

The distinction between internal and external corporate communications is a useful one, clearly differentiating between the management of communications within an organisation and those in the broader business environment.

Internal communications

Internal communications – the processes whereby employers, employees and colleagues share information with each other – take place constantly within companies, through a number of forms, many of which are informal, such as casual chats around the water cooler or hearing something of interest 'on the grapevine'. But the events that are the focus of this chapter are one element of *managed* internal communications – formal communications passing through predefined channels, which Welch and Jackson (2007) define as 'the strategic management of interactions and relationships between stakeholders at all levels within organisations'.

Effective internal communications are vital to ensuring that there is mutual understanding between management and staff. More specifically, companies rely on internal communications in order to (Pincus et al., 1991):

1   develop a shared vision of the company within the organisation;
2   establish and maintain trust in the organisation's leadership;
3   initiate and manage the change process;
4   strengthen the identification of employees with the organisation.

Using internal communications channels, companies can ensure that, for example, employees fully understand – and are engaged with – the company, its values, purposes and strategies. Internal corporate communications can also play a crucial role in the management of changes within an organisation, energising and invigorating employees for their role in the company's future direction.

The internal communications tools that are used to achieve these objectives include staff newsletters, noticeboards, emails and intranet, as well as the various types of face-to-face corporate meetings that are the focus of this chapter – such as management presentations and seminars. Face-to-face corporate communication of this type is often highlighted as the optimal channel for communicating complex information because of its ability to facilitate immediate feedback, its use of natural language and verbal and non-verbal cues, and its personal focus. For example, Cameron and McCollum (1993) note that the two-way nature of interpersonal communication channels, such as team meetings, group problem-solving sessions and supervisor briefings, enhances management–employee relationships more effectively than the use of publications.

External communications

External communications are generally defined as the sharing of information between a company and its stakeholders in the external environment, which includes the share-holders, investors and consumers already mentioned as well as other important groups in the wider community, such as government agencies and local residents. The main objective of most external corporate communications is to facilitate cooperation with these groups by building and maintaining a favourable public image for the company. The most commonly used external communications channels range from print media, such as newspapers, magazines and newsletters, through broadcast media, including radio and television, to electronic communication, including websites, social media such as Facebook and Twitter, and email. However, face-to-face business events also play a key role in the external communications of many companies, as this chapter will demonstrate.

The uses of corporate meetings

Corporate events are held by, and funded by, the countless numbers of companies or corporations worldwide that exist to make a profit by fulfilling consumers' demand for goods and services. From small, family-run, local businesses to vast multinational corporations, private-sector companies represent by far the largest sector of demand for the business events industry as a whole. Surveys consistently show that, in terms of the numbers of business events held in most countries, corporate meetings greatly outnumber all other sectors. For instance, in its survey of the Australian business events market, BECA (2015) found that 78 per cent of that country's meetings were in the corporate sector. However, although participant numbers for the most high-profile corporate events can rise into the hundreds and even thousands, the vast majority of corporate meetings involve much smaller numbers of attendees gathering together for a few hours. Nevertheless, companies' spending on meetings and events is not insignificant – estimated by Iwamoto (2011), for example, to represent 1–3 per cent of all corporate revenue.

In this book, the more *occasional* types of business events are analysed in individual chapters that are dedicated to the investigation of award ceremonies, incentive travel, exhibitions and corporate hospitality. The subject of this chapter, however, is that category of business events generally known as corporate meetings – routine gatherings that enable employers, employees and colleagues to interact with each, or allow company representatives to engage with their various external stakeholders. Despite their routine nature, such meetings are essential to the success of any company, due to their role in helping organisations to achieve their commercial goals and in fostering and strengthening effective working relationships between colleagues. As one of the basic tools available to companies for collaboration, group cohesion and communications, they play a key role in information and knowledge sharing, knowledge creation, decision-making, problem-solving and the strengthening of relationships both within and outside the company itself.

Corporate meetings take a number of distinct forms which differ from each other in several important ways, in terms of their purpose, the participants involved, the size of the group and the overall design of the event. However, the most common types of meetings are as follows.

Staff meetings

Regarded by many as an indispensable element of internal corporate communications, staff meetings are opportunities for all employees in a company, or for members of a specific department, to assemble and speak in person about various aspects of business management that cannot be easily discussed via email, for example. They offer participants the opportunity to meet face-to-face, catch up, brainstorm and have group discussions. As such, they can provide a forum for the vertical and horizontal exchange of information between employers, employees and colleagues on topics such as progress on team projects or any staff grievances. Such events can be particularly important at times of change within companies or within the market environment in which they operate – for example, for the discussion of corporate restructuring, new product developments, or new organisational strategies for the company. Face-to-face staff meetings can also be used as part of the decision-making process within companies, as employees generally feel more motivated and loyal towards the companies they work for when they are consulted on decisions affecting their jobs. Shone (2014) emphasises this aspect of staff meetings, noting that such events are often held for the purpose of making a decision and ensuring that any decision taken is the result of both a coherent process and a communal choice. In this way, decisions which are difficult to make, or which require the support – or at least the acceptance – of many people can be made in the light of the exchange of ideas expressed during the meeting.

Sales meetings

Sales meetings or sales seminars, attended by those employees whose job it is to sell the company's products or services 'out in the field', have their own particular characteristics. Rogers and Davidson (2016:5) define a sales meeting as 'a regular forum used by management to impart information, enthusiasm and team spirit to those selling their products and services'. During such events, sales figures for a particular period are generally reviewed, and the achievements of particularly high-performing sales staff may be rec-ognised and praised. The type of information imparted generally concerns changes in the company's market share, competitors' activities or new legislation that affects the selling process. Such meetings also give those present the opportunity for sales staff to share their experiences, positive and negative, of selling.

Training seminars

As companies undergo change, it may be necessary to hold training seminars to bring their managers and employees up to date on improved methods of job performance or to gain skills needed to operate new systems and equipment. Also, companies may use training seminars to introduce new staff members to corporate procedures and culture. Some of these meetings may be held on a regular basis, while others may be held when conditions dictate (Fenich, 2016). Such events may focus on increasing the participants' knowledge of subjects such as information technology, customer relations skills and employment law, but given the importance attributed to the selling function of most companies, many training seminars are designed specifically for sales staff. According to Hoyle (2002:141) the aims of sales training seminars include

> the sharpening of sales skills, the reinforcing of corporate values and philosophies, and the learning of new features of products and services to be sold. These [events are] designed ... to bolster enthusiasm and send the salesforce home with new dedi-cation to moving the product to the consumer.

Product launches

For most companies, the launching of new products is one of their main drivers of growth. In the 21st century, shorter product life cycles, faster rates of technological change, and the increasing sophistication of buyers are strengthening the relevance of new products to companies' survival and commercial well-being. Therefore, companies continuously strive to improve the range of products they sell to their consumers, either by creating new ones or by enhancing the quality of existing products. They generally take these innovations and improvements to the marketplace in the form of a product launch. Launching a new or improved product is usually an expensive undertaking for any company, involving complex manufacturing, logistical and marketing efforts, as well as sales force management. A key element in the launching of any new product is the event at which the new or improved product is finally presented to distribution networks, the press and the general public. At such events, the designers of the new car, perfume or technology application, for example, introduce it and explain its properties and fea-tures to those who will be selling it, to those who may be buying it, and to journalists in the specialist media who may write about it for their readers. Product launch events are usually short – usually a matter of a few hours – but they tend to have high production levels, often using spectacular special effects, elaborate staging, music, entertainment and celebrities in order to make the maximum impact on the audience.

Management meetings/board meetings

Every company needs to gather together its managers and other decision makers on a regular basis to develop strategies, review performances or improve their processes. Some of these management meetings are scheduled and others are spontaneous, occasionally bringing managers together on the spur of the moment to solve unexpected problems and address situations that require immediate attention. The board of directors is the governing body of a company, with responsibility for overseeing the company's activities. Board members typically meet several times a year to consider policy issues and make decisions regarding the direction of their company.

Occasionally, management and board meetings may be held off-site and for more than one day, in which case the term 'management retreat' may be used to describe them. A term previously used only to signify a temporary withdrawal from everyday life for the purpose of religious contemplation and meditation, the word 'retreat' is now commonplace in corporate language. Such events differ from routine management or board meetings in a number of ways. According to Rogers and Davidson (2016:6), the key differences are:

- Instead of moving quickly through a rigid agenda, board members spend their time at a retreat concentrating on specific long-term issues or thinking more broadly and strategically about the future of their organisation.
- Retreats are designed to spark creative thought.
- Retreats often make use of outdoor settings that are conducive to walking and reflecting on what is happening during the event.
- Time for social interaction is a vital element: teambuilding activities are often requested. Outside facilitators may be used.

Shareholders/stockholders meetings/annual general meetings

Corporate constitutions and laws usually require publicly traded companies to hold a meeting of their shareholders – or 'stockholders' – each year. At these annual general meetings (AGMs), which are usually held in the city where the company is based, senior executives present the company's annual results, informing shareholders of the previous 12 months' corporate success, or lack of it. The shareholders are invited to ask questions, to approve the annual dividend and to endorse a certain number of resolutions that will determine the company's activities in the year ahead. Every shareholder who wishes to take part in the decision-making process of the company has the right to attend such meetings and vote personally, although most choose to send in their votes by post or electronically instead. The atmosphere at such events – which can involve several thousands of participants – very much depends on the company's performance over the preceding year. As noted by Hoyle (2002), they may be highly celebratory in good times or deeply adversarial in bad times.

From the preceding review of different types of corporate meetings, it is clear that companies' reasons for holding events are wide-ranging. However, what all such events have in common is that they are all ultimately linked in some way to serving their interests, goals, and business objectives of the companies that hold them.

Beech et al. (2014) propose two systems for the classification of corporate meetings. First, they may be categorised according to the identity of the participants:

- *Internal* events are organised solely for the company's own employees. Such events include staff training sessions, management retreats and routine staff meetings.
- *External* events are attended largely by people who are not directly employed by the company funding the event. These include shareholders' meetings and product presentations.
- *Mixed* events include both employees and non-employees of the company funding the event. These include product launches and corporate hospitality days.

An alternative method is the categorisation of corporate events according to the primary *objective* for which the events are held:

- *Legal/constitutional:* internal or external meetings held for the purpose of, for instance, electing company directors or voting on business strategies
- *Commercial:* events designed directly to boost sales of the company's products or services – for example, new product presentations to clients or potential clients; or training sessions for members of the company's sales force
- *Social:* events held with the aim of strengthening bonds between staff members or between representatives of the company and its key clients – for example, management retreats, team-building events and corporate hospitality days.

In the following section, the features shared by most corporate meetings will be examined.

The distinguishing characteristics of corporate meetings

The types of corporate meetings that are the focus of this chapter share a number of characteristics that distinguish them from many of the other types of business events examined in this book.

Short but frequent

Estimating the average length and frequency of corporate meetings with a high degree of accuracy is fraught with challenges, as clearly demonstrated by the review of attempts to do so in a useful blog on this topic: https://blog.lucidmeetings.com/blog/fresh-look-number-effectiveness-cost-meetings-in-us. Nevertheless, there is a general consensus among researchers that the vast majority of routine corporate meetings last for less than one day. Regularly scheduled events such as weekly staff meetings may be of less than one hour's duration, while training seminars, product launches and shareholders' meetings may last for several hours. Meetings held off-site – not on the company's own premises – tend to be longer on average; and events involving one or more overnights, such as residential management retreats, are, by definition, often longer still. Moreover, the pervasiveness of meetings in corporate life, both scheduled and unscheduled, means that such events take place much more frequently than all of the other types of business events examined in this book. In large organisations, a corporate meeting planner may plan over 100 meetings a year, with more than one occurring on the same day in some cases.

Mandatory attendance – but at no charge to participants

Attendance at corporate meetings is usually required of company employees, who are expected to attend as part of their job responsibilities. For this reason, most corporate meetings are held during office hours, on working days. Any costs incurred in running such meetings are generally covered by the employer. For on-site meetings, these costs may be limited to the price of the refreshments offered to participants. But for off-site meetings, particularly residential events involving one or more nights' accommodation for participants, the costs can be much more substantial.

Most corporate meetings are discretionary – that is, they are subject to the decisions of management (Hoyle, 2002) in the sense that managers decide whether or not they take place (a notable exception is the annual shareholders' meeting, which is generally required by corporate mandate). As spending on meetings can represent a significant element of the overhead costs of running a business, a major consideration in the decision whether or not to hold a meeting is the extent to which it has the potential to yield benefits for the company. Meetings consume the company's resources in terms of staff time as well as the corporate finances that are required to pay for venues, speakers, staff transport and accommodation, for example. Therefore, as a direct cost to the company, they are expected to generate measurable returns on the investment they consume, usually in terms of some enhancement of the company's overall performance. As suggested by Beech et al. (2014:59),

> This may come in a variety of tangible or intangible forms – for example, increased levels of sales of the company's products, as a consequence of sales staff training sessions or an incentive trip; or a boost in staff morale and a fall in staff turnover, arising from a team-building event.

For their part, individual staff members attending corporate meetings also seek a return on their participation in such events, even though they themselves are not paying to attend. This may be the acquisition of new skills, increased level of product knowledge, or a closer working relationship with fellow employees, for example.

Due to the expense incurred in funding corporate meetings, the overall volume of such events tends to fluctuate in line with the financial performance of individual companies, with the number of meetings often declining during economic downturns as companies restrict their events activity or even cancel meetings that have already been planned. At such times, companies also need to be aware that any lavish spending on corporate meetings could be looked upon unfavourably by the press and by the companies' own shareholders.

Centralised decision-making

In corporate life, many of the decisions concerning the design and planning of meetings tend to be centralised, with the decision-making authority most often being an individual rather than a committee: the company owner or a senior manager, such as the director of the marketing department or a branch manager, for example. Once taken, the decisions concerning the different elements of the meeting – the location of off-site events, for example – are simply passed along to those with responsibility for coordinating the details: the in-house meeting planners or external agencies employed by the company for this purpose.

Short lead-times

In the events world, 'lead-time' may be defined as the length of time between the initiation of the event planning process and the actual date of the event. From the perspective of the event planners, therefore, the lead-time for any meeting is the total amount of time that is available to them for organising the event. For most business events discussed in this book, lead-times are relatively long. For example, many of the association conferences that are the subject of Chapter 3 have lead-times of several years. Due to their size and complexity, their planning processes must begin a relatively long time in advance of the dates when they are due to take place. But the situation regarding lead-times for corporate meetings is more complex: some types of corporate meetings have long planning cycles – for example, a lead-time of 12–18 months for a large shareholders' meeting; but other corporate meetings are unscheduled, impromptu events that take place at very short notice – for instance, when a sudden corporate scandal means that a crisis meeting of senior management and a press conference have to be convened within a matter of hours. More generally, in times of economic uncertainty, when many companies tend to wait until the last minute before committing to holding an event, shrinking lead-times add to the challenges faced by corporate meeting planners. Those additional challenges can include the reduced availability of appropriate venues, the reduction in bargaining powers when negotiating rates with venues and other suppliers, and a smaller pool of suitable speakers, many of whom may already be booked.

Attendance excludes spouses/partners

For their attendance at many of the events discussed in this book, participants are permitted or even encouraged to bring their spouses or partners with them. For example, those participating in association conferences are often actively urged to attend accompanied by a spouse or partner; and SMERF events of the type analysed in Chapter 4 are often family affairs as participants bring along their spouses/partners and even their children. However, with the notable exception of incentive trips (see Chapter 7), invitations to the vast majority of off-site corporate events are not extended to company employees' spouses or partners. Part of the rationale for this lies in the element of socialising and bonding between colleagues that is often an objective – primary or secondary – of business meetings. In such circumstances, an accompanying spouse or partner would be regarded as a distraction not only from the work to be done at the meeting but also from the social element – aimed at strengthening bonds between colleagues – that is often a secondary objective of off-site, residential events. During the hours outside the business programme of such events, participants are generally expected to network with each other in the interests of fostering a stronger team spirit, rather than spending time with an accompanying husband, wife or partner.

Corporate meeting planners

A wide range of decision makers may be involved in the planning of corporate meetings.

Internal staff

Within any company, one or several employees may be responsible for planning the firm's meetings. In larger companies, there may be an in-house events manager or an in-house meetings planner, or even an entire team or department in charge of organising all of the company's meetings. For those employees, event planning is their sole activity within the organisation. However, the planning of many corporate meetings is undertaken by employees for whom that activity is only one of their responsibilities among many. Secretaries, personal assistants, administrative assistants, marketing executives, and directors of training or human resources departments may also be involved in planning meetings and negotiating with suppliers such as venues, hotels, speakers and audio-visual companies. The plethora of company employees with responsibility for planning meetings can lead to a situation characterised by organisational fragmentation and a lack of transparency that makes it challenging for companies to track how much is being spent overall on such events, by whom, and using which suppliers. Recognition of this situation has led to meetings and events being labelled as one of the largest areas of 'unmanaged' corporate spending. As responsibility for booking meetings is often shared by a large number of employees throughout a company, this can result in many inefficiencies, duplications of effort and wasteful expenditure. Recently, this situation has brought corporate spending on meetings to the attention of many companies' procurement staff, whose role will be discussed later in this chapter.

External intermediaries

Companies, whether or not they employ a full-time in-house events manager, may choose to outsource the planning of some of their meetings to external intermediaries.

Venue finding services

Occasionally, the only external service required by a company may be the sourcing of a suitable venue for its meeting. In that case, the employee with responsibility for planning the meeting may use the services of a venue finding service (VFS), also known as venue finding agencies. Rogers and Davidson (2016:14) describe the role of these agencies as follows:

> VFSs generally begin by asking their client specific questions regarding their requirements for the event being planned: its date, location, the number of delegates and the budget for the event. Using these criteria, they then undertake the necessary research and produce a number of options for venues that match their client's requirements ... The VFS may also set up viewing appointments for their client.

In the majority of cases, this service is provided free to the client, as VFSs receive remuneration in the form of commission from the venues booked as a result of their recommendations.

Independent meeting planners

In cases where companies choose to outsource some or all of the meeting planning process to external agencies, they may use the services of independent meeting planners – also known as third-party planners or professional conference organisers (PCOs). These agencies offer their corporate clients a more comprehensive range of services, which may include venue sourcing, but usually extends far beyond that to include contract negotiations, hotel accommodation booking, attendee registration, and all of the logistical work that goes into organising an off-site meeting. These agencies range in size from one person working from an office based in their own home, to large, global organisations such as the MCI Group (https://www.mci-group.com/) with 64 offices in over 32 countries around the world. The relationship between a company and the agency or agencies it employs to plan its meetings can take a variety of forms, from a 'preferred' agreement between the company and one sole agency, to working with several agencies – sometimes on the planning of the same meeting. For example, a company may decide to use the services of a venue finding agency to identify a suitable venue for its event and hire a different external agency to take care of the planning and production of the event, while negotiating directly with some suppliers.

Independent meeting planners often claim that they can offer several advantages that in-house meeting planners cannot, such as:

- more extensive, specialist knowledge of event planning than in-house staff, who may have many other responsibilities, unrelated to organising meetings;
- the ability to negotiate lower rates with venues and accommodation providers, based on the volume of additional business that they can offer suppliers, from working with several different clients;
- valuable insights and experience gained from planning events for a wide range of clients, not only one company.

Nevertheless, it is generally acknowledged that there are also potential challenges associated with the use of independent meeting planners, such as:

- they are not members of the company's staff, so they may lack the deeper under-standing of internal issues that long-term employees have;
- they may be regarded as rivals by in-house events managers or in-house meeting planners concerned about losing their jobs to independent meeting planners.

Destination management companies

Another key intermediary frequently used by companies are destination management companies (DMCs), who are intermediaries based in the destination that has been chosen for the corporate event. DMCs' services are particularly useful when a meeting is being planned in a destination with which the corporate planner is unfamiliar, or which is very distant from where the planner is based, or where the local language is not spoken by the planner. These challenges can be overcome by using the services of DMCs, who bring to the meeting planning process their strong familiarity with the destination in which they are based. Competent DMCs are extremely knowledgeable about local customs, suppliers, speakers and other resources. Crucially, they are also aware of the *quality* of suppliers in the destination. Gillette and Gillette (2014) emphasise that using the services of DMCs

> can save a company's meeting planner time, money and freedom from headaches. The out-of-town meeting planner can only guess and hope for the best. Because they buy in volume, DMCs can save the organisation's meeting planner money, for the DMC has already negotiated discount prices.

The list of services that DMCs can offer meeting planners is extensive, covering elements including venue selection, participant registration, ground transportation, sightseeing opportunities, the sourcing of temporary staff, dining options, entertainment and speakers, floral arrangements, photographers, and all of the logistical tasks involved in running a meeting or other type of event. The advantages of using a reputable, well-established DMC include the fact that the staff are often creative people who can offer their clients first-hand knowledge of destinations, as well as local buying power. Rather than try to make arrangements long-distance with unknown persons and companies, it is usually more prudent for meeting planners to select a reputable DMC based in the destination to handle local logistics.

All of the intermediaries discussed here have the potential to make a valuable contribution to the corporate meeting planning process, and meeting planners are not limited to using the services of only one agency to help organise an event. One corporate meeting project can involve several intermediaries, or none at all if the meeting planner chooses to deal directly with all suppliers. Figure 2.1 indicates the different possible permutations linking buyers with suppliers.

The corporate meeting planning process

Towards the beginning of this chapter, the various forms and uses of corporate meetings were analysed, with emphasis on how such events can serve their interests, goals, and

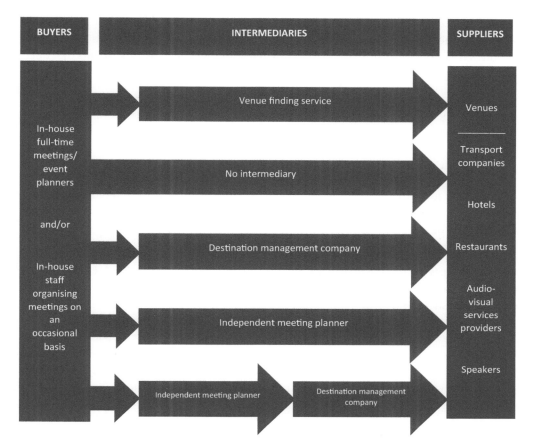

Figure 2.1
The corporate meetings supply chain

business objectives of the companies that hold them. Nevertheless, as valuable as well-planned meetings can be, it is still the case that too many meetings are seen as inefficient and a poor use of time – as a source of frustration for participants rather than a productive investment of their time and energy. The research of Rogelberg et al. (2007:20) highlights how such meetings can impair employees' job satisfaction:

> Meetings perceived as ineffective appear to have a large negative impact on how an employee feels at the end of the workday as well as on overall job satisfaction. In three different studies, the single most powerful factor in job satisfaction was how one feels about the effectiveness of the meetings he or she attends; negative feelings were exacerbated as the amount of time spent in meetings increased. Employees who attend a rash of bad meetings are stressed, dissatisfied with their jobs and more predisposed to leave.

The same authors cite research showing that, in terms of the level of productivity of corporate meetings, approximately 1 in every 7 meetings were rated as 'poor' or worse by those who attend them; and half of those surveyed saw opportunities for improvement, regarding the quality of work-related meetings. Similarly, an international survey conducted by Geimer at al. (2015) found that fewer than half of the respondents described meetings as an effective use of their time.

Given the amount of time and money that companies spend on meetings, it is clear that improving their effectiveness should be an important goal. In this section, best practice in planning effective meetings is examined.

Setting objectives

Organising a meeting without having specific objectives for it is generally regarded as a waste of valuable resources, for the company as a whole and for the individual employees who attend the event. In the corporate world, too many meetings take place simply as a weekly 'habit', for example, with no real focus or planned outcomes.

Two different types of objectives for corporate meetings may be identified. Firstly, *general* objectives: the overarching goals that justify investment in such events. The vast majority of meetings share one or more objectives of this kind, which may be summarised as (1) Learning/Communication, (2) Decision-making, (3) Networking, and (4) Motivation – inspiring the participants to have a positive attitude towards the company they work for and their role in making it successful. These general objectives frequently overlap with each other: for example, at a sales meeting, the sharing of information between participants contributes to their learning, while the coffee or lunch breaks provide opportunities for networking; and senior management may use the occasion to deliver a 'pep talk' exhorting the participants to achieve greater sales figures in the future, or may invite a motivational speaker as a source of inspiration. The relative importance of each of these four objectives varies according to the type of corporate event in question. Figure 2.2 provides examples of events and elements of events illustrating the four objectives.

For corporate meetings generally, all of the decisions made regarding their design – from the choice of venue and the food and beverage to the speakers and the overall budget allocated to the event – should be directly determined by the objective or objectives for each meeting. For example, if one of the objectives for a staff meeting is to raise morale in the company, the planner may choose to hold that meeting in a deluxe hotel in an attractive destination and to spend lavishly on food and beverage, with the aim of making participants feel incentivised and valued by their employer.

While these general objectives are helpful in describing the various purposes that can be served by corporate events, the use of more specific and detailed objectives for meetings, communicated in written form to participants in advance as part of the meeting's agenda, is widely regarded as a useful tool for increasing the effectiveness of such events. In her blog on this topic, Courtney Muehlmeier (2014) recommends that rather than using words that simply describe what the participants will be doing during the meeting – identifying, reviewing, determining, recommending, brainstorming, etc. – the stated objective for the event should clearly indicate the desired *outcome* of the event. She argues

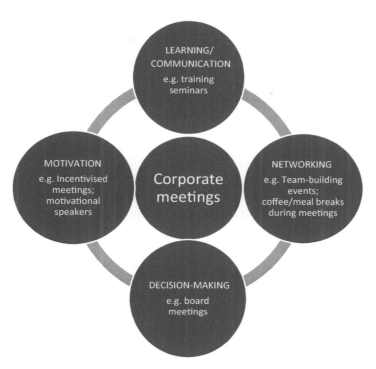

Figure 2.2
The general objectives of corporate meetings

that adding *purpose* to the meeting's stated objective better guides the direction of the discussion and makes more efficient use of the participants' time by focusing on precisely what the meeting is supposed to achieve. Effective objectives for meetings should also be time-bound, indicating a deadline or deadlines by when the outcomes should be achieved or – for more complex issues – how the matter will be progressed at subsequent meetings. Muehlmeier invites the readers of her blog to compare these two objectives for a sales meeting:

Objective #1: To talk about our sales cycle

Objective #2: To shorten our sales cycle by 1 March by collectively brainstorming ways to better handle prospects' objections to our products on 15 January, identifying the best options on 22 January, making a plan to implement on 1 February and following up on plan implementation on 15 and 22 February

Objective #2 also offers participants clear indications as to whether their meeting has been successful, as, for example, at the end of the first meeting, the question may be asked, 'Did we successfully brainstorm ways to better handle prospects' objections to our products?' If the answer to that question is 'yes', it can be concluded that that meeting's objective was met. The use of specific, results-oriented and time-bound objectives of this type can therefore provide focus and purpose to meetings, making effective use of participants' time.

When the meeting planner has developed clear objectives for a meeting, he or she can plan the event far more effectively, by being guided in every decision concerning the design of the meeting by the goals that have been identified for it. The following section of this chapter examines some of the key decisions that meeting planners take when organising corporate events.

Venues

One of the first, and most important, choices facing corporate meeting planners is whether the meeting should be held on-site (in the company's own premises) or off-site, in an external venue. Occasionally, that decision is determined by practical issues such as a lack of capacity in the company's own buildings – particularly for large meetings. But most often, the choice to hold a meeting off-site is linked to the specific objectives for that event. Rogers and Davidson (2016) list some of the most compelling reasons for holding meetings away from the participants' place of work. These include:

- The need to remove staff from the distractions of their normal working environment
- The need to encourage staff to think more creatively, to generate more innovative solutions to problems: 'it often helps to hold meetings in new environments to aid in stimulating creativity and breaking out of established ruts' (Rogelberg et al., 2007:21)
- The wish to reward or motivate staff by holding the event in an attractive location, usually with leisure elements added
- The need to keep proceedings confidential, when, for example, sensitive topics are under discussion
- The need to meet in a 'neutral' place when, for example, two companies are negotiating the terms of a merger between them.

If the meeting planner chooses to run the meeting off-site, the next decision to be made concerns the type of venue to be used. McCabe et al. (2000) demonstrate that the range of meetings venue types capable of hosting corporate events is extensive, and includes residential as well as non-residential facilities, each with its particular qualities, as indicated in Table 2.1.

Again, the choice of type of external venue may occasionally be determined by practical considerations: for example, some shareholders' meetings attract participants in such large numbers that the event can only be accommodated in a conference centre with seating for many hundreds of people; or the topic under discussion at a board meeting may be so confidential that an external venue offering exclusive hire – such as a management training centre – may be necessary.

Traditionally, hotels with facilities for meetings have been the principal type of external venue used for corporate events, and they still dominate this market. Even hotels located

Table 2.1 Venue types

Residential venues	Non-residential venues
City-centre/Central business district hotels • Business-oriented • Many facilities for meetings • Convenient access to restaurants, entertainment facilities, etc. **Suburban hotels** • Easily accessible by local companies **Airport hotels** • Cost-effective for participants arriving from different locations • Meeting rooms may be hired by the hour **Resort hotels** • Sited in desirable locations • Sporting and recreational facilities: spas, golf, etc. • May be available for exclusive hire for corporate customers **Boutique hotels** • A high standard of service and a focus on individuality • Attractive for small meetings such as executive retreats **Residential conference centres/ Management training centres** • Dedicated to hosting meetings only • Business-like atmosphere • May be available for exclusive hire for corporate customers	**Conference centres** • Can accommodate large numbers of participants • Space for exhibitions • A wide range of meeting rooms, from large auditoria to smaller breakout rooms **Unusual/unique venues** • Novelty value • Distinctive and memorable • Add interest to the event

Source: Based on McCabe et al. (2000).

close to company premises offer the advantages of external venues, as listed above; and it is not uncommon for a company to return to the same local hotel time and time again for their meetings. As indicated by Getz (2013:253), 'There is a strong tendency for corporate clients to repeatedly use the same venues, and strong links have been forged between corporations and specific hotel and resort chains for this purpose'. But the choice of *type* of hotel, from the list in Table 2.1, very much depends on the objectives for the meeting in question, as each type has its own advantages. For instance, if one of the goals of bringing employees together for a meeting is to reward them for their hard work and successful performance, a resort hotel with an abundance of leisure facilities and outstanding catering would be a logical choice.

In recent years, however, hotels operating in the corporate meetings market have increasingly faced growing competition from the category of facilities known as unusual, unique or non-traditional venues. These include castles, museums, theatres, zoos, sports stadia, theme parks and other types of facilities that have opened their doors to meetings and events as a secondary commercial activity, undertaken in parallel with their primary role as tourist attractions. Their main motivations for diversifying their offer in this way are discussed by Marr (2011), who highlights that, for many tourist and leisure attractions, the growing pressure to create additional revenue streams and the opportunity to more effectively manage the challenge of fluctuations in demand arising from the seasonality of tourism, have encouraged them to host meetings and events on their premises. The corporate meetings market has adopted unusual venues with great enthusiasm. For example, by 2015, approximately 20 per cent of all UK meetings were being held in such venues (UK CAMS, 2015). Companies' motivation for using unusual venues can be partly explained by participants' fondness for novelty: a staff training event held aboard a ferry boat, for example, is likely to be much more memorable than one held in the seminar room of a chain hotel. But Rogers and Davidson (2016:213) emphasise another benefit of unusual venues:

> From the perspective of the meeting planner, perhaps the greatest advantage of using unusual venues is that they have the potential to increase attendance levels by attracting delegates who may otherwise have declined the invitation. This is particularly important in the case of events for which there is no obligation to attend … such as press conferences, product launches and product presentations.

In general, journalists tend to receive invitations to a great number of events, and one way of increasing a particular meeting's chances of attracting such guests is by choosing to hold it in an unusual venue. For example, the use of the Design Museum in London for the launch of the new Range Rover Velar – as mentioned at the beginning of this chapter – no doubt added to the appeal of the occasion.

Seating configurations

Once a suitable venue has been identified for any corporate meeting, the planner must give some consideration to another factor that can contribute directly to the success of the event: the optimum seating plan, or seating configuration, for the participants. While for many meeting planners, the issue of where participants sit during a meeting may not be a particularly compelling factor in contributing to the effectiveness of the event, more enlightened organisers understand that where people sit in meetings, in relation to each other, can have a subtle but profound impact on the extent to which the desired goals are reached. Seating configurations can influence how well participants engage with each other and how well they absorb and retain information. Where participants are placed during meetings can also be an indication of their status and authority, as noted by Mantei et al. (1991:206), for example: 'In face-to-face meetings, the seating of people in a room is usually indicative of a hierarchy with higher status people occupying more central positions or "head of the table" locations'. More recently, research by Zhu and Argo (2013) demonstrated that seating arrangements even had a direct impact on the extent to which participants were persuaded by material presented to them at meetings. For all of these reasons, the seating arrangements for corporate events should never be left to chance. Some of the most commonly used seating arrangements for corporate meetings are shown in Figure 2.3.

Configuration name	Advantages	Uses
U-shape or horseshoe 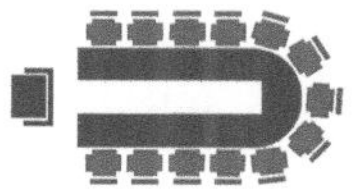	• Encourages eye contact, interaction, discussion and rapport between those present • The open end provides good visibility during presentations, while desk space enables note taking	• Training sessions
Round table 	• Non-hierarchical. Promotes a high level of interaction and participation and an equal opportunity for participants to contribute ideas in an open-discussion environment	• Brainstorming/problem-solving in small groups
Boardroom or rectangular table 	• Clarity in terms of leadership of the meeting – the leader sits at the head of the table	• Decision-making. Board meetings, small discussions and focus groups where one person facilitates
Theatre or auditorium 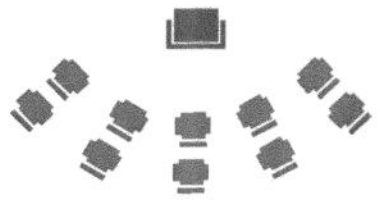	• Large numbers of participants. Good sight-lines to the stage. Allows for the maximum number of people to fit into a meeting room, seated • Appropriate for meetings of no more than two hours	• Formal presentations, lectures, keynote speakers. Product launches
Classroom 	• Desks provide space for using laptops and taking notes • Seating people in rows reduces the number of distractions and improves focus on the material presented	• Instruction, lectures and training sessions

Figure 2.3
Seating configurations

Naturally, several different seating configurations may be used at one event. For example, the meeting may begin and end with plenary sessions in theatre-style but use round tables the rest of the time, to allow brainstorming by participants.

Marketing

Because all internal participants in corporate meetings are obliged to attend as an element of their job responsibilities, the marketing of such events often consists of simply notifying those members of staff whose participation is expected. Fenich (2016) stresses that most of the marketing effort required in such circumstances is limited to sending out invitations to those who will attend and updating company websites for these events with meeting information, themes and objectives. Hoyle (2002:134) concurs, noting that the principal role of marketing, for internal meetings and events, is to clearly convey the message and the purpose of the event, rather than to encourage attendance:

> The purpose for attending is relatively easy to define. You will want to develop a marketing approach that will clearly set forth the profile of the programme, the expectations of attendee performance, and the positive results that they should anticipate.

There should be a specific message and theme for every event. For example, the marketing material for a training session would emphasise what the participants will learn and, possibly, how they should prepare for the event. Nevertheless, as Hoyle points out, although boosting attendance is not a key purpose of the internal marketing of corporate meetings, generating enthusiasm for attending certainly is.

The generating of enthusiasm is even more important in the case of marketing corporate events to those potential participants who do not work directly for the company. For example, journalists, dealers and retailers invited to a product launch are under no obligation to attend, although their participation is key to the success of such events. Therefore, they have to be persuaded to attend through a more extensive marketing effort, designed not only to create awareness and interest, but also to motivate participants to attend by creating excitement for the event. The marketing campaign could begin, for example, by sending a personal letter of invitation to media contacts, with a press release, and details of the objectives of the corporate event and its newsworthiness. The initial invitations could be followed up by reminder phone calls to as many of the invitees as possible, extending a personal invitation and strongly recommending that they attend the event.

Budget

As indicated earlier in this chapter, one distinguishing characteristic of corporate events is that they are a business expense for the companies that run them. They consume the firm's resources in terms of revenue and staff time and in return are expected to generate some form of return on this investment, usually in terms of some enhancement of the company's overall performance – such as increased levels of sales of the company's products. Companies typically set a precise budget for each of their events, based on the perceived value of the event itself – the extent to which it is expected to contribute to overall profitability. But a number of factors can cause budgets for corporate meetings to vary. For example, as McCabe et al. (2000:344) indicate,

> the purpose of the meeting will also determine how the budget is to be spent. For example, a company might budget conservatively for a meeting for shareholders, as proof that it is spending funds wisely, while a product launch might be more lavish.

Yet another variable is the company's general financial situation: budgets for events may fluctuate according to whether the firm is prospering and expanding or going through a period of austerity and cost-cutting. In any case, it is the responsibility of the planner to ensure that the costs incurred for any event do not exceed the budget allocated, but that the overall objectives for the event are nevertheless achieved.

External meetings incur expenditure over a number of areas including venue hire, speakers' fees, printed material, food and beverage, and the hire of audio-visual equipment. Planners, whether they are internal staff or intermediaries working on behalf of the company, need to be confident they have negotiated effectively to get the best rates possible from suppliers. Increasingly, planners are finding themselves guided – or even joined – in these negotiations by their colleagues in the company's procurement departments, whose influence on budgetary matters has recently expanded into their employers' spending on corporate meetings and events.

Procurement

Procurement has been defined as

> the process of finding, agreeing terms and acquiring goods, services or works from an external source, often via a tendering or competitive bidding process. The process is used to ensure the buyer receives goods, services or works at the best possible price, when aspects such as quality, quantity, time, and location are compared.
>
> (Van Weele, 2010)

Most major companies have a procurement department that is responsible for managing the firm's purchasing activity. A key role of that department is to buy all of the materials that are required for the company's production processes or daily operations. For a manufacturing company, for example, the procurement department's role could include the purchasing of raw materials such as iron, steel or plastics, as well as tools, machinery and delivery trucks, and even the company's office supplies such as photocopier paper and computers. In order to maximise the company's profitability, procurement professionals continuously evaluate whether they are purchasing these materials at the best possible price. They use money-saving techniques such as negotiating with suppliers to obtain better prices for bulk orders and investigating the possibility of purchasing materials more cheaply from alternative sources. Employees throughout the company are often required to seek the approval of the procurement department regarding the purchasing of any materials they require.

Procurement professionals' responsibilities often extend into the purchase of services as well as materials. For example, companies' spending on their staff's transient business travel has for many years been under the close scrutiny of their procurement departments, who generally work with the company's business travel managers to negotiate favourable pricing agreements with a limited number of suppliers such as airlines, hotels and car rental companies. Procurement departments have also been instrumental in drafting their companies' business travel policies that, for example, oblige staff to use the firm's 'preferred' airlines when booking flights – airlines with which the company has negotiated special discounts in return for the guarantee that its employees will book a certain minimum number of flights with those airlines in a specific period, usually a year.

More recently, companies have begun to involve their procurement departments in their purchasing of meetings-related materials and services, giving them decision-making powers over the booking of almost every element of events, from venues, accommodation and travel to catering and technology. As a consequence of this trend, a growing number of corporate meeting planners have found themselves being required to seek the approval of their company's procurement team before making bookings with suppliers – or even having responsibility for negotiating with suppliers taken from them and transferred into the hands of procurement professionals. This transition has been most successful in companies where meeting planners and their procurement colleagues have developed solid working relationships based on mutual respect, with both sides learning from each other. For example, enlightened procurement professionals have learned that, for meetings and events, the cheapest venues rarely represent the best deal in terms of achieving their meetings' objectives, and that establishing good long-term relationships with suppliers is also a factor to be taken into account in the purchasing process. Conversely, many corporate meetings managers have come to appreciate their procurement colleagues' skills in the streamlining of sourcing and contracting based on their comprehensive overview of company-wide expenditure on meetings and events.

Strategic meetings management

Companies' meeting planners, business travel managers and procurement professionals increasingly find themselves collaborating on the implementation of strategic meetings management (SMM) programmes within the companies they work for. Such programmes make use of a number of techniques designed to improve the effectiveness of corporate meetings and reduce their costs through the creation of greater transparency of spending, more negotiating power when dealing with suppliers and improved compliance with company-wide meetings policies.

The origins of SMM may be traced back to the 1990s, when large, multi-division companies implemented 'meetings consolidation' programmes to track and reduce their spending on meetings and to assist with the procurement of meeting space and hotel rooms (Corbin Ball Associates, 2009). Enabled by the advent of advanced web-based data management tools, meetings consolidation evolved into a professional discipline known by the broader term 'strategic meetings management'.

Originating in the US but gradually being adopted globally, SMM is widely considered to be a more holistic, centralised, and efficient way of managing all of a company's expenditure on meetings, giving managers greater visibility and control over their corporate events costs. In 2004, the Groups and Meetings Committee of the Global Business Travel Association (GBTA) first outlined a framework for SMM programmes and released a series of papers to guide companies through SMM development and implementation. The GBTA's definition of SMM is

> a disciplined approach to managing enterprise-wide meeting and event activities, processes, suppliers and data in order to achieve measurable business objectives that align with the organisation's strategic goals/vision, and deliver value in the form of quantitative savings, risk mitigation, and service quality.
>
> (Iwamoto, 2011)

But while the definition of SMM is relatively straightforward, in practice many different SMM models have emerged. However, there are a number of elements that are common to most of them.

Data analysis

An effective SMM programme is based upon accurate knowledge of *how much* money is being spent on a company's meetings, *by whom*, and *how effectively* it is being spent. For that reason, a starting point for many companies implementing a SMM programme is the systematic collection of data to find the answers to such questions as: Who within the company is spending money on meetings? (Sales and Marketing? Human Resources? Information Technology? ...) How much are they spending? What are the objectives for their meetings? What can be done better to help them achieve their objectives? In which destinations are meetings being held? In which venues? At what times of the year?

This form of business intelligence is essential for accomplishing two key objectives of most SMM programmes: delivering more transparent visibility into the booking of meetings activity across a company; and identifying opportunities for achieving cost efficiencies/savings. Many companies, upon gaining full visibility into their total meetings expenditure for the first time are surprised to learn how much they are spending on this activity and, in many cases, how fragmented their supplier base is: they may realise that different members of staff have negotiated different rates for identical meeting rooms in the same hotel, for example; or that throughout the company, contracts have been agreed with a number of different audio-visual suppliers for meetings, all charging different rates.

Strategic sourcing

Achieving insights into their companies' total spending on meetings often prompts managers of those companies to use that business intelligence to (1) consolidate the number of their suppliers, creating a 'preferred supplier programme' by retaining only those that can offer the most favourable value propositions, and (2) renegotiate their contracts with those retained – 'preferred' – suppliers, to obtain more advantageous rates in return for a larger volume of bookings. For example, a company may guarantee that it will hold a certain number of meetings in a particular hotel chain over a 12-month period in return for lower daily rates. This form of strategic sourcing allows companies to use their knowledge of their comprehensive meetings expenditure in order to reduce costs by fully leveraging their buying power.

Many companies further increase their negotiating power by merging the management of their meetings activity with the management of their employees' transient business travel. The integration of a company's meetings and business travel programmes offers a number of advantages, foremost among which is the ability to negotiate more competitive rates with suppliers. For example, some of the company's employees may book a certain number of nights in a hotel for their transient business travel, while others book nights in the same hotel in connection with residential meetings. Achieving insights into the overall volume of these two types of bookings allows the company to demonstrate to certain hotels that the volume of their custom is substantial enough to justify more favourable nightly rates for its employees. The opportunity to make such cost savings has persuaded a growing number of firms to integrate the management of their transient business travel with the management of their meetings operations, as an element of their SMM programmes. A 2015 survey of managers with some level of responsibility for meetings, events and/or travel in their companies found that half of them either already had created a consolidated meetings and travel programme (23 per cent) or were in the process of doing so (27 per cent) (GBTA Foundation, 2015).

Corporate meetings policies

Within most companies, various written, formal policies establish rules of conduct for employees – regarding, for example, their general behaviour, attendance, dress code and other areas related to their terms and conditions of employment. A distinction can be made between mandated policies, which are formally enforced by the decree of the company's senior management, and non-mandated policies, which are often merely 'guidelines'. In the former case, non-compliance with the company policy (i.e. doing something contrary to the policy) is likely to lead to a disciplinary sanction for the offending employee; while going against a non-mandated policy may incur no penalty at all.

Ever since business travel became a common feature of professional life, corporate travel policies have been used by organisations to communicate to employees the rules governing how they should book their business travel and submit their claims for travel expenses. The principal objectives of most corporate travel policies are to control the firm's travel costs, avoid abuses (such as employees booking flights with certain airlines to collect the air miles, even when other, cheaper flights are available with other airlines) and to keep employees safe and comfortable when they are travelling on company business. However, more recently – and often as a direct consequence of creating an SMM programme – many companies have introduced a formal *meetings policy* to guide their employees' booking of facilities and services for corporate meetings and some of the other types of business events that are the subject of this book. A key objective of such policies is to standardise and – in many cases – centralise the booking of meetings by employees. Meetings policies may be mandated or non-mandated by senior management, but common features of such policies include:

- A description of the company's meetings and events department and its responsibilities
- Details of which meetings are covered by the policy: all meetings/meetings for 20 or more participants/off-site meetings only/meetings which require a budget over a certain amount of money, etc.
- The process by which meetings should be submitted for prior review and approval – for example, meetings may be subject to review by a procurement specialist within the company, or a head of department
- Who, within the company, is authorised to negotiate with suppliers such as venues, travel companies, audio-visual production companies, guest speakers and destination management companies
- Details of which suppliers can be used – only hotels with which the company has a 'preferred partnership' agreement based on volume of bookings, for example
- An obligation to register every meeting in a company-wide events calendar
- How meetings should be paid for – by using a corporate card, for instance
- The security measures that must be put in place for meetings
- The consequences (if any) for non-compliance with the meetings policy.

Despite the growth in the number of meetings policies being implemented in recent years, they are still far less common than corporate travel policies. A study conducted by Dimanche et al. (2010), for example, found that only 33 per cent of companies surveyed had a fully mandated meetings policy, compared with 67 per cent that had a fully mandated travel policy.

While data analysis, strategic sourcing and corporate meetings policies are among the most common features of companies' SMM programmes, a number of other elements are possible, as indicated by Corbin Ball Associates (2009):

Elements of a strategic meetings management programme (SMMP)

1 Meeting design

This involves the pre-event planning of the meeting including:

- Meeting scope specification: the purpose of the meeting, the agenda, size, and cost elements.
- A formal standardised process to propose, review and approve meetings.
- Measures to encourage compliance to the above process with enforced consequences for non-compliance.

- Budget planning tools are commonly involved with meetings design, including the ability to track budgeted, actual and negotiated savings for specific meeting spend elements.

2   Strategic sourcing

Once the meeting is approved, the next step is sourcing. This involves choosing the meeting site(s) and negotiating the contracts for sleeping rooms, meeting space, travel and other event services. SMM sourcing programmes will include:

- A standardised procurement process for vendor services consistent throughout the company.
- The establishment of preferred vendors with the promise of preferred pricing/concessions for the volume of business directed to them.
- Standardised contracts and service agreements negotiated with these preferred vendors will decrease negotiation time and contractual liability.
- Usually, key performance indicators (KPI) will be set up and tracked to measure the quality of vendor performance.
- Sourcing for hotel sleeping rooms and meeting space is one of the most common elements of SMMP to be outsourced to a third-party sourcing company where, through volume purchasing, negotiating experience and standardised contracts, very competitive rates can be offered to the client, despite commissions being charged by the agencies to the hotels.

3   Corporate meetings calendar

Corporate-wide meetings calendars are also common with SMMP.

- They can help increase the visibility of meetings across the enterprise and help to avoid overlap of events.
- Calendars can help a company to avoid cancellation fees – if one division cannot use the meeting space, perhaps another can.
- Conference calendars tracking the location and participation of all company meetings can be useful in crisis management situations as well.

4   Meetings and attendee management

A significant component of tracking total meeting spend is managing the attendee registration, travel and housing expenses. Automated, web-based attendee management tools will not only track these expenses, but substantially improve staff efficiency and customer service as well. Specific components often include:

- The ability for the attendee and their guest to register for a variety of programme tracks, meals, outings and more.

- The ability for the attendee to arrange all travel matters online including air and ground transportation automatically funnelling to preferred vendors.
- The ability for planners to create arrival and departure manifests drawing real-time data directly from the travel bookings.
- Housing management including room and hotel assignment based on attendee profiles, roommate matching and other housing requirements.
- The creation of shell PNRs (passenger name records) for agency booking of travel details.
- Full hotel and flight confirmation number tracking.
- Ability for attendees to make changes to the travel records online.

When procurement principles are applied to travel arrangements through these tools, substantial savings can be accrued in addition to automating many of the management tasks and improving client service.

5   Reconciliation of expenses

When the meeting is over, the bills need to be paid. Tracking these payments is a crucial component of SMMP. The payment process should be consistent throughout the company and in compliance with standard procurement policies. Meeting expense cards (such as those offered by Visa and American Express) can simplify and streamline this process making it easier to assign specific event costs to specific budget codes.

6   Measure and evaluation

The data tallied and tracked throughout the meeting life cycle should be easily accessible for analysis. What was the average meeting cost per person? How much is the company spending annually with a specific hotel chain across all meetings? What are the meeting cost trends from year to year? What were the negotiated savings for a specific meeting? How close are the actuals to budget? These are among the hundreds of analytic questions answered through a successful SMMP. The reporting tools should be easy to use, flexible and customizable for viewing in many ways such as charts, dashboards, budget analytic comparisons and others. Good business intelligence analytics are vital to a successful SMMP. In addition to measuring meeting spend, there is a strong need to measure meeting effectiveness – or return on investment (ROI). It is not simply a question of the money spent, but also about the benefits arising from the company's spending on meetings. This requires a systematic way to convey the specific, measurable goals and objectives from the meeting owner to all meeting stakeholders. The progress toward these goals (learning, new customers, increase sales, etc.) should be measured before, during and after the event, usually by a series of carefully worded, consistent surveys.

These six SMMP elements and others can be implemented individually or not at all. Some companies adopt a full sweeping change while others do it a step at a time.

There can be little doubt that the SMM approach to overseeing companies' expenditure on their meetings and events is having a considerable impact on budgetary factors in this area of corporate communication. In future years, SMM is likely to consolidate and expand its role in helping to ensure that meetings are a sound investment for companies, rather than a liability.

Chapter summary

Corporate meetings are the largest category of business events in terms of numbers. This category includes staff meetings, sales meetings, training seminars, product launches, board meetings and shareholders meetings. This chapter set corporate meetings within the broader context of internal and external corporate communications and identified the key distinguishing characteristics of corporate meetings, including mandatory attendance and short lead-times. The corporate meeting planning process was analysed, beginning with a review of the internal and external stakeholders involved, such as procurement departments, intermediaries and suppliers, with particular emphasis on venues. The expanding role of strategic meetings management programmes was explored, focusing on their potential to provide a more effective tool for the management of companies' expenditure on meetings, giving managers greater visibility and control over their corporate events.

CASE STUDY 2.1: ASOS ASSEMBLES 2018

ASOS Assembles

Company background

ASOS (www.asos.com) is a global online retail destination, aimed at fashion-loving twenty-somethings. The company was founded in the UK in 2000 and now sells over 85,000 products including its own label, and third-party brands, and has 15.4 million active customers worldwide (ASOS Annual Report and Accounts 2017). Customers purchase goods through eight local-language websites (UK, US, France, Germany, Spain, Italy, Australia and Russia) and through the ASOS app. ASOS is also present on channels such as Facebook, Instagram, Snapchat, YouTube and Twitter. Over 70 per cent of the company's global traffic comes through mobile technology.

As at 31 August 2017, ASOS employed 3,579 people, with the majority based at the company's headquarters in Camden, North London and the Customer Care site in Watford, just north of London, with smaller teams in Paris, Birmingham, Berlin, New York and Sydney.

ASOS Assembles 2018

The ASOS Assembles 2018 event took place on 15 March of that year. It was the first time that the company had undertaken an event on such a huge scale, building on ASOS's six-monthly 'strategy days', which had previously been held in various London locations.

The venue

The ASOS Assembles event was held in Alexandra Palace in North London (www.alexandrapalace.com/), which was constructed in 1873 as a centre for education and entertainment for Victorian Londoners. The building is known as the birthplace of television, as on 2 November 1936, the world's first regular high-definition public television broadcast took place from the BBC studios at Alexandra Palace. Today, it is a multi-purpose venue, hosting an eclectic mix of live music, sport, cultural and business events. The largest room within the venue is the Great Hall, with a capacity of 10,250 (concert/reception) or 7,000 (theatre-style).

The objectives for holding the event

ASOS is expanding at a rate of approximately 30 per cent year on year, growing internationally and adding hundreds of new employees every year. This means that ASOSers (ASOS employees) are dealing with a vast amount of change inside the company. The purpose of ASOS Assembles, therefore, was to connect, familiarise and engage the ASOSers with the company's rapid development and the role they can play within that.

The participants

Over 2,000 ASOSers attended, representing all areas of the business, including ASOS's Camden headquarters, the satellite offices in Paris, Berlin, New York and Sydney, the warehouses in Barnsley and Berlin, and the company's technology hub in Birmingham.

(A separate, bespoke event was organised for colleagues at ASOS's 24/7 customer care centre in Watford in April 2018.)

The event programme

ASOS chose a personalised, festival-style structure for the event, with six break-out zones within the venue, where ASOSers could choose what they wanted to see including guest presentations on coping with growth and change; understanding the global customer; and taking action for social good, followed by a 'headline' event held at the main stage area and attended by all. Here the audience was treated to a catwalk show of ASOS's latest fashion, an on-stage interview with ASOS founder Nick Robertson and a closing speech from ASOS CEO Nick Beighton.

The aim was for every ASOSer to have their own personalised experience of the event and to spend social time with colleagues new and old.

The event organisers

An internal core project team steered the event and made the key decisions. The team included members of the Executive Board, the Communications Director, the Creative Director, and ASOS's Internal and External Events Managers. The company worked with an external event management agency, Wonderland (http://wonderland-agency.com/) to produce the event, as part of a very collaborative process.

Evaluation of the event

On the day of the event itself, comment booths around the venue allowed guests to leave feedback and questions. This was followed up by a post-event survey sent via email to all attendees, which formed the main element of the evaluation. As the event had very clear objectives from the beginning, most follow-up survey questions were designed to determine the extent to which those objectives had been reached. Social media posts using the event hashtag (#ASOSAssembles) were also used to help gauge the impact, reach and level of engagement of the event.

CASE STUDY 2.2: SIEMENS PLM SOFTWARE'S CONVERGE EUROPEAN CONSULTING CONFERENCE

The client

Siemens PLM Software, a business unit of Siemens Digital Factory Division, is a leading global provider of software, systems and services in the areas of managing the product life cycle (PLM, Product Lifecycle Management) and management of industrial operations. The company has its corporate headquarters in Plano, Texas.

Siemens PLM Software Conference

The agency

Full event management and event design was undertaken by Primary (www.primarylive. co.uk), a live communications, exhibitions and events agency based in the UK. Primary's team includes specialists in catering management and logistics, live event production, content creation and corporate communications.

Objective

The objective of the annual conference was to provide Siemens PLM Software's technical community with the opportunity to share knowledge, by:

- informing them on the latest products and industry solutions;
- sharing the company's go-to-market strategy;
- enabling them to build networks with peers from across Europe and celebrate the successes they share as a team.

The event

Some 1,100 employees from the three service areas of the business across Europe came together for the three-day event at PortAventura, an entertainment resort in Salou, on the Costa Daurada in Spain. Delegates were accommodated in three hotels across the resort, with the conference, business sessions, awards, exhibitions and networking taking place within the PortAventura Convention Centre and the final evening dinner and entertainment exclusively hosted by the newly opened Ferrari Land theme park within the resort.

The event incorporated an online registration site and an event app, and all event branding across the site included flags, signage, lighting wraps, backdrops, digital signage and billboards, as well as the bespoke custom design and building of a 12-metre LED screen.

Apart from the business content, the agenda on the first day of the event included a speech from a performance coach, app challenges and gamification, VR activities and informal networking. This was followed by an awards session complemented by aerial artistes the following afternoon, and an exciting evening of entertainment in Ferrari Land where Siemens PLM were given the first corporate exclusive hire of the theme park.

Conclusion

Primary's Managing Director Dan Stevens said: 'Working on a European Conference of this size and not only managing the event production and logistics, but also playing an instrumental role in content creation, it's quite incredible that this project was delivered by a team of just five people'.

Representing the client, Christian Wilmshoefer, VP Digital Enterprise Services, Germany said: 'It's a pleasure to work with Primary and we have the confidence everything works from a technical and logistical perspective'.

Adapted from an article by Charlotte Flach, from Conference & Incentive Travel *magazine, 14 September 2017.*

CASE STUDY 2.3: SPACEBASE

One of the first companies to apply the principles of the sharing economy to the business events market was Spacebase (www.spacebase.com).

Background

The company was founded in 2015 by German citizens Julian Jost and Jan Hoffmann-Keining together with investor and online travel pioneer, Stephan Ekbergh, a Swedish national. This was their first joint project.

'Changing the way we meet' became the goal and motivation for the three founders who, during their previous work as business consultants, took part in countless meetings and workshops held in boring and uninspiring venues. To provide meeting planners with an alternative range of venues, the Berlin-based start-up used the concept of the sharing economy to build an online booking platform enabling quick and easy rentals of office space for meetings, seminars and other types of business events.

Spacebase

Developing the Spacebase product

The platform links meeting planners with companies and individuals who have temporarily unoccupied spaces available for outside hire. These spaces range from lofts, co-working spaces and photo studios to company meeting rooms, retail space, restaurants and bars. Both sides benefit from the use of the platform. Property owners can make extra revenue from renting out unoccupied space by using Spacebase to display and promote their venues without having to set up and market their own website. Meeting planners get instant access to a large portfolio of extraordinary locations that allow for more exciting get-togethers. Spacebase is marketed through a variety of channels – offline (including events and public relations) and online. But due to the nature of the company and the product, the main marketing focus is online. In its marketing, Spacebase emphasises its offer of unusual and special venues that make meetings more enjoyable for participants, the underlying assumption being that changing from a grey office room to a more inspiring environment will spark the participants' creativity and innovative thinking, thus helping meetings become something to look forward to again.

All locations offered are handpicked by the company's location scouts and tested for their suitability to host corporate meetings. They range from more traditional conference rooms to extraordinary spaces, including a boxing ring, a vintage petrol station and an airport terminal. Just as diverse as the spaces offered on the platform are Spacebase's customers, ranging from small enterprises that are looking for one-time-only solutions for special occasions to large corporations that use the booking tool for most of their meetings.

To recruit its venues, Spacebase initially employed so-called 'country teams', which were responsible for researching locations and acquiring customers in various countries all over the world. Even though interest from both sides was undoubtedly there, managing booking requests from so many different people with such diverse requirements proved to be more difficult than expected. So Spacebase decided to shift its focus away from all types of business events to smaller meetings and workshops and to develop expertise in how to make business meetings more successful. The start-up is actively researching on creativity at work with its experiMENTAL web series (www.spacebase.com/en/experimental) to help position itself as a thought leader in the subject of the future of work.

By the third year of its operations, Spacebase had grown to a company employing 16 people at its office in Berlin, and venue bookings through Spacebase were increasing at a rate of 5–10 per cent each month. The majority of bookings were made as a result of targeted scouting by Spacebase staff.

The client base of Spacebase

A 2016 survey of the company's client base (http://www.spacebase.com/blog/2016/04/04/mice-sharing-economy-is-here-to-stay/) showed that people booking venues through Spacebase were:

- Relatively young: 50 per cent of bookers were under 30 years old
- Booking on behalf of start-ups, agencies and tech companies
- Attracted by the 'cool' venues on offer, the novelty value and the lower prices (The company claims that venues booked through Spacebase can be up to 40 per cent cheaper than hotel meeting rooms).

This selection of Spacebase's customers' comments gives insights into why they book their venue through Spacebase:

- Ramesh Chander (Programme Manager at Google): 'The unique spaces are perfect for creative workshops that really challenge the status quo'.
- Thorsten de Boer (Partner at Roland Berger): 'Unconventional strategies require new perspectives. That's why we prefer creative and unique surroundings for our meetings. Our clients share our vision and are becoming more and more interested in alternative event locations that deviate from their ordinary and grey daily office routines. Spacebase helps us find and book these trendy spaces – inspiration guaranteed.'
- Lauren Baronet (Marketing Manager at Deloitte): 'Spacebase is the perfect source to get inspiration for my next workshop venues. With the Spacebase Guarantee I can be sure the essentials will be taken care of.'

The future of Spacebase

In 2016, the company expanded to the US and established an office in New York City, making it the first European contender to challenge the American meetings industry. Further expansion to other North American cities is planned. In October 2017, Spacebase bought

Craftspace, a Hamburg start-up that focuses on renting out craft, food and creative rooms, thereby further strengthening its position in the business events venue industry. With this purchase, Spacebase became the European market leader in their field, now offering over 2,500 locations in 12 countries.

The main challenges that lie ahead for Spacebase are:

- Convincing people in the relatively traditional MICE industry to trust their brand
- Persuading customers to become loyal to the Spacebase brand and bring repeat business to the platform
- Automating the booking process to minimise the company's involvement in the communication between the booker and the person hiring out the venue.

IT'S MY JOB
PAUL BERGAMINI, PROJECT DIRECTOR,
INCITE GROUP

After studying a bachelor's degree in Events Management at the University of Greenwich I decided that the conference sector seemed to be the sensible and most vibrant of marketplaces to search for a graduate role. With an interest in advancing the interests of business, taking charge of projects and having the opportunity to mould an event from concept to delivery, it was very apparent to me from the outset that the role of conference producer was my preferred option.

Four weeks after graduating, after registering with an event industry–specific recruitment company, I was offered a position as a conference producer for TDN UK (The Development Network), a company that produces conferences for the defence sector such as: Combat Helicopter, Combat Logistics and Naval Damage Control. Our conferences focused on acquiring the key decision makers in each particular topic area – the people who are in charge of military budgets and who decide on what is procured. My role as a conference producer included researching possible topic areas for future events by conducting extensive market research and speaking to senior officials from both the military and industry. Building relationships with speakers, industry representatives and government officials was an essential part of my job and that helped me throughout the process of developing a suitable conference agenda and then locating the correct presenters to speak on each topic.

After my initial training during the first few weeks I was assigned my first conference. I began producing an event for 2016 called Electronic Warfare, in Rome. Progress was quick. My responsibilities increased which was a great boost for those who, like me, enjoy jumping into a project. After the Electronic Warfare conference, I was tasked with validating new potential events outside the military sector and established TDN's maritime sector of events with a series of new shows such as Passenger Ship Safety UK/US, Maritime Search and Rescue and Passenger Ship Sustainability.

After TDN I took a four-month career break to travel around South-East Asia and consider the future options open to me. I have now begun work as a Project Director for Incite Group assuming responsibility over our flagship event The Open Mobile Summit in San Francisco. The role is an exciting challenge and is easily the biggest event I have personally worked on, with a greater emphasis on other areas of event management I hadn't been focused on before, such as marketing. With over 50 speakers, large budgets for marketing and the necessity to amend the agenda's content year on year, it's a difficult role but one that's both rewarding and never boring!

My time at Greenwich was key to my current career path and showed me how the conference industry was a great sector to work in. The research-led projects and team exercises at Greenwich enabled me to develop a skill set that I now use in identifying new topics, markets and trends.

IT'S MY JOB
ERMAN HENDEM, GROUPS, CONVENTIONS AND EVENTS SALES EXECUTIVE, HILTON ISTANBUL BOSPHORUS

After graduating from Beykent University in Istanbul, with a degree in Tourism Management, I studied on a Master's programme in Conference Management at the University of Westminster, London, from 2010 to 2011. The postgraduate course focused on topics such as Venue Management, Conference Planning and Business Tourism Destination Marketing which provided me with specific, in-depth knowledge of the business events industry. It was an excellent experience for me to study with people from many different countries and cultures, as this provided me with a number of insights and different perspectives which I believe brought me significant professional advantages when I returned to my own country, Turkey, after completing the course.

Since graduating from the University of Westminster, I have been very satisfied with my career in business events. Since completing my military service in 2014,

I have been working in managerial positions in a cluster structure of three hotels: the Hilton Istanbul Bosphorus, the Conrad Istanbul Bosphorus and the Hilton Parksa Istanbul.

I am currently employed as the Groups, Conventions and Events Sales Executive in the Hilton Istanbul Bosphorus. My main responsibilities are handling corporate meetings as well as leisure groups, private events and outside catering. I would describe my job as acting as the interface between our clients and our hotel's operational departments. This coordinating role means that on a daily basis I am in close contact with such departments as front office, food and beverage, housekeeping and security. An important part of my job involves organising our hotel's 'Groups of the Week' meetings, which are attended by all department supervisors. At these meetings, we hold in-depth discussions of all of the events due to take place in our hotels that week, to ensure that they go as smoothly as possible.

I am also responsible for site inspections. Whenever I receive a request from a client who is considering holding a meeting or other event in our hotel, I send them my proposal and invite them to the hotel for a show-round, so that they can see our facilities for themselves. Another responsibility I have is that of arranging sales calls with potential corporate clients, visiting them in their place of work, to explain how our hotel could best host their events.

My job as a whole has given me the opportunity to apply in a real-world situation much of the general, theoretical material that I became acquainted with during my year as a student on the MA Conference Management course. My work brings me into constant contact with different types of customers, and I have learned that I need to approach each type according to their specific needs. In particular, I find that I have quite different emotional relationships with my corporate clients compared with my private clients. Corporate clients usually ask fairly predictable, technical questions about aspects such as ceiling height in the meeting rooms, the event space capacities with different room set-ups, and so on. However, those booking private events are much more variable in terms of what they need. For example, wedding couples usually start the negotiations and conversations very nervously because, this is usually the first time they have had to plan an event and they are usually not professional event organisers. In those cases, I need to handle the clients well by lowering their anxiety levels as well as understanding their specific demands.

The greatest pleasure that I get from my job is supervising how everything goes on the actual day of the event. That's when I have to work very hard in order to deliver all of the details of the event as discussed with the client. This includes everything from setting up the event space in the agreed configuration to ensuring that the food and beverage is exactly as it should be. The biggest source of pleasure for me on those days is seeing that my clients are entirely satisfied. That makes me realise that all my hard work has been worthwhile.

References

BECA (2015) The value of business events to Australia. Business Events Council of Australia.

Beech, J., Kaiser, S. and Kaspar, R. (eds) (2014) *The Business of Events Management*, Boston, MA: Pearson Education.

Cameron, G. T. and McCollum, T. (1993) Competing corporate cultures: A multi-method, cultural analysis of the role of internal communication. *Journal of Public Relations Research* 5: 217–250.

Corbin Ball Associates (2009) Strategic meetings management program implementation and idea guide. Corbin Ball Associates.

CWT/The BTN Group (2016) Driving success in strategic meetings management. Carlson Wagonlit Travel/The BTN Group.

Dimanche, F., Walcher, A., Dogra, S. and Dunton-Tinnus, C. (2010) Integration of corporate travel and meetings management. Association of Corporate Travel Executives.

Fenich, G. G. (2016) *Meetings, Expositions, Events & Conventions: An introduction to the industry,* New Jersey: Prentice Hall.

Forret, M. L. and Dougherty, T. W. (2001) Correlates of networking behaviour for managerial and professional employees. *Group & Organisation Management* 26(3): 283–311.

GBTA Foundation (2015) Meetings, events and travel programs: Consolidation drivers and barriers. Global Business Travel Association.

Geimer, J. L., Leach, D. J., DeSimone, J. A., Rogelberg, S. G. and Warr, P. B. (2015) Meetings at work: Perceived effectiveness and recommended improvements. *Journal of Business Research* 68(9): 2015–2026.

Getz, D. (2013) Event tourism: Concepts, international case studies, and research. Cognizant Communication Corporation.

Gillette, F. J. and Gillette, M. C. (2014) Destination management companies: How they work. International Society of Meeting Planners.

Hoyle, L. H. (2002) *Event Marketing – How to Successfully Promote Events, Festivals, Conventions and Expositions,* New York: John Wiley & Sons.

Iwamoto, K. (Ed.) (2011) *Strategic Meetings Management Handbook: From theory to practice,* Westport, CT: Easton Studio Press.

Jackson, P. (1987) *Corporate Communication for Managers*, London: Pitman.

Mantei, M. M., Baecker, R. M., Sellen, A. J., Buxton, W. A., Milligan, T. and Wellman, B. (1991) Experiences in the use of a media space, in Proceedings of the SIGCHI Conference on Human Factors in Computing Systems, April: 203–208.

Marr, S. (2011) Applying 'work process knowledge' to visitor attractions venues. *International Journal of Event and Festival Management* 2(2): 151–169.

McCabe, V., Poole, B., Weeks, P. and Leiper, N. (2000) *The Business and Management of Conventions*, Melbourne: John Wiley & Sons.

Muehlmeier, C. (2014) Effective meeting prep – how to sharpen your meeting objective. Available at: http://teamings.com/blog/how-to-sharpen-your-meeting-objective/.

Pincus, J. D., Robert, A. P. R., Rayfield, A. P. R. and De Bonis, J. N. (1991) Transforming CEOs into chief communications officers. *Public Relations Journal* 47(11): 22–27.

Rogelberg, S. G., Scott, C. and Kello, J. (2007) The science and fiction of meetings. *MIT Sloan Management Review* 48(2): 18.

Rogers, T. and Davidson, R. (2016) *Marketing Destinations and Venues for Conferences, Conventions and Business Events,* Oxford: Routledge.

Shone, A. (2014) Conference management – an introduction to conference and convention management. Conference Direct Publications.

UK CAMS (2015) The UK conference and meetings survey 2015. Available at: http://www.ukcams.org.uk.

Van Riel, C. B. M. (1995) *Principles of Corporate Communications,* London: Prentice Hall.

Van Weele, A. J. (2010) *Purchasing and Supply Chain Management: Analysis, strategy, planning and practice.* Cengage Learning EMEA.

Welch, M. and Jackson, P. R. (2007) Rethinking internal communication: A stakeholder approach. *Corporate Communications: An International Journal* 12(2): 177–198.

Zhu, R. and Argo, J. J. (2013) Exploring the impact of various shaped seating arrangements on persuasion. *Journal of Consumer Research* 40(2): 336–349.

3 Association conferences

Chapter objectives

On completion of this chapter the reader should be able to:

- Understand the principal activities of associations.
- Identify the distinguishing characteristics of association conferences.
- Understand the bidding process as an element of destination selection for association conferences.
- Understand the roles of the various stakeholders involved in the planning and execution of association conferences.

The countless different associations, clubs, federations and societies that exist throughout the world constitute a major segment of demand in the business events market. Association conferences are among the largest meetings held throughout the world and those of the longest duration, making them a source of considerable financial benefits to the destinations in which they are held. Before focusing on the distinguishing features of association conferences and how they are planned, this chapter begins by examining the roles and activities of these organisations.

The role of associations

Definitions

Most associations are not-for-profit, membership organisations that primarily exist to serve the interests of their members, all of whom share a common field of activity, such as a profession, a trade, or an interest in a particular cause or hobby, for example. In this chapter, the focus will be on the events held by professional and trade associations – organisations directly connected with the members' employment or economic activity. Gatherings of people whose common interest is largely unconnected with their occupation will be covered in Chapter 4.

Merton (1958:50) defines a professional association as: 'an organisation of practitioners who judge one another as professionally competent and who have banded together to perform social functions which they cannot perform in their separate capacity as individuals'. In the case of professional associations, the members are individuals working in the same profession, such as dentistry, teaching or zookeeping. The membership of trade organisations usually consists of companies operating in a particular industry, such as the hotel sector or the motor industry. The roles and activities of both trade and professional associations are similar and their ultimate goals are generally to promote the economic activities of their members, to ensure that they uphold ethical practices in the exercising of their occupation, and to support the advancement of their industry as a whole.

In this way, associations seek not only to further the interests of the individuals engaged in a particular profession or trade, but also to serve the public interest by maintaining and enforcing standards of training and ethics in their field of work. In some professions, it is compulsory to be a member of the relevant professional body; in others, it is not. This usually depends on whether or not the profession requires practitioners to have a 'licence to practise', some form of certification, or to be listed on a professional register in order to undertake that particular activity. For example, in the UK, doctors must be members of the British Medical Association in order to legally exercise their profession.

Associations operate at various geographical scales, from the local level to the global, and it is possible for individuals or companies to be members of several associations at different geographical levels. A newly graduated archaeologist based in Ireland, for instance, could join the Association of Young Irish Archaeologists while at the same time being a member of the European Association of Archaeologists as well as the World Archaeological Congress, the body representing practising archaeologists worldwide. International or national associations with large memberships – which is typically the case for professional associations – often have regional or local chapters to which their members also belong.

It is difficult to estimate with any accuracy the total number of associations, clubs, federations and societies that are in existence around the world. Particularly at the local level, many such organisations are small in terms of membership and ephemeral in terms of their lifespan. Easier to measure, due to their greater visibility and longevity, are the international associations. The *Yearbook of the Union of International Associations* (UIA, 2018) lists over 37,500 active international organisations from 300 countries and territories, with approximately 1,200 new organisations being added to that total each year. New associations are constantly created as a result of the emergence of newly recognised professions, such as acupuncturists and mediators, and the creation of new specialisations within established professions, for instance collaborative lawyers. In addition, new associations may also be created as a result of mergers of two or more existing organisations in order to pool their resources or to avoid duplication of activities and competition for members. An example of this is found in the UK, where the National Association of Jewellers was formed in 2015 through the unification of the British Jewellers' Association and the National Association of Goldsmiths, to create greater industry collaboration and benefits for members through strategic unity. Occasionally, dormant associations may be reactivated due to new threats to their field of activity. For instance, after more than a decade of inaction, the Florida Amusement Machine Association was reactivated as the Amusement Machine Owners Association of Florida in the wake of proposed changes in the state's gambling statutes that would have adversely affected certain redemption amusement games.

The management structures of associations vary as widely as the size of the membership of such organisations. Rogers and Davidson (2016) note that the management and administration of associations may be undertaken either by volunteer staff drawn from the association's own membership or, particularly in the case of large organisations, by full-time salaried staff based in the association's headquarters. However, in the past few decades a growing number of associations have chosen an alternative means of running their affairs – the use of association management companies (AMCs). AMCs are for-profit organisations staffed by skilled professionals who provide management expertise and specialised administrative services to associations in an efficient, cost-effective manner. They work from centralised office premises that serve as their clients' (the associations') headquarters, eliminating the need for those associations to invest in their own office accommodation and staff. When the AMC manages all of the activities of the association, this is known as a full-service management agreement. An alternative system is for associations to outsource only some administrative functions to AMCs, as and when the need arises. Outsourced services may include strategic planning; membership development; public affairs and lobbying; statistical research; and marketing and communication services.

Before analysing the range of activities carried out by associations, it is useful to briefly consider their historical development.

Historical background

Human beings have always had a tendency to congregate, talk among themselves, and advocate for their causes. Associations are one manifestation of this markedly human habit. Vollmer and Mills (1966) trace the origins of some of the earliest trade associations to 16th-century England and the formation of craft guilds to protect both the interests of groups of merchants and individual artisans such as shoemakers, apothecaries or candle makers. Guilds provided training in specific skills and established rules for wages and hours of work. Three centuries later, during the Industrial Revolution, many new trade associations were established as new occupations were created by the impact of industrialisation on working practices. Later, as the industrialised nations became increasingly urbanised, many professional associations were founded, including those representing medicine, law and accounting, which were created specifically to develop and enforce common standards of practice. Some of the world's oldest professional associations were formed in the second half of the 19th century and at the beginning of the 20th century. For example, the American Society of Civil Engineers was created in 1852; the Society of Accountants in Edinburgh and the Institute of Accountants and Actuaries in Glasgow were founded in 1853; and the Professional Golfers Association (Great Britain and Ireland) was founded in 1901. The rise of the professions and the development of associations are inextricably linked. Indeed, Friedman and Phillips (2004:187) maintain that associations are 'an essential component of professionalism', providing the identity necessary for workers to gain standing in their field. The link between associations and the process of professionalisation is clearly illustrated in the example of Lanosga's (2015) history of the professionalisation of journalism in the US, which began in the late 19th century. By the turn of the 20th century, journalism was well on its way to becoming a distinct occupation with its own patterns of behaviour.

> This move toward professionalisation included the establishment of trade associations such as the American Society of Newspaper Editors (ASNE) in 1922, the adoption of journalistic codes of ethics, the founding of journalism schools such as Columbia and the creation of trade magazines such as Quill, which began publishing in 1912.
>
> (Lanosga, 2015:957)

Association activities

In the modern era, one of the principal activities of most professional and trade associations is the holding of a conference – usually on an annual basis. But while such events are the natural focus of this chapter, the other activities of associations that associations undertake on behalf of their members are also worthy of mention here. These include managing public relations for the field (such as providing a spokesperson to represent its members' views on a particular matter); collecting and publishing statistics on the industry or profession – some of which may be made available to members only; advising members on technological or management issues; promoting research; publishing trade/professional journals or magazines; monitoring regulations relevant to the field; and lobbying government on their members' behalf.

The lobbying or advocacy activities of associations are designed to represent members' interests with lawmakers and policy influencers regarding legislative or regulatory proposals that could affect the activities of the membership. For instance, in 2011, the UK Automatic Vending Association successfully lobbied the British government to delay the introduction of the new 5p and 10p coins until the following year, thus allowing their members more time to update the coin mechanisms in their vending machines. It was estimated that this represented a saving of £16.8m to the vending industry (Vending International, 2011). In the US, professional associations allocate approximately 5 per cent of their total annual expenditures to providing information to Congress as part of their lobbying role (Reference for Business, n.d.).

Activities that associations carry out in the public interest are generally aimed at the maintenance of standards, and most commonly include: setting and assessing professional examinations; sponsoring quality and certification standards; issuing a code of conduct to guide the professional behaviour of members, so that the public can be assured of being treated properly; dealing with complaints against professionals; and implementing disciplinary procedures.

Hager (2014) categorises the various activities of associations in terms of the different personal reasons that motivate individual members to engage in their professional associations. He divides these into *public* engagement motivations – the *collective* benefits of association membership – and *private* engagement motivations. Public engagement motivations include the promotion of the profession/trade and increasing the public's awareness of its contributions so that it becomes a recognised and established field. Hager notes that this could include such image mechanisms as establishing and promoting a code of ethics; and lobbying on behalf of the interests of the field, including the collective membership and those served by them. The private engagement motivations are those which benefit the member as an individual. For example, professionals may join their associations for social and recreational activities and the opportunity to form friendships with other members. But more important to many members are the occupational advantages – help with job searches (through job postings), providing professional contacts, and improving members' economic conditions. Finally, Hager mentions the informational advantages that may motivate individuals to join an association. These include newsletters, journals and data services, but it is broadly accepted that associations' events are the key information services valued by most members. McCabe et al. (2000) list the events most commonly held by associations as professional updates and seminars, networking meetings, training and development programmes, as well as the annual or biannual conferences that will be the principal focus of this chapter. It is generally agreed that such events represent the most important tools at the disposal of associations in their mission to educate their members and improve professional standards in their field.

But the significance of association conferences extends beyond their information dissemination and educational role. According to ICCA (2009:3), each association conference

> plays a massively significant role in the life of that organisation: it is typically the only time when a large proportion of the members of the association physically gather together, the only time when the association is at the front of the minds of those individuals for an extended period, the only time when the association attains a concrete form and when its unique culture can be directly experienced.

In the next section, the special attributes of association conferences as business events will be analysed.

The distinguishing characteristics of association conferences

It is impossible to measure the number of association conferences that are held each year, particularly at the level of local and regional events. However, the conferences of international associations, being fewer and more visible, are somewhat easier to quantify. According to ICCA (2016), 12,212 rotating international association conferences took place in 2016, a record number captured in ICCA's annual snapshot of meetings data, with 136 additional conferences compared to the previous year. These figures indicate a doubling of the number of association meetings in a decade, from just under 6,000 in 2006 to over 12,000 in 2016.

In terms of size, budget, duration and complexity there are significant variations in the associations conference sector of business events. Meetings of local associations such as Rotary clubs may attract only a dozen or so attendees, meeting in a local restaurant for a few hours. But international associations in particular can attract vast numbers of delegates to their events. For example, the annual conferences of the European Society of Cardiology, whose members are medical professionals specialising in cardiovascular diseases, are regularly attended by over 30,000 delegates. These five-day events provide the delegates from all over Europe and beyond with an invaluable opportunity to meet and exchange ideas and information on new challenges and new techniques related to the field of cardiovascular medicine (Davidson and Hyde, 2014). Nevertheless, association conferences of this size represent only a small proportion of all association conferences. According to data published by the Union of International Associations, three-quarters of all international association meetings held between 2002 and 2017 had fewer than 500 participants; one quarter of them had fewer than 100 participants; and only 2 per cent had more than 5,000 participants (UIA 2017).

But in terms of meetings in general at which attendance runs into the high hundreds or even thousands of delegates, the vast majority of such events are association conferences. By way of contrast, corporate events of this size are relatively rare – the ASOS case study in Chapter 2 being a notable exception.

Size notwithstanding, association conferences generally have a number of important characteristics in common, according to ICCA (2013), which are discussed in the following sections.

Regularity

Most association conferences are held at regular intervals, most often annually or in alternate years. The frequency at which they are held is generally specified in the association's by-laws and regulations. In recent years, the trend has been for associations to adapt their regulations in order to hold conferences more often, as the pace at which new knowledge is being generated in many fields of activity has accelerated to the point whereby triennial or even biennial meetings are too infrequent to keep their members up to date with developments and innovations in their profession or trade. Both the International Society on Thrombosis and Haemostasis and the World Association for Medical Law Congress case studies in this chapter illustrate this trend.

Rotation

With the exception of the meetings of local organisations, association conferences rarely return to the same destination within a short time span. Rather, they change the location of their conference each time it is held. This is known as rotation. Associations operating at the national level rotate their conferences throughout the country in which the organisation and most of its members are based. For example, The Art of English, a national conference for English and literacy educators in Australia, is held in a different state or territory each year. The annual conference, run jointly by the Australian Literacy Educators' Association and the Australian Association for the Teaching of English, has followed this rotation pattern since 2017:

2017 – Tasmania; 2018 – Western Australia; 2019 – Victoria; 2020 – New South Wales; 2021 – Queensland; 2022 – Northern Territory; 2023 – Australian Capital Territory.

For international associations, with a global membership, the conferences usually rotate between continents. A typical example of this tendency is the biennial global congress of the aforementioned International Society on Thrombosis and Haemostasis, which has used the following rotation schedule:

2011 – Kyoto, Japan; 2013 – Amsterdam, The Netherlands; 2015 – Toronto, Canada; 2017 – Berlin, Germany; 2019 – Melbourne, Australia.

There are two principal reasons for the use of rotation for the selection of association conference destinations:

- To more evenly distribute the cost and effort involved in travelling to conferences among the members of the association. Rotating the conference between different destinations means that although in some years a member may have to travel relatively far in order to attend, in other years the conference may be held much closer to his/her place of residence, thereby reducing the time spent and expense incurred in attending the event.
- To make attendance more attractive to members. It is widely acknowledged that the opportunity to visit a new destination is a key motivating factor behind conference attendance. As members are under no obligation to attend their associations' events, associations must make their conferences as attractive as possible; and changing destinations for each edition of their events is an effective way of adding to their appeal.

This use of rotation as a system for choosing association conference destinations sets the association meetings market apart from the corporate events sector, where a company may well hold its meetings in the same destination and the same venue for several years – sometimes because it has negotiated a multi-year deal with the venue, earning it a more favourable rate in return for using the same venue more than once.

Long lead-times

In the international association conferences sector of business events, it is not unusual to find lead-times of 5 years or more. The sheer size of such events in terms of numbers of participants, which can run into the thousands, necessitates a long period of planning, beginning with the selection of the destination and the conference venue, as discussed below. Rogers explains that, in addition to the enormous amount of work involved in organising a large association conference, another reason for long lead-times is the more urgent need to secure the booking of a venue large enough for major events of this type: 'This is because there is a much more limited choice of venue ... Some of the larger, purpose-built conference/convention centres have provisional reservations 10 years ahead, from association conference organisers' (Rogers, 2008:43). As there are only a few venues in Europe with sufficient capacity to host a major event such as the annual congress of the European Society of Cardiology, with over 30,000 delegates, that association must choose the destinations for its conference at least four years ahead, in order to be certain of sourcing a suitable venue.

It is already evident that the above distinguishing characteristics of association events clearly distinguish them from the corporate meetings analysed in Chapter 2. A number of other contrasts between the two sectors have been highlighted by several authors (for example, Rogers, 2013; Toh et al., 2007; Oppermann, 1996) in their comparisons of association conferences with corporate meetings. The most significant contrasts identified between the two types of business events are discussed below.

Duration

While most corporate meetings last 1–2 days, association conferences typically last 2 days or more. In general, the greater the geographic spread of participants, the longer the average duration of the conference. While the conferences of local associations may last no longer than a typical corporate meeting, the annual or biannual conferences of international associations with a global membership can be four days or longer. There are several reasons for this: delegates flying long distances to attend such events need time to recover from the journey; they expect more in terms of content from the educational programme, to give them a reasonable return on their investment in terms of time and money; and they may also expect the conference programme to include significant sightseeing opportunities such as excursions, in order to let them experience the destination, particularly if they are visiting it for the first time.

Venues

While most corporate events are held in hotels (or, increasingly, in unusual venues), the venues most commonly used for association conferences are purpose-built or converted/repurposed conference centres, in the case of large national and international associations, where the sheer numbers of participants call for high-capacity venues. In the case of smaller association events, civic/municipal venues and academic venues may also be used. Shone (1998) attributes the propensity for associations to choose these latter two types of venue to the fact that the association meetings market is likely to be more price-sensitive. Rogers (2013), however, notes that in the US market, major resort hotels are often large enough to accommodate association events attracting many hundreds of participants. He also points out that where hotels are used by associations, in any country, such events often take place over the weekend, when hotels tend to offer more competitive rates. The SMERF segment of demand in particular often makes weekend bookings in hotels as venues for their conferences, as will be seen in Chapter 4.

Destination selection

In comparison with the relatively straightforward systems of venue and destination selection found in the corporate meetings sector, the process of choosing a destination for a major international association conference can be extremely complex and often takes place over a prolonged period of months or even years. For large associations in particular, a selection committee is usually created to make the decision as to where the organisation's annual conferences will be held. The system is analogous in many ways to the Candidature Process for the Olympic Games and Winter Olympic Games, with cities competing to host the event through a formal bidding process.

In the associations meetings sector, the process generally begins with an appeal to either members or destinations to submit detailed bid proposals, also known as tenders, and ends with the signing of a letter of agreement between the association and the successful destination. A summary of the basic destination selection process is shown in Figure 3.1.

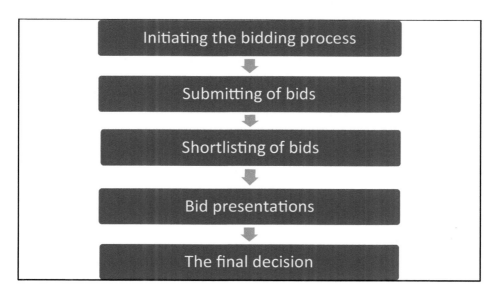

Figure 3.1
The destination selection process for association conferences

The details of a typical decision-making process for choosing the destination for a large association conference may be summarised as follows.

Initiating the bidding process

The association issues a *call for proposals* to host the association's conference for the next 'open year' (the next year for which no destination has yet been chosen). Such a call may be sent out directly to members of the association if local members are required to be the formal bidders. If this is not a requirement, the call for proposals may be issued to destinations (with city convention bureaus often coordinating the bid – see Chapter 10) or directly to individual suppliers, such as conference centres. As a set of guidelines or rules, a *bid manual* is usually made available to interested parties, specifying the required format and content of the bid document that they should submit.

The type of content usually relates to the destination itself and to the design of the conference in question:

- *The destination:* details of the proposed venue, specifying how the conference will be accommodated in the venue; accommodation information, offering a range of suitable accommodation to meet the needs of all potential delegates; transport information, including comprehensive details of incoming air routes and transport within the destination – including any public transport passes; tourist information, including a programme of pre- and post-conference tour opportunities; social programme, including proposed reception and banqueting venues; accompanying guest programme.
- *The conference:* a draft conference programme including proposed sessions and speakers; draft budget proposals; details of the destination's history or experience in the relevant sector, together with any relevant local research or cutting-edge science or technology which might strengthen the bid; details of the local representatives hosting the bid, as well as details of any eminent local, national or international figures supporting the bid. It is always an advantage to have written letters of support from these contacts. They may be local dignitaries, leading scientists or academics, government ministers or indeed royal patrons – any support of this nature is always highly regarded.

Submitting of bids

Bids must be submitted within the period specified in the bid manual. The bid document is traditionally compiled in a folder that is branded for the destination and conveys strong images and messages of the city throughout. However, according to ICCA (2014), a growing number of associations are changing from a system of printed bid materials to online bid documents, which is both cost-effective and more flexible, as bid documents can be more easily updated following negotiations or feedback.

Shortlisting of bids

Following evaluations of submitted bids by association staff, the selection committee, and any external intermediaries employed by the association to organise the conference, a shortlist is decided upon and announced. At this stage, detailed site inspections of the shortlisted destinations may be undertaken by representatives from the association and the conference organisers. The purpose of these visits is to investigate at first-hand the extent to which the city and its facilities will meet the association's requirements for its conference.

Bid presentations

Shortlisted bids are generally followed by formal presentations, typically made by one or more members of the association who are based in the destination and who are members of the bidding team. This is an extremely important element of the bidding process and represents a key factor in the final selection of the winning proposal. Convention Edinburgh, the business events destination marketing organisation of the Scottish capital, estimates that over 70 per cent of conference destinations are chosen based on the quality of the local member's bid presentation (Convention Edinburgh, n.d.). Such presentations are usually made to the representatives of the association who are responsible for choosing the winning candidate and take the form of an oral presentation based upon the material contained in the bid documents that have already been circulated. Bid presentations focus on the benefits of the proposal, essentially summarising the key elements in the document, and are followed by a comprehensive question-and-answer session.

The final decision

Once the representatives of the association responsible for choosing the winning destination have made their choice, their decision is announced, and a contract or letter of agreement is drawn up and signed by both parties. Feedback is often provided to the unsuccessful bidders, with an explanation of the rationale behind the association's conference destination selection – and, occasionally, a recommendation to bid for subsequent conferences of the association.

The International Society on Thrombosis and Haemostasis case study in this chapter provides an example of how a destination was selected as the result of a bidding process.

Financial philosophy

A further major difference between the corporate market and the association market for conferences is that while for the corporate sector conferences and meetings represent a *cost* to the company – something to be underwritten from the company's financial resources in the same way that salaries, rents, computer equipment, etc. are funded – for associations, conferences normally represent an important *source* of funds.

Rogers and Davidson (2016:7) explain that:

> this is because – again, in contrast to the corporate meetings market – [associations] charge their members for attending events. Many associations depend on the income from their annual conference to pay for many of the ongoing costs of running the association – staff salaries, headquarters rental, and so on.

A major challenge for most associations is that while most of them charge subscriptions for annual membership, these alone are rarely enough to fund all of the association's activities. On average, less than half of the revenues in the associations sector as a whole are derived from member subscriptions and fees (PARN, 2017). Profits from associations' conferences and other events such as training seminars are therefore required to close the funding gap. A key objective of most association conferences is therefore to provide a surplus of funds that can be used to support other activities of the association throughout the year.

However, the task of using conferences as a means of fundraising for associations is made more challenging due to two more key differences between corporate meetings and association events: firstly, while attendance at corporate meetings is generally mandatory for employees, being regarded as an essential element of their work, in the association meetings sector, attendance is entirely voluntary – members have the choice between participating or not participating; secondly, if they do attend the conferences of their associations, most delegates pay their own conference expenses, unlike participants in corporate meetings, whose costs are covered by their employers. One of the consequences of these two factors is highlighted by McCabe et al. (2000:58):

> Associations have to lure members to their events – in other words, the events need to be marketed. This means that programmes have to be structured to be of interest to members; sites selected for events should encourage people to attend; and partner and social programmes need to be designed to ensure that attendance at the convention or meeting is an attractive option.

One consequence of the fact that most participants at association conferences are self-funding is that such events are often more price-sensitive than corporate meetings. These issues will be revisited in the section of this chapter that examines the planning and execution of association conferences.

Legal status

For the vast majority of associations, there is a legal necessity to hold a conference for their members at regular intervals, as such an obligation is usually specified in the association's by-laws or constitution. This characteristic of association conferences makes the holding of such events more predictable than, for example, corporate meetings, which are more vulnerable to cancellation or postponement due to factors such as the state of the company's finances or of the economy in general. The level of attendance at association conferences may fluctuate according to economic or security factors, for instance, in the wider market environment, but actual cancellations or postponements are extremely rare.

Leisure component

The final contrast between corporate meetings and association conferences concerns the extent to which leisure components feature in both types of business event. While the leisure element of most corporate meetings, particularly those lasting only one day or less, is generally minimal, the longer average duration of association conferences allows more time for the *social programme* – planned leisure components such as excursions and cultural events. These elements not only let delegates enjoy the destination but also provide them with opportunities for valuable networking. The tendency for participants to use association conference attendance for *bleisure* purposes – the combining of business trips with leisure activities – is a further distinguishing characteristic of such events. This is manifested in two principal ways.

Extending the business trip for leisure reasons

Found far more frequently in association conference attendance than in corporate meeting participation is the phenomenon of delegates spending extra time at the destination before or after the event, to effectively turn the business trip into a short holiday. Many surveys of delegate behaviour highlight this factor. For example, the Finland Convention Bureau's research into (predominantly) association conference attendance in their country found that while the conferences in the survey lasted on average 3.5 days, the average stay of delegates in Finland was 5.4 days (FCB, 2017). Similarly, a survey of international delegates attending association events in New Zealand showed that they stayed in that country on average 1.6 more nights than the days they spent in attending the event. In addition to the 946,596 event days estimated to have occurred in the 2013 calendar year, 93,505 additional nights were generated as delegates extended their trips for leisure-related purposes (MBIE, 2014). While delegates extending their trips in this way may not necessarily spend their extra days in the actual conference destination, these *bleisure* activities clearly represent a significant incremental economic contribution to tourism and hospitality industries. Research by Davidson (2002) indicated that, as might be expected, the level of incidence of leisure extensions of this type increased in direct proportion to the distance between the delegate's home and the conference destination, with long-haul delegates being those most likely to spend extra days there. First-time visitors to the conference destination were also found to be more likely than average to extend their trip for leisure purposes.

Bringing guests

While participants' spouses/partners, other family members or even friends are, generally speaking, uninvited and unwelcome at most corporate meetings, they are far more often found to be accompanying delegates attending association conferences. Research findings by Hayat et al. (2014), for example, revealed that the degree to which family and friends accompany delegates was a significant difference between association and corporate events. The Finland Convention Bureau's survey offered insights into the incidence of this phenomenon in that country, showing that 25 per cent of the respondents (who were mainly association conference delegates) brought an accompanying person on their trip. The majority of them had only one accompanying person with them, and delegates from Asia were found to be the most likely cohort to have brought a guest with them (FCB, 2017).

It is reasonable to expect that there is a great deal of overlap between those delegates who extend their trips for leisure and those who bring family members or friends with them, as accompanied participants may be more motivated to spend time exploring the destination and may equally be under less pressure to return home immediately at the end of the conference.

Most of the distinguishing characteristics of association conferences discussed in this section have implications for how such events should be planned in order to maximise the extent to which they are successful. The next section of this chapter analyses best practice in this activity.

Planning association conferences

Association conference planning

As noted towards the beginning of this chapter, associations carry out a broad range of activities on behalf of their members, of which events planning is but one among many. Attracting and retaining members, lobbying, publishing reports and newsletters and financial management of the association are examples of the many other activities that must be undertaken on an ongoing basis by associations.

Nevertheless, associations' events, in particular their annual or biennial conferences, are among the most visible of their activities and one of the most significant ways in which they directly add value to their members. A wide range of individuals and organisations may assume or be given responsibility for the planning of an association's conferences, often reflecting the organisation's chosen management model.

For small, local or regional associations, the conference organisers may be unpaid volunteers drawn from the association's membership. Shone emphasises the challenges that this can pose for venue managers and their sales teams, not only in identifying who, in an association, is likely to be responsible for organising conferences, but also in dealing with organisers who may lack the necessary experience and skills: 'in consequence, sales teams may have to exert greater efforts to ensure an association conference goes smoothly' (Shone, 1998:28). For associations with full-time salaried personnel, one or more members of staff may be in charge of planning those organisations' events; and many large associations have their own in-house events department with responsibility for organising their meetings. In the case of associations that have placed some or all of their activities in the hands of an AMC, one of the key tasks frequently undertaken by AMCs is the planning of the association's conferences and other member events. In order to carry out this key function effectively, AMCs must employ staff with extensive experience and knowledge of all of the elements of association conference planning.

But associations may choose to use an alternative system for the organising of their conference: the outsourcing of all or many of the conference planning functions to professional conference organisers (PCOs) – in much the same way as companies can employ intermediaries to plan their events, as described in the previous chapter. PCOs are independent, specialist meeting planners who work on a consultancy basis, being temporarily hired by associations to organise a specific event or series of events. In return for a fee, they offer a comprehensive range of services, including: venue selection, booking and liaison; reservation and management of delegate overnight accommodation; conference programme planning, speaker selection and briefing; delegate registrations; delegates' travel arrangements; social events; and managing the budget for meetings. Many PCOs are members of the International Association of Professional Congress Organisers (https://www.iapco.org/). One such member, Bertrand Joehr, Managing Director of Symporg SA, based in Geneva, describes the role of PCOs as follows:

> PCOs are specialists. We know what details to focus on, which ideas work and which don't, what technical aspects are crucial, how much the participants drink, eat, the time needed to fill-in [sic] a 1,500-seat plenary room, etc. Our clients know what topics they have to deal with, which keynote speakers have to be invited … we take care of the rest.
>
> (IAPCO, 2018)

PCOs usually cooperate closely with the association's local organising committee and may also procure the services of a destination management company to assist them with local arrangements for the conference. However, associations generally maintain direct control over their conference's educational programme, or *scientific programme* as it is also known. This means that the association's in-house staff or volunteers retain responsibility for designing the content of the educational programme – the overall theme of the event and the individual topics to be covered – as well as the selection and management of speakers.

The choice of whether to manage conferences in-house or to outsource them to PCOs and similar intermediaries is a complex matter for associations, with advantages and disadvantages claimed for both systems. Two consecutive issues of the trade publication *Association Meetings International* debated the pros and cons of associations using intermediaries to organise their conferences, and a summary of the cases made by both sides of the argument is presented in Table 3.1.

Most probably, there is no one solution that is the most appropriate for every association. For some associations, PCOs clearly add value by acting as a professional extension to the association's in-house management team, while others opt for retaining full control of how their events are planned. Other associations may choose a middle path of outsourcing only certain conference-related functions, such as venue finding or delegate registration, to specialist intermediaries.

Some of the key tasks involved in planning association conferences will now be considered.

Table 3.1 Comparison of PCO and in-house management of association conferences

Using PCOs	In-house
PCOs have valuable specialised skills and knowledge of key factors that are particularly important for conferences that rotate destinations: cultural differences, local regulations, tax implications, etc.	No loss of association revenue, as there is no intermediary to be paid for their services.
PCOs can use their buying power and negotiating skills to cut the costs of the conferences they organise.	The association remains in complete control of its finances.
PCOs that serve a number of different associations bring their extended experience of factors such as technology and marketing, gained from working on other clients' events.	The association managers show more commitment to the conference, because, as its producers, they have a personal stake in it.
Outsourcing the conference management function to a PCO enables the association managers to focus on their primary core tasks, working in the interests of their members.	In-house management of the conference means that it can be designed in a unique manner that reflects the personality and personal touch of the association.
During the conference, the association managers are entirely free to engage with their members, without having to manage the logistical aspects of the event.	

Source: Based on AMI (2017a); AMI (2017b).

The conference programme

As previously established earlier in this chapter, it is not mandatory for members to attend association events. Many professionals are members of multiple associations, and they have a choice as to which, if any, of their associations' conferences they attend. As attendance levels play a vital role in the success of association conferences, not least due to conferences' role in raising vital revenue, those events must be designed in such a way as to attract as many members as possible. An accurate understanding of members' motivations to attend conferences is therefore essential and that understanding should guide associations in the planning of their events, beginning with the design of the conference programme.

Most association conference programmes comprise three elements:

1   The education/scientific programme – the formal, scheduled and controlled element of the event
2   The semi-formal element – one-to-one meetings, one-to-few meetings (closed, side-meetings, which are not part of the formal programme but nevertheless extremely useful for delegates)
3   The social programme – breaks, excursions, gala dinners, etc., during which informal exchanges and networking take place between delegates

The findings of researchers such as Price (1993), Rittichainuwat et al. (2001) and Fjelstul et al. (2010) suggest that education and networking are the most powerful motivators behind association conference attendance. The Decision to Attend Study of the Centre for Association Leadership (ASAE, 2017) showed that, for delegates, the most important drivers of the decision to attend association conferences was education, with 92 per cent of those surveyed agreeing on this; while 67 per cent emphasised the role played by education as a means of staying abreast of developments in their industry or profession.

Research conducted by Tourism Australia (2016) found that members' decision on whether or not to attend association conferences was closely linked to their assessment of the conference programme in terms of the papers being presented, keynote speakers and whether respected peers were attending. In that study, 'Quality programme content' was mentioned by 72 per cent of those surveyed as a factor essential to attendance; and 'Opportunities for professional networking' was mentioned by 61 per cent.

The importance of planning an attractive educational programme means that association conference organisers must critically examine their chosen themes and topics as well as the 'pulling power' of their speakers in order to ensure that they offer clear relevance and value for potential delegates. Session titles should be intriguing and challenging, and speakers should be well known in their field or respected opinion leaders, with up-to-date content and the ability to communicate it well to an audience. The social programme of the conference should contain valuable opportunities for networking, employing techniques that ensure that delegates make new contacts, for example by using a seating plan to allocate them to specific places at tables for the conference's gala dinner.

While designing a conference programme that holds great appeal for delegates is a clear priority for organisers, they also must take into account the needs of another stakeholder group – those people accompanying their spouses and partners to the conference but not attending the event themselves, known as accompanying persons (APs), or, sometimes, 'plus-ones'. Adding a guest programme of activities for APs which runs in parallel with the main conference programme can be an effective way of enhancing the overall appeal of the event. In years gone by, before it was as common for women to follow professional careers as it is today, guest programmes tended to be designed with the assumption that the vast majority of the APs would be female. So activities such as shopping, cake-decorating classes and fashion shows were common elements of such programmes. But Davidson (2002:25) notes that 'guest programmes are no longer the exclusive domain of wives or even women, as evidenced in the change in nomenclature from "wives' programmes" or "ladies' programmes" to "spouse programmes", then to the current "guest programmes"'.

But conference organisers designing guest programmes should consider other factors apart from the gender of the APs. Many of the APs are busy professional people in their own right, and they are seeking guest programmes of substance that will enrich their lives, contribute to their personal development and help them cope better with the stresses of modern life. Crocker (1999) offers a number of insights into the design of effective guest programmes, encouraging planners to familiarise themselves, in advance, with the ages, degree of sophistication and socioeconomic profiles of the APs, as well as their experience of earlier guest programmes. She advises organisers to:

- Appeal to the group's interests (antiques, churches …).
- Make it educational (classes on local culture/cuisine, investments, retirement planning …).
- Make it relevant (for example, dovetail it with the topic of the actual conference).
- Spotlight the destination (emphasise the things the city is famous for).
- Enrich the basics (do something for the group that they could not do on their own).
- Be gender-inclusive (choose topics of mutual interest, such as financial planning).

The conference destination

Following closely behind the conference programme as a motivator for association conference attendance is the destination in which the conference is held. While conference planners need to take into consideration practical matters such as there being sufficient venue space at the destination, they must also bear in mind the preferences of the potential delegates in terms of what they are seeking from the places in which the conferences are held.

Confirming the findings of previous studies by Price (1993) and Oppermann (1995), the research of Rittichainuwat et al. (2001) identified 'traveling to desirable places' as being among the top five major conference motivations, together with 'education', 'networking', 'interesting conference programmes' and 'career enhancement'. More recently, a study by the Centre for Association Leadership (ASAE, 2017) showed that, for delegates, the conference destination was the second most important motivating factor for delegates, mentioned by 78 per cent of those surveyed, with 20–30 per cent citing the destination as being the deciding factor for them – the crucial factor determining their decision on whether or not to attend.

Some insights as to what makes a destination attractive for delegates may be gleaned from Fjelstul et al. (2010), who cite evidence from a number of studies including Oppermann (1995): entertainment, scenery, accessibility; Ngamson and Beck (2000): climate and cultural attractions; and Lee and Park (2002): hotel facilities, safety, tourism outlets and accessibility. The ASAE 2017 survey highlighted the following factors as being the most important to the attractiveness of destinations, for association conference participants (ASAE, 2017):

89 per cent – transportation options

89 per cent – appears safe

86 per cent – appears clean

86 per cent – wayfinding/ease of getting around

85 per cent – welcoming, friendly people

78 per cent – service-oriented front-line

75 per cent – variety of things to see and do

69 per cent – easy to access local information

It is evident that, in their choice of conference destination, associations need to take into account the extent to which the delegates will find it attractive to visit. In its study of the 'path to purchase' behaviour of potential international association conference delegates, Tourism Australia concluded that while there is a wide range of motivations for choosing to attend an international conference, the majority of delegates are seeking a balance between destination appeal and conference content: 'for most respondents, the ideal association conference combines work and leisure. Striking a balance between opportunities to connect with peers and to discover the destination is the optimal scenario' (Tourism Australia, 2016:2). The same source identified three categories of delegates, differentiated by their attitude towards the importance of destinations in their decision to attend association conferences, as shown in Figure 3.2.

It is clear that, for potential conference attendees, destination appeal is judged on a broad range of factors. But a major challenge for international associations in particular is the fact that the appeal of any destination is not a static quality. For example, one factor that emerges repeatedly in the academic and practitioner research into this key element of association conference planning is the safety and security of the destination. Henderson's (2007:545) research into the impact of social disturbances on events led her to conclude that

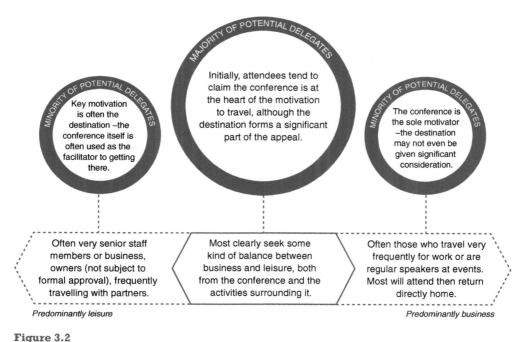

Figure 3.2
The relative importance of conference destinations in delegates' motivation to attend
Source: Tourism Australia (2016).

broader environmental, economic, political and social conditions contribute to the attractiveness of a [conference destination]. Should the overall reputation of the wider area or nation be severely tarnished in some way, particularly pertaining to stability, this could lead to lost business.

Naturally, no association would deliberately choose to hold its conference in an unstable and dangerous location; but the long lead-times that are necessary in this sector of business events mean that the degree of security can deteriorate considerably between the time the destination was chosen and the actual date of the conference. For example, the Middle East and Africa Duty Free Association was obliged to cancel the 2017 edition of its conference, which was due to be held in Beirut, due to the resurgence of political uncertainty in the region. The 400 delegates who had registered for the event were informed that it would be rescheduled and relocated (Pentol, 2017). The conference was eventually held in Dubai at the beginning of 2018, but with the intention of returning to Beirut at a future date.

The image of any destination may also alter significantly due to political changes that suddenly and unexpectedly reduce its appeal for delegates. An example of this phenomenon was seen in 2016, with the passing of a controversial anti-LGBT (lesbian, gay, bisexual, transgender) law by the North Carolina state government, overturning an ordinance previously passed by Charlotte's city council to extend rights to that city's LGBT community. The negative impact of the new law (named HB2) soon became apparent as associations and other groups expressed their opposition to it by cancelling their events in the state in order to register their protests. The CEO of the convention bureau with responsibility for promoting Raleigh, the state capital, as a conference destination said:

> We continue to receive concerns from definite and tentative groups regarding HB2. We also have a great deal of concern about those groups that were going to consider Raleigh and North Carolina but have now taken us off their list of consideration due to the bill.

He reported that the Greater Raleigh Convention Centre had lost six firm bookings worth an estimated US$2.4m, and that a further 16 bookings worth an estimated US$44m were also in jeopardy. One example of the direct impact of the legislation was the relocation of the Community Transportation Association of America conference which was due to bring 1,000 people to Raleigh in June 2018, but was moved to Baltimore instead, resulting in a loss of US$1.7m for North Carolina (Kasperkevic, 2016).

The conference budget

With most participants at association conferences being self-funded, the affordability of any such event is a key consideration for planners, who must take into account the ability of their association's members to pay for attendance, while at the same time, the necessity for the event to make a profit. The actual cost of attending association conferences has been identified as a key inhibitor by several authors including Henderson (2007), Fjelstul et al. (2010) and Rittichainuwat et al. (2001).

Nevertheless, it is difficult to generalise regarding the extent to which association conferences are price-sensitive, as this depends on a number of factors including the spending power of the delegates and their expectations in terms of comfort and services. For instance, it is reasonable to speculate that there was a considerable difference in the per-delegate cost of attending the 2018 conference of the American Judges Association held at a luxury resort in Hawaii and the fee for participating in the Australian Catholic Students Association's annual conference held that same year in an academic venue, Queen's College in Melbourne.

But as these examples suggest, one way of controlling costs is to select destinations and venues where prices are commensurate with the association members' ability to pay. The use of civic/municipal venues, academic venues, and hotels offering lower rates at weekends is widespread for associations with less than lavish budgets for their events.

As well as controlling costs in this way, association conference planners also have at their disposal two further means of boosting their events budgets and therefore the probability that they will make a profit from their conferences: sponsorship and exhibitions.

Sponsorship

A technique commonly used by planners is to earn additional revenue by recruiting sponsors for association conferences. A successful marriage between the association and the sponsors can and should add value to all stakeholders. One condition of this win-win arrangement is that the organiser of the conference targets potential sponsors who are appropriate to the theme of their event. For example, it would rarely be suitable for alcohol or tobacco companies to sponsor the conferences of medical associations.

The list of components of association conferences that can be funded through sponsors' financial support is long and varied: Wi-Fi in the venue, delegates' conference bags, name badges and lanyards, lunches, coffee breaks, the gala dinner, travel expenses and accommodation for the conference's keynote speaker, bursaries or travel grants for early-career researchers or for delegates from emerging nations. And conference sponsorship does not always involve the sponsors donating money; they might equally donate goods (conference bags or bottles of wine for the gala dinner, for example) or provide their services (such as audio-visual or registration) for free. From their side, sponsors' motivation for sponsoring conferences usually derives from their wish to reach their target market(s) and to get increased exposure for their brands though access to key opinion leaders and delegates.

The search for sponsorship generally begins with the conference organisers creating a sponsorship proposition – a document that shows potential sponsors how their sponsorship of the conference would benefit their companies or organisations. It should include the theme of the conference and an estimate of the number of delegates expected to attend the conference, as well as their demographic profiles, as the value of the potential benefits to the sponsors is usually influenced by the number of people who will learn about the sponsorship, the prominence it is given at the conference, and how well the characteristics of the expected participants align with the market segments targeted by the sponsor. While large conferences are clearly attractive to sponsors, it is not necessarily the case that smaller events lack appeal for them. In an interview for the Exo Ordo blog, Nicole Giacomini, a PCO based in Lausanne, said 'It depends on the quality of delegates. We organise the annual meeting of Swiss neonatologists. Even if there are only 100 or 200 participants, they're the best of Switzerland. So, for sponsors, it's the place to be' (McCurry, 2017).

The proposition should also include details of the sponsorship packages on offer, in particular, specific examples of how sponsors will be given exposure at the conference. This might include the sponsor's name and logo appearing on a plaque or banner, on volunteers' T-shirts, on the conference website, or on the conference mobile app. The package might also include the opportunity for a representative from the sponsoring company to address the delegates at the conference. If this is limited to, for example, a five-minute speech at the dinner being sponsored by the company, this is, generally speaking, uncontroversial. But requests from a potential sponsor to make a longer presentation at the conference itself must be treated with caution, as such speeches can quickly turn into promotional product presentations, which may provoke a negative reaction from delegates.

The advantages of conference sponsorship, for associations, are considerable, particularly in helping them manage their budgets for such events. But organisers must always ensure that any sponsorship involvement in the programme is balanced with event integrity and delegate appeal.

Exhibitions

Exhibition fees – the income generated from the sale of exhibition stands or space – represent another useful source of additional revenue for association conferences. Many such events host an exhibition in the same venue, where goods and services linked to the theme of the conference are displayed on exhibitors' stands. The two main reasons for integrating an exhibition into a conference are that, firstly, exhibitors get access to well-targeted delegate contacts and the opportunity to meet key prospective customers; and, secondly, that the presence of an exhibition running in parallel with the conference gives delegates an additional reason for attending, as they can update themselves on the latest products, technologies and services relevant to their occupation. Depending on the size of the conference, the *quantity* of visitors to the exhibition may be considerably less than the numbers found at stand-alone trade shows of the type discussed in Chapter 8 of this book; but the *quality* of visitors is often superior, as they tend to be specialists with a clear interest in their specific profession or trade.

Nevertheless, in order to attract exhibitors and ensure that they get a satisfactory return on their investment, conference organisers must make efforts to be honest with them concerning their chances of making sales during the event. They should, for example: be frank about the opportunities that exhibitors will have to interact with delegates – exhibitors must understand that the conference will almost certainly take priority and that there will be long periods when there is no traffic in the exhibition; organisers must also strive to achieve a balance between the number of exhibitors and the number of delegates – one stand for every ten delegates is generally considered to be about right; and they should provide generous time in the conference programme for coffee breaks and buffet lunches served in, or close to, the exhibition area.

Hoyle (2002) emphasises that when marketing exhibition space, conference organisers should ensure that they provide potential exhibitors with the following information:

- History and growth of the show and its buyer attendance.
- Testimonials from exhibitors and buyers attesting to the economic viability of the event.
- Credibility and purpose of the sponsoring organisation.
- Qualifying the association's buyer base, through quantitative and qualitative research. While numbers of people in the aisles are important, the exhibitors will want to know the profile of the potential buyers: their professional level, spending authority, specific product interests and needs, and demographic characteristics.
- Defining the role of exhibitors in the overall conference programme. Are they welcome to attend seminars, social events and general sessions? These are important opportunities for additional customer contact and value-added benefits of supporting the organisation. Many association exhibitors who are relegated to restricted convention participation react negatively to the 'second-class citizen' syndrome.
- Preparation of a clear and concise exhibitor prospectus, outlining rules, regulations and other requirements of exhibiting.

Organisers can also assist exhibitors in the following ways: by providing delegates with a good-quality, informative programme with details of each exhibitor and their products/ services; by holding combined social events for exhibitors and delegates; by making public announcements about specific activities taking place in the exhibition zone; and by locating a meeting place, such as a cyber-cafe, in the centre of the exhibition area. Associations with large conference teams may even appoint a member of staff with special responsibility for looking after exhibitors' needs.

For associations, a key advantage of attracting revenue from sponsors and exhibitors for their conferences is that it is usually paid early in the conference planning cycle, unlike delegates' registration fees which tend to be paid later, occasionally just before the conference begins. This is of considerable help to the organisers' cashflow, as funds are required long in advance of the conference in order to pay for items such as the deposit on the venue, the building of the conference website, the developing of the conference app and marketing material.

Marketing the conference

Associations have a number of target markets for their conferences, including members, exhibitors and sponsors. In the final section of this chapter, the focus is on how associations endeavour to attract delegates to their events, with the emphasis on promotional activities.

The marketing objectives

Given the voluntary nature of association conference attendance, the effective marketing of such events is essential in ensuring their success in terms of attracting a sizeable proportion of the membership and ensuring the profitability of the conference. And persuading members to participate in their associations' conferences is particularly challenging when there are many other competing demands on their financial resources or on their free time. At such times, it can be particularly difficult for potential delegates to justify the investment of time and money in conference participation.

Moreover, the objectives of association conference marketing extend beyond the generating of registrations, to encompass the building of engagement with and excitement for the event itself. All of these objectives can be achieved, in part, by identifying a strong and convincing *theme* for the conference that encapsulates the value and content of the event into one statement and strategy – and differentiates it from previous editions. For associations, some of the most successful themes chosen for conferences reflect key changes in the trade or profession or challenges faced by practitioners. For example, the theme chosen for the 2018 conference of the British Institute of Energy Economics was *Innovation and Disruption: the energy sector in transition*. In the same year, the theme of the European Educational Research Association conference was *Inclusion and Exclusion, Resources for Educational Research?*, chosen to focus the presentations and discussions on the challenges faced by educators in a continent witnessing the arrival of increasing numbers of migrants and refugees.

Promotional activities

Promotion is essential in generating potential delegates' awareness of any association event, their desire to participate, and their conviction that the investment of their time and money will yield sufficient benefits for them to justify the outlay.

Used correctly, promotional marketing messages have the power to inspire potential delegates to register for the conference, but in order to do so, they must clearly convey the selected theme for the event as well as the multiple benefits of attending the event. These will certainly give prominence to the unique educational programmes that the event will offer the delegates, as for most of them this will be the primary motivating factor. Hoyle (2002:126) offers the following advice regarding the marketing of the educational benefits:

> emphasis should be placed on the credibility of presenters, in particular, their bios, academic and professional credentials and designations, and a capsule of the content to be presented. 'This is what you will learn' is the benefit that must be carried in the message.

In addition to the educational benefits, other factors such as the opportunities for networking and career enhancement, as well as the prospect of experiencing the attractions of a desirable location should also be emphasised in promotional messages.

A variety of channels, both online and offline, may be used to transmit the marketing messages. Online channels include email, websites and social media, while offline channels include printed brochures and advertising or press release coverage in magazines and other periodicals. But whichever channels are used, the association's mailing lists are an indispensable tool in reaching out to potential delegates. Membership databases and the contact details of previous participants generally form the core of such mailing lists, but it is essential that associations not only constantly update these lists but also remain vigilant in their search for new audiences for their promotional messages. Indeed, they need to ensure that the promotion of their events extends beyond the actual association to the entire trade or profession.

Furthermore, Kovaleski (2011) stresses that, for maximum effectiveness, rather than sending out the same messages to all of the people on their mailing lists, associations should adapt their messages to each target segment, speaking to each of them in a different voice, about different issues. He identifies six different segments of potential attendees:

- Members who do not usually attend meetings
- New members
- Members who often attend
- Former members
- Non-member professionals near the meeting site
- Non-members in overlapping industries.

According to Kovaleski, once the principal segments have been identified, a different communication strategy should be created for each one. For example, for those who often attend the conferences, the message might be what is new in the forthcoming event. For new members, many of whom will be young professionals, the message might be delivered with a different voice and a clearer focus on career advancement.

In terms of the timing of sending out promotional messages about the association's conference, a multi-level approach to marketing the event, using a staggered system of communication, is generally followed. A typical schedule for communicating information about the conference is shown in Table 3.2.

Table 3.2 Association conference communications schedule

8–10 months ahead	'Save the date' or 'teaser' messages
4–6 months ahead	A brochure outlining the preliminary conference programme
2–4 months ahead	Final brochure, with final programme outline, a list of speakers and a registration form
2–6 weeks ahead	A reminder message

Source: Based on Silvers (2004).

Commentators generally agree that, for association conferences, marketing should begin well in advance of the events themselves. For example, in her blog, MacKinnon (2016) advocates that associations should

> as a general rule of thumb, begin marketing next year's conference ... before this year's event is over. If your conference has an app, encourage all participants to download it and send out 'save the date' push notifications before this year's event is over. Extend special rates to this year's participants if they register for next year's event by a specified deadline.

Any important deadlines should be emphasised in the marketing communications, for example time limits for submitting proposals for delivering presentations at the conference, or for qualifying for discounted, early-bird registration fees.

Social media

Most associations have enthusiastically incorporated social media into the promotion of their conferences. For example, many have launched a LinkedIn or Facebook group to engage members throughout the year and to market the association's events. Interest in association events can be generated on these platforms in a number of ways, such as the hosting of Twitter chats, and pre-event webinars featuring keynote speakers and the facilitators of the breakout sessions. First-time delegates can be given an idea of what to expect at a forthcoming conference by the creating of a Q&A (questions-and-answers) blog post based on interviews with a few of the previous year's delegates, during which they discuss what they are looking forward to in the upcoming event and share their best networking tips, and advice of how to get the most out of the conference. The online audience can be expanded by the association asking speakers, exhibitors and sponsors to promote the conference on their own social media channels, websites and blogs. In fact, some associations formalise this as a requirement by including promotion clauses in speaker, exhibitor and sponsor contracts.

The conference website

The conference website is the key information source used by potential and actual delegates to guide them throughout the process of deciding whether or not to attend, and, if they do decide in favour of participating, to provide them with all of the details they require to prepare for their trip and their experience of the event. As a resource that is consulted at several points in the decision-making process, website content should inspire, inform and facilitate the decision to attend. As a bare minimum, it should provide information on the delegates attending, key speakers, networking opportunities and programme content. The conference website should be visually appealing and offer a 'one-stop shop' for delegates to plan their trip. This includes information on the destination itself, including accommodation, public transport and attractions.

However, research undertaken by Tourism Australia (2016) found that the expectation that conference websites would provide all the information required by the delegates is often not met, with many respondents in their survey expressing the view that conference websites currently fail to deliver. More specifically, many of them felt that the websites focused on the conference programme but provided little or no information about the destination, and why the delegate should choose to attend the event there. Links to further information sources on the destination were also felt to be lacking even though they were highly desirable.

Offline channels of communication

In common with most organisations, associations have found email to be a boon for their communications with members, being faster, cheaper and greener than traditional outreach methods. But some are finding that with members now being bombarded with email, they are seeing lower opening rates, meaning that a proportion of their promotional messages are not being read by recipients.

The challenge of communication clutter – or overload – was confirmed as a key challenge by the president of the American Society of Association Executives (Naylor.com, 2014) who advised associations to do more to prioritise their messages. Regarding messages relating to their events, he expressed the opinion that

> we tend to over-communicate when the additional communication isn't likely to yield results. For instance, we tend to promote our meetings too much. If someone hasn't responded to your [repeated] earlier emails about an upcoming meeting, then sending them another 10 emails about the same meeting isn't going to help attendance and could backfire on you.

Kovalski (2011) maintains that in certain cases, the pendulum is swinging back to 'old school' promotional tactics such as direct mail and telemarketing. Direct mail, for instance, has higher open or view rates than email, and while it is more expensive, it is more effective than email, according to the author. He cites the example of the Electronic Retailing Association in Arlington, Virginia, whose vice president of marketing always sees an upsurge in conference registrations immediately following the telemarketing campaign he targets to executives.

Just as it is advisable for associations to segment their promotional messages, they should also segment the communication method. While some members may prefer brochures and direct mail, others, perhaps young professionals, may favour e-communications.

The final chapter of this book further explores the use of technology by the business events industry in general.

Chapter summary

This chapter began with a history of professional and trade associations and a review of the principal activities that they provide for their members including advice, education, lobbying and the collecting and publishing of data. The distinguishing characteristics of association conferences were analysed, many of which contrast with the features of corporate meetings discussed in Chapter 2, in terms of size, duration, lead-times, marketing and the destination selecting process. The system of bidding to win association conferences was described, followed by an analysis of best practice in association conference planning and marketing and the different roles of the various stakeholders involved in these processes.

CASE STUDY 3.1: THE INTERNATIONAL SOCIETY ON THROMBOSIS AND HAEMOSTASIS IN MONTPELLIER

ISTH in Montpellier

The International Society on Thrombosis and Haemostasis

Thrombosis refers to abnormal, possibly life-threatening blood clots that form in arteries or veins. Worldwide, one in four people die from causes related to this disease. Haemostasis is the process that causes bleeding to stop through coagulation – the first crucial stage of wound healing.

Founded in 1969, the International Society on Thrombosis and Haemostasis (ISTH) is a global not-for-profit membership organisation advancing the understanding, prevention, diagnosis and treatment of thrombotic and bleeding disorders. The Society is dedicated to transformative scientific discoveries and clinical practices, the development of young professionals and the education of physicians, scientists and allied health professionals worldwide. Today, the ISTH is the leading thrombosis- and haemostasis-related professional organisation in the world, with more than 5,000 members in 94 countries.

The ISTH holds two principal types of meeting: a biennial global Congress and meetings of its Scientific and Standardisation Committee (SSC), which are held at least annually, either in conjunction with an ISTH Congress or as a free-standing meeting. In May 2016, the ISTH Council announced the Society's decision to hold its global Congress on an annual basis from 2020 onwards, due to the increasingly rapid advances in science as well as in laboratory technology and treatment approaches, and the greater need for global collaboration, knowledge exchange and education.

ISTH's SSC is a permanent committee of the Society. It has independent authority over its scientific programme and reports to the ISTH Council. It is made up of 20 topical sub-committees in addition to two standing committees and its own executive committee. Through collaborations with related organisations, the SSC develops and recommends standards relevant to the fields of thrombosis and haemostasis. Many of the standards developed by ISTH's SSC are adopted by the World Health Organization (WHO) as International Standards.

Meetings of the ISTH SSC bring together the best experts in the world and are a living platform for clinical and scientific working groups that provide the foundation for future breakthroughs.

Recent meetings of the SSC:

2010: Cairo, Egypt

2011: Kyoto, Japan (in conjunction with the XXIII ISTH Congress)

2012: Liverpool, England

2013: Amsterdam, The Netherlands (in conjunction with the XXIV ISTH Congress)

2014: Milwaukee, USA

2015: Toronto, Canada (in conjunction with the XXV ISTH Congress)

2016: Montpellier, France

2017: Berlin, Germany (in conjunction with the XXVI ISTH Congress)

Montpellier as a conference destination

With a population of over 434,000, Montpellier is France's eighth largest city and is situated in the south of that country, close to the Mediterranean coast. Each year, Montpellier hosts over 500 business events – representing some 1.5 million attendees, exhibitors and visitors. In 2016 the ICCA rankings showed Montpellier to be France's third most popular destination for international association conferences, after Paris and Nice.

The Montpellier Convention Bureau

The Montpellier Convention Bureau's (MCB) (http://www.bureaudescongres-montpellier.com/Montpellier-Convention-Bureau) team of seven meetings industry professionals act as a key interlocutor representing Montpellier as a business events destination. It receives its funding from the Montpellier Méditerranée Métropole, an intercommunal structure, centred on the city of Montpellier as well as its network of 95 partners. In return for their support for the convention bureau, the partners receive a number of benefits. These include: increased visibility through all the MCB's online and offline publications, additional exposure in the national and international business events press, the MCB's dedicated newsletters, and Requests for Proposals from qualified enquiries. The MCB organises two meetings each year to report back to its partners on its activities, to inform them about major business events coming to Montpellier and to share with them the MCB's global strategy to promote Montpellier worldwide as a conference destination.

The MCB is an active member of national and international networks of major conference cities, including the CFTAR (Club Français du Tourisme d'Affaires Réceptif), France Congrès and ICCA (International Congress and Convention Association).

The services they offer to conference organisers include:

- Assistance with Requests for Proposals, by orientating organisers towards the most suitable local partners
- Organising inspection visits
- Acting as an intermediary between organisers and the Convention Bureau's partners as well as with the local authorities
- Promoting forthcoming conferences on the Convention Bureau website, their social networks and at key points in the city.

The International Society on Thrombosis and Haemostasis SSC, in Montpellier 2016

Following ISTH's normal selection process, the Society's Council selected Montpellier as the host city for its 2016 SSC Meeting four years earlier, at the Council meeting in Liverpool (2012). It had been Montpellier's third attempt to bring an SSC meeting to the southern French city. Montpellier was one of six destinations that bid for the 2016 meeting, and the city was shortlisted with two other destinations for final presentation to the ISTH Council in Liverpool.

There were two principal partners responsible for putting together Montpellier's bid for the 2016 SSC Meeting: Enjoy Montpellier, the company responsible for managing the four principal venues in the city – Le Corum, the Sud de France Arena, the Exhibition Centre and Le Zénith Sud (Enjoy Montpellier is now known as Montpellier Events – www. montpellier-events.com/) – and the ISTH's Local Organising Committee, which comprised ISTH members based in France as well as one from Geneva. At the time when this bid was made, the Montpellier Convention Bureau had not yet been established, but the

Sales and Marketing service of the local Tourist Board was already working with Enjoy Montpellier, and in that capacity helped to organise the site inspections of the city for the ISTH and then to put together a Montpellier Méditerranée Métropole welcome pack for ISTH members.

Having learned from previous unsuccessful attempts, the two principal partners put forward a strong bid, highlighting the geo-strategic importance of France in the fields of thrombosis and haemostasis as well as clearly communicating the local hosts' strong scientific/educational/legacy vision, which included a strong outreach element involving not only practitioners in Southern Europe but also in North Africa and the wider Mediterranean. These aspects of the bid were instrumental in leading to its success.

The Local Organising Committee also paid special attention to committing itself to the changing requirements of the ISTH (greater central organisation from the Society's headquarters in the US; certain programme format changes and of course the increasingly strict adherence to compliance rules and regulations).

What were the advantages and challenges of holding the 2016 SSC Meeting in Montpellier? Thomas Reiser, Executive Director of the ISTH explains them here:

> The size and location of Montpellier provided a number of benefits but also some challenges. Montpellier is a very attractive destination from a tourism point of view. In addition, it is home to one of the oldest universities and medical faculties in Europe and has a strong tradition in medicine and science. It also provides – particularly for an event the size of the ISTH's SSC meetings – an excellent fit, as it is a smaller city with a convention centre right at its heart, which allows participants to fully enjoy both the congress and the city, get together outside the official functions of the meeting and combine the serious sides of learning and scientific exchange with networking and an authentic experience in an inspiring environment.
>
> With the help of the Montpellier Convention Bureau, the ISTH strongly communicated all of these advantages in its promotion for the meeting, finding the right balance between the tourism opportunities and the 'business' aspects of the event, in order not to contravene the increasingly strict compliance rules that govern scientific conferences.
>
> One challenge arose from the fact that Montpellier is not ideally connected in terms of international or even domestic French flights, which made it less than straightforward for some of the participants to get there. They came from over 70 countries, many of which were outside Europe. Apart from longer travel times, it also resulted in higher airfares for some. ISTH and the local organisers countered this by strongly communicating the excellent train connections, which many participants ultimately took advantage of.

Another issue was that while the city offered sufficient hotel rooms for the size of the Congress, the room block had to be spread over many different properties. While for the individual traveller, this was less of an issue, it created challenges for the Society's sponsors and exhibitors who prefer to book their groups into one property. This challenge was resolved by the Society and the appointed PCO, Colloquium (www.colloquium-group.com/), by strategically selecting the properties offered in the official room block and by strong customer management. This particular challenge turned into a benefit as it made it attractive for individuals and supporters to utilise the official room block.

Another challenge to be overcome was the layout of the convention centre, Le Corum (www.montpellier-events.com/en/The-Corum/Presentation). Located ideally in the middle of the city, it was purpose-built but did not quite fully fit the exact requirements of the Society/Meeting. It was also not quite as modern as some other venues, particularly in first-tier cities. However, through excellent teamwork, several site visits, and close collaboration with the Convention Bureau, the centre staff and Colloquium (who had already managed many meetings in that venue over the years – which was one of the main decision criteria for using them), the programme format of the meeting and exhibition was adapted to best fit the venue, resulting in an excellent experience for attendees and sponsors alike. The venue ultimately provided an ideal environment for participants and exhibitors/sponsors to interact, network, discuss and elevate their own professional performance and that of the field as a whole.

SSC 2016 turned out to be the most successful ISTH SSC meeting to date, with over 2,000 attendees, the highest number of abstracts and most exhibitors at an SSC meeting – a >20 per cent increase in all aspects over the previous high mark. Montpellier offered an outstanding mix of Mediterranean hospitality, professionalism and an effective environment for scientific discourse.

The programme consisted of a wide range of plenary sessions, education sessions and sessions of each of the subcommittees of the SSC. For early-career professionals, the Society offered a 'Trainee Day' on the morning before the start of the official meeting, as well as masterclasses throughout the event. Overall, the conference offered a fascinating debate on current diagnostic and therapeutic challenges and opportunities. The discussions on new approaches and standards will enable the medical community to better work together on solutions centred on the patient.

Having overcome the challenges (and no meeting is without its challenges), most of which the attendees and exhibitors/sponsors were entirely unaware of, the ISTH SSC 2016 meeting received some of the best feedback we have ever had from participants and sponsors alike, in terms of the experience they had, the value the meeting provided, and how it benefited their work.

That is ultimately what we all strive for!

CASE STUDY 3.2: THE 23RD WORLD CONGRESS OF MEDICAL LAW IN BAKU

WAML in Baku

The World Association for Medical Law

The World Association for Medical Law (WAML) (http://wafml.memberlodge.org/) was established in 1967 by Professor R. Dierkens from the Faculty of Law at Ghent State University, whose work in the 1960s focused on multicultural issues related to medical law. His vision was to establish a professional association where medical and legal professionals could devote their energies to this new discipline.

The WAML's main objectives are:

- to encourage the study and discussion of problems concerning medical law, and their possible solution in ways that are beneficial to humanity;
- to promote the study of the consequences of new developments in medicine and related sciences;
- to address any matters that involve issues of medical and health law;
- to provide political leadership and advocacy for medical law professionals;
- to encourage research and development in medical law and related fields.

The WAML is affiliated with the WHO (World Health Organization), UNESCO, ICC (International Criminal Court) and a number of national professional medico-legal organisations. The association's headquarters are located in Los Angeles, California.

The World Congress of Medical Law

Meetings of the WAML have the title World Congress of Medical Law (WCML), and they play a key role in helping the association achieve its objectives through enabling the presentation and discussion of learned papers and the exploration of the results and recommendations of scientific enquiries. At WCML gatherings, participants are able to:

1   encourage the study and discussion of current problems in health law and bioethics as well as possible solutions, in ways that benefit humanity and advance human dignity;
2   promote the study of the legislative, jurisprudential and ethical consequences of changes and developments in medicine, healthcare and related sciences;
3   address sundry matters involving issues of medical law, bioethics and legal medicine.

The first WCML was held in Ghent, Belgium in 1967. Between 1967 and 1994, WAML congresses were held in three-yearly intervals, and then biennially, and – starting from 2014 – annually, at the destinations shown below:

Israel (1994)

South Africa (1996)

Hungary (1998)

Finland (2000)

The Netherlands (2002)

Australia (2004)

France (2006)

China (2008)

Croatia (2010)

Brazil (2012)

Indonesia (2014)

Portugal (2015)

USA (2016)

Azerbaijan (2017)

Israel (2018)

Japan (2019)

Canada (2020)

The locations for the World Congresses of Medical Law are chosen by the WAML's Board of Governors. Destination proposals may come from individual cities, countries, national associations, the Executive Committee and Board members. Initially, the Executive Committee considers all proposals, before they are discussed at the meetings of the Board of Governors, where the final decision is taken.

The 23rd World Congress of Medical Law in Baku

The 23rd WCML was held in Baku, Azerbaijan from 10–13 July 2017. This was the first time in its 50-year history that the conference had been held in the heart of Eurasia, at the eastern edge of Europe and on the cusp of Central Asia.

In the JW Marriott Absheron Baku Hotel, on the shore of the Caspian Sea, the world's largest lake, about 400 leading specialists in medical law, bioethics and legal medicine from 50 different countries met to exchange their experience and knowledge of the latest developments in medical law. The largest group of delegates, with 48 participants, came from Russia, while there were over 30 delegates from Azerbaijan and from China. Delegations of between 10 and 22 participants came from the USA, Turkey, Israel, Belgium, Kazakhstan, Indonesia and Saudi Arabia.

The 2017 Congress, with the theme of 'Medical Law, Bioethics and Multiculturalism', was remarkable for two main reasons, beyond the large number of delegates. First, the event marked the 50th anniversary of the founding of the WAML. Second, this was also a very important event for Azerbaijan because it was the first scientific world congress on that scale ever held in the country, enhancing Azerbaijan's reputation as a destination for international business events. All costs regarding travel, accommodation, tours, visas, venue and Congress registration were paid by the WAML and Congress participants.

Advanced promotion of the Congress – attendance-building

Beginning in October 2016, the WAML administration staff regularly updated the Congress website (http://wafml.memberlodge.org/event-332060). A Call for Abstracts was announced, with a deadline of 1 March 2017. Other information placed on the website included welcome messages from the Programme Chair, Prof. Dr Vugar Mammadov, in English, Azerbaijani and Russian. The programme brochure, poster and Save the Date card were prepared and printed in these three languages. A short movie, *Welcome to Azerbaijan,* photographs of the venue, pre- and post-Congress tours packages and instructions about discounted hotel registration were also placed on the Congress website.

The 23rd WCML was also promoted through presentations given by the Programme Chair, and distribution of printed materials at the following national and international conferences during the period October 2016 to March 2017:

- The Silk Road Forensic Consortium Symposium at Xi'an Jiaotong University and Xi'an International Studies Universities, China
- Two Russian national conferences in Moscow: the National Conference of Medical Law of the Russian Federation and the National Congress of Forensic Medicine of the Russian Federation
- The 2nd Saudi International Conference of Forensic Medicine and Sciences in Riyadh, Saudi Arabia
- The 1st International Conference on Medical Law in Astana, Kazakhstan with delegates from the CIS (Commonwealth of Independent States) nations

Four committees were formed to carry out the preparations for the Congress: the Honorable Scientific Committee, consisting of 16 members; the International Scientific Committee of 28 members; the Local Scientific Committee of 16 members; and the Abstracts Review Committee. In April 2017 the Award Committee was formed from three WAML Governors and two members of International and Local Committees to select from about 35 papers the winners of the Young Scientists Competition for the best oral presentation and best poster. A key partner for the 2017 Congress was Azerbaijan's leading destination management company, PASHA Travel. The DMC was responsible for visa arrangements, flight tickets and accommodation out of the venue, hotel transfers and pre- and post-Congress tours. PASHA Travel prepared five optional pre- and post-Congress tours that were advertised on the website. The objective of these tours was to help participants discover the history, culture and tourist attractions of Baku and Azerbaijan, such as the Old City and Shirvanshah Palace, UNESCO heritage Gobustan and Ateshgah as well as tours to regions such as the Caspian Sea, Gabala, Sheki, Lahij, Quba, Khinaliq and the oldest Jewish settlements of Krasnaya Sloboda. More than 250 participants took these tours. About 150 e-visas were issued to delegates visiting the Congress from most countries of the world, with the required documents being submitted online to the DMC, who then arranged for the visas to be issued as PDF files.

The official carrier of the Congress was Turkish Airlines, who provided discounts of up to 20 per cent on flights for participants at the WCML.

The congress programme

10 July

In the evening, a Welcome Reception for registered Congress participants was held in the Marriott Hotel, where delegates met old friends and became acquainted with new colleagues.

11 July

On Day 1 of the Congress, all keynote speeches and oral presentations were given in the main ballroom of the Marriott Hotel. There were three keynote speeches and an Opening Ceremony with a talk by Prof. Henry Lee, 'New Concepts in Criminal Investigation' and a presentation by Dr Suha Al-Fehaid, 'The Medieval Contribution of Arabs and Muslims in Forensic Medicine and Toxicology'. In the Opening Ceremony, a formal greeting and welcome from the Azerbaijan state was given to the Congress by the Minister of Health of Azerbaijan, Prof. Oqtay Shiraliyev. There was also an award presented to Mrs Mehriban Aliyeva, the First Vice-President of Azerbaijan, UNESCO and ISESCO Goodwill Ambassador, and President of Heydar Aliyev Foundation as recognition of contributions made into the development of Medical Law, Bioethics and Multiculturalism. She was awarded the 'WAML 50th Golden Anniversary Award' and WAML Diploma in acknowledgement of her unique achievements in these fields and in recognition of her enormous efforts in serving to promote multicultural dialogue between different religions and civilisations in order to enhance the spirit of tolerance and strengthen global peace and security.

12 July

On Day 2, oral presentations were given in the hotel ballroom as well as in an adjoining room. Papers were read from 09:00 until 18:30, with moderators keeping presenters to time. There were three sessions on 'Bioethics and Medical Law Education', one session on 'Bioethics, Religion and Multiculturalism' and four sessions on 'Challenges of Medical Law and Legal Medicine in the XXI Century'. In the evening, a gala dinner and award ceremony took place in the Marriott Hotel. The awards were given for best oral and poster presentations at the Congress, as well as for Young Scientist.

13 July

On Day 3, more oral presentations were given, in two rooms. There were three sessions on 'Bioethics and Medical Law Education', three sessions on 'Bioethics, Religion and Multiculturalism', and one session on 'Challenges of Medical Law and Legal Medicine in the XXI Century' as well as a session for poster presenters who gave short platform speeches.

Abstracts of the WCML presentations were published in the *Medicine and Law* Journal, Volume 36, Number 2, printed copies of which were distributed to all participants at the Congress.

IT'S MY JOB
MATHIAS POSCH, PRESIDENT
AND PARTNER, INTERNATIONAL
CONFERENCE SERVICES LTD

When I finished my high school studies, I had a few ideas of what I would eventually want to do in the world of work, but didn't really have a dream career in mind. But growing up in a region of Austria that relies heavily upon tourism, I felt that this would be a good route to think about, so I enrolled in the College for Tourism Management in Innsbruck.

As important as the college was for giving me a good overview of the tourism industry as a whole, I would say that my internship was probably one of the most important parts of my education that year, and definitely one that defined my career. To tell the truth, when choosing where to do my internship, my priority was not so much on the job itself but rather its location. That's why I chose an internship at the San Francisco Visitors and Convention Bureau, as this was a city that I had always wanted to visit. During my internship, I realised that the tourism field was much broader than I had thought and that there were many more opportunities in it than I had previously envisioned. What fascinated me more than anything else was the conference business, as it combined two major interests of mine: my passion for learning new things; and my love of organising and making budgets work. I was fascinated by the sheer variety of groups holding conferences and the potential to get to work with some of the world's best and brightest experts in so many different fields.

When I returned to Austria, I finished my degree and eventually started looking for a job in Vienna. I researched various companies that managed conferences and applied for the one I felt was the leader in the Austrian market – Mondial Congress. After only one interview, I was hired and started work just a few days later. The salary and job title were completely unimportant to me at that point – all I wanted was to get my career started.

At Mondial, I worked hard from day one and soaked up as much knowledge as possible. I never had a problem with self-confidence and as I took on every job that was presented to me, I soon ended up working long hours and on projects that really challenged me – I didn't mind. It filled me with pride that I was given the opportunity to prove myself, and I made it my goal to climb up the career ladder quickly. That's exactly what happened. By proving my value early on, my boss understood my potential and rapidly promoted me so that I ended up being the Head of Operations over a team of about 20 people within just three years. Although this may seem like a rapid progression, it is somewhat normal in the conference industry, which is an excellent platform for people who are diligent and prepared to work hard in order to move up quickly in their careers.

The next big milestone in my life came when I received an offer to change jobs and move to Canada. This prospect represented a huge upheaval for me and at first I was inclined to turn it down as I felt quite happy in Vienna. Part of me, however, was intrigued by the opportunity and felt that it was a great chance to gain some more valuable experience and then perhaps return to Austria 3–4 years later. The position that was offered to me was to take over a PCO company with 11 employees in Vancouver – an interesting and daunting opportunity for someone like me who was still so young and had less than five years' direct experience in the conference industry. But I accepted the job nonetheless. So, after finishing up at my old job, I received my visa in late 2006 and moved to Canada to become Managing Director of International Conference Services (ICS) (http://www.icsevents.com/). ICS has been providing conference, events and incentive programme management solutions for over 40 years, and in that time has built up a varied and international client base that now includes prestigious organisations such as the International Association for the Study of Lung Cancer, the Human Proteome Organisation, and the International Society for Diseases of the Esophagus. Although the company primarily manages association conferences, it also manages online meetings and webinars, which in some cases attract up to 3,000 participants.

Once I started at ICS, through a string of events, I ended up managing the company on my own within the first few months. It was challenging and often extremely frustrating in my first year to not only find my bearings in a new company but to actually lead it, manage and unite a team (where everyone was older than me), win our clients' trust and secure enough new conference business for the years ahead. This was so demanding that there were days when I simply wanted to give up, return to Austria and to a job that I knew and had mastered. My stubbornness and pride, however, wouldn't let me do that. So I decided to work hard, overcome obstacles by facing them head-on and identify areas in the company that needed change, and then make a plan for those changes.

One of the most helpful things that I did during that time was consulting a business coach. He helped me to focus on a long-term strategy for the company and helped me formulate my own ten-year plan. As part of the plan, we defined together a 'Big Hairy Audacious Goal' (BHAG), which was a defined goal for the company that seemed unachievable at the time but was something big to aim for. As much as I found it daunting, that goal gave me the vision and guidance I needed to align the team and everybody else associated with ICS and to get them to focus on the same goals. It was a significant change not only for the company but also for me personally, as it gave me a purpose and a clear roadmap. I became a partner at ICS just a year after I joined, and have since managed the company.

In my career, my hard work and dedication were not always rewarded – there has been a considerable number of setbacks and disappointments (and I am sure that more of those lie ahead) – but in order to succeed in business, as an owner or an employee, I believe that it is essential to have a positive outlook and try to find opportunities where they are sometimes difficult to see. The BHAG that I formalised in 2007 was scary at the time, but it was something that defined my career – I believe that if you're not a little scared, you are not pushing yourself far enough to keep your job interesting. And I am proud to say that we didn't just achieve everything outlined in the ten-year plan but exceeded the BHAG by quite a degree.

Today ICS has more than 60 employees in six offices in North America and Europe, managing meetings in over 30 countries. Most importantly, we have changed our structure to be less of a one-man show and more a company run by a team of young, very engaged professionals who are not just executives of the company, but – like me – its actual owners. Most of the people on the Executive Team started with me at an entry level (one as an intern, another one as my assistant), and hard work, dedication and unquestionable loyalty made them executives and partners in the company that they gave so much to.

I believe strongly in the power of a positive attitude, hard work, dedication and loyalty (to the company/your staff/your clients) and that we are in an industry where these values really matter and can get you anywhere. Eleven years after I started in the company, I am proud to be embarking upon yet another chapter of my career – redefining my role to empower others and focus on the international growth of our company. This is an exciting industry and my path might not be applicable to everyone, but if you take just three things away from my story, those should be: Go for it, push yourself and always find something that excites you in your job.

IT'S MY JOB
SHANI KUPERSHMIDT, MEETING
PLANNER, KENES GROUP

My professional career began when, at 18 years of age, I served for two years as a Foreign Affairs commander with the Intelligence Corps of the Israeli Army. Following my army service, I travelled in Asia, visiting China, Thailand and Nepal, before returning to start my BA in Political Science and Communications at Tel Aviv University. At university, I had my first experience of planning business events when I took part in a fellowship programme, organising a humanitarian aid conference in Tel Aviv for over 60 medical students from all over the world. The conference was a great success and I was fascinated by the adrenaline and excitement I got personally from organising this event. After graduating in 2012, I was looking for a job in the meetings industry when a friend sent me the details of a position with the Kenes Group (http://kenes-group.com/) as a Programme Coordinator. I immediately applied, even though I didn't have much relevant experience – and I got the job! I think they chose me because they saw that I was highly motivated and eager to learn. In addition, I believe I was a good fit for Kenes' company culture: service-oriented, a 'people person' and the ability to pay attention to details.

The Kenes Group is one of the world's leading professional conference organisers, specialising in medical conferences and association management services. Founded in Tel Aviv in 1965, and now headquartered in Geneva, Kenes has hosted over 3,000 conferences in more than 100 cities around the globe, with over 120,000 participants per year. Kenes is the only global PCO dedicated to medical and scientific events and has a team of over 300 professionals in 29 offices on four continents, serving over 120 long-term clients. I am based in Tel Aviv, but travel frequently overseas, for site visits and conferences.

As Programme Coordinator, my job was to create, manage, and implement scientific programmes for conferences. The scientific programme is the core of any medical conference: the professional medical content which consists of lectures, new research presentations and sometimes hands-on workshops. It was also my responsibility to lead client relationships with senior stakeholders at international medical associations. In that role, I act as the main point of contact for the scientific committee and serve as an advisor to help translate the scientific programme's needs and requirements into a feasible plan taking into account all logistical and technical aspects.

Most of my training was 'on the job', and my first conference was for 11,000 participants in Barcelona, the 2014 European Congress of Clinical Microbiology and Infectious Diseases. It was an amazing experience, seeing many months of detailed planning and preparation come to life during the actual event. After working on about ten conferences as a Programme Coordinator during my first 18 months with Kenes, I was ready for my next challenge. I realised that I wanted to be involved more with the logistics and planning aspect of the events. At the time, as the result of an organisational change within Kenes, the position of Meeting Planner was created, and I found myself being promoted to this position. As Meeting Planner I am now responsible for the planning and management of all aspects of the conference:

- Managing conference production and logistics, negotiations with suppliers, pricing, supervision of the conference operational Gantt chart, as well as setting schedules for supporting departments
- Managing the conference budget
- Leading the conference operational team of >10 colleagues
- Managing the conference on-site.

I enjoy working on conference projects because this means that every few months my routine changes, which brings great variety to my job. I love the travelling, visiting new places and meeting new people that comes with managing the conferences on-site.

Some examples of conferences that I planned recently are:

- The 9th International Conference on Advanced Technologies & Treatments for Diabetes, in Milan
- The 34th Annual Meeting of the European Society for Paediatric Infectious Diseases, in Brighton
- The 36th Annual European Society of Regional Anaesthesia and Pain Therapy Congress, in Lugano
- The 9th Congress of the World Federation of Paediatric Intensive & Critical Care Societies, in Singapore.

I sometimes stay a few days longer at the conference destination after the event has ended, to have a short vacation. But I often find that I'm too exhausted for that, because my work is very challenging, both physically and mentally. The four weeks of preparations before the actual conference are very stressful. And then, once on-site my colleagues and I are on our feet for on average 14 hours a day, with early mornings, late nights and social events in the evenings. We walk around the venue constantly, making sure everything is going on as it should. If it's a large venue I can easily walk over 15 kilometres in one day, for five days in a row.

The most challenging part of my job is the stress. This is a very exacting industry, and whenever any report on the world's most stressful jobs is published, we meeting planners are usually right behind firefighters, police officers and pilots. There is enormous pressure to deliver flawlessly these large-scale and long events with complex operations, while meeting deadlines and budgeting goals, and dealing with countless logistical and technological challenges. We also have to take into account many cultural differences. We work all over the world, and planning a conference in Europe is nothing like planning one in Asia or the US. But we need to make sure that no matter where the conference is taking place, our own high standards are met. Working in a stressful environment is just something we get used to – and some people in the business events industry would probably say that it makes them work even better, by keeping them on their toes!

References

AMI (2017a) Look in the mirror. Association Meetings International, October.

AMI (2017b) House rules: PCOs strike back. Association Meetings International, December.

ASAE (2017) Decision to attend study. The Centre for Association Leadership.

Convention Edinburgh (n.d.) Ambassador Programme Conference Organisation. Available at: https://www.conventionedinburgh.com/media/101022/ambassador-programme-toolkit.pdf.

Crocker, M. (1999) Great expectations: No longer can assumptions be made about what your attendees' guests want or even who they are. Meetings & Conventions, June.

Davidson, R. (2002) Leisure extensions to business trips. *Travel and Tourism Analyst*, October.

Davidson, R. and Hyde, A. (2014) *Winning Meetings and Events for Your Venue*, Oxford: Goodfellow Publishers.

FCB (2017) Delegate survey. Finland Convention Bureau.

Friedman, A. and Phillips, M. (2004) Balancing strategy and accountability: A model for the governance of professional associations. *Nonprofit Management & Leadership* 15: 187–204.

Hager, M. A. (2014) Engagement motivations in professional associations. *Nonprofit and Voluntary Sector Quarterly* 43(2): 39–60.

Hayat, A., Severt, K., Breiter, D., Nusair, K. and Okumus, F. (2014) Attributes influencing meeting planners' destination selection: A case of Orlando, Florida. *Event Management* 18(2): 195–205.

Henderson, J. C. (2007) Hosting major meetings and accompanying protestors: Singapore 2006. *Current Issues in Tourism* 10(6): 543–557.

Hoyle, L. H. (2002) *Event Marketing*, New York: Wiley & Sons.

IAPCO (2018) The added value of PCOs. Available at: https://www.iapco.org/app/uploads/2018/04/Boardroom-AM-interviews.pdf.

ICCA (2013) A modern history of international association meetings. International Congress and Convention Association.

ICCA (2014) International association meetings: Bidding and decision-making. International Congress and Convention Association.

ICCA (2016) Statistics report – country & city rankings. International Congress and Convention Association.

Kasperkevic, J. (2016) North Carolina's anti-LGBT law could cost the state millions in lost revenue. *The Guardian*, 19 April. Available at: https://www.theguardian.com/us-news/2016/apr/19/north-carolina-anti-lgbt-law-bathroom-bill-hb2-economic-losses.

Kovaleski, D. (2011) 10 big ideas for marketing your association meetings. *MeetingsNet*, 1 February.

Lanosga, G. (2015) The power of the prize: How an emerging prize culture helped shape journalistic practice and professionalism, 1917–1960. *Journalism* 16(7): 953–967.

Mackinnon, S. (2016) Association event marketing checklist: 8 strategies to market your association. Available at: https://www.eventmobi.com/blog/association-marketing-checklist-8-strategies-market-association/.

McCabe, V., Poole, B., Weeks, P. and Leiper, N. (2000) *The Business and Management of Conventions*, Milton: John Wiley & Sons.

McCurry, D. (2017) Conference sponsorship packages 101. Available at: https://www.exordo.com/blog/conference-sponsorship-packages-101/.

MBIE (2014) Convention delegate survey report. New Zealand Ministry of Business Innovation and Employment.

Merton, R. K. (1958) The functions of the professional association. *American Journal of Nursing* 58(1): 50–54.

Naylor.com (2014) John Graham on mobile, agility and association pay. Available at: https://www.naylor.com/associationadviser/john-graham-mobile-association-careers-advocacy/.

Oppermann, M. (1995) Professional conference attendees' and non-attendees participation decision factors. *Society of Travel and Tourism Educators* 7(1): 25–37.

Oppermann, M. (1996) Convention cities: Images and changing fortunes. *Journal of Tourism Studies* 7(1): 10.

PARN (2017) Financial benchmarking for professional bodies. PARN Global.

Pentol, A. (2017) MEADFA 2017 conference cancelled due to political uncertainty. Available at: https://www.dfnionline.com/latest-news/meadfa-2017-conference-cancelled-due-political-uncertainty-13-11-2017/.

Price, C. (1993) An empirical study of the value of professional association meetings from the perspective of attendees. Unpublished doctoral dissertation, Virginia Polytechnic Institute and State University, Blacksburg.

Reference for Business (n.d.) SIC 8621 professional membership organizations. Available at: http://www.referenceforbusiness.com/industries/Service/Professional-Membership-Organizations.html.

Rittichainuwat, B. N., Beck, J. A. and Lalopa, J. (2001) Understanding motivations, inhibitors, and facilitators of association members in attending international conferences. *Journal of Convention & Exhibition Management* 3(3): 45–62.

Rogers, T. (2013) *Conferences and Conventions: A global industry*, 3rd edn, Oxford: Routledge.

Rogers, T. and Davidson, R. (2016) *Marketing Destinations and Venues for Conferences, Conventions and Business Events,* Oxford: Routledge.

Shone, A. (1998) *The Business of Conferences,* Oxford: Butterworth-Heinemann.

Silvers, J. R. (2004). *Professional Event Coordination,* Hoboken, NJ: John Wiley & Sons.

Toh, R. S., Peterson, D. and Foster, T. N. (2007) Contrasting approaches of corporate and association meeting planners: How the hospitality industry should approach them differently. *International Journal of Tourism Research* 9(1): 43–50.

Tourism Australia (2016) New research on association conference delegate behaviour.

UIA (2017) International meetings statistics report 58th edition. Union of International Associations.

UIA (2018) *The Yearbook of International Organisations.* Union of International Associations.

Vending International (2011) Successful lobbying by automatic vending association delays implementation of new coinage until 2012. Available at: http://www.vendinginternational-online.com/successful-lobbying-by-automatic-vending-association-delays-implementation-of-new-coinage-until-2012/.

Vollmer, H. M. and Mills, D. L. (eds) (1966) *Professionalization,* Englewood Cliffs, NJ: Prentice Hall.

4 SMERF meetings

SMERF meetings in the 21st century

- Twenty-five years after the Gulf War, the Combat Engineer Regiment of the Canadian Army held a two-day reunion in Edmonton, Western Canada to commemorate a significant event in its history, the successful disarmament and disposal of high explosive munitions following the end of hostilities.
- During the Chinese Spring Festival, six generations of the Ren family gathered in their hometown of Shishe village, in Zhejiang province, for a reunion attended by 500 family members, resulting in one of the biggest family photographs in human history.
- An event to celebrate the 2,561st anniversary of the birth of Buddha took place in Ho Chi Minh City, Vietnam, attracting many thousands of Buddhist dignitaries, monks, nuns and followers.
- Over 900 former students of the London Business School attended the annual three-day alumni event in London. Alumni who graduated over 25 years ago enjoyed the special privilege of having brunch with the Dean of the Business School.

Chapter objectives

On completion of this chapter the reader should be able to:

- Understand the importance of the human need for communities and a sense of community.
- Appreciate the features of the different types of events included under the SMERF sector.
- Recognise the features that distinguish SMERF events from other types of meetings.
- Recognise the most effective approaches that may be taken by venues and destinations wishing to attract SMERF events.
- Understand the processes involved in planning SMERF events.

A sense of community

The preceding chapters in this book have primarily focused on meetings and conferences that are closely linked to the participants' occupations. By way of contrast, most of the events analysed in this chapter have little or no direct connection with the participants' employment, but instead are linked to the various *communities* to which they belong. This sector of the events market is often known by the acronym SMERF, which is used to designate the face-to-face meetings of social, military, educational, religious and fraternal communities. The term has been widely used in the US events market for several decades but is now being adopted more widely outside that country. Participants attend SMERF events because they have a close personal connection to and passion for a particular community to which they belong. Before analysing SMERF events in detail, this chapter begins with an assessment of what 'community' means, as it is precisely a sense of community that primarily motivates most people to attend such events.

The need for companionship and social interaction is habitual to most people. Through membership of communities, people support each other, communicate and learn from others. The idea of a community stems from people's need to congregate and share the positive and joyous aspects of life or lean on others in times of need. However, the nature of human communities, which was initially based on geographical proximity, has changed with time to focus more on social cohesion and common values rather than physical closeness. This has resulted in a paradigm shift in the definition of community, which, with technological advances, has further evolved to include online or virtual communities (Rotman et al., 2009).

Nevertheless, academics have found it challenging to construct a comprehensive definition of 'community'. But most commentators differentiate between *place-based communities* (such as neighbourhoods) and *communities of interest*, in which members congregate around something they care deeply for (for example, a group of like-minded individuals united by their passion for owning and riding Harley-Davidson motorcycles). The types of events covered in this chapter are the gatherings of communities of the latter type – whose members share a special interest, who identify with a certain idea, or more generally, who happen to share a common context or experience, such as belonging to the same family, having studied at the same educational institution or having served in the same military regiment.

Blanchard and Markus (2004) are among the many authors who note that a widely accepted feature of successful, thriving communities, whether place-based or constructed around a common interest, is their ability to generate a distinct 'sense of community' (SOC), characterised by members' mutually supportive actions and their emotional attachment to the community and other members. It has been demonstrated that a greater bond and an SOC are created where interaction leads to a positive shared emotional connection among group members; and in turn, a well-developed SOC may create greater participation in and feelings of belonging to a community, and increased commitment to it (Rotman et al., 2009; Abfalter et al., 2012). Our understanding of the specific characteristics of an SOC has been enhanced by the descriptive framework developed by McMillan and Chavis

(1986), which has been widely accepted for studies of both place-based communities and communities of interest.

Their SOC framework has four dimensions:

- *Feelings of membership:* feelings of belonging to, and identifying with, the community
- *Feelings of influence:* feelings of having influence on, and being influenced by, the community
- *Integration and fulfilment of needs:* feelings of being supported by others in the community while also supporting them
- *Shared emotional connection:* feelings of relationships, shared history and a 'spirit' of community.

In the 21st century, the concept of SOC has also been applied to the context of online or *virtual* communities of interest – groups of people who interact primarily through electronic communication channels such as computer bulletin boards and social networks. The concept of a sense of virtual community (SOVC) has been developed to describe members' feelings of identity, belonging and attachment to online groups. But the ability of face-to-face meetings to generate valuable SOC has also been extensively harnessed by online communities, as noted by Schubert and Koch (2003:2), who emphasise that 'even in communities that began as pure virtual communities, the members tend to ask for and arrange physical meetings'. As a result, the distinction between offline and online communities is becoming blurred as a growing number of the physical groups that meet regularly in real life also profit from a virtual platform for ongoing communication between members; and online communities increasingly organise face-to-face events as a way of boosting their SOC and giving members a deeper connection to each other. For example, in June 2012, a small group of Australians from different professions who wanted to join Rotary International (a global not-for-profit community service club) but could not commit to attending physical meetings every week because of family and work commitments, created the Rotary eClub of Greater Melbourne (www.rotaryeclubgreatermelbourne.org.au). This is an online community dedicated to collaborating on projects around the areas of polio eradication, health and hunger, water and education. Three months later, the initial 27 members held their first face-to-face meeting at a restaurant in Melbourne. One member describes the impact of the event:

> It was an interesting and fun event because it was the first time that I had met many of my fellow club members. Sure, we had met online, and I knew them only from their tiny profile photo and member biography, but it was like meeting up with old friends. We finally put faces to names and the connection was set! Afterwards, (the day after the event), you could see the Facebook Friend Requests in my inbox as we all became friends with our social media and put this new friendship into another realm altogether. We also had the opportunity to meet our 'other halves' and together we saw that there was a real spirit and excitement about being involved in something so new and innovative.
>
> (Activate Learning Solutions, 2012)

The final chapter of this book includes a discussion of virtual events, but this chapter examines face-to-face meetings of communities of interest and their role in strengthening the affective bonds between community members.

The SMERF meetings market

SMERF events have long been recognised by venues and destinations worldwide as a distinctive segment of demand for meetings, to the extent that many venues and destination marketing organisations (DMOs) now have dedicated staff, with responsibility for targeting the organisers of these gatherings. The SMERF segment of demand is considered by many to be simply a useful 'catch-all' category, comprising all events that cannot be classified as corporate, association or political meetings. But even within the SMERF segment itself, there are important nuances between the five sub-segments, each of which displays its own distinguishing characteristics.

Social meetings

The APEX Industry Glossary (2008) defines social meetings as 'lifecycle celebrations' such as weddings, bar/bat mitzvahs, anniversaries and birthdays, to which Host (2012) adds class or family reunions, the meetings of social clubs and fundraisers. Holloway and Humphreys (2016) further expand the range of gatherings under this sub-segment to include the meetings of collectors and hobbyists. Ritual, conviviality and shared enthusiasms are the motivating factors behind social meetings, and the degree to which they are successful largely depends on the extent to which they generate pleasure and a reinforced sense of community for the participants.

Military meetings

The events in this sub-category are entirely distinct from the highly confidential meetings of serving military personnel coming together to discuss strategies in war situations. Rather, as defined by Holloway and Humphreys (2016), this segment largely comprises the reunions of *veterans* – people who previously served in the armed forces during periods of conflict. The intensity – and sometimes the tragedy – that frequently characterise such conflicts means that those who lived through them often find comfort and therapeutic benefits in reuniting with their fellow servicemen and servicewomen at regular intervals to recall their wartime experiences. Veterans who were deployed together or who served in the same unit or combat area almost inevitably forged strong bonds with each other, bonds which often helped them endure during the most challenging times, and those bonds are reinforced through regular attendance at events of this type. Military reunions, therefore, are largely nostalgic events that allow veterans to re-forge the connections between them, rekindle past friendships, share stories and heal from past experiences. To facilitate the reminiscing, a room in the venue for the display of memorabilia is often requested, and such events are frequently accompanied by ceremonies to commemorate those comrades who did not survive the hostilities.

According to Anderson (2014), attendance at these events can be as small as 25 or as large as 250, and they are typically four to five days long, which distinguishes them from the shorter average length of SMERF events. This sub-segment displays two other unique characteristics:

- Military reunions are often held in cities where military installations are present. For example, McGee (2015) identifies Pensacola, Florida as a major destination for US military reunions, due in part to the large number of military-related venues in the area, such as the National Aviation Museum and the Wall South, a half-size replica of the Vietnam Veterans Memorial in Washington, DC and the presence of the Naval Air Station Pensacola.
- Out of respect for veterans, some venues waive the fees that they would normally charge for room hire, and the event expenses may be further offset by some charitable organisations donating money or items.

Clearly, with the passage of time, the number of World War II reunions is gradually decreasing in all of the countries where such events have taken place on a regular basis. But, reunions of men and women who fought in conflicts such as Korea, Vietnam and the Gulf War, for example, will undoubtedly continue to create demand for this sub-sector of the SMERF market for some time to come.

Educational meetings

Those who attend educational events are generally school teachers, university lecturers and academic researchers who meet in order to share the results of their research in a particular subject area, as well as to discuss new challenges and other developments affecting the teaching of their specialist subjects. A further category of participants in education meetings are education administration staff, employed in schools, colleges and universities, who also meet for the purpose of sharing expertise and best practice in their profession. To this extent, the education sub-segment of the SMERF market is the one that most closely resembles the type of professional association conferences discussed in Chapter 3, as the motivation behind attending such events is generally work-related. This makes the education sub-segment something of an anomaly in the SMERF market, although it does share many of the other characteristics that distinguish this market from other types of meetings.

Religious meetings

Meetings in this sub-segment bring together people who share the same faith. At such events, worship and prayer are often combined with debates and workshops during which topical issues relating to the participants' particular religion are discussed. Religious meetings vary enormously in size, from weekend retreats of a dozen or so participants to the gatherings of many thousands in vast arenas to listen to charismatic religious leaders. According to Host (2012), it is common for religious organisations to require that their meeting planners in this sub-sector have a degree of familiarity with their faith and an understanding of specific rituals and rites.

While the key motivation behind attending religious meetings is clearly a spiritual one, participation is also partly fuelled by the wish to experience the type of conviviality and sense of community found in other types of SMERF events. Religious events often include some form of community service component, for example allowing attendees to work directly with local charities or engage in on-site projects, such as organising donation drives.

Fraternal meetings

Reunions or homecomings of university alumni or fraternities and sororities are usually classified as belonging to this sub-segment. Research has shown that alumni retain emotional attachments to their alma maters based on relationships established while they were students (Dolbert, 2002), and regular face-to-face events can be effective in nurturing the relationships of alumni with each other and reinforcing their attachment to their alma maters. As many alumni chapters are interested in raising money for student scholarships, their reunions are often designed toward that end, incorporating revenue-earning activities such as golf tournaments or wine tasting, the proceeds of which go towards supporting disadvantaged students.

The meetings of philanthropic and socio-political organisations are also widely classified under the fraternal sub-segment which includes the events held by groups such as Rotary International, Lions or Elks Clubs, the National Organization for Women or the World Wide Fund for Nature. A common objective of the meetings of such groups is to help train their members and volunteers, build a sense of community and further their cause, issue or concern.

The distinguishing characteristics of SMERF meetings

While each of the SMERF sub-segments is unique, all five of them share a number of common characteristics that distinguish these events from other types of meetings. These characteristics present opportunities as well as challenges for venues and destinations competing to host SMERF events. While it is difficult to generalise in terms of a market as diverse as this one, the following features are commonly considered to be representative of the SMERF segment.

Participants

As a general rule, the groups of people participating in SMERF events are far less homogenous than those attending work-related meetings. Participants from widely differing age-groups and socio-economic backgrounds may be found attending the same social or religious event, for example. But two noticeable features of SMERF events in terms of their participants are, firstly, the widespread tendency of delegates to bring their spouses, partners or families with them and, secondly, their propensity to extend their trips for leisure purposes, effectively turning the event trip into a couple's or a family's holiday.

Planners

Certain specialist professional meeting planners exist to organise events for different sub-sectors of this market. For example, in the US, a number of specialist events planners such as Military Reunion Planners (https://www.militaryreunionplanners.com/about.html) cater exclusively for the military reunions market. And in North America planners who organise events for the religious sub-segment of the SMERF market have created their own association, the interfaith Religious Conference Management Association (www.myrcma.org/) which has its own certification programme, the Certified Faith-based Meeting Professional.

But in general, the SMERF segment is distinguished by the amateur status of a large proportion of the planners of such events. Many of these meetings are held by organisations that are run by volunteers, in their spare time; and events in the social category are often organised by family members, many of whom may be planning an event for the first time. This presents a number of challenges for destinations and venues endeavouring to attract SMERF events. For example, the task of identifying those with responsibility for choosing sites for such events can be difficult, as their planning role is rarely reflected in their job titles; and the volunteers in any case often change from year to year, or from location to location of the event. Moreover, given the fact that many planners of SMERF meetings lack experience and technical knowledge of the logistics and marketing of events, they often require extra guidance from DMO and venue staff.

As most SMERF groups do not use the services of professional conference organisers (PCOs) and destination management companies (DMCs) in the planning of their events, the task of quantifying the actual numbers of meetings in this sub-sector is all the more challenging, as many such events take place 'under the radar'. But larger SMERF events are far more visible partly due to the fact that, as indicated by Host (2012), SMERF organisations with larger and/or complex events are increasingly turning to professional planners for their logistical and contractual expertise.

Price-sensitive but dependable

Due to the fact that most SMERF events are entirely unconnected with the attendees' employment, most participants are self-funding, with financial support from the participants' employers being a common feature of educational meetings only. For that reason, suppliers tend to regard most SMERF sub-segments as being fairly price-sensitive, with planners often finding creative ways to save money on items such as room rates, food and beverage packages, meeting space rental, parking fees, and audio-visual equipment. For example, in order to adhere to their personal budgets, participants may opt to share hotel rooms; and they may even bring their own food and beverages. Furthermore, the fact that many religious groups do not consume alcohol eliminates a significant revenue source for hotels and other suppliers. As a result of such economy measures, hotels often consider SMERF meetings to be among their least profitable customer segments.

However, on the other hand, SMERF events are generally regarded as a dependable segment of the meetings market, because the commitment and enthusiasm of the participants mean that, even in recessionary times, these events are far less likely to be cancelled than corporate meetings; and attendee numbers are often more stable than those found in the association market. Reveron (2013) noted that 'While the SMERF segment isn't the largest, it is dependable, and continues to meet during the good times and the bad economic times, with little attendee falloff. SMERF groups most often have loyal attendees.' Because such groups continue to book meetings even in the harshest of economic climates, they deliver a steady stream of income to the venues and destinations in which they are held. Furthermore, that income is supplemented when participants bring their spouses, partners or families and extend their trips, for leisure purposes.

Timing

The non-vocational nature of most SMERF events means that they are generally held outside the normal working week, notably over weekends, when participants are free to attend. Moreover, for budgetary reasons, they often take place in off-peak periods, during shoulder seasons and at other times when demand from the corporate and associations segments is lower and venues are offering more favourable rates. The weekend and off-peak bookings of SMERF groups provide venues and destinations with welcome revenue, and hotel employees with work during what would otherwise be challenging periods in terms of business. Some venues and destinations therefore tend to regard SMERF groups as 'fillers' that are willing to hold their events at times when business would otherwise be slow.

Destinations and venues

Again, for budgetary reasons, SMERF events are often held in second- or third-tier cities, where average prices are lower than those found in capital cities and major centres of population, making the meetings more financially accessible for participants. Organisers often seek venues that offer value for money, such as universities, many of which have the added advantage of having on-site budget accommodation, in addition to a range of meeting rooms of different capacities. However, the majority of SMERF events are held in hotels, due to the convenience and often the financial advantages of having all elements of the meeting under one roof.

But some authors have indicated that the heterogenous nature of many SMERF groups, in terms of the financial resources available to individuals for spending on their attendance, means that cities offering a wide variety of accommodation options make attractive destinations for this sub-segment. Chavis (2015) gives the example of Pigeon Forge, a mountain resort city in Tennessee being considered an appealing option for such groups as it is a second-tier city with 'the attractiveness of a wide variety of lodging options at varying rates. Through the availability of 13,000 lodging units in the city, attendees can choose from a diverse portfolio of hotels, motels, chalets, cabins and campgrounds.' A further characteristic of successful SMERF destinations is their ability to offer a range of family-friendly attractions to satisfy those extending their trips for leisure purposes.

Targeting and servicing the SMERF market

As SMERF events often fill those dates that are less likely to be booked by associations or corporations, it represents an attractive market segment for destinations and venues. For that reason, many DMOs and venues have sales personnel designated to sell specifically to this particular segment of demand, supported by a range of marketing tools and techniques. It can be an advantage if those members of staff with specific responsibility for working with the SMERF market are able to work at least one or two evenings a week and occasionally at weekends, as many planners of SMERF events have 'day jobs' of their own and therefore tend to focus on their event planning tasks when they are at home in the evening or at weekends. It is at those times that they are most likely to need to interact with SMERF specialists in DMOs and venues.

Destination marketing organisations

To support their efforts in marketing themselves to the SMERF market, DMOs have a range of techniques at their disposal, including the following:

- *Information:* DMO websites can create pages aimed directly at SMERF groups, outlining the facilities and services available to them. An example of this is the website of the DMO of Irving, Texas, where SMERF planners can find out about how that organisation's staff can help them with site selection, event planning and activity coordination: https://www.irvingtexas.com/meetings/meeting-groups/smerf-groups/.
- *Incentives:* In order to motivate SMERF meeting planners to choose their cities, some DMOs offer a range of incentives to participants, primarily designed to save them money. McGee (2015) lists some possible incentives as: free passes to cultural attractions, discount rates on city-owned venues for special events, and free passes for transportation within the destination. Irving's DMO goes further, offering SMERF planners a range of complimentary services, which include name badges, registration personnel assistance, and visitor bags and brochures, as well as room night incentives for qualifying groups.
- *Training:* As has been noted earlier in this chapter, SMERF event organisers often have little or no formal meeting planning training; they can be volunteers or family members organising an event for the first time. Reveron (2013) reports that some DMOs are reaching out directly to those who plan SMERF meetings by offering them training in event planning. It gives the example of the Lee County Convention & Visitors Bureau in southwest Florida, which sponsors complimentary planning workshops every April and October, attracting 40–60 attendees. The workshops feature planning experts who offer advice in areas such as budgeting and creative activities for attendees, and information on understanding, for example, the differences between full-service and limited-service hotels; how to negotiate with directors

of sales and catering; how to set up a food and beverage budget; and how to put together a committee in charge of deciding on activities and banquets.

Hotels

In her blog for Cvent (https://blog.cvent.com/), Sarah Vining (2014) notes that since, in most cases, the organisers of SMERF events are not professional planners, hotel sales staff need to nurture the relationship more and provide extra reassurance to make these clients feel comfortable and secure about the outcome of their event. She considers that an effective SMERF marketing strategy for hotels is to include the services of a dedicated in-house personal conference manager in the meetings package – someone who will take care of all logistical elements and ensure the event runs smoothly. Vining also recommends that hotels offer the services of an on-site audio-visual team, as SMERF groups are reassured by the knowledge that an audio-visual technician will be present during their events to deal with any malfunctions or to answer general questions.

Bowden (2017) gives the example of a hotel that is successful in winning SMERF business, the Renaissance Riverview Plaza Hotel in Mobile, Alabama, where the relationship between hotel staff and the planner is considered to be the most important element for the success of such events. She quotes the hotel's director of sales and marketing:

> Understanding that a large portion of SMERF planners may be relatively new to their role or will likely have many other responsibilities is crucial. The salesperson and the event manager need to partner with them from the beginning to make sure their meeting process starts off on the right track. This partnership continues throughout the entire process, from the sales to planning to event phases. Partnering with them from the start will give them a sense of assurance that you have their best interest at heart. You sometimes have to educate them in hotel terminology and explain to them what contractually they are obligating themselves to. Discuss their meeting history, explain attrition and cancellation, offer alternate dates that may reduce the overall costs and offer menu suggestions that will also reduce their costs.

Conference centres

While hotels are the type of venue most commonly used for SMERF events, they do not have the monopoly in this market. Some events, for example religious gatherings, require the capacity offered by conference centres due to the sheer numbers of participants. Fraternal events too can be so large that only conference centres have the room to accommodate them. For instance, over 20,000 members of the Alpha Kappa Alpha Sorority from all over the world converged on Atlanta in 2016, for the organisation's week-long biennial conference, which was held at the Georgia World Congress Centre.

But conference centres are increasingly targeting the social sub-sector of the SMERF market. According to Welly (2011),

Conference centres are playing host to more and more SMERF events, particularly weddings, which can largely be attributed to two factors: the economic downturn, which has made conference centre sales staff go after a more varied type of business; and the increasingly luxurious amenities available, which makes them more appealing destinations for weddings, family reunions, and those scrapbooking conventions.

The same source quotes the senior vice president of sales and marketing of Benchmark Hospitality International, a company that manages an extensive portfolio of resorts, conference centres and hotels: 'Conference centres are very different than they were five years ago. They started as very serious meeting spaces. Now you have that serious approach if you want it, but they are set up more like luxury resorts.' As a result of this diversification of their facilities, many conference centres actively market themselves for weddings and social events by highlighting different features of the property – which can even extend to naming the venue differently for each market segment. Welly gives an example of this, from a venue in Santa Cruz, California, citing the director of sales:

> We go by two different names, really. Fifteen years ago, we used to be recognised as the Chaminade Executive Conference Centre. We dropped 'executive' for group business, and we are really just known as Chaminade. For leisure business, including SMERF and weddings, we go by Chaminade Resort and Spa.
>
> (Ibid.)

Bowden (2017) summarises her advice to venues and destinations competing to win SMERF business as follows:

- Express your willingness to work within tight budgets. This often involves providing planners with a list of potential meeting dates when pricing can be more flexible, but also can include scaled-down menus and lower audio-visual costs.
- Establish one liaison from the property and/or the DMO. Some SMERF event planners are volunteers and others often have several roles within their organisation, so the destination staff can make the planning process more efficient by having just one key person to contact for all issues related to the event.
- Be upfront and accurate about the distance and time it takes to get from the airport to the destination and provide ample information about area transportation options.
- Provide planners with information about nearby attractions and special events that will be occurring while they are in your community. There are many ways that SMERF groups can save money by arranging some of their events at an affordable off-site venue, such as a city park or entertainment centre. Additionally, some SMERF groups have been able to incorporate a local festival or evening concert into their agenda by knowing the details about these programmes in advance.
- Be aware of the specific needs of the group and explain how your destination staff will address those needs. For example, a reunion involving retired military personnel might require more than the usual amount of equipment to assist people with disabilities.

Planning SMERF events

Marketing SMERF events

Host (2012) is among several authors to highlight a similarity between the SMERF market and the association market in terms of their marketing approaches to potential attendees. In both cases, members are under no obligation to participate – although in the case of lifestyle events such as weddings and anniversaries there is usually a reasonable expectation that close family members will be present. But due to the voluntary nature of attendance at most SMERF events, planners, in common with those organising associations' conferences, must provide an appealing programme to attract registrations. The process begins with the choice of destination which, in common with destinations used by other sectors of the business events market, should have a positive image, should be easily accessible to most potential participants both geographically and in terms of affordability, and should offer the appropriate facilities for SMERF groups discussed earlier in this chapter, including a wide range of accommodation options, opportunities for attendees to extend their visits, and a variety of family attractions.

Advance notice of the dates, locations, topics, programme and speakers for the event must be circulated several times prior to the event using a similar range of online and offline tools to those used by associations, as described in the previous chapter. The advent of social media tools such as LinkedIn, WhatsApp and Facebook has made the task of identifying and contacting potential attendees for events such as school reunions or university homecomings much easier. An illustration of the power of such tools is provided by Anderson (2014) who cites the president of the Reunion Friendly Network, a trade organisation that connects volunteer military reunion planners with hotels and other suppliers. She notes that social media platforms have allowed for increased connection among military members, something that was a problem area for reunion planners in the past, and this has improved attendance. Nevertheless, in the case of the military reunions market, more traditional, paper-based forms of communication continue to play a role, due to the advanced age of many in the targeted audience which means that in some cases promotion through the social media may not reach them. As most Korean War, World War II and Vietnam War veterans are now over 65 years old, communication tools that cater to the more mature audience should be chosen.

Effective marketing is a key factor in building attendance at all events, but it is particularly important for the SMERF market, as the prospect of an event attracting large numbers of attendees strengthens the planner's arguments when negotiating with hotels and other suppliers.

Budget

The budgetary limitations that are a feature of most SMERF events make it imperative that planners have basic skills in negotiating with suppliers such as venues and caterers. A degree of give-and-take on both sides of budget negotiations is essential, and planners generally find that they are able to work within their financial restraints if they are prepared to be flexible on the dates or the location (or both) of their events. But it is vital that, when negotiating rates, it should be made clear that there should be no *hidden* costs. SMERF planners are usually seeking an all-inclusive price from their suppliers, and do not appreciate unexpected charges in the final bill, for items such as parking or cloakroom fees, that they believed were covered in the quoted price. One way to ensure this is for suppliers to use contracts that are particularly easy to understand by non-professional planners.

Beginning the negotiations as early as possible in the planning cycle is essential to securing favourable rates from suppliers, as evidenced from the following advice from a SMERF events planner:

> A main challenge to controlling costs is working with hotel partners. We try to keep hotel total charges within a person's budget. We focus on keeping room rates, and food and beverage costs as reasonable as possible, but you still want value. With food and beverage, I usually ask for tastings to make sure hotels aren't cutting too many corners. To get what you want, you have to start planning further out. Many SMERF planners don't do that.
>
> (Reveron, 2013)

The same source describes a further method that may be effective in reducing SMERF meeting costs. The annual two-day New England Synod Assembly meeting, a religious gathering which represents the six New England states and two New York state counties, attracts more than 500 attendees including lay and clergy members as well as spouses and retired pastors. In order to secure favourable rates for this event, the planner negotiated a series of one-year deals to meet in Springfield, Massachusetts each year from 2011 until 2014. She describes how she had some leverage in negotiating because the Greater Springfield Convention & Visitors Bureau which actively targets the SMERF market, showed that it really wanted the event.

Timing

The strategic timing of SMERF events to coincide with days of the week or periods of the year when venues' rates are lower has already been highlighted as a feature of this market segment and is probably the principal consideration to be taken into account by planners when choosing dates for their events. However, other factors may also come into the decision. For example, for events at which children accompany their parents, school holiday schedules must be taken into consideration.

But occasionally, budgetary factors are not the main point to be considered when choosing dates for SMERF events. For instance, Reveron (2013) reports how the New England Synod Assembly changed its meeting days to improve attendance and attract more young people, citing the event's planner:

> We used to meet on Thursday, Friday and Saturday and attracted a lot of older and retired people. We moved it to the weekends so we can get more young working adults that don't have to take all that time off from work. We also try to have sessions and events like community work projects that appeal to younger people.

It is evident that the SMERF sector of events offers challenges as well as advantages for destinations and venues. But making an effort to gain a deeper understanding of the special characteristics of this market can bring these suppliers significant rewards in terms of adding more social, military, educational, religious and fraternal events to their business portfolios.

Chapter summary

This chapter focused on the sector of the events market known by the acronym SMERF, which is used to designate the face-to-face meetings of social, military, educational, religious and fraternal communities. It began with an assessment of what is understood by 'community' and the type of 'sense of community' that is a primary motivation behind attendance at SMERF events. A distinction was made between place-based communities and the types of 'communities of interest' that gather at SMERF events. The features that distinguish SMERF events from other types of meetings were examined: the profiles of their participants, as well as their timing, price sensitivity and the types of destinations favoured by those who plan such events. On the supply side, the techniques used by destination marketing organisations to attract SMERF events to their cities were explored, with emphasis on the specialised information, incentives and training that they offer planners of these events.

CASE STUDY 4.1: THE 81ST NATIONAL ASSOCIATION OF FREE WILL BAPTISTS CONVENTION, LOUISVILLE, KENTUCKY

Ryan Lewis, NAFWB Convention Manager

The National Association of Free Will Baptists

The Free Will Baptist denomination is a fellowship of evangelical believers, comprising more than 2,400 churches in 42 US states and in 14 other countries. Its origins can be traced to the influence of the Baptists of Arminian persuasion who settled in the US from England. In Nashville, Tennessee, on 5 November 1935, representatives of two separate associations of Free Will Baptists met and created the National Association of Free Will Baptists (NAFWB), which is now the largest of the Free Will Baptist groups.

The Executive Office of the NAFWB, located in Antioch, Tennessee, exists to serve the national body, various boards, state organisations, local churches and individual members of the association. The duties of the Executive Secretary and his staff include the coordination and planning of the NAFWB's annual national convention.

The 2017 National Convention

The 2017 National Convention of the NAFWB took place between 16–19 July in Louisville, Kentucky with the theme 'Equipping the saints'. The various components of the event comprised: business elements (such as the meetings of various NAFWB committees and boards); educational elements (a seminar programme); a series of youth competitions (bible studies, art, drama and music); a worship component (religious services for different age groups); and an exhibition (displays of denominational enterprises and stands offering church-related services and products).

Interview with Ryan Lewis, the NAFWB Convention Manager

Q: Who attends the annual FWB Convention?

Ryan Lewis: Many of our attendees are pastors, obviously, but we also get a lot of lay people. It's a very family-oriented event. And many young people attend with their parents, to take part in the competitions. So our age range is literally from birth to death. I was already very familiar with the convention even before I got this job, because I've been going to it every year since I was born.

Q: In general, how do you choose the destinations for the convention?

Ryan Lewis: There's a long lead-time for our conventions. We usually know at least five years in advance where each convention will be held. The process begins with an invitation from the FWB state-level organisation. When they invite us, they don't necessarily have a city in mind, but in any case, most states have usually only one or two, maybe three, cities that could accommodate our event, which generally attracts between 4,500 and 5,000 participants. So, we need approximately 1,000 hotel rooms and a lot of meeting space. When we receive invitations from any of our state-level organisations, we do our research and make a site visit to make sure that our convention would work well in the city or cities proposed. As this is a religious meeting, most of the participants are paying for their own attendance, so we have to work within a limited budget. For that reason, most often the choice of destination comes down to the question of cost. We are looking for best value for the money that our attendees spend. After the site visit, I then make a presentation to our board, and they usually accept my recommendation.

We don't follow a rotation pattern as such. The vast majority of FWBs are located in the south-east of the US. We've held our convention in Phoenix, Arizona and Anaheim, California, but on those occasions, we found that our attendance was lower than usual. This wasn't a reflection of the cities themselves, but rather due to the fact that, with most FWBs living east of Oklahoma and south of Ohio, travelling to Phoenix or Anaheim meant taking a flight, which added to the costs of attending. Even when we used cities on the edges of the south-east of the US, such as Oklahoma City, Cincinnati or Tampa, our attendance levels were adversely affected by the location of the destination. Approximately 85–90 per cent of attendees drive to the convention in their own vehicles, in church vans or in chartered buses. So most of the time, we choose a convention city that's within a day's drive of where most of our attendees live.

Q: Why was Louisville chosen as the destination for your 2017 convention?

Ryan Lewis: The Kentucky state organisation of the FWBs expressed an interest in hosting the 2017 convention. They successfully raised some money to support the convention in their state, and so we selected Louisville – really because it's the only city in Kentucky with the physical capacity to host our event. Our convention had already been held there several times before, and so we knew that the city was a good 'fit' for our event.

In terms of the actual venue for the convention, we encountered a significant challenge about 2 years before the actual convention. We were told then that the city of Louisville had decided to demolish their principal venue, the Kentucky International Convention Centre (KICC), and completely remodel it as part of an expansion and renovation project – and that this was programmed to take place between 2016 and 2018, which included the year of our convention. In other words, the convention centre that we thought we'd be using would be unavailable at the time of our event. So we looked at the alternatives, which basically consisted of either moving the 2017 convention to a different city or moving it to a different venue within Louisville. The alternative venue proposed to us by the KICC was inappropriate for two reasons: firstly, as a huge arena, it was far too big for our purposes; and secondly, that venue was a highly unionised facility, meaning higher labour costs, which would have been a challenge for us, given our budgetary constraints.

But finally, the city of Louisville stepped up and told us they wanted to make this right with a plan that would not incur extra costs for us. The solution was to hold our convention in the Galt House Hotel, a large convention hotel in the city. We had already used the Galt House Hotel during previous editions of our convention in Louisville, but only as an overflow property for a couple of hundred rooms. That's because it's located about four blocks away from the KICC, and our main hotels were much closer to the convention centre. But in 2017, all of our attendees were accommodated in the Galt House Hotel – over 1,000 rooms per night – and most components of our convention were also held in the hotel. We used every inch of their available meeting space, but we still needed more. So our evening youth worship services, which attract about 2,000 participants – were held in a nearby performing arts centre, The Kentucky Centre; and adult services and the general worship sessions were held in a multi-purpose sports arena, the KFC Yum! Centre. That area has 22,000 seats, of which we only needed about 4,000, but we made it work, by arranging seating on the floor of the arena, rather than using the raked seating.

Q: Did you use the services of the local Convention Bureau in Louisville?

Ryan Lewis: Yes, we rely heavily upon the CVB (Convention & Visitors Bureau) in every city we use. They are our first point of contact. When we have narrowed our choice down to one state and a couple of cities, the CVBs are the first people we approach. There's not a city I have ever encountered where the CVB didn't ask 'How can we help you?' when they know that we are bringing our convention to their city. The support they offer is not necessarily monetary. Sometimes it's a question of sharing their useful connections with us, for example hotels and transportation. I don't know the shuttle companies in Louisville but the CVB do, and they did a fantastic job in recommending suppliers like that. CVBs sometimes provide financial aid or incentive packages for our conventions, but for the main part we just depend on them to provide us with the answers we need.

Q: Do many of your attendees extend their convention trips for leisure purposes?

Ryan Lewis: Absolutely. As the participants are already taking some of their own vacation time to attend and are paying their own expenses, many of them use the opportunity to do that. So in the days immediately preceding the convention and the days following the convention, we find that we have a lot of pick-up in terms of extra hotel nights. We tend to choose cities that offer lots to do for families. For example, when we were in Tampa, Florida, a lot of people took the opportunity to visit Disneyland which was about an hour's drive away from there. The convention programme from Sunday–Wednesday is very intensive, so attendees don't have much time for tourism-related activities during the actual event. That's why so many of them come in a couple of days early or stay later, afterwards.

Q: What are the main challenges of organising the NAFWB annual convention?

Ryan Lewis: We always face the challenge of finding hotels that are affordable. Managing a block of pre-booked rooms and avoiding attrition charges means trying to successfully predict attendance levels – which can be difficult. Finding downtown area eating places for 4,500–5,000 people on a limited budget is another challenge. Our convention includes very few catered functions, so attendees have to find restaurants and other food outlets by themselves. What makes this particularly challenging is the fact that many downtown restaurants don't open at weekends, as there are no business customers.

Q: What is the main innovation you have seen in the convention in your time as an organiser of the event?

Ryan Lewis: Within the national association, we have various national departments, such as the Missions Agency, a Publishing House and our College. Our seminar programme began a few years ago when one department came forward with suggestions for speakers that they thought would be beneficial for our convention's audiences. Other departments began to pick up on that trend, and also began providing us with speakers on topics of interest to the attendees. So now we offer an extensive seminar programme each year, so the convention is much more of a learning experience for attendees. Before this development, the convention programme comprised only business sessions and worship; but now attendees can go back to their churches with useful information for their future ministry activities. Over recent years, the educational element of the convention has grown and has given people an additional reason to attend, as well as for the fellowship and the experience. It gives our convention more of a buzz, which is appreciated by all.

References

Abfalter, D., Zaglia, M. E. and Mueller, J. (2012) Sense of virtual community: A follow up on its measurement. *Computers in Human Behaviour* 28(2): 400–404.

Activate Learning Solutions (2012) Meeting my online community service network face-to-face for the first time. Available at: https://activatelearning.wordpress.com/2012/08/20/meeting-my-online-community-service-network-face-to-face-for-the-first-time/.

Anderson, E. (2014) SMERF meetings evolve. *MeetingsToday.com*, November 2014.

Blanchard, A. L. and Markus, M. L. (2004) The experienced sense of a virtual community: Characteristics and processes. *ACM SIGMIS Database: The DATABASE for Advances in Information Systems* 35(1): 64–79.

Bowden, A. (2017) SMERF events: What destinations need. What planners want! ConventionSouth.

Chavis, S. (2015) SMERF meetings: Destinations that appeal to government and non-profit groups. ConventionSouth, June.

Dolbert, S. C. (2002) Future trends in alumni relations. Proceedings of 16th Australian International Education Conference, pp. 1–14.

Holloway, J. C. and Humphreys, C. (2016) *The Business of Tourism*, Harlow: Pearson Education.

Host, W. R. (2012) Special markets, in Pizam, A. (ed.) *International Encyclopedia of Hospitality Management*, 2nd edn, London: Routledge.

McGee, R (2015) Yes, SMERF is still a thing. PCMA Convene, 1 December.

McMillan, D. W. and Chavis, D. M. (1986) Sense of community: A definition and theory. *Journal of Community Psychology* 14: 6–23.

Reveron, D. (2013) SMERF meetings. Available at: http://www.themeetingmagazines.com/acf/smerf-meetings/?post_type.

Rotman, D., Golbeck, J. and Preece, J. (2009) The community is where the rapport is – on sense and structure in the YouTube community. Proceedings of the Fourth International Conference on Communities and Technologies, pp. 41–50.

Schubert, P. and Koch, M. (2003) Collaboration platforms for virtual student communities, in System Sciences, 2003. Proceedings of the 36th Annual Hawaii International Conference on System Sciences, IEEE.

Vining, S. (2014) Does your hotel have the best SMERF marketing strategy? Available at: https://blog.cvent.com/events/event-marketing/smerf-marketing-strategy/.

Welly, K (2011) Conference centres get SMERF-happy. *Successful Meetings*, 1 March.

5 Awards ceremonies

Awards ceremonies in the 21st century

- At the annual Academy Awards ceremony, the Oscars are presented to actors, directors, producers and film professionals who worked on the previous year's best films. The ceremony was inaugurated in 1929, and the event's broadcast now draws more than a billion viewers worldwide.
- Since 2012, the Game Rangers Association of Africa has held its annual Rhino Conservation Awards Ceremony in South Africa, to recognise and honour the committed efforts of individuals and organisations involved in the protection of this endangered species.
- The Building and Architect of the Year Awards ceremony in the Mansion House in Dublin celebrates the outstanding work carried out by Ireland's leading architecture practices. At the inaugural event in 2017, nearly 300 architecture and construction industry figures came together to celebrate their industry's excellence and creativity.

Chapter objectives

On completion of this chapter the reader should be able to:

- Appreciate the importance of public recognition and the celebration of achievements.
- Understand the uses and impacts of awards ceremonies.
- Recognise the distinguishing characteristics of awards ceremonies.
- Understand the processes involved in planning awards ceremonies.

Recognising achievement

In the worlds of business, culture, academia and sports, awards are a widespread phenomenon, satisfying individuals' vital need for social recognition and esteem on the one hand and our fundamental desire to celebrate others' outstanding achievements on the other. The bestowing of medals, titles and trophies for outstanding feats on the field of battle, in the arts or in the sports arena – or for other significant accomplishments – is a practice that finds its origins in ancient times. Many of the magnificent statues, stone columns and arches that were presented to exceptional individuals many centuries ago in the classical civilisations as trophies for their achievements are still standing today. Urde and Greyser (2015) trace back the custom of conferring cultural awards to the 6th century BC, in Greece, noting that in the early Renaissance period, the practice became common, with the rise of royal and national academies such as the French Academy founded in 1672. Another key institution in France, the *Société d'encouragement pour l'industrie nationale* (Society for the Encouragement of National Industry), founded in 1801, had a different objective – that of promoting economic development by the granting of inducement awards for innovations in the fields of technology and manufacturing (Khan, 2015).

In the modern world, awards are ubiquitous, providing the recipients with public recognition for anything from one particular accomplishment, such as writing a highly acclaimed novel, to a lifetime of good works. They may be bestowed upon an organisation, a team or an individual.

Frey and Gallus (2017) suggest four reasons for the enduring popularity of awards: Firstly, awards convey *appreciation* and *recognition*, which boost our self-evaluation and assure us that our activity is valued. Secondly, awards establish a *special relationship* between the donor and the recipient, a bond of loyalty which brings with it the assumption that both parties share common goals and mutually support each other. Third, awards often bring *material* advantages as well as social benefits. For example, an undivided Nobel Prize earns the recipient a windfall of around €900,000, while the winner of the Man Booker Prize for the best novel originally written in English and published in the UK receives the sum of £50,000. Fourth, and most importantly, award recipients gain social status because, unlike a cash bonus in salary, for example, awards are invariably given in a public ceremony, in an atmosphere of public celebration and elation, attended by the winners' own reference group. In this way, receiving an award in the presence of one's peers and colleagues satisfies the recipient's fundamental need for status and esteem that authors such as Huberman et al. (2004) and Brennan and Pettit (2004) have identified as being important drivers of performance for significant numbers of people in the workplace.

It is clear that individuals can be presented with awards at almost any point in life, from a school prizegiving to post-retirement, as in the case of Lifetime Achievement Awards. Moreover, given the great popularity of awards and prizes, there are very few areas of human endeavour and professional activity in which they are not used.

Table 5.1 lists, with some well-known and less well-known examples, the principal domains in which awards are regularly bestowed.

Awards abound in the business events industry itself, as a means of recognising the work of the many suppliers and intermediaries who are active in this sector. Awards categories range from Best Conference Centre and Best Convention Bureau to prizes for innovations in meetings industry technology and for environmentally sustainable exhibition centres. There are even awards for outstanding awards ceremonies, such as the Best Awards Event, one of the prize categories in the annual Conference Awards held in London or the Awards Event of the Year prize, at the PPA (Professional Publishers Association) Connect Awards in the same city.

Table 5.1 Types of awards

Type	Examples	Donor/presenting organisation
State orders and decorations		
	British Order of the Garter	The British Sovereign
	Legion of Honour	The French Republic
	Congressional Gold Medal	The United States Congress
Arts, media and fashion		
	The Academy Awards (Oscars)	Academy of Motion Picture Arts and Sciences
	The Pulitzer Prize	Columbia University for Joseph Pulitzer
	Elle Style Awards	*Elle* magazine
Sports		
	Wimbledon Tennis Trophies	All England Lawn Tennis Club
	Webb Ellis Cup (Rugby World Cup)	International Rugby Football Board
	Sports Personality of the Year	BBC
Religion		
	Beatifications and Canonisations	The Roman Catholic Church
	Green Church Awards	The Church Times
	South Carolina Baptist Pastor of the Year	South Carolina Baptist Convention
Voluntary and humanitarian sector		
	The Florence Nightingale Medal	International Committee of the Red Cross
	Guardian Charity Awards	*The Guardian*
	Humanitarian Overseas Service Medal	The Australian Honours Secretariat
Academia		
	Nobel Prizes in Physics and Chemistry	Royal Swedish Academy of Sciences
	Fields Medal in Mathematics	International Mathematical Union
	Fellow of the Royal Society	The Royal Society
Business		
	World Entrepreneur of the Year	Ernst & Young
	Businesswoman of the Year	Businesswomen's Association of South Africa
	Young Banker of the Year	Chartered Institute of Bankers

Source: Adapted from Frey and Gallus (2017), with additional material by the author.

The most high-profile prizes are awarded by the vast range of business events associations, industry publications and trade show organisers. Table 5.2 lists some of the most prestigious awards in this industry. However, below the national and international levels, business events–related awards may also be conferred by individual cities, as is the case, for example, at the Prague Convention Bureau Ambassador Awards Evening (see the case study in Chapter 10) as well as by individual companies, such as the Qantas Business Travel Awards which include prizes for the Best Meeting Rooms in Australia and Best Conference Venues in Australia.

Despite their ubiquitous nature and their distinct characteristics, awards have been largely disregarded by the academic community, focusing on events studies and the

Table 5.2 Examples of business events industry awards

Donor/presenting organisation	Name of award/ ceremony	Objective of award
International business events associations		
Professional Convention Management Association (PCMA):	Chairman's Award	To honour an individual or an organisation for their unique achievements or contributions to the meetings industry in the previous year
Society for Incentive Travel Excellence (SITE) Recognition:	Crystal Awards Programme	To honour the top tier of world-class organisations that excel in designing unique and memorable incentive programmes that deliver measurable business results for their clients
The Global Association of the Exhibition Industry (UFI)	Marketing Award	To reward the best marketing initiatives undertaken by exhibition professionals
The International Congress and Convention Association (ICCA)	Best Marketing Award	To recognise the excellence and outstanding achievements of organisations in their effort to market their destination or product
Business events industry publications		
Meetings & Incentive Travel magazine	Meetings & Incentive Travel Industry Awards	To reward excellence of service and product
China MICE magazine	China MICE Industry Golden Chair Awards	To commend hotels, destinations, airline companies and travel agencies for their performance
Revista Eventos	Ciao	To honour Brazil's leading event professionals and most creative and innovative event agencies

Business events exhibitions		
IBTM World	Lifetime Achievement Award	To recognise exceptional contributions to the business events industry.
IMEX	Academy Award	To honour individuals who have served the meetings and incentive travel industry exceptionally well
AIME	Rising Star Award	To recognise the next generation of industry greats, shaping the future of MICE across Asia-Pacific

Source: Compiled by the author.

social sciences more widely. In his typology of event forms, Getz (2007) classifies awards ceremonies under 'Arts and Entertainment', together with other planned events such as music concerts, theatre and dance shows. For this author, this classification places awards ceremonies, as events, 'largely in the realm of hedonistic consumption' (Getz, 2007:37), and the association of awards ceremonies with entertainment will be explored later in this chapter. In a different academic discipline, economics, the study of awards has in recent years gained some momentum, according to two of the most active researchers in this field, Frey and Gallus (2017). Currently, however, the extant literature on awards is dominated by studies focusing on the Nobel Prizes, Academy Awards, book, food and academic prizes (Harrison and Jepsen, 2015). Frey and Gallus (2017) admit, therefore, that the field is still wide open for future research, and they make a number of suggestions for awards-related topics that, in their opinion, are worthy of further research. These include analysing the impacts of awards on the recipients' self-esteem; determining the optimal number of awards for different activities and areas; the deliberation process of award givers; and the reactions of non-recipients of awards. Harrison and Jepsen (2015) add to the list, noting that there is a dearth of scholarly research on the impact of winning an external work-related award in the corporate or business sector. Some of these topics will be explored in the rest of this chapter.

The distinguishing characteristics of awards ceremonies

Worldwide, some of the most watched programmes on television are awards ceremonies, such as the Academy Awards, at which the Oscars are presented, or the Grammy Awards which recognise the year's best recordings, compositions and artists in classical, jazz, country and popular music categories. But not all awards ceremonies have red carpet entrances, with thousands of guests gathered in a glittering gala atmosphere and global television coverage. Awards events can also be national, regional or local in their reach.

Indeed, the majority of awards ceremonies are smaller, in-house events, held for the purpose of honouring the achievements of colleagues working for the same employer – for example to mark a specific milestone in an employee's career, such as 25 years spent working for the company, or to bestow awards with titles such as Salesperson of the Year or Employee of the Month upon members of the company's staff. Such presentations may constitute little more than a drinks reception in the office canteen on a Friday afternoon, and, as such, barely figure on the radar of the events industry, as the services of external suppliers and intermediaries are not often used. These events may be categorised as *internal* business award ceremonies.

The more high-profile, *external* business awards ceremonies, however, tend to be industry-wide, in which case members of the same profession or sector of activity gather to celebrate the notable achievements of their colleagues. Some institutions hold an annual awards event to recognise outstanding work; others present awards only occasionally, and only in response to truly outstanding achievements. But, whatever the scale or frequency of such ceremonies, the same elements tend to be present: some form of dinner or banquet, entertainment, the actual presentation of the awards, followed by networking and after-dinner dancing.

Awards ceremonies make a clear statement about achievement, honouring people for their past performance and successes, as most clearly seen in lifetime achievement or post-mortem awards. This distinguishes them from the type of incentive awards that are analysed in Chapter 7, which are used to motivate people to improve their performance over a period of time in the future. More broadly, an awards ceremony may be regarded as the culmination of a more extensive awards programme, which, generally speaking, has one or more objectives. According to Silvers (2004:324), 'The objectives may be based on sculpting desired behaviour, motivating specific actions, increasing productivity, promoting certain agendas, attaching importance to accomplishments, and /or providing important revenues to the sponsoring organisation'. Award programmes' effectiveness in reaching some of these objectives is examined in the next section of this chapter.

First, however, it is necessary to consider a key element of any awards programme, the adjudication process. A transparent and fair adjudication process is essential to the credibility of any awards programme. Award winners may be selected through a system based on their performance as measured against the performance of other nominees, on their level of contribution, or through a system based on nomination or consensus. Entry procedures and selection criteria must be clear, and the judging process must be impeccably fair. The adjudication process almost always involves the recruiting of judges or adjudicators to decide who will win particular awards. Clearly, it is important that these people are experts in the field and can judge independently and fairly across a range of candidates. Silvers (2004:327) maintains that

> If the awards programme is a competition, the jury or judging committee should be selected carefully to ensure that they are qualified to evaluate the submissions entered, preferably a panel of industry or professional peers, and that they are recognised as reputable and ethical individuals.

However, a glimpse at the history of awards programmes is sufficient to show that the strictest standards of probity have not always been observed. The adjudication process of the aforementioned *Société d'encouragement pour l'industrie nationale* (SEIN) was considered to have fallen short of the ideal, by at least one researcher:

> Throughout its first century most of the administrators, committees, and members of SEIN were drawn from the elite circles of aristocrats, scientists, politicians, professors, bankers, and wealthy manufacturers, who were not all necessarily qualified to gauge inventive merit. Jury or committee membership may in part have been offered as an honour, rather than as a means of obtaining the most technologically-qualified personnel.
>
> (Khan, 2015:8)

To this day, accusations of flaws and biases in the judging of awards programme candidates continue. The judging of the Oscars, for example, has been subject to accusations that it merely reflects the results of 'politically-contaminated opinions' (Jeacle, 2014:164, quoting Simonton, 2004).

In order to boost levels of trust, accuracy and integrity in their adjudication processes, some awards programme administrators draw upon the services of third-party auditors as official scrutineers of the judging system. According to Jeacle (2014), harnessing the power of audit as a legitimating tool in this way can be particularly effective when a well-known audit firm – namely one of the 'big four' (PricewaterhouseCoopers, Deloitte, Ernst & Young and KPMG) – is recruited to fill the role of official scrutineer. Using the example of the annual film awards ceremony of the British Academy of Film and Television Arts (BAFTA), Jeacle describes the scrutineer duties undertaken by the audit firm Deloitte as: checking that the systems and processes around the voting system have been followed; confirming the results according to the voting; and keeping the details of the winners secure and confidential in sealed envelopes until the actual event. Her research results suggest that the presence of an external auditor bestows additional value and credibility on BAFTA award results, highlighting the power of the auditor's stamp of approval as a legitimating tool. However, it is highly likely that this power has been somewhat diminished following the fiasco of the 2017 Oscar ceremony. On that infamous occasion, an employee of PricewaterhouseCoopers – the firm which had overseen the Academy's ballot-counting process for the previous 83 years – handed the wrong envelope to the presenter of the awards, resulting in chaos and confusion on stage as the wrong Best Picture winner was announced.

The value of awards ceremonies

The value for participants

Awards ceremonies are occasions for celebration and applause. For all guests, they provide opportunities for relaxation and enjoyment, a break away from the everyday work routine. At the same time, as well as celebrating the successes of individuals, awards ceremonies provide the participants with the chance to mark the important contribution made by their company, organisation or industry as a whole to the business, cultural, tertiary or scientific world in which it operates. This form of shared experience is a key part of the value of such ceremonies.

However, participants include two distinct categories of guest: winners and non-winners. To be successful, awards ceremonies must add value to both groups.

Winners

Clearly, winners, as the centre of attraction at awards ceremonies, bathe in the glow of the approbation and applause of those present at the event. And the added renown they receive can be greatly multiplied beyond the walls of the venue if the ceremony is being followed by the media.

But beyond the acclamation they receive at the moment of being presented with their prizes, what other types of value do awards bring to winners? A number of academic researchers have focused on the financial success that an award can create, particularly in the creative industries. Their basic premise is that awards can function as a form of 'signalling device', indicating the *quality* of a book or film that has been selected by expert judges as worthy of a prize. The hypothesis is that the award, by encouraging the public to see the film or buy the book, indirectly contributes to the financial success of the creative talents that produced it. However, although they generally agree that the role of awards as a signalling device seems particularly important in the cultural industries, where the actual quality of products is often difficult to determine prior to consumption, researchers differ in their assessment of the extent to which awards contribute to financial success.

Ginsburgh (2003) acknowledges that film and book awards have a positive impact on the financial success of the actors and authors, but concludes that while prize-winning movies most often become box office successes, there are no long-term differences in terms of financial success between book award winners and titles that were shortlisted but did not win. In other words, the fact of being shortlisted brought non-winning books the same commercial benefits as the winning titles.

Ponzo and Scoppa (2015) found evidence of substantial financial benefits resulting from Oscar nominations and awards for best picture and best actor/actress. Their research also demonstrated that the most prestigious Italian literary award, the *Premio Strega*, awarded annually to the year's best Italian work of fiction on the basis of voting by a jury of experts, had a highly significant influence on book sales, with most of the impact occurring in the weeks following the announcement of the prize. However, they do acknowledge that part of this impact may be a consequence of the indirect effects caused, for example, by increased marketing efforts of publishers for books which have won prizes. Ginsburgh (2003) focuses on the quality of the evaluations of candidates for the Oscars and the Booker Prize. He found that while their verdicts (i.e. the awards they bestow) may affect commercial success in the arts, expert juries were often poor judges of an oeuvre's fundamental aesthetic quality. Gemser et al. (2008:45) concur to a degree, at least in respect of mainstream films:

awards in themselves are not that effective as signals of quality for mainstream films, irrespective of whether they are consumer, expert, or peer selected. Other signals of quality such as advertising and screen intensity may spur ticket sales to a much greater extent.

However, by way of contrast, the authors postulate that with regard to independent films, relative lack of word of mouth and comparatively limited marketing budgets may increase the importance of winning awards for increasing ticket sales.

In the world of business, awards may act as indicators of quality when they are considered signals of the recipient's expertise and skills. Harrison and Jepsen (2015) note that prize-winning individuals, in their résumé and on social media platforms such as LinkedIn, often refer to their awards in order to distinguish themselves from others. These winners, therefore, may be seen to be using their awards as a means of signalling their skills and abilities to recruiters and hiring managers. However, the authors found no clear evidence that, in business, winning an award has the effect of automatically advancing the recipient's career:

> We do not know whether award winners would have been successful without the award win. When skills are recognised by an award, the individual's career success may be a result of the award or a result of the skills they had that led to the award. In theory and in practice, those receiving the award already possess the skills to be successful. In other words, we do not know to what extent winning an award is a cause or effect of a successful career.
>
> (Harrison and Jepsen, 2015:29)

Non-winners

In order to offer value to all participants, awards ceremonies need to appeal to the wider audience, which includes those who are not there to receive an award, and those who are not closely connected to potential award winners. Highlighting the challenge that this creates for event designers, Silvers (2004:325) quotes Steve Kemble of Steve Kemble Event Design in Dallas, Texas:

> We all love award ceremonies, but in so many situations, we have to remember that half the audience couldn't care less about that portion of the programme. They didn't submit entries; they're not receiving an award; they didn't participate; they're just there for the party! The burden is then on us as event designers to develop ways to make the entire programme more interesting (and, we hope, to entice them to participate or enter next year).

An imaginative solution to the challenge of engaging the non-winners during the prize-giving element of award ceremonies is illustrated in the Sensix case study in this chapter.

The value for presenting organisations

In the corporate world, award programmes and ceremonies offer a range of benefits to the individual companies that use this form of employee recognition. Award programmes can help underpin and reinforce the entire motivational culture and ethos of a company, demonstrating in a very public manner that it is an organisation in which hard work is correctly rewarded. As well as showing the recipients of the awards that their work is valued, awards ceremonies remind other employees that their good work will be rewarded if they too strive for excellence. If the ceremony is reported by the media, it also serves as a useful source of positive public relations for the company.

When awards ceremonies are held to recognise achievements at the broader level of a profession as a whole, the publicity they generate can serve as a useful means of drawing attention to the importance of the field in which the activity takes place. For example, the European Union Prize for Women Innovators, with its awards ceremony held each year in the European Parliament in Brussels, is designed to boost the public awareness of the contribution of women researchers to entrepreneurship and to encourage entrepreneurial women to become innovators.

Europe urgently needs more innovators to stay competitive in the coming decades and to spur economic growth. The large number of well-educated women who, for various reasons, including lack of awareness, do not consider entrepreneurship as an option, represents a tremendous untapped pool of innovation.

Awards have a strong potential to drive innovation through the recognition of achievements and the promotion of role models. Therefore, the European Commission (EC) created in 2011 a Prize for Women Innovators to increase public awareness of this issue and to encourage women to exploit the commercial and business opportunities and become entrepreneurs.

The EC wants to highlight the outstanding achievements of women innovators who have (co-) founded a successful company and brought an innovation to market and benefited from research and innovation funding from the public or private sector.

The Commission will award up to three 'EU Prize for Women Innovators' awards and one 'Rising Innovator Award' (female innovators – aged 30 years or under – at the start of their careers) following a European-wide contest.

First Prize – €100 000

Second Prize – €50 000

Third Prize – €30 000

Rising Innovator – €20 000

Source: European Commission (n.d.).

The existence of awards for particular professions has been credited with the raising of standards within those fields. For instance, Lanosga (2015) discusses how the awarding of Pulitzer Prizes has been influential in raising the quality of professional journalistic reporting practices by helping to determine standards of quality for newspapers, as well as nurturing the practice of exposés and encouraging certain topics for investigation.

> Recognition through prizes – particularly the Pulitzer Prizes, which represent professional affirmation of the highest order – is certainly not the only influence over journalistic behaviour, but it is a significant one that adds context to our current understanding of how that behaviour developed in the twentieth century.
>
> (Lanosga, 2015:4)

Awards ceremonies as forums for activism and protest

The publicity generated by awards and awards ceremonies is clearly of considerable value to the individual prizewinners as well as to the companies and professions that benefit from the public relations generated by the media coverage of such events. However, the media's interest in awards ceremonies is not always to the benefit of the presenting organisations. For example, Reid (2006) describes how the MTV Europe Music Awards became politicised when they were hosted in Edinburgh in 2003. This was due to a large public subsidy given to MTV to part-fund the event's temporary structure and the outside broadcast costs of a simultaneous live concert in Edinburgh's city centre Princes Street Gardens. Although the subsidy was intended to generate local economic benefits by helping to portray Edinburgh in a new light as part of the city's ongoing repositioning strategy, local media were very critical. The local newspaper in particular emphasised the event's cost and disruption, the inappropriate actions of public officials, and MTV's ticket allocation to corporate clients.

For many observers of, and participants in, high-profile awards ceremonies that attract the attention of the world's media, the temptation to use such occasions as forums for protest and activism has increasingly proved to be irresistible. For example, in the weeks leading up to the 88th Academy Awards ceremony, industry pundits, critics and bloggers alike took to the trending hashtag #OscarsSoWhite to protest about what they perceived as the exclusion of actors and artists of colour in key awards categories. The following year, at the 2018 Golden Globes ceremony, also held in order to honour achievements in the film industry, many of the attendees wore black in support of Time's Up, an initiative aimed at combating sexual harassment and supporting gender parity across a multitude of industries. Several of the award winners used their time in the spotlight to address the issue of sexual harassment and gender inequality in their acceptance speeches.

It can be a severe test of the organisers' skills to maintain an appropriate tone for award ceremonies, when they are faced with the challenges of tackling such sobering issues within an event format that is also widely expected to have a celebratory character.

The market for awards ceremonies

As stated towards the beginning of this chapter, awards and awards ceremonies are ubiquitous, and they continue to proliferate to the extent that some commentators have expressed the view that there are already too many in some sectors. Even some actors have reported suffering from awards season fatigue (Block, 2014). New professions and new specialisms within professions add to the burgeoning list of awards ceremonies as they create their own events to celebrate the achievements of their colleagues. Inevitably, many of these new awards ceremonies are in the technology field, such as the PropTech (Property Technology) Innovation Award Ceremony which was launched in Berlin in 2017, or the first Scotland Women in Technology Awards Ceremony which took place the same year.

In this section, the principal stakeholders in the market for awards ceremonies are investigated.

Demand

The sources of demand for awards ceremony events is extremely varied, with a diverse range of donors, presenting organisations and awarding institutions generating business for intermediaries and suppliers in this market. Awards ceremonies recognising the achievements of public sector employees do take place, but in most countries their numbers are limited and budgets are generally moderate, due to the need for governments not to be seen spending public funds without sound justification.

In the corporate world, individual companies requiring external events for the bestowing of awards upon their colleagues constitute a major share of the demand for such ceremonies, which are often annual occasions with a significant emphasis on celebrating and partying.

Professional associations of the type discussed in Chapter 3 represent another category of demand for awards ceremonies, whether at the local, regional, national or international level. Such ceremonies may be organised as stand-alone events or may be held as a component of the association's annual conference, often as part of the gala dinner.

The various elements of the media, such as magazines and broadcasters, are a further source of demand, with events held to celebrate the winners of, for example, the BBC's annual All in the Mind Awards and the Food & Farming Awards. Again, these ceremonies may be stand-alone, or they may be held during other types of business events such as conferences or exhibitions. For instance, since 1992, *Global Finance* magazine has compiled an annual ranking of the World's 50 Safest Banks. The banks highest up in the list are presented with awards at special ceremonies held during the annual meetings of the International Monetary Fund and the World Bank, ensuring widespread media coverage.

The charity and voluntary sectors also constitute a major part of the market, often using awards ceremonies as a way of acknowledging the efforts of their volunteers and the outstanding contributions of colleagues who give back to their communities. Such events also provide third-sector organisations with the opportunity to raise funds to support their causes. The revenue may arise from the sale of tickets for the event, or the event itself may include some fundraising activities. For example, the Eagle Nature Foundation which is based in Illinois and campaigns for the protection of the bald eagle and other endangered species, combines its annual awards ceremony with a fundraising luncheon featuring raffles and an auction.

A final category of demand is that generated by event management agencies creating and running their own awards programmes and ceremonies as commercial ventures designed to earn revenue for the owners of such events. It is common for such agencies to specialise in running awards ceremonies for specific industry sectors, such as the communications and advertising industries, the retail sector or information technology.

Suppliers

The stakeholders supplying facilities and services for awards ceremonies include the great variety of venues that may host such events. Although hotel ballrooms are often the default choice for such events, other types of venues are often chosen due to the prestige that they bring to the event. Historic properties, museums, opera houses and theatres can lend a touch of opulence to awards ceremonies; while sports stadia may be selected as venues due to a connection with the presenting organisation. For example, the Guyana Netball Association has held its annual awards ceremony at the National Gymnasium, a sports venue in the nation's capital, Georgetown.

Food and beverage is another key component of most awards ceremonies. This may be supplied by the venue or, as is often the case with non-traditional venues, may be brought into the event by outside caterers.

The appearance and the quality of the acoustics in the venue are vital elements of the success of awards ceremonies. As with catering, these may be supplied by the venue or brought in, often by an event production company that takes care of the sound, lighting, staging, rigging, power and audio-visual elements of the ceremony. Less tangible, but no less important, are the growing number of specialist cloud software programs that help organisers manage the entire applications and evaluations processes online. Suppliers such as Award Force (www.awardforce.com) provide such software as well as online backup to those using it.

Finally, not to be overlooked are the men and women whose job it is to act as hosts for the event, keep it running smoothly and to time, read out the names and descriptions of the winners, and introduce speakers. A variety of titles are used in connection with these suppliers, including Master of Ceremonies (or MC/emcee), host, toastmaster or compère. Their essential role is to help the audience feel engaged with, and informed about, everything that is happening during the event.

Intermediaries

Although some organisations may undertake to organise their awards programme using in-house staff from the events department or the marketing team, for example, the specialist nature of awards programmes means that most presenting institutions use the services of intermediaries to design and execute the event.

A wide range of intermediaries and agencies offer their services to clients in this market. A few may specialise entirely in running awards ceremonies, but most are also involved in managing a variety of business events of the types covered in this book. They have titles such as event designers, event agencies and event management companies, and most of them are full-service agencies, using their experience and expertise to ensure that their clients' awards ceremonies are entirely successful. Their role is to act on behalf of their clients, selecting and negotiating with the full range of suppliers.

The role of a full-service awards ceremony management company is analysed in the next section.

Designing and delivering awards ceremonies

Just as with any other type of business event, the designing and execution of awards ceremonies must meet the goals and objectives of the presenting organisation, whether it is an individual company, an association, charity or another type of institution. The attendance levels and tone of these events are key contributors to their success.

The websites of two London venues often used for the hosting of awards ceremonies offer general advice regarding the desired tone of such events:

> Awards ceremonies are a celebration of talent, success and achievement, so when planning this kind of event, it's important that it's upbeat, exciting and well attended. Ensuring the event is well attended by respected peers and industry experts will add weight and authority to your event, making it a more sought-after event in general.
>
> (https://www.senatehouseevents.co.uk)

> Award shows do not all have to be as lavish or as glamorous as the Grammys and the Oscars, but they do have to deliver an unforgettable experience for attendees. This can pose a unique set of challenges, which means they must be approached differently from other corporate events. For starters, you need to ensure that the award show is memorable and engaging for all attendees whilst meeting the needs of the client and any sponsors. The competitive nature of the awards ceremony planning industry ... means that you have to be innovative as well as deliver the basics with genuine aplomb – and all on a budget too! The pressure to produce an award ceremony that is better than the previous year is also a major factor.
>
> (http://20bedfordway.com/)

The rest of this chapter examines best practice in the design and execution of awards ceremonies.

Budget

Budget considerations largely depend upon the financial model for the awards ceremony in question. As is the case for most types of corporate event, the funding of the ceremonies of individual companies represents a cost to that company, with funds generally coming from the marketing budget or the human resources budget, or both. Regarding the awards ceremonies of associations, on the other hand, as is the case for association conferences, such events are usually expected to at least break even, or preferably to make a profit for the association.

Two other categories – the awards ceremonies of charities and those of event management agencies running their own awards programmes as commercial ventures – are clearly expected to make a profit. Tickets are sold for such events, and sponsorship packages are created as a further source of revenue.

The size of the budget available for the design and execution of the event represents a key determining factor in the selection of the following facilities and services.

Venue

In addition to budgetary considerations, the choice of venue will also be determined by two other influencing factors: the size of the event in terms of the number of guests and the level of formality. Small external corporate awards ceremonies, for one company only, can be held in a private room at a local restaurant, for instance. Informal ceremonies, for example to recognise community service, can be held in a school gymnasium or sports centre; while the potential venues for more formal events would include hotel banqueting rooms or historic properties that lend a touch of dignity and kudos to the event.

An eventbright.co.uk blog emphasises the importance of the venue impressing and delighting the guests:

> You should look for somewhere with a degree of 'wow factor'. By their very nature, award shows are supposed to be exciting and glamorous and generate pre-event anticipation. Choosing a unique venue can help raise interest, so don't dismiss unlikely venues out of hand – creative lighting and set dressing can totally transform a space. Just be sure to check with your audio-visual supplier that the space will work from a practical standpoint with regards to acoustics etc. and that no guests will have an obstructed view of the stage. Of course, it's reassuring if the venue has hosted awards before and you could ask to see photos or talk to the organiser to see how it all worked.
>
> (Eventbrite, 2015)

Entertainment

As celebratory events, awards ceremonies are largely expected to provide some form of entertainment. This element is particularly important for the non-winners at the event, who expect more than simply listening to a long list of award winners' names and looking on as they have their photographs taken. The Senate House website offers the following suggestions: 'Consider hiring local bands, celebrities, dance groups, musicians, magicians; anything that will entertain your guests whilst awards are not being presented. Professional entertainers help create a buzz at your event and also facilitate networking by creating a relaxed atmosphere' (University of London Venues, 2014).

But, of course, it is essential that a balance is struck between the type of entertainment provided and the dignity of the event. If the principal objective is to show respect for the people being honoured at the event, the value of their awards can be diminished if the ceremony involves elements of over-frivolous and irreverent entertainment.

Food and drink

Most formal award ceremonies follow the format of a sit-down dinner, with guests either dining before the awards are presented or during the presentations. One convincing argument for waiting until after the meal before presenting the awards is that by doing so, the clatter of dishes and glasses does not interfere with the awards speeches.

Vikki Kennedy, Event Manager at The International Centre, Telford, UK, offers advice that takes into account the perspective of the caterers:

> It is helpful if you can stick to timings and serve the starter and main course without having awards in-between as it guarantees the quality of the food. There is nothing more stressful for the catering team than awards overrunning between courses.
>
> (Eventbrite, 2016)

There are also budgetary considerations to be taken into account regarding the provision of food and drinks. Generally, alcoholic drinks are provided throughout the event to reinforce its celebratory nature of the event, but to avoid these becoming a major drain on the budget, one option is to offer wine throughout the meal, but have guests pay for their own drinks for the rest of the event (University of London Venues, 2014).

Hosts and speakers

The event organisers, when deciding who should be chosen for the critical role of host or hosts, must remember that the role of host is vital for both setting the correct tone for the event and maintaining the energy levels in the room throughout the evening. Nick Gold, the Managing Director of Speakers Corner, emphasises the importance of the pre-event briefing between organisers and hosts:

> Organisers need to be clear in communicating their requirements regarding delivery. This includes the pace of the awards, the extent of interaction with the winners, and whether or not an autocue will be used. Most importantly, but often overlooked, is the ability to hold an audience's attention when 90% are tempted to switch off

(normally once their award category of interest has passed). To create a needed lift at this point, make sure that your host of choice is able to keep the energy flowing in the room. It will help to make the night even more memorable.

(Eventbrite, 2016)

It is generally agreed that hosts should be charismatic, likeable, respected and knowledgeable, but, in addition, their duties require them to be excellent performers too:

> As part of the awards presentation, they will need to present a clear and engaging narrative as to why the recipient has won the award. A few things to be aware of are the importance of pronouncing the award recipients' names correctly and holding and presenting the awards with body language that imparts the award-giving with the gravity it deserves.
>
> (20Bedfordway.com, n.d.)

As well as a host or hosts, one or more speakers are often recruited to add value to the award ceremony's proceedings. The Senate House website makes the case for including a relevant inspiring speaker in such events:

> This could be someone who has won the award previously, or who is closely linked to the content of the awards. The added value of a good speaker will offer a further reason for your guests to attend the event.
>
> (University of London Venues, 2014)

Other considerations

Networking opportunities

The facilitating of networking opportunities is an effective way of adding value to awards events, as guests generally seize the chance to mingle in a pool of relevant peers. Networking can take place throughout the event, from a pre-dinner drinks reception and during the meal, to an after-ceremony networking drinks/dessert.

During these socialising periods in the programme, it is useful to have some form of animation which can be used as 'ice-breakers' – something for the guests to comment upon at the beginning of their conversations. One possibility is the use of television screens playing short videos featuring those who have been nominated for awards. This brings an extra dimension into the event, giving guests more of an insight into each nominee. The videos can also include messages from the event's sponsors.

Photography

Given the celebratory nature of awards ceremonies, it is customary to capture the events' key moments on film, which can subsequently be shared with sponsors, on social media and kept for posterity by the award winners. Often, the photography can begin long before the actual awards are presented, as suggested by the Gigsalad blog:

Hire some photographers to stand outside and flash photos at your guests. Paparazzi are the bane of celebrities' lives, but to a regular person, for one night, it'll make the experience memorable. Plus, the professional photos make great party favors for your guests.

(Clark, 2015)

Naturally, there should be at least one photograph of each winner with their trophy, but not necessarily on the stage. Many ceremonies have an offstage area where the official photographs can be taken, usually against a backdrop that prominently features the presenting organisation's logo. But, most awards ceremony planners take care to make sure that it is not only the winners who appear in photographs. London-based events planners visionevents suggest that,

Roaming cameras can capture great footage throughout the event, including any interviews with sponsors/guests/winners, and create a fabulous post-event highlights video for you to share on your website, or use as promotional tools to secure those all-important sponsors for future years.

(20Bedfordway.com, n.d.)

Raffles and auctions

Another way of engaging guests, while at the same time raising useful funds, either for the presenting organisation or to support a separate charitable agenda, is to have raffles or auctions with donated prizes. For example, at the annual Meetings & Incentive Travel Industry Awards in London, funds are raised for the UK events industry's own charity (Meeting Needs, n.d.).

It is generally good practice to announce at the end of the event how much has been raised, as this can boost the feel-good factor in the room. If the final figure raised is not immediately available, the good news can be shared through follow-up communication, such as a press release.

Table planning

Regarding the issue of how guests are seated for the ceremony, there are two factors to be taken into consideration: networking opportunities and, for award winners, ease of access to the stage when they are presented with their prizes.

One option open to planners is to sell tickets via entire tables, which has the advantage of allowing guests the option of purchasing a whole table for their group. This leaves the networking in their hands and allows them to invite others to the event as their guests. Selling individual tickets is also a useful option, as it is an effective way of filling spaces on tables that have only been partly booked. In this way, individuals or small groups can choose where they would like to sit, for networking purposes.

To save valuable time during the ceremony, careful thought must also be given to the ease with which the stage may be accessed and exited by those receiving their awards. Long gaps in the proceedings as award winners make their way to the stage can cause the event to lose its momentum. Furthermore, Vikki Kennedy, Event Manager at The International Centre, Telford, offers a useful piece of advice on using seating arrangements to maintain the engagement of guests: 'Ensure all the winning tables are evenly distributed around the room, otherwise those placed at the back and sides soon work out they are not going to win and lose interest' (Eventbrite, 2016).

Trophies

The event planner may be required to choose and arrange for the purchase of the award trophies. This task requires considerable thought as the trophy represents the tangible symbol of recipients' achievements. There are many options available, including framed certificates, medals, plaques and statuettes as well as trophies made of metal, glass, crystal, wood, acrylic or ceramics. Contemporary awards such as those made of glass or crystal are preferred by many companies and businesses because of their elegant appearance and stylish designs.

Nevertheless, other factors apart from appearance must be taken into account. There are budgetary issues to be considered if each trophy is to be engraved with the holder's name and the donor's logo. In addition, there are practical considerations: for example, if award winners are travelling home by plane after the event, the weight and size of their trophies may complicate their luggage arrangements.

Chapter summary

This chapter began with a discussion of the importance of awards as a form of public recognition of the achievements of individuals, teams or organisations, satisfying the recipients' fundamental need for status and esteem. The range of awards and types of awarding bodies was explored, including awards presented to business events stakeholders. The chapter highlighted the paucity of academic research into this topic and reproduced the suggestions of Frey and Gallus (2017) for possible research topics linked to awards and awards ceremonies. The characteristics of awards ceremonies were explored, focusing particularly on the adjudication process. The value of awards as a 'signalling device', indicating quality in the cultural and business worlds, was discussed, as well as their role in raising standards within professions and drawing attention to particular issues. In addition, the role of awards ceremonies as forums for activism and protest was analysed, noting the challenge that this creates for organisers of such occasions. There followed a review of the various stakeholders in the market for awards ceremonies: sources of demand, including the corporate, association and the charity and voluntary sectors; suppliers, including venues and technology support; and the full-service agencies who organise such ceremonies for their clients. The chapter concluded with a review of the awards ceremony planning process.

CASE STUDY 5.1: THE FOOTBALL BUSINESS AWARDS

Football Business Awards

Background

Football in the UK has developed into a multi-billion-pound business. In 2015, a report by consultants Ernst & Young estimated that the Premier League, the UK's top football league, and its clubs contributed £3.36 billion to the nation's GDP, supported employment of more than 100,000 jobs, and added around £2.4 billion to UK government coffers through tax receipts (EY, 2015).

The Football Business Awards (http://footballbusinessawards.com/) are designed to recognise the essential role that business plays in football, the positive impact of football on the community, and the vital role played by the businesses which serve the football industry in the United Kingdom. The Football Business Awards ceremony is a national event at which all the football industry's achievements off the pitch are celebrated at the end of each year. It is also a significant annual networking event for the industry.

The Football Business Awards were created in 2012 by a partnership of three events professionals who, alongside their events expertise, combined their valuable individual knowledge of football, PR and awards ceremonies.

Venue

For the first four editions of the Football Business Awards, the ceremony was held at the Chelsea FC (football club) Stamford Bridge's 1,400m² Great Hall events space in southwest London. The inaugural event attracted 450 senior representatives from clubs and businesses working in football – not only from the UK but from around the world. Four years later, attendance figures had risen to 550, as the event became more widely established.

The 2016 ceremony was held at the Emirates Stadium in north London, home of the Arsenal FC. And for the first time, in 2017, the event was held in a non-football venue, Tobacco Dock (http://tobaccodocklondon.com/) in London, ten minutes' walk from Tower Hill. By the fifth edition of the ceremony, the organisers were of the opinion that it no longer needed a football venue as a foundation, as it was well enough established to stand on its own, independent of any football club.

Award categories

The award categories cover a broad range of football business and commercial issues, and are open to clubs and to any business connected to football. In deciding upon which award categories to offer in any particular year, a priority for the event's organisers is to achieve a balance between awards for clubs and awards for businesses serving clubs. When a category is seen to be popular, it can be split into more nuanced categories the following year. The organisers also understand that, financially, Premier League clubs dominate so they work hard to ensure that achievements at all levels of the game are recognised. To that end, the award categories are regularly reviewed in order to give small clubs and businesses more of a voice.

The categories for 2017, with the entry fees, are shown below:

2017 Categories (The entry fee is £225 + VAT per submission or £395 + VAT for two entries)

Best Professional Service Business Serving Football

Agency of the Year

Best Business Serving Football – up to £2m turnover (non-professional service)

Best Business Serving Football – over £2m turnover (non-professional service)

Best Club Marketing Initiative – Premier League

Best Club Marketing Initiative – non–Premier League

Best Football Club Hospitality

Best Use of Technology in Football (not club specific)

Best Use of Technology in a Football Club

Football Brand of the Year

Innovation Award

Stadium of the Year

Best Football Community Scheme

Best Corporate Social Responsibility Scheme

Best Non-match Day Use of Venue

Best Fan Engagement by Club

Sponsorship/Partnership of the Year

Best Brand Activation Involving Football

fcbusiness Magazine CEO of the Year Award

Judges

The award judges change each year, but the organisers tend to look for people who are senior and have credibility in the football industry. Originally, a broader base of judges was used, comprising football club CEOs, as well as senior business and marketing professionals involved in football; but this has evolved into a panel of judges who are predominantly football club CEOs.

Sponsorship

Support for the awards ceremony comes from two different types of sources: category sponsors, who, in return for their sponsorship, gain considerable exposure; and partners, who have a broader involvement in the event. Both category sponsors and partners benefit greatly from the networking opportunities at the event.

In 2017, there were two category sponsors:

Smith & Williamson is an independently owned accountancy and investment management group which has a dedicated sports team providing specialised advice to assist sports professionals to effectively manage their financial affairs.

Visual Elements is Tobacco Dock's in-house lighting, rigging and audio-visual team, with extensive experience in providing equipment and technical advice for organisers of live events, exhibitions, conferences and roadshows.

There were three partners in that year:

The London Sporting Club: the UK's first ever invitation-only members' club for people who play professional sport and those at the highest level in the business of sport.

StreamAMG (Advanced Media Group): suppliers of global digital media solutions to European companies. One of the company's main sectors is the sports industry.

fcbusiness: the business magazine for the UK and Republic of Ireland football industry, serving as a practical guide to those involved in the business of running a football club at every level.

The ceremony

The ceremony is generally held in the month of November but finding the optimum date for this event is often challenging, given that football is a very busy and travel-intensive industry.

The Football Business Awards ceremony begins with networking drinks, followed by a welcome speech from the hosts. Entertainment and a three-course dinner are then provided, and these are followed by the actual awards. A final networking drinks session completes the evening's programme. Prices for the 2017 ceremony are shown below:

Table for 10 – £3,250 + VAT

Table for 12 – £3,750 + VAT

Individual place – £350 + VAT

Five places – £1,625 + VAT

Premium table for 10 – £3,750 + VAT

Premium table for 12 – £4,250 + VAT

Premium tables are located in premier positions and include two bottles of champagne per table.

CASE STUDY 5.2: SENSIX COMMUNICATIONS & EVENTS: INVOLVING THE NON-WINNERS AT AN AWARDS CEREMONY

Sensix

The material in this case study is adapted from a blog by Michael Caplan, founder and Creative Director of Sensix Communications & Events, which was originally published on www.specialevents.com. Sensix Communications & Events (http://sensix.com/) is an event planning and meeting production company with offices in Montreal and Toronto and over 30 years' experience in the business events sector. Here, the company's founder and Creative Director, Michael Caplan, describes how Sensix rose to the challenge of involving the non-winners in attendance at an awards ceremony.

The challenges

Awards ceremonies are always so boring for the majority of the audience – the 'non-winners'. Even the Oscars – with top Hollywood writers, mega-talent on stage and major production budgets – can bore you to tears.

How can we possibly make corporate awards exciting?

That's the challenge we were recently faced with – creating an exciting awards ceremony for 600 people at their annual sales force event with a total of 60 awards in 13 categories and 37 presenters!

We also had to:

- Shorten the duration of the awards from previous years and leave more time for partying
- Lower the budget from the previous years
- Make the winners feel honoured
- Involve the non-winners.

The solutions

We ended up synthesising the most powerful elements of movie premiere excitement with a rock concert vibe to create a truly exciting award show without any hired entertainment.

It worked like this:

Total group recognition started from the outset as guests were given the red-carpet treatment and high-fived and cheered all the way into the awards room by a receiving line of their senior managers. A live film crew made all the guests feel like movie stars.

Inside, guests found stadium-style seating, bringing everyone nice and close to the non-stop action that was about to begin. When the first award was announced, it was just like any other award show – the winner's name and bio popped up on screen and a spotlight followed the winner in the audience and projected their live image ... But then all hell broke loose! As the winner made his way to the stage, a party dance hit filled the air and a classic Hollywood movie clip was projected in sync with the music.

These clips featured dance scenes and inspirational moments, from movies such as *Dirty Dancing* to *Chariots of Fire*, as well as famous cinematic expressions such as 'I'll be back', to add some humour.

The solution to audience boredom: The non-winners became part of the show! They rose to their feet, cheering and clapping for the winner to the beat of each new song and seeing how fast they could identify the movie clip that appeared on-screen.

Sixty ovations in a row in 60 minutes – before the audience had time to realise it, an hour flew by and the last set of awards was being presented.

No one had to just clap politely as they endured the endless monotony of long winner bios and thank-you speeches at this awards ceremony.

The celebratory atmosphere was cemented with a final group award – Sales Team of the Year. These 14 winners, along with eight presenters and the top company executives, were cheered on by the audience as the awards climaxed with a boisterous confetti explosion.

Why it worked

Having the awards presented in one quick 60-minute burst before dinner rather than breaking them up into segments between courses solved many of our challenges.

We were able to harness the collective 'kinetic' energy felt at the beginning of an award show and not let it be dissipated throughout the evening. The high energy generated at these awards was maintained during the dinner and dancing since everyone was now free to party.

Costs were lowered by eliminating the need for a professional emcee or hired entertainers. Time was also saved by not having to add injections of entertainment between courses to keep the audience's interest.

And of course, the winners – for whom this event was being held in the first place – felt very honoured during this award ceremony. The lights, the music and the classic movie moments gave them each their 45 seconds of fame in the spotlight. (Yes, that's three times the classic 15 seconds.)

What ultimately made this award ceremony exciting? It felt like a party for each and every person, winners and non-winners alike, from the opening of the first envelope to the last. The pace was lightning-fast . . . no speeches, no lulls and no boredom.

CASE STUDY 5.3: THE ASIA PACIFIC SCREEN AWARDS

Background

Covering one-third of the earth, the 70 countries and areas of the vast Asia Pacific region stretch from Egypt in the west to the Cook Islands in the east, from Russia in the north to New Zealand in the south. Between them, these countries are home to 4.5 billion people and produce half of the world's films.

The annual Asia Pacific Screen Awards (APSA) (www.asiapacificscreenawards.com) were established in 2007 to recognise and promote the cinematic excellence and cultural diversity of the Asia Pacific region. They are now the region's highest accolade in film.

Headquartered in Brisbane, Australia, the APSA are supported by Brisbane City Council and managed by the economic development board, Brisbane Marketing. They are endorsed by UNESCO and FIAPF – the International Federation of Film Producers Associations. With UNESCO, APSA aims to build a greater understanding of diversity across cultures. Through the collaboration with FIAPF, the awards share the common interests of Asia Pacific film producers in promoting their films to a global audience.

Since the awards' inception, thousands of feature-length films have competed in the APSA, films that demonstrate a wide range of diversity – each telling a story from its country of origin.

APSA aims to:

- Acclaim filmmaking in the Asia Pacific region that best reflects its culture, origin and cinematic excellence
- Award the people behind this excellence
- Promote this outstanding work in film to a global audience in order to broaden the market appeal of such works
- Encourage collaboration between filmmakers
- Develop, through film, greater understanding of the region's various cultures
- Take the creativity of our neighbouring cultures in the vast Asia Pacific region to the world.

Awards are presented for the following achievements:

- Best Feature Film
- Best Animated Feature Film
- Best Documentary Feature Film
- Best Youth Feature Film
- Achievement in Directing
- Best Screenplay
- Best Original Score
- Achievement in Cinematography
- Best Performance by an Actress
- Best Performance by an Actor
- Jury Grand Prize.

Additional awards are presented for outstanding achievement:

- FIAPF Award for outstanding achievement in film in the Asia Pacific region
- Cultural Diversity Award under the patronage of UNESCO – The United Nations Educational, Scientific, and Cultural Organization (UNESCO) Award for outstanding contribution to the promotion and preservation of cultural diversity through film

- Young Cinema Award in partnership with NETPAC (Network for the Promotion of Asian Cinema) and Griffith Film School (GFS) recognises the abundant emerging talent of the Asia Pacific.

The APSA competition

Each year, approximately 300 feature-length films participate in the APSA competition.

The APSA judging process is conducted in three phases to view the nominees, deliberate and determine the winners.

1   Submitting Member Organisations are enlisted to put forward four films to represent their country or area. These films are shortlisted by a Features Selection Panel. The APSA Secretariat and International Nominations Council are also empowered to invite films to ensure the broadest representation possible from the 70 countries and areas engaged by APSA.
2   The International Nominations Council deliberates and votes to choose the nominees in seven award categories – Best Feature Film, Achievement in Directing, Best Performance by an Actor, Best Performance by an Actress, Best Screenplay, Achievement in Cinematography and the Cultural Diversity Award, under the patronage of UNESCO. Selection panels of experts drawn from the relevant industry fields determine nominees in the Youth, Animation, Documentary and Best Original Score categories. The FIAPF Award and Young Cinema Award winners are also determined at this stage.
3   APSA appoints the following Juries to determine the winners in their relevant categories, which are announced at the Awards Ceremony:

- International Jury
- Youth, Animation, Documentary International Jury
- Music in Film International Jury
- Cultural Diversity International Jury.

The APSA ceremony

Each year, more than 1,000 key film industry luminaries from across the Asia Pacific region gather to honour the best films and filmmakers in that region. The ceremony is webcast live from the Brisbane Convention and Exhibition Centre. Representatives from each of the nominated films attend the ceremony and are presented on stage along with the Nominations Council, International Jury and special guests. Recipients of an Asia Pacific Screen Award receive a unique work of art to acknowledge their achievement – a symbol common to all cultures and civilisation – the urn, the vase or the vessel, designed by Brisbane artist Joanna Bone.

In the past, special guest performers have included Demi Im, Tenzin Choegyal, Katherine Philp, number one Japanese R&B star Ai, internationally renowned Erhu virtuoso Ma Xiaohui and William Barton, Australia's leading didgeridoo player and composer.

CASE STUDY 5.4: THE SERBIA TOURISM FLOWER AWARD

Serbia Tourism Flower Award

Background

The Tourism Flower Award ceremony ('Turistički cvet') is organised each year by the National Tourism Organisation of Serbia (NTOS) (http://www.serbia.travel), which was founded in 1994 as a government agency to promote and improve tourism in the Republic of Serbia in both the domestic and foreign tourism markets.

The Tourism Flower Award was created in 1982 with the aim of stimulating innovation and competitiveness in the domain of tourism in Serbia. Awards are traditionally given for significant achievements in raising the quality of tourist services and products, as well as for contributing to the development, improvement and promotion of tourism in Serbia.

Award categories

The different categories for the awards have changed several times, but for the past few years, they have been given to:

1   The best tourist local organisation in Serbia
2   The best tourist event
3   The best inbound tourist agency

4   The best (a) hotels; (b) other types of accommodation
5   An organisation or individual for contributing to the improvement of tourism and raising the quality of tourist services

The ceremony

Around 300 people are invited to the ceremony each year, from various state institutions, companies and agencies active in the tourism sector, as well as representatives from the media, educational and culture sectors. A number of celebrities and figures of national importance are usually in attendance. For example, the 2017 edition of The Tourism Flower Award ceremony was attended by Rasim Ljajic – Deputy Prime Minister of the Republic of Serbia, and Minister of Trade, Tourism and Telecommunications. Prizes were awarded by the NTOS Director, Marija Labović.

To highlight the importance of tourism for Serbia, the ceremony is generally held on World Tourism Day, as celebrated by the United Nations World Tourism Organization.

The venue for the award ceremony changes from year to year in order to draw more attention to the award and give more prominence to the venues chosen to host this event. The NTOS usually selects a venue which holds some significance for the country's tourism offer: for example, a new or particularly successful hotel, a concert hall or a museum, which this way gains additional attention.

The judging process

Tourism businesses choose categories for which they want to apply. There is a formal procedure for each candidate. They must provide a written explanation of why they consider they deserve an award, supported by material such as photographs, an audio-visual recording of up to five minutes, advertising material, etc.

The judges are recruited from various fields: academics specialising in tourism education and research, CEOs of different tourism-related trade associations, such as hotels, tourism agencies and travel journalists.

IT'S MY JOB
MATT RILEY, FOUNDER AND CEO OF
THE CONFERENCE AGENCY, LTD

I discovered the world of events when I got my first job after college, at the South Carolina Bar Association, the mandatory association for the state's lawyers and judges. I worked in the Continuing Legal Education division, coordinating small seminars focused on various legal topics. As a student, I had worked on the front desk of a hotel, so I had basic venue and customer service knowledge, and I quickly learned how to work with volunteers and navigate the association setting. As time went by, I was promoted to dealing with larger seminars, distance learning and eventually the association's annual conference, which includes an awards ceremony.

The South Carolina Bar offers various awards focused on distinguished service to the association, pro bono legal services provided for the common good, and even awards for teachers involved in the organisation's mock trial programmes that give high school students a taste of the legal profession. The awards are presented during a plenary session at the Annual Bar Convention, which is attended by roughly 1,000 of the top lawyers and judges in the state.

I was struck by the make-or-break nature of a job that revolved mostly around one big moment (the awards ceremony and the convention) where, for a short period of time, all eyes would be on the organisation and my work. At first, the thought of that kind of command performance seemed very stressful to me, but over time, I learned that what determines success and failure in that moment has much to do with the planning that takes place in the months leading up to it. What I had initially found unnerving ultimately became very rewarding, and I took great pride in each success-ful awards ceremony, knowing that what looked easy on site at the event was actually the culmination of my many months of hard work and thoughtful preparation behind the scenes.

After about six years at the Bar association, I began looking for new challenges. I had become involved in the South Carolina Society of Association Executives, and to a lesser extent, in the parent body, the American Society of Association Executives (ASAE). Both associations were excellent resources for making connections and find-ing job listings. I initially limited my job search to Columbia, South Carolina, as my wife had started a business there and we preferred not to move. However, the number of association jobs in the state was small. Each week, I would visit the ASAE career centre webpage, only to find 2–3 new association jobs, typically none of which fell into my strength areas (events and education). But occasionally I would take a look at the job listings in Washington, DC, the hub of most national US associations, and I would see dozens of new jobs every week.

I talked to my wife about expanding my job search beyond Columbia, which would mean that we would have to sell our house, and that she would have to walk away from a business that she had built herself and guided through some very challenging times, personally and professionally. Somewhat to my surprise, she was completely in agreement. Though her business was continuing to grow, she was ready for a new adventure, and for some time she had been dreaming of going back to school to get an MBA and learn the academic theories behind some of the business principles she had already been dealing with as an entrepreneur.

152

Within a week of expanding my job search, I had an interview at the National Court Reporters Association (NCRA) in Washington, DC, and within a couple of months my wife and I were relocating for me to start my new job. In addition to being responsible for organising a convention which drew 1,200 stenographers from across North America, my new responsibilities also included organising:

- An executive retreat for 200 company owners in resort locations such as southern California and Florida.
- A legislative fly-in (in the US, a legislative fly-in is an event where association members from all over the country fly to Washington, DC to meet face-to-face with legislators and talk to them about the association's key issues). It is considered to be very effective because the legislators are hearing from actual constituents rather than paid lobbyists and it also helps to develop the leadership pipeline of the organisation.
- A specialised technology conference that embraced innovative formats and technologies.

In terms of the awards presented at the NCRA's annual convention, these included not only the usual Distinguished Service Award and other similar honours for exceptional contributions to the profession, but also medals for the top performers in several skill-based contests. These contests judged stenographers on their speed and accuracy in using their specialised steno machine to convert speech to text. Because the entire profession is based on the stenographer's speed and accuracy, NCRA members are passionate about these contests (dating back to 1909) and a high level of admiration and outright celebrity is enjoyed by the winners.

After six years with the court reporters, I had come to oversee not just the association's events portfolio, but also its continuing education offerings, school programmes, and its extensive list of professional qualifications. I was reporting to the CEO and working with the board, proposing new projects, managing large budgets, and interpreting the results back to the volunteer leadership of the organisation. I enjoyed working with board members who were enthusiastic about their profession, but who also trusted and relied on me for expertise on event planning and association management.

Around that time, my wife was offered an irresistible job opportunity that involved us relocating to London, so I finally got a chance to reciprocate the support that she had shown for me when we moved to DC. As we lived in a hotel for a month with our cat, waiting for all of our worldly possessions to arrive by ship, she took on the challenge of launching a new hotel brand in Europe and I started The Conference Agency (www.theconferenceagency.com), an events planning business with a strong focus on association conferences, awards ceremonies and executive retreats. While I had a couple of clients from the US (former association colleagues and acquaintances), in Europe I had no network and minimal venue and destination knowledge.

I became an avid attendee of networking events for both events professionals and association professionals, co-founded a web-based TV show focused on innovation in the events industry (The Future in 15 Show: http://thefuturein15.com), and accepted every collaboration and partnership I could find in this collaboration-driven events industry. As my client base grew, I began to receive hosted buyer invitations that allowed me to make contacts with venues, destinations and suppliers. As an avid traveller, both work and personal trips also became opportunities for me to expand my destination knowledge.

Being a founder and solopreneur showed me how much I had taken for granted all the resources that had been available to me as an in-house meeting planner. In addition to planning events for clients, I found myself also needing to 'work on the business', investing time into new client acquisition, finances and so on. A fellow small business owner and I were recently commiserating about the cyclical nature of our growth, jumping back and forth between business development and then back into operations to care for those new clients. Fortunately, my connections (both old and new) have provided me with a stable of freelancers and other small businesses that I can call in for projects as needed, allowing me to act as a virtual agency, leveraging much larger resources when needed. This kind of strategy and creative thinking are the most enjoyable parts of agency ownership for me.

The latest series of awards ceremonies that I'm planning for a data science association includes the Data Creativity Awards, the Data Start-up Challenge Awards, and the Smart Data Awards events. But the main event is the Data Science Hackathon Award, which is tied to a hackathon, where teams from all over the world will attend the association conference and be given 24 hours to tackle a challenge issued by the event's corporate sponsors. The finalists selected by the jury will compete in a final round assisted by mentors who are top industry experts, and the winning team will be announced at a sumptuous gala dinner to close the event.

While the trappings around it may change, industries and communities will always feel the importance of recognising excellence in their midst. The moments created for this need to be engaging and flawlessly executed – and that is the responsibility of the awards ceremony organiser.

References

20Bedfordway.com (n.d.) How to organise an awards ceremony. Available at: http://20bedfordway.com/news/how-to-organise-an-awards-ceremony/.

Block, A. B. (2014) Too many awards shows? Emphatically yes, say veteran actors. Available at: https://www.hollywoodreporter.com/news/oscars-veteran-actors-say-are-685485.

Brennan, G. and Pettit, P. (2004) *The Economy of Esteem: An essay on civil and political society,* Oxford: Oxford University Press.

Clark, J. (2015) Planning an elegant award ceremony. Available at: https://www.gigsalad.com/blog/award-ceremony/.

European Commission (n.d.) Topic: EU Prize for Women Innovators 2018. Available at: http://ec.europa.eu/research/participants/portal/desktop/en/opportunities/h2020/topics/h2020-swfs-2016-2017-35.html.

Eventbrite (2015) How to organise a killer awards show in 10 simple steps. Available at: https://www.eventbrite.co.uk/blog/organise-a-killer-awards-show-ds00/.

Eventbrite (2016) 6 experts reveal the secrets to hosting a successful awards night. Available at: https://www.eventbrite.co.uk/blog/hosting-a-successful-awards-night-ds00/.

EY (2015) The economic impact of the Premier League. Available at: https://www.ey.com/Publication/vwLUAssets/EY_-_The_economic_impact_of_the_Premier_League/%24FILE/EY-The-economic-impact-of-the-Premier-League.pdf.

Frey, B. S. and Gallus, J. (2017) Towards an economics of awards. *Journal of Economic Surveys* 31(1): 190–200.

Gemser, G., Leenders, M. A. and Wijnberg, N. M. (2008) Why some awards are more effective signals of quality than others: A study of movie awards. *Journal of Management* 34(1): 25–54.

Getz, D. (2007) *Event Studies: Theory, research and policy for planned events*, Oxford: Butterworth-Heinemann.

Ginsburgh, V. (2003) Awards, success and aesthetic quality in the arts. *Journal of Economic Perspectives* 17(2): 99–111.

Harrison, B. and Jepsen, D. M. (2015) The career impact of winning an external work-related award. *Journal of Vocational Behavior* 89: 21–31.

Huberman, B. A., Loch, C. H., Önçüler, A. (2004) Status as a valued resource. *Social Psychology Quarterly* 67(1): 103–114.

Jeacle, I. (2014) 'And the BAFTA goes to [...]': The assurance role of the auditor in the film awards ceremony. *Accounting, Auditing & Accountability Journal* 27(5): 778–808.

Khan, B. Z. (2015) Inventing prizes: A historical perspective on innovation awards and technology policy. *Business History Review* 89(4): 631–660.

Lanosga, G. (2015) The power of the prize: How an emerging prize culture helped shape journalistic practice and professionalism, 1917–1960. *Journalism* 16(7): 953–967.

Meeting Needs (n.d.). Available at: https://www.meetingneeds.org.uk.

Ponzo, M. and Scoppa, V. (2015) Experts' awards and economic success: Evidence from an Italian literary prize. IZA Discussion Paper No. 8765.

Reid, G. (2006) The politics of city imaging. A case study of the MTV Europe Music Awards Edinburgh '03. *Event Management* 10(1): 35–46.

Silvers, J. R. (2004) *Professional Event Coordination.* Hoboken, NJ: John Wiley & Sons.

University of London Venues (2014) Planning an awards ceremony. Available at: https://www.senatehouseevents.co.uk/features/planning-awards-ceremony.

Urde, M. and Greyser, S. A. (2015) The Nobel Prize: The identity of a corporate heritage brand. *Journal of Product & Brand Management* 24(4): 318–332.

6 Political meetings

Chapter objectives

On completion of this chapter the reader should be able to:

- Understand the principal uses of meetings in the political process.
- Identify the distinguishing characteristics of political meetings.
- Understand the different aspects involved in the planning and execution of political meetings.

The uses of political meetings

Ever since the time of the *contiones* – a type of political meeting held in ancient Rome – and the regular assemblies held in the *agora* as part of the democratic process of Athens in classical times, governments and other political organisations have held events to debate policies, choose candidates and announce new initiatives or measures. In the modern era, such events have become an important element of political communication and policy-making for governments and, in the case of public political meetings, a key part of civic engagement and political participation for citizens.

Meetings are held at all levels of government, from the regular meetings of parish councils and local authorities through national government events such as the annual political party conventions, to the high-profile conferences of international bodies such as the European Commission, the United Nations, the G20 and the World Economic Forum. But, regardless of the level at which they take place, political meetings generally focus on achieving one or more of the following objectives: negotiations, public relations, policymaking and fundraising.

Negotiations

While political meetings for the purpose of negotiating are held at all levels of government, it is the high-level summit conferences that feature most significantly in the public consciousness, as decisions made or announced during these events have the potential to change the course of history and the lives of countless people. The most high-profile of such events are attended by heads of state and their ministers, accompanied by hundreds of bureaucrats and other government officials. Thousands of journalists cover these events, for the most momentous summits, and millions of people around the world watch the proceedings and debate the results. Participation in such events can range from the superpowers only to all nations, regardless of their political and economic weight.

The term 'summit' for a conference between high-level negotiators was first coined by Winston Churchill in 1950, but the practice of summits (known as 'summitry') is as old as diplomacy itself. Most history textbooks describe events where emperors, kings or chiefs came together to settle disputes, make peace or divide up a kingdom after the death of a monarch. For example, in 1807, Napoleon and Alexander I of Russia met on a raft in the middle of the River Niemen in East Prussia to discuss relations between their two states; and the Versailles Peace Conference was a meeting of the victorious Allied Powers following the end of World War I to set the peace terms for the defeated Central Powers.

In modern times, summits have become a common element in international politics, and extensive periods of time are reserved in the diaries of world leaders for scheduled conferences of various international organisations and for bilateral and multilateral meetings with other heads of state and their entourages. These range from regional events such as the APEC (Asia-Pacific Economic Cooperation) meetings and the conferences of the African Union to global or world summits, including the Earth Summit in Rio de Janeiro or the annual World Economic Forum in Davos. Although most of the decisions announced at summit meetings have already been agreed in advance, often following protracted negotiations by civil servants, much of their value lies in their ability to attract the international media spotlight on to the issues under discussion and to the measures announced at the actual summit.

Weilemann (2000) suggests two essential criteria for a meeting to qualify as a summit. The first is executive participation, diplomacy at the highest possible level. Participation at summits may include not only state leaders, but also leaders of international or transnational organisations such as NATO or the European Union. The second is that summit meetings are distinguished by the form of personal contact, meaning that participants communicate face-to-face. According to Weilemann, this is significant, because it is more difficult and usually involves a ceremonial dimension that represents a greater commitment of time, energy and political risk than is present in, for example, a telephone call between heads of state.

The most momentous summits are those that are held in a context of hostilities between nations. In his history of the great summits of the 20th century, Reynolds (2007) notes the significance of those that were held to arbitrate between the forces of war and peace, encounters that could spell life or death for millions: Chamberlain and Hitler at Munich in 1938; Churchill, Roosevelt and Stalin at Yalta in 1945; and, reflecting the politics of the Cold War, Kennedy and Khrushchev in Vienna in 1961, Nixon and Brezhnev in Moscow in 1972, and Reagan and Gorbachev in Geneva in 1985. According to Reynolds, the key elements that facilitated or necessitated such grand summits were: the advances in air travel, which allowed for timely meetings; weapons of mass destruction, which raised the stakes; and modern mass media, which turned summits into global spectacles. Dunn (2016) links the growth of modern-day summitry to the rise of serious political crises and the threat of potentially catastrophic wars, in which circumstances the speedy conclusion of grave international problems was at a premium. 'The feeling developed among politicians that diplomacy in the nuclear age was too important to be left to the diplomatists. Thus developed the trend for greater involvement by political leaders in the detailed process of international dialogue' (Dunn, 2016:5).

However, Dunn also notes that the practice of summitry has consistently been resented by professional diplomats, who have continuously warned of the dangers of amateurism. He quotes the English diplomatist Harold Nicholson who, writing in 1939, expressed the firm view that:

> Repeated personal visits [between high-level politicians] should not be encouraged. Such visits arouse public expectation, lead to misunderstandings and create confusion. The time at the disposal of these visitors is not always sufficient to allow for patience and calm deliberation. The honours which are paid to a minister in a foreign capital may tire his physique, excite his vanity or bewilder his judgement. His desire not to offend his host may lead him with lamentable result to avoid raising unpalatable questions or to be imprecise regarding acute points of controversy.
>
> (Dunn, 2016:4)

Public relations

Two types of events may be covered by the rubric of 'public relations': political party conferences and press conferences. Both are central means by which political parties communicate with the general public.

Political party conferences

Annual political party conferences or party conventions are part of the rhythm of political life, usually taking place at a time of the year when the normal business of governing a country is in suspension. For example, in the UK the party conference season is the period of three weeks in September and October of each year, when the House of Commons is in recess. They were originally designed as events at which politicians and grassroots party members gathered to debate and vote on policies, and hear their leaders speak. But since the latter part of the 20th century, many of these events have developed into highly controlled and stage-managed spectacles designed for the maximisation of favourable media coverage of politicians and their parties, particularly in the US but increasingly too in other advanced democracies. According to McNair (2011), in the US, where this change in the role and function of the party gathering began, the Democratic and Republican conventions have embraced, with unabashed enthusiasm, the principles of showbusiness:

> Meaningful political debate and manoeuvring takes place behind the scenes, while in its public manifestation the convention functions as a huge signifier of whatever it is that the party that year is selling. In Ronald Reagan's re-election campaign of 1984, the Republican convention was dominated by an emotional film of Ron and Nancy, accompanied by the adulation of convention delegates and (by extension) the American people. All this was communicated, through media coverage, to the audience.
>
> (McNair, 2011:128)

The same author notes that in the UK in the 1980s, when showbusiness entrepreneur Harvey Thomas was employed to design the annual Conservative Party conferences, the stages on which conference speakers and party leaders sat were constructed with the same attention to form and colour coordination as a West End stage set. At the 1983 conference, the first following the Thatcher government's victory in the Falklands, the stage resembled a great, grey battleship, on which the Tory leadership sat like conquering admirals (ibid.). In a further attempt to inject excitement into UK political party conferences, high-profile guest speakers have increasingly been invited to speak at these events, including Nelson Mandela and Bill Clinton for the Labour Party and US Senator John McCain for the Conservative Party (BBC News, 2007).

But much of the business of political party conferences takes place away from the main hall and the gaze of the media. For example, there are fringe meetings – often in hotels near the conference centre – which are smaller, more informal sessions, normally with a panel of three or four speakers debating a topical issue and taking questions from the audience. Each conference also offers exhibition facilities where business, industries and other groups can have stands and use the opportunity to raise their profile and lobby political parties.

Press conferences

In most Western democracies, political press conferences – or 'news conferences' as they are also known – are an institutionalised form for communication between leading politicians and journalists. They usually take place on the initiative of politicians for the announcement of policies, programmes, decisions, etc., but also for handling more specific, and often more challenging, events such as accidents, catastrophes or political scandals (Eriksson, 2011). Press conferences normally follow a predictable structure of an uninterrupted speech made by the politician or politicians, followed by an interactional phase comprising a typical question and answer session in which the journalists ask questions and the politicians provide answers. While the majority of such events are single-party press conferences, most commonly between the party leader and the assembled journalists, there are also press conferences involving political leaders from more than one country, which have an international platform, rather than national-level press conferences which are solely concerned with domestic policies. An example of such a press conference is the one that followed President Macron of France's first meeting with the German Chancellor Angela Merkel, during which both leaders pledged to work together to implement European Union reforms. Such events are normally used as a mediatisation of political action, which is meant to give voice to a joint statement on the outcome of political meetings, often to tell the rest of the world that the meeting was successful and useful to both the parties engaged in talks (Bhatia, 2006).

From the perspective of politicians, press conferences are an opportunity for them to set media agendas and thus influence public debate, particularly during election campaigns, by making public statements before audiences of journalists, which are then transmitted by print and broadcast media to the wider citizenry. McNair (2011:132) emphasises the importance of this form of media management for politicians, noting that 'in general, news conferences are designed with a view to maximising coverage. Hence, they will be put on in time to be reported on key news bulletins and at locations accessible to journalists'.

From the point of view of the media, press conferences are opportunities for journalists to hold politicians to account for their words and actions – a task that is widely regarded as a core democratic function of journalism – often described as the *watchdog* role of the media. But the effectiveness of political press conferences as elements of the democratic process have been called into question. As Eriksson (2011) points out, on such occasions it is the politician or politicians who control the event, notably by choosing who, among the journalists present, gets to ask a question: several journalists are present and they have to compete for the chance to ask questions, which puts the politician in a position from which he or she can control the interaction and choose the next questioner. Clayman (2006:251, in Eriksson, 2011) underlines that, in comparison with the one-to-one interaction in news interviews, press conferences 'entail a substantial shift in the interactional balance of power that favours the public figure over the journalist'. One basic premise for this shift is that it is the politicians who, with their staff, organise these events and invite the journalists, often at short notice. In addition, the topical agenda, through the introductory speech, is set by the politicians, not by the journalists themselves.

Policymaking

The policies and priorities of government are rarely formed in the media spotlight that accompanies summits, political party conferences and press conferences. Neither, in most Western democracies, are policies developed by politicians alone. In this section, the role of meetings and special forums in involving experts and the general public in policymaking is examined.

Advisory commissions and task forces

In the political and policy landscape, advisory commissions and task forces are perhaps the most widely used convening structures. Tepper's (2004:524) study of these structures notes that such bodies are typically set up to study a problem or issue, have a fixed duration, tend to be well funded and staffed, and are often composed of distinguished individuals: 'In fields as diverse as health care, nuclear energy, economic competitiveness, and race relations, governors and presidents have called upon commissions of experts to produce reports geared toward diagnosing problems and prescribing remedies'.

The following three examples of bodies created to advise governments demonstrate the range and variety of issues discussed:

- In 2011, in an effort to combat childhood obesity, the US Congress directed the Federal Trade Commission, together with the Food and Drug Administration, the Centers for Disease Control and Prevention and the US Department of Agriculture, to establish an Interagency Working Group of federal nutrition, health and marketing experts to develop recommendations for the nutritional quality of food marketed to children and adolescents.
- In 2014, the government of Malta set up the Food Waste Working Group to study the issue of food waste on the Maltese islands and to develop an action plan for mitigating this problem for their nation.
- In 2017, in response to the forecast that over the following 30 years, the population of Auckland, New Zealand was expected to increase by up to a million people, the city's mayor set up a Housing Taskforce to identify barriers to building new homes at a speed and scale needed to meet the demand caused by the city's population growth. Later the same year, the Mayoral Housing Taskforce Report was published, with a series of recommendations.

However, although such meetings are ubiquitous in the policy process, the extent to which they effectively influence governments' policies has often been questioned. According to Tepper, many believe that such convenings are simply symbolic responses to problems, allowing politicians to deflect attention away from their own inability to adequately address intractable problems. By convening such meetings, politicians can appear to be doing something, while in fact they are simply postponing an indefinite future decision (Tepper, 2004:533).

Participatory governance meetings

A second category of political gatherings designed to shape the policies of governments, particularly at the local and national levels, is that of so-called participatory governance meetings, which are distinguished by the fact that they are open to members of the public. A typical example of such events would be the 'town hall meetings' held in the US, at which local residents generally present ideas, voice their opinions and ask questions of the elected officials or political candidates. As events that give members of the public the opportunity to be heard directly by politicians and their civil servants, this type of public meeting may be regarded as an important element of participatory democracy and a key part of civic engagement and political participation which can directly impact upon important public policy decisions.

McComas et al. (2010) describe the range of purposes served by these meetings: some are held primarily to provide information, others to obtain public input into decisions or recommendations, and still others to build consensus around proposed planning initiatives, for instance. An example of a major experiment in participatory democracy is provided by Pogrebinschi and Samuels (2014) in the form of Brazil's National Public Policy Conferences (NPPCs), which have provided widespread opportunities for grassroots participation to shape important national policies on subjects such as health, public security and the rights of the elderly. According to the authors, 'about seven million people participated in at least one of the NPPCs held between 2003 and 2011, which is about five percent of Brazil's adult population' (Pogrebinschi and Samuels, 2014:321).

At the municipal level of government, Llewellyn (2005) describes the expansion in practices of participatory local governance in the UK, where local authorities have established a range of mechanisms for consulting the public, including citizens' juries, focus groups and area assemblies. His research has as its main focus the area assemblies held in North London – open, regularly convened public meetings where local residents question councillors and officers discuss issues such as education, social services and transport. They are held in school halls, churches, council buildings and libraries, where, typically, audiences sit in rows facing a small panel of speakers. Llewellyn contrasts the free, open and spontaneous public discourse of such meetings with the more stage-managed, controlled interactions that characterise most broadcast TV debates and press conferences.

Fundraisers

Very few political campaigns can be successfully waged without monetary donations from supporters. Fundraiser events exist to generate revenue for an individual political candidate, cause or party, and to allow candidates to meet important members of their community. They can take the form of an elegant dinner in an upscale hotel, a cocktail reception or even a low-key barbecue in the garden of one of the candidate's political supporters. Guests are selected on the basis of the financial contribution that they are likely to make; and the costs of the event are kept as low as possible by using venues and other suppliers who support the candidate or cause, since the objective is to raise, not spend, money. Douglas and Gregory (2009) note that high-profile political guest speakers are often invited to fundraisers, to garner additional attendance and income at the event, even though, with their packed schedules, particularly during election campaigns, they are somewhat prone to confirming or rescinding their invitation at the last minute. The same authors report that, because of their political nature, fundraiser events are generally required to respect the stringent legal regulations that apply to the financing of political organisations. For example, in the US, the Federal Elections Commission (FEC) closely tracks monetary and in-kind contributions to political parties. These FEC regulations and other finance laws, such as the Honest Leadership and Open Government Act of 2007, make managing the budget a primary concern for the organisers of fundraiser events.

However, what is acceptable practice in countries such as the US is prohibited in other political systems. For example, in Japan, political donations to individual politicians or their personal fundraising organisations have been illegal since 2000. Instead of basing their campaign funds on contributions from the private sector, members of the Diet (the Japanese parliament) must rely on their party headquarters and local and regional branches as their main sources of funding. To further ensure an independent money base for political parties, they are also entitled to receive government subsidies based on their share of seats in the Diet and on election results (Blechinger, 2000).

The time spent by politicians in raising funds in this way has often been called into question. One US senator is said to have complained that the considerable amount of time and energy spent on fundraising 'pushes out more worthwhile activities such as discussing the issues, meeting with ordinary voters, and legislating' (Tam Cho and Gimpel, 2007:255). Nevertheless, the effectiveness of this form of political event is rarely challenged, particularly in the US, where far more money is raised at face-to-face events than through direct mail solicitation.

The distinguishing characteristics of political meetings

There are four major characteristics that distinguish political events from other segments of the meetings and events industry, including the additional skills required particularly of political event professionals, beyond the standard skills employed in the planning of other types of meetings and events. Douglas and Gregory (2009) highlight these distinguishing characteristics as follows:

Short lead-times

Political events can have very short lead-times, similar to those often found in the corporate meetings sector. For example, press conferences following a terrorist attack or another type of crisis may have to be organised in a matter of only one or two hours.

During national electoral campaigns, when scheduling is rarely done more than a few days in advance, the harried process of planning events takes place within a context of a constantly nuanced shifting of the political context of the moment and the fluid nature of politicians' schedules. Political meeting planners therefore operate in an environment of considerable pressure regarding the logistics of such events, from sourcing suitable venues at very short notice to making last-minute travel arrangements for VIP participants.

Media scrutiny

Media scrutiny is a factor that is essential to the success of political events. In common with red carpet events and other gatherings that attract celebrities, political events necessitate the careful handling of the press on an ongoing basis. One reason for this is the widely acknowledged fact that the purpose of most political events is rarely the event itself, but rather to garner the media's attention and therefore that of the public at large. Another reason is offered by Bhatia (2006), who maintains that courting the press and feeding the egos of journalists can help ensure more favourable coverage for politicians, making the introduction of their policies – or alterations to existing ones – easier to accept by the electorate. Since, in most countries, the media have a crucial impact on citizens' levels of trust in politicians, political events strategies need to incorporate effective media management strategies. The same author discusses the interdependency between politics and the media, suggesting that they share a paradoxical relationship whereby although each needs the other to survive, or rather thrive, each side at times tends to demonstrate considerable hostility towards the other.

Heightened security

The security presence found at political events is usually much more extensive and thorough than in other sectors of the business events industry. Since political figures tend to very often be highly public, highly polarizing personalities, they are subject to a battery of risks that are rarely encountered in other forms of meetings. According to Everwall (2015), these range from benign protest pranks – 'glitter bombing', pie-throwing and general heckling – to violent attacks. As a result of this, political event planners tend to approach security in a very different manner from other intermediaries in the event industry. At high-profile political events in particular, the security agencies are generally far more specialised and their staff more highly trained. Dangerous and disruptive guests are dealt with in a much harsher fashion and may even see charges pressed against them.

As emphasised by Getz (2007:36), 'Most political and state events are security nightmares. When leaders assemble or governments meet, … the media pay close attention – and so do those people who want to protest or disrupt'. Summit meetings in particular have been known to attract violent demonstrations. The high-profile nature and the magnitude of such events, combined with the presence of the media, frequently makes them targets for demonstrators and others with less legitimate intentions. Ever since the 'Battle in Seattle', the 1999 World Trade Summit meeting during which violent street protests led to 600 arrests and US$3 million in property damage, security has been a prime concern for summit meetings. And as terrorist threats have increased, the costs have soared (Austin, 2010).

Protests during summits and official responses to those protests are key themes of Henderson's (2007) case study on the 2006 meetings of the Boards of Governors of the International Monetary Fund and the World Bank Group held in Singapore. She notes that mass demonstrations prone to violent eruptions have become closely associated with these occasions, with many taking part claiming to be members of anti-globalisation movements dedicated to fair trade, the cancellation of the debts of the world's poorest countries and curbs on corporate power. Environmental and animal rights activists, other advocacy or pressure groups, and anarchists and nihilists of assorted descriptions, are also in regular attendance, each group pursuing its own agenda. Although, as Henderson stresses, violent tactics are openly favoured by only a small minority, protests can threaten to interfere with formal proceedings if hostility is sufficiently intense. The G20 case study in this chapter analyses the protests that have accompanied past meetings of that group of nations.

But Henderson also notes that official responses must be carefully assessed and implemented to strike a satisfactory balance between the widely accepted right to peaceful protest and the maintenance of law and order. The point at which that balance is struck very much depends upon the political culture and the stage of development of civil society of the destination. Countries with more authoritarian regimes, with strict regulations on public assembly, may even be chosen as destinations for political events by planners wishing to minimise the risk of serious disruption from protestors.

High levels of security at political meetings are also made necessary by the ever-present threat of terrorist activity in the modern world. The memory of the bombing of the UK Conservative Party conference in Brighton in 1984 by the Irish Republican Army serves as a salutary reminder that high-profile political gatherings need to be defended from those who would seek to use such events for their own sinister purposes.

Budgetary restraints

Given that attendance at events by government employees is generally funded from the public purse, limitations are often set on how much may be spent on meetings at which all or most of the participants are people working for government agencies. A case of such limitations was highlighted by Rein (2014) who reported that, following what were considered to be examples of excessive spending on events by certain US federal departments, government agencies had to submit reports to their inspector general on any conference costing more than US$100,000 and include details of the number of participants, the purpose of the event and a breakdown of food and other costs.

Chavis (2015:24) confirms the types of spending limitations that must be taken into consideration by those planning government events in the US:

> Budgetary restrictions are always top-of-mind for meetings and events, but this is especially true for government groups, which must follow specific parameters laid out by the US General Services Administration. Specifically, government entities must adhere to per-diem rates for hotel stays and may also face restrictions as to food, beverage and entertainment options.

Special skills set for political event planners

Many political event professionals argue that the set of competencies required to meet the specific challenges of organising events in the political world is more extensive than for the planning of other types of events. Douglas and Gregory (2009) highlight the importance of the following skills and attributes for the organisers of political events:

- *Interpersonal and communication skills:* many elected officials and politicians have a reputation for their huge egos, and the most effective way of accommodating these demanding personalities and ensure a successful event is to employ well-honed interpersonal and communication skills to keep these key stakeholders at their ease.
- *Diplomacy* is also essential in the political environment. Political event professionals must be firm but polite and not at all fazed by the important people around them.
- *A high level of commitment:* politics and the hospitality industry are two sectors known for their long hours and tendency to require employees to often work evenings and weekends. Political event planning blends these two fields and demands a high level of commitment to the job. Eighteen-hour days are the norm for organisers of political events in the weeks before an election, for example.

To these distinguishing characteristics of political event planners may be added the view held by some in the events industry that many of those planning events in this sector share a specific professional background. For example, a commentator writing in the Everwall (2015) blog maintains that the vast majority of political event managers started out in a career or volunteer position tied in some way to their political party of choice. According to him,

> They were campaign office volunteers, perhaps; or canvassers, or political aides. The important thing is that they worked in the political climate of their city or region for some time. In so doing, they established a network of political connections – connections which would prove vital in the growth of their career.

> Likely as not, they started small. Maybe they organized a simple rally or helped plan a parade ... Eventually, they began to make a name for themselves, and were chosen to plan larger and more varied events for their party.
>
> (Everwall, 2015)

In some instances, political events organisers have created their own professional associations, in recognition of the particular demands placed upon those who choose this career path. For example, in the US, the Society of Government Meeting Professionals (http://www.sgmp.org/) has the mission of enhancing and promoting the expertise of government meeting professionals, and the objectives of improving the quality of, and promoting the cost-effectiveness of, government meetings.

Planning political meetings

From the preceding pages of this chapter, it should be clear that, for political events, there is considerable variety in terms of the length of such events and the budgets available for them. For government events in particular, such as press conferences, budgets are usually closely scrutinised, since public money is being used. Procurement regulations must therefore be respected concerning aspects of political events planning such as venue selection and hospitality provision.

More broadly, a number of valuable insights into the planning of political meetings may be gleaned from the research of Douglas and Gregory (2009) into the work of the 'Advance Teams' in the US political events world. These events professionals organise and execute events for high-ranking, prominent politicians who tend to make more public appearances than other politicians and therefore require their own security detail. Advance Teams play their most significant role in US national electoral campaigns, where they are responsible for coordinating politicians' trips across the country and executing several events – such as campaign rallies – during those multi-day trips.

According to Douglas and Gregory, Advance Team professionals fall into several organisational roles. The 'lead' oversees the entire operation and supervises team members assigned to handle the following aspects of the event.

The press

The press members of the Advance Team are responsible for all press logistics including acquiring Internet access at the venue, managing press buses, designating separate press entrances, and procuring food for them when necessary. The Everwall (2015) blog emphasises the importance of providing appropriate facilities for the press attending political events, adding press boxes, press risers (raised platforms for TV cameras and press photographers) and multiple cameras to the list of amenities expected. The commentator concludes that any 'political event in which there isn't space for the press is considered to be a significant gaffe and will undoubtedly reflect poorly on you as an event planner'.

Crowd management

The two tasks of building the crowd before the event and managing them on site are the responsibility of the crowd management members of the Advance Team. Most pre-event crowd-building takes the form of local outreach – encouraging members of various organisations to attend, promoting the event through the local media and on the Internet, and using the personal connections of opinion leaders in the community. Inside the venue, the staging of the crowd must create the appearance of a well-attended event and provide the perfect 'cut shot' for the cameras. This includes constructing the crowd seated behind the speaker in such a way that they reflect the diversity of the audience and help to convey the message of the event.

Site coordination

The site coordinator leads the venue selection process and then coordinates with the venue manager and suppliers to prepare the venue. In reality, in order to construct successful events in a very limited time frame, the constantly travelling Advance Teams often use local contacts to find appropriate venues more swiftly than through the traditional request for proposal (RFP) process.

Two key selection criteria, according Douglas and Gregory (2009), are that the venue must be photogenic and that, visually, it should help to convey the message of the event. For example, an event promoting a bill supporting green energy initiatives could be held in a 'green' building equipped with solar panels. As already mentioned above, it is important for the event to look well attended on TV and in press photographs, because crowded events convey a positive image of support and enthusiasm for the speaker, initiative or movement. Consequently, the venue must be small enough to appear crowded, regardless of actual attendance, but large enough to accommodate everyone present. The set-up of most venues for political events is generally determined by the programme format and crowd size. Most site coordinators prefer large, open venues for political rallies and speeches rather than facilities with fixed seating arrangements, as the flexible spaces allow them the freedom to create a crowded cut-shot for the press photographers.

Security is of paramount concern at venues for political events, especially for those with high-profile speakers. At the destination level, some cities actively promote themselves as being safe places for political events: the Dutch city of The Hague, for example, promotes itself on the CVENT blog as a city with considerable experience in hosting high-profile conferences and welcoming international leaders:

> As The Hague is the international city of Peace & Justice, the Dutch Royal city and the seat of the Dutch government, it frequently has prominent guests, which in turn leads to a high level of security in the city.
>
> (CVENT, 2017)

At the level of the event venue, the Advance Team works closely with the police and security agents to ensure that the venue, members of the press and the attendees are all cleared for security at least one-half-hour before the event begins.

Transport coordination

Transport coordination includes taking responsibility for the motorcade, the procession of vehicles used to transport politicians from one event to the next. The people in charge of transport coordination plan and coordinate the routes for multi-stop trips. Some of their other duties include selecting and managing the drivers and vehicles in the motorcade. They are also in charge of all the transportation for the staff, travelling press, politicians and other officials. The size of the motorcade is dependent on the size of the event and the media coverage expected. A typical motorcade length is from 8 to 12 cars, plus a coach bus and two additional staff cars if the event is part of a multi-stop bus tour.

Rooms overnight coordination

Douglas and Gregory (2009) describe how those members of the Advance Team who have this responsibility handle all hotel logistics for multi-day trips. Their most critical duties are procuring the accommodation, handling the billing and distributing room keys to the staff and press.

It is clear that with the political stakes so high and with a considerable media presence and the ever-present security threats, the planning of political events leaves no room for error, making this career one of the most demanding in the events industry as a whole.

Chapter summary

This chapter focused on the four principal objectives of political meetings: negotiations, public relations, policymaking and fundraising. The role of summit conferences in political negotiations was discussed, highlighting their key characteristics of executive-level participation and face-to-face interaction. The public relations role of political party conferences and press conferences was analysed, followed by a review of the role of advisory commissions, task forces and participatory governance meetings as policymaking instruments. The use of fundraising events to raise revenue for political candidates, causes and parties was considered, with reference to its contentious nature in some countries. The chapter then highlighted the distinguishing features of political events: short lead-times, media scrutiny, heightened levels of security and budgetary restraints. The special skills required of political event planners were discussed, and the chapter ended with a review of the various tasks involved in planning political meetings.

CASE STUDY 6.1: THE G20 SUMMIT MEETINGS

The G20

The G20 (or the Group of 20, as it is also known) is an international forum for the governments and central bank governors from the world's 20 major economies. It has its origins in the 1970s, when the leading industrialised economies created an annual forum for the discussion and development of a system of global governance to respond to the various crises, financial and other, that were threatening the orderly growth of the world's economic system. Beginning in the 1970s, the 'G' system began as the G6, the G7, then the G8 (the US, Japan, Germany, UK, France, Italy, Canada and Russia) as new countries were added to the group.

In the 1990s, the G20 was created because of the desire to develop a more effective, inclusive forum to deal with the challenges of a rapidly globalising world and to mobilise the rising capabilities of emerging economies, particularly those located in Asia. Its members are Argentina, Australia, Brazil, Canada, China, the European Union, France, Germany, India, Indonesia, Italy, Japan, Mexico, Russia, Saudi Arabia, South Africa, South Korea, Turkey, the UK and the US. Between them, these countries, recognised for their role as powerful drivers of the world economy, represent 85 per cent of global GDP, 80 per cent of international trade and 65 per cent of the world's population.

But for the first ten years of its existence, the importance of the G20 was far less than that of the G8, as G20 meetings' participants were finance ministers and central bank governors, while heads of state and government attended G8 Summits. However, after a decade of acquiring an increasingly influential role on the world stage, the G20 formally replaced the G8 as the pre-eminent platform for executive-level deliberation in 2009. And while the 'G' system originally focused exclusively on the governance of the global economic system, it has increasingly addressed a wider range of issues such as terrorism, global warming and global health.

G20 Summits

The Group of 20 has no formal organisational structure, permanent secretariat or indeed any permanent staff of its own. It has a rotating presidency that is responsible for setting the agenda every year and organising all of the meetings and events during that period. Much of the important business of the G20 takes place in informal meetings throughout the year, but the most well-known G20 event is the annual Summit. These are generally held on an annual basis, but the G20 Summit was held twice a year in both 2009 and 2010, when the global economy was in severe crisis. The destinations for these Summits since 2008, together with the key topics discussed and actions taken, are shown in Table 6.1.

Table 6.1 G20 Summits since 2008

Year	Destination	Key topics/actions
2017	Hamburg, Germany	Climate change; global trade
2016	Hangzhou, China	The Paris climate change agreement; the war in Syria
2015	Antalya, Turkey	The terrorist attacks in Paris; the war in Syria
2014	Brisbane, Australia	Russia's attack on the Ukraine; global economic growth; Ebola
2013	St Petersburg, Russia	The war in Syria; stimulating global economic growth
2012	Los Cabos, Mexico	The eurozone debt crisis
2011	Cannes, France	The Greek debt crisis
2010	Seoul, South Korea	Agreement to stop the currency wars, primarily between China and the US
2010	Toronto, Canada	Government debt reduction
2009	London, UK	G20 leaders pledged US$1 trillion to the IMF and World Bank to help emerging market countries ward off the effects of the recession
2009	Pittsburgh, US	A new Financial Stability Board was created, to establish common financial regulations for all G20 countries
2008	Washington, DC, US	The 2008 financial crisis

Source: Adapted from Amadeo (2018).

The Summits are attended by the executive leaders of the G20 member states, although Spain as a permanent non-member invitee also participates. Representatives from other countries may also attend Summits at the invitation of the host country, and it has become customary for the Chair of ASEAN (Association of Southeast Asian Nations) and representatives of the African Union and NEPAD (New Partnership for Africa's Development) to be present at these events. Each annual Summit is chaired by the host country, which also has the responsibility for establishing an agenda in consultation with other members. To relay the proceedings of the G20 Summits via the world's media, journalists also attend in vast numbers. For example, almost 5,000 journalists were present during the 2017 G20 Summit in Hamburg.

Despite their ability to attract the world's most politically powerful leaders, G20 Summits are often criticised for their lack of substantive outcomes in terms of effective measures and solutions to world problems. But it is generally agreed that they at least provide national leaders with the opportunity to get to know each other better on a personal level, and that these enhanced personal relationships can lay the groundwork for more successful future, often bilateral, cooperation between G20 participants.

Protests at G20 Summit meetings

G20 Summits have traditionally attracted large numbers of protesters seeking to express their anger over a wide range of issues such as global economic policy, the banking system and bankers' remuneration and bonuses, and climate change. The right to demonstrate is a basic right in a democracy, and many people choose to exercise that right when the world's media are focused upon the G20 Summit destination. The economist Kimberly Amadeo, writing in www.thebalance.com, claims that protesters object to the G20 leaders concentrating mainly on economic and financial interests and globalisation. According to her, they usually want to persuade the G20 leaders to focus on one or more of these issues (Amadeo, 2018):

- Poverty – for example, in Toronto, 2010, some protesters were against the G20's focus on fiscal responsibility and austerity at the cost of social programmes. Some were also opposed to the over C$1 billion cost of the meeting itself, which was borne by Canadian taxpayers. (For more details, see Monaghan and Walby, 2012.)
- Climate Change – some protesters want the G20 to refocus on global warming as a priority.
- Gender Equality – protesters believe that the G20 countries need to pay more attention to rights for homosexuals and provide funding for family planning, including abortions.
- Immigration – protesters want more open borders for immigrants fleeing humanitarian and climate crises.

Although the clear majority of protesters are peaceful, G20 demonstrations have also been known to attract certain radical factions intent on violence and criminal damage, and for that reason they are usually met with large police presences. For example, at the 2011 G20 Summit in Cannes, when about 10,000 protesters gathered to decry what they regarded as corporate greed and the modern financial system, they were met by 12,000 French riot police.

Clearly, the cost of ensuring security at G20 Summits represents a major outlay for the host nation. For instance, according to a report compiled by the University of Toronto's G8 and G20 Research Groups in 2010, the cost of hosting the 2010 G8 and G20 summits in Toronto was C$1.1 billion, of which C$933 million was spent on security measures.

The 2014 G20 Summit in Brisbane, Australia saw the deployment of 6,000 police officers and 1,900 troops, the establishment of a no-fly zone in a wide area over the convention centre, and the enforcement of special rules that gave more power to police officers and prevented people from entering certain areas of the city. Australia spent about A$100 million (US$87 million) on security alone during the Brisbane Summit.

However, as has been seen too often at meetings of the G8 and the G20, lavish spending on security brings with it no guarantee that such events will pass off peacefully. At the 2017 G20 Summit in Hamburg, about 100,000 protesters gathered in the city to take part in over 30 planned demonstrations in the days before, during and after the event. But violent clashes between protesters and the police began when officers dressed in riot gear intervened as protesters tried to enter the 'red zone', a blocked-off area close to the Summit venue. In the three days that followed, protesters lit bonfires in the streets, torched cars and looted shops, as tension between demonstrators and police escalated. According to the Hamburg Police, out of the 20,000 police officers deployed throughout the Summit, 476 officers were injured. At least 186 protesters were arrested and 225 were detained over the three days of the Summit. The cost of the damage to property in Hamburg ran into millions of euros.

Security at the G20 in Hangzhou, China 2016

The security situation surrounding the previous year's G20 Summit could hardly be more of a contrast with that witnessed in Hamburg. The 2016 G20 Summit, the 11th meeting of the Group of 20, was held on 4–5 September in Hangzhou, the capital city of East China's Zhejiang province and home to over nine million citizens. The Hangzhou meeting was the first G20 Summit that China had ever hosted, and was only the second Summit held in Asia since 2008.

In China, hosting the Hangzhou G20 summit was regarded as a valuable opportunity for the country to show its growing dominance on the world stage, to enhance its 'soft power' and to enable it to play a bigger role in global governance. It was also seen as an opportunity for President Xi Jinping to demonstrate his diplomatic credentials. At the grassroots level, local residents overwhelmingly supported the hosting of the Summit in Hangzhou, as shown in the results of a survey conducted by the Zhejiang University of Technology: over 97 per cent of the respondents said that they took great pride in Hangzhou being the destination for the Summit, and most of them promised to improve their civic behaviour ahead of it (Shoufeng, 2016).

With so much at stake, in terms of China's international reputation, a range of extraordinary measures were introduced to ensure a trouble-free Summit. A report by Ben Westcott, for CNN, Blue skies and police vans: China prepares to host its first G20 Summit (2016), describes

Hangzhou as being in a state of 'virtual lockdown', before and during the conference. Police officers and security guards were stationed every five to ten metres at popular attractions such as the city's West Lake. Organisers also recruited over one million citizen volunteers to provide various services and security assistance during the Summit. There were increased security checks on inbound travellers and parcels arriving in Hangzhou, as well as more frequent checks on residents' identification cards. Passengers were even asked to drink some of their bottled water before boarding public transport. To ensure food security, a 7,450-square metre storehouse was built to hold the 900 tons of food for Summit guests and personnel.

But the local authorities also took some radical steps to guarantee that their city was looking its absolute best for the world's media. In order to ensure that Hangzhou was free of crowds and heavy traffic, local residents were granted a seven-day holiday during the G20 summit. To lure them out of town, citizens were offered discounted tours to destinations outside Hangzhou and free admission to tourist attractions in nearby cities. Furthermore, in an effort to ensure that the sky over Hangzhou appeared crystal clear and blue during the G20 Summit, 225 factories in five provinces were ordered to stop working before and during the Summit, in much the same way that factories in Beijing were shut down to curb pollution during the capital's hosting of the APEC (Asia-Pacific Economic Cooperation) meeting in 2014. That action gave rise to the use, in China, of the expression 'APEC Blue' to indicate something wonderful but fleeting.

CASE STUDY 6.2: THE ST. PETERSBURG INTERNATIONAL ECONOMIC FORUM 2017

The St Petersburg International Economic Forum

The St Petersburg International Economic Forum

The St Petersburg International Economic Forum (SPIEF) is a leading communications platform for the discussion of contemporary trends in the global economy. It offers a valuable opportunity for government officials, business people and experts to exchange opinions on current international and Russian affairs. As well as developing the substantive agenda for the event, the Forum also offers participants advice, information and expert support, helps to promote business projects, attracts investment and supports social entrepreneurship and charitable projects.

The key theme for the 2017 SPIEF was 'Achieving a New Balance in the Global Economic Arena'. Over 500 leading experts from Russia, Europe, the US, Australia and Asian countries helped develop the Forum's programme, including representatives from a range of economic schools, development institutions and business communities from around the world. More than 900 moderators and speakers addressed social and economic development issues, energy and transport, health and the environment, culture and tourism, and science and education.

The 2017 edition of the SPIEF attracted a record number of participants – over 14,000, including business people, representatives of international organisations, officials, experts, academics and journalists from more than 143 countries. Among the attendees were the heads of 700 Russian and 400 international companies. Companies from the US, Germany, China, Italy and Japan were widely represented.

As the Forum is held under the auspices of the President of the Russian Federation, the main event of SPIEF 2017 was a plenary session involving the Russian President Vladimir Putin, the Indian Prime Minister Narendra Modi, the Federal Chancellor of Austria Christian Kern, and the President of Moldova Igor Dodon. The event was also attended by many other high-ranking political figures, including the UN Secretary-General António Guterres, the Secretary General of the Organization of the Petroleum Exporting Countries (OPEC) Mohammed Sanusi Barkindo, the Prime Minister of Gabon Emmanuel Issoze-Ngondet, the Prime Minister of Mongolia, Jargaltulgyn Erdenebat, the Prime Minister of Dominica, Roosevelt Skerrit, and the Acting Prime Minister and Minister of Foreign Affairs of Serbia, Ivica Dačić. Many foreign representatives and companies use the SPIEF as a tool for promoting their investment projects. In 2017, this opportunity was particularly taken up by the guest country, India, as well as by the Republic of Serbia, which built their own exhibition spaces within the Forum's exhibition area, the SPIEF Investment & Business Expo.

The SPIEF programme featured 127 events, including panel sessions, roundtables, TV debates, business breakfasts and business dialogues. Forum side events included a B20 meeting, BRICS and Shanghai Cooperation Organisation summits, as well as a special session of the 19th World Festival of Youth and Students, which was held in Sochi in October 2017. The Forum is usually a regular meeting place for Nobel Prize laureates, and for the 2017 edition, they held a special session, 'New Frontiers in Scientific Advancement', in cooperation with the Russian Academy of Sciences.

SPIEF 2017 saw the signing of 475 investment agreements, memoranda of agreement and statements of intent, worth a total of RUB 1,817.9 billion – and this figure only includes those agreements whose value has been announced publicly. The most significant agreements signed at SPIEF 2017 included:

- an agreement between the Linde Group, a German chemical company, and the Russian TAIF Group to build a new ethylene plant as part of Nizhnekamskneftekhim, valued at RUB 600 billion;
- an agreement between Rosatom and the Nuclear Power Corporation of India to build the fifth and sixth units of the Kudankulam Nuclear Power Plant, valued at RUB 239.4 billion;
- a statement of intent between the City of St Petersburg, the Eurasian Development Bank and VTB Bank to invest in the construction of the Eastern High-Speed Diameter, a highway crossing over the river Neva between Fayansovaya and Zolnaya Streets, valued at RUB 150 billion.

Planning the SPIEF

The 2017 SPIEF was organised by the Roscongress Foundation (http://roscongress.org/en), a major organiser of congress and exhibition events that was founded in 2007 with the aim of facilitating the development of Russia's economic potential and strengthening the country's image by organising world-class business events. Over the past decade, the Roscongress Foundation has held more than 450 events including the Eastern Economic Forum in Vladivostok, the Russian Investment Forum in Sochi, Russian Energy Week in Moscow and other important events.

A representative from the Roscongress Foundation provided the following insights into the planning of the 2017 SPIEF:

All key decisions regarding the organisation and running of the event, including the event's location, are approved at a meeting of the St Petersburg International Economic Forum Organising Committee which is typically made up of representatives from ministries, agencies and organisations with an interest in SPIEF preparations.

From its inception in 1997 until 2006, SPIEF was held at the Tauride Palace in St Petersburg. It then moved to the Lenexpo Exhibition Complex where it was held until 2015. Since 2016, the Forum has been held in the ExpoForum Convention and Exhibition Centre, which opened in October 2014 and which is three times larger than the previous venue.

A great many different things need to be taken into account when organising an event on the scale of SPIEF. The first thing that needs to be drawn up is a project preparation schedule, which includes the budgeting system, an extensive invitation campaign targeting both Russian and international participants, and preparation of the business programme and the event venue. It is important to make sure that no compromises are made when it comes to security and the quality of services provided to event participants. This includes information support, hotel booking services for the Forum period, arranging catering at the venue and the impeccable handling of logistics, from the provision of transport for Forum participants to clear signposting at the venue.

We take extra security measures to ensure safety at the SPIEF. This includes the involvement of the fire and rescue departments, emergency services, security forces and essential services.

There is an emergency services headquarters at the Forum venue. Emergency and repair units of Lenenergo (one the largest electric power distribution and network companies in Russia), Vodokanal (the water company supplying St Petersburg), TEK (the Fuel and Energy Complex of St Petersburg) and PetersburgGas are on duty 24 hours a day. The city reserves 20 ambulances, two emergency helicopters and 1,500 beds in 12 hospitals especially for the Forum. Security levels at Pulkovo Airport are also increased before and during SPIEF. A checkpoint is set up near the exit from the Pulkovskoye Shosse street leading to the airport, to inspect motor vehicles.

We had to ensure that the needs of the world's media were also taken care of. Over 3,000 journalists from 800 media organisations representing 45 countries took part in the 2017 SPIEF. The plenary session was streamed by 83 TV channels in Europe and Africa belonging to the European Broadcasting Union. In addition, the plenary session was broadcast by the Indian state broadcaster Doordarshan (21 national channels and 11 satellite channels). NBC broadcast sessions throughout the US, and in China, reports were shown from the SPIEF venue. A total of 28 TV crews from leading global channels broadcast live from St Petersburg.

We would like to give a special mention to the fact that it is not only Roscongress Foundation employees who make SPIEF possible, but a large number of volunteer students, schoolchildren and young professionals. This is a valuable experience for volunteers, giving them the opportunity to communicate with people of different nationalities and cultural backgrounds, show hospitality, practise foreign languages, gain new knowledge, develop leadership qualities, make useful acquaintances and, last but not least, experience being part of a huge team of professionals. Roscongress now has a team of 20,000 volunteers.

IT'S MY JOB
LUCIE ČAPKOVÁ, ASSOCIATION
MEETINGS MANAGER, PRAGUE
CONVENTION BUREAU

I was born and bred in Prague and, apart from a short spell spent in England, I have always lived in the capital of the Czech Republic. After leaving school, having passed exams in Tourism and Hotel management, I left for England where I worked as an *au pair* for two years. Upon my return to Prague, I studied for a bachelor's degree in Tourism, Hotel and Spa Management at the College of Tourism, Hotel and Spa Hospitality, while working in hotels at the same time. I worked for high-profile international hotel chains, including the InterContinental and Mandarin Oriental, both of which are in the historical city centre of Prague, but on different sides of the Vltava river, each targeting different segments of clients. My 12 years' experience at the InterContinental Prague included six years within the sales department, where I was employed as a Convention Sales Manager. In that job, I oversaw local and international markets and also looked after the conference groups once the contract has been signed by the client. That role included active event planning and being on site for the organisers during the event or conference itself. I then moved to the Mandarin Oriental Prague to take up a position named In-house Meeting Manager, which was more about active sales work, targeting the local market. The hotel was much smaller, but the role of orchestrating successful events was still an important part of my job.

In both hotels I looked after diplomatic events, although the types of event differed slightly from one hotel to the other. The InterContinental Prague is located on the river bank close to the Old Town Square, has 372 bedrooms and a very flexible conference area of 14 function rooms; the Mandarin Oriental Prague is set in a tranquil location in a district called the 'Little Quarter', which includes many large renaissance or baroque palaces transformed into embassies, ambassadors' residences or ministry buildings. The hotel itself is a former monastery, with 99 bedrooms and only one main banqueting hall and an adjacent function room.

The types of events at the InterContinental were mostly either national days receptions organised by the ambassadors, panel discussions attended by Czech politicians or ad hoc meetings during official visits of European or international politicians. More intimate diplomatic events were held in Mandarin Oriental, as the hotel premises offered more privacy. The nearby ministries often used the private area of the restaurant or function space for lunches when the relevant minister was hosting VIPs' visits to Prague for the signing of official documents, for example. And the hotel's bedrooms were used for the accommodation of important government guests of the nearby embassies. Most importantly, the hotel was often chosen for its location and its prompt, but discrete service.

The principal challenge that I had to deal with in both hotels was security. Through practice, for example, I learnt that not all ministers were entitled to have the same type of security. The level of security required depended on several factors, such as whether the event was organised by a non-government organisation and diplomat where the politician was only a guest; whether it was a local or foreign individual; and whether it was an official or private visit. Based on these criteria and others, the security measures differed. Most challenging was the actual arrival in the hotel of the politicians or diplomats that were the hosts of these events. The fastest and most direct access to the event had to be secured for them, to keep them away from prying eyes. Inquisitive guests and particularly any media representatives asking about the event and its attendees had to be dealt with firmly but politely. Checks on the premises were usually carried out by the politicians' own security staff, who often wanted to check areas such as the hotel entrance, bathrooms, meeting room, kitchen and indeed any area the VIP might enter. The hotels I worked in had their own security staff who were usually on site during these types of events, and they worked in partnership with the politicians' staff.

Protocol factors were another challenge for me at the beginning, as I had no prior knowledge of these, and had to learn them through experience. I found that during the planning it was vital to ask questions about protocol and not to presume anything. The more diplomatic events I organised, the easier it was, as I learnt how to ask the right questions at the right time. My job was made easier by the fact that at many events the person in charge of the diplomatic group had a written 'minute by minute scenario' that included details of the correct protocol to be observed. As they usually shared that information with me, it meant that I did not have to worry about knowing what the correct protocol for that occasion was.

The most challenging event I looked after was for a Chinese delegation attended by the governor of Sichuan province. The language barrier was a major challenge, as the group leader did not speak English very well, and so meetings with the client about the arrangements for their event were extremely protracted and complicated. Whenever I asked about any logistical matters, such as the required security, protocol, greetings on arrival, or even about the flowers they wanted in the venue, the answer from the client's side was always that that decision had to be made by their superiors, who were not present at the planning meeting but who nevertheless had to be consulted for a decision. Depending on the decision to be made, prior approval had to be sought by phone or by email to higher-ranking managers, some of whom were based in Prague and some in Sichuan. On the day of the event, many details were still unresolved with the client, and I felt great frustration at the fact that I did not have the final details and timings of the event ready to be communicated to the hotel management, head of departments and service staff. It was then that I really experienced what truly professional colleagues I was working with, as they demonstrated great patience and flexibility in order to make that event a success.

Despite all the exciting times I had in those roles, meeting international and local celebrities, politicians, sportspeople, writers, etc., I recently decided to take a rest from event planning and to look for a job where I could still utilise the valuable experience I gained from working in hotel sales and event management. By good luck, I was approached by the Prague Convention Bureau who were looking for someone with extensive knowledge of business events and our city. After a 1.5-hour interview with the managing director I was offered the job of Association Meetings Manager. In this role, I now provide objective assistance and advice about Prague's hotels, venues and opportunities for social events to the organisers of association conferences. I can honestly say that I am thoroughly enjoying selling the facilities and services of the entire destination rather than those of one property only.

References

Amadeo, K. (2018) What does the G20 Do? World leaders address terrorism, climate change and economic crises. Available at: https://www.thebalance.com/what-is-the-g20-3306114.

Austin, I. (2010) Canadians dismayed by meetings' costs. *International Herald Tribune*, 28 June.

BBC News (2007) What happens at party conferences? Available at: http://news.bbc.co.uk/2/hi/uk_news/politics/6993552.stm.

Bhatia, A. (2006) Critical discourse analysis of political press conferences. *Discourse & Society* 17(2): 173–203.

Blechinger, V. (2000) Corruption through political contributions in Japan. Submitted for a Transparency International Workshop on Corruption and Political Party Funding, La Pietra, Italy, October.

Chavis, S. (2015) SMERF meetings: Destinations that appeal to government and non-profit groups. ConventionSouth, June.

CVENT (2017) Event security is now more important than ever. Available at : https://blog.cvent.com/events/venue-sourcing/event-security-now-important-ever/.

Digance, J. (2005) Intergovernmental conferences: The CHOGM experience. *Journal of Convention & Event Tourism* 7(3–4): 65–83.

Douglas, M. R. and Gregory, S. (2009) Not all politics are local: exploring the role of meetings and events coordinators in the political arena. *Journal of Convention & Event Tourism* 10(2): 134–145.

Dunn, D. H. (ed) (2016) *Diplomacy at the Highest Level: The evolution of international summitry.* Basingstoke: Palgrave Macmillan.

Eriksson, G. (2011) Follow-up questions in political press conferences. *Journal of Pragmatics* 43(14): 3331–3344.

Everwall (2015) What's involved in planning a political event, exactly? Available at: https://everwall.com/blog/whats-involved-in-planning-a-political-event-exactly/.

G8 and G20 Research Groups (2010) G8 and G20 Summit costs. Available at: http://www.g8.utoronto.ca/evaluations/factsheet/factsheet_costs.pdf.

Getz, D. (2007) *Event Studies: Theory, research and policy for planned events,* Oxford: Butterworth-Heinemann.

Henderson, J. C. (2007) Hosting major meetings and accompanying protestors: Singapore 2006. *Current Issues in Tourism* 10(6): 543–557.

Llewellyn, N. (2005) Audience participation in political discourse: A study of public meetings, in Sociology. *The Journal of the British Sociological Association* 39(4): 697–716.

McComas, K., Besley, J. C. and Black, L. W. (2010) The rituals of public meetings. *Public Administration Review* 70(1): 122–130.

McNair, B. (2011) *An Introduction to Political Communication,* London: Routledge.

Monaghan, J. and Walby, K. (2012) 'They attacked the city': Security intelligence, the sociology of protest policing and the anarchist threat at the 2010 Toronto G20 summit. *Current Sociology* 60(5): 653–671.

Pogrebinschi, T. and Samuels, D. (2014) The impact of participatory democracy: Evidence from Brazil's national public policy conferences. *Comparative Politics* 46(3): 313–332.

Rein, L. (2014) Federal travel and conferences: Spending down, as lawmakers consider more restrictions. *The Washington Post*, 14 January.

Reynolds, D. (2007) *Summits: Six meetings that changed the twentieth century,* New York: Allen Lane.

Shoufeng, C. (2016) G20 Summit needs tighter security, period! Available at: http://www.chinadaily.com.cn/opinion/2016-07/29/content_26263730.htm.

Tam Cho, W. K. and Gimpel, J. G. (2007) Prospecting for (campaign) gold. *American Journal of Political Science* 51(2): 255–268.

Tepper, S. J. (2004) Setting agendas and designing alternatives: Policymaking and the strategic role of meetings, in Review of Policy Research, July.

Weilemann, P. R. (2000) The summit meeting: The role and agenda of diplomacy at its highest level. *NIRA Review* 7(2): 16–20.

Westcott, B. (2016) Blue skies and police vans: China prepares to host its first G20 Summit. Available at: https://edition.cnn.com/2016/08/30/asia/china-hangzhou-g20-2016/index.html.

7 Incentive travel

Incentive travel in the 21st century

- Mercedes-Benz USA took 400 of its top-selling dealers to the Caribbean island of St Lucia for the company's annual incentive trip. The participants were lodged in the 5-star Capella Marigot Bay Resort and Marina. Their programme of activities included two excursions, the first by catamaran to Pigeon Island to explore its historic Natural Park, and the second to Tikaye Beach to snorkel in its famed coral reef. Other activities were rum tasting, a cooking demonstration and an art class with local St Lucian artists.
- Axa Life Insurance ran an incentive trip to Bangkok as a reward for its top salespeople. One of the highlights of the trip was dinner in the famous Rose Garden attraction. The aim was to boost sales of the company's insurance policies and provide an opportunity for participants to network and exchange ideas.
- Daisy Distribution, a leading UK mobile phone distributor offered its distribution partners the opportunity to win a place on a three-day incentive trip to Iceland that included a jeep tour and snowmobiling. The winners were those partners who sold the highest volume of Samsung premium devices during a six-month competition period. The incentive programme resulted in a 69 per cent increase in sales of the Samsung product.

Chapter objectives

On completion of this chapter the reader should be able to:

- Recognise the importance of generating, recognising and rewarding high levels of performance in the workplace.
- Understand the use and value of incentive travel, as well as the potential disadvantages.
- Appreciate how incentive trips are designed, including the roles played by all suppliers.

Motivation in the workplace

It is a central theme of industrial and organisational psychology that incentives can improve workers' effort and performance. Therefore, in the corporate world one of the most important functions of management is to motivate, recognise and reward those who are vital to the ongoing success of their companies. Most company owners and managers understand that high levels of staff motivation lead to increased workplace performance, productivity and loyalty of their employees, which in turn help their companies to grow and become more profitable. In recognition of this fact, many companies introduce some form of employee incentive or motivation programme to boost the productivity levels of their workforce. Such programmes usually offer a range of monetary and non-monetary rewards to high-performing staff, as well as employee recognition awards of the type that were discussed in Chapter 5.

Formally defined, incentive programmes are 'plans that have predetermined criteria and standards, as well as understood policies for determining and allocating rewards' (Greene, 2011:219). The rewards are generally contingent upon the recipients' level of performance and productivity in the workplace. In terms of the categorisation of awards proposed by Frey and Gallus (2014), incentive programmes are *confirmatory* awards: the eligibility criteria are fixed, and the prizes are awarded when the specific criteria, fixed in advance, are reached or surpassed. For example, a company may offer their employees the prospect of being rewarded by an all-expenses-paid trip to a luxury resort, in return for reaching a specific performance target at work over a given period of time.

Monetary and non-monetary rewards are forms of 'extrinsic motivation', one of the two main determinants of human behaviour in organisations identified by Deci and Ryan (1985) in their self-determination theory. The extrinsic motivation to carry out a task well comes from the prospect of receiving some external reward for doing so – for example, an increase in salary or enhanced job benefits, such as a larger office. This may be contrasted with the other main determinant of behaviour identified in the self-determination theory, intrinsic motivation, which consists of the worker's passionate interest in the work they do and the pleasure and satisfaction they derive from that work. When employees feel intrinsic motivation, the work itself is its own reward.

Although workplace incentive programmes have been widely adopted by a broad range of sectors of the economy, a number of authors have highlighted potential drawbacks inherent in the use of such motivational systems.

Zoltners et al. (2012) express the view that incentives can create undesired consequences, including an organisationally unproductive, short-term focus among salespeople that leads to a counterproductive culture that actually damages company performance.

> When incentives are a large portion of sales force pay, salespeople and sales managers often obsess about making their monthly or quarterly numbers, and spend too

little time developing future selling skills or building long-term customer relationships ... The right combination of decisions – such as how to size and structure the sales team, how to find and develop the best sales team talent, and how to coach and manage the team for success – has a much higher impact on company results than do incentives.

(Zoltners et al., 2012:172).

To this general concern may be added the criticisms identified by Achtziger et al. (2015) that extrinsic incentives can even be responsible for crowding out the intrinsic motivation of employees and putting them under undue pressure.

Shinew and Backman (1995) also suggest that incentive reward programmes may result in a number of perverse or unanticipated outcomes, including reduced cooperation among employees before, during and after a contest period; a decline in morale because the contest was perceived to be unfair; and post-competition period slumps. According to the same authors, there is also the danger that rewards will lose their extra incentive value if used too often, thereby becoming a routinely expected component of the compensation package. More fundamentally, they suggest that performance improvement systems in general may fail to reward the behaviours that have the greatest impact on the long-term success of the sponsoring company. This challenge arises from the fact that the planning of incentive programmes tends to be led by ease of measurement. As management seeks to establish simple, concrete and quantifiable standards against which performance is measured, this approach, according to Shinew and Backman (1995), may result in the rewarding of behaviours (usually sales of the company's products) that have limited application to overall organisational effectiveness while excluding those that are more complex. While the activities of a company's salesforce may be relatively straightforward to quantify, general cooperation among colleagues and the inventiveness of the Research & Development department are examples of behaviours that may not be rewarded simply because they are difficult to measure. They may, however, be just as important to a company's survival and success as its sales record.

Gold (1996) suggests that a potential threat to the continuing growth of workplace incentives arises from the fact that they are driven by companies' conviction that their employees 'could do better', or in other words, that they are not working to their full capacity. The theory behind incentives of any kind is that employees can be urged on to even greater efforts on behalf of the company if they are rewarded for their achievements. But, Gold claims, in the increasingly competitive world of modern commerce, where employees are under increasing daily pressure to achieve better results, such as higher sales figures, it is no longer the case that there is a great deal of unused potential in the system. As a growing number of those in employment are finding that they have to work at full capacity just to hold on to their jobs, the incremental returns from sending staff on incentive trips, for example, may diminish to the extent that such rewards are no longer cost-effective.

The distinguishing characteristics of incentive travel

For over a century, managers and business owners have used the prospect of winning a lavish, all-expenses-paid trip to an appealing or exotic destination as a motivational tool for their staff in order to develop their capacity, capability, expertise, commitment and ultimately their performance in the workplace. With its strong focus on fun, entertainment and sports or cultural activities, incentive travel is the sector of business events that most resembles the type of leisure travel normally undertaken by individuals in their own time, unconnected with their employment.

However, despite their superficial similarity to high-end holidays, incentive trips represent a distinctive type of experiential reward that belongs firmly in the category of business events due to the directly work-related objectives of most incentive programmes. These objectives are mentioned in the following two definitions:

- 'Incentive travel is a self-funding marketing activity that employs unique travel experiences to reward people who achieve exceptional business performance.' (The Society for Incentive Travel Excellence)
- 'Incentive travel programmes are a motivational tool to enhance productivity or achieve business objectives, in which participants earn the reward based on a specific level of achievement set forth by management. Earners are rewarded with a trip and the programme is designed to recognise earners for their achievements.' (The Incentive Research Foundation).

Incentive travel programmes, therefore, are internal competitions offering the sponsoring company's employees the opportunity to win memorable and enjoyable trips to attractive destinations, usually funded entirely by the sponsoring company. The explicit aim is to encourage employees to meet *challenging* business objectives. This type of reward usually takes the form of group travel, with participants travelling with other award winners, and often with their own spouses or partners, too.

Incentive trips typically include a wide range of enjoyable spectator or participative activities, such as wine-tasting tours, hot-air balloon rides, white-water rafting, spa treatments, fine dining or bungee jumping. They may also include an educational or work element. Rogers (2008:69) notes that

> this can involve visits to factories and businesses in the same industry sector as that of the award winners, team-building programmes, and a conference-type session with an award presentation ceremony and announcements of corporate plans, designed to encourage the incentive winners to reach future performance targets.

Increasingly, participants in incentive trips also undertake some form of corporate social responsibility activity while at the destination, and this will be discussed later in this chapter.

A variety of terms are used to describe the participants on incentive trips, including 'earners', 'award winners' and 'qualifiers'. These terms indicate a fundamental characteristic of incentive travel, which is that places on such trips are obtained as a result of winning a competition that includes clearly stated individual and/or group targets or quotas, set by the company. Those who reach or exceed the targets are rewarded with a place on the incentive trip. For companies that have adopted incentive travel as an element of their employee motivation programmes, the incentive travel competition is often an annual event, anticipated with much excitement by the workforce.

Clearly, in order to motivate those competing to win places on incentive trips, the travel experience on offer must be of an extraordinary nature, featuring first-rate transport, accommodation and food and beverage elements as well as a range of exceptional activities. Incentive travel budgets, therefore, are usually extremely lavish. The 2017 Incentive Research Foundation Outlook Study (IRF, 2017) reported that the largest concentration of incentive travel budgets was between US$3,000 and US$4,000 per person, accounting for 36 per cent of the survey. The next two largest responses were for higher budget ranges: US$4,000–US$5,000 at 19 per cent; and greater than US$5,000 at 2 per cent. While such high levels of spending may seem extravagant, the benefits of running an incentive travel programme almost always outweigh the cost of implementing it. A successful incentive programme should be 'self-liquidating', meaning that it pays for itself through, for example, creating increased profitability for the sponsoring company due to incremental sales growth or the achievement of some other key business objective.

The value of incentive travel

Incentive travel has a long history of being used as a motivational tool. Ricci and Holland (1992) trace back the origins of incentive travel to the US company National Cash Registers of Dayton, Ohio (now part of AT&T) which, in 1906, awarded 70 salespeople diamond-studded pins and a free trip to the company headquarters. In 1911, the same company's top sales staff were rewarded with a free trip to New York. Joppe et al. (2002) also trace the origins of incentive travel back to the early years of the 20th century but note that it did not really become widespread as a reward option until the 1950s, with the development of commercial jet travel.

But long before the first incentive trips were awarded to high achievers, companies were attempting to motivate their employees through other means, notably monetary rewards. Latham (2012), for example, identifies, in the work of Frederick Winslow Taylor, one of the earliest expressions of the notion that performance which leads to rewards leads to satisfaction. In the early 20th century, Taylor, an engineer, developed a 'scientific management' approach to running a business, a key principle of which was the offering of monetary incentives to workers. 'In short, Taylor believed that employees should be paid substantial bonuses for goal/task attainment because compensation for work done efficiently and effectively, he believed, leads to satisfied employees.' (Latham, 2012:14) Incentive travel, therefore, is one of several methods available to management to motivate their workforce to achieve high levels of performance in their work. Monetary awards such as cash bonuses, profit-related pay schemes and stock options have long been used as motivational tools, but other possible awards for high achievers are merchandise, gift cards or vouchers.

The principal distinction between incentive travel and the other possible awards is that incentive travel is an *event* – it is experiential in nature. In the 21st century, a growing body of evidence supports the contention that many people derive more enduring satisfaction from their experiences than from their material purchases. Authors such as Van Boven and Gilovich (2003) identified a strong worker preference for experiences rather than tangible goods because experiences are more open to positive reinterpretations, are a more meaningful part of one's identity, and contribute more to successful social relationships. Caprariello and Reis (2011) refined this hypothesis, suggesting that it is *social interaction* experiences in particular that are a more effective source of sustainable happiness than spending money on material goods. These findings are generally held to apply to higher-income individuals – those who have reached a certain level of affluence. For such people, it has even been demonstrated that offering them more money in return for improved performance was counterproductive. Fisher (2005) highlights the findings of Victor Vroom, who discovered that for workers who had reached a specific level of material comfort, offering them more money in return for improved performance actually impaired their performance as it created unproductive stress and reinforced the view of the workforce that management regarded staff as mere economic units, to be manipulated like plant and machinery to create higher profits.

The many benefits of incentive travel both for participants and for the sponsoring companies are widely acknowledged by many authors (for example, Van Dyke, 2010a; Fenich et al., 2015). These may be summarised as follows.

Value for participants

Incentive travel offers participants:

- a *more memorable* prize than monetary awards. Cash bonuses, for example, are easily spent and often the reason for winning the reward (extra hard work) is forgotten as soon as the money is gone. Well-designed incentive travel can have a more lasting effect, due to the vivid memories created from the experience itself.
- opportunities for *networking and socialising* with other top performers and often with senior management.
- *professional development.* When a work-related element is included, this provides participants with opportunities to increase their knowledge through training, for example.
- *rest and relaxation.* Incentive trips can help stressed-out high performers unwind and re-charge in preparation for the next business cycle.
- *'trophy value'.* Being rewarded by a luxury trip in return for the effort invested and results achieved not only creates a certain pride and feeling of triumph, but it gives recipients something that they can talk about freely with family, friends and

neighbours. Money has far less 'trophy value' as in most cultures it is unacceptable to openly discuss one's earnings and bonuses.

It can be seen that travel as a reward owes much of its effectiveness to the fact that it has the potential to respond to some of the individual employee's own intrinsic needs. It has been suggested by Ricci and Holland (1992) that, for the individual, an incentive trip has the potential to satisfy the following four categories of travel motivation:

- Physical motivation (rest, health, sport, etc.)
- Cultural motivation (the desire to experience other cultures)
- Interpersonal motivations (to meet other people)
- Status and prestige motivation (the highly visible attention and status conferred upon award winners).

Value for sponsoring companies

Beyond helping companies to reach their 'hard' targets – usually to increase sales volume and profits – incentive travel offers sponsoring companies many 'soft' benefits. It:

- *facilitates communication and bonding* between employees. Co-workers who know each other well are more likely to work well together. The type of shared experiences and memories that an incentive trip can provide can be instrumental in building better-performing teams in the workplace.
- *reinforces the company's corporate culture*. Particularly for recent recruits to the company, spending extended periods of time with colleagues can be effective in inculcating in them the values and behaviours that contribute to the unique social and psychological environment of the organisation.
- *strengthens company loyalty and improves staff retention rates*. When employees feel connected to a company and appreciated by it, they are far less likely to seek employment elsewhere. Well-designed incentive trips can enhance the participants' level of engagement with their employer and their desire to continue working for that company.
- *motivates non-winners*. When colleagues return from their trips excited and keen to share the fascinating descriptions of their experiences, this can have the effect of stimulating other colleagues to work harder in order to be rewarded during the company's next incentive programme. For the company, this represents a lasting benefit which would not arise from simply giving the most productive members of staff a cash bonus, for example, since, as previously stated, the recipients would be less likely to discuss that type of reward with their colleagues.

Nevertheless, despite the numerous benefits arising from the use of incentive travel as a motivational tool, it is still the case that the majority of companies still opt for using monetary rewards. For example, Jeffrey et al. (2013) highlight the widespread use of gift cards by companies seeking to motivate their staff. Part of the reason for the popularity of monetary rewards is no doubt the convenience and simplicity of that form of reward, as opposed to the complex process of offering an incentive trip as a prize for the high-achieving employees. Incentive travel as a motivational tool may bring additional challenges, one being the obvious disadvantage that such trips remove the highest-performing members of staff from the workplace for a few days, rendering them wholly unproductive during their absence. Incentive travel also brings with it the risk of winners being disappointed, if the trip is poorly designed or if it is affected by unforeseen circumstances such as a strike or bad weather conditions.

But despite these potential drawbacks, incentive travel remains one of the key elements of business events, and an analysis of the market for this sector now follows.

The market for incentive travel

Demand

It is important to distinguish between those who are the actual buyers of incentive trips and those who are the recipients or end-consumers.

Buyers

Regarding the buyers of incentive travel, it is clear that they are overwhelmingly *private sector* enterprises. Motivational tools of any kind, monetary or non-monetary, are very rarely used in the public and non-profit sectors. This is partly due to the difficulty in identifying and measuring the exact output and performance of those employed as, for example, teachers, social workers or doctors (Burgess and Ratto, 2003). But there is also widespread evidence to suggest that those who choose to work in the public and non-profit sectors are generally driven by *intrinsic* motivation, as defined at the beginning of this chapter. Motivation for work in the public sector is widely characterised as relying on, for example, the employee's feeling of accomplishment, sense of public duty or the general satisfaction derived from working in the public interest and doing good for others and society (Park and Word, 2012). Indeed, a number of psychologists and sociologists have demonstrated that offering monetary and non-monetary rewards to public sector and non-profit employees can often be counterproductive, because they can actually undermine the vital intrinsic motivations of those workers (Georgellis et. al., 2010).

Analysing private sector incentive travel buyers in terms of industry sectors, it can be seen that there is little change, from year to year, in those types of businesses that invest most in this form of business event. The major buyers of incentive programmes were identified in the Incentive Research Foundation Vertical Market Study as (Van Dyke, 2010b):

*   Electronic computer/component manufacturing
*   Pharmaceutical preparations/manufacturing
*   New car dealers
*   Telecommunications resellers

- Commercial banking
- Insurance agencies and brokerages.

The fact that these industries all operate in extremely competitive sectors, where maintaining or increasing market share demands constant exhortations to greater efforts on the part of the salesforce, makes them the natural sources of demand for the vast majority of incentive trips. Fisher (2005) adds another reason for this: 'Automobiles, pharmaceuticals, computers and life insurance all benefit from a high margin, thereby making it possible to invest more of the accrued profit ... in staff' (Fisher 2005: 15).

Considering the main buyers in national terms, it is the US (the country that first used travel to motivate employees) which is still considered to be the world's largest consumer of incentive travel products, followed by the major European economies. But as other emerging nations, particularly those in South-East Asia, develop their economies, a rapidly growing number of their companies are adopting the practice of motivating their employees through incentive travel programmes. The president of the Society of Incentive Travel Executives (SITE) made this point when discussing the outbound incentive business from Asia:

> [Incentive travel in China] is in a maturing phase, a very high growth phase and one that the regional and world's destinations are counting on for boosting their tourism economy. The challenge I have observed is that in China, incentive travel is a relatively new concept and there are not that many incentive companies at the same level as in Europe and the US. In some cities, these types of businesses don't even exist. This is not to say incentives are not being organised, but corporates are doing it themselves and using local travel agents to book trips to a destination for a group of winners. This is how the industry starts, and as the requirements from corporate clients become more sophisticated, so specialised companies will emerge to meet the needs.
>
> —(Chan, 2013)

Recipients

One particular category of employee in particular is frequently the principal beneficiary of their company's motivation programmes: the salesforce. Successful business owners understand that for their companies to grow and prosper, it is not enough to simply create and manufacture strong, desirable products or services. They must also find effective ways of motivating their sales teams to sell to their customers; because without an effective salesforce, most companies are doomed to fail. For that reason, incentive travel is most often used with the basic objective of increasing sales. In the survey of US companies conducted by Jeffrey et al. (2013), almost 80 per cent of the target audience for incentive travel programmes were found to be sales employees.

Managers and business owners have long used the prospect of winning a lavish, all-expenses-paid trip to an appealing or exotic destination as a tool to motivate those who are responsible for selling whatever their company produces. But such rewards are not only extended to internal sales staff. Many companies sell their products and services through two types of distribution channels:

1   The direct sales model – the company's in-house sales staff sell directly to clients.
2   The channel sales model – the company's goods and services are sold indirectly, by independent, third-party sales 'channel partners', the company's independent distributors, dealers, vendors or retailers.

For example, most motor manufacturers hold franchise agreements with third-party dealerships that they rely upon for sales of their automotive products as well as providing service and after-sales representation to customers.

The channel sales model of distribution brings with it many advantages to the companies that take this approach to selling. It can provide a much wider geographical reach for their businesses and get their products or services in front of many more prospective buyers than would be possible by using their in-house salesforce only. For example, a network of local channel partners can help a company establish a presence in a new region or market with a fairly low initial investment. There is no need for it to incorporate and manage new companies, advertise locally, hire people in remote locations or manage new offices (Kirov, 2017).

Taken together, internal sales staff and external channel partners, are by far the most prevalent category of recipients of incentive travel awards. However, extending the reach of incentive programmes beyond sales teams and channel partners would appear to be growing as a practice. Joppe et al. (2002) identified an increasing trend towards including non-sales staff in incentive programmes, as a means of achieving the non-sales business objectives of the sponsoring company such as reducing staff turnover or improving health and safety levels by cutting the amount of working time lost through workplace accidents. The trend appears to be sustained, as Van Dyke (2011:1) noted:

> Progressive firms are breaking old paradigms. The Incentive Research Foundation (IRF) is seeing companies implement aggressive approaches in the effort to focus all employees on behaviours that drive business success. One such shift is the increasing inclusion of non-sales employees in group travel award programs – an award element traditionally reserved for only quota-carrying sales people.

There may also be another convincing reason for including non-sales staff in incentive programmes. Ting (2016) supports the case for doing so, citing the words of Susan Adams, Senior Director of Engagement for Dittman Incentive Marketing:

> Rewarding only sales can generate an 'us-versus-them' culture, instead of one where everyone's contributions are valued and recognised. Demonstrating appreciation for the efforts of those supporting the sales process will go a long way to ensuring that everyone is working toward the same goals and reaping the rewards of achievement.

Suppliers

In common with the other forms of business events covered in this book, incentive travel makes use of the services and facilities of the travel and hospitality industries. But incentive travel suppliers expand beyond the accommodation, catering and transport sectors, to include the full range of tourist attractions, recreation and activity providers that are required to service incentive trips. Another distinguishing feature of incentive travel is that, unlike, for example, the conference or exhibition sectors, no additional infrastructural facilities are required for tourism destinations that wish to be active in the incentive travel market. Destinations aspiring to attract this type of business event have no need to construct the conference or exhibition centres that are essential to hosting those other types of business events.

Clearly, one important attraction of this market for the destinations in which incentive trips take place is the fact that it brings business and healthy profits to those suppliers selling high-end products and services, such as rooms in 5-star hotels and tables in high-class restaurants. In recognition of the importance of this market, many suppliers have created their own dedicated incentive travel departments to sell into and service this market. From hotels and cruise ship operators to airlines and other forms of transport such as the Eurostar train service, specialist staff are recruited to fulfil the extremely high expectations of their incentive travel clients, providing faultless standards of service and attention to detail.

In the incentive travel market, the transport element is often not seen as simply a means to an end – getting to the destination – but as part of the incentive experience itself, characterised by pleasure, exclusivity and uniqueness. For that reason, many transport operators make particular efforts to ensure their incentive passengers feel special. For example, companies using the Eurostar as transport for their incentive trips have a wide range of benefits to choose from to make their award winners feel privileged. These include in-carriage branding with the company logo, on-board entertainment and personalised on-board welcome messages for their groups.

But it is the airline sector which is used most frequently to convey incentive winners to their destinations, and a key feature required of the airlines, by incentive travel organisers, is flexibility and at least a basic understanding of how incentive programmes work. To take just one example, with airlines that have no real understanding of how incentive programmes work, purchasing tickets can be problematic, as the passengers' names are not available until the winners of the incentive programme have been selected. On the other hand, more enlightened airlines have been known to provide dedicated group check-in facilities for their award-winning passengers.

Intermediaries

The incentive travel sector of business events, perhaps more than any other, is one where the use of intermediary agencies is widespread. The complexity involved in creating, administering and promoting incentive programmes, as well as designing and delivering the actual trip, means that only a very small proportion of sponsoring companies undertake to plan the entire incentive programme using their own in-house staff. The vast majority of companies outsource these tasks to one or more intermediaries, some of which may specialise in organising incentive travel events and some of which offer that service among others.

The range of intermediaries dealing directly with sponsoring companies to provide them with different levels of incentive travel–related services was identified by Ricci and Holland (1992):

- *Full-service incentive marketing companies* which handle both travel and merchandise fulfilment for their clients' incentive programmes
- *Full service incentive houses* which are similar to incentive marketing companies but specialise in incentive travel, and do not deal with merchandise rewards
- *Incentive travel fulfilment houses* which primarily arrange incentive travel trips with some incentive promotion services
- *Travel agents* with an incentive division where the agency specialises in providing incentive travel programmes but offers no marketing services
- *Retail travel agencies* offering typical travel arrangement services that can help deliver incentive trips.

Intermediaries active in this field vary from one-man/woman businesses to vast multinational conglomerates such as Maritz Travel, the AIM Group International or CWT Meetings & Events, for whom incentive travel is only one part of their business.

However, regardless of their size, many of the intermediaries identified by Ricci and Holland (1992) use the services of destination management companies (DMCs), whose role in the context of meetings and conferences was described in Chapter 2. DMCs may be thought of as the 'creative packager' of the incentive travel experience at the destination, as well as being the manager of all of the logistical elements of the incentive trip, ensuring that all arrangements run smoothly. When working for clients or other intermediaries in the incentive travel market, DMCs are required to use their vast amount of local knowledge, expertise and contacts to turn the other stakeholders' ideas into reality. Incentive trips demand of DMCs their full creativity and resourcefulness to deliver the type of unforgettable experiences that incentive earners expect from their trips.

Figure 7.1 shows the various permutations of intermediaries linking the sponsoring companies with the suppliers of facilities and services for their incentive trips. As can be seen, the supply chain between buyers and suppliers can vary in length, depending on the number of intermediaries involved, if any.

The next section of this chapter explores the typical range of tasks that are undertaken by full-service incentive marketing companies or full-service incentive houses on behalf of their clients.

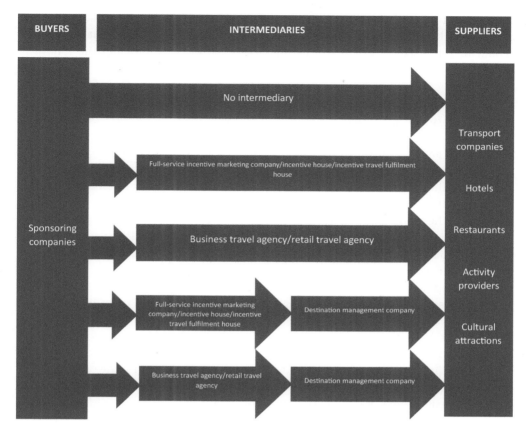

Figure 7.1
The use of intermediaries in incentive travel

Designing and delivering incentive travel programmes

To the outsider, they make look like extravagant upmarket holidays, but behind the fun and excitement of incentive trips lies a lengthy period of detailed planning and designing of the whole incentive programme, to ensure that the sponsoring company's objectives are met in full. In this section of the chapter, the entire process of designing incentive programmes is analysed.

Research and target-setting

The extent to which any incentive programme is successful in boosting motivation and performance naturally depends on how well the entire programme is designed and promoted. The design process begins with in-depth research into the sponsoring company's business and the collection of data that will guide later stages of the process by determining which members of the workforce should be incentivised – and what targets they should be set. Fisher (2005) calls this the 'human audit', and provides the following guidelines:

1   Analyse company performance over the previous five years in terms of sales, profits and return on investment. This may need to be done by division or by product group.
2   Classify and quantify the personnel and their impact on company growth. It is important to clarify each group's strategic task and value to the company.
3   Within the sales function, identify the distribution of sales per salesperson, month by month, and the overall distribution of individual performance.
4   Within the administrative function, clarify any objective measures of performance, such as retention rates, absenteeism and throughput.
5   Catalogue all previous attempts at 'motivating' any teams or groups or divisions of the company, together with any data on improved performance.
6   Talk to all department heads about morale, motivation, performance standards and incentives, with the aim of agreeing a broad statement of the prevailing views.

This detailed research into the sponsoring company's internal workings should result in a clear view of what the objectives for the incentive programme should be, and to whom it should be directed. The next step is to decide upon the objectives for the programme. If the human audit has been sufficiently rigorous, it should be possible to identify specific goals for specific groups of employees within the company. Within the sales department, for example, the type of targets to be met in order to qualify for a place on the incentive trip could include:

*   Increasing sales overall
*   Increasing sales of specific products
*   Increasing sales to particular clients
*   Increasing sales in specific local regions
*   Introducing new products or services
*   Increasing market share.

Naturally, for the purposes of meaningful measurement, the targets must be quantitative. They must also be fair, simple, achievable, realistic but challenging – and clear. In order to be fully equitable, they must take into account local market conditions. For example, an automobile company cannot fairly expect the same sales growth volume from a car dealer in a small town as from a large dealer in the capital city. If the targets do not reflect reality, they may backfire and demotivate the participants. But when employees feel that the targets are reachable, they are more likely to buy into the programme and work harder to reach the goals set. Palmer (2012), writing in *Incentive Magazine*, argues that it is employees' perception of fairness that has the biggest impact on their satisfaction with their employers' incentive programmes.

Deciding on the reward system

The incentive trip destination

Designing the incentive travel programme also involves, at an early stage, deciding upon what will be the most appropriate travel award to offer as a prize. The incentive destination is clearly one of the strongest motivating factors for employees and choosing one that inspires all of them to work hard to win a place on the trip brings significant challenges. But if the incentive house fails to identify a destination which fully inspires the company's employees, the programme is unlikely to succeed.

Fisher (2005:140) emphasises the importance of the destination's image, which must be strong and positive:

> Cities like London, Paris and New York are bona fide world players as far as the image of the destination is concerned. They need little explanation and offer a wide range of attractive features to many levels of participant in many cultures.

But he notes that other, less well-known destinations can be successful for incentive programmes, if they are correctly promoted to potential qualifiers. 'Some cold and windy destinations in northern Europe are irresistible to people who live in hot climates simply because they represent an alternative lifestyle.' (ibid.:141)

The decision-making process generally begins with the incentive house establishing a short-list of possible destinations, in discussions with the sponsoring company, their client. A number of factors are taken into account: the employees' aspirations, the budget available, ease of access, the demographic profile of the likely participants, and where the company's recent incentives were held.

Joppe et al. (2002) note that destinations sometimes become popular for incentive travel following hallmark events, such as the Olympic Games or the FIFA World Cup, because of the extra exposure they receive. Indeed, it is not uncommon for such destinations to attract incentive travel groups during the major events they host, especially if there is a link between the sponsoring company and the event, such as the automotive industry and the Formula One Grand Prix.

A further determining factor to be taken into account is the possible links between the sponsoring company itself and the destination. This could be in terms of the company's products or services – a technology company might choose to reward its high achievers with a trip to San Francisco to visit Silicon Valley, for example. Or the company might select a destination because it has a branch or local office there, a visit to which could constitute a work-related element of the incentive trip.

But whatever the destination, a basic requirement, naturally, is that the destination should be perceived as being entirely safe and politically stable. Any hint of danger or political volatility can disqualify an incentive destination overnight, as no one will work hard for the prospect of winning a trip to somewhere that is potentially hazardous. For example, in the 2017 Incentive Travel Report (C&IT, 2017), 73 per cent of intermediaries said that for security reasons Turkey was no longer a destination that they would propose to their clients.

A single-tier or multi-tier award structure?

Often, the conclusion of the incentive travel house's research is that it is appropriate to offer more than one incentive travel product to the company's employees: a multi-tier award system, rather than one that is single-tier. For example, in a multi-tier award structure, employees qualifying for the first-tier award could be entitled to a merchandise reward or a gift card, rather than a travel product; those reaching the second-tier level of qualification could win a trip to a domestic destination; while those qualifying for the third tier award could win a trip to a short-haul international destination; and those qualifying for the highest tier award could win a trip to a long-haul international destination.

There are two convincing reasons for using a multi-tier award system of this kind. First, it offers at least a partial solution to the problem created when employees perceive that the same people within the company win the incentive trip every year, as can often be the case in an all-or-nothing, single-tier structure. According to research findings of the Society for Incentive Travel Excellence, this perception is problematic because it can discourage non-earners from trying harder the following year. It can also create an environment in which some employees thrive, and others stagnate (SITE, 2013).

Secondly, having a multi-tier award system avoids the problem of employees becoming complacent and working less hard once they have reached the qualifying target in a single-tier system. With multi-tier awards available to high achievers, the momentum to keep performing well in the workplace is maintained until the employee qualifies for the top level of award.

Spouses and partners of award winners

The influence of employees' spouses and partners on their commitment to working hard in order to win a place on the company's incentive trip has been emphasised by several researchers. For example, the vast majority of employees interviewed by Shinew and Blackman (1995) indicated that the support of their spouses or partners was a major consideration to them in their decision whether or not to participate in their employers' incentive programmes. To enlist this domestic support to the greatest degree possible, spouses and partners are frequently included as participants in the trip, based on the belief that they will then be more tolerant of the extra hours that the employees had to work in order to qualify for the trip. Fenich (2015:154) illustrates this point in a quote from a representative of a company using incentive travel:

> Because spouses or guests are included and there are a lot of repeat participants, the relationships get driven much deeper than one might anticipate. Because now we have spouses who become friends and we have spouses who begin to encourage their spouse, who is producing business for us, to produce more.

Designing the itinerary

There is no such thing as an 'off-the-peg' incentive trip itinerary. Each trip must be tailored to the precise needs of the incentive group, taking into account previous incentive trips that they may have experienced. Much of the skill of the incentive marketing company or incentive travel house, therefore, lies in designing a travel experience which, every time, surprises, delights and impresses the – often very demanding and well-travelled – incentive travel winners. In other words, incentive trips must provide the 'wow!' factor.

Fenich et al. (2015:148) emphasise the importance of emotional appeal: 'Memorable incentive travel programmes are measured by their emotional level of intensity. This includes the emotions an employee feels before, during, and after the trip.' Producing this emotional appeal can be achieved through itineraries that offer the following characteristics:

- *Uniqueness:* no incentive trip should be like any other. Itineraries should not be predictable, but rather, full of surprises and special events. Innovative ideas are the lifeblood of this sector, and organisers must continuously produce creative and original elements to thrill participants. The unexpected arrival of the company's managing director by hot-air balloon, for the final evening's gala dinner, for example, would be a memorable way to conclude an incentive trip.
- *Fantasy or exotic experiences:* incentive trips often include the opportunity for participants to try out novel sporting activities, such as clay-pigeon shooting, falconry or hang-gliding. A skilled incentive travel house will be able to include in the programme some activities which the participants will not have already tried but may have always wanted to.
- *Exclusivity:* at the end of the trip, the participants should have the impression that they have had privileged access to exclusive places and people. If a tourist attraction such as Madame Tussauds is visited, then it must be unlike the visits made by the general public: for example, a champagne breakfast may be held there before opening time, or the visit could include a behind-the-scenes look at how the wax models are made. Use is often made of celebrities, to achieve this effect. For example, guided tours of the destination are all the more memorable if the guide is a well-known actor or sportsperson who happens to live there.
- *Activities:* few incentive trips leave participants to lie on the beach day after day. Activities and sports are included as a way of making the trip more memorable and dynamic. Given that award winners are, almost by definition, often competitive by nature, much use is made of competitions and team games, such as beach Olympics, mini hovercraft races and talent competitions.

But recently, an additional factor has emerged as a characteristic of incentive trips: *corporate social responsibility* (CSR). In the 21st century, it has become increasingly common to incorporate a worthwhile volunteering activity into the itinerary, such as planting trees to help the environment, or helping disadvantaged local people by renovating school classrooms. *Conference & Incentive Travel* magazine's 2017 Incentive Travel Report

(C&IT, 2017) identified a resurgence in the number of incentive travel itineraries that included a CSR element as a way of enabling participants to give something back to the destination. The Goodyear case study in this chapter provides an outstanding example of a CSR activity on an incentive trip.

Promoting the incentive travel programme

Once the incentive programme rules have been devised and the destination and itinerary have been agreed upon, the next step is for the incentive travel house to carry out a communications campaign within the company, to promote the competition and the prize to the employees concerned. In general, this campaign begins with a 'kick-off' event to announce the details of the programme to those members of staff selected to participate and to motivate them to strive to qualify for the trip on offer. Such events work best when they create maximum employee buy-in through generating genuine excitement for, and interest in, winning a place on the trip. Visuals such as images and videos of the destination are often used at kick-off events, sometimes combined with opportunities to sample food and beverages from the chosen incentive destination.

But although the main promotional effort should be at the launch of the incentive programme, it is vital to continue promoting the programme throughout the period of the competition. According to SITE (2013), for an incentive programme to be effective, it must include an effective communication and feedback strategy: 'If the company frequently promotes their incentive travel programme and its goals, it will be on employees' minds more often. Also, ongoing feedback will encourage employees to continue to put effort into the programme.'

Throughout the duration of the incentive programme, the incentive travel house monitors employees' performance, and periodically sends them reminders of the desirability of the prize, in order to continue to spur them on to greater achievements and to avoid the sagging of enthusiasm. These reminders are known as 'teasers', and may take the form of brochures or postcards of the destination being sent to employees at work or to their homes. Even more creative teasers have been used. An agency once sent small bottles of sand to participants to remind them that the prize they were competing for was a trip to an exclusive oasis resort in the Sahara.

The final task to be undertaken before the actual trip is to select and nominate the winners. Announcing the winners is often done at an in-company event, such as a reception or lunch, to make maximum impact and to give the qualifiers the recognition they have earned.

Delivery of incentive travel programmes

It goes without saying that after all of the meticulous planning and promotion, the actual trip must at least meet, but preferably exceed, the expectations of the incentive programme winners. To the greatest extent possible, they must be made to feel like VIP guests, as a recognition of their status as qualifiers, and the incentive trip experience should feel quite different from an upmarket package holiday in the same hotel and destination. Fisher (2005) suggests a number of techniques for enhancing the incentive trip participants' experience. These include:

- *Off-airport check-in:* at the airport of departure, the incentive travel house can arrange for participants' luggage to be checked in at a nearby hotel, so that they do not have to queue up with other passengers at the terminal.
- *Pre-selected seats on the aircraft:* while booking seats with the airlines, the incentive travel house can negotiate particular seats by the window or by the aisle, or seats with additional legroom, for example.
- *Charter flights:* in the event of a suitable scheduled flight not being available at the times and dates required, or not having enough seats for the group in question, an alternative – although expensive – option is to charter a plane.
- *Quick check-in at the hotel:* by prior arrangement with the hotel, qualifiers are able to collect their keys from a dedicated check-in desk, separate from the main hotel reception desk, avoiding lengthy queuing.

Silvers (2004:124) mentions additional services that hotels might provide for the convenience of incentive travel participants:

> For incentive groups, the professional event coordinator may arrange a concierge desk exclusively for the event's guests, special delivery of specific newspapers and magazines, or reserved tee times at a golf course. If the incentive guests are receiving numerous souvenir items and gifts, a special shipping service might be prearranged so they do not have to carry them home in their luggage.

A further factor contributing to the participants' feelings of being privileged during incentive trips is the presence of senior management on those trips. Indeed, the opportunity to spend quality time with those higher up the workplace hierarchy is commonly regarded as a key attraction in the incentive travel award. According to Van Dyke (2010a):

> To meet the business objectives of the incentive travel program, it is important to have the executive management team included in the incentive travel program. The CEO, Presidents, Vice Presidents, and Regional Directors of each corporate division are referred to as 'hosts', (and) ... the primary responsibility of the host is to show earners how much their outstanding contributions to the company are appreciated. All participating hosts are ... required to attend all of the events, mingle with the winners and engage in all business sessions ... This allows the host or manager to learn first-hand from top performers and get feedback from their employee categories on issues that may be of interest for improvement or development. This opportunity not only allows management to build a personal relationship with their top performers, but also allows top performers to build a relationship with other top performers within the corporation.

Finally, throughout the delivery of the programme, it is essential to record photographic or video material of the destination, the accommodation and all of the fun, exotic activities undertaken by the participants. This material subsequently serves two purposes: first as a way of keeping the memory of the trip fresh in the minds of the participants, in order to encourage them to maintain their high levels of performance when they return to work, with the aim of qualifying for the following year's incentive trip; and secondly for taking photographs and making videos to inspire and encourage non-qualifiers. 'Video (etc.) will ensure that non-qualifying colleagues will get to see what went on and, we hope, encourage those colleagues to qualify during the following year.' (Fisher, 2005:159)

Chapter summary

This chapter began by analysing the role of incentives in the workplace as a form of extrinsic motivational tool, reviewing the strengths and drawbacks of such systems. Incentive travel as a motivational tool was then defined and its characteristics described. Its strengths and drawbacks were compared with those of monetary rewards. The roles of the various stakeholders in the incentive travel market were reviewed: sources of demand, suppliers and intermediaries operating in this market. Next, the design, promotion and delivery of incentive trips were described, with emphasis on the factors determining the choice of destinations and the unique factors to be taken into account in the design of incentive travel itineraries.

CASE STUDY 7.1: SAGE PLATINUM ELITE 2017

Sage Platinum Elite

The client

Sage is a global technology company that describes itself as 'the market and technology leader for integrated accounting, payroll and payment systems' (www.sage.com). The company has over 13,000 employees across 23 countries, providing technology-based solutions for well over 6 million customers across the globe.

The event and its objectives

Sage Platinum Elite 2017 was the company's second annual incentive event, organised for the company's top performers. Their first took place in 2016 in St Lucia, and following the success of that event, the 2017 incentive programme was announced.

Sage Platinum Elite 2017 was organised to reward the company's highest performing employees from all of their offices globally. Only 140 winners and their spouses/partners/guests were invited, from their entire global workforce. Sage used this opportunity to reward their employees for their hard work, dedication and productivity throughout the year. In addition, they also used the event to launch the following year's incentive programme. This was in order to motivate employees to continue driving sales in order to meet and exceed targets so that they could once again have the opportunity of winning the upcoming year's trip, which in 2018 was held in Mexico.

The destination and the programme

Sage Platinum Elite took place in Dubai, United Arab Emirates, between 2 and 6 February 2017 at the Madinat Jumeirah Resort (www.jumeirah.com/en/hotels-resorts/dubai/madinat-jumeirah/), which includes three exclusive hotels, 29 traditional summerhouses and a number of villas, as well as its own private beach.

The group exclusively booked 14 villas on the property with each villa containing 9–11 rooms spread over two floors. Each cluster of villas had its own private pool and direct access to the beach, 300 metres of which was privatised for Sage Platinum Elite. This exclusive area was renamed 'Sage Village' and throughout the programme, the Sage Platinum Elite logo was liberally displayed on everything from the bottles of water to the signposting within the Sage Village.

The five-day programme was as follows:

- Day 1: Arrival, time at leisure and Welcome Dinner
- Day 2: Optional activities and dine-around
- Day 3: Private Polo match and Desert Adventure with dinner in the desert
- Day 4: Optional activities and Farewell Dinner
- Day 5: Time at leisure and departure.

The destination management company

24 Degrees (http://24degrees.com/) is a destination management company (DMC) specialising in creating tailored experiences for groups visiting Dubai, Abu Dhabi and Oman.

Founded in 2010, 24 Degrees counts among its clients multinational companies and industry sectors including automotive, pharmaceutical, financial services, sports and film production. The company attributes its success to the strong relationships it has with local suppliers, which enable it to deliver innovative products at reasonable prices. Its services include an online registration and delegate management system, event planning and execution, logistics, exhibition build and sales, team building and motivational experiences.

How 24 Degrees supported this event

As Sage's selected DMC, 24 Degrees sourced a shortlist of hotels and liaised with the chosen hotel on behalf of their client. Through its network of relationships and buying power in the market, 24 Degrees was able to secure a preferential group rate for Sage Platinum Elite. 24 Degrees also arranged and executed two site inspections with the client, during which both sides were able to finalise the various elements of the programme.

- Shortlisted hotels
- Venues
- Restaurants
- Off-property activities
- Desert experience.

24 Degrees had full responsibility for the group's arrival experience and ground transportation to the hotel. This included a VIP 'meet and greet' service by which participants were met as soon as their flights arrived at Dubai International Airport and taken to a private lounge for refreshments and to relax while their immigration formalities were handled. 24 Degrees arranged pre-arrival visas for over 100 participants. Upon completion, they were escorted through and assisted with duty-free shopping and luggage handling. Each winner and their guest were then escorted to their own luxury sedan and transferred to the hotel.

In collaboration with the respective teams at the hotel, 24 Degrees arranged all F&B (food and beverages), audio-visual and entertainment options for the group's Welcome Gala. This was originally planned to be held at an outdoor venue on the property; however, due to inclement weather, the DMC was forced to move it to an indoor venue within two hours of the time set for the beginning of the Welcome Gala.

24 Degrees was also in charge of the sourcing, contracting, planning and execution of all daily activities which included boating, auto racing, golf and Dubai city tours. A dine-around was also planned for the group whereby each participant and his or her guest could select their desired dining establishment from a list of seven, all of which were sourced, negotiated and contracted by 24 Degrees.

Day 3 of the itinerary for the group was a complete surprise to the winners and their guests. A private polo match was arranged for the group by the 24 Degrees team. It included F&B throughout the day, as well as Sage's company branding being displayed throughout the polo grounds. After the match, 73 luxury 4 × 4 vehicles took the entire group into the desert for an evening that included dune bashing (a form of off-road driving on sand dunes), camel riding and an exclusive dinner under the desert stars. 24 Degrees handled the set-up of the dinner and the F&B requirements, as well as the extensive entertainment options which included falcon shows, fire dancers, a four-piece Arabic band and henna artists.

The Farewell Dinner on the final evening was also sourced, negotiated, planned and executed by the 24 Degrees team. Once again using their well-established relationships and buying power, the DMC was able to secure for their client the use of the brand new terrace of the Burj Al Arab, which describes itself as the world's most luxurious hotel. With exclusive use of the Burj Al Arab terrace, Sage was one of the first companies to use this venue after it was transported to Dubai from Finland where it was constructed. As well as organising all of that evening's F&B requirements, 24 Degrees also arranged a four-minute fireworks show that was synchronised to the music playing during the event. All permissions and safety procedures required for this by the government were also handled by 24 Degrees.

Finally, on the day of the group's departure, all transfers from the hotel to the departure terminal at Dubai International Airport once again used luxury sedan transportation.

Other services provided by 24 Degrees, for the Sage event included:

- Branding throughout the programme
- Printing arrangements for menus and gift cards
- Professional photographers and videographers throughout the programme
- Arranging licences and permissions for the entertainment throughout
- Room-drops and gifts for all of the guests every night
- Company-branded bottles of water throughout the programme – over 9,000 bottles in all.

CASE STUDY 7.2: GOODYEAR INCENTIVE TRIP

Goodyear incentive trip

The client: Goodyear

The Goodyear Tire & Rubber Company (www.goodyear.com) started in 1898 with just 13 workers producing bicycle and carriage tyres and quickly grew to become one of the world's largest tyre companies. Today, Goodyear is headquartered in Akron, Ohio and has facilities across the world, with annual sales of more than US$15 billion. In addition to Goodyear brand tyres, the company produces other well-known international brand names, including Dunlop, Kelly, Fulda, Sava and Debica, and its non-tyre business provides rubber products and polymers for a variety of markets.

The event management agency: BCD Meetings & Events

BCD Meetings & Events (BCD M&E) (www.bcdme.com) is an independently managed operating company of the BCD Group, a privately owned company founded in 1975. It is a global meeting and event management agency with its headquarters in Chicago and locations in over 40 countries across the Americas, Europe, Middle East, Africa and Asia Pacific. BCD M&E has a combined global workforce of more than 1,000 and an annual sales volume of approximately US$850 million.

The local DMC: Amstar DMC Mexico

Amstar DMC (www.amstardmc.com) is a leading destination management company and MICE team operating in Mexico, Jamaica, the Dominican Republic, Costa Rica and Hawaii. It employs more than 1,200 travel professionals, and has its corporate headquarters in Cancun, Mexico and Punta Cana, the Dominican Republic. Amstar DMC is a division of the Apple Leisure Group, which specialises in the sales of leisure travel packages to Mexico, the Dominican Republic and Jamaica.

The SITE Crystal Awards Recognition Programme

The SITE Crystal Awards Recognition Programme honours organisations that excel in designing unique and memorable incentive programmes that create extraordinary motivational experiences and deliver measurable business results for their clients. Sponsored by the IMEX Group, which operates B2B exhibitions for incentive travel, meetings and events, the SITE Crystal Awards Recognition Programme is the most prestigious form of recognition in the global incentive travel industry.

In 2016, BCD M&E won a SITE Crystal Award for 'Most Impactful Effort toward Corporate Social Responsibility as Part of an Incentive Programme' at the Crystal Awards Recognition Ceremony held during that year's SITE Global Conference in Panama City, Panama. This case study analyses how BCD M&E designed the Goodyear incentive programme, with particular emphasis on the corporate social responsibility (CSR) element.

The incentive programme

Goodyear runs an annual 'Goodyear Champion' incentive trip for customers and associates in its Americas region (the US, Canada and Mexico). In 2016, the trip took place in Puerto

Vallarta, Mexico. That year, for the first time ever, a CSR component was integrated into the programme to help bring the participants together and make a positive impact on the lives of local community members through a lasting contribution – building a new playground for a local school in need.

Goodyear's goal for the incentive trip was not only to reward but to connect participants from across the region in a meaningful way. They wanted to bring customers and associates together to celebrate the company, unite them with a common purpose and build engagement among them as well as with the local community – who are ultimately the company's customers.

The participants in this programme were extremely varied and included dealers, distributors, Goodyear executives, children, parents, teachers, media and even government officials. And with participants coming from North America as well as Mexico, there was also a range of different cultures and languages represented. But the overarching common goal was to provide local schoolchildren with a safe environment to play in, while emphasising the importance of teamwork, patience and environmental and cultural awareness.

The entire programme was fully customised by BCD M&E for Goodyear, who had a say every step of the way to make sure that the results would be something that not only served the purpose of executing a CSR activity but something that everyone would be proud of.

Working with their local partner Amstar DMC Mexico, the event management agency was able to provide seamless coordination for the client. The behind-the-scenes work that was done locally with the government and Board of Education in order to select and prepare the school was invaluable. However, the complexity of planning the programme was intensified by the fact that at the planning stage the local government was in a period of transition with a new mayor and staff taking office (including a new Board of Education) and the schools were on their annual summer holiday, meaning there had to be continuous follow-up and communication with local stakeholders.

The DMC helped secure approval from the Board of Education and identify a school in need. They also brought in a local contractor and jungle gym supplier to both prepare the playground area and help install the equipment. In addition to the jungle gym and a swing set, the playground also included a pyramid of Goodyear tyres that were brightly painted. This creative use of the client's product in the construction of the school playground had the effect of strengthening their brand in the region. The CSR initiative also demonstrated best practices by recycling used tyres and repurposing them in the construction of a playground for about 1,000 pupils who previously only had a single soccer field for recreation.

The CSR activity made a considerable impression on the participants as it was unlike anything that they had previously experienced on incentive travel programmes. They were divided up into different groups in charge of various activities based on their abilities, and given corresponding colour-coded bandanas. For example, there was a team who were responsible for the heavy lifting, digging holes and putting the jungle gym pieces together. Another group was in charge of setting up tables and chairs and helping the caterers with lunch. In this way, all participants were able to contribute in a meaningful way to the overall success of the CSR initiative. The Goodyear team was able to rally around the project, creating a sense of camaraderie amongst customers and associates, while giving back to the community they were visiting. After constructing the playground, a celebratory BBQ for the entire community was held. The mayor of Puerto Vallarta, Arturo Davalos Peña, attended the event and spoke about the benefits of education and the generosity shown by Goodyear toward his community.

Conclusion

The CSR element of the Goodyear incentive programme created an opportunity outside the corporate setting for team members to work together and give something back to the local community. The engagement among associates created by undertaking the tasks necessary to constructing the playground translated to engagement back at the office, creating the more unified team that Goodyear wanted. It also increased brand value in the region as it demonstrated collaboration between the brand and consumers to improve the quality of school amenities in the community. The return on investment for Goodyear was substantial, taking into account overall customer satisfaction and the fact that the overall approval rating from participants was 99 per cent.

Reflecting on the impact of the programme, Martin Rosales, Goodyear's managing director in Mexico, said:

> We worked together with our North American distributors to provide a better future for those little kids in Mexico. It was a unique experience. It was very clear that we – the associates – are not the only ones who protect the company's good name. Our customers do it as well. It was an example of the synergies we can create within the Americas and how powerful this new region will be.
>
> (SITE, n.d.)

IT'S MY JOB
STÉPHANIE STRIKA, INCENTIVE PROJECT MANAGER, EXPERIENCE SCOTLAND

I have always been passionate about languages and travelling, so after graduating with a degree in History from Lyon 3 University in 2005, I trained to become a tourist guide in France. After getting my licence, I worked in a tourism agency based in Burgundy as a guide and tour leader, organising tours to Italy for French tourists and accompanying them on those trips.

As I enjoyed working with groups so much, I was delighted when I got the opportunity to work as a project manager with Un Monde Bleu, a DMC (destination management company) in my home city, Lyon, in France. This DMC specialised in river cruises but also offered tailor-made programmes in this area of France for leisure groups, working mainly with the American and German markets.

I was recruited partly because of my knowledge of the destination, which I got to know very well as a guide; but also, my previous experience in an agency was an asset because it meant that I knew already how to put together tours, how to sell them to clients, and how to implement them by booking all of the services required. This role of project manager was extremely varied, and I enjoyed it very much. I discovered that this type of work is not only about the clients, but also (and I would say, above all) about suppliers. It is essential to have excellent people skills and to build relationships with suppliers, because they are your main ally in difficult situations.

After five enjoyable years of working in my city, I decided to move to Scotland to experience a new adventure and to improve my English, and that's where – through an advertisement on LinkedIn – I found my dream job, working as Incentive Project Manager in a DMC specialising in incentive travel – Experience Scotland (http://www.experiencescotland.co.uk/).

In this job, one of the first things I learned was how different it is to be working with corporate groups, compared with the leisure groups that I was more used to, particularly in terms of the expectations of incentive clients.

Why is incentive travel so demanding for those employed in this sector? In my opinion, this is for two main reasons:

- Incentive trips are generally short and intended to make an impression on the participants. You constantly have to source new venues or activities, to be as creative as possible and always one step ahead, to amaze your clients. My experience has taught me that in incentive travel, you can never stop being creative and thinking out of the box – even though sometimes it is difficult to get what you have in mind, because the suppliers are not always happy to do things differently. I've also learnt that what looks great in your opinion is not necessarily exciting for other people. That's why it is really important to understand the requirements of your clients and to try to focus on your clients' tastes, which can be different to your own, depending on their culture or background. But the fact that your clients (usually people working for an incentive company, sometimes accompanied by the end-client) usually come ahead of the group for a site inspection gives you a good opportunity to better understand what they are looking for. This is the moment when you can adjust your offer, if necessary.
- With incentive groups, you need to pay a level of attention to detail that you don't necessarily have with leisure groups. An incentive event is not only a way for companies to reward their employees – it is also a way for them to build their image and reinforce their brand through the events they offer to their staff. So there is no second chance – everything must be perfect when the participants

arrive. Every little thing counts and needs to be arranged in advance: the decoration of the tables for the gala dinner, the logo of the group displayed wherever possible, the quality of the food of each meal, the service of the guides, the music during the party after dinner, the quality of the photographs of the event, the standard of each bedroom, the backup – in case of bad weather – for outdoor activities. And, of course, you have to make sure that everything runs smoothly according to the schedule.

As a consequence, I find that organising incentive trips means working under a lot of pressure. You try to coordinate every supplier involved and also to please your client (who is generally under a lot of pressure, too), trying to arrange last-minute changes or to fix problems. You stay with the group from the beginning to the end of the trip. This job requires you to be organised, patient, firm sometimes, diplomatic most of the time – and passionate about what you do! If you like what you are doing and you try to deliver the best service, your clients will see it and you'll always be rewarded for that.

What is great for me about my job is that I never stop learning. Every week is different and it is anything but boring. My job takes me to places that I would never have visited myself. And I find that in an interesting way, I am never 'off-duty' because even during my free, personal time, I am always thinking about how this restaurant that I just tried, for example, could be used by future incentive groups.

For me, incentive travel is not just a job, it's a way of life. And I wouldn't dream of working in any other sector.

IT'S MY JOB
EDA OZDEN, DIRECTOR OF BUSINESS
DEVELOPMENT, MEPTUR, TURKEY

It is hardly surprising that I chose business events as my profession, as my parents have been active in this industry for almost as long as I can remember. My father owns an incoming agency and my mother is the founder of Turkey's first and largest inbound destination management company (DMC), Meptur (www.meptur.com.tr). I consider myself very fortunate to have been given the opportunity, from an early age, to be directly exposed to so many experiences in the business events industry.

For example, in the early '90s, soon after my mother's DMC business was founded, it organised events for the Chief Executives Organization in Istanbul and Ephesus. As part of the conference programme, my mother planned an evening in one of Istanbul's oldest churches – a dinner with a ceiling fire show as its highlight. This was the first time anybody had ever dared to do something this bold in the UNESCO World Heritage old citadel of Istanbul and it gave me an invaluable insight into the lasting effect that an 'experiential evening' can leave on the attendees. I understood that night the difference between working in tourism and working in the MICE industry.

While my plan was not always to join the industry, my destiny led me to this point. After studying International Relations at the George Washington University Elliott School of International Affairs in Washington, DC, I graduated in 2007 and decided to spend some time backpacking around South America on my own. This trip to Peru and Bolivia was the first ever that I had organised on my own, and it built my confidence more than any other experience I had had until that point. It also taught me that what makes any trip impactful isn't its level of luxury but the unique experiences, personal engagement and cultural enrichment it offers.

Continuing my education, I then went on to study a master's degree in Law, Globalization and Development at the School of Oriental and African Studies (SOAS), in London. While writing my thesis in the summer of 2009, my mother saw I was working very hard and so she decided to reward me with a trip to Iceland to attend that year's SITE (Society for Incentive Travel Excellence – http://www.siteglobal.com/) Global Young Leaders Conference. For me, this was a life-changing experience. I found the SITE event so inspirational and felt such a strong connection with the other participants that I decided right then that the time had come for me to go back home and join the family company.

Because of my strong proficiency in the English language, my knowledge of Turkey as a destination and passion for the business events industry, the sales and marketing side of my work came easy to me, and I found that I was soon able to write detailed incentive travel proposals in response to RFPs (requests for proposals) from potential clients. However, it took me longer to acquire the logistical skills that my company required from its employees. Learning to remain calm in moments of crisis, delegating and managing relationships with clients, and understanding the specific requirements of each industry we were dealing with, such as the codes governing pharmaceutical events, for example – all of this proved to be a much bigger challenge for me. I soon understood just how much technical knowledge our industry requires and the importance of keeping up with all of the constant changes it is going through, legally, technologically and environmentally.

My career in business events has been marked by many highs and lows. One of my worst moments came when the private yacht that I had booked for a small but very high-budget incentive group got caught in a storm in Turkish waters, making some of the participants very sick indeed. My agency contact yelled at me loudly and at some length in the lobby of the Four Seasons Bosphorus, and when we got back to the hotel I broke down in tears. A colleague of mine then came to calm me down. He said, 'Never bow your head down unless it is your own fault; and even then, stay strong, find a solution and keep on smiling'.

My best moment came during a sales call in Beijing, at the office of a global pharmaceutical meeting organiser. Just as I began introducing our company and Turkey as a destination, a British client who had worked with us before stopped me and said 'Let me tell you about Eda's company. I was once hosting a meeting in Istanbul, there was a snow storm and the roof of the restaurant that our group was heading to actually collapsed. Eda's colleague found a similar alternative restaurant, with an identical menu for the same price before coming to me with news of the problem. That is what service is and that is why you always use a DMC. Because when everything is going smoothly, nobody needs support.'

Today I find myself in an excellent position, in respect to my career in incentive travel. I sit on the Board of Directors of SITE Global, and I get regular invitations to speak at conferences and tradeshows across the world, for example the SACEOS Singapore MICE Forum, the SITE GB Chapter Incentive Summit, and Event Biznes in Warsaw. I've also had the honour of being named as a 'Millennial to Watch' by *Meeting & Conventions* magazine.

But while things are going well for me personally, the destination I sell, Turkey, on the other hand is undergoing the worst tourism crisis in its history. A few years ago, my company was able to pick and choose which RFPs we would respond to. But now that the Turkey of 2017 is perceived as unstable and at risk of violence, selling this damaged brand has proved to be a completely new challenge. While finding creative short-term solutions for our company, I am also having to build entirely new strategies to diversify our future. On a day-to-day basis, it is hard at times to be motivated. But I remain optimistic, remembering that Istanbul is a 4,000-year-old city that has weathered much bigger storms in that time. The fact that the MICE sector globally is set to boom in the future also calms my nerves.

I don't see this industry as a profession but rather a way of life which has its joys and satisfactions as much as it has its struggles.

IT'S MY JOB
MICHELLE MUSCAT, SENIOR ACCOUNT
MANAGER, DESTINATION MARKETING
SERVICES, SYDNEY, AUSTRALIA

Even before leaving school, I knew that I wanted to work in tourism, so from 2005–2009 I studied for a degree in Business Management, majoring in Tourism, at the University of Western Sydney. Throughout my studies, I was particularly drawn to the business events sector, and I had the opportunity to engage in a few internships during my studies to get a taste of what a career in this field would really involve.

One internship sticks in my mind. In 2007, I worked alongside the team responsible for organising the Dalai Lama's visit to Sydney, part of his Australia Tour that year. I worked directly with a team that had a wealth of experience of organising medium- to large-scale events. Focusing on the logistics of planning a one-day event attracting 6,000 participants was an excellent learning experience for me. I was given the responsibility of coordinating all the stallholders and exhibitors, which meant that I had to cross-check stall regulations and ensure that all exhibitors had the correct paperwork. Most importantly, this role gave me the opportunity to interact with a diverse mix of local businesses, and I quickly realised that although the organising of events was interesting for me, I found more satisfaction in the client services side of the job.

Another internship involved me working with a municipality, Fairfield City Council in southwest Sydney, to develop a Tourism Marketing Plan and Calendar of Festivals and Events for the Bonnyrigg Town Centre, one of the suburbs of Fairfield. The initiative was put in place to attract visitors from neighbouring suburbs and further afield, to boost economic growth for small businesses and other organisations in the area. Since Bonnyrigg has more places of worship and greater religious diversity than any other area in Sydney, the Tourism Marketing Plan and Calendar of Festivals and Events placed great emphasis on cultural and religious festivals. This internship was an opportunity for me to implement some of what I had learnt throughout my degree, and I very much enjoyed engaging with a wide range of business and community groups.

Upon graduating from the University of Western Sydney, I decided that my goal was to find work in either a tourism board and/or a convention bureau. In 2011, my ambition was realised when I joined my local business events marketing organisation, Business Events Sydney (http://businesseventssydney.com.au/) as a Sales Research Executive. In this role, I was responsible for researching and engaging with associations, academics, industry professionals and renowned medical institutions to identify bid opportunities for Sydney, and most importantly find out who could be the bid leaders – people working in Sydney who were experts in their field. This was a fascinating aspect of my work, as I was dealing with people who were literally saving lives by researching a cure for cancer, inventing the next smartphone, or discovering new micro-organisms, for example. My role involved asking them to consider investing some of their time towards working with Business Events Sydney to bid for a major congress, conference, or study tour to be held in our city, a process that at times could be run over four years. To say I learnt a lot in this role would be an understatement. At times, I found myself googling subjects ranging from nanotechnology to biomolecular sciences to familiarise myself with these topics before holding a conversation with potential bid leaders who were experts in these fields.

While at Business Events Sydney, I was mainly involved in the association conferences, while my colleagues in another team were looking at incentives, focusing on bringing incentive programmes from China and South-East Asia into Sydney. This turned out to be an area that I would become increasingly interested in.

In 2014, I changed employer and changed my role, moving closer to the incentive travel sector of business events. Destination Marketing Services (DMS) (http://www.destinationmarketing.com.au) is a sales and marketing representation office linking Australian and New Zealand business event planners with a global network of destination management companies (DMCs), operating in more than 80 countries across the globe, including some of the world's most exotic and cutting-edge destinations. Founded in 1992, DMS represents the largest portfolio of DMCs in the Australian and New Zealand market.

As an Account Manager in the company (and, following my promotion in 2016, Senior Account Manager), I am responsible for connecting local PCOs, incentive houses and corporate agencies with reputable DMCs from around the world. I find the client relationship side of things extremely interesting, but what I love most is the marketing – putting together marketing campaigns and e-newsletters and using social media to show Australian and New Zealand business event planners all of the exciting programmes, concepts and experiences that our DMC partners can put together in their respective destinations. One day I can be talking or writing about Bali, the next day Argentina, then Ireland and South Africa – or sometimes all of them in one day! Being able to promote so many amazing destinations is one of the best aspects of my job. And in this role, I have had the opportunity to travel the world, to enhance my destination knowledge and experience at first hand the excellent products that our DMC partners can provide for outbound business events from Australia and New Zealand.

But it certainly is the case that there are a few challenges that we are facing, working in the incentive travel sector:

1   Growing competition in an unregulated world. One of the main challenges we are now faced with is the increased competition from new companies claiming to offer DMC services, especially in emerging incentive destinations. DMCs are generally unregulated in most countries, so it is more and more difficult for distant PCOs and incentive houses to know if they are always dealing with the type of financially stable, reliable and reputable partners of the kind that we represent at DMS.

2   Global events. Natural disasters and terrorist atrocities can have an immense impact on the incentive sector, as travel to certain destinations becomes perceived as a risk, rather than a reward for exceptional performance. Given the high level of spending on companies' incentive programmes, cancellations or merely a lack of interest can have a detrimental effect on the economy of destinations affected by life-threatening events, whether natural or man-made.

So why do I do what I do? Why I am so passionate about the incentive industry? Well, whether I am linking up with a partner for a teleconference at 07h00, sitting down for a meeting, boarding a flight, opening my emails at 22.00, I know that I wouldn't dream of doing anything else. On a Sunday night, I never think 'I wish I didn't have to go to work on Monday', because I am yet to have a day in my job when I haven't learnt something new.

I always had an idea of what my 'dream job' would be, and now I finally feel that I have found it.

IT'S MY JOB
LLUÍS AMAT, DIRECTOR, KLASS
REPRESENTACIONES TURÍSTICAS, BARCELONA

I studied Economics and a postgraduate degree in Tourism Management. After university, for my first job, I was in charge of sales and marketing in Spain for Hurtigruten, a cruise boat along the Norwegian coast. Later I was a tour leader for Spanish groups all over the world.

In 2006, I saw an important business opportunity. I always felt that destination management companies (DMCs) operating in foreign destinations lacked sufficient understanding of the outbound Spanish market for business events, and that many business events buyers based in Spain had inadequate knowledge of DMCs operating in certain foreign destinations. In the leisure tourism market, the role of intermediary between buyers and suppliers is generally filled by tour operators. But for the MICE market, the products offered by tour operators are, in my opinion, often inappropriate as most of them see their role as one of selling packages rather than customising travel products for their clients.

So, for the MICE market, I created my company, KLASS Representaciones Turísticas (http://www.klass.com.es/), located in Barcelona, to directly connect DMCs based in other countries with the market for outbound business events from Spain. KLASS represents ten foreign DMCs, mainly based in European destinations, who offer tailor-made products for the business events market and who are seeking business from Spanish incentive houses. Each of the DMCs I represent has a minimum of ten years' experience and each one is a leading DMC in their destination, selected on the basis of their creativity, their quick responses to requests and their adaptability to the Spanish outbound market for business events.

The DMCs that I represent are located in the following destinations: Austria, Hungary, Czech Republic, Germany, Belgium, Portugal, Italy, Malta, Croatia, Slovenia, Greece, Argentina and Colombia.

In order to improve the Spanish business events organisers' understanding of the services and products offered by our foreign DMCs, we use a number of communication channels including newsletters, advertisements in the publications *PUNTO MICE* and *EVENTOPLUS*, sales calls, attendance at IMEX Frankfurt and IBTW World in Barcelona, workshops and fam trips to the destinations I represent.

As a key intermediary between the Spanish incentive and conference organisers and the DMCs I represent, we have to add value to both types of client. We support our Spanish clients by sharing with them our expert knowledge of the destinations, as well as our creative ideas for business events held in those places. Naturally, all products are genuinely tailor-made, and all of the accommodation, restaurants, venues and activities that we propose are selected with the business events organisers' clients in mind. We want those clients to feel that the planning and design of each one of their business events is unique and offering the best value for money. For that reason, we provide a follow-up service which includes finding out to what extent the client's incentive trip or conference was effective in helping them reach their targets for that business event. I want to make sure that the client feels that the choice of one of my DMCs and the destination was the right one for them. That is one of the means of attempting to secure repeat business from each client.

From the perspective of the foreign DMCs I represent, KLASS is an extension of their own sales teams, helping them to find additional business from Spain by connecting them with Spanish incentive and conference organisers and supporting them throughout the whole process. I cover all types of business events but in particular the incentive travel market, where enormous creativity and à la carte products are required, to make those events a success.

The part of my work that brings me the greatest pleasure is bridging the gap between agencies and DMCs by introducing them to each other and working daily with different cultures. Naturally, I have to choose my DMCs carefully, in each destination, but I very much enjoy the research that I have to do before choosing. My plans for the future are to keep my company focused on just a few, select destinations, rather than over-expanding and becoming too global.

References

Achtziger, A., Alós-Ferrer, C., Hügelschäfer, S. and Steinhauser, M. (2015) Higher incentives can impair performance: Neural evidence on reinforcement and rationality. *Social Cognitive and Affective Neuroscience* 10(11): 1477–1483.

Burgess, S. and Ratto, M. (2003) The role of incentives in the public sector: Issues and evidence. *Oxford Review of Economic Policy* 19(2): 285–300.

C&IT (2017) Incentive Travel Report. Conference & Incentive Travel. Haymarket Media Group.

Caprariello, P. and Reis, H. (2011) To do, to have, or to share: the value of experiences over material possessions depends on the involvement of others, in Dahl, D. W., Johar, G. V. and van Osselaer, S. M. J. (eds) *Advances in Consumer Research*, volume 38, Duluth, MN: Association for Consumer Research.

Chan, K. (2013) Trends in Asia's incentive sector, in *MICE Biz*, 8 April.

Deci, E. L. and Ryan, R. M. (1985) *Intrinsic Motivation and Self-Determination in Human Behavior,* New York: Plenum.

Fenich, G. G., Vitiello, K. L., Lancaster, M. F. and Hashimoto, K. (2015) Incentive travel: A view from the top. *Journal of Convention & Event Tourism* 16: 2.

Fisher, J. G. (2005) *How to Run Successful Incentive Schemes,* London: Kogan Page.

Frey, B. S. and Gallus, J. (2014) Awards are a special kind of signal. CREMA Working Paper No. 2014–04.

Gold, J-P. (1996) Un marché en plein mutation. Tourisme d'affaires. *Les Cahiers Espaces* 45.

Greene, R. J. (2011) *Rewarding Performance: Guiding principles, custom strategies.* New York: Routledge.

Incentive Federation (2016) Incentive marketplace estimate research study. Available at: http://www.incentivefederation.org/wp-content/uploads/2016/07/Incentive-Market-place-Estimate-Research-Study-2015-16-White-Paper.pdf.

IRF (2017) The 2017 Incentive Research Foundation Outlook Study. Available at: http://theirf.org/research/irf-2017-outlook-study/2020/.

Jeffrey, S. A. and Adomdza, G. K. (2011) Incentive salience and improved performance. *Human Performance* 24: 47–59.

Jeffrey, S. A., Dickinson, A. M. and Einarsson, Y. F. (2013) The use of incentives in organizations. *International Journal of Productivity and Performance Management* 62(6): 606–615.

Joppe, M., Martin, D., Shaw, D. and Miyagi, N. (2002) *Challenges and Opportunities of Incentive Travel*, Toronto: Ontario Tourism Marketing Partnership.

Kirov, M. (2017) Direct sales vs channel sales: Pros, cons, and balance. Available at: https://www.saleshacker.com/channel-sales-direct-sales-strategy/.

Latham, G. P. (2012) *Work Motivation: History, theory, research and practice*, Los Angeles: Sage.

Palmer, A. (2012) Incentive trips add value. *Incentive Magazine* 186(6): 39.

Park, S. M. and Word, J. (2012) Driven to service: Intrinsic and extrinsic motivation for public and non-profit managers. *Public Personnel Management* 41(4): 705–734.

Ricci, P. R. and Holland, S. M. (1992) Recreation as a motivational medium. *Tourism Management* 13(3): 288–296.

Severt, K. S. (2012) Channel incentive travel: A case study. Available at: http://theirf.org/research/channel-incentive-travel-a-case-study/114/.

Shinew, K. J. and Backman, S. J. (1995) Incentive travel: An attractive option. *Tourism Management* 16(4).

Silvers, J. R. (2004) *Professional Event Coordination,* Hoboken, NJ: John Wiley & Sons.

SITE (n.d.) Most impactful effort toward corporate social responsibility as part of an incentive program. Available at: https://www.siteglobal.com/page/bcd-meetings.

SITE (2013) Incentive travel: The participant viewpoint. Available at: http://www.site-global.com/p/cm/ld/fid=62.

Van Boven, L. and Gilovich, T. (2003) To do or to have? That is the question. *Journal of Personality and Social Psychology* 85(6): 1193–1202.

Van Dyke, M. (2010a) The anatomy of a successful incentive travel program. Available at: http://theirf.org/research/anatomy-of-a-successful-incentive-travel-program/107/.

Van Dyke, M. (2010b) Vertical Market Study. Available at: http://theirf.org/research/incentive-research-foundation-vertical-market-study/145/.

Van Dyke, M. (2011) Critical findings for recognition travel programs. Available at: http://theirf.org/research/critical-findings-for-recognition-travel-programs/119/.

Zoltners, A. A., Sinha, P. and Lorimer, S. E. (2012) Breaking the sales force incentive addiction: A balanced approach to sales force effectiveness. *Journal of Personal Selling & Sales Management* 32(2): 171–186.

8 Exhibitions

Exhibitions in the 21st century

- The China International Beauty Expo was held as a three-day event at the China Import & Export Fair Complex in Guangzhou, displaying a vast range of cosmetics and other beauty products. The exhibition extended over an area of 300,000 square metres and attracted almost 4,000 exhibitors and just under 1 million visitors.
- Intersolar India, an exhibition for the global solar energy industry, took place at the Bombay Exhibition Centre in Mumbai, focusing on the areas of photovoltaics, energy storage systems and solar thermal technologies. There were 235 exhibitors and around 12,000 visitors attended the event, which was accompanied by a conference focusing on the same themes, with 100 speakers and over 800 attendees.
- During one weekend, over 40,000 people attended the *Salon du Mariage*, France's largest wedding fair, held in the Porte de Versailles exhibition centre in Paris. More than 200 exhibitors presented wedding-related goods and services, from dresses and flowers to chauffeur-driven limousines and honeymoon holidays in exotic locations.
- IBTM World, a leading global exhibition for the business events industry, took place in the Fira Gran Via exhibition venue in Barcelona, with over 3,000 exhibitors ranging from conference venues and convention bureaus to destination management companies and hotels with meetings facilities. The visitors were buyers of business events services and facilities, including conference organisers, incentive houses and meetings planners from all over the world.

Chapter objectives

On completion of this chapter the reader should be able to:

- Understand the use and value of exhibitions as a sales and marketing medium.
- Recognise the distinctive characteristics and value of exhibitions as business events.
- Understand the roles of the key stakeholders in the exhibitions market.
- Appreciate how exhibitions are planned and implemented.

Marketing communications

A wide range of tools are available to anyone involved in marketing any product or service. These tools are traditionally divided into four categories: product, price, place and promotion, which, together, constitute what is commonly known as the marketing mix. In recent years, it has been widely acknowledged that these four categories of marketing tools work most effectively when they are integrated with each other in such a way that the product or service is marketed in an entirely coherent and consistent manner (De Pelsmacker et al., 2007).

The promotion – or marketing communications – element of the marketing mix includes all of the instruments that a company or organisation uses to communicate with its target groups in order to promote itself and its products. Marketing communications have been more broadly defined as 'the means by which a supplier of goods, services, values and/or ideas represent themselves to their target audience with the goal of stimulating dialogue leading to a better commercial or other relationship' (Egan, 2007:1). This definition serves to emphasise the idea of an organisation reaching out to its audiences, whether the organisation is a commercial, not-for-profit, government or other type of collective seeking to establish a dialogue.

Marketing communication channels include advertising, direct marketing, branding, personal selling, online/digital media, printed materials, PR activities and sales presentations. Kotler and Keller (2009) distinguish between mass (or 'non-personal') communication channels, which carry marketing messages without personal contact with the targeted audiences (such as advertising), and personal communication channels, which involve two or more people communicating directly with each other (such as personal selling). Channels in the latter category provide opportunities for individualising the marketing message and receiving/giving feedback. In order to achieve their objectives most effectively, the vast majority of marketing managers use a mix of personal and non-personal marketing communication channels.

As a powerful face-to-face sales and marketing medium, exhibitions represent an important component in the marketing communications mix of companies and organisations worldwide. They may be considered as representing both categories of communications channels: personal – because of the direct personal selling by sales personnel working on the exhibition stand (or 'booth' in US English); and non-personal – because the presence of, and design of, the stand itself serves as an advertisement, generating greater awareness of the company and its products (Gopalakrishna and Lilien, 1995).

This chapter explores their role as large-scale business events that bring together sellers and buyers in the same place at the same time, with a range of mutual benefits to all participants.

The distinguishing characteristics of exhibitions

Definition and terminology

Exhibitions, in the sense of business events as opposed to displays of artistic works, are events that are held regularly in a specific location at a specific time of the year to showcase a particular sector of industry or commerce and to facilitate the buying and selling process. Practically any product or service imaginable, from a tractor to a ski holiday and from a laptop computer to a jet aircraft, if it can be bought and sold, has its own regular exhibition or exhibitions somewhere in the world. These events are 'shop windows', where, on a regular basis – most often annually – those who produce the products or services can display them, explain them, and sell them to customers and potential customers.

Kirchgeorg et al. (2005:ix) define an exhibition as

> a temporary market event, held at intervals, where a large number of buyers (attendees or visitors) and sellers (exhibitors) interact for the purpose of purchasing displayed goods and services, either at the time of presentation or at a future date.

At these events, the exhibitors and visitors are often joined by another group of participants, those in the relevant print, digital and broadcast media, as exhibitions are usually extremely newsworthy events, with companies often choosing them as occasions on which to launch new products, for example, in the media spotlight.

As is still the case for most elements of the business events industry, universally accepted terminology for the exhibitions sector has not yet been realised. Terms such as exhibition, trade show, trade fair and exposition (or expo) are used interchangeably by many academics as well as practitioners. In this chapter, the generic term exhibitions will be used most often, but a useful distinction will be made between two contrasting types of exhibitions.

Trade shows/fairs or business-to-business (B2B) shows/fairs

At these events, the exhibitors are generally confined to one industry or to one specific segment of a particular industry, and visitors are restricted to those seeking to purchase products or services for use in their businesses or professions – industrial printing equipment, agricultural machinery, or specialist software packages for accountants, for example. Attendance is often by invitation only, with pre-registration usually required. Trade shows may be held in conjunction with the conference of a professional industry group or association, as described in Chapter 3.

Examples of large-scale trade shows are the annual WASMA international trade show held in Moscow, where manufacturers display equipment and technologies for waste management, recycling and water treatment; and the Print Tech and Packaging Show in Bangkok, where exhibitors showcase their products in the fields of printing and packaging.

Consumer shows/fairs, public shows/fairs or business-to-consumer (B2C) shows/fairs

At these events, exhibitors display a wide variety of products and services, with the intention of selling them directly to the end-users. Consumer shows are open to the general public, who generally pay an entrance fee, and they feature any products or services which the visitors may purchase for their personal consumption, from cars and kitchen appliances to holidays and investment opportunities. The motivation for attending these events is usually a personal interest in what is being sold, combined with the opportunity for an excursion with friends or family. Consequently, according to Bathelt et al. (2014), B2C shows are more often more hedonistic in character than trade shows.

Examples include The Ideal Home Show at the Olympia exhibition centre in London, where visitors can see and buy a vast range of furnishings and equipment for their homes and gardens; or The Technology and Gadget Expo in Melbourne, Australia, which showcases products including home entertainment systems, monitoring and security systems, and home automation appliances such as smart lighting controls.

However, there is a third category of exhibitions, sometimes known as mixed shows, which are open for trade visitors as well as public visitors, often on different days. For instance, the week-long International Paris Air Show – the world's largest aerospace show, begins as a B2B event, as the first four days of the show, held at Le Bourget airport near Paris, are reserved for trade visitors. But it becomes a B2C event for the following three days, when it is open to the general public.

However, both main types of exhibition, B2B and B2C, differ significantly in the patterns of travel they stimulate. Consumer exhibitions tend to attract large numbers of visitors, but most of them attend for only one day and are drawn mainly from the local or regional area. Very large or very specialised trade fairs, on the other hand, generally attract visitors and exhibitors from a great number of countries and are regarded as important stimulators of international inbound business tourism for the host destinations.

Given the business events theme of this book, this chapter will focus on B2B exhibitions.

Before a closer investigation of the value of such events and the structure of the market, the historical context of this type of business event will now be considered.

A historical perspective

Exhibitions have been an essential sales and communication tool for many centuries. Morrow (2002:31) describes how, in the ancient world:

a fair was a temporary market where buyers and sellers gathered to transact business. The fair afforded the opportunity to barter and sell goods and services within a particular region and became the central distribution point for entire geographical areas. Fairs concentrated supply and demand in specific locales at specific times.

According to Gopalakrishna and Lilien (2012), the tradition continued through medieval times, when artisans and villagers exhibited their wares at local fairs. Those fairs were a convenient way for local producers to gain access to large numbers of potential buyers who came to attend the events from neighbouring towns and villages.

In the modern era, the first industrial-scale exhibitions appeared in the form of 'world fairs', such as the Crystal Palace Exhibition of 1851 (officially called the 'Great Exhibition of the Works of Industry of All Nations') in London's Hyde Park. Opened by Queen Victoria, the first international trade fair was openly accessible by the general public as well as industrialists, and its commercial success generated many others. Those include the New York World Fair of 1853 and the *Exposition Universelle* in Paris, which was visited by over 32 million people in 1889 and by over 48 million in 1890 (Dee, 2011:xx). The vast scale of these world exhibitions and others like them is worthy of note. Van Wesemael describes them, by 19th-century standards, as being mega-projects for which there were no precedents:

> The organisers alleged that they were presenting an international and comprehensive overview of the best, most up-to-date and most promising innovations and developments from as many countries as possible and from every conceivable field of human activity. With this aim in mind, they gathered ever-increasing numbers of exhibits and visitors from all over the world at one central location that had been specially constructed for the occasion, albeit temporarily, so that the public could view, study and enjoy the objects in optimum fashion.
>
> (Van Wesemael, 2001:19)

Often, the architectural design of the purpose-built exhibition venues was just as exciting as the events taking place inside them, and many are still standing today. For example, the Eiffel Tower was constructed as the central attraction and entrance arch for the 1889 *Exposition Universelle* in Paris; and the 1951 Festival of Britain exhibition, held on London's South Bank, left the Royal Festival Hall as a legacy (Dee, 2011).

By the early 20th century, exhibitions were firmly established as regular fixtures in the business calendars of the industrialised nations, and the practice of affixing trade shows to the conference programmes of professional and trade associations was spreading. In the 21st century, the number of trade shows worldwide continues to grow and occupy a prominent position in commercial life. Demand for exhibitions comes from almost every sector of human activity, commercial and non-commercial, from embroidery to oil exploration; but the most frequently exhibited industrial sectors are shown in Table 8.1.

Table 8.1 The principal industrial sectors for exhibitions		
Agriculture	Energy	Home decoration
Art	Equipment and technologies	Leisure
Automobile	Fashion	Medicine
Beauty	Food	Natural environment
Business	Furnishings	Services
Construction	Furniture	Sports
Education	Health	Technology
Electronics		Tourism

Source: nTradeshows (n.d.).

In response to increasing demand, the global supply of exhibition space in venues has also grown – by 1.2 per cent on average per year since 2011. According to the Global Association of the Exhibition Industry, there are now 1,217 large-scale exhibition venues (those offering gross indoor exhibition space of over 5,000 square metres) throughout the world, providing, between them, a total of almost 35 million square metres (UFI, 2017).

The value of exhibitions

For exhibiting companies and organisations, having a presence at an exhibition seldom comes cheap. The stand has to be hired or purchased, transported to the event and set up. It has to be staffed by company employees, whose travel and accommodation costs have to be paid. Costs that are directly linked to the exhibition stand itself may only account for as little as one third of the total costs for exhibitors, with the remainder being spent on local hotels, transport and so on (AUMA, 2006). Nevertheless, despite the considerable investment they can necessitate in terms of time, expenditure and human resources, the enduring presence and proliferation of exhibitions in the commercial world would appear to testify to their ongoing appeal for all participants.

The benefits of participation in these business events, for exhibitors and visitors, take two principal forms: sales-related and non-sales-related.

Sales-related benefits

The main purpose of most exhibitions is ultimately to generate sales, and exhibitions are widely recognised as an effective sales channel in today's business environment where face-to-face sales opportunities are increasingly rare. Without such events, the supporters of exhibitions maintain, the efficiency of trade would be severely diminished. Exhibitions help stimulate domestic trade and they promote exports when they are attended by foreign visitors. Conversely, attendance at exhibitions overseas can help companies enter new geographical markets for their products and services.

Exhibitions offer exhibitors invaluable access to a self-selected group of buyers and potential buyers and the opportunity to meet many of them in person. As the visitors choose to come to the exhibition of their own accord, exhibitors are engaging in a non-intrusive form of marketing known as 'permission marketing' – an approach to selling goods and services in which potential customers explicitly agree in advance (in this case by attending the exhibition) to receiving marketing information.

Smith et al. (2003) classify visitors' motives into buying and non-buying objectives. The buying objectives include seeing new products or services, gathering technical information, comparing exhibitors' products and services and, in many cases, ultimately acquiring them. Exhibitions enable visitors to observe a broad range of products and services at first hand, under one roof, and within a relatively short period of time.

A major benefit of having the products physically on display, as opposed, for example, to them appearing in the pages of a catalogue or on a website, is that visitors can see, handle, compare, assess by demonstration and (depending on the product) even smell and taste them – a particular advantage of exhibitions for industries such as food and drinks, cosmetics or fabrics. By touching fabrics, fashion designers, for instance, can gather information not available through sight, for example on softness or warmth. For that reason, it is often said that one reason for the appeal of certain types of exhibitions is their ability to stimulate all five senses of the visitors. Indeed, some authors have suggested that there is a danger of sensory overload at such events. According to Rinallo et al. (2010), the exhibition environment can be so rich in sensorial stimuli – sounds, noises, odours, colours, signs, physical objects, the crowd – all of which carry information and compete to attract visitors' attention, that the result can be the sensorial overwhelming of visitors, who are exposed to a volume of stimuli that they simply cannot process meaningfully.

However, beyond facilitating the immediate buying and selling process of at-show transactions, exhibitions offer exhibitors a range of other sales-related benefits. These include the opportunity to increase their visibility in the market, find new potential clients through high-quality leads, and strengthen existing customer relationships. Being present at exhibitions can also generate media coverage for companies and organisations, particularly when they use such events to launch new products. As already mentioned, it is a widespread practice for companies to launch new products at exhibitions, as they know that the relevant media will be present and interested in reporting what the company is initiating.

Some authors argue that exhibitions are particularly effective for the promotion and sales of newly launched products and services. Kay and Ap (2008), for example, in their analysis of exhibitions as a marketing promotion medium, maintain that exhibitions are the most important forum for the dissemination of information about products during the initial stages of the product life cycle – creating 'interest' and 'awareness', but that later in the life cycle other kinds of promotional media (such as advertisements, roadshows, cold calls, relationship marketing and direct marketing) can be more effective sales techniques.

The opportunity for direct, face-to-face, two-way communication that exhibitions offer participants also means that exhibitors can use such occasions to gather valuable marketing information by seeking feedback from visitors to their stands on their products or services. By way of judicious questioning, exhibitors can glean useful information on visitors' opinions of their products and services – why they purchase (or do not purchase) them, and what modifications in terms of design, price, etc. the visitors would find desirable.

Finally, market intelligence of a different type is available to exhibitors during trade shows in the form of their competitors' stands and activities. Exhibitions provide an opportunity for participating exhibitors to monitor the competition in their market, which they often do by visiting the other exhibitors' stands to take note of new products and prices, and probe staff for technical details of what is being displayed. For the sake of discretion, these visits to competitors' stands are often carried out under the guise of 'mystery shoppers', exhibitors posing as visitors, so as to elicit the maximum amount of information from their unsuspecting competitors.

Non-sales-related benefits

The value of most exhibitions extends far beyond facilitating the marketing process and sales transactions. Exhibition organisers usually add a range of ancillary elements to these events, to make them more attractive to, and productive for, all participants.

Education

Most exhibitions position themselves as events that facilitate learning, innovation, knowledge creation and knowledge exchange between exhibitors, industry experts and visitors. In doing so, they are continuing a long tradition of exhibitions acting as a valuable source of education and training. For example, in the UK, the 19th-century Royal Horticultural Society Shows, where gardeners from all around the country assembled to examine the latest equipment and tools of their trade, were also an important part of the network through which expertise and knowledge of gardening techniques were disseminated.

In the modern era, learning at exhibitions takes two forms: informal (casual or planned face-to-face communications with peers who are in similar professional roles); and formal (scheduled seminar programmes offering presentations and educational sessions from industry leaders, experts and gurus). Both forms contribute to helping participants build the skills they need to advance their careers and keep pace with industry trends. Formal education and training sessions can take place in meeting rooms located either among the exhibition stands on the show floor itself, or in another zone of the exhibition venue, sometimes on a different floor altogether, to avoid noise interference. But according to Friedman (2016), the current trend is towards more educational sessions being offered in areas on the show floor, perhaps as a response to attendees' lack of time and their unwillingness to walk some distance off the show floor to seminar rooms.

Many exhibitions include educational courses designed to contribute to the professional certification of attendees. In most countries, professions such as medicine, nursing, law, engineering and financial advice require practitioners to participate in continuing education programmes for a certain number of hours every year in order to keep their certificates, or licences to practise, current. Exhibitions therefore often include such educational programmes as a means of adding an important motivator for visitors to attend. In some cases, the mere fact of attending an exhibition, even if no formal education is provided, can contribute to visitors' and exhibitors' professional certification. For example, in the US, Building Operator Certification (BOC) is the leading training and certification programme for building engineers and maintenance personnel. In order to keep their BOC qualification valid, holders must accumulate a certain number of 'maintenance points' each year; and one of the ways of earning such points is by attending a relevant exhibition.

Regarding the educational components of exhibitions generally, Han and Verma (2014) note that although these opportunities are positively viewed by both visitors and exhibitors, it is visitors who are the more motivated by the educational elements, while exhibitors are primarily focused on transacting business and developing contacts. Nevertheless, the importance of exhibitions as a source of education and training cannot be overemphasised. Indeed, Damer et al. (2000) and Geigenmuller (2010), cited in Bathelt et al. (2014:2), claim that

> such learning opportunities are, perhaps, the main reason why trade shows … continue to thrive in the age of the World Wide Web and social media, despite experimentation and commercial attempts to substitute these events with virtual trade fairs and other forms of online professional interaction.

Social events

Networking between participants occurs naturally on the exhibition stands and in the aisles between the stands, and this represents a major aspect of the value of such events, creating new contacts, maintaining existing connections and helping companies develop trust and rapport with their customers. But to boost the opportunities for networking, many exhibitions include social events such as welcome receptions and party evenings during which participants can meet on a more informal basis. Rinallo et al. (2010) call these elements 'relational opportunities' – simply put, one of the reasons for participants attending exhibitions is to meet new people and see old friends, exhibitors and visitors alike. Exhibitions thus permit participants to establish or maintain social bonds with key actors in their business and occupational networks.

Rinallo et al. (2010) go further, arguing that the regular frequency of exhibitions, coupled with the repeated presence of a large number of exhibitors and visitors, make them 'organisational rituals' that foster a sense of community among participants, who often view attendance as a social necessity that goes beyond utilitarian motivations.

Entertainment

Seldom explored in the research into exhibitions, however, is the element of entertainment they can offer to visitors, who may lack the means or the intention to buy the goods on display, but who nevertheless enjoy looking at aircraft or boats, for example, as the focus of a day out with friends and family. By the very nature of the products on display, the entertainment value of certain categories of exhibition is extremely high: for example, Gamescom in Cologne, the world's largest exhibition for interactive games and interactive entertainment, or the annual Salon du Chocolat in Paris. As a general rule, it is likely that the entertainment value of B2C events is higher than that of B2B exhibitions.

However, there is evidence that a demographic variable may apply, regarding this aspect of exhibitions' value. Kozak and Kayar's (2009) research into visitors' objectives for exhibition attendance identified entertainment and vacationing as factors but found that the entertainment factor differed significantly in importance among age groups, with visitors aged 22 and younger rating 'having a good time' a more important factor than the 39–46 age group in their sample. The importance of entertainment as a motivation for attending exhibitions particularly among younger visitors was confirmed by Mensah and Lestyo (2012).

The market for exhibitions

Demand

Demand for exhibitions comes from two distinctive groups of participants, each with their own specific requirements from the events they attend.

Exhibitors

The exhibitors in this market are primarily those companies and organisations who pay to display their wares at such events. From multinational manufacturing groups to one-man/woman businesses selling craft jewellery or consultancy services, all sizes of companies in all sectors of industry and commerce are served by specialist exhibitions promoting their particular product or service. The sheer diversity of such events and those who exhibit at them can be seen in Table 8.2, showing the list of exhibitions scheduled for one month in one venue, the Dubai International Convention and Exhibition Centre.

As was noted earlier in this chapter, for certain industry sectors such as automotive, construction and electronics, exhibitions are one of their preferred marketing communications channels, and a considerable proportion of such companies' sales and marketing budgets are spent on exhibiting at the relevant events.

Prior to making a decision to participate in an exhibition, companies usually seek information on the organiser's track record and verify attendance figures of previous events and the extent to which the event is supported by the industry sector. Once the decision to attend has been taken, in order to get the maximum benefit from their attendance, most exhibitors undertake some form of promotional activity to draw attention to their presence at the event. This could take the form of:

Table 8.2 Exhibitions at the Dubai International Convention and Exhibition Centre in March 2018

27 February–1 March Leatherworld Middle East (B2B)

27 February–1 March Dubai International Pharmaceuticals and Technologies Conference and Exhibition (B2B)

27 February–1 March Dubai Drink Technology Expo (B2B)

27 February–1 March GESS – Global Educational Supplies & Solutions

27 February–1 March Paperworld Middle East and Playworld Middle East (B2B)

27 February–3 March Dubai International Boat Show (B2C)

28 February–1 March Offshore Arabia Exhibition & Conference (B2B)

5–7 Dubai International Humanitarian Aid & Development Conference & Exhibition (B2B)

6–8 Middle East Electricity Exhibition (B2B)

6–8 AGRA Middle East Exhibition (for the agriculture, veterinary, equestrian and horticulture industries)

10–12 Hemaya International Forum & Exhibition on Drug Issues (B2C)

11–13 Innovation Arabia Conference 2018 (for the business and financial sectors) (B2B)

12–13 Middle East Rail (B2B)

12–14 Dubai International Wood & Wood Machinery Show (B2B)

13–15 Careers UAE 2017 (B2C)

15–17 Dubai International Horse Fair (B2C)

18–21 Arablab Exhibition (for the laboratory and instrumentation Industry) (B2C)

19–21 Dubai World Dermatology and Laser Conference and Exhibition (B2B)

19–21 Middle East Coatings Show (B2B)

26–29 INDEX – International Design Exhibition (B2B)

26–29 Surface Design Middle East (for the building and facilities management industries) (B2B)

26–29 Workspace at Index (B2B)

26–29 Big 5 Heavy (for the building and facilities management industries) (B2B)

Source: Dubai World Trade Centre (n.d.).

- Notifying existing and potential customers of their participation in the event, using direct mail or email
- Undertaking advertising in the relevant trade or consumer publications
- Organising some activity to draw visitors to the stand – for example, live demonstrations of their products, a competition (such as a prize draw) or featuring a celebrity (occasionally termed an 'attractor').

While this form of preparation is clearly a key factor determining exhibitors' degree of success in attracting visitors to their stands, the knowledge and exhibiting skills of the individual staff members working on the stand have a direct influence on exhibitors' level of performance during the event. In an ideal situation, company employees working in three different functions should be present on the stand, in order to be able to respond most effectively to different types of visitor, with different types of enquiry, at different stages in the sales cycle: technical staff, sales staff and marketing staff. In reality, particularly in the case of small companies with only one or two representatives present on the stand, each of those individuals has to have knowledge of all three of these functions.

But many exhibitors face significant challenges in engaging visitors, and this can lead to low exhibitor satisfaction, even at events with very high visitor numbers. Therefore, in addition to their professional knowledge, exhibitors need a range of specific skills to ensure that their performance on the stand is optimal. These exhibiting skills include everything from body language and initiating contact with visitors to the stand, to recognising and dealing with different categories of visitors. A wide range of sources of exhibiting skills training is available in the form of seminars, workshops, webinars, blogs and training manuals. Some exhibition organisers also offer training and tips for successful exhibiting on their websites, as it is clearly in their best interest that exhibitors have as successful an experience as possible of their events. UFI & Explori Global Exhibitor Insight (2017) confirm that organisers can counter the poor performance of some exhibitors by offering them training programmes and actively working with them to help them showcase innovation and launch products. Their research showed that events that offered exhibitor training saw a 23-point boost in NPS (Net Promoter Score – a measure of how likely exhibitors are to recommend events) compared with exhibitions that did not.

Visitors

From the perspective of both the organisers and the exhibitors, the success of any exhibition depends upon its ability to attract the right quantity and quality of visitors.

Also called the 'audience' for the event, the visitors are those who invest their time and money to attend the exhibition, either as trade buyers or, in the case of B2C shows, as members of the general public. Their experience of the exhibition must be of the highest quality, or they will neither return to subsequent editions of the event nor recommend it to friends or colleagues.

For this reason, provision must be made for their various needs: refreshments, toilets, and rest areas, as well as adequate signage and printed or digital exhibition guides. In addition, those exhibitions attracting an international audience may need to provide an interpreter service and multilingual information staff. Visitors to B2B events in particular are likely to judge an exhibition by the quality of these various services.

A number of authors have attempted to categorise exhibition visitors according to their motivations for attending or their patterns of behaviour at these events. For example, Godar and O'Connor (2001) categorise visitors as follows:

- 'Buyers': those with influence on a purchase decision. They may be further divided into 'current buyers' – already purchasing – and 'potential buyers' – in a new-buy situation.

- 'Non-buyers': they have no direct influence on purchase decisions but have been sent to the exhibition, for example as a reward from their employer in the form of a trip or a day out of the office in return for their favourable performance in the workplace.

The authors emphasise the importance of exhibitors determining to the greatest extent possible which of these two categories each visitor to their stand falls into, in order to achieve the most fruitful interaction with them. In this way, the exhibitors can use their limited resources more effectively by prioritising and giving more attention to those visitors who are most likely to be of commercial interest to their companies.

Ueding (1998) focuses on visitors' patterns of behaviour, identifying four possible categories:

- Type A – 'intensive trade fair user': utilises exhibitions as an important source of information, particularly current market developments; is highly communicative and uses exhibitions for serious networking; attends many exhibitions and every visit is planned in detail; in contrast to the other types, they tend to complete a sales transaction during the event.
- Type B – 'special-interest trade fair user': prepares in advance and uses the visits intensively, carefully considering products or services, but does not transact business directly at the fair.
- Type C – 'trade fair stroller': Uses trade fairs primarily as an instrument to observe the market; has little contact with exhibitor personnel and does not intend to buy.
- Type D – 'pragmatist': does not have any specific aim such as transacting business or making a purchase; is very passive, seldom stays for more than a day and is oriented to other sources of information.

Suppliers

Venues

The basic requirement for the hosting of an exhibition is the venue – the hall in which the event is held. The venue owner's role as a key supplier in this market is to provide covered exhibition space with access for transport to deliver on site, visitor reception facilities, car parking and a variety of support services ranging from catering to first-aid and from security to cleaning. Jin and Weber (2013) emphasise the critical role played by exhibition venues, as the quality of their facilities and services, together with the skills and knowledge of the venue staff, can directly influence exhibitors' satisfaction with, and behavioural intentions towards, a particular exhibition.

A range of types of venue, with various ownership and management structures, may be used for the hosting of exhibitions. The most visible venues are the large, purpose-built exhibition centres that are generally used for the hosting of major B2B and B2C shows. These vast exhibition complexes, situated in and around major cities and conurbations, provide the extensive surface areas required by large, international events attracting many thousands of visitors. Given the enormous amount of land they cover, finding a location for such venues can present city planners with considerable challenges. Lawson (2000) describes the range of sites that may be used, from redundant railway stations and sidings, in disused industrial or docklands areas ('brown' land sites), or on low-value agricultural land, disused airports or exhausted mineral workings. He emphasises the importance of easy access from the international airport and city, junctions to the main highway network and an integrated system of frequent and fast public transport designed to carry the large numbers of visitors attending exhibitions. In addition, he notes the need for good landscaping and associated development (business, research and/or science parks, hotels, shops, institutional and commercial buildings, recreation facilities) in order to generate an attractive image and viable services around the exhibition centre.

Many large exhibition centres are part of multi-purpose complexes – often combined with conference centres of the type discussed in Chapter 3, enabling them to host exhibitions run in parallel with conferences. But, even when an exhibition centre is a stand-alone facility, it can usually be used to host other types of events apart from exhibitions, such as entertainment events, university graduation ceremonies, etc. Indeed, many exhibition centres depend on these other types of activity for essential income.

But exhibition and conference centres are not the only type of venue in which exhibitions are held. Agricultural shows, for example, require expansive outdoor areas for the animals and farm machinery they exhibit; and air shows displaying civil and military aircraft are usually held at airports, often taking the name of the airport venue. For example, the Australian International Airshow is also known as the Avalon Airshow, named after the venue, Avalon Airport, in the state of Victoria. Other facilities offering exhibition space include hotels and sports venues such as the Emirates Stadium in London which offers 1,372 square metres of exhibition space available for hire outside of match days.

While many exhibition centres are owned and managed by private sector entrepreneurs such as property companies or exhibition organisers, the majority of large venues of this type are owned and managed by the public sector – usually municipal authorities. Developing exhibition venues is seen as an attractive investment by some governments, due to the potential benefits the exhibition industry may bring to their community, in the form of employment and profits for local hospitality and transport businesses, for example. France, Germany and Italy, three of the world's most successful exhibition destinations, are examples of countries that rely heavily upon public sector support to build and operate exhibition centres.

However, it is often argued that exhibition venue operation is complex and calls for the type of commercial creativity and robust facility management services that may not be readily available in the public sector. For that reason, the financial resources of the public sector are often combined with the talents of the private sector in order to successfully build and manage these venues. Liu and Wilkinson (2014) identify two existing delivery models used for publicly owned venue development: direct public funding, ownership and management; and public funding and ownership, but with management by the private sector. An example of the latter model would be the Sydney Convention and Exhibition Centre, which is publicly owned but with management outsourced to a company called Convention Centre Management Pty Ltd. The same authors, however, acknowledging the challenges of sourcing sufficient public funding for venue development requiring considerable capital investment and operating costs, explore an alternative funding system, public–private partnerships (PPPs) which have been introduced by some governments as innovative delivery models to bring forward venue projects.

In terms of the geographical locations of the world's exhibition centres, some useful indications are provided by the annual global surveys of large (gross indoor exhibition space of over 5,000 square metres) venues carried out by UFI, the Global Association of the Exhibition Industry. Their 2017 survey indicated that, of the world's five largest indoor exhibition centres, three are in Europe and two are in China:

1   Messe Hannover, Hannover, Germany – 463,275 square metres
2   National Exhibition and Convention Centre (Shanghai), Shanghai, China – 404,400 square metres
3   Messe Frankfurt, Frankfurt/Main, Germany – 366,637 square metres
4   Fiera Milano, Milan, Italy– 345,000 square metres
5   China Import & Export Fair Complex (Pazhou Complex), Guangzhou, China – 338,000 square metres

Source: UFI (2017).

Regarding the location of large exhibition venues by world region, Europe retains its global lead on available venue capacities with 45 per cent of the global market share, well ahead of the Asia-Pacific region with 23.7 per cent and North America with 23.5 per cent. Nevertheless, while the growth trend in the supply of venues is worldwide, it is the Asia-Pacific region that is at the forefront of new development, with almost 25 per cent growth between 2011 and 2017, driven primarily by China, compared with a global average growth of just over 7 per cent over the same period.

In terms of individual countries, the US remains the market with the greatest amount of exhibition venue space available (19.8 per cent of global capacity), with China (16.6 per cent) and Germany (9.3 per cent) completing the top three. These three, plus Italy and France, each offer more than 2,000,000 square metres of total gross indoor exhibition space; and taken together, these markets account for almost 60 per cent of the total world indoor exhibition space (UFI, 2017).

Exhibition contractors

While venues provide the space in which exhibitions are held, in order for an exhibition to take shape, that space must be transformed into a physical selling environment, in other words filled with the exhibition stands that are indispensable to such events. This is the role of exhibition contractors, also known as exhibition services contractors – or simply, contractors. These are the professionals who arrive at the event in advance of the exhibitors and leave after the exhibitors have returned home at the end of the event.

The principal services provided by contractors are the design, hire, installation and maintenance of exhibition stands, followed by their subsequent dismantling. On behalf of the exhibitors, they look after all elements connected with the stand, including lighting, flooring and furnishing, audio-visuals, signage and freight handling. It is the contractors' responsibility to ensure that the structure of the stand is safe and that it complies with the detailed regulations supplied by the exhibition organiser or venue, as well as those imposed by local authorities or fire officers.

Morrow (2002) distinguishes between *exhibitor-appointed* contractors (EACs) and *general service* contractors (GSCs). EACs are firms that have a contractual relationship with individual exhibiting companies for the production of their exhibition stands. GSCs are designated by the exhibition organisers, and their responsibility goes beyond the design and construction of individual stands, to include creating the exhibition floor plan and layout, hiring and coordinating staff such as photographers and entertainers, and constructing the staging for exhibition seminar programmes.

An important part of the work of contractors begins a long time in advance of the exhibition, with the design of the stand. In the 21st century, standardised modular unit stands or 'shell schemes' are increasingly rare, as individually designed and customised stands are rapidly becoming the norm – as a visit to practically any modern exhibition will demonstrate. Exhibition stands have been termed 'three-dimensional marketing tools', due to their role in representing the brand and character of the exhibiting company. With visitors inevitably comparing an exhibitor's stand with those of the company's competitors at the same event, the importance of having a stand that is both visually appealing and accurately representative of the company's brand has been universally recognised. In order to design stands that are attractive and informative as well as practical and conforming to safety regulations, the contractors must work with several experts such as specialist architects and graphic artists.

Stands that effectively contribute to the success of the exhibition experience for exhibitors and their visitors must fulfil a number of functions. Rinallo et al. (2010), in a survey of exhibition stands at ten events, found that the principal functions to which stand space was dedicated were as follows:

- *Product display* – products were present on practically all stands and most of the stand space (60 per cent on average) was dedicated to their display.
- *Professional interaction* – the vast majority of stands in the sample (about 70 per cent) featured spaces dedicated to professional interaction, consisting of desks in open spaces, closed offices and meeting rooms. On average, around 34 per cent of total space was dedicated to this function.
- *Socialising* – a large proportion of stands in the sample included socialising areas of various kinds, including bars (65 per cent), café areas (10 per cent) and relaxation corners (24 per cent). On average, around 6 per cent of the total space was dedicated to this function.

In terms of overall design, the authors found that the majority of stands (73 per cent) could be considered 'open', in the sense that they presented no physical barriers to entry, thus permitting visitors passing by to easily look at the interiors of the stands and the products on display. They also found that many exhibitors (25 per cent on average) hosted various types of in-stand events, including product demonstrations (particularly at technology trade shows), social events (for example, cocktail hours in the evenings) and entertainment events (such as comedians, cabaret artists) as ways of attracting crowds of visitors.

Intermediaries

Exhibition organisers

When examining what contributes to a successful exhibition experience, it is possible to make a distinction between the 'hardware', represented by tangible aspects such as the exhibition venue and individual stands, and the 'software', represented by intangible factors such as the knowledge and skills of the key stakeholders. Exhibition organisers are key stakeholders whose expertise is essential to the success and economic sustainability of any exhibition. Also known as exhibition producers/managers/owners, they are the professionals who create, organise and implement exhibitions, managing the overall visitor and exhibitor experience. Morrow (2002), from a US perspective, identifies two principal types of exhibition organisers. Writing in terms of exhibition 'ownership', she distinguishes between exhibitions owned (and organised) by *associations* and those owned (and organised) by *entrepreneurs*. Association organisers assume the responsibility for managing the type of exhibitions that run in parallel with association conferences, as a source of additional revenue for the association itself (arising from the selling of stand space to exhibitors, as discussed in Chapter 3) and as a means of adding value to their members attending the conference. Entrepreneurial organisers, who occasionally use the term 'independent organisers' to describe themselves, vary greatly in size, from one-man/woman operations to huge multinational conglomerates. Lawson (2000) notes how horizontal integration has led to the creation of large, international exhibition organiser groups – often with interests in publishing and other media. For example, Reed Exhibitions, the world's leading exhibitions business, has a staff of 3,000 exhibition specialists running a portfolio of over 500 events in 41 countries, attracting more than 7 million participants (www.reedexpo.com).

In countries such as China and many of those in continental Europe, a third category of exhibition organiser is active in this market – government-linked organisers, whose motivations for running exhibitions are usually connected with the local economic benefits that they generate. For example, Messe Frankfurt Exhibition GmbH is the exhibition organiser arm of Messe Frankfurt, a holding company owned by the City of Frankfurt/Main (60 per cent) and the federal state of Hessen in which Frankfurt is located (40 per cent). Responsible for organising events in 30 different locations worldwide, Messe Frankfurt Exhibition GmbH has in particular used their organisation's experience and expertise to help develop the exhibition market in China, Russia, India, Dubai and Turkey (www.messefrankfurt.com).

A list of the world's leading exhibition organisers, in terms of annual revenue, is shown in Table 8.3.

Table 8.3 Revenue of exhibition companies worldwide (€millions)*

	2016	2015	2014
Reed Exhibitions (GB)	1,277.4	1,183.0	1,104.0
UBM plc (GB)	830.6	855.5	561.1
Messe Frankfurt (D)	647.0	647.8	554.2
GL events (F)	452.6	456.0	409.8
Messe Dusseldorf (D)	442.8	302.0	411.5
Messe München (D)	428.1	277.4	309.4
Informa (GB)	358.3	356.1	248.7
Emerald Expositions (USA)	340.4	281.0	225.4
Messe Berlin (D)	309.4	242.0	269.4
Deutsche Messe (D)	302.3	329.3	280.6
NürnbergMesse (D)	288.0	203.7	228.7
Koelnmesse (D)	274.0	321.2	231.2
HKTDC (HK)**	237.6	243.6	188.0
Fiera Milano (I)	221.0	337.3	242.7
Ascential plc / i2i Events Group (GB)	210.1	204.0	177.3
VI PARIS (F)	196.7	283.0	303.8
Coex (ROK)	195.2	217.0	163.1
Fira Barcelona (E)	165.0	148.0	152.6
Tokyo Big Sight (JP)	n/a	160.1	159.5
Landesmesse Stuttgart (D)	158.5	120.6	142.1
ITE Group (GB)	155.8	183.1	223.7
BolognaFiere (I)	132.4	119.0	120.0
Svenska Massan Goteborg (S)	131.0	128.9	97.4
Comexposium (F)	126.6	108.5	129.3
IEG Italian Exhibition Group (I)	124.8	n/a	n/a
dmg :: events (GB)	122.6	128.1	128.0
SNIEC Shanghai (CN)	121.1	115.7	139.0
Amsterdam RAI (NL)	120.2	126.2	119.7

Artexis Group (B)	114.9	107.0	92.8
Jaarbeurs Utrecht (NL)	111.1	133.3	131.6
Hamburg Messe (D)	110.9	61.8	99.8
IFEMA Madrid (E)	105.6	97.6	93.2

* If possible, without revenue in business areas outside the exhibition and congress sector.

** Exhibitions and missions

Source: AUMA (n.d.).

Although the first two are British – Reed Exhibitions and UBM – Germany is the country with most exhibition organiser businesses appearing in the top ten ranking. Of the 33 exhibition companies with revenues of more than €100 million, nine are located in Germany and six in the United Kingdom. It is clear that, overall, European companies dominate this ranking: only five of the 33 companies are based outside Europe: Emerald Expositions (USA), Hong Kong Trade Development Council, Coex (Korea), Tokyo Big Sight, and SNIEC Shanghai.

Following this review of stakeholders that are active in the exhibitions market, it is evident that, in order to become truly successful, exhibitions must satisfy the aims and objectives of all of these stakeholders. The final section of this chapter examines how exhibition organisers attempt to achieve that goal.

Organising exhibitions

The challenges for organisers

Exhibition organisers are interested in developing events that provide high levels of positive outcomes for exhibitors and visitors, while at the same time making a profit for themselves and increasing repeat business in the form of a growing number of satisfied exhibitors and visitors returning to each edition of their exhibitions. Gopalakrishna and Lilien (2012:227) explain how these three key stakeholders must be satisfied, for any exhibition to be successful:

> The show managers, who organise and manage the event, transact with exhibitors for the sale of floor space and to provide other fee-based show services. They want exhibitors to have a successful experience, such that they will return to exhibit again at a future show. Exhibitors will return to a show only if the attendees they were able to attract to their booth were of good quality and the interactions led eventually to successful outcomes. Similarly, attendees will want to return only if they felt that they had a cost-effective experience that enabled them to find products/solutions from alternative suppliers.

Events that fail to attract and satisfy sufficient numbers of exhibitors and visitors and earn a profit for their organisers are eventually withdrawn from the market, to join the unknown number of exhibitions that arrived at the end of their life cycle after experiencing a period of decline that was either gradual or, in some cases, abrupt. There are many reasons for exhibitions going into decline, and the best efforts of organisers can be undermined by factors beyond their control – for instance, the general state of the global or national economy, or a government's introduction of visa requirements that can have the effect of restricting how many foreign exhibitors and visitors are able to attend the event.

But the main factor influencing the degree of success of any exhibition is widely recognised to be the general market performance of the sector that it serves, with the level of profitability of exhibitions paralleling the overall success of the sectors they cover. Challenging market conditions for potential exhibitors generally have a negative impact on the events serving their industry. For example, a downturn in the market for luxury watches, and growing competition from electronic and smart watches, were suggested as directly contributing to the dramatic shrinking of Baselworld, the world's leading watch exhibition, in 2018 (Doerr, 2017).

Another reason for the decline and eventual failure of exhibitions is the arrival of a directly competing event. The trade show Interstoff (*stoff* means 'fabric' in German) dedicated to clothing fabrics closed in 1999 after a 40-year run in Frankfurt, because a new exhibition aimed at the same market, Premiere Vision, had been inaugurated in Paris, widely regarded as the fashion capital of the world. After a few years of losing growing numbers of exhibitors and visitors to its French rival, the Interstoff trade show was permanently withdrawn (Rinaldo and Golfetto, 2015). In some cases, the cause of an exhibition's decline and final withdrawal comes as a result of several factors. For example, one of Germany's earliest computer exhibitions, Systems, based in Munich, closed in 2009 after a run of 40 years, due to competition from another German IT exhibition, CeBIT, combined with the impacts of the financial crisis of that period (Riedl, 2010).

To avoid their exhibitions entering the decline phase in the life cycle, organisers must be constantly assessing the markets served by their events. Jin and Weber emphasise that the role organisers play in the exhibition industry has been evolving as a result of the gradual transformation of the function and operation of exhibitions: 'Organisers now need to spot industry trends, develop innovative exhibition concepts in line with market requirements, and help exhibitors establish lasting communication with their customers' (Jin and Weber, 2013:9, quoting Heckmann).

Delivering successful exhibitions

Exhibition organisers are responsible for the production of events, from their conception to their completion. Within the organising team, there are three main roles: marketing, sales and operations.

Marketing

The launch of every new exhibition comes as the result of a perceived 'gap' in the market, between which exhibitions are available and which should be. In the exploratory stages for a new exhibition, the marketing team is responsible for researching the relevant sector of the industry at which the exhibition is aimed, in order to:

- find out if there is sufficient demand for the new exhibition;
- create leads for the sales team to follow up and convert into paying exhibitors;
- assess where the marketing team should focus its promotional activity.

If the research indicates that there is sufficient demand for a new exhibition, the marketing team then creates a promotional campaign, the nature of which will depend on whether the exhibition is a B2B or B2C event. They use a combination of magazine or journal adverts, posters, direct mail, online communications tools and other promotional channels to maximise publicity and attract as many visitors as possible to the event. For B2B events, they may create a *hosted buyers programme*, which means that the organisers will fund the exhibition-related travel and accommodation costs of pre-qualified buyers, selected because of their purchasing power and purchasing history, on condition that they undertake to engage with exhibitors through a pre-determined number of pre-scheduled appointments.

Sales

Sales professionals on the organising team are responsible for generating all non-ticket revenue for an exhibition, from selling stand space to finding sponsorship. However, their task begins with promoting the conceptual package of the exhibition to potential exhibitors in order to convince them to buy stand space for the event. Selling stand space for a *new* exhibition is a considerable challenge for sales staff, as they have no bargaining power with the exhibitors based on the performance of previous editions. Exhibitors, therefore, are able to extract many favours, such as price discounts and prime corner locations. However, with successful, established exhibitions, the exhibitors are generally less demanding on the price front and would rather have a favourable location than a price discount. (Kay and Ap, 2008). The layout of the exhibition floor plan is vital. Han and Verma note that it can be difficult to determine where to place specific exhibitors to keep everybody satisfied:

> Placement is often first-come, first-served. Beyond that, it is often based on price and other related factors. But when determining placement, focusing on satisfaction among exhibitors is important, as competitors may not want to exhibit next to one another. On the contrary, it is helpful to place exhibitors with similar products in one area of the tradeshow for attendees' convenience.
>
> (Han and Verma, 2014:244)

Morrow (2002) stresses the importance of giving equal weight and attention to both stand space sales and attendance promotion, because, without a solid exhibitor base, visitors will not come; and without qualified visitors, companies will not buy exhibition space.

Operations

The operations team is responsible for organising the logistical elements of the exhibition. Their tasks begin with the selection of the destination and venue in which the exhibition will be located. In doing so, they will take into consideration many of the criteria used by the organisers of large association conferences, as discussed in Chapter 3, such as accessibility, security and general appeal for visitors. A further criterion that can be a determining factor in this process is the presence at the destination of businesses that are active in the market for the products or services that are the focus of the exhibition in question. For example, part of the rationale for holding the world's largest automobile exhibition, the International Motor Show (Internationale Automobil-Ausstellung) in Germany is no doubt the fact that that country's vast automobile industry is widely regarded as the most competitive and innovative in the world.

Once the venue has been booked, the exhibition operations staff must ensure that all the necessary general service contractors are hired, and that all required services are provided for exhibitors and visitors, from signage and broadband connections to catering facilities. Planning the exhibition's education programme is a key task, and one that is growing in importance as this element of such events assumes more prominence in the visitors' motivations for attending exhibitions. Han and Verma strongly emphasise this:

> To ensure that attendees feel like they are getting a return on their investment, the tradeshow must remain fresh, present new ideas, and offer distinctive value. In that regard, tradeshows should provide something that the attendee cannot get anywhere else, such as a prominent keynote speaker, designated areas where people can meet each other, and educational sessions on innovations.
>
> (Han and Verma, 2014:243)

As the opening date for the exhibition approaches, the operations team coordinates the build-up of the event and makes sure that everything is in place ready for the opening, including an effective and efficient registration area. During the exhibition, the team liaises with exhibitors, contractors and visitors to monitor that they are satisfied and deal with any difficulties that may arise.

It is clear from the above list of tasks that while some require the exhibition managers to be highly organised and detail-oriented, others call for them to develop a deep strategic understanding of the evolving exhibition industry and, most importantly, to be able to use that knowledge to implement innovative strategies for success.

Chapter summary

This chapter presented exhibitions, trade shows and trade fairs as components of organisations' marketing communications strategies, an element of the marketing mix. The history of exhibitions was discussed, and distinctions between consumer (B2C) events and trade (B2B) events were made. The benefits of and motivations for exhibition participation by both exhibitors and visitors were highlighted, and the key stakeholders in the exhibitions market were identified. There was a discussion of the different categories of visitors and the various types of venues that can be used to host exhibitions. A step-by-step analysis of the various stages of organising an exhibition was undertaken, and reasons for the failure of certain exhibitions were reviewed.

CASE STUDY 8.1: CAFÉX, CAIRO

Caféx

Background

The B2B exhibition Caféx (http://cafex-me.com) describes itself as 'The Specialised Fair for Café & Restaurant Equipment, Supplies, Furnishings & Services'. The exhibition's organisers, Events Middle East Ltd, launched the show in Cairo, Egypt in 2014 as a hub for the café and restaurant industry in the Middle East region – 'a place where all levels of the supply chain meet, share and learn'. The show was launched against a background of a wave of entrepreneurism in that region, a boom in the number of new café and restaurant openings, and a growing interest, on the part of many entrepreneurs, to open a café or restaurant of their own. These developments in Egypt's food and beverage (F&B) industry were taking place despite the political instability and unrest that was prevalent in that country at the time. Noticing these trends, Events Middle East Ltd conceptualised the Caféx exhibition. And Cairo, as a city with a strong café culture, was the logical destination for such an event.

The venue for the exhibition is the Cairo International Convention Centre (http://www. eeca.gov.eg/), which is centrally located, with parking facilities for around 1,200 vehicles, five exhibition halls, fully furnished kitchen cafeterias, three large boardrooms and mobile interpretation units for exhibitors and visitors.

Since 2014, Caféx has grown to become one of the largest events for Egypt's F&B industry, setting a benchmark in innovation and organisational techniques in that country's exhibition industry and demonstrating strict adherence to international standards for the exhibition industry.

Stakeholders

As a start-up, Events Middle East Ltd operates with limited resources. There are, in all, six employees, including the financial manager. For that reason, the company has a relatively flat structure, with all employees taking responsibility for selling, marketing and implementing the exhibitions. Caféx was launched and entirely executed by only three members of staff.

The Caféx exhibitors are providers of any goods and services that are relevant to anyone planning to start, develop or expand a café or restaurant. These range from designers and furniture suppliers, to equipment and food traders and consultants.

Caféx's targeted visitors are the existing owners, decision makers, and operators of cafés and restaurants from all over Egypt and the Middle East region, as well as future investors and new entrants in this market.

The Caféx marketing campaign

Caféx is promoted via the following channels.

Social media

The Caféx organisers make extensive use of social media to raise and maintain interest in the show from year to year. They find that their use of social media is the most cost-effective and targeted form of promotion, enabling them to target the exact audience demographic they are seeking to contact.

- The Caféx Facebook page: http://www.facebook.com/cafexegy
- The Caféx Instagram page: https://www.instagram.com/Cafex.egypt/

Digital advertisements and articles

- On websites: Yellow pages – Cairo 360 – Cairo Scene
- On mobile apps: MGP and Bogo Plus.

Outdoor advertising

- 50 banners on Salah Salem, the main road in Cairo
- 50 banners on 15 May Bridge, one of Cairo's busiest bridges over the River Nile
- 75 billboards in the Mohandeseen, Masr El Gdeeda and Nasr City districts of Cairo.

Print advertisements

- In the national press: Ahram Newspaper – two ads; and Standout Magazine – four ads
- Posters in cafés and restaurants across Egypt.

The broadcast media

During the five days leading up to the opening day of Caféx, there were advertising spots on the following radio stations: Nile FM – Nogoum FM – Radio 90/90.

Direct marketing

- 50,000 invitations are distributed throughout Egypt to Caféx's network of F&B outlets
- Flyers are distributed throughout Egypt.

Geofencing

Geofencing technology was used to send locally targeted messages to the mobile devices of potential visitors in the following areas of Cairo, one week before the show:

- Nasr city
- Zamalek
- Mohandeseen
- New Cairo
- 6 October City.

Bulk SMS

100,000 text messages were sent to Orange, Vodafone and Etisalat subscribers announcing that Caféx was imminent, with the dates and location of the show, and mention of the benefits of attending, including the educational element of the show.

The goal of each year's marketing campaign is to attract as many suitable visitors as possible to Caféx. To measure the success of each element of the marketing campaign, the organisers analyse the responses to the question, 'How did you know about us?' that appears on the registration forms the visitors complete. The results of the analysis demonstrate that for the first four editions of the exhibition, Facebook was the most successful marketing tool of all.

The Caféx education programme

Caféx is more than a marketplace where goods and services are bought and sold. Within the show, the Caféx Forum is a series of lectures, seminars, discussion panels and workshops on F&B industry-related topics, during which some of Egypt's most successful F&B entrepreneurs share their stories and advice with visitors and exhibitors alike.

In order to enhance the educational element of Caféx, in 2016 Events Middle East partnered with Endeavor Egypt, part of the Endeavor Global group that supports the growth of its entrepreneurs' companies throughout their business life cycle by developing and providing a comprehensive array of services ranging from a mentoring network to facilitating access to capital (http://endeavoreg.org/model/). Using its resources and network, Endeavor organises the education programme for Caféx and manages the speakers.

The Egyptian Barista Championship

Another important element of Caféx is the annual Egyptian Barista Championship (EBC). During this event, designed to show off the F&B industry's hidden talents, Egypt's top baristas compete to win the title of the Best Barista in Egypt. This involves demonstrations of skills in, for example, mixing innovative (non-alcoholic) signature drinks, using latte art and making the perfect espresso. Egypt's first EBC was launched at Caféx 2014, and has been going strong and constantly evolving since then. This element of Caféx is supported financially each year by sponsors, who use their association with the EBC to promote their brands.

The evolution of Caféx

The objectives of Caféx have evolved with each new edition, and each year has seen different objectives for the show.

Cafex 2014

- To introduce Caféx to the general public through a teaser campaign
- To attract as many new audiences as possible
- To create general interest and curiosity within the café and restaurant industry and engage it with Caféx.

Caféx 2015

- To position Caféx as the café and restaurant industry's principal gathering in the region
- To tackle industry-related issues and show how Caféx can help solve them, thereby reinforcing the desired market position for the exhibition
- To raise brand awareness.

Caféx 2016

- To consolidate exhibitors' and visitors' awareness of the Caféx brand and how the event is of use to the industry
- To extend the exhibition's focus to entertainment and creativity, as a means of sustaining attendees' attention more effectively than by merely talking about the industry and the role of Caféx within the industry
- To focus the show's marketing principally on industry professionals rather than the general public
- To extend the event's geographical reach beyond Cairo and Alexandria
- To position Caféx as the 'hub of the café and restaurant industry'.

Caféx 2017

- To fully engage the social media audience, as a means of creating a buzz around Caféx
- To attract as much attention as possible and achieve maximum engagement by using unorthodox and even controversial posts on social media channels
- To create an organic viral reach
- To create a media buzz
- To launch a new concept 'Carnevale', a family-day-out zone at the show, with music, food, drinks, a 'kids' corner' and a bazaar selling handicrafts, home accessories, beauty and personal care products.

Table 8.4 indicates the growth of Caféx in terms of the number of exhibitors, the space rented out to exhibitors and the number of visitors.

Table 8.4 The growth of Caféx				
Edition	Number of exhibitors	Gross space (square metres)	Number of Halls used in the venue	Number of trade visitors
2014	65	4,000	1	4,000
2015	90	5,000	1.25	5,500
2016	100	7,000	1.5	7,000
2017	120	10,000	2	10,000

Source: Events Middle East Ltd.

Looking to the future, the organisers' strategic aim is to develop Caféx into an international brand, and to be able to franchise it to exhibition organisers operating in other countries.

CASE STUDY 8.2: INPRINT, THE INDUSTRIAL PRINT TECHNOLOGY EXHIBITION, MUNICH

InPrint

The Mack Brooks Exhibitions Group

The Mack Brooks Exhibitions Group is an independent, privately owned trade show organiser, established in 1965. The company has its European headquarters in St Albans, England, and offices in the USA, China, Thailand and India. The Mack Brooks Exhibitions Group owns and organises leading international trade fairs and B2B exhibitions, events and conferences around the world in specialised industry sectors. The portfolio of events covers specialised technology areas including airport technology, chemicals, civil infrastructure, paper, film and foil converting, corrugated and carton manufacturing, fastener and fixing technology, metal working, polyurethanes, printing, rail technology, sheet metal working and water technology. The company's major trade fairs, such as EuroBLECH, the world's leading sheet metal working technology exhibition, bring together more than 1,600 manufacturers and suppliers with some 60,000 trade customers.

One of the company's latest exhibitions, InPrint, focuses on technology for industrial printing.

What is industrial printing?

Even if we are largely unaware of it, we are surrounded in our everyday lives by examples of products that use industrial printing:

For functionality: our smartphones, washing machines, cars and computers all depend on the use of, for example, printed touchscreens or circuit boards for their functionality.

For decoration: industrial printing plays a major role in the decoration of our environments, such as floors and wall coverings and furniture – for example, the printing of a wood finish effect on laminate flooring or the printing of an airline's logo on the exterior of its planes.

For packaging: innovative and imaginative packaging helps manufacturers sell more of their products. With innovations in special inks for printing on high-end luxury products as well as the increasingly visible direct-to-shape inkjet evolution, this segment is an exciting and buoyant one within industrial printing.

InPrint

The launch edition of InPrint (http://www.inprintshow.com/germany) was held in 2014 in Hanover, before moving to the Munich Trade Fair Centre in Germany in 2015. The concept was to provide a focused technology platform connecting state-of-the-art printing technology with experts from the manufacturing sector seeking to learn about and invest in cutting-edge technology, components and services for specialty, screen, digital and inkjet printing. InPrint was designed to respond to a need for a specialist platform where these two sectors could connect.

Market research for the exhibition, prior to its launch

Prior to the launch of any exhibition, it is essential for the organisers to gain a clear understanding of the market, as well as key trends. Part of this process, in the case of InPrint, involved speaking to industry leaders in order to understand the areas of growth and whether there was a need in the market for an exhibition focusing on industrial printing. The organisers in this case ran a series of Development Group Meetings – discussions with selected industry leaders – to determine if they would be ready to support a new event like InPrint.

The organisers also looked closely at the size of the market and its growth potential, as well as the costs of running such an exhibition and its potential profitability. Much of the pre-launch research focused on identifying a unique visitor and exhibitor profile to determine if the exhibition would really create a new platform for which exhibitors have a genuine need and that would provide something unique and valuable to visitors. It was also necessary to look at potentially competing exhibitions that were already established in this industry sector. It was found that most of the existing exhibitions for the printing industry had a different focus, with an emphasis more on commercial printing technology. On the other hand, established manufacturing exhibitions tended to cover a broad range of processes, of which printing was not or only one of many aspects covered at such shows.

The organisers concluded that there was great potential for an exhibition that uniquely focused on innovative industrial printing technology, connecting print technology manufacturers with printing experts from the manufacturing industry, over a broad range of sectors. In this way, InPrint was born.

The exhibitors and visitors

The exhibitors are leading international companies who wish to showcase their state-of-the-art technology, components and services for functional, decorative and packaging printing. These include, for example, manufacturers of:

- Machinery and printing systems
- Print heads, screens and other special parts
- Ink, fluids and chemicals
- Materials and substrates
- Hardware and software solutions

Among the products on show on the exhibition stands are specialty, screen, digital and inkjet printing equipment, solutions and processes for printing on metal, plastics, foils, textiles, glass, ceramics, woods and other substrates, equipment for processing and finishing, inks, fluids and chemicals, materials and substrates, as well as software solutions and other services for the industrial printing sector.

As a technology event exclusively dedicated to industrial print technologies, InPrint attracts senior decision makers from diverse areas of the manufacturing industry who are seeking customised solutions to enable them to generate new possibilities and new revenue in their industrial production processes. In particular, the show attracts:

- Strategic production professionals who are looking for ways to improve production capacity, flexibility and output within their plants, including in-house print professionals, R&D Directors, Chief Technology Officers and Production Directors and Designers.
- Industrial print production companies that produce decorative or functional print solutions for integration into a larger manufacturing process.
- Original equipment manufacturers, integrators and developers looking for partners and technologies to integrate and create new machinery solutions for industrial print production.
- Traditional print companies – commercial and graphic art print houses looking to adopt new techniques and technologies to generate new revenue streams.

The first three editions of InPrint in Germany welcomed professionals from a wide range of industries including aeronautics and aerospace, automotive, ceramics and glass, flooring, furnishing and interior décor, medical, and packaging and containers. The visitors included representatives from a broad spectrum of companies such as Airbus, BMW, Hugo Boss, Kraft Foods, Procter & Gamble, Roche Diagnostic and Villeroy & Boch.

These visitors represent a target group which the exhibitors rarely meet at other events, but a target group that is highly interesting and valuable to them. Printing digitally within the manufacturing industry is still fairly new, and with technology developing there are many opportunities and ever-more applications opening up. So the exhibitors have a great interest in connecting with these representatives from the manufacturing sector. And, in turn, with a growing number of companies operating in the manufacturing sector seeking to start adopting print technology or improve their existing processes, it is very useful for them to have a very focused platform dedicated to that industry.

InPrint is an international event, in terms of both exhibitors and visitors. Among the visitors, the largest individual group is from Germany, the host nation (as is the case for most exhibitions), followed by other European countries, and then visitors from other continents. With regards to exhibitors, fewer than half are from Germany.

Key facts on InPrint 2017

- 153 exhibiting companies from 18 countries, 63 per cent international, 37 per cent national
- Top exhibitor countries: Germany, Great Britain, Italy, Switzerland, The Netherlands, Belgium, Austria, France, USA, Portugal
- 3,000 visitors from 63 countries, 52 per cent national, 40 per cent Europe, 8 per cent North and South America, Asia, Africa, Australasia
- Top visitor countries: Germany, Italy, Great Britain, Austria, Switzerland, Spain, The Netherlands, France, Poland, Russian Federation
- 4,900 net square metres

Marketing InPrint to exhibitors and visitors

To market InPrint to exhibitors, Mack Brooks staff begin by contacting exhibitors from the previous edition of the show, to inform them about the next event's dates and offer them the opportunity to rebook their previous stand space. To these companies, as well as to potential new exhibitors, InPrint is marketed via direct mailings, both printed and electronic, sales calls and face-to-face meetings. In addition to these methods, the organisers regularly visit industry events, for example Drupa, K Show and Fachpack, to stay up to date with the market trends, engage with stakeholders in that market, and network with those active within it. Attendance at such events also brings useful opportunities for promoting the event to potential exhibitors. For exhibitors, there is also an active blog, regular webinars and meetings, to keep the organisers connected with the market.

Mack Brooks is a very visitor-driven company, so the company's visitor promotion campaign is usually substantial, in recognition of the fact that the key for a successful show is to attract the right audience to the exhibition. InPrint invests in an extensive marketing campaign to bring the top industry professionals from relevant industrial sectors to the exhibitors' stands. Precise measures include:

- Personal invitations and direct mailings tailored to representatives in the most important industry sectors
- A worldwide print and online advertising campaign in trade publications
- Regular online newsletters sent to an international distribution list
- Regular press information sent to international trade media
- A multilingual website and visitor information, for example an extensive Show Preview

Exhibitors are also provided with a range of free marketing tools to support them in promoting their presence at InPrint and invite their own current and potential customers to their stand at the show. These include:

- Free printed and online promotional material, such as branded banners for the website or email signature, most of which can be personalised
- Online marketing packages to increase their presence online, for example an exhibitor list with profile, product photographs and a listing of their product categories
- Free visitor vouchers for their customers
- Free press service to inform the trade press about their innovations
- Advertising and sponsorship opportunities at the venue, the Munich Trade Fair Centre

For further engagement with both exhibitors and visitors and for keeping them updated on news around the show, InPrint has a strong presence on social media channels and networks, such as:

- Facebook (https://www.facebook.com/InPrintShow/)
- Linkedin (https://www.linkedin.com/showcase/9478082)
- Twitter (https://twitter.com/inprintlive)
- YouTube (https://www.youtube.com/channel/UC9uYflxRV6wg6OwzR7xxxvA)

Education at InPrint

The InPrint conference programme is a key component of the show, and is generally in line with the three focal points of the show – functional, decorative and packaging printing. At each edition, over 60 sessions on two stages explore the latest technological developments, exciting new applications, trends and key areas, through presentations, panel discussions and specialised Tech Talks.

The conference stages are located on the show floor, at the heart of the exhibition space. They are deliberately designed to be open to the rest of the show, to emphasise that it is an integral part of the exhibition and encourage participation by visitors and exhibitors alike. For the InPrint community, learning and knowledge exchange are important, and some exhibitors consider stands next to the stages as prime space, since this gives them many additional possibilities to interact with the visitors, as well as more exposure during the show.

The organisers believe that especially for a small-sized show like InPrint, having a conference programme really does provide added value for the visitors, and increases the time the visitor stays at the exhibition. The open design allows for and encourages 'popping in and out', which avoids people being away from the stands for extended periods.

Challenges encountered

The organisers of InPrint have identified the following challenges in launching the show

1   Initially, being a launch show was a major challenge. Launching any new exhibition clearly means that no one has heard of it; no one is familiar with the concept; there is no data available; and there is no guarantee concerning which visitors – and how many visitors – would be attending.

2   In the case of InPrint, the organisers had to work hard in order to clarify the exact profile of the show. The industrial print sector is still developing and somewhat ill-defined, even to those who are active within it. This means constant evaluating and re-evaluating of the show's profile to ensure that it remains valid, relevant, clear and plainly distinguished from potentially competing exhibitions.

3   Competition from existing shows. Companies usually have a huge choice of shows and events to attend – with, it must be remembered, exhibitions being just one (though very important) element in their marketing mix. Even though different exhibitions have their unique profile and focus, there often is some element of overlap with the profile of another show. This adds to the challenges for a comparatively young show such as InPrint to be recognised and acknowledged.

4   Budgetary constraints. In a context of increasing budget awareness and growing emphasis on measuring return on investment, companies are constantly reviewing which shows they attend, and that makes the task of winning exhibitors even more challenging. This is particularly the case for InPrint, which was launched fairly recently and whose target market for exhibitors includes many prospects who themselves are at the developmental stage and therefore very risk-averse, and have budgetary constraints.

Organisers are faced with the fact that stand space costs are not the only investment an exhibitor will have to make. Taking part in an exhibition is complex and costly and requires further investment, for example in accommodation and stand building, as well as human resources. Especially for an exhibition where machines are brought on site, the logistics are often complex and expensive too. Spending on exhibitions is initially an uncertain expense for companies, as return on investment (ROI) can only be judged a while after the end of the show and is often not even directly measurable at all.

Measuring the success of InPrint

The degree of success of the exhibition is measured each show year by looking at key figures such as visitor and exhibitor numbers, square metres sold, and revenue generated.

But the visitor quality and the general satisfaction with the show from exhibitors and visitors alike are also very important. To measure these factors, the organisers conduct exhibitor and visitor surveys, asking for feedback on key indicators and also requesting input for potential improvements and developments. For each show, a Close of Show Report is produced, which reviews and summarises each area and element of the show cycle, and an internal list of improvements and 'lessons learnt' for the following edition is compiled.

The development of InPrint since its first edition

Industrial printing is an emerging sector, so the development of the show is driven by and reflected in the development of the market. While individualisation of many products and materials was previously mainly possible for small individual batches or on a made-to-order basis, innovative printing applications now enable long-term mass customisation within the industrial production process. The industry has moved from the initial hype over the sheer potential of new technologies to a more pragmatic and practical understanding of the opportunities and challenges. Consumer behaviour is changing rapidly, calling for customised products that reach the markets faster than ever before. Retailers need a swift and flexible production to meet these demands and improve their business agility. There is a growing community of innovators looking to open up new markets and to form new partnerships that will lead to the development of powerful printing solutions capable of improving the manufacturing processes. What we can see as a result of this year's show is that InPrint is clearly evolving from a developmental networking event into a networking and trade exhibition, with increasing sales activity on the show floor and a larger number of concrete solutions having been demonstrated by exhibitors on their impressive stands than at previous shows.

Future plans for InPrint

After its third edition in Germany, InPrint is now more well known and recognised as an important business platform for print applications in industrial production. The further growth potential of the show of course relates to how fast technologies will change in the future. To develop InPrint further, existing and additional exhibitors who are on the forefront of developments will be encouraged to use the platform to present their latest technologies. With the new Innovation Awards programme, InPrint recognises smart and powerful printing solutions that can help transform the manufacturing sector. The broad spectrum of award entries at the last show demonstrated the enormous scope of practical solutions that are currently being developed which indicates that industrial print is reaching a new level. The organisers will also keep working to increase recognition in the visitor communities to attract more high-quality visitors. InPrint has a key role in forming this community, and with market consolidation the show is expected to be a stronger vehicle for sales by gradual evolution.

In addition, InPrint has already been launched in other markets and took place in Italy in 2018 and the USA in 2017, both regions to which InPrint will return in the future.

CASE STUDY 8.3: FASHION & LIFESTYLE EXPO, SKOPJE

Fashion & Lifestyle Expo

Ognena Ristovska is the General Manager of the Macedonia-based events company, Momentum Inc. In this interview, she discusses her company's Fashion & Lifestyle Expo event.

When and why did you create Momentum?

Momentum Inc. (www.momentum.mk) was created in April 2015 in Skopje, with a visionary concept for the design and organisation of events through the application of two principles: a unique purpose and flawless execution.

Our driving force is the improvement of the quality of life in our community, through events. Our goal is to create unique, memorable and intense experiences for everyone who attends a Momentum event. I believe that the execution of an event is truly an art, and that the charm and memorability of our events lie in the subtle details that demonstrate our commitment and sincere desire to reach our goals as we strive to achieve perfection in our work.

As is probably the case with many ideas, Momentum was a spur-of-the-moment decision. At one moment in time all of the elements came together – namely, what I was most passionate about (fitness and health); what I most loved doing and was best at doing (organising events); what was clearly beneficial for the community and a cause that drives me (health and the prevention of illness); and what was becoming a trend (a healthy and active lifestyle). The alignment of all of these elements persuaded me that it was the right time to launch my own events agency, Momentum, and create our first event, the Health, Fitness & Wellness Expo (https://www.facebook.com/hfwexpo/).

Most events agencies are involved in planning events for their various clients, where the concept is already established and the events are executed with the clients' own objectives in mind. But, in addition to operating along the lines of this traditional model, Momentum also gives form to and designs, plans, implements and evaluates its own events, entirely in its own name and for its own purposes. And that makes us unique in Macedonia.

Why did you create the Fashion & Lifestyle Expo?

The Fashion & Lifestyle Expo (http://www.momentum.mk/?page_id=2082) is the second event, after the Health, Fitness & Wellness Expo, that Momentum realised as its own concept and project. We felt that we needed to step up with a more serious show, on a different scale, to show the public and the market that we could work on an event with a different theme and different content. Again, when designing the event's theme and concept I began with a topic that was attractive to me personally, something that I would personally enjoy being involved in.

The fundamental idea was to create an event for anyone that wanted to challenge the status quo and everything that is neutral, ordinary and boring in daily life. From the beginning, this project had as its purpose the creation of an event that helped stimulate a sort of 'shift' in everyday living by presenting an event that was itself avant-garde and unusual. The Fashion & Lifestyle Expo celebrates products and services that go beyond the 'everyday' by appealing to people in search of authenticity, uniqueness and even the avant-garde in what they buy.

Bearing in mind that in Macedonia we are fairly restricted by our market size and potential, before launching the event we needed to assess the market for the Fashion & Lifestyle Expo. In particular, we had to research potential products and services that would be appropriate for being exhibited at such an event, as well as the target audience to which these products and services would be presented. The conclusion of our research was that, despite operating in a market of limited size, we would nevertheless be able to bring together sufficient exhibitors and visitors to make this event viable. Regarding competition from similar events in Macedonia, we looked closely at two events that were targeting a market similar to that which we had in mind. The first of these was the Fashion Weekend Skopje, but the focus of this event is purely fashion and fashion shows by local designers. The second was the Skopje Design Week. This is an event that overlaps to some degree with certain areas of the Fashion & Lifestyle Expo such as the design of furniture and appliances. But we remained convinced that the Fashion & Lifestyle Expo's unique selling point would lie in presenting a comprehensive range of fashionable, exciting and innovative products and services, from cars and jewellery to interior design, kitchen appliances and food and wines. Consequently, we decided to go ahead and develop the concept for the first Fashion & Lifestyle Expo in 2016.

What kind of exhibitors and visitors do you target for the event, and how do you market the event to them?

We target exhibitors from various industries: high-level world fashion, automotive, consumer electronics, experience design (deep, sensory and engaging experiences), interior style (home decor, bed and bathroom, kitchen), architecture, decorative accessories, luxury goods, watches and jewellery, cosmetics and perfumes, travel, action and sports, books, vintage and craft, paper and packaging, food and drink (products, appliances and packaging).

Regarding the visitors, we target people who are focused on quality, who are looking for novelty and uniqueness, who value quality service and relationships, and who are attracted by brands that are aligned with their desire for social status.

To reach exhibitors, the event is marketed via direct sales – direct phone calls, face-to-face meetings and emails – to explain why this exhibition is a place where they should position their products and services, what type of visitors it attracts, and what are the benefits that they will gain through participation. These direct contacts to exhibitors as well as applications for participation take place over a two-month period, usually 4–5 months before the actual event. For visitors, we use all available channels, with support from over 25 media partners, including Web portals, print media, TV and radio shows, and print materials. Posters and flyers are distributed throughout Skopje, and for the second edition, we also used a billboard advertisement. We rely heavily on social media, including a Facebook page for the regular fans of the event in general. We create a different Facebook page for each edition when we announce the programme. We also use Instagram, as it is well suited to the type of visually artistic and cultural content generated by the exhibition. And we post regular blogs about the event on Momentum's blog.

What are the major challenges in running the Fashion & Lifestyle Expo?

There are many challenges associated with this event. Firstly, we are very limited by the market size and potential. There are only a few companies and individuals offering products and services suitable for exhibiting at the event. This is compounded by the fact that many companies' marketing budgets have been cut as a result of the economic situation in Macedonia. So even when there is considerable interest in participating, some potential exhibitors decide not to, because they cannot afford it.

The second challenge is connected to the first – the low prices that we need to maintain in order to attract exhibitors, since many of them struggle to afford to exhibit at this event even with very reasonable prices for booth space hire. This creates a huge challenge for us to provide a high-quality and full programme of performances, to decorate and animate the event with different activities, as well as to provide the level of human resources and logistical support that is required for an event such as this.

The third one would be finding a suitable location – as Skopje is a fairly small city with limited capacities and venues, many of which have been used very often for events such as weddings or conferences and which are therefore already known to the general public in a very different context. The size of the venue is also very important, as we need a hall that is big enough (but not too big) to accommodate the number of participating exhibitors and visitors. There is also the technical issue of finding a venue with access for all of the merchandise to be exhibited, some of which is heavy and voluminous. Most venues in Skopje do not have facilities for the receiving of such goods. As an illustration of the problem, for the first edition of the Fashion & Lifestyle Expo we had the challenge of lifting two very expensive cars – a Jaguar and a Porsche – up three sets of stairs and through the front door of the venue (the Macedonian Opera and Ballet), which was only 1 cm wider than the width of the Porsche!

The fourth challenge would also be the sheer novelty of the Fashion & Lifestyle Expo concept and the need to explain it to the general public. Many people have initial difficulty in understanding what kind of event this is, what types of products and services will be showcased, and what are the potential benefits to them of attending. This was a particular problem for the first edition in 2016, as that year we had no photos, videos or testimonials from a previous edition and we were still in the process of positioning this event in the market.

How did you overcome these challenges?

In order to recruit sufficient numbers of exhibitors from a very small pool of suitable companies, we realised that we needed to perform very well in direct sales, to achieve a large rate of success. For example, from a pool of 200 companies, we had to attract at least 40 exhibitors, which is a 20 per cent success rate. In addition to our use of direct sales, we can also rely on positive press coverage and public relations, positive experiences from previous exhibitors, as well as recommendations and word of mouth, all of which add to our success in attracting exhibitors. We also understand the need to have a high rate of repeat business from exhibitors, since we do not have a wide pool from which to replace any companies who may discontinue their exhibiting. This means that all exhibitors need to be very satisfied with the event, since we want them to come again the following year.

To maintain interest in the event, we aim to offer something different in each edition. For example, for the second edition, we chose a very different and unexpected location – the foyer of the Macedonian Opera and Ballet. That space is unique. With its white marble and broken asymmetrical walls, it is the perfect space for the exhibition and an anything-but-ordinary experience. After facing several logistical problems in the first edition such as the one already mentioned (physically getting all of the equipment and exhibits into the venue), for the second edition we devised a specific action plan for the exhibition set-up, with a strict timeline and directions for every exhibitor, telling them when and through which entrance to enter the building. This time, all went well, and we brought in all of the exhibits in a record three hours.

Regarding the challenge that comes with running a new, innovative event that is entirely unfamiliar to the target audience, we found that the solution lay in patiently explaining the concept to potential exhibitors and visitors to bring the idea closer to them and familiar-ise them with it. More specifically, we found it useful to determine their interests and then to emphasise a part of the programme or exhibition that has some link to those interests. Overall, the most difficult part has been getting the visitors and exhibitors to take that initial decision to attend. We have found that, once they have experienced the Fashion & Lifestyle Expo, their comments have been nothing but positive. Those who are unsure as to what exactly will be happening at the event are usually very positively surprised by the fullness and variety of the programme, the products and services on show and everything they can see and do at the event.

How has the Fashion & Lifestyle Expo changed since the first edition – and why has it changed?

Following the successful second edition of the event, I can say that it is now much more clearly positioned and that it has achieved an audience that recognises its value and would visit again and recommend it to a friend. This is very important because this is the audience we need to make the event viable, and because word of mouth is the best way to attract visitors for an event such as this one. The second edition of the Fashion & Lifestyle Expo was larger than the first. We had approximately 25 per cent more exhibitors (34 for the second edition, compared with 27 for the first one). There was a fuller range of products, services and brands on display at the booths, and the design and visual presentation of all the booths was much improved. Content-wise, the programme has been significantly upgraded from only one main stage with half a dozen presentations per day, to six locations, including: the main stage where the principal performances and shows take place; a Food & Drink Corner with presentations and tastings of seafood, wine, chocolate and coffee; a Fashion & Lifestyle Café, which was decorated as an actual café, with a specific programme of presentations of coffee, sweets and books, including book signings and promotions, chocolate, coffee and tea promotions; a Creative Hall for hands-on workshops on topics ranging from DIY clothes design and photography to modular bicycles; a Beauty Bar where make-up and cosmetic workshops took place with professional staff from the Make-Up Academy, as well as an Open Backstage before the fashion shows, and a Gallery, where we had over 50 designers from the International Fashion Institute Izet Curi exhibiting their designs, an exhibition of paintings of young artists and an exhibition of photography.

As a result of these improvements, this year's exhibitors and the programme of activities had a lot more to offer visitors and the range of things to do and see was broad enough to attract a much wider audience, with everyone finding something of interest to them.

How do you measure the success of the event?

The success of the event is measured in several ways:

- The exhibitors complete an evaluation form, with various questions relating to the success of their exhibition experience, such as the amount of promotional material distributed, new subscriptions to their newsletters, new club memberships, the degree of participation in the activities they offered at their booths, and the volume of sales made at the exhibition (if they chose to sell).
- Post-event telephone interviews are done with each exhibitor to solicit their feedback on various issues such as: the exhibition's preparation and planning, the programme, the logistics, public relations and publicity, the visitors, as well as technical issues such as set-up, stage, sound and even the basic concept and suggestions for future editions.
- The number of visitors. For the second edition, we had almost 4,000 visitors which was satisfactory for an event the size and scope of the Fashion & Lifestyle Expo.
- Press clippings mentioning the event. This year, we had over 60 of these, which is a good number bearing in mind the limited number of media outlets in our small country.
- Internal feedback and evaluation is carried out among the Momentum Inc. team as well as with other stakeholders such as audio-visual equipment suppliers, performers and the venue.

All of these evaluations together add up to one complete general picture of the success of the event and each edition.

What are your plans for the future of the Fashion & Lifestyle Expo?

Our intention is that the Fashion & Lifestyle Expo should continue to offer an innovative, avant-garde and exclusive programme and range of exhibitors each year. Ultimately, we aim to make the event international in scope, by attracting international exhibitors, performers and visitors who will possibly trigger international cooperation between foreign and local participants in our event.

IT'S MY JOB
HELGA BOSS, EXHIBITIONS
MANAGER, MESSE DORNBIRN

I studied Economics at the University of Innsbruck and graduated in 2003. My majors were Tourism as well as Finance. During university, I had a part-time job in an events agency, and that experience convinced me that I would love to work in this industry. I come from Austria, and we Austrians are well known for the high quality of our customer service. So it comes very naturally to me to focus on what clients want and what makes them happy.

My first full-time job in the events industry came after my graduation when I was employed by the President of the University of Innsbruck to organise all of the university ceremonies as well as incentive events for members of staff of the university. This was at a time when organisers of conventions and congresses were beginning to look for venues that were alternatives to traditional convention centres. At the same time, universities in Austria needed more money as they were facing cuts to their funding. Therefore, we started to hire out our lecture rooms as conference venues, especially for meetings of scientific disciplines that were relevant to research being carried out at the University of Innsbruck. I still can remember my first scientific conference at that university. It was the European Congress of Entomology – all about insects. For me, working with the professors, who were extremely knowledgeable about the insect world, but had little idea of how to organise a conference was fascinating. I very much enjoyed the challenge of supporting the university's scientific staff in this way.

In December 2006, I moved to Vorarlberg, the province west of Tyrol, situated beside Lake Constance in a very attractive region where four countries' borders meet: Germany, Austria, Switzerland and Liechtenstein. There, I began working for the convention centre in Bregenz, called the Festival House (Kongresskultur Bregenz GmbH) (http://www.kongresskultur.com/en/). Within German-speaking Europe the annual Bregenz Festival is very famous for its large-scale operatic performances which take place on a specially constructed floating stage on the part of Lake Constance which is just beside the Festival House.

When I began working there, the venue had just undergone a major renovation and enlargement resulting in the provision of meeting rooms ranging from the Great Hall, with a capacity of 1,656 guests in theatre-style seating, to a variety of multifunctional rooms offering natural daylight and a view over the lake.

My first job for the venue was project manager for conventions and congresses. Just after the renovation, business in the venue was going very well simply because of the availability of the new meeting rooms. But it became clear that, for the future, a strategic sales process would be required, to sustain that level of business. Therefore, my boss gave me the challenge of being responsible for sales for the convention centre. It was then that I began working with our new and very young destination marketing organisation, the Convention Partner Vorarlberg (http://www.convention.cc/en/). We worked very closely together, jointly attending meetings of the International Congress and Convention Association, visiting potential customers within the three neighbouring countries and inviting key accounts to attend the Bregenz Festival as our guests.

In 2011, I began my Master's in International Marketing and Sales at the Vorarlberg University of Applied Sciences, while continuing to work at the Festival House. By the time I graduated in 2013, I had moved into a new job, this time in the exhibition industry. In September 2012, I began working for the Messe Dornbirn, the exhibition centre and organiser of trade fairs in Vorarlberg (https://www.messedornbirn.at/).

The Messe Dornbirn was a very traditional company. Its main consumer show – the Herbstmesse – was created just after World War II, when people were keen on seeing new products and buying them. The company gradually expanded its range of events to include a public fair, the Schau! in the Spring; an art exhibition, Art Bodensee, in the Summer; Intertech, an international B2B technology exhibition; and one for church facilities, the Gloria, the only church trade fair throughout all German-speaking countries (https://gloria.messedornbirn.at/themen-aussteller/). But by 2012, the Messe Dornbirn company was facing financial difficulty as the life cycle of these events went into decline. We found ourselves with two sinking cash cows, the Herbstmesse and the Schau!, a very poorly attended art exhibition and a declining international technology exhibition. The Gloria did not succeed in Dornbirn and was subsequently licensed to the Messe Augsburg.

The new CEO of the company, who recruited me, gave me the power and authority to make changes and introduce innovations for the company. In particular, Dietmar Stefani gave me the responsibility for the creation and launch of a new event – the Gustav – an international consumer show for products that are characterised by a high level of craftsmanship, quality materials and durability (https://gustav.messedornbirn.at/die-gustav/). This was a very challenging task, and I can say that never before in my life had I had to work so hard to sell exhibition space. But it became an instant success as a show, and everyone – visitors and exhibitors – was satisfied with this new event.

After building up the Gustav, I handed it over to another project manager. Today, the event is still a successful consumer show – not yet exactly a cash cow, but one sign of its success is that we recently signed a contract with an exhibition company in Zurich, giving them a licence to run a Gustav Zurich. Hopefully more destinations will follow!

Besides being responsible for the Gustav, I was the head of the department in charge of all fairs except the two main ones, Schau! and Herbstmesse. Our objective was to make sure that all of the Messe Dornbirn's special-interest fairs made a positive contribution to the company's operating profits, something that we finally managed to do very successfully. The hardest decision was to let our declining Intertech show go, after the 2013 edition, due to the poor response from potential exhibitors, and start to develop a new trade fair in the field of smart textiles in its place. But we were convinced that Intertech had no future – and in discontinuing the event, I learned that it needs far more courage to bury a failing trade fair than to develop a new one.

In 2014, when we started a campaign to hire out our rooms and halls to event organisers and exhibition organisers, I took over this challenge. At the same time, we started to reconfigure six old halls into four new exhibition halls. But the following year, after a restructuring of the company, I concentrated completely on events sales because of the know-how that I had built up in that field while employed at the Festival House in Bregenz.

It was certainly a challenge to create a marketing and sales strategy from zero. The first thing I did was to look carefully at how we could use the halls most profitably, by focusing on the projects that brought in the most money.

In June 2015, I said goodbye to my beloved work to start a new challenge – that of having a baby and becoming a first-time mother. When I returned to the company after 18 months, I found that there had been many staff changes at the Messe Dornbirn, including a new CEO. But a new opportunity came my way when the project manager of our two main public fairs, Schau! and Herbstmesse, resigned, and I stepped into his shoes. Working with a very young and motivated team, I can say that we are succeeding in making these two events more profitable for the company, by targeting new market segments in both exhibitors and visitors.

But I have other responsibilities in my current job. First, I am preparing two young employees to take over the challenge of the project management of these two consumer shows. At the same time, I am establishing a department for the hosting of exhibitions in our new halls. This means creating price lists, sales documents, photographs and much more, to explain our venue to organisers of trade fairs and consumer shows. Throughout German-speaking Europe, we at Messe Dornbirn are well known for our ability to run excellent consumer shows. Our challenge now is to demonstrate that we can also host successful trade fairs.

And, finally, I am responsible for new business development. In that role, I need to consider: which events will bring in the most money in the future? What are the trends within the business? What are the main trends within our society and how can we translate these topics into the running of successful events in our venue? The exhibition market is changing rapidly, and we have no choice but to evolve in step with it, or preferably one step ahead. But I am convinced that we can do this, even though we are a small company. This – along with our very favourable geographical position – gives us a sound competitive advantage.

I honestly love the work I do. There are no problems, only challenges to be solved. I would say that there is practically no other industry in which you have to be so completely up to date as in the exhibition industry. I love training and mentoring young members of staff, because they are the future of this industry, and they bring us ideas for what lies ahead in this world of ours.

References

AUMA (n.d.) Revenue of exhibition companies worldwide (more than Euro 100 million). Available at: http://www.auma.de/en/Seiten/Default.aspx.

AUMA (2006) Die Messewirtschaft Bilanz 2006, AUMA, Berlin.

Bathelt, H., Golfetto, F. and Rinallo, D. (2014) *Trade Shows in the Globalizing Knowledge Economy*, Oxford: Oxford University Press.

De Pelsmacker, P., Geuens, M. and Van den Bergh, J. (2007) *Marketing Communications: A European perspective*, London: Pearson Education.

Dee, R. (2011) Sweet Peas, Suffragettes and Showmen: Events that changed the world in the RHS halls, Andover: Phillimore & Co.

Doerr, E. (2017) Breaking news: Baselworld 2018 will be up to 50% smaller! Up to half the exhibitors gone and 3+ halls closed. Available at: http://quillandpad.com/2017/11/09/breaking-news-baselworld-2018-will-50-smaller-half-exhibitors-gone-3-halls-closed/.

Dubai World Trade Centre (n.d.) Event calendar. Available at: http://www.dwtc.com/en/Events/Pages/default.

Egan, J. (2007) *Marketing Communications*, London: Cengage Learning EMEA.

Friedman, J. F. (2014) Future trends: Impacting the exhibitions and events industry. International Association of Exhibitions and Events.

Friedman, J. F. (2016) Future trends: Impacting the exhibitions and events industry. International Association of Exhibitions and Events.

Godar, S. H. and O'Connor, P. J. (2001) Same time next year – buyer trade show motives. *Industrial Marketing Management* 30(1): 77–86.

Gopalakrishna, S. and Lilien, G. L. (1995) A three-stage model of industrial trade show performance. *Marketing Science* 14(1): 22–42.

Gopalakrishna, S. and Lilien, G. L. (2012) Trade shows in the business marketing communications mix, in Lilien, G. L. and Grewal, R. (eds) *Handbook on Business-to-Business Marketing*, Cheltenham: Edward Elgar Publishing.

Han, H. and Verma, R. (2014) Why attend tradeshows? A comparison of exhibitor and attendee's preferences. *Cornell Hospitality Quarterly* 55(3): 239–251.

Jin, X. and Weber, K. (2013) Developing and testing a model of exhibition brand preference: The exhibitors' perspective. *Tourism Management* 38: 94–104.

Jin, X., Weber, K. and Bauer, T. (2012) Relationship quality between exhibitors and organizers: A perspective from Mainland China's exhibition industry. *International Journal of Hospitality Management* 31(4): 1222–1234.

Kay, A. L. K. and Ap, J. (2008) Exhibition organisers: Thriving & surviving in the China market. Proceedings of the International Convention & Exposition Summit (ICES). Hong Kong Polytechnic University and the University of Nevada Las Vegas (UNLV).

Kirchgeorg, M., Dornscheidt, W., Giese, W. and Stoeck, N. (eds) (2005) *Trade Show Management: Planning, implementing and controlling of trade shows*, Wiesbaden: Conventions and Events: Gabler Verlag.

Kirchgeorg, M., Springer, C. and Kastner, E. (2010) Objectives for successfully participating in trade shows. *Journal of Business & Industrial Marketing* 25(1): 63–72.

Kotler, P. and Keller, K. L. (2009) *Marketing Management*, 13th edn, Upper Saddle River, NJ: Prentice-Hall.

Kozak, N. and Kayar, C. H. (2009) Visitors' objectives for trade exhibition attendance: A case study on the East Mediterranean International Tourism and Travel Exhibition (EMITT). *Event Management* 12: 133–141.

Lawson, F. (2000) *Congress, Convention and Exhibition Facilities: Planning, design and management*, London: The Architectural Press.

Liu, T. and Wilkinson, S. (2014) Large-scale public venue development and the application of public–private partnerships (PPPs). *International Journal of Project Management* 32(1): 88–100.

Mensah, C. and Lestyo, E. (2012) Visitors' objectives for attending a regional trade fair in Ghana. *European Journal of Social Sciences* (31)4: 496–506.

Morrow, S. L. (2002) *The Art of the Show*, Dallas, TX: IAEM Foundation.

nTradeshows (n.d.) Worldwide trade shows, sector to sector. Available at: https://www.ntradeshows.com/sectors/.

Riedl, T. (2010) Aus nach 40 jahren. Available at: https://www.sueddeutsche.de/digital/computermesse-systems-aus-nach-jahren-1.530785.

Rinallo, D. and Golfetto, F. (2015) Internationalization and knowledge-based strategies of European trade show organizers in Asia: The case of Messe Frankfurt, in

Rinallo, D., Borghini, S. and Golfetto, F. (2010) Exploring visitor experiences at trade shows. *Journal of Business & Industrial Marketing* 25(4): 249–258.

Smith, T., Hama, K. and Smith, P. (2003) The effect of successful trade show attendance on future show interest: Exploring Japanese attendee perspectives of domestic and offshore international events. *Journal of Business & Industrial Marketing* 18(4/5): 403–418.

Ueding, R. (1998) Management von Messebeteiligungen: Identifikation und Erklärung messespezifischer Grundhaltungen auf der Basis einer empirischen Untersuchung, Frankfort: Peter Lang.

UFI (2017) World map of exhibition venues. Global Association of the Exhibition Industry.

UFI & Explori (2017) Global exhibitor insight. Global Association of the Exhibition Industry.

Van Wesemael, P. (2001) *Architecture of Instruction and Delight: A socio-historical analysis of world exhibitions as a didactic phenomenon (1798–1851–1970)*, Rotterdam: 010 Publishers.

9 Corporate hospitality

Corporate hospitality in the 21st century

- As a 'thank-you' to some of their key clients, *Meetings & Incentive Travel* magazine invited over 50 buyers and suppliers, including corporate event planners, to a hospitality day at Ascot racecourse, near London. The guests enjoyed a day of horse racing, a champagne reception, complimentary bar, lunch and afternoon tea.
- Guests of Mercedes-Benz enjoyed excellent views of the motor racing at the Australian Formula One Grand Prix from the VIP hospitality suite overlooking the Melbourne Grand Prix Circuit. Team Vodafone McLaren Mercedes drivers Lewis Hamilton and Heikki Kovalainen were on hand to entertain guests – both on the track and in person.
- Through its ten-year sponsorship deal with the Kia Oval international cricket ground in London, the OCS Group invited its key customers, associates and employees to enjoy high-profile cricket matches from the comfort of the OCS executive boxes at the venue.

Chapter objectives

On completion of this chapter the reader should be able to:

- Understand the role of relationship marketing strategies.
- Understand the distinguishing characteristics of corporate hospitality.
- Recognise the potential benefits offered by corporate hospitality as well as the challenges it can present.
- Appreciate the range of stakeholders active in the corporate hospitality sector.
- Understand key factors to be taken into account when planning corporate hospitality events.

Relationship marketing

Practically all organisations use some form of marketing to reach their customers and persuade them to buy their products and services. When customers purchase any product or service, they may be said to be engaged in a *transaction*, the term used to describe the form of marketing that was predominant for most of the 20th century: transactional marketing. As a business strategy, transactional marketing typically focuses on the winning of a steady stream of new customers to maximise the company's market share and sales volume.

However, over the past few decades most companies, recognising that their dependence on short-term transactional marketing alone may not be enough to enable them to compete successfully in the marketplace, have also adopted a *relationship marketing* approach, centred on engaging with their customers in order to retain them and develop mutually satisfying, long-term, ongoing relationships with them (Buttle, 1996). Consequently, rather than focusing on capturing a large number of separate transactions, a growing number of companies are now making deliberate efforts to keep their existing customers and maintain their relationships with them through a series of interactions designed to foster customer loyalty and long-term engagement. In terms of marketing strategy, the rise of relationship marketing means that in essence 'the focus is, therefore, on the relationship rather than the transaction' (Palmer et al., 2005:316).

Relationship marketing strategies are designed to extend the 'lifetime value' of customers, an approach based on the expectation that the longer the company/customer relationship lasts, the more profitable it becomes for the company. A further rationale for the widespread move toward the use of relationship marketing is the high cost involved in acquiring a continuous stream of new customers making 'one-off' purchases only – the transactional marketing approach. This phenomenon has been well documented in estimates of the costs of acquiring new customers compared with those associated with keeping current customers. For example, Peppers and Rogers (1996) assert that it typically costs five times as much to acquire a new customer than it does to retain an existing one.

Companies using relationship marketing strategies generally invest in ongoing contacts with their customers, in order to create stronger customer engagement and loyalty. That loyalty can be rewarded and strengthened through companies providing their customers with a range of benefits including loyalty schemes, such as airlines' frequent flyer programmes, 'club' membership, discounts and promotional offers, 'valued customer' bookings, free gifts and special offers. The different levels of engagement between companies and their customers are often depicted in the 'ladder of loyalty' developed by Christopher et al. (1991) and represented in Figure 9.1.

In ascending order, the 'rungs' of the ladder of loyalty consist of prospect, purchaser, client, supporter, advocate and, ultimately (although rarely), partner (at which stage the customer has formally joined forces commercially with the company in question). The creators of this scheme state that it portrays how relationship marketing, when used effectively, can move new, transactional customers (purchasers) up the ladder to become clients who make regular purchases, and then progressively into becoming strong supporters and, finally, advocates who are deeply committed to the company and its products and who also influence other people's views of the company and its products through positive word of mouth, not only purchasing the companies' products for themselves but also sharing their satisfaction with others.

- **Partner:** Someone who has the relationship of partner with you.
- **Advocate:** Someone who actively recommends you to others, who does your marketing for you.
- **Supporter:** Someone who likes your organisation, but only supports you passively.
- **Client:** Someone who has done business with you on a repeat basis but may be negative, or at best neutral, towards your organisation.
- **Purchaser:** Someone who has done business just once with your organisation.
- **Prospect:** Someone whom you believe may be persuaded to do business with you.

Figure 9.1
The ladder of loyalty
Source: Christopher et al. (1991).

A wide range of benefits and rewards are used by companies to propel their customers up through this hierarchy, and it is common for companies to use different rewards for different market segments, depending upon the value of each market segment to the overall profitability of the company. This chapter explores a specific relationship marketing tool that is widely used by companies seeking to boost the quality of their relationships with some of their most profitable B2B customers and with other key stakeholders: corporate hospitality.

The distinguishing characteristics of corporate hospitality

Privileged access to sporting and cultural performances for the elite is a practice that has existed since the earliest civilisations. The Colosseum in Rome (AD 80) was designed with separate entries for noblemen, politicians, knights and other dignitaries, leading to the best-placed viewing platforms, closest to the action, from which they could enjoy the spectacle and the continuous provision of food and beverages (Hopkins, 2011).

In the modern world, corporate hospitality, also sometimes known as corporate entertainment or B2B hospitality, is used as a form of experiential B2B marketing, consisting of companies inviting their highest-value customers and other key stakeholders to join them, at no charge, at enjoyable events. The general aim of such invitations is to help the host companies to deepen their relationships with existing customers or to start to bond with potential new customers. When companies and the guests interact in a social setting, outside of the usual business environment – with its sometimes formal and adversarial overtones – they can relate to each other much more readily as human beings and discuss business in a low-threat environment.

In this sense, corporate hospitality experiences are one example of the business events that take place in what Crowther (2011) calls a 'marketing space', a notion which he depicts as 'a transient reality where representatives of an organisation come together physically, and in a planned manner, with a gathering of existing and future customers, clients, and wider stakeholders' (Crowther, 2011:68).

Corporate hospitality experiences, usually lasting one day or less, can be either active (participative) experiences – as in the case of guests taking part in a golf day or sailing excursion, for example – or passive (spectator) experiences, such as attending prestigious performances of operas or ballet, or a day at Roland-Garros during the annual French Open tennis tournament.

Mintel (2008) suggests a classification of corporate hospitality events according to the types of activity that is their main focus:

- Spectator sports (for example, football, rugby, golf)
- Participatory events (for example, helicopter rides, rally driving, sea-fishing excursions)
- Cultural events (for example, concerts, exhibitions, film premieres)
- Other events (for example, visiting leisure attractions or imaginative surprise events).

But whatever the attraction or activity, corporate hospitality is generally characterised by a generous amount of lavish entertainment being on offer for the guests. It would be a very rare corporate hospitality event at which champagne and fine wines did not flow abundantly, accompanied by the finest catering, all expertly served up to create a memorable culinary experience. In the case of spectator events, either premium seats, located close to the performance/game, or enclosed VIP suites (or 'boxes') are used to provide corporate hospitality guests with excellent views of the event as well as a high standard of comfort. Walzel (2014:300) describes the key features of VIP boxes at sports events:

> VIP boxes are often closed-off rooms with a glass front with a view into the sports facility as well as seats in and/or directly outside the VIP box. Guests in the VIP box are offered food and drinks before, during and after the sporting event. A separate bar, kitchen, coat area and toilet for each VIP box increase convenience. Compared with premium seats, VIP boxes offer a more private atmosphere. Companies usually hire VIP boxes for several years and can often design them ... in accordance with their corporate design.

It goes without saying that this level of comfort and service can be extremely costly for the host companies. For example, access to a private VIP suite on Wimbledon's Centre Court can cost over €5,000 per person for a view of the men's singles final.

But, despite its emphasis on lavish enjoyment, the objectives behind corporate hospitality are entirely serious and closely connected to the host companies' key business objectives. Those objectives are invariably concerned with forging and fostering good quality relationships with the host company's key stakeholders, both internal and external.

Six main groups of stakeholders may be invited to participate as guests at corporate hospitality events:

- Actual and potential customers and suppliers
- Intermediaries and agents likely to buy or recommend the host company's products or services
- The financial community, including investors and potential investors
- Key 'influencers' or advocates: representatives of the general media and trade journalists; politicians – local and national
- Members of the local community liable to influence or be affected by the host company's operations
- 'Internal' customers: the company's own staff.

When corporate hospitality events are organised for a company's own staff, there is inevitably a significant level of similarity between these events and the incentive travel awards described in Chapter 7. The employer may have similar aims and objectives for both types of event: motivating staff or rewarding them for achieving their work-related goals – such as meeting their sales targets. However, one key distinction between incentive travel and corporate hospitality is that while an incentive trip usually includes at least one overnight stay, corporate hospitality experiences rarely do. Since the use of incentive travel to motivate staff has been explored in detail in Chapter 7, this chapter will deal specifically with the more common use of corporate hospitality – as an *external* marketing tool.

The benefits of corporate hospitality

As corporate hospitality events typically bring hosts and guests into proximity for several hours, in an informal, relaxed atmosphere, they create numerous opportunities for one-to-one contacts or 'face time' with each other. Many argue that this personal and immediate quality of corporate hospitality is particularly important at a time when advances in technology mean that companies are engaging virtually with their audiences for much of the time. Used effectively, therefore, this form of business event has the potential to bring a number of possible benefits to the host companies. A survey of UK companies using corporate hospitality, carried out by Bennett (2003) highlights the key uses and benefits perceived by those organisations, as shown in Table 9.1.

While most of the benefits listed are self-explanatory, number 4, 'Preparing the ground for follow-up contacts', means that the objective of inviting some guests to a corporate hospitality event is to charm them to the extent that any follow-up sales calls from the host company will be more favourably received by them. The links between corporate hospitality and the companies' relationship marketing strategies are confirmed by the

Table 9.1 Uses of corporate hospitality

Benefit	Mean	Standard deviation
1 Retaining profitable customers	4.3	0.9
2 Building relationships with existing clients	4.2	0.8
3 Developing loyalty and trust among customers	3.9	0.9
4 Preparing the ground for follow-up contacts	3.6	1.1
5 Increasing direct sales	3.4	1.3
6 Developing corporate image and identity	3.4	0.9
7 Gaining new customers	2.3	1.1
8 Winning back profitable customers	2.0	0.7

Note: Five-point scales — 5 = very important benefit, 1 = not at all important

Source: Bennett (2003).

fact that the three most important benefits in the list focus on retaining customers and developing ongoing relationships with them.

Walzel (2014) identifies a similar range of benefits, but divides them into three separate, but linked, categories:

- the *cognitive* effects: generating more information/awareness about the host company's products or services
- the *affective* (emotional) effects: improving guests' attitudes towards the host company – image-building; increasing guests' loyalty to the company and giving it a competitive edge
- the *conative* (behavioural) effects: increased sales from, and brand-switching by, the guests.

Indeed, following this categorisation, the cognitive effects might be said to apply in two directions – not simply the guests learning about the host company's products and services but also the company gaining useful market intelligence from guests' feedback during the conversations that take place during the corporate hospitality event. Crowther (2011:77) notes that:

> An organisation's customers, clients, and wider stakeholders present a considerable resource for learning and intelligence, to then positively influence decisions across the organisation's departments. This intelligence could be something as obvious and immediate as customer feedback and feed-forward, or the much more strategic endeavour focused upon the consultation of wider stakeholders to inform future marketing strategy.

Most corporate hospitality events take place in an environment conducive to this two-way exchange of information between hosts and guests.

The challenges in using corporate hospitality

Bribery

Given the considerable sums of money that companies normally spend on entertaining their corporate hospitality guests, this form of business event has inevitably come under the scrutiny of lawmakers responsible for anti-corruption legislation designed to prevent bribery and other forms of corruption. The higher the spending, the more likely the gift is to be regarded, by the law, as a form of bribe offered by the company to the recipient. For example, a construction company spending lavishly on a luxury weekend trip for someone (and his/her spouse/partner) who is involved in selecting the winner of a tendering process, in which the company is bidding to win a contract, may be open to suspicion of making a blatant attempt to influence the recipient's opinion in their favour. Indeed, whenever an invitation to any event has the appearance of being an inducement or a reward in connection with a business deal, the legitimacy of that invitation may be called into question, with possible legal consequences for both the host and the recipient.

In countries around the world, new or tightened anti-corruption laws, such as the 2010 Bribery Act in the UK, have had an impact on corporate hospitality, with companies having to plan their use of such events with a lot more care in order to avoid making themselves vulnerable to prosecution for being involved in corrupt practices. The UK's Bribery Act, widely considered to be among the toughest anti-bribery and corruption laws in the world, outlines two general offences covering the offering, promising or giving of a bribe (section 1) and the requesting, agreeing to receive or accepting of a bribe (section 2).

However, initial concerns that providing or accepting any corporate hospitality might, under the terms of the Bribery Act, be illegal appear to have been unwarranted, as the Act clearly recognises that hospitality can be an established and important part of doing business and building and maintaining relationships. Nevertheless, it also warns that spending on corporate hospitality must be proportionate and reasonable. Coates (2016) outlines the measures that UK companies must take in order to remain compliant with the law. They need to implement and enforce clear, practical and easy-to-understand policies, ensuring that colleagues – in particular budget holders and those who purchase hospitality – are fully trained and understand their requirements and responsibilities, as well as the implications of non-compliance, both to the individual and to the company as a whole. Specifically, Coates (2016) advises companies to follow these three steps:

1 Due diligence

Carrying out due diligence beforehand will enable bookers of hospitality to be better placed to make more informed and ultimately more successful investment decisions. Research who will be the beneficiary of the entertainment and what their level is within their organisation, ensuring you fully understand the relationships between the recipient and your company – particularly if it involves high-profile organisations or individuals. It is also essential to ensure that the recipient is entitled to receive hospitality under the laws of their country.

2 Transparency

By placing openness and transparency at the heart of their buying practices, organisations will be able to develop a compliant hospitality programme, placing commercial resonance and best practice behind why they choose certain business entertainment. Ensure evidence of all expenditure when purchasing hospitality has been correctly documented and recorded by all parties. If expenditure on a hospitality experience is significant, then sign-off will be required from senior management and must be secured before going ahead with the purchase.

3 Corporate responsibility

Corporate responsibility can be enhanced through booking official hospitality packages, whereby providers are contracted by governing bodies to design, develop, market and sell hospitality experiences on their behalf. More often than not, the revenues generated by these programmes are invested back into the event or sport, enabling hospitality bookers to measure and report back on how they are contributing to their organisation's wider corporate responsibility policies.

Potential conflicts of interest

In 2012, a proposal to introduce plain packaging for cigarettes was being considered by the UK Parliament, as a measure primarily designed to deter young people from starting to smoke (a measure that finally came into force in 2016). That year, *The Telegraph* newspaper (http://www.telegraph.co.uk/) revealed that some of the Members of Parliament (MPs) who were firmly opposed to the Department of Health's proposal had accepted corporate hospitality from a major tobacco company, Japan Tobacco International (JIT), the owner of some of the UK's most popular cigarette brands. Six of the MPs who signed a letter calling for the Department of Health to abandon its proposal to introduce plain packaging for cigarettes had accepted hospitality invitations from JIT in the form of tickets and lunch at the Royal Chelsea Flower Show, each worth over €1,200. JIT also offered corporate hospitality to MPs in the form of tickets for the opera festival at Glyndebourne and test match cricket at the Oval in London. The article cites Martin Dockrell, Director of Policy at the anti-smoking campaign group Action on Smoking Health, as saying: 'This is how it works: a couple of MPs take a "little harmless hospitality" from big tobacco. It's all very cosy. Next thing, those MPs are having a word with other MPs and the tobacco company gets its letter to the health secretary. Job done.' The MPs receiving the corporate hospitality denied that there was any conflict of interest.

Extravagance

Due to the lavish nature of most corporate hospitality experiences, the generous budgets often allocated to this form of experiential relationship marketing can become vulnerable to being reduced or even eliminated, during economic slowdowns, a fact noted by Mintel (2008), for example, who observe that as a marketing tool, the budgets reserved for hospitality functions tend to be among the first to be reviewed when the economy slows down.

High spending on champagne-fuelled prestigious sports or cultural events may appear to be particularly insensitive when, for example, some of the company's staff have just been made redundant. Minnaert's (2009) research showed that, in those times of economic crisis, companies were becoming more cautious about how their spending on corporate hospitality was being perceived by their shareholders, the public and the media. One of the people she interviewed commented: 'People have the money, but they don't want to be seen spending it. They can't be seen spending thousands of pounds if the staff wages are frozen for a year.' (Minnaert, 2009:49).

Conflicting audiences

At most cultural and sports events, the venue's desire to earn revenue from the corporate hospitality guests must be balanced against satisfying the needs and expectations of the loyal fans and true aficionados. But many examples suggest that this balance is not always achieved. For example, at Wimbledon there has long been controversy over the large number of corporate hospitality seats being left vacant during matches, despite the fact that some tennis fans have to queue for many hours to get tickets – and some are turned away empty-handed. Turner (2015) interviewed several members of staff at Wimbledon who lamented many corporate hospitality guests' lack of interest in tennis ('Some were saying they hate tennis, and one had never heard of Djokovic'), saying that many of them seemed to prefer to eat and drink in the on-site hospitality marquees rather than take their prime-location seats at the tennis courts.

It has become increasingly clear that sports clubs that ignore the reaction of their supporters to corporate hospitality extravagance do so at their peril. For although corporate hospitality is a lucrative aspect of many such clubs' finances, the loyalty and the revenue provided by members of the public are also essential. Experience has shown that football clubs, for example, are not always sufficiently aware of the danger of antagonising fans who notice that the best views and best facilities are reserved for corporate guests, and that occasionally the luxury boxes are only partly filled with people, many of whose attention is not focused on the game in play.

Warren and Warren (2015) provide a colourful image of marked differences in attitude to watching an ice hockey game, for the two contrasting audiences:

> Fans are not the only buyers of season tickets. While this family passionately cheers on their team, two seats over, in the same arena, at the same game, a man and a woman passively take in the hockey game as they discuss the manners by which

their respective businesses can help the other achieve a variety of corporate objectives. Neither of these two people paid for their ticket to the game. The tickets were provided to the man at his office as tool to do business, and he invited a major client to the game in an effort to jumpstart a [business] relationship.

(Warren and Warren, 2015:4)

Genuine football fans' anger tends to intensify in the run-up to FIFA World Cup tournaments, when they can find it difficult to get tickets for matches due to the widespread allocation of corporate hospitality packages. Murray-West's (2006) investigation into corporate hospitality packages allocation for that year's World Cup in Germany included an interview with the chair of the Football Supporters Federation who expressed the opinion that most of the recipients of such packages were not real football fans. ('For a lot of them, it's a status thing. It would be interesting to know how many matches they usually watch.') The same interviewee expressed the view that the large number of World Cup tickets sold for corporate hospitality 'feeds the black market', with tickets available on the online auction site eBay for many times their face value.

But a defence of the role played by corporate hospitality sales in football clubs' finances was given by Tottenham Hotspur's sales manager (Croft, 2001) who, while admitting that there was some resentment from certain sections of the club's fan base at the idea of corporate hospitality, stressed that without the extra revenue, fans' tickets would cost a lot more: 'If corporate guests weren't bringing in the millions, then we would have to find that money somewhere else'.

The corporate hospitality market

Buyers

As the name '*corporate* hospitality' suggests, this is a form of business event that is almost exclusively employed in the private sector. While public sector officials and political representatives may from time to time find themselves, as stakeholders, being invited to corporate hospitality events, for obvious reasons of probity and accountability this is not generally a tool used by organisations funded through the public purse.

In terms of the principal sources of demand for corporate hospitality, the key sectors are very similar to those listed in Chapter 2 for corporate meetings in general, with large financial firms and pharmaceuticals prominent among them. However, in recent years, new industries such as information technology and gaming have begun to create additional demand for corporate hospitality. In the 21st century, a pattern has emerged showing that a growing number of small and medium-sized enterprises are booking corporate hospitality events. Croft (2001) is one of many industry observers to notice that an increasing number of smaller companies are using corporate hospitality as part of their marketing mix. He cites, as an example, the observation of the sales manager for Tottenham Hotspur:

Ten years ago, it was just big companies which used corporate hospitality facilities at football matches; now small companies are doing the same. Further growth in our market will continue to come from small to medium-sized companies. It's more difficult to sell to blue-chip businesses as they have to go through 40 levels of management to get approval.

Sponsorship

Companies with large budgets often combine corporate hospitality with sponsorship deals that include corporate hospitality access to the event for the sponsoring company. Walzel (2014) notes that as a prominent corporate hospitality presence at the event in question often forms part of sponsorship agreements, this presents an important argument for purchasing sponsorship packages and/or initiating sponsorship engagements. In some cases, sponsors may even obtain exclusive rights to official corporate hospitality at the event.

Effectively, sponsorship of, and offering corporate hospitality at, particular events and venues are activities which reinforce each other's impact for those companies in a position to combine the two. For example, a company which becomes the sponsor of a particular football team can enjoy the twin advantages of:

- being associated in the minds of spectators with a game and team they admire, thanks to the advertising on the players' kits and around the stadium;
- impressing the company's key stakeholders through their access to the corporate entertainment facilities at the football ground as well as the chance to meet the players in person, etc.

But although football may provide the most obvious examples, other sports and cultural activities also attract sponsorship deals combined with corporate hospitality. For example, until 2015, through American Express's annual sponsorship of Mercedes-Benz Fashion Week, the premier fashion event in North America (now named New York Fashion Week), American Express cardmembers were invited to an exclusive cardmember-only show at the Fashion Week venue, the Lincoln Center in New York. Guests were given exclusive access to the American Express Skybox, a lounge-style viewing room, in which they could enjoy appetisers, cocktails, a close-up view of the catwalks and the opportunity to mingle with famous fashion designers.

Suppliers

Events and venues

Drake (2008) partly ascribes the growth of corporate hospitality during the past few decades to supply-side factors, notably the rise in number, quality and range of major events, which have created many more opportunities for corporate hospitality to be used as a marketing tool. In the UK, for example, this phenomenon was witnessed in 2014 and 2015, when that country hosted a number of high-profile events including the 2014 Commonwealth Games, the Ryder Cup and the 2015 Rugby World Cup, all of which drove further investment in corporate hospitality packages.

It is clear that the motivation for major events opening their doors to corporate hospitality clients has been financial. Corporate hospitality programmes provide a major revenue source for the owners of sporting and cultural events throughout the world. Indeed, Drake contends that many special or hallmark events would struggle to exist on a regular basis without the support of corporations who consistently provide them with financial support through patronage in terms of attendance, sponsorship and hospitality (ibid.). Titlebaum et al. (2013) estimated that some professional sports organisations generate 50 per cent of all their ticket revenues from luxury suites and premium seating, with the majority of premium ticketing customers being corporations.

Spectator sport is generally held to be the largest sector within the corporate hospitality market, in terms of spending. For example, Cooper (2013) estimated that it accounted for approximately 85 per cent of total expenditure on corporate events in the UK. The connection between corporate hospitality and sports is long-established. One commentator, Crofts (2001), links the origins of corporate hospitality in the UK to the early 1970s when the organisers of the Open Golf Championship gave permission for a catering tent to be erected at the event. Other sports events, seeing this form of hospitality as a means of generating extra revenue, followed suit. But, despite the popularity of spectator sports, there are many signs that the corporate hospitality market is diversifying, and one indication of that is the fact that the use of cultural events to entertain companies' stakeholders is growing in popularity.

Cooper (2013) gives one example of this trend:

> Xerox's corporate activity is not restricted to sport, which can be polarising for an audience. It has also partnered with Cirque du Soleil for the past three years, offering clients the opportunity to see the show, but also to meet some of the artists who perform or do a question-and-answer session with them.

For venues, corporate hospitality is a market with many attractive features, not least the fact that it is one of the most high-spend, high-yield sectors of business events. Many venues regard corporate hospitality as a means of using spare capacity to increase their revenues, quite considerably in many cases. Venues such as football stadia and racetracks with VIP boxes and corporate hospitality suites find that these can be a lucrative source of revenue even during non-match/non-race days, when they can be hired out for other types of business events and social events such as conferences, product launches and dinner dances.

In many cases, the venues used for corporate hospitality already include all of the services and facilities required to provide for the comfort and entertainment of the client's guests.

But often a considerable number of ancillary services are required, such as marquee hire, security staff, lighting and floral arrangements for decoration. An event held in the grounds of a stately home, for example, will call for the services of a number of different suppliers beyond the venue itself.

Catering and activity providers

Beyond the principal beneficiaries of corporate hospitality, the events and venues where they are held, another key category of suppliers is the catering sector. Given the importance placed on high-quality food and beverage for corporate hospitality events, it is common practice for venues to outsource the catering element to companies ranging from local caterers to multinational corporations such as Aramark and Sodexo which offer specialised catering services for corporate events.

But the range of companies engaged in supplying facilities and services for corporate hospitality is extremely wide, and they include what Minnaert (2009) calls 'activity providers' – small companies offering activity or entertainment options for these events. Her diverse list of such providers includes: a big band and DJ service, outdoor activity centres, wine tasting companies, cooking class instructors, a rugby club, a murder mystery agency, an after-dinner speaking service, a yoga retreat, a corporate drumming class and a health spa.

Intermediaries

There are two types of intermediary active in the corporate hospitality market: those working on behalf of buyers and those working on behalf of suppliers.

Agencies working on behalf of buyers

Due to the considerable expense involved in paying for the hire of the required facilities and services, host companies' spending on corporate hospitality events generally represents a significant financial investment. But, those companies are also investing much of their reputation in the corporate hospitality event going successfully, and this can mean taking a considerable risk: by offering corporate hospitality, an organisation is putting itself 'on show' to the people it values and who are important to its continuing success. If anything goes wrong during the event, it is those valued guests who witness the failure, to the considerable embarrassment of the host. For these reasons the planning of any corporate hospitality event must be extremely meticulous and rigorous.

That is precisely why most companies entrust the planning and organisation of their corporate hospitality events to specialist intermediaries – external agencies with the specialist skills and knowledge required to design the event and liaise with the various suppliers. During the event, that leaves the host company to concentrate on their guests, without having to worry about the many logistical aspects of the event.

Intermediaries in corporate hospitality include:

- Specialist agencies, dealing exclusively with the organisation of corporate hospitality events
- Agencies also operating in associated sectors such as product launches, conferences, team-building exercises and incentives
- Business travel management companies offering a corporate entertainment service in addition to their other services
- In-house corporate hospitality organisers employed by the venues themselves, to package specific programmes for corporate clients.

The size of intermediary organisations varies from one-person operations to multi-national conglomerates, for which arranging corporate hospitality is just one element of a much wider portfolio of business. According to Minnaert, corporate hospitality intermediaries offer their clients different levels of assistance ranging from full-service to simply sourcing tickets for an event. One of the respondents in her survey estimated that

> in the UK alone, there are 300–400 corporate hospitality agencies, and 95–96 percent of them are very small. Many simply act as a broker and buy and sell products that are offered by suppliers or by larger corporate hospitality agencies.
>
> (Minnaert, 2009)

Agencies working on behalf of suppliers

These agencies specialise in supporting events rights owners in developing their corporate hospitality products and selling corporate packages for their events. In return for an agreed fee paid by the rights owner, agencies take over the responsibility for the sale of the corporate hospitality tickets and the operational implementation of the events. Acting as the official resale agency, these intermediaries then contact potential customers in order to sell the corporate hospitality packages to them.

Clearly, given the considerable sums of money involved, it is in the interest of host companies to purchase their corporate hospitality products from trustworthy agencies with a proven track record of experience in packaging and selling the type of activity they are seeking for their guests. This sector of business events is characterised by too many cautionary tales of companies being duped by fraudsters selling fake tickets to high-profile events. Buyers are generally advised to avoid being the next victim of such scams by only purchasing tickets directly from the event organiser or from legitimate vendors who are members of a regulatory body, such as STAR (the Society of Ticket Agents and Retailers), in the UK.

Planning corporate hospitality events

Objectives

As with many of the other types of business events under consideration in this book, one of the first steps to be taken when planning corporate hospitality events is to determine the *objectives* for the event in question. Some possible objectives for such events were implied in the section of this chapter focusing on the benefits of using corporate hospitality, but, by way of reiteration, the actual corporate hospitality objectives given by Drake's (2013) respondents were:

- Relationship-building with guests
- Personalised communication with guests
- Access to people who may be a source of new business
- Educating guests about new products/services
- Profile and brand building
- Gaining useful market intelligence from guests.

Nevertheless, Drake, in common with many other researchers in this field, notes that despite the importance of determining the objectives that companies seek from their corporate hospitality events, many such programmes either lacked objectives entirely or those commissioning these events had not clearly defined them and communicated them to others within their organisation (ibid.).

A useful comparison has been made in the academic literature between objectives that reflect a strategic use of corporate hospitality (part of an integrated long-term plan) and those that are indicative of a tactical use of such events (focused on a quick win or other short-term objective). Data gleaned from Bennett's (2003) survey appeared to suggest that UK companies (particularly those in the financial services sector) were largely adopting a strategic approach to their use of corporate hospitality, as indicated by their use of a number of specific actions, including:

- Spending on corporate hospitality at constant levels, in real terms, from year to year, not only in profitable times. Strategic users of corporate hospitality may even spend *more* on corporate hospitality during financial downturns in order to strengthen and maintain their relationships with major clients.
- Conducting formal research to identify and target key customers to invite to corporate hospitality events.
- Establishing clear objectives before selecting an event and choosing whom to invite.
- Integrating corporate hospitality into marketing communications programmes.
- Using corporate hospitality to leverage sponsorships.
- Explicitly linking events to the corporate image and identity of the organisation.

In addition to sound research into the host companies' objectives for the corporate hospitality events, it is generally accepted that certain fundamental conditions must be fulfilled for those events to successfully achieve their aims (Sodexho, 2001):

- Making sure that the target guests attend
- Achieving a good mix of people, both guests and employees
- Finding the appropriate venue
- Excellent organisation
- Providing high-quality catering and service

- Providing enjoyment and fun for guests
- Creating an original, exclusive, interesting and memorable event
- Finding the right event for the right people.

Certain of these factors will now be elaborated upon, to illustrate their significance in the corporate hospitality planning process.

Choice of event/activity

The choice of the particular event or activity that forms the focus for any corporate hospitality experience is a key factor determining the degree of success of this form of relationship marketing, in terms of yielding the best acceptance rates from the invited target market. Many academic researchers as well as practitioners agree that choosing high-profile sports or cultural events can be effective in persuading guests to accept the host company's invitations. In the words of one marketing practitioner, quoted by Drake (2013:241), 'It has to be an event of significance, a big brand event'.

But while a ringside seat at the Moscow State Circus or a close-up view of the Rugby World Cup final from the comfort of a VIP box will always attract guests, a growing number of host companies are taking steps to offer corporate hospitality experiences at events that reflect their company *brand* through an appropriate 'brand fit' between the event and the brand of the host company.

Cuddeford-Jones (2014) offers two examples of firms that plan their corporate hospitality events in terms of this type of brand fit. The tyre company Michelin uses its natural link with motorsport by offering corporate hospitality on its stands at several prominent racing events such as Le Mans, Silverstone and Goodwood. She cites Michelin UK's marketing director for passenger and light truck tyres Alexander Asklov:

> We put our main focus on the Goodwood events because they reflect our premium brand values. The big investment is on the stand which is a large presence. It shows our products to consumers who we don't normally get to engage with, as we sell through distributors. But it also gives us a chance ... to invite key clients and discuss new developments.

Spanish beer brand Estrella Damm uses its exclusive sponsorship deal with FC Barcelona by inviting a few select guests – wholesalers and bar owners from various countries – to come to that team's football matches in Barcelona. Cuddeford-Jones quotes Genna Burchell, brand manager for Estrella Damm distribution company Wells & Young's, who explains:

> It's a really important part of our corporate hospitality package when we're looking to meet up with customers that this would appeal to. It reinforces the Barcelonan heritage of the beer, creating differentiation in a crowded market, as well as giving us an opportunity to reinforce relationships that ultimately increase our market penetration.
>
> (Ibid.)

As well as identifying an event that has a close match with the host company's brand, it is essential that the event should also be one that is attractive to the company's target audience of guests. The challenge of finding events with a broad appeal has been intensified by the growing number of women working at managerial levels in most countries around the world. One of the key findings of the research undertaken by Drake (2013) indicated that events which would continue to draw corporate hospitality audiences needed to be those offering cross-gender appeal. So while sport still accounts for the great majority of corporate hospitality events, there is growing interest in cultural experiences including first-night shows, art exhibitions and theatrical events such as performances of *Cirque du Soleil*.

The choice of guests and hosts

At any corporate hospitality event, it is important to have an appropriate mix of people, notably, the right guests and suitable representatives from the host company's own staff. It is also essential to establish a suitable ratio of hosts to guests, as most guests will expect to spend some time in discussion with the hosts.

Guests

Key to the success of an event is ensuring that the right audience attends. If the host company is spending thousands of euros per guest, then clearly it is important that those people should be of an appropriate level of seniority and should have some decision-making capability. Guests should be invited well in advance of the date of the event, to avoid losing out to other, competing, companies that may invite them to the same event. In order to derive optimum value from the event, the host company should establish at least one important outcome for each guest – what it is that the company wishes to achieve from the conversations that will take place with each guest on the day. Given that corporate hospitality experiences are first and foremost *social* gatherings, it is unlikely that those desired outcomes will include something as ambitious as the signing of a sales contract or a formal agreement of any kind. But other, 'softer', outcomes could include arranging a subsequent appointment with the guest, agreeing on a follow-up call to discuss business, or gaining a valuable introduction to an important colleague of the guest.

Hosts

The success of any corporate hospitality experience also depends upon the performance of the members of the host company's management team who are present at the event. Effective preparation is essential. According to Alison Morris of Huthwaite International, experts in sales, negotiation and communication skill development:

> At the event itself, it is critical to assign the right people to key roles and in each case clearly define responsibilities and expectations. This means ensuring the right people are on hand, from the initial 'meeters and greeters' to the 'statues' – those who should typically stay in one place and to whom invitees are brought. Everyone

involved needs to be aware that, even though the event may appear to be primarily social – or even casual – it is a shop window for the host company.

(Pharmafield, 2004).

She offers the following advice to corporate hospitality hosts:

At a social event you are not seeking to transact business. What you are trying to do, by contrast is gain information, extend relationships, perhaps give some information about yourself or make some progress in a major deal. The key to success therefore centres on influencing rather than selling. Yet this is a social event. You can't 'influence' all the time, for that would be crass; it's outside the rules, which are that you have got to have some fun! This is precisely why effective influencers make a conscious distinction between 'social' and 'purposeful' conversation. They devote an appropriate amount of air time to each and switch seamlessly between the two modes of communication. Similarly, they recognise the value of both the 'push' style of persuasion or influencing – that is, giving information and putting forward ideas – and the 'pull' style of asking questions and building on others' ideas, depending upon the topic or situation in question.

(Ibid.)

Another commentator emphasises the importance of achieving balance in hosts' interactions with corporate hospitality guests: 'Don't go too overboard on business talk. The trick is to create an entertaining and enjoyable experience not to break your guest down with sales talk when he is trying to watch Maria Sharapova serve.' (Craik, 2015)

Representatives of the host companies can – and should – learn these skills. Bennett noted that satisfaction with corporate hospitality was higher among businesses that formally trained their staff how to perform at such events: 'This suggests the desirability of incorporating dedicated corporate hospitality training into mainstream interpersonal skills training programmes' (Bennett, 2003:239).

Chapter summary

This chapter began with a general discussion of relationship marketing and established corporate hospitality – also known as corporate entertainment or B2B hospitality – as a technique used by organisations to achieve their relationship marketing objectives, notably forging stronger connections with their high-value clients. The way in which lavish spending incurred by companies using corporate hospitality can create problems linked to the possible perception of bribery or extravagance, by corporate stakeholders was discussed, as were the issues surrounding possible clashes of interest with genuine sports fans. The chapter analysed the various stakeholders operating in the corporate hospitality market, underlining buyers' use of sponsorship and the importance of hallmark events as a focus of these occasions. The roles of the different intermediaries in this market were reviewed. The chapter ended with a review of best practice in planning corporate hospitality events.

CASE STUDY 9.1: THE INVESTEC DERBY AT EPSOM DOWNS RACECOURSE

Epsom Downs

Epsom Downs Racecourse

According to Mintel (Spectator Sports – UK – October 2016), horse racing is Britain's second largest spectator sport, after football. This makes it a popular choice of corporate hospitality activity. One of the UK's best-known horse racing venues is located on Epsom Downs, a large stretch of hilly countryside in the county of Surrey, close to London. Epsom Downs Racecourse (http://epsom.thejockeyclub.co.uk/) is situated on the North Downs, located 30 minutes from central London by train. It is part of The Jockey Club, the largest commercial group in British horse racing. In addition to Epsom Downs, the Jockey Club owns 14 other leading racecourses in the UK, including Aintree, home of the Crabbie's Grand National; Cheltenham, stage for the prestigious Cheltenham Festival; and Newmarket, the home of horse racing. Epsom Downs Racecourse hosts 11 race days each year, including one of Britain's best-known national sporting events, The Investec Derby Festival.

The Investec Derby Festival

The Investec Derby Festival is held over two days each year, the first Friday and Saturday of June. The name of the event derives from the international specialist banking and asset management group, Investec, who became the event's sponsor in 2009, with a sponsorship deal that was extended in 2017 until 2026. That year, Investec also launched a new partnership with Steinhoff International, owners of the Poundland chain of shops and activated the 'Poundland Hill' for racegoers to enjoy free entertainment on the famous 'Hill' area of the racecourse.

The first day of the Investec Derby Festival, Friday, is known as Ladies' Day and it generally attracts around 50,000 spectators. The main race on the opening day of the Festival is the Investec Oaks. The Saturday, popularly known as Derby Day, is when approximately 100,000 spectators gather at the Epsom Downs Racecourse to enjoy a spectacular day of racing. The main race on Derby Day is the Investec Epsom Derby itself. These two races are among the most prestigious of Britain's five classic horse races, the others being the 2000 Guineas Stakes; the 1000 Guineas Stakes; and the St Leger Stakes. The Derby, which is run over a distance of 2,420 metres, is held in such high esteem that in 2012 the Queen chose to open her Diamond Jubilee celebrations at this race, confirming its status as one of the UK's most popular sporting events.

Corporate hospitality at the Investec Derby Festival

Being present at the Investec Derby Festival is one of the UK's most sought-after corporate hospitality experiences. The venue's corporate hospitality packages allow guests the opportunity to enjoy every aspect of this iconic racing occasion in style. Within the venue, different packages are available in three separate locations:

The Tattenham Straight Suite

This glass-fronted structure suite is positioned alongside the final 200 metres of the racetrack, giving guests a clear view of the pivotal point on the course. Private tables are available for ten guests.

The Winning Post

The Winning Post is a contemporary-styled marquee located close to the finishing line and directly opposite the Royal Box. Bookings are taken for private tables of eight.

The Queen's Stand

The restaurant Chez Roux @ Blue Riband offers a four-course a la carte menu designed and delivered by celebrity chefs Albert Roux OBE and Michel Roux Jr. Private tables for two or more guests are available.

Beyond the standard packages, there are a large number of ways in which the corporate hospitality experience can be personalised and enhanced for guests. For example, some corporate clients request complete refurbishments to their hospitality spaces, displaying their company brands throughout the room and hiring their own teams, chefs or entertainers to host their guests. Other possible add-ons include the possibility of guests landing a helicopter on site or being chauffeur-driven to their location in a Bentley.

However, there is one constant: dressing up formally is obligatory for all guests and strict dress codes are enforced during the two days of the Investec Derby Festival:

Ladies' Day:

- Gentlemen must wear a jacket, collar and tie.
- Ladies are asked to wear a fascinator or hat.
- Jeans, sports shorts, denim or trainers are not acceptable.
- Children should be dressed smartly.

Derby Day:

- Either black or grey morning dress with a top hat, service dress or full national costume is obligatory for gentlemen.
- Ladies must wear formal day dress, or a tailored trouser suit, with a hat or substantial fascinator.
- Children should be dressed smartly.

While horse racing naturally takes centre stage, there are many other sources of entertainment on offer at the Epsom Downs Racecourse during the Investec Derby Festival. During the day, guests are able to observe and interact with some of the UK's top mixologists and chefs or relax in the hot tubs and seating lounges, which allows guests to spend time with each other on a personal level. During the racing season, music takes centre stage during the official after-parties and concerts which, in the past, have featured performers such as Sarah Cox, Madness, Boyzone, James Blunt and Blondie.

Selling corporate hospitality packages

The Epsom Downs Racecourse corporate hospitality team is made up of six full-time employees whose job it is to promote re-bookings and sell new spaces. The corporate hospitality market for the Investec Derby Festival widens to a global catchment area, with boxes being the most popular spaces and often selling out first, followed by grandstand suites where companies can book an entire room for corporate awaydays, or entertaining clients. A huge proportion of the boxes are sold to Dubai- and Qatar-based companies, many of which have business interests in British horse racing through racehorse breeding, ownership and sponsorship. This adds a new dimension to the sales process, with cultural issues needing to be taken into consideration.

Epsom Downs Racecourse's official hospitality partner is Keith Prowse, who sell all the corporate hospitality packages for the venue. Keith Prowse acts as official hospitality provider for many venues and stadia across the UK. For the Investec Derby Festival, key account managers who are familiar with the venue and the products are assigned by the company to ensure a consistent sales approach, leading through to on-the-day delivery.

The racecourse regularly invites prospective corporate clients to a taster day at the racecourse, during which they are able to sample the corporate hospitality packages offered by the venue. This has proved to be a valuable sales technique for the racecourse and has resulted in new business on every occasion.

It takes 13,000 casual hospitality staff to deliver a successful event, including waiting staff, bar staff and room managers, as well as 40 managers from across the Jockey Club to oversee the operation and maintain Jockey Club standards. There are 102 chefs on site, with 30 kitchen porters ensuring food is delivered to every table seamlessly.

Challenges

Challenges to the Investec Derby Festival include competition in the marketplace, with many other large sporting venues also gearing up for their biggest events of their year at a similar time to the Derby, in a relatively saturated marketplace. Long-term sales agreements and rebooking offers help Epsom Downs Racecourse face up to the competition and maintain a busy diary. In order to remain competitive, it is also essential that the racecourse does not stand still, and there are constant reviews in the food offering, furniture, customer journey and overall experience taking place during the year to ensure that the event grows year on year.

IT'S MY JOB
EMANUELA STIGLIANI, CORPORATE HOSPITALITY MANAGER, FEDERAZIONE ITALIANA RUGBY

In 2001, I graduated with a degree in Communication Science from the University of Trieste, my home town. My thesis was on the theme of the main sports event in Trieste, 'La Barcolana', which is a huge regatta, with over 2,000 sailing boats participating together in the same race.

During my final year at the University of Trieste, I moved to the Universitat Autònoma de Barcelona through the Erasmus exchange programme. Directly following that experience, I studied for a master's degree in Sports Marketing and another in European Public Relations in Rome.

My interest in working in the events industry began while I was still a student. I was working part-time as a cashier in an arthouse cinema (in Trieste) when my boss asked me to organise an event for directors and actors, at the cinema and in other locations in the city. I enjoyed this experience very much, and found that organising events suited my character, as I am generally pragmatic and well organised.

My first job after graduation was in an events and communication agency in Rome, called FUN. I had just finished my probation period when the agency acquired a new client who was sponsoring the 'Casa Azzurri' (the hospitality venue that forms the focal point for Italians following their national team) during the 2002 FIFA World Cup, which took place in South Korea and Japan. I was chosen to travel to Japan to organise everything, even though I had practically no experience of corporate hospitality. It was an unforgettable time in my life. In just one month I had to manage so many things and work with so many different people, both Europeans and Japanese, from politicians to CEOs, from waiters to graphic designers, hotel managers, singers and models. The logistical operations were truly international, and due to the time zone difference, I found myself working with Japanese partners by day and Italian colleagues during the night, leaving me only three or four hours each night for sleeping. It was a huge challenge for me, but I learned so much from that experience –personally, professionally and socially.

After three years of working with that agency and then a short spell spent organising training courses and workshops for the World Wildlife Fund in Barcelona, I was employed as Corporate Hospitality Manager by the Italian Rugby Federation, FIR (Federazione Italiana Rugby) in Rome, and I have been working in that job ever since.

In 2006, the FIR was going through a period of rapid development. With the addition of Italy into the Six Nations Championship, rugby in Italy was changing from an amateur sport into a professional one. At that time, there was no Event and Marketing Department within the FIR, so we based our initial events activity on what other members of the Six Nations were already doing. We began by creating an entertainment village outside the Stadio Flaminio, the venue for the Six Nations tournament home matches in Rome. We then introduced the first corporate hospitality packages for sale during the Six Nations rugby matches held in Italy.

In 2012, the FIR moved the Six Nations games from the Stadio Flaminio to the Stadio Olimpico, which is part of the vast Foro Italico sports complex in Rome. With its huge hospitality area, this new venue created exciting opportunities for expanding corporate hospitality events, and that became my responsibility from the beginning.

There is no such thing as a typical working day for me at the FIR. My duties depend on which phase we are in, regarding our corporate hospitality offers.

The cycle begins with me creating our new range of corporate hospitality packages, planned in detail, with a clear business plan. During this stage, I do all the necessary research for new ideas, holding many meetings within the FIR and with suppliers to negotiate prices. I then need to focus on communicating our offer to the market. So I work on updating my database and preparing the new brochure, newsletter and website, which are launched at the moment we open sales.

After that, the commercial phase begins: contacting old clients and meeting new ones to explain why our services could be of interest to them. This can include inviting them on venue tours in order to help them experience the impact of our stadium. This sales work is my responsibility and mine alone, as we do not work with any external agencies but rather organise everything internally. Within the FIR, the Corporate Hospitality team works closely with the Marketing Department, who deal with anything related to sponsorship and partnership.

The final phase is the actual delivery, which includes everything from managing the distribution of tickets to organising accreditation passes for participants and giving them the required information on security, etc. This is the most adrenaline-filled phase, with many hours of work per day, a lot of stress and a thousand things to do in a very short time.

Overall, my job brings me much personal satisfaction – and a few challenges too. I especially enjoy the production aspect of corporate hospitality. With the Italians' love of good food and beverages, it is important for us to offer the very best in catering. I love researching ideas for new dishes as well as using imaginative furniture and decor in order to surprise and delight our clients. That is the most creative part of my job.

The main challenge is a commercial one – companies in Italy are not as used to investing in PR and corporate hospitality as companies in other countries. So we need to work harder to win business in the Italian market than we do in the British or French markets, for example, from which clients come more easily.

My advice to anyone wishing to succeed in a career in corporate hospitality would be:

- Always plan ahead!
- Be customer-focused.
- Be precise and clear in communicating with all of your stakeholders, internal and external.
- Always be positive and develop a can-do attitude. Nobody likes to work with negative people.
- Take care of every detail. They are all very important.
- Be prepared to do everything, from simple operational jobs to dealing with people in high positions of authority.
- Think creatively. Corporate hospitality is very much about finding solutions.
- Be ready to work in a team, learn multitasking, and be very flexible and cool under pressure.
- Ask for help from other professionals when you need to. You cannot know everything.

References

Bennett, R. (2003) Corporate hospitality: Executive indulgence or vital corporate communications weapon? *Corporate Communications: An International Journal* 8(4): 229–240.

Buttle, F. (ed.) (1996) *Relationship Marketing: Theory and practice*, London: Sage.

Christopher, M., Payne, A. and Ballantyne, D. (1991) *Relationship Marketing: Bringing quality, customer service, and marketing together*, Oxford: Butterworth-Heinemann.

Coates, S. (2016) Corporate hospitality: A balance between business and pleasure. Available at: https://squaremile.com/features/corporate-hospitality-business-and-pleasure/.

Cooper, L. (2013) Putting the wow factor into hospitality. *Marketing Week*, 31 July.

Craik, D. (2015) The definitive guide on the best approach to corporate hospitality. Available at: https://realbusiness.co.uk/hr-and-management/2015/04/28/the-definitive-guide-on-the-best-approach-to-corporate-hospitality/.

Croft, M. (2001) Perfect pitch. *Marketing Week*, 29 March.

Crofts, A. (2001) *Corporate Entertaining as a Marketing Tool*, Chalford: Management Books 2000 Ltd.

Crowther, P. (2011) Marketing event outcomes: From tactical to strategic. *International Journal of Event and Festival Management* 2(1): 68–82.

Cuddeford-Jones, M. (2014) Corporate hospitality: Boost your formula for winning over allies. *Marketing Week*, 30 April.

Drake, C. N. (2008) Corporate hospitality: An effective tool of influence or an executive extravagance? Towards a conceptual framework. CAUTHE 2008: Tourism and Hospitality Research, Training and Practice.

Drake, C. N. (2013) Maximising effectiveness of corporate hospitality programmes at Australian special events. *International Journal of Event and Festival Management* 4(3): 236–248.

Flyn, C. (2012) MP opponents of plain-packaging for cigarettes accepted hospitality from tobacco giant. Available at: https://www.telegraph.co.uk/news/politics/9361730/MP-opponents-of-plain-packaging-for-cigarettes-accepted-hospitality-from-tobacco-giant.html.

Hopkins, K. (2011) The Colosseum: Emblem of Rome. Available at: http://www.bbc.co.uk/history/ancient/romans/colosseum_01.shtml.

Minnaert, L. (2009) Corporate hospitality in times of an economic downturn: A case study of corporate entertaining in the UK, in Celuch, K. and Davidson, R. (eds) (2009) *Advances in Business Tourism Research*, Arnhem: ATLAS Publications, pp. 41–51.

Mintel (2008) Corporate hospitality (Industrial report), May. London: Mintel.

Morgan, R. M. and Hunt, S. D. (1994) The commitment-trust theory of relationship marketing. *Journal of Marketing* 58: 20–38.

Murray-West, R. (2006) £14,000 World Cup packages to sell out, *The Telegraph*, 19 January.

Palmer, R., Lindgreen, A. and Vanhamme, J. (2005) Relationship marketing: Schools of thought and future research directions. *Marketing Intelligence & Planning* 23(3): 313–330.

Peppers, D. and Rogers, M. (1996) As products get smarter, companies will have to focus on relationships. Forbes ASAP Supplement, 69.

Pharmafield (2004) Making corporate hospitality work for you. Available at: www.pharmafield.co.uk/features/2004/04/Making-corporate-hospitality-work-for-you.

Sodexho (2001) Survival Guide to the Season, Paris: Sodexho.

Titlebaum, P., Lawrence, H., Moberg, C. and Ramos, C. (2013) Fortune 100 companies: Insight into premium seating ownership. *Sport Marketing Quarterly* 22(1): 48.

Turner, C. (2015) Wimbledon's empty seats blamed on corporate guests choosing wine and steak over tennis, *The Telegraph*, 8 July.

Walzel, S. (2011) Corporate Hospitality bei Sportevents – Konzeption eines Wirkungsmodells, Wiesbaden: Gabler Verlag.

Walzel, S. (2014) Events management and the hospitality industry, in Beech, J., Kaiser, S. and Kaspar, R. (eds) *The Business of Events Management*, London: Pearson Education.

Warren, C. J. and Warren, C. (2015) Industrial marketing in sport: Understanding season ticket renewal across account types. *International Journal of Sport Management, Recreation and Tourism* 20: 1–19.

Destination marketing for business events

Chapter objectives

On completion of this chapter the reader should be able to:

- Understand the role of convention bureaus as destination marketing organisations.
- Distinguish between the different models of governance and funding for convention bureaus.
- Understand the range of marketing techniques employed by convention bureaus.

A history of convention bureaus

The considerable economic – and other – benefits that business events can bring to the destinations in which they are held have created a situation in which there is often intense competition to host the types of events covered in this book. With an abundance of competing destinations and venues available for the hosting of conferences, incentive trips and other types of business events, effective marketing strategies are key to winning them and reaping the benefits of hosting them. A range of different stakeholders may be involved in marketing their services and facilities to the planners of business events. For example, the organisers of a major conference may choose to hold it in a particular destination as a result of the efforts of the marketing team of an international hotel chain with a property in that city. But the major responsibility for marketing destinations as locations for the hosting of business events most often lies with those destination marketing organisations (DMOs) known as convention bureaus. Over a century of professional destination marketing has demonstrated that an effective convention bureau can be crucial to the overall success that any destination has in attracting business events. This chapter explores the possible structures, funding models and marketing activities of convention bureaus, but begins with a historical perspective on the development of these organisations that have come to represent a major force in the marketing of destinations for business events.

The origins of business events destination marketing are often traced back to an article by the journalist Milton J. Carmichael, who, in February 1896, wrote in the *Detroit Journal*:

> During the past few years Detroit has built up a name as a convention city, delegates coming from hundreds of miles, manufacturers holding their yearly consultations around our hotels, and all without any effort on the part of the citizens, or any special attention paid to them after they got here. They have simply come to Detroit because they wanted to ... Can Detroit, by making an effort, this year secure the holding of 200 or 300 of these national conventions during the year of '97? It will mean the bringing here of thousands and thousands of men from every city in the union ... and they will expend millions of dollars.
>
> (Ford and Peeper, 2007:1107).

In the same article, Carmichael argued that local businesses should join forces to begin a formal and organised promotion of Detroit as a desirable convention destination, in order to attract more business events. As a result, less than two weeks later, on 19 February 1896, members of the Chamber of Commerce joined with the Manufacturers Club to form a new organisation, The Detroit Convention and Businessmen's League, which had the objective of promoting that city as 'a desirable convention destination' (ibid.:1107).

This model was soon followed by other cities, in North America and beyond, that were motivated to attract business events because of the economic benefits they offered as well as the opportunity to project a favourable image of the destination in order to attract inward investment. In 1915, the International Association of Convention & Visitor Bureaus was founded, with the aim of enabling the exchange of information about the meetings industry among its membership and to encourage sound professional practices within the industry. When the association held its first meeting in 1920, there were 28 member cities (Gartrell, 1994). Almost a century later, that association, by now known as Destinations International (https://destinationsinternational.org/), reported that it had members representing 575 destinations (Destinations International, 2017). And while the majority of Destinations International members are DMOs located in North America, other national and international associations of convention bureaus, such as the Association of Australian Convention Bureaux and the Asian Association of Convention and Visitor Bureaus, have been created as convention bureaus throughout the world have proliferated.

A small minority of those convention bureaus operate at the national level, promoting their countries as a whole to the organisers of business events (for example, the German Convention Bureau, the Finland Convention Bureau, and the Thailand Convention and Exhibition Bureau); and an even smaller number of convention bureaus are responsible for marketing a specific region of a country (for example, the Hauts-de-France Convention Bureau, which markets eight major business events cities in the north of France). But the vast majority of convention bureaus are local, marketing an individual city or metropolitan area as a destination for business events.

In North America, the term 'convention and visitor bureau' (CVB) is in common use. According to Gartrell (1994) the term CVB generally refers to DMOs with responsibility for developing, promoting and maintaining their image as an attractive destination, not only for organisers of business events but also for leisure visitors. By way of contrast, in other continents the term 'convention bureau' is generally reserved for organisations that are almost exclusively involved in winning business events such as conferences and incentive trips for the destinations they represent, while the marketing of the same destinations to the *leisure* market is usually the responsibility of organisations with titles that often include the word 'tourism'. For example, while the Spanish city of Valencia is marketed to the leisure market by Valencia Tourism, a separate, but linked, organisation, the Valencia Convention Bureau, is responsible for promoting the city to the business events market.

According to Vallee (2008:162), a convention bureau's tasks most commonly include working to:

- solicit, qualify and confirm groups to hold meetings, conventions and trade shows in the area it represents;
- assist meeting groups that have confirmed through attendance building and convention servicing;
- manage the destination brand through awareness building and customer relationship management;
- market the destination through targeted promotional and sales activities;
- facilitate relationships between meeting manager and travel trade buyers and sellers, with sellers generally composed of local businesses offering products and services;
- service visitors, including convention delegates, in the destination to encourage them to stay longer and see more of the area.

These tasks will be explored in detail later in this chapter, following an analysis of how convention bureaus are governed and funded.

The governance and funding of convention bureaus

The organisational structures, governance and funding mechanisms of convention bureaus vary enormously between and within individual countries. However, most of them are linked, to a greater or lesser degree, to the local governing authority of the territory they represent, essentially as a source of all, or some, of their funding. The vast majority of convention bureaus representing individual cities or local authority administrative areas may be categorised under one of the following three models of governance and funding, as described by Whisenant (2012).

The convention bureau as a government agency

Convention bureaus operating under this structure are usually a department within local government, reporting either directly to the political leadership (the mayor, for example) or to a local government manager or administrator. They often work with an appointed oversight or advisory committee made up of government representatives and stakeholders representing the business events industry, such as venue managers, hoteliers and DMCs.

The convention bureau as an independent agency

In this model, convention bureaus are free-standing, independent agencies, most often not-for-profit organisations, with their own governing board of directors who hire the executive director, establish and oversee the policies and procedures of the organisation, and give overall direction to the convention bureau's programme of work.

The funding for these convention bureaus and their programmes of work comes primarily from local governments who enter into a contracted arrangement with the convention bureau to provide marketing activities for the destination and pay for such services through local taxation receipts. Independent convention bureaus may also have other revenue streams, such as receipts from advertising in its publications and on its website, and in some cases, membership fees.

Independent convention bureaus may be non-membership organisations or may be membership-based. Non-membership independent convention bureaus provide services to all business events stakeholders in the destination; membership-based independent convention bureaus (sometimes referred to as 'pay-to-play' convention bureaus) provide limited services to all stakeholders in the destination while providing a much higher level of service and benefits to their members.

The convention bureau as a function of a Chamber of Commerce or other economic development agency

The task of promoting a city as a business events destination is often undertaken as a function, division or department of the city's Chamber of Commerce or other economic development agency (EDA). In these cases, the Chamber/EDA usually acts on a contractual basis, with funding for the marketing programme coming from the local government. In some cases, the Chamber also makes a financial commitment to the programme, most often through personnel and/or office-related costs.

Table 10.1 shows the advantages and disadvantages of these three convention bureau governance and funding models.

In the US, a major source of income for convention bureaus is the local transient or hotel occupancy tax that local authorities can charge visitors. As revenue collected in this way is used to fund the marketing of the destination, it directly supports the marketing activities of the relevant convention bureau or goes towards funding the construction and operation of conference centres. However, this system of collecting hypothecated

Table 10.1 Advantages and disadvantages of convention bureau (CB) governance and funding models

	Advantages	Disadvantages
The CB as a government agency	• Direct accountability to the funding source • Direct line of administrative supervision (reporting directly to one person) • Utilises administrative, personnel and accounting systems already in place in local government • Interaction and coordination with other local government departments • Some cost savings (office space rental, administrative costs, etc.) • Agency is perceived as neutral, not favouring any one stakeholder interest • Overall long-term organisational stability • Personnel benefits (insurance, retirement, time off, etc.) on a par with local government employees	• Possibility of political influence on the CB's programme of work and/or staffing decisions • If not involved in an advisory/oversight capacity, industry stakeholders may feel excluded from the decision-making process

(*Continued*)

Table 10.1 (Continued)

	Advantages	Disadvantages
The CB as an independent agency	• Independent CBs tend to be less bureaucratic in structure and are free to operate more on a business model • Members of independent CBs' board of directors tend to be individuals who have experience in the business events industry and who have a direct vested interest in seeing the work of the CB being successful • CB staff are directly accountable to a board of directors for carrying out the agenda and programme of work established by the board • Salary and benefit programmes in independent CBs tend to be closer to market equivalency, making it easier to attract and retain experienced and qualified professionals • Since they are not government agencies, independent CBs have the freedom to develop non-tax revenue streams	• Local government may feel a sense of diminished control of a programme of work they are largely responsible for funding • If non-tax revenues become an overly important source of CB funding, a larger portion of management and time resources may have to be directed to that function rather than to the primary function of marketing the destination • If a membership-based CB model is used, there is an inherent structural bias towards marketing and promoting members over non-members, often leading to dissatisfaction among non-members • Membership-based CBs often have to allocate personnel resources to a Membership Director/Manager, whose responsibility it is to recruit and retain members and to provide member services rather than the function of marketing the destination
The CB as a function of a Chamber of Commerce or other economic development agency (EDA)	• If the Chamber/EDA has good standing/reputation in the community, that good standing lends credibility to the CB and to its programme of work • Chambers/EDAs generally represent a very broad cross-section of a community's business, government and civic leadership, and those resources, skills and influence in the community can be made available to assist and enhance the work of the CB • There is often a cost saving for both the Chamber/EDA and the CB through the sharing of administrative, personnel, and operating expenses	• Chambers/EDAs and CBs have somewhat different missions and objectives • Chambers/EDA boards of directors are not generally experienced in or focused on the development of their city as a business events destination • If the Chamber/EDA does not have a good standing/ reputation in a community, that lack of good standing can be detrimental to the programme of work of the CB • In communities with multiple Chambers of Commerce, the placement of the CB within any one Chamber can lead to feelings of favouritism, exclusion or preferential treatment towards one community over another on the part of the CB

Source: Adapted from Whisenant (2012).

taxes to subsidise the costs of destination marketing has not been widely adopted outside the US, in part due to concerns about making destinations more expensive and therefore less competitive. In most countries, contributions from local authorities and members' fees remain the two major sources of funding for convention bureaus.

The marketing activities of convention bureaus

In previous chapters, the roles of various intermediaries operating on behalf of *buyers* have been examined – for example, PCOs, DMCs, incentive houses and exhibition organisers. But convention bureaus may be considered as intermediaries acting on behalf of *suppliers* in their destinations – conference centres, hotels, restaurants, conference interpreters and all of the other businesses that benefit when a business event is hosted in their city. Naturally, most suppliers engage in their own marketing activities in their effort to win business. But the marketing of the destination as a whole is generally the remit of the convention bureau and its primary function. In order to attract business events, convention bureaus focus their marketing efforts on gaining the attention and interest of the professionals who choose – or influence the choice of – the destinations for the meetings, incentive trips, etc. that they organise. This section of the chapter examines the range of traditional marketing tools used by convention bureaus to influence the decisions of meeting planners, incentive organisers, etc. in their favour. Chapter 14 of this book, which focuses on technology, includes an analysis of the technology-based tools that convention bureaus may use to supplement their use of the marketing techniques described in the rest of this chapter.

A collaborative approach

As the content of the previous chapters of this book demonstrates, the business events industry is one that is composed of many different stakeholders at several levels, playing various roles. The success of any convention bureau's mission primarily depends on the active support of the various stakeholders operating in the destination. Therefore, a key role of most convention bureaus is to facilitate collaboration between the various components operating in their destination by playing a leadership and coordinating role. Wang (2008) highlights the importance of this role, observing that convention bureaus are often expected to provide leadership in initiating, managing and maintaining their destination's marketing networks. This requires them to be skilful in coordinating partnerships between the public and private sectors, between normally competing entities such as hotels, restaurants and attractions, and other diverse constituents within the community. Such partnerships are at the core of collaborative destination marketing. According to Wang:

> collaborative destination marketing arrangements ... involve a number of stakeholders (both public and private) working interactively on a common issue or problem domain through a process of exchange of ideas and expertise and pooling of financial and human resources ... Examples of collaborative destination marketing may include joint promotion campaigns, participating in co-op programmes for trade

shows and advertising, organising familiarisation tours … information and market intelligence sharing, and contributing to destination events, among others.

(Ibid.:191)

The principal collaborative marketing techniques will now be analysed, beginning with destination branding and positioning.

Destination branding and positioning

While the concept of branding has been applied to corporations and consumer products for many decades, the practice of destinations formulating brand strategies only began to appear during the 1990s, when DMOs started applying the concepts and techniques of product branding into their own operational field.

Now, it is widely considered to be a critical mission for each DMO to develop a coherent brand image that clearly positions its destination in the marketplace as a viable and desirable location for tourism and events of all kinds. Brand development is now generally accepted as an indispensable tool in enabling DMOs to present their destinations as places that are distinctive, memorable and clearly distinguished from their competitors. This widespread adoption of destination branding as a technique is in stark contrast to early practices in destination marketing, which relied upon the promotion of product features alone as a means of differentiating places from their competitors. But as so many destinations can now offer attractive features such as good accessibility, a range of venue and accommodation options and interesting things to do or see, the need for individual destinations to distinguish themselves from competing cities has become critical. The process of branding and positioning a destination therefore goes far beyond the simple promotion of the destination's features to disseminating strong, convincing messages about its unique character.

Destination branding seeks to influence the mental image that visitors hold for any individual country or city. Destination image has been defined as the 'expression of all objective knowledge, impressions, prejudice, imaginations, and emotional thoughts an individual or group might have of a particular place' (Lawson and Baud-Bovy, 1977, cited by Milman and Pizam, 1995). The image that any person may have of a particular destination usually depends on various factors, most of which are beyond the control of DMOs, including how the media present the country or city in question and the stories that visitors to the destination tell their friends and family upon returning home. But effective branding can also influence which associations are held about any destination and how strongly they are held. A favourable destination image is a key element in the decision-making process of anyone choosing a location for a business event and for potential participants (if attendance is optional) considering whether or not to attend.

Harrill (2005:33) offers a succinct guide to the steps to be followed by any DMO seeking to brand its destination:

- Supported by marketing research, first, define the unique selling points that separate your destination from the competition.
- Then produce and prioritise a series of crisp and clear motivational messages ... that address the positive visitor characteristics of the community.
- Next, craft a market 'positioning statement' that describes the destination and separates it from other competitors.
- Finally, consider creating a new theme line and graphic logo for the destination that supports the positioning statement.

However, various authors have emphasised the unique challenges involved in branding any destination. Morgan et al. (2010), for example, focus on the constraints to destination branding presented by the lack of control over the destination product and marketing programmes, comparing this with the branding of consumer products, for which a single organisation directs the product development and marketing activities. In the case of complex, multi-attributed destinations such as entire countries or cities, the DMO itself has little or no control over the features and quality of the product it is responsible for marketing. Features such as the destination's geography and climate and the social/demographic make-up of its residents cannot be changed in response to consumer demand. Even as far as their destinations' facilities and services are concerned, DMOs have only minimal control over the supply, quality and pricing of essential elements such as venues, accommodation and transport links.

Moreover, for any destination, its branding is made more complex by the great diversity of stakeholders and how suppliers promote their own facilities and services through their individual marketing programmes which may or may not be in harmony with the overall destination brand. Baker and Cameron (2008) highlight the challenges created by the issue of multiple stakeholders operating in any destination and the complex relationship among them which can present an obstacle for an effective destination branding process. Overcoming these challenges and creating a strong, unified destination brand involves the DMO gaining the cooperation and collaboration from all stakeholder groups, and in particular the suppliers.

A further challenge for those seeking to brand a destination is the existence of diverse target groups. Individual cities, for example, may promote themselves as attractive places in which to study, invest or retire, as well as places to visit. Furthermore, even within the single category of visitors, it is clear that multiple target groups exist, including various types of leisure tourists and, closer to the theme of this book, those choosing destinations for business events and those attending them.

A survey of the academic and practitioner literature on destination branding reveals that, despite the importance of business events for destinations, almost all of the research on this topic focuses on the leisure tourism market. One notable exception is the research undertaken by Hankinson, who contrasts the brand image attributes that are relevant to both target groups, observing that in the case of leisure tourism, visitors are interested in the touristic potential of the place, while those seeking destinations for business events have other types of requirements such as a wide choice of venues, central locations, everything in close proximity, etc. (Hankinson, 2005). But the same author goes on to note that some of the brand image attributes considered important in the field of leisure tourism are also valued by business events participants: physical environment, accessibility, strength of reputation and the characteristics of the local population. He explains this overlap by the fact that business events participants have the same interests and expectations as leisure tourists at certain times during their trips – namely, during the hours when they are not engaged in their business-related activities.

Harrill (2005:34) also emphasises the overlap between the destination attributes that hold an appeal for leisure tourists and those that are attractive for planners of business events:

> When meeting planners are asked what their top reason was for choosing a particular destination, the answer is universally the destination itself. This means that planners choose meeting destinations (after they are comfortable that adequate convention facilities are available) based on the unique appeal of the particular destination – the community's personality, culture, heritage or qualities that distinguish it from other communities. Thus, when attempting to motivate meeting planners, convention bureaus should wrap their convention product and meeting 'hardware' with their positioning statement and compelling leisure tourism benefits.

Hankinson concludes that in branding their destinations for business events planners, DMOs must remember that organisers' decisions for choosing a destination for business events will not be based primarily on the touristic characteristics of the place but more on the functional attributes required by the event (quality of the conference facilities, the choice of venues, the quality of hotel accommodation and accessibility). The ambience-related attributes have an important role in the selection process, but the functional attributes are still the first decision criteria.

The academic and practitioner literature on destination branding provides very few case studies of destinations that have attempted to brand themselves with the specific aim of targeting the business events market. Nevertheless, it is the case that a few cities have created taglines or 'theme lines' – defined by Pike (2005) as a public articulation of a destination's brand positioning strategy – that hold a certain appeal for the business events market. The Polish city of Wroclaw, for example, has 'The Meeting Place' as its slogan; and Manchester's convention bureau uses the tagline 'Where Great Minds Meet'. A further example was created in 2016 when, following their city's hosting of the G20 Summit, Hangzhou's DMO, Business Events Hangzhou, introduced a new logo and tagline as part of its branding of the city as a business events destination. The trade press reported that 'Hangzhou is now China's first city with an official MICE destination brand, and with the new tagline, "Hangzhou, Inspiring New Connections", the city hopes to become a leading MICE destination globally' (M&C/Asia, 2016).

To what extent might a destination's leisure tourism brand even be counterproductive in terms of how it is perceived by business events organisers? It might be argued that destinations that position themselves by emphasising the laid-back, easy-going, 'mañana,

mañana' personality of the destination may inadvertently make themselves somewhat less attractive to business events organisers for whom guaranteed efficiency, promptness of delivery and immediate solving of problems are qualities they seek. A similar issue is highlighted by Anholt in his introduction to the ETC/UNWTO Handbook on tourism destination branding (ETC/UNWTO, 2009:13) where he cautions that (a focus on leisure tourism) may create 'a skewed, "soft", leisure-oriented nation brand which conflicts with the country's reputation as an exporter of quality products, a serious political player, a technological power, or a suitable destination for investment'. Certainly, more research into the potential for leisure/business destination 'brand clash' is required.

The rest of this chapter focuses on some of the key marketing activities that convention bureaus use in order to win business events for their destinations. As has been noted in this section, DMOs have very limited control over the destination 'product'. Therefore, their effective use of the 'promotion' element of the marketing mix is all the more fundamental to their success. Moreover, the destination's brand should run consistently through all of any convention bureau's marketing communications; and, for its marketing communications programme to be successful, it must enjoy the proactive participation of the destination's suppliers, in terms of their own marketing communications.

Advertising

Despite the considerable cost of advertising, it remains one of the most widely used techniques employed by convention bureaus to enhance awareness of their destination brand and motivate business events planners to consider their country or city as locations for their future conferences, incentive trips, etc. Pike (2004:142) describes the four generally accepted stages in the design and implementation of any advertising campaign as follows:

- Setting the objectives, which include those relating to sales targets and communication purpose
- Budget allocation decisions
- Message decisions, including both the content of the messages and the type of medium
- Campaign evaluation.

In terms of objectives for convention bureau advertising, the most common communications purpose is to promote the destination to their target audiences, the planners of business events, who are the decision makers – or at least the influencers – when destinations are chosen. The target audience may be further defined and refined in terms of geography (local, regional, national, international), and by event types (corporate meetings, association conferences, incentive travel, government events, etc.). But, regardless of the geographical target, convention bureau advertising is entirely B2B, designed to raise business events organisers' awareness of and interest in the destination. Regarding the medium or media selected to convey their advertising, the use of the broadcast media (television, radio and film) is rare, but convention bureaus make extensive use of a wide range of trade publications, many of which exist in print and in online versions, as their readership includes business events planners in search of information and inspiration. Most trade publications of this type have a national coverage, in terms of their readership, and, in common with most magazines, they are dependent on advertising revenue for their continued existence. Convention bureaus as well as venues are among their principal sources of that advertising revenue. A list of business events online trade publications is shown in Table 10.2.

Table 10.2 Business events online publications
Africa https://www.businesseventsafrica.com/digital-magazines/
Americas https://www.meetingstoday.com/
Asia http://www.bizeventsasia.com/ http://www.miceinasia.com/ http://www.cei.asia/ http://www.mixmeetings.com
Asia-Pacific http://www.ttgmice.com/magazine-post/
Australasia https://www.cimmagazine.com/ http://mice.net.au/
Austria http://acb.at/Start/TagungStart/Magazin
Belgium http://mice-magazine.com https://www.eventnews.be/nl/ https://www.eventplanner.tv/
Central and Eastern Europe http://mice-cee.com/
Central and Southeast Europe http://kongres-magazine.eu/
China www.micechina.com
Finland https://eventolehti.fi/in-english/
Germany http://www.tw-media.com http://www.mep-online.de/ www.cimunity.com www.MICEboard.com https://www.events-magazin.de/ http://www.convention-net.de/ http://www.trade-fairs-international.com/tfi/ https://www.businesstraveller.de/
Greece www.xeniosworld.com

India
http://micetalk.com/
https://www.miceworldindia.com/

International
http://boardroom.global/magazines/
http://www.meetingsinternational.com/
http://www.destinationmice.com/
www.conferencemeetingsworld.com
http://www.meetingsnet.com/

Italy
http://www.meetingecongressi.com/it
https://www.eventreport.it/
http://www.qualitytravel.eu/
http://www.mastermeeting.it/

Poland
http://thinkmice.pl/

Russia
www.miceandmore.org
https://event.ru/

South Africa
http://www.theevent.co.za/

Southeast Europe
http://kongres-magazine.eu/

Spain
https://www.eventoplus.com/en/publications/
http://puntomice.com/

Sweden
http://www.meetingsinternational.se/
https://www.meetingsinternational.com/ (English version)

Switzerland
https://abouttravel.ch/author/mice-tip/
https://www.eventemotion.ch/

US
http://www.pcmaconvene.org/magazine/
http://www.meetings-conventions.com/
http://www.meetingsnet.com/digital-edition
http://www.smartmeetings.com/magazine
http://www.eventmarketer.com/
http://www.tsnn.com/
http://www.exhibitoronline.com/magazine/
http://www.themeetingmagazines.com/
https://www.collaboratemeetings.com/magazine/

Often, the tasks associated with advertising, from setting objectives and producing designs, to choosing which media to use and evaluating the campaign, are undertaken by full-service advertising agencies, working on behalf of the convention bureau. Such agencies are generally selected as a result of a competitive tendering process and, in addition to their work on the convention bureau's advertising, may also assist it with other marketing communications techniques such as public relations services, publications and direct mail campaigns.

Public relations

Defined by Holloway (2004:339) as 'a series of communications techniques designed to create and maintain favourable relations between an organisation and its publics', public relations (PR) is another powerful element of the marketing communications mix available for use by convention bureaus. PR is the name given to the various methods that an organisation may use to disseminate positive messages about its products, services or overall image to its customers, and to other stakeholders in the community. Two of the most commonly used PR tools are press relations and lobbying. In the context of destination marketing, the former is used by convention bureaus with the aim of increasing awareness of the destination and creating a favourable impression of it in the eyes of potential clients. Lobbying, on the other hand, is generally aimed at political leaders and others who have direct power over the funding of convention bureaus such as key businesses that support the convention bureau – all of whom should be kept informed of the bureau's activities and successes.

Press relations tools include the issuing of media releases and media conferences, maintaining a library of images and video footage of the destination for use by journalists, and the production of media kits for journalists, giving basic details and statistics about the destination.

Many authors compare advertising (unfavourably) with PR in terms of its potential for creating a favourable, credible image of the destination. For example, they point to the greater credibility of positive editorial coverage in business events trade magazines as compared with that of purchased advertising copy in the same publications. However, McCabe et al. (2000) demonstrate how the two can work together effectively when convention bureaus supplement their advertisements with a corresponding 'editorial story' in the same publication. The advertisement sets the general tone of the destination and gives exposure to its brand, while the more detailed information about the destination provided by the editorial copy lends more credibility. For that reason, the overall package sold to convention bureaus by publications often includes both the advertisement and the accompanying editorial copy.

As in the case of their use of advertising, many convention bureaus choose to employ an external agency to handle their PR.

Familiarisation trips/educational tours/press trips

As an element of experiential marketing, actual visits to destinations by business event organisers are widely considered to be one of the most powerful techniques for educating meeting and incentive planners about destinations' assets for the hosting of their events. Known as familiarisation trips (usually abbreviated to 'fam' trips) or educational tours, these are free (or heavily discounted) trips of a few days' duration offered by convention bureaus to pre-qualified intermediaries such as meeting planners or incentive organisers.

These intermediaries are invited on a speculative basis, the expectation being that they will be impressed by what they experience while visiting the destination and will consequently consider it as a potential location for their future events. Fam trips are normally planned as a group activity, with the size of the group ranging from six to eight people (occasionally more) and the length of the visit being between two and four days. During these trips, the participants follow a busy schedule of activities that typically includes visits to a variety of venues and accommodation providers, as well as the opportunity to meet other suppliers based in the destination. Occasionally, the business events planners may be joined by journalists from the trade press, who are invited in the expectation that they will subsequently write a feature article on the destination in their publications. When the group is exclusively composed of journalists, the event would be known as a press trip, but the objective would be the same: to allow participants to directly experience the destination for themselves, with the aim of creating a favourable impression and boosting brand awareness of the destination that will lead to positive publicity and future business.

Clearly, the planning and funding of fam trips and press trips can be costly in terms of consuming the time and financial resources of the host convention bureau. But local suppliers, such as hoteliers, and national airlines often provide the accommodation and transport for such visits as a means of supporting the marketing activities of their convention bureau.

The power of fam trips as a marketing tool is highlighted in two recent studies, Kourkouridis et al. (2017) and Buckley and Mossaz (2016), although both focus on the use of fam trips for retail travel agents, rather than for business events intermediaries. Nevertheless, these studies demonstrated the efficacy of this marketing tool, with Buckley and Mossaz (2016:137) concluding that 'direct and emotional personal experiences exert far greater influence in ... decision processes, than any written or numerical information'.

In order to be fully effective, it is generally accepted that fam trips must follow a certain number of guidelines. Gartrell's (1994:201) advice on this matter includes the following:

- Keep the fam tour small in number to provide individualised attention. The clients will be far more receptive to this format than being part of a larger audience.
- Invite planners who have similar meeting needs; this will make it easier for the bureau to present information that is homogenous...
- Be sure to maintain close liaison with fam tour guests prior to arrival, providing them with highlights of the fam tour, information on participants, what to bring and wear.
- In setting the final itinerary, blend a mixture of business and pleasure; equally important is providing some free time for the guests to do things they wish.
- Involve the bureau's membership... Clients are looking not only at the destination's physical capabilities but also at the spirit of cooperation and rapport a bureau has with its members and the community.

However, it might be argued that the most important criterion of all for a successful fam trip is the careful selection of guests, to ensure that only qualified business events planners are invited. Unfortunately, there are frequent cases where abuses of the fam trip system take place as a result of bogus planners joining the fam trip group of otherwise bona fide guests. This problem will be further examined in Chapter 13, on the theme of ethics in the business events industry.

Exhibiting at trade shows

In Chapter 8, the many uses of exhibitions were explored, with an emphasis on the advantages that they offer for exhibitors and visitors. The business events industry itself has made extensive use of dedicated business events exhibitions for several decades, and a wide range of such B2B events now exists at different geographical levels – regional, national and global – bringing together buyers, suppliers and intermediaries active in all sectors of this industry.

At these events, the exhibitors are generally suppliers of facilities and services for business events, such as venues, transport companies, conference interpretation services, providers of technology-based tools for business events, as well as manufacturers/distributors of meetings-related merchandise ranging from delegate badges to conference bags. But convention bureaus are also major exhibitors at these B2B trade shows, where many of them are present on highly visible, imposing stands that are decorated to reflect the brands of their destinations and to attract the attention of exhibition visitors.

The visitors to these exhibitions are in general people with a specialist interest in acquiring knowledge of the facilities, services and products that are presented on the exhibition stands and which they need to be familiar with in order to effectively carry out their professional duties. Although exhibition visitors include a wide range of professionals including meetings industry journalists, specialist consultants, as well as academics and students specialising in events management, the majority of visitors – and those clearly of most interest to exhibitors – are people whose professional role includes the selecting of destinations, venues and other facilities and services for their business events. They may be, for example, in-house meeting planners or PCOs or incentive travel organisers. At many business events exhibitions, certain visitors have the status of 'hosted buyers'. The hosted buyers system was described in Chapter 8, for exhibitions in general. In the specific context of business events exhibitions, Davidson and Hyde (2014) describe hosted buyers as visitors who have been qualified by the exhibition organisers as valuable, bona fide, meetings planners actively seeking destinations and venues for their events. The travel and accommodation expenses they incur in attending the exhibition are paid by the exhibition organisers – funded from the fees paid by the exhibitors. In return for their expenses being paid in this way, the hosted buyers are obliged to attend a certain number of appointments with exhibitors. They may choose which exhibitors they wish to meet according to the profiles provided by exhibitors in the show catalogue; but exhibitors can also request appointments with those hosted buyers whom they have specifically identified as potential clients. These appointments may take the form of one-to-one meetings between exhibitors and hosted buyers or presentations made by exhibitors to groups of hosted buyers on the stand.

For convention bureaus, exhibition attendance offers many advantages, which Gartrell (1994:194) summarises as follows:

> Trade shows ... allow for one-on-one contact. Convention bureau representatives are able to meet with specific individuals who represent their target markets, assess their meeting requirements and needs, maintain or develop awareness about their destination and the development of facilities and resources, and simply maintain a rapport and relationship with present and past clients. The fact that [convention bureau] staff are present and visible becomes an important factor in a destination attaining recognition and credibility among meeting planners. There is no question that trade show participation is costly; but it should be looked upon as an investment and a necessary part of any convention bureau's marketing mix.

These same advantages may be enjoyed by individual suppliers exhibiting at business events trade shows. Often such suppliers – for example, venues and DMCs – may be invited to exhibit on the stands of their local convention bureaus, with those stands playing the role of 'umbrellas', under which not only representatives from the DMO but also individual suppliers based in the destination may be found. Those suppliers who opt to share a stand with their convention bureau, rather than having their own – separate – stand, may enjoy several advantages, described by Davidson and Hyde (2014):

- The cost will generally be lower than exhibiting independently, as the expense incurred in the design, transportation, construction and storage of the stand, as well as the hiring of the exhibiting space, will be shared among several exhibitors.
- Benefiting from any investment that the convention bureau makes in terms of pre-exhibition promotion to attract visitors to the stand.
- Benefiting from the extra visitation on the stand created by any events (receptions, 'happy-hours', cocktails, etc.) organised by the convention bureau.
- Exposure to the hosted buyer groups that come to the stand to attend presentations given by the convention bureau. Although these presentations are generally destination-focused, there can sometimes be the opportunity for suppliers to have a slot within the overall presentation, to introduce themselves and their facilities or services. Many convention bureaus also provide lunch on their stands for hosted buyers groups, and that gives the suppliers a further opportunity to mingle and network with these important prospects.

Table 10.3 provides a listing of national and international exhibitions for the business events industry.

With such a plethora of specialist exhibitions for the business events industry, the question arises as to which exhibition or exhibitions a convention bureau should attend for maximum return on the investment. The answer to the question generally depends on the specific market or markets that the convention bureau intends to target. According to Gartrell (1994:195):

Table 10.3 Major business events exhibitions

Exhibition	Focus	Location	Website
Academic Venues Show	UK	London	http://www.academicvenueshow.co.uk
ACE of MICE	Turkey, International	Istanbul	http://ameistanbul.com/
AIBTM	US, International	Orlando	www.aibtm.com
AIME	Australia, Southeast Asia	Melbourne	www.aime.com.au
Association Solutions Marketplace	US	Rotates	https://annual.asaecenter.org/expo.cfm
Best of Events	Germany	Dortmund	www.bo-e.de
BIT	Italy	Milan	www.bit.fieramilano.it/en
BNC Shows	UK, International	London	http://bnceventshows.com/
Business & Meeting Solutions	Belgium, Benelux	Brussels	www.business-meeting-solutions.com
China Events (MICE) Industry Fair	China, International	Shanghai	http://fortuneforum.dx226.ccjjj.net/
CIBTM	China	Beijing	www.cibtm.com
Convene	Baltics	Vilnius	www.convene.lt
Conventa	Southeast Europe	Ljubljana	www.conventa.si
Conference and Hospitality Show	UK	Leeds	https://www.chs18.co.uk/
Destination Showcase	US, International	Washington	https://destinationsinternational.org/2018-destination-showcase
EMITT	Turkey	Istanbul	www.emittistanbul.com/en
Eventit	Scotland	Glasgow	www.eventit.org.uk/
Expo ! Expo !	US	Rotates	https://www.iaee.com/events/
ExpoEventos	Latin America	Buenos Aires	www.expoeventoslatinoamerica.com/
FIEXPO	Latin America, Caribbean	Santiago	www.fiexpolatinoamerica.com/
GIBTM	Gulf	Abu Dhabi	www.gibtm.com
ibtm Africa	Africa	Cape Town	www.ibtmafrica.com/
ibtm Americas	Americas	Mexico City	www.ibtmamericas.com/
Ibtm China	China	Beijing	www.cibtm.com/
ibtm World	International	Barcelona	www.ibtmworld.com/

IMEX	International	Frankfurt	www.imex-frankfurt.com
IMEX America	US, International	Las Vegas	www.imex-america.com
Incentive Works	Canada, International	Toronto	www.incentiveworksshow.com/
International Confex	UK, International	London	www.international-confex.com
IT&CMA	Asia	Bangkok	www.itcma.com
IT&CM China	China	Shanghai	www.itcmchina.com
MBT Market	Germany	Munich	www.mbt-market.de
MCE CEE	Central, Eastern Europe	Budapest	www.europecongress.com
Meetings Africa	South Africa	Johannesburg	www.meetingsafrica.co.za
MICE Forum	Russia, International	Moscow	www.miceforum.ru/
Meetings & Events Summit	Spain, Portugal	Madrid	http://www.grupoeventoplus.com/wp/misummit-en/
MITM Americas	Americas	Rotates	www.mitmevents.com/
MITT	Russia	Moscow	www.mitt.ru/en
Réunir	France	Paris	http://salon.reunir.com/
Salon Bedouk	France	Paris	www.salon.bedouk.com
Square Meal Venues and Events	UK	London	www.venuesandevents.co.uk
SuisseEMEX	Switzerland	Zurich	www.suisse-emex.ch
The Meetings Show	UK, International	London	www.themeetingsshow.com
UITT	Ukraine	Kiev	www.uitt-kiev.com/en

Once that is known, it is possible to ask whether a given trade show will have the kind of prospects a convention bureau wishes to target. If not, then there should be some concern as to the value of that trade show in light of the goals sought by that bureau ... Bureaus have only limited resources and must be very prudent when identifying and selecting trade shows for their marketing mix.

Clearly, the geographical distribution of exhibitions is a factor to be taken into account by convention bureaus in their decision whether or not to attend. For example, the management of the convention bureau of a small provincial town may conclude that exhibiting at their country's national trade show for the business events industry would be the best investment of their resources, as their principal target market is meeting planners based in their own country. On the other hand, for major cities with brands that enjoy worldwide recognition and hotels and conference centres capable of hosting the events of international associations, attendance at exhibitions with a global coverage would be a logical choice. Such trade shows attract large numbers of exhibitors and visitors from many countries. For example, the 30th anniversary edition of IBTM World – which took place at Fira Gran Via, Barcelona, in November 2017 – attracted around 3,000 exhibitors from over 150 countries. Approximately 10 per cent of the exhibitors were DMOs, and the visitors included almost 3,500 buyers. In all, over 74,000 appointments took place during the three-day event, setting a new record for the exhibition (IBTM, 2017). That edition of IBTM World was attended by hosted buyers from corporations including L'Oréal Active Cosmetics, Montblanc, Mars Incorporated, Gucci, Volvo, Shell and Microsoft, and associations including International Stereoscopic Union (Germany), European Health Management Association (Belgium), The Optical Society (United States), European Society of Ophthalmology (United Kingdom) and UEFA (Switzerland).

Ambassador programmes

Also known (particularly in North America) as 'Local Hero' programmes or 'Bring It Home' campaigns, ambassador programmes represent another useful technique employed by convention bureaus to attract business events to their destinations. The experience of many convention bureaus has demonstrated that a well-developed and well-supported ambassador programme can be an effective tool in helping their cities stand out as attractive business events destinations, in particular for association conferences. In Chapter 3, it was noted that the majority of association events that rotate between cities or countries involve a competitive bidding process in the selection of their destinations. Many such processes require bids to be submitted by local or national supporters, either as individuals, as part of a bidding group, or as part of a formal chapter or other sub-group of the association. Ambassador programmes, which are generally created and administered by convention bureaus, can help influence the decision-making process in the favour of the cities that run them. Such programmes work through the convention bureau identifying, recruiting, training and supporting local professionals who have a certain status in key sectors such as medicine, technology or academia and who are in a position to influence, either directly or indirectly, the choice of destination of their associations' conferences. When recruited into the ambassador programme of their city, they are accorded the status of someone who has the power and knowledge to act as a representative of the destination in order to attract conference business to it. Convention bureaus equip their ambassadors with extensive knowledge of their cities' assets as conference destinations, so that they are able to use that knowledge to strengthen their case when lobbying their associations. As well as knowledge, most convention bureaus offer the members of their ambassador programmes a range of support services to facilitate the bidding process. These include assistance with: venue selection – sourcing potential venues to match the association's requirements; bid document preparation and presentation; an accommodation booking service for delegates; and inspection visits by members of the conference committee.

Naturally, an individual may choose to act independently to lobby their professional association to attempt to entice the conference planning committee to bring the event to his or her city. But Association Management International (2012) suggests the following reasons why such individuals may benefit from acting as a member of their local convention bureau's ambassador programme:

Those within associations who opt to become an ambassador will find themselves far better equipped to encourage their association's conference to come to their local area:

- As part of a network of ambassadors there are opportunities to share best practice experiences and forge valuable relationships at networking events throughout the year.
- There is also an opportunity to increase valuable skills with practical advice and support to make organising a conference much easier.
- Finally, one of the most compelling reasons why ambassadors are drawn to the role is the opportunity to increase the profile and recognition of any university or institution they may belong to as well as their own profile within the association.

A key role of the convention bureau is to maintain levels of enthusiasm and motivation among its ambassadors, as the process of lobbying and bidding for association conferences can take several years. Rogers and Davidson (2016) describe some of the techniques used by convention bureaus to help achieve this, including the publishing of regular newsletters for their ambassadors and keeping them informed of developments at the destination such as new venues, hotels and forthcoming events of interest. Another technique is the hosting of regular ambassador dinners, which act as recruiting and networking events, providing opportunities for ambassadors to meet each other, exchange innovative ideas for attracting conferences to the destination, and congratulate successful members of the programme.

The activities of the Prague Convention Bureau's Ambassador Programme are described in a case study in this chapter.

Bidding for events

In Chapter 3, the analysis of how destinations are selected for large-scale association conferences included a description of the system by which destinations participate in bidding for such events as part of a competitive tendering process. Convention bureaus are generally closely involved in the bidding process on behalf of their destinations, as their 'umbrella' role makes them obvious candidates to lead the bidding team, either bidding on behalf of the destination as a whole or assisting members of the association's local branch in their goal of winning the conference in question.

As described in Chapter 3, the process usually begins with the publication of a bid manual by the association that is seeking a destination for one of its future conferences. In response, convention bureaus with an interest in winning the event for their destinations assume responsibility for coordinating a city-wide response by compiling a detailed, customised bid document. Rogers and Davidson (2016:164) list the types of information generally included in a bid document:

- Letters of invitation (for example, from the mayor or other civic or government dignitary inviting and welcoming the conference)
- Details of convention bureau services and support
- Information on the host city, covering its location, climate, geography, culture, history, economy; its experience and reputation as a conference destination; testimonials from satisfied conference organisers; its opportunities for entertainment, cuisine, arts and culture, recreation and shopping
- Access and transport – how to reach the destination by air, road and rail
- Venues and accommodation: photos of and data on the main conference centre; details of major hotels; a map showing the location of the main venue(s) and hotels
- Details of local DMC services
- Budgetary details: quotations for the different elements of the conference, including details of financial support or subvention, if available
- Tours and excursions: details of city tours, and ideas for pre- and post-conference excursions.

ICCA (2014) adds that convention bureaus can supplement the bid document with a large range of information and marketing materials and can provide promotional films and brochures that provide colour and excitement to the bid, as well as useful factual information.

A case study in this chapter describes the Lucerne Convention Bureau's successful bid to bring the 2017 conference of the European Lift Association to their city.

Harnessing local expertise and knowledge

With many thousands of associations issuing bid manuals each year in their quest to identify suitable destinations for their conferences, it would not be cost-effective, in terms of the use of its resources, for any convention bureau to bid for every conference that declares itself to be in search of a destination. For that reason, they are increasingly adopting a strategy of bidding only for those conferences that have the best 'fit' with the destination, notably those events that closely match the city's 'intellectual capital'. Davidson (2016) observes that in recent years, a new approach to marketing destinations for business events has emerged, as a growing number of convention bureaus are beginning to understand that, in addition to important factors such as price, accessibility and having the appropriate infrastructure for the hosting of meetings, the existence of local economic and scientific expertise can deliver an important competitive advantage when attempting to attract association and academic conferences. In order to strengthen their bids for business events, convention bureaus are seeking to differentiate their destinations by developing strategic alliances with their local knowledge industries – such as universities and research institutions – and local businesses to promote the city or region as a destination for the meetings and conferences of associations representing those industry sectors that are active in their particular destination. This harnessing of cities' local industrial and research expertise represents a major shift from simply marketing the destination's meetings infrastructure hardware to promoting its intellectual software as well. This new concept in destination marketing depends upon convention bureaus adopting a strong partnership approach to winning business events for their cities. Most commonly, they have to work with their colleagues in economic development, inward investment and education departments in order to reach out to local companies, organisations and research centres.

For example, the Convention Bureau of Hamburg, representing a city with a strong presence of companies operating in the logistics and transportation sectors, began to leverage the presence of those companies in order to promote the destination to meeting planners seeking destinations for large-scale business events in the global transportation industry. An early success of the Hamburg Convention Bureau, working in partnership with local transportation companies, was the winning of the IATA World Passenger Symposium in October 2015 (DMAI, 2016).

The reason why this approach is so effective in winning conferences is partly because planners are attracted by the idea that, when their industry is present in the destination, local experts can be invited as speakers at their conferences; local specialists working in the field of the conference topic can boost delegate numbers; and local research centres, laboratories or factories can provide interesting sites for conference excursions.

The German Convention Bureau publishes the annual Meeting & Event Barometer that provides details of developments in the conference and events sector of that country. The 2016 edition showed that, for meeting planners, local expertise in the sector was becoming a critical factor to be taken into account in the choice of destination for their business events. Of the organisers surveyed, 73.7 per cent believed that partnering their events with local companies and research organisations in their sector was becoming increasingly important (GCB, 2016). The same report showed that city convention bureaus in Germany were increasingly geared to this approach. Accordingly, in 2012, one-third of them had integrated regional fields of competence into their marketing campaigns, while these figures rose to 44.4 per cent in 2015 (ibid.), demonstrating that DMOs' cooperation with established scientific and business institutions in the sector has increased substantially in recent years.

Convention bureau services for business events planners

The involvement of convention bureaus in any business event is not usually limited to simply winning that event for their destination. It is in the interest of the convention bureau – just as it is in the interest of the event planner – that the conference, meeting or incentive trip is regarded as successful by as many stakeholders as possible. Successful business events can considerably enhance the reputation of the destination through positive word of mouth among events planners, which is in itself an extremely effective form of marketing. For that reason, most convention bureaus offer planners – at no cost – a range of types of service before, during and after the event, representing a form of 'one-stop shop' that provides various kinds of support that save event organisers time and money – and reduce their stress levels.

As Harrill (2005:7) explains,

> Once the event has been booked, the convention bureau changes from sales organisation to service superstar. In this role, the convention bureau becomes a consultant and can assist the planner in several ways. Especially if the planner lives outside the area, a convention bureau can be his or her eyes and ears in identifying facilities, vendors, speakers and more.

He adds that convention bureaus can also act as an effective liaison agent between planners and local government officials when special permits are required.

> For instance, if a pyrotechnics convention wishes to stage a fireworks display on its closing night, … it will need the convention bureau to acquire approval from the police, public works [department] and the mayor's office … The convention bureau should have strong, ongoing relationships with each of these groups and a track record of successful events with which to advocate for the necessary permits.
>
> (Ibid.)

The same author notes that most convention bureaus can also offer assistance to meeting planners who wish to begin their events with an official welcome ceremony, as they are often able to be instrumental in arranging for key local government officials to appear and address the participants – a role that is often relished by officials for whom the occasion provides a useful photo opportunity that can assist in future election campaigns.

According to Tinnish (2007), the range of services and support that a convention bureau can provide to business events planners includes the many actions listed in Table 10.4.

All of the marketing activities outlined in the preceding pages are generally described in convention bureaus' annual marketing plans, which provide details of the organisations' objectives, strategies and marketing programmes for the year ahead, usually with the relevant costs and timelines for each activity. An example of such a document is provided in Figure 10.1, which shows the 2018–2019 Marketing Plan of the Yukon Convention Bureau (YCB), which promotes Canada's westernmost territory as a destination for conferences and incentive travel.

Table 10.4 Convention bureau assistance for event planners

Bid development	Destination expertise	Convention planning
• Develop bid strategy • Develop bid documents • Secure provisional room and venue allocations • Coordinate and serve as host for site inspections • Help negotiate with venues	• Distribute Request for Proposals (RFPs) to multiple hotels, eliminating the need for the planner to contact each individual property • Provide expertise on local products, venues and services • Distribute Meeting Planner's Guides with complete information on the destination and the CB's members • Access to local, industry and government contacts • Suggest itinerary planning	• Secure welcome letters from government, officials and agencies • Book government officials as speakers • Introduce local fire, police officials or other government officials to incorporate into the planning team • Aid with protocol-related programmes • Provide local media contacts (newspaper, radio and TV) • Provide inventory control for hotel room blocks • Arrange greeters at the airport or signs throughout the city • Secure space at the city's convention centre • Connect the meeting manager with potential sponsors from the local business base that might seek visibility at the event • Provide shuttle services (potentially complimentary)

Attendance building	On-site event support	Post-event support
• Draft news and press releases for the upcoming event • Provide promotional materials (brochures, pre-show mailers, videos, slides, and photographs) • Produce email blasts • Recommend pre- and post-event itineraries • Market the destination through 'prior-year conventions' to create excitement for the next annual event	• Supply on-site support personnel including: – Registration personnel – Hall monitors – Tourist guides for attendees • Provide attendees with personalised hotel maps • Establish a courtesy/concierge booth near the meeting's registration area where attendees can make dinner reservations, etc.	• Post-event housing information on pickup, cancellations and no-show percentages • Survey attendees about their experience, using various methods including handheld PDAs, kiosks and written surveys

Source: Based on Tinnish (2007).

YCB – 2018/2019 Marketing and Sales Calendar

Month	Events/Workshops	Trade Shows	FAM	Est. Partner Costs	Bill Date
April	MPI The Event -Apr 12-14			Individual	n/a
May	YCB AGM May 23rd				n/a
June	BEC – Sales Event – June 13/14 MPI BC – Year End Gala **TBA**	BEC Seattle, WA June Sales Lunch – Vancouver – June 13th		-Approx $750 *less TCMF 50% - Open to MPI members – $75	30 days TCMF – partner does own
July	Membership Tour/Drive – Yukon			Open to YCB Partners	n/a
August	Membership Tour/Drive – Yukon wide (July –Aug)	Incentive Works – Toronto Aug 13-16	Private FAM- Grace Ng (IMEX) Aug 23-26	IW: $10-12k / split cost with partners of 3+ *less TCMF 50%	30 days TCMF – partner does own
Sept		Can.Cham.Comm Thurderbay – 2021 Bid Sales Mission	Fall FAM Sept 11th-15th	CCC - Individual	n/a
Oct	TBA – (if needed) Mid Oct Sales Luncheon Ottawa	CSAE Ntl Oct 24-26		CSAE: $10-12k / split cost with partners of 3+ *less TCMF 50%	30 days TCMF – partner does own
Nov	PCMA – Victoria Nov 17-21 w/ Sales Luncheon		Red Carpet Tour		
Jan		Tete a Tete, Destination Direct & MPI Gala Ottawa TBA Late Jan/Feb		TaT: $17-19k split cost with partners of 3+ *less TCMF 50%	30 days TCMF – partner does own
Feb	Bravo Awards – Feb 28	GOWest - TBA		GW$3-4k split cost with partners of 3+ *less TCMF 50%	GW -30 days TCMF – partner does own YCB Seeking Title Sponsor of $4000
March			Winter FAM Tour		

Figure 10.1
YCB – 2018/2019 marketing and sales calendar

Chapter summary

This chapter began with a history of convention bureaus, a type of destination marketing organisation specialising in promoting cities, regions or entire countries as places where business events can be successfully hosted. Convention bureaus were defined as intermediaries working on behalf of the business events suppliers in their territory.

The different governance and funding models for convention bureaus were discussed, with the strengths and weaknesses of each. The various marketing tools employed by convention bureaus were reviewed, with best-practice guidelines for each: destination branding and positioning, advertising, public relations, familiarisation/press trips, exhibitions and ambassador programmes. The role of convention bureaus in the bidding process was discussed, with an analysis of how they are harnessing their local intellectual capital to bid for conferences on subjects linked to their cities' industrial/ knowledge infrastructure.

CASE STUDY 10.1: THE EUROPEAN LIFT ASSOCIATION CONFERENCE IN LUCERNE

European Lift Association
© John Gale – Creative Spark Design Partnership.

Lucerne

With a population of approximately 84,000, Lucerne is the capital of the canton of Lucerne and in many respects the most important city in Central Switzerland. It is the cultural centre of the region and the fourth largest Swiss agglomeration. Lucerne's above-average quality of life and proximity to the country's commercial and financial centres make it a popular place to live and work. Access to the city is through its rail connections (half-hourly services from, for example, Zurich and Bern), by air (it is approximately one hour by road/rail from Zurich or Basel Airports), boat and road (A2/A4 motorways).

Lucerne as a business events destination

A plentiful supply of hotel accommodation and an extensive variety of venues add to the attractiveness of Lucerne as a business events destination. Venues include the KKL Luzern (Culture and Convention Centre Lucerne) designed by the star architect Jean Nouvel; and a notable unusual venue, the Swiss Museum of Transport – Verkehrshaus. In terms of natural attractions, the city's location on the shores of the lake and the nearby Alpine peaks provide opportunities for excursions and team-building events.

Lucerne Convention Bureau

Within Lucerne Tourism, the city's destination marketing organisation, the Lucerne Convention Bureau is the department responsible for promoting the city and region of Lucerne as a destination for business events. In addition to marketing Lucerne as a business events destination, it offers conference planners three different types of support: organisational, financial and marketing. On their website, the details of these different types of support are listed:

Organisational support

- Analysis of conference requirements:
  We will be glad to analyse your request and advise on which venues would be most suitable for your conference.
- Consultation:
  As a mediator between you and the Lucerne specialists, we put you in touch with expert service providers such as conference venues, hotels and professional conference organisers.
- Bids:
  We provide professional destination marketing, for example in a bid book or a PowerPoint presentation.
- Site inspection:
  We will be happy to organise a site inspection to meet your requirements.
- Partners:
  We will be glad to recommend professional destination management companies (DMCs) and professional conference organisers (PCOs).

Financial support

- Conference funding:
  Lucerne Tourism and its partners actively support conferences. Funding is available depending on the scale of the event.
- Reduced-rate public transport ticket for Lucerne:
  Benefit from a free ticket for public transport when booking a hotel in the city of Lucerne. The ticket is valid in the zone 10 and is for 2nd class travel (excluding

boat trips) for the duration of your stay from the day you arrive to the day of your departure.

- Partnership with Swiss:
  Swiss supports international conferences in Switzerland as the official carrier. We will be glad to advise and put you in touch.
- VAT refund:
  Foreign companies can obtain VAT refunds. See luzern.vat.taxback.com for details.
- Free handling for small-scale events:
  We provide free quotations for small-scale events or when only one service partner is involved.

Marketing support

- Advertising materials:
  We will be glad to provide you with a range of advertising materials such as photographs, films, brochures and city maps of Lucerne. Destination brochures are available to you to provide your event participants with information in advance.
- Invitation letters:
  We will be more than happy to organise a letter of invitation from the government or letters of support from local industry.
- Give-aways:
  We will be glad to offer suggestions of local give-aways as mementos for participants.

The Lucerne Convention Bureau is a partnership organisation. Within Lucerne itself, the principal partners are fifteen hotels, nine venues, two outdoor partners and one DMC. In addition, from the Lucerne region as a whole, there are thirty hotels that are also partners of the convention bureau.

The fees from partners and support from the city government are used to fund the activities of the Lucerne Convention Bureau.

The European Lift Association

The European Lift Association (http://ela-aisbl.eu/) is a non-profit making international association with its headquarters in Brussels. It represents the lifts, escalators and moving walks associations that are active in the European Union, the European Free Trade Area or in any country that is a member of the Council of Europe, whether they are national associations or sector-specific associations.

The objectives of the ELA include:

- Promoting quality, safety and the highest technical standards and encouraging technical progress in the fields of manufacturing, installation and maintenance of lifts, escalators and moving walkways

- Participating in all dialogues and to represent its members vis-à-vis public or private, national, EU and international organisations dealing, directly or indirectly, with issues related to lifts, escalators and moving walks
- Participating in the formulation of codes, standards, regulations, instructions or other notifications, regarding lifts, escalators and moving walks, together with national, EU or international organisations, and to supervise the implementation thereof.

The annual conference of the ELA plays a key role in assisting the association to achieve its objectives, by promoting the education of its members as well as communication between them and other stakeholders in the wider lifts, escalators and moving walkways community in Europe. Attracting around 100 participants each year, the ELA annual conferences are generally held in hotel venues, in European capital cities. But for the 2017 conference, the ELA chose a second-tier city, Lucerne, as the destination. In the years preceding 2017, the ELA conferences were held in the following locations:

- 2016 Radisson Blu, Rome
- 2015 Hyatt Regency, Paris
- 2014 Mövenpick Hotel, Amsterdam
- 2013 Grand Hyatt Hotel, Istanbul.

Bringing the ELA conference to Lucerne

Isaline Grichting works as the Sales & Marketing Manager (MICE) at the Lucerne Convention Bureau. Her role is to win association events for the city. Here, she describes how she helped bring the 2017 conference of the European Lift Association to Lucerne:

'The headquarters of Schindler, one of the biggest lift companies in the world, is in Lucerne, and that was the main reason why I thought that the European Lift Association could be persuaded to hold their conference in this city. Looking at the ICCA Association Database, I saw that the conference had never been held in Switzerland, and that prompted me to contact the ELA president in Brussels to ask him if Lucerne/Switzerland would be an option for a future conference. He responded positively but informed me that the invitation to hold their conference in Lucerne should come from a Swiss member of the association. So, after some research, I found the details of Jorge Ligüerre, the vice-president at Schindler Elevator Ltd (Switzerland) who is a member of the Verband Schweizerischer Aufzugsunternehmen (VSA), the Swiss Association.

'I then contacted him to ask if he would work with me to bid for the conference, and he readily agreed to this.

'I helped the VSA to make a detailed offer for the hosting of the ELA conference in Lucerne, including identifying the most suitable venue and hotels for the event. On this occasion, there was no bidding process, as Lucerne was the only city that made an offer for the hosting of the 2017 conference. So the whole process was fairly straightforward.'

The conference

The theme of the 2017 ELA conference was 'Lifts & Escalators – our part in the Digital World'. It was held in the Radisson Blu Hotel, Lucerne, from 24 to 25 April, and 100 participants attended. Most of the event took place in the hotel's meeting rooms, but the Gala Dinner was held in the Museum of Transport (Verkehrshaus).

Stella Bedeur, Senior Manager of the ELA Secretariat, made the following statement shortly after the conference took place:

'The 2017 ELA conference was a major success. All of our delegates appreciated the organisation of the event, the meeting rooms at the Radisson Blu Hotel, the speeches at the conference, the trip on the lake, as well as the gala dinner at the Verkehrshaus. Those participants who had an opportunity to visit Lucerne before or after the conference fell in love with the incomparable charm of that magnificent city. We can truly say that this conference in Lucerne was a "Grand Cru". We are extremely grateful to the Lucerne Convention Bureau for their excellent support in making our conference such a success.'

CASE STUDY 10.2: THE PRAGUE CONVENTION BUREAU AMBASSADOR PROGRAMME

Prague Ambassador Awards Evening 2018

Background

The project originated in 2010 as an initiative of the Prague Convention Bureau (www.pragueconvention.cz) and its members, with the aim of supporting the organisers and hosts of international conferences in Prague. The programme directly supports the activity of the 'Congress Ambassadors', who are generally individuals or groups (for example, the collective staff of a university department) who have the ability to influence the choice of destination of a future international association conference. They can be:

- Czech Republic-based scientists, physicians, and other experts who are members of international associations
- High-ranking representatives of international companies based in the Czech Republic

Whenever, with their assistance, a bid to bring a conference to Prague is successful, Congress Ambassadors subsequently assume the role of one of the chief organisers of the events (for example, the congress president, or an active member of the scientific, preparatory or organisational committee).

Objectives

The objectives of the Prague Convention Bureau Ambassador Programme are:

- To increase the number of conferences being held in Prague and throughout the Czech Republic
- To increase the competitiveness of the Czech Republic internationally
- To demonstrate the appreciation and acknowledgement of Congress Ambassadors for their contributions to the Prague and Czech Republic conference industry
- To promote Czech science and research, including key branches of the Czech economy, throughout the Czech Republic and internationally.

Within the Prague Convention Bureau, a dedicated member of staff is responsible for overseeing the operations of the Ambassador Programme. She describes her role as follows:

'My name is Markéta Růtová, and my job title at the Prague Convention Bureau is 'External Relations Manager – Ambassador Programme'. I have been working in the business events industry for 20 years, and my previous jobs as a Professional Conference Organiser, a Project Manager and a Hotel Marketing and Sales Manager have provided me with valuable experience in corporate and association conferences. Most importantly, I was born in Prague and I know the city extremely well.

Marketa Rutova

'My overall role is to act as a bridge between our convention bureau's services and those who are interested in making use of our services, in order to increase the level of local recognition of the Prague Convention Bureau. Reaching out to, and cooperating with, academic institutions is an essential part of my role as manager of our Ambassador Programme, as it is well known that a local academic's advocacy effort within his or her professional association can play a key role in bidding to win the right to host an international conference. My aim is to provide our Ambassadors with supporting activities that can lead to a successful bid. Essential to this process is identifying potential Ambassadors, by finding synergies between their (and their institutions') objectives and the goals of the Prague Convention Bureau. If they are not already members of their relevant international associations, we encourage them to join; and if they are already members, we encourage them to become active members. I also organise our annual Ambassador Awards Gala evening. It's extremely varied work, and I enjoy it very much.'

Support for Congress Ambassadors

Through the Prague Convention Bureau Ambassador Programme, Congress Ambassadors are provided with a range of support designed to facilitate their role in bidding for and organising conferences. This includes:

- Easier access to information and financial resources
- Easier access to marketing materials and destination presentations
- The assistance of a professional team to help with the process of bidding for an international conference
- Access to direct contacts with local conference organisers and other suppliers
- Networking opportunities.

Congress Ambassadors also have access to the support provided by the official Ambassador Programme Patrons. These are Ambassadors whose valuable contribution to the Czech conference industry has previously been recognised at an Ambassador Awards Gala Evening. The support of such Patrons takes the form of educational seminars during which they share their practical experience of bidding for and organising conferences.

One example of an extremely proactive Patron of the Prague Convention Bureau Ambassador Programme is Professor Vladimir Tesař, Head of the Department of Nephrology in the First Faculty of Medicine of Charles University in Prague. Professor Tesař holds a prominent position in the international scientific community, partly due to his membership of several key international associations. He has served as a member of the European Renal Association – European Dialysis and Transplant Association (ERA-EDTA) Council and a member of its Scientific Advisory Board; and he is currently the Chair of the ERA-EDTA Immunonephrology Working Group and the Chair of the Scientific Committee for the 55th ERA-EDTA Congress in Copenhagen in 2018. From 2014–2017, he was President of the International Society of Blood Purification. From 1999–2004, and again from 2010–2012, he served as Chair of the Czech Society of Nephrology (CSN), and he has been re-elected Chair of the CSN for the period 2018–2020. In addition to these roles, he is also a member of the International Society of Nephrology (ISN) and the American Society of Nephrology (ASN).

For many years, Professor Tesař has capitalised on his involvement in scientific associations to bring a number of international medical conferences to Prague. These include the International Vasculitis and ANCA (Anti-Neutrophil Cytoplasm Antibodies) Workshop in 2003, the European Peritoneal Dialysis Meeting in 2005, the annual conference of the International Society for Blood Purification in 1999 and again in 2007, and above all, one of the largest conferences ever to be held in Prague, the ERA–EDTA Congress in 2011. This is how he describes his role in bringing conferences to Prague:

'My role in bringing medical conferences to Prague was very specific and will be probably not be easily repeated in the future as it was related to the sudden change of the political system in our country occasioned by the break-up of the Soviet Union in 1991. As communication between the former communist countries and Western Europe was interrupted (or at least hibernated) for more than 40 years, there was suddenly considerable interest in organising medical meetings in my country in the early 1990s. But as we were a relatively unknown destination for the wider European medical community, we had to start with smaller meetings and workshops which helped us in building mutual confidence and gradually gaining experience and expertise in hosting conferences. Organising several smaller meetings of between 50 and 300 participants also gave the Czech medical community the opportunity of becoming involved in many European and worldwide networking activities relating to different areas of renal disease, leading to our participation in a number of interesting scientific projects. Our growing experience in hosting conferences finally resulted in us being given the opportunity to host the 2011 Congress of the European Renal Association – European Dialysis and Transplant Association (ERA – EDTA), with almost 9,000 registered participants. As the 2011 meeting was generally considered to be a great success, our objective now is to have the privilege of hosting it in Prague once again, over the next few years. We also remain dedicated to organising many smaller CME (continuing medical education) courses, workshops and conferences here in this city.

'My motivation for acting as a Patron for the Prague Convention Bureau Ambassador Programme stems from my belief that it is important to share my experience of bringing conferences to Prague with colleagues from other branches of medicine – especially those without previous experience in the field of organising medical meetings – to help them better to succeed with their bids. What I also very much appreciate about the Prague Convention Bureau Ambassador Programme is the opportunity it offers for useful discussions between the representatives of biomedicine in our city and the people involved in Prague's conference industry. These discussions help us to better understand each other and to optimise our collaboration. My role as Patron also gives me the chance to motivate younger colleagues and opinion leaders so that, over the next few decades, we can build upon what has already been achieved in terms of winning conferences for our city. Finally, of course, it is worthy of mention that the nature of the city of Prague itself helps us in our task of bringing conferences here, as it is a charming city with a rich history and cultural life, making it an attractive destination for repeated visits of our colleagues from all over the world.'

IT'S MY JOB
TAUBIE MOTLHABANE, EXECUTIVE
DIRECTOR, THE TSHWANE
CONVENTION & VISITORS BUREAU

I grew up and went to school and university in the North West province of South Africa. I hold a BA in Communications from the University of the North West in South Africa, and an MSc in Global Marketing from the University of Liverpool in the UK.

My first job was in public relations at the North West Consumer Council in 1990. This was during my last year of university study. I then went on to work in television as a researcher, scriptwriter and presenter for a magazine programme. I was a sub-editor of a local newspaper for a while and then moved back to public relations and communications.

My introduction to business events was 20 years ago when I joined the South African Broadcasting Corporation as Chief of Staff in the office of the CEO: Television. A couple of years later, I was recruited by the South African Reserve Bank as their Head of

Conferences and Protocol. My career in business events continued when I joined (in 2009) the Business Tourism Unit of South African Tourism, the organisation responsible for marketing South Africa as a tourism destination globally. This is where I fell in love with business events and destination marketing as a career.

The time I spent at SA Tourism offered me many insights into the workings of the business events industry. Meeting international meeting planners, destination management professionals and fellow destination marketing professionals opened my eyes to the extent and importance of this wonderful industry and how convention and visitors bureaus play a crucial role in the marketing of countries and cities for business events.

My career journey led me (in January 2016) to the Tshwane Convention & Visitors Bureau, which was a newly formed destination marketing unit for South Africa's capital city, Tshwane (popularly known as Pretoria). The role of Executive Director has been an interesting and challenging one for me.

One challenge has been the fact that the city of Tshwane was relatively unknown as a destination for business events, so our aim here at the Convention & Visitors Bureau has been to build a strong brand that can compete with better-established South African city brands such as Cape Town, Johannesburg and Durban. Our goal is to work more closely with the business events industry to improve the brand visibility and the appeal of Tshwane.

We are helped in achieving this goal by the fact that the city has a very strong and unique offering in the South African and broader African landscape. Being the seat of government as well as a centre of new scientific research and knowledge development is a great advantage. Most government departments' headquarters are based in our city and this means that attracting academics, scientists and researchers is easier for our city than for our competitors in South Africa. The Tshwane Convention Bureau's focus has therefore been to attract more professional association conferences and government meetings. This drives a lot of business events into our city.

As a department within the municipality, the Tshwane Convention Bureau is 100 per cent funded by the state. At this stage, there is no membership programme in place, although this is one of the strategic future focuses of the Bureau. We are a team of 23 people whose daily functions include providing visitors to the city with tourism information, engaging with the tourism trade to package, market and sell Tshwane as a business events destination. We also support business events planners to enable them to seamlessly plan events in the city.

My particular responsibilities include the development and implementation of a tourism strategy for the city; high-level stakeholder engagement and management; and lobbying meeting planners and decision makers to attract more business events to the city.

I serve on the Tourism Curriculum Advisory Board of the University of South Africa; the Executive Committee of the Tshwane branch of the Southern African Association of the Conferencing Industry (SAACI); and I am a member of the South African National Convention Bureau's Business Events Coordinating Forum.

What do I like most about my job? I love the ever-changing pace of this industry. One of the biggest changes I have seen over the past few years is the serious entry of the African continent into the business events sector. In terms of winning international events, Africa is becoming a real contender, and I find that very exciting and very satisfying on the personal level.

I also enjoy the travelling that my job brings me. Through my job, I regularly travel to business events exhibitions such as IBTM China in Beijing, China; IBTM World in Barcelona, Spain; IMEX in Frankfurt, Germany; Meetings Africa, in Johannesburg, South Africa; and meetings of the international associations such as the ICCA Congress in Hyderabad, India. I also recently travelled to Sochi, Russia to do delegate boosting and marketing of the World Choir Games coming to Tshwane in 2018. I love to travel, and I feel fortunate that I have a career that gives me the opportunity to do what I love.

IT'S MY JOB
BIRGITTE NESTANDE, PROJECT MANAGER EVENTS, NORWAY CONVENTION BUREAU

I was born in Oslo, Norway 32 years ago. I always knew that after leaving school I would spend some time studying abroad, and that's exactly what I did. I spent one semester in Natal, Brazil, on a university foundation course, studying subjects such as philosophy and ethics. It was a wonderful experience, which I shared with the man who is now my husband, Christian, who is also a Norwegian citizen.

But living in Natal also inspired me to study tourism at university. I was fascinated to see how the city used its status as a major tourism destination to help alleviate poverty and promote development, and this was the origin of my interest in studying tourism. Therefore, after my time in Brazil, I enrolled on a BA Tourism and Planning degree at the University of Westminster in London.

Business events – or, as it was known at the University of Westminster, business tourism – was one element of my degree course. But I wasn't motivated to focus on that aspect of the programme until, in the second semester of my course, I participated in a short study trip to Cambridge, UK. During that trip, my classmates and I visited that city's famous university, where the Events Manager explained to us how the university facilities were marketed for use as meetings venues outside term time, bringing business visitors to Cambridge and earning additional revenue for the university.

I was fascinated to learn that meetings and events could be a way of stimulating tourism and bringing economic benefits to destinations, and so I deliberately chose courses in that area. In the second year of my studies, I opted to take a course in Business Tourism, and the following year I chose a course in Conference Planning. Between them, these two courses convinced me that this was an industry that I definitely wanted to work in.

After graduating in 2009, I returned to Norway and began to look for jobs there. Knowing of my ambition to work in business events, one of my professors had advised me to contact the Norway Convention Bureau (NCB) (www.norwayconventionbureau.no), the organisation responsible for promoting my country as a destination for meetings and events. So even though no vacancies were being advertised, I sent an application letter to the NCB. It turned out to be a very fortunate move on my part, because I immediately received a positive response from them, telling me that they had just received funding from the government to create two new positions in their organisation. After an interview in the NCB offices, I was offered a job – and I have been there ever since.

To begin with, my duties mainly involved me in doing research – identifying key contact persons in Norway, such as scientists, doctors and professors, who regularly attend conferences and who might be persuaded to become possible hosts for conferences in Norway – in other words, to become our conference ambassadors. I also worked on developing our statistics. The NCB was, and still is, a very small organisation in terms of the number of staff employed there (currently three), so everyone who works there is expected to cover a variety of tasks, from designing marketing material and working on our website to helping formulate our strategy. I'm probably the member of staff who is most interested in technology, so I tend to do those kinds of jobs.

My job has grown as the responsibilities of the NCB have expanded over the years. International travel has become an important element of my work. For example, I work on the NCB stand at the annual IBTM World exhibition in Barcelona and IMEX in Frankfurt. The NCB also exhibits at IMEX America in Las Vegas, where we exhibit in the Scandinavian Pavilion, collaborating with the other Scandinavian and Nordic countries. But my colleagues usually attend that event. I also regularly visit our five main target markets – the UK, Sweden, Germany, France and the Netherlands – to work on B2B events and carry out sales calls to potential clients – business events organisers based in those countries. As the NCB is a member of the International

Conference and Convention Association (ICCA), I have also had the opportunity to participate in several of their sales and marketing training events and attending the annual ICCA congress in countries outside Norway. But much of the important work I do is based in my home country. For example, I regularly organise fam trips in collaboration with our Norwegian city destinations. Generally, the city-based convention bureaus request fam trip programmes, and we work with them on that, identifying potential participants and helping them with logistical elements of those trips. We are helped in some of these tasks by our overseas-based staff. For instance, for the UK market, we use the services of a colleague based in Visit Norway's London office. She helps with recruiting participants for fam trips, organising events in London, and planning sales calls in the UK.

Over the years, there have been several important changes in the funding of the NCB. The organisation began in 1989 as a department within Visit Norway, the public sector funded destination marketing organisation for my country. But the department was closed in 2001 as a consequence of government cuts in funding. However, the main cities in my country wanted to continue benefiting from the services of a national organisation with the mission to attract international association conferences to Norway. So they hired a person to organise the Norway stand at the IBTM World and IMEX exhibitions, and that led to the establishing of the NCB as a private sector company in 2005. From 2009, following an injection of state funding for the NCB, it subsequently became a public sector–private sector partnership which is partly 'owned' by the Norwegian meetings industry, who hold a share in the company, and partly funded by the Norwegian government through Visit Norway/Innovation Norway.

In 2018, the NCB merged with Innovation Norway (IN) (http://www.innovasjonnorge.no/), the state body responsible for helping develop all kinds of industries in my country through the promotion of entrepreneurship, inward investment, exports and tourism. The merge made sense in many ways. We had already been collaborating successfully with IN for several years, and in Norway, IN is far more widely recognised than the NCB (although we continue to use that title for our organisation especially abroad), which makes it easier for us to, for example, approach potential conference ambassadors. Another benefit of merging with IN and being based in their offices is that funds that we previously spent on running the NCB office can now be invested in marketing activities that directly benefit our partners.

What do I most enjoy about my work? Certainly, I love the travel aspect, both internationally and within my own country. In Norway, I travel widely to experience our destinations and the fascinating products they offer for business events, so that I can share these with our potential clients in order to inspire them. For example, I recently found myself husky sledging in the archipelago of Spitsbergen, situated between northern Norway and the North Pole in temperatures of minus 20 degrees! I also enjoy the very supportive and collaborative environment we work in, where colleagues freely share their knowledge and experience, even with potential 'competitors'. For instance, the relatively new manager of the Trondheim Convention Bureau has recently been receiving a lot of valuable advice and support from the more experienced manager of the Stavanger Convention Bureau. I also like the fact that there is close collaboration with the convention bureaus of other Nordic countries. As a general rule, people in our industry are positive, enthusiastic and pleasant to work with, and I enjoy that very much.

In fact, there is very little that I don't enjoy about my job. But I do find doing the paperwork for claiming my travel expenses somewhat tedious at times. And it's true that from time to time I have to deal with people who are a little difficult to collaborate with. But I find that although those experiences test me, I am continually getting better at successfully coping with that particular aspect of my work. This is very much a people industry, which I believe is what makes it fun, interesting and educational to work in.

IT'S MY JOB
OLIVIER PONTI, MANAGER,
RESEARCH, AMSTERDAM MARKETING

I studied Economics at the Sciences-Po university in Paris (at the same time as Emmanuel Macron, who famously went on to hold the high office of President of France), and I then did a Master's course in Tourism Development at the University of Paris 1 (Pantheon-Sorbonne).

Within the broad array of activities related to tourism, what attracted me most was the area of research as a source of useful market intelligence. I felt this area suited both my studies and my analytical mind. I was also convinced that research would be an extremely varied activity. Tourism is such a diverse sector that it provides an endless supply of excellent research topics and material. One day, you can be working at the macro level, analysing how shifts in the global economy are affecting the competitiveness of a specific destination compared to its competitors. The next day, you can be working at the micro level, examining millions of transactions to distinguish patterns which could enable a destination marketing organisation to sell more City Cards.

I started being active in the field of business events research in 2004 when I was employed as Research Manager for the Paris Tourism and Convention Board (Office du Tourisme et des Congrès de Paris). Very surprisingly, for a conference destination as important as Paris, at that time, we didn't keep track of the number of meetings taking place in the French capital each year; and our understanding of trends in the sector was limited to the statistics produced annually by the International Congress and Convention Association (ICCA) and the Union of International Associations (UIA). That year, together with my colleagues from the Convention Board, we collected data from all major meeting venues in the city and produced a report focusing on congresses (their seasonality, number of participants, type of venue, type of meeting, etc.). We sent Microsoft Excel sheets for the venues to complete, keeping the methodology as simple as possible in order to facilitate the participation of all types of meeting venues in our survey, whether large or small. The report we produced was a major breakthrough, and the Paris business events sector was so delighted with these new insights that we decided to repeat and expand the project in the following years. The 'Congress Study' (Enquête Congrès) became a key building block for the understanding of the sector and is still being produced today. Since it has been produced on an annual basis for so many years, my colleagues in Paris are now able to identify trends over a long period of time, and therefore achieve a much better longitudinal understanding of developments in the performance of Paris as a congress destination.

In 2007, I moved to the Netherlands after being recruited by the Amsterdam Tourism & Convention Board (Amsterdam Toerisme & Congres Bureau). (The Amsterdam Tourism & Convention Board was later merged into Amsterdam Marketing, the city marketing organisation of the Amsterdam Metropolitan Area.)

As well as being interesting for me from the point of view of developing my career, this move was also closely aligned to my personal objective of moving to the Netherlands, as my partner comes from that country. Even so, I spoke very little Dutch in 2007, and although this was not a particular handicap (it is possible to work professionally in the Netherlands with a good level of the English language, which I already had), I focused on immersing myself in the Dutch language during the first six months of taking up my new job. Today, I am entirely comfortable with using Dutch as my language of work.

My new colleague, Marc Horsmans, Director of the Convention Board, told me that he was a fan of what I had done in Paris and that he would like me to do something similar in Amsterdam. I promised him that we would do even better! The situation in Amsterdam was comparable to the one in Paris several years back: basically, no data. So, with financial support from a committed group of hoteliers, we began collecting information about all of the meetings taking place in the city, whether they were corporate, non-corporate, national or international. We presented the results of this work in the form of well-designed reports including a lot of infographics; we organised events to share our insights; and we developed new ways of spreading our knowledge among meeting professionals, such as audio presentations. The objective was to make the Amsterdam meeting sector as a whole much better informed, so that our partners could make information-based decisions, for example when working on their business plan or their strategy.

The project was very successful, and we have been building on it ever since, with the publication of an annual report entitled 'Key Figures: Amsterdam as a Conference Destination'. Our expertise in data collection has been widely acknowledged beyond the city of Amsterdam itself. For example, in 2014, the report was nominated for the ICCA Best Marketing Awards; and in 2015, it won a United Nations World Tourism Organization (UNWTO) Ulysses Award for Innovation in Research and Technology. We continue to experiment with innovative ways of presenting the data to our partners, for example by exploring the possibilities offered by photo-infographics and multimedia online magazines. The response from our partners in Amsterdam has been extremely positive, and this is very motivating for me. Typical of the comments we receive is this feedback from the General Manager of a major hotel in the city: 'This report assists my organisation – and many others – to prepare our business plans, and gives us a better understanding of how Amsterdam is growing in the meetings and conventions industry'.

In 2010, I was involved in another important research project: the launch of the European Cities Marketing (ECM) Meeting Statistics Report (www.europeancitiesmarketing.com). The starting point of this project was the realisation that if convention bureaus in Europe really wanted to understand what was going on in their own destination, they should be able to benchmark themselves against the results of competing destinations. Besides, it was clear that convention bureaus needed data that went beyond the rankings published by ICCA and the UIA, which focus only on international non-corporate meetings with specific criteria. I was attracted to this exciting research project both from the point of a meetings industry professional in Amsterdam but also as chairman of the ECM Research & Statistics Group. As was the case in Paris and Amsterdam years before, we decided to start small by collecting the data through a survey using Excel sheets. After a pilot involving ten cities was very positively received by ECM members, the project was repeated on a larger scale in each of the following years. By 2017, 48 cities were involved in the survey and the data was being collected via a dedicated online platform.

Another highlight of my career came in 2013, when I was invited by the Course Director of the ECM Summer School to join the faculty. Pier Paolo Mariotti wanted to give market intelligence a more prominent role in the Summer School curriculum and thought that the students (usually young professionals active in the various branches of the meetings sector) could benefit from my expertise. I gladly accepted and began giving presentations on the latest trends and developments, with guidance on how to collect and analyse good data, based on the concrete example of how I use research to make Amsterdam more competitive as a business events destination.

One illustration of how my work makes Amsterdam more competitive came when, as I analysed the results of the 2012 ECM Meeting Statistics Report, I realised that compared to its competitors, Amsterdam was barely exploiting the city's meeting venues other than the hotels, universities and convention centres. The data showed that there was a real opportunity for Amsterdam's theatres, museums, tourist attractions and historical monuments to enter the market as venues for meetings of fewer than 500 participants. The report also showed that this segment (<500 participants) was on the rise. Taking this into account, we (Amsterdam Marketing) decided to work more closely with the city's 'non-traditional' venues and help them take their first steps as meetings locations. Two years later, 27 per cent of meetings in Amsterdam were taking place in this type of venue, while traditional meeting locations were still going strong. In other words, we had managed to expand the supply of venues in Amsterdam, and demand rose as a consequence of that action.

How is research evolving now? In the past few years, there has been much talk of 'big data' and how it could become a game changer in practically all fields of the world economy, including business events. I believe that this is largely true. In the past 15 years, I have witnessed the explosion of data and seen how some analytically minded companies have turned this into a powerful competitive advantage: think of Google, Booking.com or Uber, to name just a few. The conclusion I draw from this is that the need for people able to analyse data in our industry and turn it into actionable information will keep growing. The burning question for me is: how many companies currently active in business events have already understood the importance of big data and are ready to make the necessary investments in the technologies and skills which can enable them to benefit from these powerful new tools?

References

Association Management International (2012) Association Management 12(3). Available at: http://www.associationmanagement.co.uk/Documents/AMI%20Vol12%20Ed3.pdf.

Baker, M. J. and Cameron, E. (2008) Critical success factors in destination marketing. *Tourism and Hospitality Research* 8(2): 79–97.

Blain, C., Levy, S. E. and Ritchie, J. R. B. (2005) Destination branding: Insights and practises from destination management organisations. *Journal of Travel Research* 43: 328–338.

Buckley, R. and Mossaz, A. C. (2016) Decision making by specialist luxury travel agents. *Tourism Management* 55: 133–138.

Davidson, R. (2016) Harnessing local expertise and knowledge: A new concept in business tourism destination marketing. Proceedings SITCON 2016 – Singidunum International Tourism Conference. Singidunum University, Belgrade.

Davidson, R. and Hyde, A. (2014) Winning Meetings and Events for Your Venue, Oxford: Goodfellow Publishers.

Destinations International (2017) Annual report 2017: A year of progress. Destinations International.

DMAI (2016) The Evolving role of DMOs in a shifting marketplace. Destination Marketing Association International.

Doyle, M. (2005) Catch me if you can – screening for fam abusers. *Corporate & Incentive Travel*, January.

Dwyer, L. and Mistilis, N. (1999) Development of MICE tourism in Australia: Opportunities and challenges. *Journal of Convention & Exhibition Management* 1(4).

ETC/UNWTO (2009) Handbook on tourism destination branding. European Travel Commission and World Tourism Organization.

Ford, R. C. and Peeper, W. C. (2007) The past as prologue: Predicting the future of the convention and visitor bureau industry on the basis of its history. *Tourism Management* 28(4): 1104–1114.

Gartrell, R. B. (1994) Destination Marketing for Convention and Visitor Bureaus, Dubuque, IA: Kendall/Hunt.

GCB (2016) Meeting & event barometer report. German Convention Bureau.

Hankinson, G. (2005) Destination brand images: a business tourism perspective. *Journal of Services Marketing* 19(1): 24–32.

Harrill, R. (2005) Fundamentals of destination management and marketing. Educational Institute of the American Hotel & Lodging Association/International Association of Convention & Visitor Bureaus.

Holloway, J. C. (2004) Marketing for Tourism, Harlow: Prentice Hall.

IBTM (2017) IBTM World celebrates 30th anniversary in record style. Press Release, 30 November.

ICCA (2014) International association meetings: Bidding and decision-making. International Congress and Convention Association.

Kourkouridis, D., Dalkrani, V., Pozrikidis, K. and Frangkopoulos, Y. (2017) Familiarisation trip-fam trip: An effective tool for touristic promotion and development. The case of the fam trips organized by TIF-HELEXPO in the context of the International Tourism Exhibition 'Philoxenia 2016' & 'Philoxenia 2017'. *Tourism Research Institute* 16(1): 239–248.

M&C/Asia (2016) Hangzhou launches MICE destination brand. *Meetings & Conventions/ Asia*, 13 December.

Milman, A. and Pizam, A. (1995) The role of awareness and familiarity with a destination: The central Florida case. *Journal of Travel Research* 33(3): 21–27.

Morgan, N., Pritchard, A. and Pride, R. (eds) (2010) *Destination Branding: Creating the unique destination proposition*, Oxford: Butterworth-Heinemann.

Pike, S. (2005) Tourism destination branding complexity. *Journal of Product & Brand Management* 14(4): 258–259.

Pike, S. and Page, S. J. (2014) Destination marketing organizations and destination marketing: A narrative analysis of the literature. *Tourism Management* 40: 202–227.

Rogers, T. and Davidson, R. (2016) *Marketing Destinations and Venues for Conferences, Conventions and Business Events*, Oxford: Routledge.

Tinnish, S. (2007) Tips for innovative meetings and events (T.I.M.E.) topic: CVBs – an innovative partner. SEAL Inc.

Vallee, P. (2008) Convention and visitors bureaus: Partnering with meeting managers for success. In G. C. Ramsborg, B. Miller, D. Breiter, B. J. Reed, & A. Rushing (eds), *Professional meeting management, comprehensive strategies for meetings, conventions and events*, Chicago, IL: Kendall/ Hunt, pp. 161–178.

Wang, Y. (2008) Collaborative destination marketing: Roles and strategies of convention and visitors bureaus. *Journal of Vacation Marketing* 14(3): 191–209.

Whisenant, J. (2012) Convention and visitor bureaus organizational models. The Crossroads Company.

11 Business events knowledge

Business events knowledge in the 21st century

- With support from the SITE Foundation, the Society for Incentive Travel Excellence undertook an extensive job analysis study to define competencies for incentive travel professionals at the Coordinator, Manager and Director levels.
- Destinations International partnered with George Washington University to design and deliver a new and improved version of its Professional in Destination Management certificate programme for entry-level professionals.
- One of the keynote speakers at the Global Events Congress in Warsaw was Jadwiga Berbeka, a Professor at Cracow University of Economics and an academic specialist in the business events industry.
- 60 middle- and upper-level managers from nine different countries participated in the 9th International Summer University for Trade Fair Management at the Cologne Exhibition Centre, where the theme was 'Cutting-Edge Services – Tipping the Scale for Exhibition Success'. The annual ISU is an initiative of the University of Cologne's Institute of Trade Fair Management, Koelnmesse and UFI, the Global Association of the Exhibition Industry.

Chapter objectives

On completion of this chapter the reader should be able to:

- Understand the process of professionalisation as it applies to the business events industry.
- Appreciate the role of academia in creating and disseminating knowledge relevant to business events.
- Appreciate the importance of developing a body of knowledge and competency standards for business events.
- Understand the various sources of professional development and research for the business events industry.

335

The professionalisation of the business events industry

Over the past few decades, many of the management-level roles within the business events industry have made momentous strides towards becoming recognised as professions in their own right, requiring highly specialised skills and knowledge. This trend towards professionalisation contrasts markedly with the previous status of the men and women employed in these roles, as even towards the end of the 20th century, much of the work associated with business events was still regarded as simply consisting of administrative, logistical functions. For instance, the role of meeting planners was widely perceived as basically comprising a series of logistical tasks such as making reservations for accommodation, food and beverage, and transportation – secretarial functions which were supervised by those in more executive, strategic roles (Goldblatt, 2005).

But in the present century, the worldwide expansion and increased prominence of business events as an important element of commercial, political and associative life has resulted in the growing recognition of the specialised knowledge, skills and competencies of those employed in the various managerial roles within this industry. To continue with the specific example of meeting planners, Sperstad and Cecil (2011) illustrate this trend by noting that there has been a paradigm shift from their role being limited to the handling of meetings logistics, and the ordering of meetings components, to them becoming meetings designers or meetings 'architects' – strategic creators of the meeting experience, focusing, among other aspects, on measuring the impact of the meeting experience in terms of business results.

As the landscape of the business events industry has evolved, specific sets of knowledge, skills and competencies have been developed for the various management-level roles that exist within the various sectors, from meeting planners, DMCs and exhibition organisers to venue managers, incentive travel executives and destination marketing managers. Consequently, each of these activities is now able to make a convincing claim to be considered a profession in its own right, bringing a number of benefits for a wide range of stakeholders including governments, clients, the professional bodies and their members.

Most definitions of what constitutes a profession focus on a set of objective traits that any group must demonstrate to be considered a profession. Greenwood (1957), for example, argued that a profession must have the following elements:

- A systematic body of theory or knowledge
- Authority and credibility
- Community sanction, or regulation and control of its members
- A code of ethics
- A professional culture, or a culture of values, norms and symbols.

It is clear that a precise definition of any discipline's unique body of knowledge represents a vital step towards it being defined as a stand-alone profession. This most often takes the form of an agreed body of knowledge that drives the recognition and growth of the discipline and helps to ensure that the professional job title in question is used only after the necessary competencies have been acquired and verified through formal qualifications, usually regulated by professional bodies.

This chapter analyses the progress made towards the definition of a body of knowledge for business events as an important building block in the march towards the professionalisation of this industry. It begins by examining the role of formal education in that process.

The role of formal education in business events

As the business events industry has expanded around the world, the demand for qualified employees has grown, and higher education has become one of the principal mechanisms by which many of these employees are first equipped with the knowledge they require for employment in business events organisations. Several authors highlight the connection between the growing provision of university courses in business events subjects and the professionalisation of this industry. For example, in Baum et al. (2009), Mair explicitly links the increasing recognition of events management as a profession to the growth in the supply of event management training courses and degree qualifications. Similarly, Getz (2007) considers that the acceptance of events management as a profession is associated with the increasing number of graduates in events management as well as holders of designations from certifying professional associations.

As early as 1989, in the US alone, 19 colleges and universities were offering academic courses that related specifically to the business events professions, with the most common course titles being 'Meetings Management', 'Meetings and Conventions Management' and 'Convention Management' (Meetings & Conventions, 1989). Nevertheless, MacLaurin, in Weber and Chon (2002:79), voiced the opinion that formal educational provision for this industry had not kept up with its expansion, noting that 'the [business events] industry has grown rapidly in recent decades, supported by tremendous infrastructure and technology advancements, yet the improvements in education and professional development programmes are, if evident at all, only sporadic and ad hoc'.

One decade later, the global situation looked very different, according to Sperstad and Cecil (2011), who observed that

> the number of academic programs in institutions of higher education now offering meeting planning or event management courses is exploding. Significant interest from students and the demand from the market have driven rapid growth in academic programmes at all levels. Academic programmes offering certificates, associates, bachelors, masters, and PhDs are being introduced and enhanced all over the world.

It seems that as the business events industry was maturing and becoming more recognised, colleges and universities were seeing the potential for defining this subject within their programmes. A study by Cecil et al. (2011) estimated that there were over 200 programmes in North America offering one or more courses in meeting or event management, in academic departments ranging from hospitality, business and tourism to events management and communication.

Accompanying the expansion in provision of business events-related courses in higher education, a supporting knowledge infrastructure has developed alongside, facilitating and validating university teaching and research in these subjects.

More specialised textbooks and academic journals

Although a limited number of specialist textbooks were available in the 1990s (for example, *Meetings, Conventions, and Expositions: An introduction to the industry* by Montgomery and Strick (1994) and *The Business of Conferences* by Shone (1998)), it was in the first decade of the 20th century, as interest in business events as a scholarly subject developed among educators, that a growing number of university-level textbooks were written on this theme. In the English-speaking world, one of the first of these was the seminal work, *The Business and Management of Conventions* by McCabe et al. (2000). This was followed closely by *Business Travel and Tourism* by Swarbrooke and Horner (2001), *Conferences and Conventions* by Rogers (2003), *Business Travel: Conferences, incentive travel, exhibitions, corporate hospitality and corporate travel* by Davidson and Cope (2003), and *Meetings, Expositions, Events and Conventions: An introduction to the industry* by Fenich (2004). Textbooks such as these – and the many that followed – played a key role in supporting business events education in universities worldwide.

In addition, the growing number of educators choosing business events as a focus for their scholarly activities were able to publish their research findings on this theme in specialist academic journals such as *The Journal of Convention and Event Management* as well as in the more general events management publications such as the *International Journal of Event and Festival Management* and *Event Management*. Many academic researchers, however, chose to publish their findings in travel and tourism-themed journals, such as *Tourism Management* and the *Journal of Travel Research* (Mair, 2005).

More specialised academic conferences

An additional channel for the dissemination of business events educators' research is the specialised academic conferences that have become regular forums for the sharing of knowledge on this subject. For instance, an established annual event for academic researchers and lecturers, as well as for practitioners specialising in business events, is held under the auspices of ATLAS – the Association for Tourism and Leisure Education. The ATLAS Special Interest Group for Business Tourism (www.atlas-euro.org) holds an annual conference for the dissemination of best practice in business events education and research. Educators' research on business events themes is also regularly presented at the growing number of academic conferences on events in general such as the biennial

Global Events Congress and the annual meeting of the Association for Events Management Education (AEME) in the UK (www.aeme.org/).

More involvement by the professional associations

The professional associations in business events have increasingly acknowledged the value of higher education courses in this subject, through a number of initiatives designed to welcome their students as members and enter into a dialogue with university educators. At the international scale, for example, Meeting Professionals International and the Society for Incentive Travel Excellence offer Student and Faculty membership packages at special rates; and the International Association of Conference Centres offers a range of advantages for students, including scholarships, funding students' participation at IACC conferences, and a global internship programme.

More support from business events exhibitions

In recognition of the role played by formal education in disseminating knowledge relating to this industry, some of the major international exhibitions have taken steps to support the work of academics and encourage students specialising in this field.

For example, each year at their trade shows in Frankfurt and in Las Vegas, the organisers of IMEX, in partnership with the International Association of Exhibitions and Events, run a two-day Faculty Engagement Programme, a conference bringing together business events educators with industry experts to enable both parties to learn from each other.

However, despite these important advances in how higher education is contributing to the dissemination of knowledge relating to the business events industry, a number of challenges have still to be overcome before the contribution of universities worldwide can be considered to have reached its full potential. Prominent among these challenges is the task of convincing employers that academics have a valuable role to play in preparing the next generation of managers for careers in the business events industry. Part of the solution to this challenge is undoubtedly for the academic community to increase mutual understanding between education and the business events industry. Encouraging lecturers to spend periods in that industry to gain work experience can provide them with valuable insights into industry issues, as well as giving them the opportunity to persuade employers of the value of specialist education. Similarly, inviting practitioners into universities to give presentations on the work they do is another useful way of increasing mutual understanding. But a clear priority for those designing and teaching courses in business events is to ensure that, to the greatest extent possible, the content of such courses includes the body of knowledge considered by practitioners in this industry to be essential for a successful career. The following section of this chapter explores the process leading to the definition of a body of knowledge for the business events industry.

Defining the body of knowledge for business events

Curriculum development

Since the development of the earliest educational programmes in business events-related subjects, academics have been mindful of the need to ensure that the material taught by them should effectively equip students for careers in that industry. One of the first attempts to define the skills and knowledge most valued by business events managers was undertaken by Chon (1990), who conducted a survey in order to identify what they believed should be included in university courses in meetings management. The top five items considered by the respondents as being most important for inclusion in such courses were: (1) budgeting; (2) skills of negotiating with facilities; (3) establishing meeting design/objectives; (4) planning with convention services; and (5) selecting sites and facilities. Additionally, to an open-ended question in which the respondents were asked to provide suggestions for 'other important skills which meetings managers need to possess', the majority of the respondents commented that 'financial management and accounting skills' and 'communications and people skills' were the most important. A further conclusion of the survey was that such courses needed to be supported by a number of business and interdisciplinary courses in order to enhance students' understanding of a broad range of subjects, including human resources, finance, operations, marketing, administration, as well as communications and psychology.

Twenty years later, universities involving local practitioners in the development of their curricula for business events programmes of study had become generally recognised as good practice. For example, Jones (2010:154) describes the process of developing the first business events degree programme in Hong Kong, at Hong Kong Polytechnic University's School of Hotel and Tourism Management:

> One approach to developing a new programme and its curriculum would have been to use the subjects that had already been created in the US. However, as clear differences exist in the nature of the business events industry between North America and Asia, simply mirroring the curriculum developed in the US was not necessarily the best way to proceed in developing a new degree in Asia ... We started by creating a task force we called the Convention and Event Management Task Force made up of industry professionals. The Task Force was comprised of 12 members that included representatives from corporate meetings, exhibition organisers, exhibition service contractors, incentive companies, tourism commission and bureau officials, convention and exhibition venue operations and sales, hotel sales, hotel convention services, and the related media.

Highlighting the competencies that the industry expected for entry-level graduates was the focus of a co-creation session entitled 'What Should an Entry-Level Manager Know to be Successful in the Industry?' The ensuing discussion of what that meant to the Task Force members shaped the core of how the competencies desired from the curriculum would be determined. The final subjects identified for inclusion in the curriculum were as follows:

- Convention Sales and Service
- Catering and Banquet Service Management
- Events Tourism and Management
- Meeting Management
- Special Topics in Convention and Events
- Convention Venue Management
- Exhibition Management
- Special Event Project I and II (a two-semester subject).

The final approval of the new degree was given by the academic body at Hong Kong Polytechnic University and the degree was launched in August 2009, with strong support from the local business events industry.

Competency standards

The rationale for identifying the skills and knowledge required by business events professionals extended beyond academics' aspiration for their educational programmes to reflect the demands of the industry. Towards the end of the first decade of the 21st century, there was still no general agreement as to the standards of competency required to successfully perform many of the critical functions in defined business events work settings. As indicated by Cecil et al. (2013), although the global business events profession had grown into a major worldwide industry, it had not yet formally defined the role of its professionals. The next stage in the evolution and maturation of the industry was to be the development and release of an internationally recognised and accepted set of competency standards.

In this context, a competency may be defined as the capability to apply or use a set of related knowledge, skills and abilities. According to Parry (1996), a competency typically demonstrates four characteristics:

1   A cluster of related knowledge, attitudes, skills and other personal characteristics that affect a major part of one's job
2   Correlates with performance on the job
3   Can be measured against well-accepted standards
4   Can be improved via training and development

One of the first attempts towards developing competency standards relevant to business events professionals was made in 2008, when the Canadian Tourism Human Resource Council, in cooperation with industry representatives from 20 other countries, created the Event Management International Competency Standards (EMICS). These standards drew upon certain aspects of the Events Management Body of Knowledge (EMBOK), which had been developed for the management of events in general (Cecil et al., 2013). The EMICS described in detail the skills, knowledge and attitudes sought by employers and clients when obtaining professional services to plan, implement and evaluate different types of events. They covered a number of different domains, including: strategic planning, project management, risk management, financial management, human resources, meeting or event design, site management and marketing.

In 2011, the Canadian Tourism Human Resource Council in collaboration with Meeting Professionals International (MPI) essentially used these standards as a foundation to create the first globally recognised set of competency standards developed specifically for business events. Known as the Meeting and Business Event Management Competency Standards (MBECS), they built upon the existing EMICS and added new knowledge, skills and abilities that were specifically applicable to business events professionals. The finished MBECS document proposed 12 domains with 33 skills and 100 sub-skills (MBECS, 2011). In terms of the domains, the MBECS maintain that in order to perform effectively, business event managers must be competent in strategic planning; project management; risk management; financial management; administration; human resources; stakeholder management; meeting or event design; site management; marketing; professionalism and communication (ibid.). The full MBECS Curriculum Guide may be downloaded from: https://www.mpiweb.org/docs/default-source/Research-and-Reports/MBECS-Guide-APP-2-Standards.pdf.

Sperstad and Cecil (2011) suggest how the body of knowledge enshrined in the MBECS may be useful to those employed in the business events industry as well as to those designing formal educational programmes. In the first case, it allows current and prospective professionals to map a career path for their personal development and growth and may be used as a platform for best practice and benchmarking. These competency standards also offer the business events industry as a whole: the prospect of improving practices through the creation of occupational job and salary standards; the recognition of the expertise of professionals through the body of knowledge and portable credentials; the development of a career ladder for professional and personal growth; providing more focus to human resource practices, such as creating job descriptions, roles and workplace training programmes; and separating the skilled from the unskilled and the professional from the non-professional employee.

In the second case, the authors suggest that by aligning their educational programmes with the MBECS, the academic community is better equipped to prepare students with the skills and knowledge needed to compete in the 21st-century employment marketplace. They also maintain that a competency-based curriculum tied to a body of knowledge adds credibility when the course content reflects the knowledge and skills determined by professionals in the field and documented in the MBECS. Finally, Sperstad and Cecil (2011) highlight the potential for useful reciprocity, expressing the opinion that through academics incorporating these standards into their higher education curricula, the body of knowledge itself is further formalised.

Professional development for the business events workforce

In a constantly evolving industry that is directly impacted by developments in areas such as technology, legislation, demographics and adult learning, the ongoing professional development of those employed in business events is essential, not only to enable them to keep abreast of changes in the market environment but also to maintain and improve their professional competence, to enhance their career progression, or simply to satisfy their interest in lifelong learning. This section focuses upon the range of opportunities for professional development available to business events practitioners.

The role of the professional associations

The involvement of MPI in developing the MBECS is but one example of how the relevant professional associations have contributed – and continue to contribute – to the knowledge base of those employed in the various sectors of the business events industry. For practically all of the associations, regardless of the geographical level at which they operate, the continuing education of their members is a major priority, not only for the benefit of individual members but to raise the level of professionalism in the industry as a whole. Typically, most international and national associations provide opportunities for knowledge transfer at their annual conferences and chapter meetings, through seminars and presentations by industry experts. But the advent of webinars – 'Web seminars' – has enabled associations to offer presentations, lectures or workshops transmitted over the Web throughout the year as opposed to only at their annual gatherings.

A few examples of the professional development provision on offer from some of the principal international associations serve to demonstrate the range of opportunities open to practitioners:

- The International Congress and Convention Association (ICCA) runs an annual Forum for Young Professionals, which brings together 35 young business events professionals from a diverse array of backgrounds. Over three days, the selected applicants are given networking opportunities, educational sessions, social activities and valuable guidance from influential figures in this industry. According to the ICCA website (https://www.iccaworld.org/), 'Participants will complete the FYP with a wealth of knowledge, a stronger network within the meetings industry, and enhanced professional skills'.
- European Cities Marketing (ECM), the association for city marketing organisations in Europe, runs an annual Summer School, a valuable learning opportunity for all professionals working in convention bureaus, conference centres, DMCs and meeting planning. The Summer School is described on the ECM website (www.europeancitiesmarketing.com/) as follows: 'Ongoing education is a success factor for future business, whether you belong to an important or second tiered destination. It's a crucial task for top management ... to train every employee continuously. The

ECM Summer School sets out the background and context of the Meetings Industry (key players, exhibitions, press, social media, sustainability, clients, intermediaries, RFP and decision-making processes) with a focus on European and international best practices.

- International Association of Professional Congress Organisers (IAPCO) (https://www.iapco.org/) runs three educational EDGE seminars each year in different regions worldwide for participants ranging from young professionals to senior management. Each seminar provides tailor-made learning opportunities, and numbers are capped to maximise participants' interaction and networking opportunities with industry leaders and faculty.

Going beyond the direct provision of professional development opportunities such as these, many business events associations make a valuable contribution to professional development through the activities of their educational foundations – bodies that are supported through financial endowments and operated at arm's length from the associations. For example, the educational foundations of MPI, PCMA, SITE and Destinations International are valuable sources of educational scholarships, grants and research funding for members and non-members. The generosity of eminent business events veterans such as Albert Cronheim (IAPCO) and Vanessa Cotton (MPI UK & Ireland Chapter) is another source of scholarships to be used for the purposes of professional development.

Other sources of professional development

While the contribution of the business events industry associations to the professional development of practitioners is considerable, other organisations also provide education and training opportunities.

- *Exhibitions:* it is rare indeed for a business events-related exhibition not to include an educational programme that provides visitors and exhibitors useful opportunities to attend seminars at which they can learn from experts, gurus and researchers speaking on topics of current interest. For example, at The Meetings Show in London each year, approximately 70 seminars are on offer on a free-to-attend basis.
- *The trade press:* many trade publications offer their readers – and others – access to specialist training. For example, the publishers of M&IT (Meetings & Incentive Travel) magazine (http://www.meetpie.com/) offer a series of training webinars which are tailored to the business events industry and designed to provide suppliers and buyers with a better understanding of the market. Topics of individual webinars include: social media for the events industry; the Bribery Act; data protection; and venue contracts.
- *Consultants and training companies:* a wide range of professional development opportunities are delivered by individuals or companies with varying degrees of specialisation in the business events industry offering bespoke or off-the-peg training for all occupational levels from operations to management. Popular topics include customer service and venue sales skills.

Occupational certifications

A further contribution of the main industry associations in the field of professional development for the business events industry has been the developing of specific occupational certifications. In any industry, certifications represent a public, formal and official recognition of an individual's occupational skills. For individuals, therefore, certification attainment not only offers the possibility of them boosting their pay and enhancing their self-esteem, but most importantly represents a way for them to formalise their skills acquisition and a verification of their ability to accomplish identified tasks at a particular level of proficiency. But a system of occupational certification also offers advantages for other stakeholders. For employers, certification makes the quality and quantity of individual job applicants' skills clearly observable, and therefore they increasingly rely upon certifications as a means of differentiating among applicants. According to Crawford and Mogollón (2011), for firms, certification should decrease the transaction costs of selecting and placing workers, improve the ability of managers to match skills to tasks, and increase the effectiveness of outsourcing by making it possible to identify competent external suppliers. Ultimately, from an employer's perspective, a system of certification may thus enhance organisational performance, promote continuous improvement of efficiency, and increase productivity and profits.

Within the business events industry, certifications have proliferated recently, usually at the initiative of the professional associations. Programmes leading to these certifications are often run by the associations themselves, sometimes cooperating with industry partners or universities (Weber and Chon, 2002). However, unlike in other professions such as healthcare, where certification or a licence is required as a condition of employment, occupational certification in the business events industry is entirely voluntary, meaning that individuals may choose whether or not to certify.

Certifications offered by some of the principal international associations active in the business events industry are listed in Table 11.1.

Table 11.1 Events industry certifications

Certification	Managing organisation(s)	Website
Certified Association Executive (CAE)	ASAE & The Centre for Association Leadership (ASAE)	https://www.asaecenter.org/programs/cae-certification
Destination Management Certified Professional (DMCP)	Association of Destination Management Executives (ADME)	http://www.admeinternational.org/aws/ADME/pt/sp/accreditation_certification
Certified Meeting Professional (CMP)	Event Industry Council (EIC)	http://www.eventscouncil.org/CMP/CMPApplicants.aspx

(Continued)

Table 11.1 (Continued)

Certification	Managing organisation(s)	Website
Certified in Exhibition Management (CEM)	International Association of Exhibitions and Events (IAEE)	https://www.iaee.com/cem/
Certified Facilities Executive (CFE)	International Association of Venue Managers (IAVM)	https://www.iavm.org/cve/cve-overview
Certified Government Meeting Professional (CGMP)	Society of Government Meeting Planners (SGMP)	https://www.sgmp.org/cgmpbenefits
Certified Destination Management Executive (CDME)	Destinations International	https://destinationsinternational.org/cdme
Certified Incentive Travel Professional (CITP)	Society for Incentive Travel Excellence	https://www.siteglobal.com/page/certification

In parallel with the system of certifications of the main international associations, a number of *national* associations' certifications have also been developed. One such example is the MEA (Meetings & Events Australia), the main body representing the industry in that country, which offers its members certification as Accredited Meeting Manager and Accredited In-House Meeting Manager. Another example, the Certified Croatian Meetings and Events Professional award of the Croatian Meeting Professionals Association, is the subject of a case study in this chapter.

Within the business events industry, many believe that in the near future, certification will be a professional *requirement*, not just a choice. In the meantime, as awareness of the existing certifications grows among employers, an increasing number of them are specifying, during the recruitment process, the need for applicants to have an appropriate certification. Furthermore, some associations actively recommend that priority in hiring be given to those members who have achieved recognised occupational certifications. For example, the MEA, mentioned above, 'highly recommends' that employers and clients use those members who have achieved the designations Accredited Meetings Manager and Accredited In-House Meetings Manager.

Research on the business events industry

No body of knowledge can ever be static. It must develop over time, as the industry it serves matures; and it must evolve by taking into account the new findings of researchers, in particular those focusing on best practice.

One challenge for the business events industry, often highlighted by commentators, is the lack of systematic and regular research to produce useful insights and reliable data. Rogers and Davidson describe this dearth of market intelligence as one of the legacies of the industry's relative immaturity. However, they continue by noting that 'while many gaps still remain, some genuine progress is being made in gathering better market intelligence and there are increasing numbers of best practice examples from around the world, which themselves deserve recognition and emulation' (Rogers and Davidson, 2016:253).

Before considering the remaining gaps in our knowledge of this field, it is useful to review the various sources of research that help expand our knowledge of business events. The variety of stakeholders described earlier as being providers of professional development are also in many cases active in commissioning and undertaking research projects. For example, in terms of exhibitions, each year at the IBTM World (http://www.ibtmworld. com/) trade show in Barcelona, the findings of the researchers of the Trends Watch Report are launched, highlighting current trends in the business events industry and predictions for the state of the market in the year ahead.

Industry associations and their associated foundations are other key sources of research. At the international level, for example, the SITE Foundation sponsors ongoing research on topics relating to the incentive travel market (https://www.siteglobal.com/page/research); and the International Association of Conference Centres (http://www.iacconline.org/) regularly publishes research reports on venue-related themes such as 'The Meeting Room of the Future' and 'Trends in Nutrition and Delegate Wellbeing'. And at the national level, the associations are also active in commissioning research. For instance, the Business Visits & Events Partnership, an umbrella organisation representing leading trade and professional organisations, government agencies and other significant influencers in the business visits and events sector in the UK, is a source of much insightful research of relevance to that country and beyond (https://www.businessvisitsandeventspartnership. com/research-and-publications/research/category/4-bvep-research).

Trade publications also contribute directly to our knowledge through, for example, reader surveys or through the commissioning of research reports such as the annual British Meetings & Events Industry Survey which is commissioned by CAT Publications and carried out by specialist researchers The Right Solution, with the support of sponsors (http://www.meetpie.com/staticpagedisplay.aspx?code=bmeis_sponsorship).

Academic research

There can be no doubt that there has been a recent increase in both the quantity and quality of academic research focusing on the business events industry. But this growth has been slow in coming. In one of the first reviews of academic research into business events, Yoo and Weber (2005) declared that, despite strong growth in flows of global business tourism over the previous quarter century, it remained under-represented in tourism scholarship as a whole. A similar conclusion was reached by Lee and Back (2005) in their review of convention and meeting management research between 1990 and 2003. Five years later, Stetic and Simicevic (2010) still considered that business events had not attracted the attention of a number of researchers that was commensurate with the economic importance of the industry.

Moreover, authors were generally in agreement that the extant academic research had focused almost exclusively upon the developed world. Yoo and Weber (2005), for example, examining the regional focus of the articles in the review of the academic research, found that more than half of the articles had a focus on North America (although they also identified a developing trend towards the publication of more articles focusing on Asia and Australia). A decade later, Rogerson (2015) observed that most academic papers on business events still related to economically advanced countries, with the bulk of the literature dealing with North America, Pacific Asia and Europe.

However, new insights were provided by Mair's (2012) review of the academic business events literature from 2000–2009. While acknowledging in this publication that researchers in the business events field still considered that there was a general lack of literature, she raised the question of whether it was reasonable to highlight a dearth of research overall, or whether the field had progressed to a stage where it was more helpful to identify specific research strengths and gaps. The results of her review of academic papers published on business events-related themes revealed that, in terms of research focus, meeting planners were the subject of the highest number of articles, followed some considerable way behind by papers focusing on meeting suppliers, attendees and destinations. The two most popular research sub-themes she identified were the evaluation of satisfaction (with the destination, the event and the service quality), followed by articles on technology as it impacts upon business events, the attendee decision-making process, and the meeting planner/association site selection process.

But perhaps the most valuable contribution of Mair's review is her highlighting of important research gaps. She identifies these as:

- The social and environmental impacts of business events
- Climate change and events
- Incentive travel
- Qualitative research (into, for example, the meanings that individuals attach to business events, or about their experience of attending a business event).

It is clear that the analytic skills and enquiring spirit of those in the academic community equip them well in terms of their potential to add significantly to our knowledge of business events. Only by increasing the quantity and the quality of research into this still under-researched field can academic researchers truly realise that potential and make their full contribution to our knowledge of this industry.

Chapter summary

This chapter began by noting the paradigm shift as business events employment has moved from the logistical to the strategic level while the industry has undergone a process of professionalisation. Links were made between this process and the expansion of business events-related programmes in higher education. The contribution of universities to the development of a body of knowledge for business events and of a set of general competency standards was examined. The theme of continuing education for the business events workforce was developed, noting the contributions of the professional associations in terms of direct provision of educational opportunities as well as the provision of support by the associations' educational foundations. The contribution of other sources (exhibitions, the trade press, consultants and training companies) was also described. The expansion of occupational certification for business events professionals was analysed, noting the advantages of such systems for employers and employees. The chapter ended with a review of the various sources of research into business events, encompassing the valuable contribution of academics in this domain.

CASE STUDY 11.1: THE CERTIFIED CROATIAN MEETINGS AND EVENTS PROFESSIONAL PROGRAMME

CCMEP

The Croatian Meeting Professionals Association

The Croatian Meeting Professionals Association (CMPA) (www.cmpa.eu/en/), which was founded in 2011 as a non-profit organisation, is the premier professional association for meetings, incentives and events organisers in Croatia. Its mission is 'to develop and enhance the professional status of meeting and event organisers and increase the recognition given to its members and to CMPA as the leading representatives of the profession in Croatia'.

Continuing education has been one of the CMPA's priorities since the beginning, and since 2011 it has held regular educational seminars (approximately two per year) for business events professionals in Croatia. But, going one step further in its efforts to improve industry standards, in 2015 the CMPA decided to launch a national certification programme for meeting industry professionals – entitled the Certified Croatian Meetings and Events Professional.

The Certified Croatian Meetings and Events Professional

The programme was inspired by two existing examples of training provision: the European Cities Marketing Summer School (www.europeancitiesmarketing.com/ecm-summer-school/) and the Events Industry Council's Certified Meeting Professional designation (www.eventscouncil.org/CMP/AboutCMP.aspx).

The CMPA's supporting partners in the project were the Zagreb Faculty of Economics and Business (Department of Tourism), the Croatian Chamber of Commerce and EFAPCO – the European Federation of Associations of Professional Congress Organisers (www.efapco.eu/default.asp), of which the CMPA is a full member.

The CCMEP was created by a working group comprising seasoned industry professionals who met face-to-face 15 times to develop the programme. The group members were: Jasmina Bilac, ProConventa PCO; Ivica Covic, VIP Travel, DMC&PCO; Zeljka Cuturic, Esplanade Zagreb Hotel; Ranko Filipovic, PerfectMeetings.hr, PCO&DMC; Goran Pavlovic, Opatija Convention Bureau; Debora Petrovic, Importanne Resort; Slaven Reljic, Coral Group, DMC; Braco Suljic, AS Congress Service; and Aleksandra Uhernik Djurdjek, Eventfully Croatia, Destination Specialist. The result of the group's deliberations was a 60-page syllabus and a four-day curriculum.

The programme consists of two sections:

1 Meetings and events organisation – two days

- Who is who in the meetings industry
- Types of events and their planning
- The project management process, including: project planning; setting up an agenda; project budgeting; programme launching; carrying out the programme; programme follow-up; technology in events; incentive travel special features
- Glossary of industry terms.

2 Croatia as a MICE destination – two days

- Croatia as a MICE destination: its strengths and weaknesses
- Panel discussion with the convention bureau directors of the Croatian premium MICE destinations
- Group work which results in oral and PowerPoint presentations, including budgets, as bids to three different clients (association meeting, corporate product launch, top incentive travel programme)
- One-hour online exam based on the four days' lectures and a handbook encompassing the project (70 per cent correct answers are required to pass)
- Certificate and badges distribution to those who successfully completed the programme.

Each of those who successfully completes the CCMEP receives a certificate and a badge, as well as eight Events Industry Council Continuing Education hours.

Once acquired, the certificate is valid for five years, after which a re-certification is manda-tory. To apply for a re-certification, a certificate owner must attend at least 60 percent of the educational events organised by the CMPA during the five-year period of their certificate's validity.

CCMEP graduates

By 2018, three cohorts of business events professionals had successfully completed the programme and acquired CCMEP designations. They came from all fields of the industry: PCOs, DMCs, hotels and venues, audio-visual and other technology companies, convention bureaus, academia and the public sector – and all levels of responsibility, from experienced senior staff to their young, aspiring colleagues.

Two testimonials from programme attendees indicate their enthusiasm for the project:

'I am very happy to have participated in the first round of the Certification programme and can only recommend it, as it is a great opportunity to learn about new trends, and to exchange knowledge and experiences with colleagues from the industry. Finally, it helps you freshen up on industry terms, work processes and all that you come across in your daily work routine. Naturally I have encouraged my co-workers to get certified and am happy to say that we now have 3 team members who are Certified Croatian Meetings & Events Professionals.'

Marina Raic-Bobic, 360°incentives & MoRe, DMC/PCO

'As one of the first Certified Croatian Meetings & Events Professionals, I can say that this certification process gave me a lot in my daily work. In this constantly changing environ-ment, it is extremely important to educate yourself on a daily basis. So this structured certification programme came as a great solution and gave me some new insights, tips and tricks for our industry – and refreshed some already known facts. Excellent programme – and I would like to recommend it to everyone in events!'

Nikica Zunic, Penta, PCO

Further developments

An offshoot of the CCMEP programme was launched in spring 2018, designed for a public sector audience rather than industry professionals. The content of this one-day programme is a summary of the basic facts included in the full CCMEP programme. The aim is to make people in the public sector aware that the design and planning of the various kinds of meet-ings they might be involved in are underpinned by a whole industry of professionals and their associations.

A second programme evolving from the CCMEP is one that will be designed to meet the needs of educational institutions dealing with the business events industry, either through their teaching of students with an interest in a career in this industry or as researchers.

CASE STUDY 11.2: THE UFI EXHIBITION MANAGEMENT DEGREE

EMD

Background

In 2006, UFI (http://www.ufi.org/), the Global Association of the Exhibition Industry, in cooperation with the Cooperative State University in Ravensburg, Germany, created the UFI Exhibition Management Degree (UFI-EMD) for exhibition industry professionals. The objective was to offer participants the opportunity to develop valuable management skills applicable to the management of exhibition centres and the development of successful trade shows. The UFI-EMD focuses on the transfer of knowledge in the form of sound management skills, strategic thinking and well-developed professional expertise based on best practices in the exhibition industry.

UFI is the global association of the world's leading tradeshow organisers and exhibition centre operators, as well as the major national and international exhibition associations and selected partners of the exhibition industry. UFI's main goal is to represent, promote and support the business interests of its members and the exhibition industry.

The Steinbeis Transfer Centre (STZ) is part of the Steinbeis Foundation, which is a worldwide initiative focusing on technology and knowledge transfer. It was founded in Germany in 1971 with the goal of making scientific knowledge available to the entire global economy. The Cooperative State University in Ravensburg, Germany was founded in 1978 and now cooperates with more than 150 companies working in the events industry. The STZ–ECE (Steinbeis Transfer Centre–Exhibition Convention and Event Management at the

Cooperative State University, Ravensburg, Germany) partnership is responsible for the EMD's curriculum development and the selection of experienced international teachers to provide the course instruction. The staff of STZ–ECE also take care of the content, presentation and logistical aspects of the UFI-EMD programme. UFI is responsible for the marketing, quality control and certification of this course.

As a rule, local hosts of the EMD support the UFI programme. They are UFI members and manage the programme on site. The hosts promote the UFI-EMD in their region. As an example, the Macau Fair and Trade Association (MFTA) advertises the programme in the Pan-Pearl River Delta and the Guangdong–Hong Kong–Macau Greater Bay Area as well as in the countries and regions along the Belt and Road. TCEB, the Thailand Convention and Exhibition Bureau, supports the EMD in South-East Asia.

The first edition of the EMD programme was run in Thailand in 2007. Since then, 19 editions of the programme have been offered in nine different cities (Bangkok, Istanbul, Macau, St Petersburg, Riyadh, Dubai, Doha, Bangalore and Hanover) resulting in 490 graduates from 32 different countries.

Target audience

The target audience for the UFI-EMD consists of:

* Organisers of exhibitions and conventions
* Associations and government institutions – for example, the TCEB, MFTA, the QTA Tourism Authority, and the Dubai International Exhibition and Convention Centre
* Managers of exhibition and congress centres
* Senior and mid-level project managers responsible for the development and operation of exhibitions.

The participants are required to have an acceptable level of English language skills.

Educational programme

The educational programme is divided into four modules totalling 150 hours, comprising one on-site, face-to-face four-day module, and three e-learning modules that allow participants to continue their learning experience from a distance, supported by an online learning platform. From the list of modules on offer, each participant composes an individual programme for himself/herself, based on their specific interests as an organiser, venue operator or service provider. The content of the modules is shown in Table 11.2.

A renowned group of international instructors and exhibition industry experts lead the course on site and manage the e-learning sessions, ensuring individual contact and support for all participants during the online modules. A group project undertaken by the attendees completes the e-learning collaboration.

Table 11.2 UFI Exhibition Management degree modules

Module 1
Basics in Exhibition Management I On-site module (36 hrs)

1.1 Introduction into the exhibition industry

This module provides an overview of the exhibition markets and the service orientation of the industry. The basic terminology is introduced. This introduction to the MICE industry is practice-oriented. Economic aspects of the industry are also explained.

1.2 Exhibition Marketing + Sales Management

This module explores the principles of marketing and marketing instruments, with a special focus on communication tools. Each aspect is examined in relation to the specific concerns of the exhibition industry. Media planning, promotion to visitors and exhibitor recruitment are studied. Sales means the creation of value. The students learn how to determine target groups, create sales concepts and efficiently use sales instruments.

1.3 Project Management

Project management is a critical skill for successful exhibition managers. The module content includes: theory and principles of project management, project structure, exhibition objectives and concepts, project development and controls.

1.4 Risk Management

Risk management must be implemented during the exhibition process. Today it is accepted that risks are an integral part of any project. In this module, participants develop an understanding of the factors involved and the means of controlling risk.

Module 2
Advanced Studies in Exhibition Management I E-Learning module (24 of 36 hrs)

2.1 Intercultural Management

Globalisation is the current trend in all areas of contemporary society. As exhibitions bring together people from all parts of the world, project management should be well versed in the principles of intercultural management. These are addressed thoroughly in the UFI-EMD course.

2.2 Exhibitions from the exhibitor's perspective

Exhibitors are one of the key customer groups for an exhibition organiser. Organisers must offer services which meet the needs of exhibitors. UFI-EMD participants learn how to coordinate activities and services to successfully meet these goals.

2.3 Special Event Marketing

Special events are often used as promotional activities to launch brands, products and companies. They are initiated at exhibitions by exhibitors or by organisers. UFI-EMD participants examine ways to develop special events with a win-win result for all.

2.4–2.6 Service Partners of the MICE Industry

Exhibition organisers cooperate with a variety of exhibition service providers. All partners must work to develop a mutually beneficial and supportive network system: service strategy and organisation; stand design and building; catering.

2.7 Information Management

The core competence for exhibition organisers is often said to be his/her databank of personal contacts with exhibitors, visitors and representatives of different organisations. UFI-EMD participants learn how to carefully manage this material and profit from its potential.

1.5 Joint Project

The participants determine several joint projects that must be undertaken during the face-to-face and the e-learning modules. The subjects will be directly relevant to the industry and may be linked to the special interests of certain attendees. These assignments will be undertaken through group work.

Module 3: Advanced Studies in Exhibition Management II E-Learning module (24 of 36 hrs.)

3.1 Finance, Accountancy and Treasury

The exhibition manager is responsible for the profits achieved within the exhibition project. Sound knowledge of cost management is a requirement and must include the principles of cost control, finance, budget management, accounting and treasury management.

3.2 Market Research

Exhibitions are an excellent source for market research. Many exhibitors and visitors representing a market segment meet at a single location at the same time. This provides an ideal opportunity to undertake specific market research. Market research techniques and objectives are studied in this section.

3.3–3.4 E-Marketing – Social Media – Public Relations

The Internet has become an essential tool to launch exhibitions and congresses. Content: Setting-up an e-marketing plan; digital marketing trends, e-channel strategies and e-marketing-mix; e-models; social media marketing; social media channels and strategies; content marketing and engagement strategy. Introduction to public relations tools, planning and evaluation options as they relate to the exhibition industry.

3.5 Service Partners of the MICE Industry

Exhibition organisers cooperate with different service providers. All partners build a network. The relationship between agencies providing promotion, incentives, events and travel are related in this course to the exhibition industry.

2.8 Venue Management I

Exhibitions require large and expensive infrastructure and facilities. This may be privately or state-owned. This topic examines the 'how to' of professional facility administration and management, including technical and infrastructure facility management: operations, maintenance, energy, safety and waste disposal.

Module 4: Advanced Studies in Exhibition Management III E-Learning module (24 of 36 hrs.)

4.1 Management Strategy

Exhibition organisers and venue managers must develop strategic plans, which reflect corporate evolution. Companies must plan for long-term growth and profitability. New events must be developed. Strategic management is an important part of the company's management process.

4.2 Customer Relationship Management (CRM)

CRM is one of the most important aspects of today's marketing environment. Customer satisfaction and customer loyalty are frequent objectives for exhibition companies. Participants will evaluate a variety of CRM approaches.

4.3 Sponsoring

Sponsors contribute increasingly to exhibition revenues. Sponsorships can provide financial and barter advantages to all parties. This topic will explore ways of developing balanced sponsorship opportunities.

4.4 Special Event Management

The planning and realisation of special events is closely related to the exhibition industry. Therefore the principles of special event management should be well understood by exhibition managers.

4.5 Exhibition Logistics

Three types of logistics are explored: Exhibitor logistics (the transport and the information flow during the mounting and dismantling of stands); visitor logistics (the guidance of visitors on the exhibition ground); and logistics for international stand building companies.

(Continued)

Table 11.2 (Continued)

3.6–3.7 Congress Management – Interpretation

The planning and operation of congresses and auxiliary events is closely related to the exhibition industry. Exhibitions are often a part of congresses and vice versa. The principles of congress and event management must be well understood by exhibition professionals. Interpretation is an essential part of international events. The students learn how to plan and consider interpretation tools as a necessary service within their events.

3.8 Venue Management II

Venues must optimise their business units (i.e. exhibitions, congresses and other events are single units of the overall product portfolio). Participants learn how to manage the facilities from the commercial side. Facility management process; investments; make-or-buy; controlling; sales management; destination management; management concepts. Special areas: e.g. destination marketing.

4.6 Sustainability

Sustainability in the exhibition industry has become a vital issue for all organisers and their service providers. Sustainability is about people, planet and profit in a true, fair and clean way.

Evaluation procedure

The Exhibition Management degree is awarded to participants who have successfully completed all four modules within a period of three years. If any participant is not able to complete all modules in one region, they are invited to participate in another UFI-EMD programme hosted in a different region.

The UFI-EMD community

The UFI-EMD community on LinkedIn (https://www.linkedin.com/groups/3814830/profile) is designed to enable UFI-EMD participants and alumni to stay connected with each other and with the programme instructors before, during and after the completion of the programme.

The UFI-EMD community serves as a platform for participants, alumni and instructors to receive and provide support, collaborate online or share experiences, opinions and know-how with other specialists in the exhibition industry. Community members can start discussions that are of particular importance to them, ask questions and share their opinions and work experiences with other exhibition industry professionals.

The UFI alumni network

UFI-EMD graduates also have the opportunity of enhancing their professional network through collaborating and connecting with fellow participants and professors via the UFI Alumni Network. The network is exclusively reserved for all graduates of the UFI-EMD programme (successful completion of all four modules), participants of the UFI International Summer University (ISU) and instructors of both UFI education programmes.

In the future, UFI intends to offer this programme in other key languages, such as Chinese and Arabic.

CASE STUDY 11.3: EDINBURGH NAPIER UNIVERSITY'S MSC IN BUSINESS EVENTS

Edinburgh Napier University

Named after John Napier, the brilliant 16th-century mathematician and philosopher, Edinburgh Napier University first opened its doors to students in 1964 as Napier Technical College. The institution evolved into a modern, ambitious and innovative university located in Edinburgh, Scotland's capital city. By 2017, it had achieved the position of the top university in the UK for adding value to students (Guardian University Guide 2017) as well as winner of the prestigious Queen's Anniversary Prize, which recognises institutions for internationally acclaimed research. The University recognises and celebrates diversity and strives to achieve its vision which is to be 'an enterprising and innovative community renowned internationally, with an unrivalled student learning experience'.

The University's strong links with industry create many opportunities for work-related learning for the majority of its students, from internships and work shadowing to live projects and experiences abroad. A key element of the University's Strategy 2020 is to deliver an excellent personalised student experience through providing opportunities for students to undertake accredited work-related and developmental experience as part of their overall educational experience. Consequently, there has been a move toward offering educational programmes that are created in collaboration with industry and taught by academics and industry professionals who are experts in their fields. This helps provide students with the practical skills and insights they need for securing graduate employment. In 2017 Edinburgh Napier University's Destination Leaders Programme won the Times Higher Education Leadership and Management Award for Employee Engagement.

The Edinburgh International Conference Centre

The provision of a major conference venue in Edinburgh was originally proposed in the 1980s in response to a surge in demand for conferences throughout the world at that time. The objective of attracting more business events to the city underpinned the vision and mission for the Edinburgh International Conference Centre (EICC) as set by the City of Edinburgh Council in 1993: 'to procure the successful and continued operation of the Conference Centre in a global market place with national and international customers so as to maximise the economic benefit to the city of Edinburgh'.

Opened in 1995, the EICC became the first conference venue in the world to utilise revolving auditoria to optimise events space. By 2010, it became clear that the sustained success of the EICC had created a demand for increased events space, and so construction on an extension to the venue began. In 2013, the new extension opened, effectively doubling the venue's capacity. Since its opening, the EICC has welcomed 1.3 million delegates from more than 120 countries, generating £545m of economic impact for the city region. Of the EICC's clients, 66 per cent are repeat customers (http://www.eicc.co.uk/about-eicc/facts-figures-vision/). Recently they have refreshed their vision and focus 'to create an environment which inspires ideas that change the world'.

The EICC is still owned by the City of Edinburgh Council but operates as an independent commercial venture.

Origins and development of the MSc in Business Events

The EICC has been a long-time supporter of Edinburgh Napier University through providing on-site visits, guest lectures and employment opportunities for both current students and graduates. As part of a wider discussion regarding collaborative opportunities between the EICC and the University, initial discussions focusing on the MSc in Business Events commenced in early 2016. The next 12 months saw extensive negotiations between the two organisations that concentrated on programme content, assessment methods, the target market, opportunities for joint delivery of modules and, crucially, the opportunities for programme participants to undertake a period of work experience at the EICC. This resulted in the development and agreement of the final programme that was put forward for validation in May 2017 (see Figure 11.1 below). The programme was initially launched as a one-year, full-time programme in September 2017, with the aim of offering part-time and more flexible modes in the future. Taught at Edinburgh Napier's Craiglockhart Campus, participants enjoy all of the facilities necessary for their academic development, while having structured opportunities to regularly interact with members of staff at the EICC.

The programme

The course is designed to prepare students for a range of careers in business events, such as corporate event planner, meetings planner, conference and exhibition organiser, business event manager or incentive travel planner. But graduates could also use their knowledge and skills to work for a destination marketing organisation, or in a range of venues such as a conference and exhibition centre, hotel or visitor attraction.

Students study modules that are specifically focused on elements of the management of business events (such as Business Skills and Sustainable Conference and Event Management), more generic management modules (such as Tourism Marketing and Experience Design and Management), and modules focused on research (such as Research Methods and Dissertation). Throughout the programme, managers from the EICC deliver guest lectures to students – particularly concerning sustainability and project management.

In the second trimester of the programme, students have the opportunity to undertake a three-week placement at the EICC. During this time, students spend time in all seven operational areas of the organisation and work alongside departmental managers as a means of developing an understanding of the role, responsibilities and constraints of both the position and the organisation. Students also have the unique opportunity to work alongside the chief executive and gain first-hand experience and understanding of the strategic direction

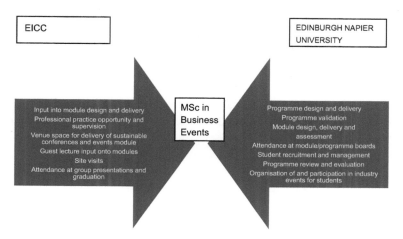

Figure 11.1
Development of the MSc in Business Events

of the organisation. Students can request the opportunity to specialise in one of the seven operational areas by asking to spend more time in whichever area is of most interest to them. This provides the opportunity to develop a greater in-depth understanding of a particular area and can also provide additional background for future research interventions that may be necessary for successful completion of their dissertation in the third trimester.

IT'S MY JOB
DR. NELLIE SWART,
SENIOR LECTURER AT THE
UNIVERSITY OF SOUTH AFRICA

Following my education at schools in South Africa's North West Province, I studied at the University of Pretoria, and in 2007 I was awarded my MCom in Tourism Management. The title of my dissertation for that degree was 'Service Quality: A survey amongst convention consumers at the CSIR (Council for Scientific and Industrial Research) International Convention Centre'. During my studies, I worked as a volunteer at a conference, and that experience made me realise that I had a passion for the operational aspects related to the business tourism industry. I still enjoy the planning of business events and the satisfaction I derive from their execution.

Following my studies at master's level, I moved to the University of Johannesburg, where I completed my doctoral studies in 2013, being awarded the degree of Doctor of Commerce (DCom) in Leadership Performance and Change for my thesis entitled 'A Business Tourism Service Quality Scorecard for Predicting Tourist Retention'. This study focused on ways of determining how business tourists think about service quality, how they experience service delivery, and how this impacts upon their intention to visit a destination in future. Today the model has been refined and applied in the annual research I do for HuntEx (see below).

While studying towards my MCom in Tourism Management in Pretoria, I was also teaching tourism to undergraduate students at the University of South Africa (UNISA) in that city. Similarly, in parallel with studying towards my DCom at the University of Johannesburg, I was also employed full-time as a lecturer there. The empowerment of people with knowledge is a priority in South Africa. My experiences of teaching at UNISA and at the University of Johannesburg showed me that I have natural ability to relate to students and enjoy transferring my skills and knowledge to them. I do not measure my success in the awards I receive, but in the achievements of the students I educate.

I am now a Senior Lecturer in Tourism at the University of South Africa, in the Department of Entrepreneurship, Supply Chain, Transport, Tourism and Logistics Management.

Ever since I began teaching, I have always ensured that I continually gain practical experience through involvement in project work, both within the business events industry and within academia. This is because I believe that it's essential for me to keep my own knowledge regularly updated with regard to the requirements of the ever-changing business events industry, complemented by sound academic research.

On the academic side, I frequently speak at educational conferences and author or co-author accredited journal articles, book chapters and accredited conference proceedings articles. A few recent examples of my publications on business events topics are as follows:

- Swart, M. P. and Engelbrecht, W. H. (2017) Expo market segmentation variables as moderators of expo technology acceptance. *African Journal for Physical Activity and Health Sciences*, June (Supplement): 170–183.
- Swart, M. P. (2016) Re-inventing experiential value and satisfaction behaviour in business tourism experiences, in Sotiriadis, M. and Gursoy, D. (eds) *Managing and Marketing Tourism Experiences: Issues, challenges and approaches*, Bingley: Emerald.
- Swart, M. P. (2016) Expo Product Satisfaction as a mediator between Expo Promotion and Expo Retention. Conference proceedings of the XXXIII Pan Pacific conference held in Miri, Malaysia. Conducted by the Pan Pacific Business Association (PPB) (ISBN: 1-931649-27-6).

One example of the research that I regularly conduct on behalf of the business events industry is the work I have undertaken each year since 2011 on behalf of HuntEx (www.huntex.net), an international consumer exhibition for hunters and sport shooters, held each year at the Gallagher Convention Centre in Midrand, South Africa. In 2017, my research focused on the experiences of female hunters, the marketing and product offerings at the expo as well as the experience of visitors when using the HuntEx mobile application during the expo.

I strongly believe in the power of associations to make positive changes in education and in the tourism and business events professions. For that reason, I invest a considerable amount of my time in active membership of associations that are relevant to my interests. I am an executive committee member of the association Tourism Educators South Africa (TESA), and the Southern African Association for the Conference Industry (SAACI) Tshwane branch. I am also currently a faculty member of Meetings

Professional International (MPI). As a representative of these associations, I have been an invited panellist at the annual IMEX-MPI-MCI Future Leaders Forum (FLF) since 2015. The FLF was developed to encourage students worldwide to consider careers in the meetings and incentive travel industry. The South Africa FLF is held in Johannesburg during South Africa's principal exhibition for the business events industry, Meetings Africa (https://www.meetingsafrica.co.za/).

Another of my external activities is my involvement as Programme Leader in the Executive Development Programme for Women in Tourism (EDP for WiT), commissioned by the National Department of Tourism (NDT). The EDP for WiT initiative is a transformation intervention to position black women in tourism management, and for consideration at executive management level.

As well as teaching and researching in the field of business events, I also organise conferences on a regular basis. I learned many of the practical skills needed by conference organisers when, in 2010, I studied to gain the professional certification, Certified Meetings Professional (CMP), awarded by the Events Industry Council. Here are a few examples of events that I have recently organised:

- 2014 Tourism Educators South Africa Student Conference hosted by UNISA
- National Department of Tourism: 2015 Annual Tourism Lecture hosted by UNISA
- 2016 Economics Curriculum Lekgotla, hosted by UNISA and the University of the Witswatersrand, sponsored by the City of Tshwane
- UNISA Teaching and Learning Festival (20–21 October 2016)
- The 6th International Tourism Studies Association (6–8 August 2018).

It's certainly true that all of these activities keep me extremely busy. But I sincerely believe that they bring real benefits to my teaching in the form of up-to-date events industry knowledge and contacts. I believe that it is simply impossible to capture all the aspects of the business events industry in any textbook, so I share my event experiences in 'Nellie's Words of Wisdom' with my students, in an attempt to sensitise them to some real-life issues and how I have handled them. Recently I have been very encouraged by prominent public recognition of the work that I do in being a bridge between events industry education and the industry. In 2017, I was named one of South Africa's 'Top 40 Women in MICE' at an annual award ceremony that forms part of *Meetings* magazine's Women's Month celebrations. *Meetings* magazine is one of the most widely read publications in the South African business events industry. The women were recognised for their ability to motivate their peers in the industry, the amount of revenue they generate or their passion for the industry. I was extremely proud to be the first academic ever to receive this honour. And at the UNISA Women's Forum 'Women of the Year' award ceremony, I was thrilled to receive the accolade 'Defying Gravity' which is given to female employees of the University in recognition of their going far beyond the expectations of their job.

IT'S MY JOB
DR. JUDITH MAIR, SENIOR LECTURER IN EVENT MANAGEMENT, UNIVERSITY OF QUEENSLAND

After studying for a degree in Languages (Interpreting and Translating) at Heriot-Watt University, Edinburgh, I completed my MSc in Tourism in 1995. I wanted to work in the tourism industry, and as a proud Scot, I spent ten years promoting tourism in Scotland, working for VisitScotland, The Edinburgh Woollen Mill and Scotsell Scottish Holidays. As part of all these jobs, I represented my various employers at many trade shows, and loved the buzz and excitement of exhibitions. This sparked my interest in the non-leisure aspects of tourism. So when I decided to go back into academia, it was the study of business events that most appealed to me. From 2000 to 2005, I studied for my PhD at the Scottish Hotel School, part of the University of Strathclyde in Glasgow. I took conferences as my specific PhD focus, and investigated how people decide which conferences to attend. Entitled 'Towards an Attribute-Based Model of the UK Association Conference Attendance Decision-Making Process', my PhD examined the consumer behaviour of conference delegates when deciding whether to attend association conferences. I was surprised by how little academic research there was in the area at that time, although this has increased exponentially over the past ten years or so, particularly as people recognise the economic (and other) importance of the business events sector.

Once I had completed my PhD, I emigrated to Australia and was lucky enough to begin work at Victoria University in Melbourne, with a team of eminent academic business events specialists, including Professor Leo Jago and Professor Marg Deery. I was successful in obtaining a Postdoctoral Research Fellow position, working on a project on business events and climate change/environmental sustainability, which really set me up in my research career and helped me to become a business events expert.

Since that time, I have continued to research and publish in the business events area, keeping my particular interest in environmental and social sustainability, although I have expanded my focus to encompass a number of different types of events and festivals. I enjoy writing and editing academic papers and books, especially as, when compared with other types of events, there are relatively few publications focusing on business events. Some of my best-known academic papers are:

- Mair, J. and Thompson, K. (2009) The UK association conference attendance decision-making process. *Tourism Management* 30(3): 400–409.
- Mair, J. and Jago, L. (2010) The development of a conceptual model of greening in the business events sector. *Journal of Sustainable Tourism* 18(1): 77–88.

- Mair, J. (2010) Profiling conference delegates using attendance motivations. *Journal of Convention and Event Tourism* 11(3).
- Mair, J. (2012) A review of business events literature 2000–2009. *Event Management* 16: 1–9.
- Rittichainuwat, B. and Mair, J. (2012) Motivations for attending consumer shows. *Tourism Management* 33: 1236–1244.
- Ramirez, D., Laing, J. and Mair, J. (2013) Exploring intentions to attend a convention: A gender perspective. *Event Management* 17(2): 165–178.
- Mair. J. (2015) Incentive travel: A theoretical perspective. *Event Management* 19(4): 543–552.
- Mair, J., Jin, X. and Yoo, J. (2016) Exploring the site selection decisions of incentive travel planners. *Event Management* 20(3): 353–364.
- Mair, J. and Frew, E. (2016) Academic conferences: A female duoethnography. *Current Issues in Tourism* 1–21. Available at: https://doi.org/10.1080/13683500.2016.1248909.

In 2014, I published my first textbook, *Conferences and Conventions: A research perspective*, which was a great personal achievement. This was followed in 2018 by the publication of a second textbook, *Festival Encounters – Theoretical Perspectives on Festival Events*, written by myself and Michelle Duffy.

I now teach Events Management at the University of Queensland, specialising in courses on event operations and strategic management. And while these courses are not exclusively about business events, I always like to illustrate my lectures with plenty of examples from conferences and meetings. In 2015, along with colleagues, I contributed to a textbook for event management students entitled *Events and Sustainability* which is a very useful resource for anyone interested in encouraging more sustainable behaviour at events.

Of course, business events is a challenging area of research – particularly in relation to data collection. There are few standardised measures in the business events industry, and there are issues of commercial confidentiality which *can* make getting accurate statistics tricky. There are also challenges in terms of getting funding for research in this area, but I am working hard to overcome these obstacles.

I keep up to date with developments in the business events industry mostly through trade associations and publications, such as those released internationally by ICCA, but also national associations such as Business Events Australia (an arm of Tourism Australia) and the Business Events Council of Australia. Of course, I also like to keep up to date with all the new academic research in the business events area – I am particularly interested in developments in the study of the 'beyond tourism' benefits of business events, which I can see becoming a key part of the study of this field in the future.

References

Baum, T., Deery, M., Hanlon, C., Lockstone, L. and Smith, K. (eds) (2009) *People and Work in Events and Conventions: A research perspective*, Wallingford: Cabi.

Beaulieu, A. F. and Love, C. (2005) Characteristics of a meeting planner: Attributes of an emerging profession. *Journal of Convention & Event Tourism* 6(4): 95–124.

Cecil, A., Fenich, G. G., Krugman, C. and Hashimoto, K. (2013) Review and analysis of the new international meeting and business events competency standards. *Journal of Convention & Event Tourism* 14(1): 65–74.

Cecil, A., Reed, B. and Reed, L. (2011) Meeting management programs in US higher education. *Journal of Convention and Event Tourism* 12(3): 179–205.

Chon, K. S. (1990) A systematic evaluation of four-year college courses in meetings and conventions management. *Hospitality Research Journal* 14(2): 459–465.

Crawford, M. and Mogollón, M. P. (2011) Labor competency certifications in commercial occupations: A literature review. Washington, DC: World Bank Education.

Davidson, R. and Cope, B. (2003) *Business Travel: Conferences, incentive travel, exhibitions, corporate hospitality and corporate travel*, Harlow: Pearson Education.

Getz, D. (2007) *Event Studies: Theory, research and policy for planned events*, London: Butterworth Heinemann.

Goldblatt, J. J. (2005) *Special Events: Event leadership for a new world*, 4th edn, New York: Wiley.

Greenwood, E. (1957) Attributes of a profession. *Social Work* 2(3): 45–55.

Jones, D. L. (2010) Developing a convention and event management curriculum in Asia: Using blue ocean strategy and co-creation with industry. *Journal of Convention & Event Tourism* 11(2): 154–158.

Lee, M. J. and Back, K.-J. (2005) A review of convention and meeting management research 1990–2003 – identification of statistical methods and subject areas. *Journal of Convention & Event Tourism* 7(2): 1–20.

Mair, J. (2012) A review of business events literature. *Event Management* 16(2): 133–141.

MBECS (2011) Meetings and business events competency standards. Canadian Tourism Human Resources Council.

Meetings & Conventions (1989) A guide to meeting planning courses. A Supplement to *Meetings & Conventions*, December: 43–48.

Montgomery, R. J. and Strick, S. K. (1994) *Meetings, Conventions, and Expositions: An introduction to the industry*, New York: Wiley.

Parry, S. B. (1996) Just what is a competency? (And why should you care?). *Training* 35(6): 58.

Quinn, B. (2013) *Key Concepts in Event Management*, London: Sage.

Rogers, T. (2003) *Conferences and Conventions: A global industry*, 1st edn, Oxford: Butterworth Heinemann.

Rogers, T. and Davidson, R. (2016) *Marketing Destinations and Venues for Conferences, Conventions and Business Events*, Oxford: Routledge.

Rogerson, C. M. (2015) Unpacking business tourism mobilities in sub-Saharan Africa. *Current Issues in Tourism* 18(1): 44–56.

Shone, A. (1998) *The Business of Conferences: A hospitality sector overview for the UK and Ireland*, Oxford: Butterworth Heinemann.

Sperstad, J. and Cecil, A. K. (2011) Changing paradigm of meeting management: What does this mean for academia? *Journal of Convention & Event Tourism* 12(4): 313–324.

Stetic, S. and Simicevic, D. (2010) Business travellers – an important segment of tourism development in Serbia, in *Mass tourism vs niche tourism: Cyprus 2010 ATLAS conference.*

Swarbrooke, J. and Horner, S. (2001) *Business Travel and Tourism*, Oxford: Butterworth Heinemann.

Weber, K. and Chon, K. S. (eds) (2002) *Convention Tourism: International research and industry perspectives*, Binghamton: Haworth Hospitality Press.

Yoo, J. J-E. and Weber, K. (2005) Progress in convention tourism research. *Journal of Hospitality & Tourism Research* 29: 194–222.

12 Sustainability for business events

> ## Sustainability for business events in the 21st century
>
> - The Metro Toronto Convention Centre works with local charity organisations by donating leftover materials from events, including delegate bags and any food not consumed during the event.
> - The incentive trip of the telecommunications company Optus to Ho Chi Minh City, Vietnam, included a CSR component, run in partnership with the non-profit organisation Habit for Humanity. Participants spent two days helping to build six homes for local villagers and repairing and painting two schools.
> - By making significant upgrades to its heating, water and ventilation installation systems, LED light retrofits, and upgrades to its roof and windows, the World Forum venue in The Hague saw total energy costs reduced from €1 million in 2006 to €440,000 in 2016.
> - Part of the legacy of the Royal Australian Chemical Institute Centenary Chemistry Congress in Melbourne was the event's School Outreach Programme that brought together 750 students from across the state of Victoria for a once-in-a-lifetime opportunity to learn from the acclaimed British chemistry professor, Sir Martyn Poliakoff, one of the speakers at the conference.

Chapter objectives

On completion of this chapter the reader should be able to:

- Understand the basic principles underlying sustainability as a concept.
- Appreciate the impacts of business events on the natural environment.
- Understand the steps taken by the business events industry to 'green' itself.
- Appreciate how business events can be leveraged to create a social legacy.
- Understand the support provided by formal, voluntary standards and business events industry associations.

A history of sustainability

The concept of sustainability can be traced back to an international conference. In 1972, at the United Nations Conference on the Human Environment in Stockholm, industrialised and developing nations debated which was more important: environmental protection or economic development (UNEP, 1972). The debates at the Stockholm event gave birth to the notion that environmental protection and economic development were both inextricably linked. In 1987, the Brundtland Commission, a group appointed by the United Nations to propose strategies for improving human well-being without threatening the environment, published its report, which contained the definition of sustainable development still widely used today: 'Development that meets the needs of the present without compromising the ability of future generations to meet their own needs' (WCED, 1987). Five years later, at another conference, the concept was expounded in 27 principles in the Rio Declaration on Environment and Development, a significant outcome of the Rio Earth Summit, the UN Conference on Environment and Development held in Rio de Janeiro. By the end of the 1990s, a definitional term drawn from financial accounting was widely adopted in definitions of sustainability: the 'triple bottom line' (TBL) (Elkington, 1994), which went beyond the traditional corporate measures of profits, return on investment and shareholder value to include environmental and social dimensions. When the Global Reporting Initiative, a coalition of investors, activists, business and other organisations, issued its Sustainability Reporting Guidelines for organisations in 2002, the concept of the TBL of economic efficiency, environmental integrity and social equity, commonly called 'the three *P*s' – people, planet and profit (or, occasionally, prosperity) – was employed throughout the document, consolidating its widespread acceptance as a framework for measuring organisations' activities' impact upon the world.

In the 21st century, businesses are under increasing pressure from a diverse range of internal and external stakeholders, who expect higher levels of accountability and transparency with regard to firms' economic, social and environmental performance. Adding to the weight of these community expectations are two additional factors: the fact that in most parts of the world, environmental protection is enshrined in regulations and building codes, which companies must respect; and the public's growing awareness of and concern about environmental and social issues, fostered in part by the widespread use of social media as a communications tool.

As a result, there is an ever-increasing emphasis being placed on sustainability issues by organisations in general, and more specifically on issues associated with reducing the negative environmental and social outcomes of their business activity. As studies such as McKinsey's annual global survey, The Business of Sustainability, demonstrate, a growing number of companies are actively integrating sustainability principles into their business practices, in the pursuit of goals that range from reputation management and energy saving to retaining and motivating employees.

This chapter explores how the business events industry has endeavoured to incorporate sustainability practices into its management and operations with the aim of minimising its negative impact on the environment and maximising the positive effect it can have on the host communities. First of all, the commentary of academics and the actions of different business events stakeholders regarding the 'planet' aspect of sustainability will be considered, as this is the overwhelming focus of most of the literature on this theme. Next, business events industry sustainability initiatives aimed at benefiting local 'people' will be examined.

The 'profit' element of the TBL will be taken as 'a given' here. The financial bottom line objective is the one that all companies share, whether or not they subscribe to the TBL philosophy. When considering the question of profit from a sustainability perspective, the idea is that a company remains financially sustainable, generating profits that not only flow to the CEO and shareholders but also sustain the community as a whole, through providing employment, for example, which in turn supports other local businesses.

Terminology

The terms 'sustainable' and 'sustainability' are not the only ones used in discussions of this topic by academics and practitioners. Other terms used interchangeably with 'sustainable' include 'responsible', 'green', 'environmentally friendly', 'corporate social responsibility', 'corporate philanthropy', 'corporate citizenship' and 'eco-friendly'. However, rather than covering all three elements of sustainability as represented in the TBL, the use of certain of these terms limits their range to only the 'planet' (e.g. 'green') or the 'people' (e.g. 'corporate philanthropy') aspects. Henderson's (2011:247) verdict on the use of this terminology serves as a reminder of the need for commentators to take into account all aspects of sustainability: 'it is clear that much of the thinking behind the use of these terms is over-simplistic and that all three elements of sustainable development should be addressed by those wanting to manage activities in a sustainable manner'. This echoes the conviction of Getz (2009) who advocates that any definition of sustainability should integrate the environmental component with the sociocultural and economic roles embodied in the TBL approach.

Given that there is very limited agreement on the formulation, meaning and subsequent operationalisation of the term 'sustainability' as it is applied to events, in this chapter a 'sustainable' business event will be defined as one that incorporates sustainable practices into its planning, management and operations, encompassing not only environmental responsibilities or concerns, but also economic and social sustainability.

Business events and the natural environment

Events of all types create impacts on the environment that can be both positive and negative. On the one hand, the environmental improvements that business events may generate include urban clean-up programmes in preparation for the hosting of a major conference; environmental regeneration schemes based on the construction of new conference venues in previously neglected and derelict areas; and urban conservation initiatives featuring the reconversion into conference facilities of historic buildings that may otherwise have been demolished (Rogers and Davidson, 2016).

On the other hand, the negative impacts of business events on the natural environment are not negligible, even though very few of them could be categorised as 'mega-events', the impacts of which are the focus of much of the academic research on this topic.

In fact, conforming to impeccable standards of sustainability represents a considerable challenge for the business events industry, being contingent as it is upon the facilities and services of the transport and hospitality sectors, both of which have significant, well-documented impacts on the environment. In Chapter 1, some of the negative impacts of business events on the natural environment were discussed, with emphasis on the effects of participants' travel on air quality and the consumption of natural resources occasioned by the construction and operation of large-scale venues. In addition, there is the energy consumed in heating and cooling venues as well as in the preparation of participants' meals. To these impacts may also be added the issue of waste management as it applies to conference and exhibition centres. Business events bringing together large assemblies of people into a concentrated area over a short period of time can generate large quantities of waste: energy waste, food and beverage waste, and solid waste. Exhibitors at trade shows, for example, produce vast amounts of waste material in the form of the packaging used to transport material to their stands, floor coverings, laminates, etc. And much of the collateral material that they provide to exhibition visitors, in the form of brochures, for example, is later discarded by them, further adding to the volume of waste generated by these events.

Acknowledging the significant footprint that business events can leave on the natural environment, this industry has been increasingly responding to pressure to demonstrate its sustainable or 'green' credentials, and since the early 1990s interest in designing greener meetings and events has been growing among business events professionals. However, despite the magnitude of this issue, the amount of academic research that has focused specifically on sustainability in the business events industry has been minor, in particular when compared with the very extensive discussions of tourism-related sustainability issues in academic publications. As observed by Merrilees and Marles (2011:361):

> Business events are rarely studied in terms of their green practices. The presumption may be that commercial and financial considerations dominate and therefore environmental considerations are secondary. The situation in practice is unknown because of the relatively few previous academic studies of green business events.

There have been, nevertheless, a few notable contributions to the literature on this theme. Most of these focus on the meetings sector of business events: Park and Boo (2010) conducted a study of green attitudes associated with two US conventions, mainly from the perspective of the participants but also from the viewpoints of the meeting planners and the convention suppliers. Further valuable insights resulted from the research of Draper et al. (2011), Mair and Jago (2010), and Mair (2011). The most conceptual of these contributions is that of Mair and Jago, who examined the process of corporate greening and developed a model of greening in the business event sector which highlights the factors that influence an organisation's choice to position itself along a spectrum ranging from 'very green' to 'not green at all'. Their model begins with organisational objectives and values, in an economic context, guiding drivers (benefits) and barriers (such as regulations) and further facilitated by media, culture and eco-champions, ending with different degrees of green practice.

One of the very few investigations into the environmental impacts of the exhibitions sector of the business events industry is Merrilees and Marles's (2011) study based on the annual International Boat Show held in Sanctuary Cove on Australia's Gold Coast. Highlighting and evaluating the show's environmental practices, this is a constructive case study example of how green practices may be introduced into an exhibition business event.

Going beyond the limited academic literature on this topic, there is a substantial body of published material issued by business events associations and other organisations providing advice to practitioners seeking to boost their sustainability credentials. The greatest part of this material by far centres on 'greening' actions and initiatives. One of the most authoritative and comprehensive sources of such advice is the Green Meeting Guide published by the United Nations Environment Programme (UNEP, 2009), which includes detailed checklists of what can be done to make this form of business events more 'environmentally friendly'. It focuses in particular on the most common type of meetings – small and medium-sized meetings with up to 200 participants – and is structured to support those individuals and teams who are responsible for the organisation and the logistics related to such events. In that publication, a green event is described as one that is organised in such a way that:

- emissions of greenhouse gases, such as CO_2, are minimised, and unavoidable emissions are compensated for;
- natural resource consumption (including water and energy) is minimised and demand is adapted to available local resources;
- waste generation is avoided where possible and remaining waste is reused and/or recycled;
- biodiversity, water, air and soil resources are protected;
- minimal environmental damage is caused while preparing and implementing the meeting;
- the local community benefits economically, socially and environmentally both during and after the meeting, with local sustainable development encouraged to the extent achievable;
- the above principles are applied in purchasing goods and services for the meeting, the selection of the venue, transportation, catering and accommodation arrangements;
- the awareness of participants, staff service providers and the local community in sustainability issues is increased, with the greening aims and measures communicated clearly to all;
- local hosts, regional and national authorities, sponsors, citizens groups, NGOs, business and technical experts are involved to the greatest extent possible in order to comply with and support the above-stated principles.

(UNEP, 2009:9)

The next section reviews the steps taken by the various business events stakeholder groups to introduce greening measures into their operations.

Destinations

Several academic commentators have emphasised the growing importance of the greening of a location as a decision-making factor for meeting planners (Lee et al., 2013; Whitfield et al., 2014). Mair (2011) also notes that destinations' sustainability credentials are an important factor in conference buyers' decision-making processes, citing as evidence the fact that, increasingly, as an element of bid documents, there is a section on the environmental performance of the destination, in which such factors as 'a compact and walkable city-centre (thus reducing the need for transfers by car or coach for delegates), a good public transport system, and venues and facilities with good sustainability credentials' may be emphasised.

A growing number of destinations, as represented by their convention bureaus, have adopted greening as an element in the branding of their city or country for business events. For example, Thailand, through the work of the Thailand Convention and Exhibition Bureau (TCEB), was the first country in Asia to use the greening of its business events industry as a positive marketing tool. Going beyond branding, in 2008 the TCEB developed and implemented the innovative Green Meetings Guidelines to take that country's business events professionals along the path of becoming greener. The Thai business events industry adopted TCEB's Green Meetings Guidelines so thoroughly that Thailand is now regarded as one of the most outstanding nations for the hosting of environmentally friendly business events. Building upon this initiative, in 2016 the TCEB launched its five-year Thailand MICE Sustainable Destination Master Plan to further strengthen the country's competencies as a green destination (http://micesustainability.com/).

At the level of individual cities, a growing number of destinations have seized the opportunity to position themselves as suitable locations for green business events. One example is that of Berlin, for which, since 2009, the Berlin Green Meetings platform has been offering information about Berlin hotels and tourist companies that actively implement sustainable measures in their businesses. This initiative of the Berlin Convention Office of VisitBerlin aims to establish the German capital as an environmentally conscious and sustainable destination (https://convention.visitberlin.de/de/sustainable-meetings-berlin).

Details of the green initiatives of another city-level convention bureau are given in the case study in this chapter describing the Glasgow Convention Bureau's 'People Make Glasgow Greener' campaign.

Venues

The role of venues as key suppliers for business events means that if a conference or exhibition, for example, is to be regarded as green in any credible manner, the conference centre, hotel or exhibition centre itself must use green practices in their building design, management and operations. A growing number of venues, therefore, have adopted such practices in recent years, in response partly to market pressures and partly in order to give themselves a competitive advantage. Much is known about the steps taken by large, purpose-built, venues and international hotel chains to operate at reasonable levels of sustainability. But Mair (2011) raises the question of whether the situation for smaller venues is similar and concludes that this is yet another gap in the available research on this topic.

The most common types of green initiatives undertaken by larger venues, are described in the annual Green Venue Report (https://greenview.sg/green-venue/), a survey of conference centre and exhibition centre sustainability practices. The 2017 Green Venue Report includes data for 66 venues from 14 countries and lists the most widespread green practices as being waste reduction (including food waste), energy and water conservation. The report noted that almost all the venues in the global survey of self-selected conference and exhibition centres were proactively marketing their green commitment and programmes to planners and other stakeholders, with 92 per cent of the venues having a Web page or website section dedicated to sharing the venue's sustainability practices.

As the principal type of venue for the hosting of corporate events, hotels have also adapted to the need to develop and demonstrate green credentials. Accordingly, many hotel chains as well as individual properties have introduced schemes to demonstrate their commitment to sustainability. As an example, the Four Seasons chain introduced its Greening Meetings programme, through which each of their properties offers the services of a Green Team that can provide insights to meeting planners on ways in which their events can do more to spare the environment. The hotels in the chain offer the following features as standard:

Meeting services:

- All meeting correspondence is sent electronically, including sales proposals, catering menus and banquet orders, except for legal documents where hard copies are required.
- Clients are provided with opportunities to donate their decorations and display materials to local organisations.
- Dry-erase boards are provided as an alternative to flip charts.
- Recycling bins are placed in all meeting rooms.
- Temperatures in meeting rooms are set conservatively to save energy.
- Local printing services can be arranged on behalf of clients to lower transportation emissions.

Food and beverage services:

- China and silverware are used instead of disposable plating and utensils.
- Condiments are served in bulk rather than in individual packages.

- Menus are planned around abundant, local, seasonal and artisanal ingredients.
- Chefs create menus with more vegan and vegetarian options to lower greenhouse gas emissions associated with animal farming.
- Leftover food is composted or donated.

Source: Four Seasons (n.d.).

Exhibition centres, due to their sheer size and the exhibitors' heavy use of materials, are generally faced with considerable scope for the greening of their activities and those of their clients. Han and Verma (2014) identify an original measure in the form of the Green Aisles introduced in some trade shows, where there is a specific area for exhibitors who want to be identified as 'green'. The authors report that this approach has been hugely successful, as, for some events, these aisles have sold out almost immediately. Furthermore, they add that many exhibitors are no longer using paper and brochures but rather are using flash drives and quick response (QR) codes for collateral material.

Further insights into the greening measures that may be introduced by exhibition centres are provided by the comprehensive steps taken by Cologne trade fairs (Koelnmesse), which we discuss below (extracted from Koelnmesse, n.d.).

Energy efficiency

The energy balance in the trade fair halls and the administration building are being continuously improved. Electricity and gas consumption is being effectively reduced and power is being used only to the degree that is actually required. For example, during periods when there is no trade fair activity, the lighting fixtures in the halls are controlled by presence sensors. Areas that receive a generous amount of daylight were incorporated into the halls during construction. Ventilation control is set up to respond to the air quality. When it comes to cooling the halls, two positive measures are important: Koelnmesse has increased the energy efficiency of the air-conditioning equipment and has also completely converted to environmentally friendly refrigerants.

In addition to this, Koelnmesse is investing in energy-saving technology as part of its modernisation programme 'Koelnmesse 3.0'. One of the important measures consists of the company's own combined heating and power station, which will work according to the combined heat and power principle to produce both electrical energy and heat. This new energy concept will serve to reduce annual CO_2 emissions by 3,200 tons in the first year alone, which equals the emission of approximately 410 single-family homes.

Recyclables management

The Koelnmesse waste concept ensures that refuse from the materials used for stand construction is separated according to waste type in the purest possible manner.

Significantly, more than 90 per cent of the waste generated in a year is recycled. In addition, many stand elements – such as carpeting and individual walls – are reused at a number of trade fairs.

Traffic guidance and mobility

During large trade fairs, Cologne experiences an unavoidable increase in traffic. With the close cooperation of the traffic department of the city of Cologne and through the promotion of local public transport, Koelnmesse's logistics concept ensures that exhaust emissions and negative influences on street traffic are significantly reduced. Logistics experts use modern technology to manage the traffic related to stand construction and dismantling. For example, lorries with a gross vehicle weight of 3.5 tons and more are directed to a specific parking area immediately next to the exhibition centre. In this way, lines of lorries waiting on the street with their engines running are avoided, eliminating damaging emissions.

Koelnmesse encourages the use of the public transport network. Event admission tickets are valid for travel on trains, trams and buses of the Verkehrsverbund Rhein-Sieg (VRS). The Köln Messe/Deutz train station as well as a tram stop are located only a few steps away. The use of public transport is not only practical for trade fair participants; it also reduces street traffic, thus protecting the environment.

Source: Koelnmesse (n.d.).

The important role played by 'smart transportation' options in reducing traffic is also emphasised by Guillot (2013), who notes that the addition of bicycle lanes, greater use of public transportation and more walkability means a more enjoyable convention district that is less cluttered with traffic and cars. He remarks that at some venues, such as the Anaheim Convention Centre, visitors can use bicycle-sharing services that allow rentals by the day or hour.

It is clear that, for all types of venue, the introduction of some green measures requires a degree of financial investment. Some of the venue managers who responded to the Maritz Future of Meetings survey on this issue expressed concern over the increased expenditure incurred, with comments such as 'green initiatives can be tricky, based on the cost of organic and local food options as well as the extra steps in food composting/measurement, etc.' and 'it takes money to upgrade venues to meet green standards. For example, it can be challenging to find the capital for a new green roof' (Maritz, 2012). However, Kang et al. (2012) express the view that as well as reducing their negative impact on the environment, venues adopting green practices can also benefit from cost savings in the long run – although they do admit that there are some who hesitate to invest in green practices because of the difficulty in measuring whether their investment is financially beneficial.

In an interview on this point, Brian Tennyson, principal of convention centres at LMN Architects in Seattle, is less ambivalent on this question, contending that 'green design initiatives have moved directly to the realm of cost savings as facility managers see that upfront investments can produce substantial savings down the line and pay off in relatively little time. Green design equals energy savings and that equals cost savings' (Guillot, 2013).

Although the vast dimensions of some large-scale venues have been mentioned as a source of potential damage to the natural environment, in some cases, the extensive area covered by large-scale conference and exhibition centres has been converted into an opportunity. In recent years, some of the flat roofs covering these buildings have been 'greened' by the planting of vegetation, thereby creating a number of environmental benefits such as rainwater retention, increasing roofing membrane life, increasing biodiversity and habitat, and reducing noise and air pollution (Getter and Rowe, 2006). Consequently, a growing number of conference centres, such as the Grimaldi Forum in Monaco, are using the spaces available on their rooftops to develop greening projects. A case study in this chapter offers the example of how Montreal's flagship convention centre turned its roof space into a valuable asset for the environment.

Buyers and participants

It is evident that a considerable amount of supplier-side initiatives have been taken in the drive for destinations and venues to be – and to appear to be – green. Many of these initiatives have been taken in collaboration with business event planners. For instance, the International Centre in Ontario created a Sustainable Event Guide, a resource and tool for planners to guide them toward planning a more sustainable event. And at the World Forum venue in The Hague, sustainability is discussed throughout the planning process. The venue has created an easy checklist for event organisers to follow, ensuring that they take advantage of sustainability programmes and practices in place at the venue (Greenview, 2017).

There is a measure of evidence that buyers are motivated by such initiatives. For example, Mair and Jago (2010) noted that increasing demand from conference buyers for more environmentally friendly or sustainable options was being reported. A further sign of this interest in green issues on the part of buyers is the fact that a growing number of Requests for Proposals now stipulate sustainability practices and ask potential suppliers about their core company values (UNDP, 2018). Some commentators go further in their analysis of buyers' preferences in terms of green venues and other suppliers, contending that initiatives such as green building design, recycling programmes, energy-efficient features and water-conservation systems are no longer simply features that are desirable – they are features that are *expected* (Guillot, 2013).

Buyers such as conference organisers may choose to take their own initiatives, to make their events greener. For example, a growing number are opting to attempt to make their business events 'climate-neutral' by compensating for the CO_2 emissions arising from participants' travel and other event-related factors. Bossdorf et al. provide this example from colleagues employed at the Institute of Plant Sciences and Oeschger Centre for Climate Change Research of the University of Bern:

Recently we hosted a medium-sized three-day ecology conference ... with 125 participants from 14 countries. To make the conference 'greener', we chose local food for catering, avoided disposable tableware, and printed materials on environmentally-friendly paper. We inquired regarding each conference participant's means of transportation and entered all conference details into the CO_2 calculator for events provided by http://www.myclimate.org, which estimated the total emissions caused by our conference as 11.5 tons of CO_2. Sixty-six percent of these emissions were due to travelling, whereas food and accommodation accounted for 18 percent and 13 percent, respectively; and the remaining 3 percent were due to printed material and waste. To bring the carbon balance of our meeting back to zero, we invested €280 into carbon offset projects.

(Bossdorf et al., 2010:61)

While such initiatives are well intentioned and a further indication of meeting planners' wish to minimise the impact of their events on the environment, nevertheless, as indicated by Mair (2011), the practice of voluntary carbon offsetting as a means of mitigating the carbon emissions from air travel is far from straightforward. This is due, among other factors, to the complexity and variability of such schemes, and the fact that they place the onus for offsetting on the travellers rather than the polluters (the airlines).

The ultimate test of the worth of the types of green initiatives described above is the extent to which the end-users of business events – the participants – value them. Surprisingly little is known about participants' attitudes towards this aspect of sustainability. However, Park and Boo's (2010) study found that participants generally have a positive attitude towards 'green' events. They also found that they are willing to use public transport where possible and have a positive attitude towards attending conferences closer to their places of residence. Similarly, Han and Hwang (2017) concluded that as individuals' environmental awareness increases, attendees have been increasingly well disposed towards conferences that incorporate sustainable practices into their management and operations. Davidson's (2010) review of the characteristics of the younger generation of meetings and incentive travel participants identified their heightened concern over the environment as being a distinguishing feature likely to determine their preferences regarding participation in business events.

Nevertheless, there is less consensus and evidence regarding the issue of buyers' and participants' willingness to pay extra for conferences that respect sustainability principles, thereby subsidising the extra expense incurred by some venues in their greening measures. Park and Boo (2010) identified an unwillingness among participants to pay extra; but the results from Sox et al.'s (2013) exploratory study of 74 meeting planners' and 76 participants' sustainability concerns suggested that both groups were willing to pay more for meetings held at sustainability-certified venues.

There is little doubt that more research is required to answer this question and many others, as it would appear that only limited progress has been made since Laing and Frost (2010:265) highlighted the need 'to explore aspects of behaviour of green event-goers, including their motivations, the influence of their green interest on their decision-making processes with respect to attending events, and their expectations as to the 'green' content of events'.

Business events and social legacy

While, as has been shown, much of the sustainability-related discussion in the academic literature focuses on the planet-centred greening of events, there has been much less investigation of the role of events in the context of the 'people' element of the TBL. Smith (2009) admits that social needs are recognised as the least explored element of Brundtland's definition of sustainable development. However, he notes that there has been some progress in terms of the amount of research identifying the potential of *major* events to generate a range of positive social effects including: reinforcing collective identities; uniting people; improving self-esteem; increasing civic pride; raising awareness of disability; inspiring children; providing experience of work; encouraging volunteering; increasing participation in sport; and promoting well-being/healthy living. But other commentators have noted that such discussions in the academic literature centre mainly on the social impacts of *sports* events – and in particular the mega-sports events that cities stage on a one-off basis, such as the Olympic and Paralympic Games and the FIFA World Cup (Chalip, 2006; Misener and Mason, 2006; Cornelissen et al., 2011).

Very little of this discussion of the social impacts of mega-sports events is relevant to the role of business events in fostering social sustainability within the communities in which such events take place. By comparison with any type of mega-events, whether sports or cultural, most meetings, exhibitions, etc. are much smaller in scale, far less visible to the host community, less commercialised, and open only to an invited group of participants. But, despite the absence of a substantial body of academic research into the potential of business events to generate positive social effects, this is a theme which has been discussed extensively by business events practitioners in the trade press, often in terms of 'corporate social responsibility', 'corporate philanthropy', 'corporate citizenship', or – the term that will be employed here – 'social legacy', more commonly known in US English as 'community legacy' or 'community service'.

In this section of the chapter, the focus will be less on the general social impacts of business events – whether positive or negative – and more on the social initiatives actively and deliberately pursued in conjunction with business events. Here, Chalip's (2014:6) concept of social leveraging is a useful point of reference, defined as 'the collection of strategies and tactics employed to enable the generation of desired legacies'. The distinction between social legacy and social leveraging is valuable, with leveraging being construed as a means towards legacy. Applying the concept to the context of sports events, Chalip contends that

> social leveraging endeavours to focus event stakeholders' attention onto targeted social issues by (a) aligning the event with those social issues, (b) aligning values

between social issues and focal sport subcultures, (c) lengthening visitor stays (to lengthen their engagement with the targeted issues), and (d) enticing attendees' engagement with targeted social issues. Social leveraging also seeks to use event media to (a) showcase social issues via event advertising and reporting, and (b) use the event in issue-related publicity.

(Ibid.:5)

While confronting all of these social issues is not generally feasible for most business events, it is clear that events such as meetings and incentive trips in particular have the potential to be a genuine force for good, in terms of what they can do for the benefit of certain elements of their host communities, in particular the disadvantaged members of those communities.

How can business events be leveraged in order to produce desired social legacies? In his analysis of this topic, Davidson (2009) attributes part of the growth in interest in the social legacy of business events to the younger generation of participants, who are 'uncomfortable with the type of 'conspicuous consumption' that can characterise such events when they feature bountiful, premier wining and dining and lavish entertainment – often against a background of the deprivation of disadvantaged communities or in developing countries'. According to the author, heightened social awareness, particularly among younger, 'Generation Y' participants, and their desire to somehow 'make a difference' and 'give something back' to the communities where their corporate meetings and incentive trips take place, has been a key factor in the growth of social legacy initiatives accompanying business events, and it is one of the key trends driving the design of such events today. He links this phenomenon to the growing interest in volunteerism (or 'volun-tourism') as a form of community service that promotes goodwill and is also personally fulfilling, adding that, for many participants, the social legacy element has also become an essential part of the 'experiential' dimension of participating in a meeting or incentive trip. These elements take a number of different forms.

Different types of social legacy initiatives

Donations to charities

Rogers (2008:321) notes that: 'A successful business event can be marked with a "legacy" initiative, for example with a corporate donation to a sustainable project, or by fundraising among delegates, possibly with top-ups by the venue, agency and other suppliers'. This is one of the most common ways in which business events are leveraged to leave a legacy in the destinations where they take place. Participants may be invited to donate to a local charity or another worthy humanitarian cause at the time of registering for the event or, more commonly, at the conference or incentive trip gala dinner, often after viewing a video presentation describing how their contributions will be used. From the point of view of the event organiser, the appeal in this approach to leaving a social legacy lies in its relative simplicity and its minimal impact on the time taken out of the principal focus of the business event.

Construction/renovation projects

Davidson (2009) notes that, for business events lasting a few days, where there is less pressure on participants' time, a more 'hands-on' approach to leaving a social legacy may be used, when participants can volunteer to take a day or half-day out of the event's proceedings to directly work on a project. This can range from landscaping the garden of a local retirement home to constructing a library in a nearby village school. Construction/renovation projects may even be included in the event's actual programme, as seen in the example of Swedish communications and events company Inspiration, which arranged for participants in one of its events to build new park benches for the Stockholm City Mission, over pre-dinner drinks and canapés (Emdén, 2008).

Many participants in business events are more motivated by 'outreach' activities, which give them the opportunity to meet and interact directly with local people. This approach works particularly well when part of the objective is to raise participants' awareness of social issues impinging on the local community. An example of this approach was seen in Vancouver: at the International Urogynaecological Association's (IUGA) Annual Meeting held in June 2017. The meeting's organisers incorporated a free Public Health Forum at which four regional experts and one patient came together in front of an audience to speak about important health issues affecting women. The panel addressed the issue of pelvic floor health and provided an open forum for questions from the audience (Beauchamp, 2017).

When those attending business events include participants who are renowned experts in their field, another valuable type of outreach activity can add to the event's social legacy. This takes place when such participants volunteer to take time out from the event they are attending, to share their knowledge and skills with people in the local community, for example by offering master classes for medical professionals in local hospitals.

Advantages and challenges

It is clear that, when used effectively, these activities can have a positive impact on the lives of people living and working in the destinations where business events take place. And this is clearly something that applies to all destinations where a section of the population suffers from some form of social or economic disadvantage – not only developing countries. Furthermore, including social legacy activities in meetings and incentive trips can also considerably enhance the image of individual companies and the business events industry as a whole, by demonstrating their social awareness and desire to 'make a difference'. This form of reputational management is particularly important at times when the general economic context means that the media and company shareholders are alert to any corporate events that appear to be too lavishly funded.

But leveraging business events for reasons of leaving a social legacy is not without its controversy and pitfalls. While it is often presented as an enlightened approach by corporations eager to demonstrate their corporate philanthropy, it is sometimes criticised as a public relations cover for 'business as usual' or, worse, a collection of initiatives that are designed to distract consumer and watchdog attention away from business practices that are actually detrimental to communities in some way (Davidson, 2009). 'Greenwashing', is frequently used as a term of criticism for a manufacturer or service provider that makes a claim about the environmental benefits of its product/service without foundation. Companies that incorporate social legacy activities into their business events need to avoid having similar accusations levied against them. Pinchera (2008) highlights this risk in the context of corporate social responsibility (CSR) and offers the following advice:

- To avoid 'CSR washing,' [organisations should] tie [efforts] into their own organisational goals, mission and vision. This shows that the organisation is serious.
- CSR efforts should also be long-term. Community activities or investments that don't have any staying power are obviously headline-driven.
- The biggest warning sign is a company that aggressively boasts about its activities. Most corporations that are truly committed to CSR practices understand that CSR is an evolution, so you don't often see these companies bragging about what they do, they tend to share stories and their best practices but also focus a lot on what they can do better.

Elaborating upon Pinchera's first point, it would appear that business events-related social legacy activities work most effectively and are most convincing when they take place within the wider context of the company's existing CSR policy. This lends coherence and continuity to such activities, focusing, where they exist, on the company's established contacts and the causes that it already donates to on a regular basis.

Sensitivity to the plight of disadvantaged local communities is another factor to be respected when social legacy activities are being planned. While the desire to engage in outreach activities and make actual contact with local people is generally commendable, it is vital to avoid any impression that the event participants are 'slumming' in any way or motivated by voyeuristic curiosity. Emdén (2008:75) cites the CEO of a Swedish events company with experience in including social legacy elements in their clients' events: 'It's important not to go and see people in misery because it leaves a bad taste in the mouth. Rather like shanty-town tourism in South Africa, and that's not pleasant'.

Furthermore, in situations where a company has no established contacts with charities or other worthy causes, the choice of the recipient or recipients of the benefits of its social legacy activities must be handled carefully. Meetings and incentive planners may have very limited knowledge of the local situation, and they therefore need to act in close partnership with destination stakeholders who are in a position to understand what causes are most deserving and what can be achieved in the limited time that participants in business events can dedicate to such activities. Some convention bureaus have played a valuable role in bringing together meetings and incentive planners with local agencies representing charitable causes. As interest in offering social legacy activities as an add-on element of business events has grown, a growing number of convention bureaus have taken on the role of key intermediary in bringing together the interested parties. One example of this is seen in the service offered by the Glasgow Convention Bureau in the form of a section on their website called 'Leave a Lasting Legacy'. A range of add-on activities for business events participants is proposed, 'providing a platform for delegates to interact with the local community, businesses and academics, organising a charity bike ride around the city or to the picturesque shores of Loch Lomond or setting up green team building activities' (Glasgow Convention Bureau, n.d.). This chapter's case study on the Glasgow Convention Bureau provides further details of its sustainability initiatives. A similar resource for planners organising business events in North America is the Giving Good portal (http://givinggood.com/) for event organisers seeking to find, vet and book 'community impact' projects. This resource enables planners to connect with other event organisers, get additional information from destination marketing organisations or contact charities and other community impact projects directly. By 2018, Giving Good covered more than 40 destinations featuring over 200 community impact projects.

But it is perhaps the limited *time* that is available for these types of social legacy activities that has exposed them to most criticism, with some stakeholders actively questioning how much can really be achieved, given the short duration of most business events. Smith and Fox (2007), for example, highlight the limitations of using an event as the focus of social projects, noting that support for such projects tends to wane once an event has ended. Further questioning of the sustainability of these initiatives has come from within the charity community, with Eileen Heisman, President/CEO at the US-based National Philanthropic Trust underlining the transient nature of the impact of some business events' social legacy:

> What is it that you can do that is possible? If you go to an after-school programme and play with the kids, you're going to have a one-time impact that is going to evaporate really quickly. If you tutored for one day, that would be nice, but a kid who can't read well needs to be tutored for six months.
>
> (Russell, 2013)

Indeed, far from such activities being useful, many charities complain that one-off actions of the type favoured by some corporate groups are actually time-consuming and disruptive to their own activities, creating more problems than they solve.

Russell (2013) cites further criticism from Claire Smith, vice president of sales and marketing for the Vancouver Convention Centre and board liaison to PCMA's CSR Task Force, who stressed that planners need to keep

> the needs of the community in the foreground rather than sort of as an afterthought. I think … we want to do good, but we are almost lazy about it. We want to feel good that we have done something, but we actually do not want to get our hands dirty. And we want an activity that is fun. So we build bicycles for a school, and that is really lovely – but do those kids really need bicycles? And we are doing it almost like a team-building activity, so it is more really about us than it is about them. I think what we really need to be leery of is giving people things they don't need. And I think that we do it because it's easy, and it feels good. But if people don't need that, then it really is tokenism.

Nevertheless, despite these challenges, it is evident that there is a vast amount of goodwill and a growing sense of social justice on the part of many business events participants that can be leveraged to enable such events to be a catalyst for the improvement of the lives of people living in the places where they take place. Furthermore, when social legacy actions of the type discussed above involve outreach activities that bring participants into direct contact with members of the host community, there is considerable potential for mutually enriching encounters. But the numerous criticisms and pitfalls described here suggest that much more research and planning by events organisers is required to ensure that their social legacy efforts make the best impact possible. That should include more evaluating of the performance and effectiveness of the charitable organisations they consider supporting; focusing less on what makes participants feel good about themselves and more on the needs of the actual beneficiaries of their community service work. Effective planning also entails looking at the particular skill sets of the business events participants and connecting them to a genuine need in the host community. Finally, there should be more emphasis placed on leveraging the longer-term social benefits for communities from the business events taking place in their localities, which means planners strategising beyond a single event and its impacts.

Support for business events sustainability initiatives

In the final section of this chapter, two types of external support for business events professionals seeking to develop sustainability measures will be examined.

Voluntary standards

In response to the growing concern over the environmental impacts of business activities in general, a number of voluntary standards have been developed over the years to guide organisations in their adoption of sustainable practices. Through systems of external, third-party verification these standards may be used to indicate the extent to which any organisation is operating according to sustainable principles. Two of the first to be developed were the Eco-Management and Audit Scheme (EMAS) created in 1993 by the European Commission and the ISO 14001 developed in 1996 by the International Organization for Standardisation (ISO). Both of these standards serve to demonstrate that organisations complying with them have voluntarily implemented a structured management system consisting of a number of stages defining organisational policies, procedures and practices related to environmental issues. According to Guizzardi et al. (2017), the motivation for organisations to meet formal environmental standards such as these can be twofold:

1   to positively react to demand and pressures from different stakeholders concerned with ecological issues; and/or
2   to obtain a competitive advantage as a result of implementing a recognised environmental management system.

The range of bodies adopting these standards includes organisations operating in the events industry in general and in business events in particular. But more recently, a growing number of formal, voluntary standards have been developed specifically by – and for – the events industry to provide planners and suppliers with specifications for producing events in a more sustainable manner.

One of the first of these was ISO 20121, a process-based, international *events management system* standard designed to support organisations in the event industry by specifying the practices that they need to have in place in order to improve the sustainability of their services, products and/or general activities. The history of ISO 20121 is linked to London's hosting of the Olympic Games in 2012. After that city won the bid to host the Games, it became apparent there was no formal framework for implementing sustainability at events, in venues and for suppliers. This led to the development and launch of the British Standard for Sustainable Event Management BS 8901, which was designed to provide a framework for organisations seeking to develop a management system based on the issues relevant to them. Following the launch of BS 8901, there was considerable evidence to suggest that such a standard was also in great demand outside the UK, principally within Europe and the US. This response resulted in BS 8901 being the proposed framework as a starting draft for ISO 20121, the international standard which was eventually launched in 2012 for the use of events organisations throughout the world.

Specifically, ISO 20121 requires organisations to:

- Identify their issues in relation to their event management operations
- Outline their commitments to sustainability in the form of a sustainability policy
- Develop SMART objectives and targets in relation to sustainability
- Train their staff on sustainability
- Engage their suppliers on sustainability
- Develop a sustainability communications plan
- Monitor and measure their success
- Audit and review their documentation.

By becoming ISO 20121 certified, organisations are able to demonstrate that they care about the social, environmental and economic impacts of the events that they organise or host, while gaining formal recognition for the sustainability of their services and products. The particular benefits of certification have been described as:

- Boosting employee motivation, attracting the best talent and improving retention
- Enhancing reputation and strengthening relationships with key clients, suppliers, partners and other external stakeholders who hold similar values
- Achieving cost savings with respect to material consumption, waste and energy
- Reducing carbon emissions over the entire event supply chain
- Strengthening the position of the organisation within the community.

There has been widespread adoption of ISO 20121 throughout the global events industry. In the case of organisations operating in the business events industry, encouragement and support for the implementation of these standards has occasionally come from convention bureaus motivated to boost the sustainable credentials of their destinations. For example, the Thailand Convention and Exhibition Bureau offers financial support and resources to Thailand's business events suppliers implementing ISO 20121, and the organisations having achieved certification include the Hat Yai International Convention Center, the Plaza Athenee hotel in Bangkok, and the Queen Sirikit National Convention Center (QSNCC). In terms of major business events, the World Expo 2015 in Milan was the first universal exposition with a certification for event sustainability complying with the international standard of ISO 20121 (Guizzardi et al., 2017).

As awareness of the ISO 20121 standard spreads, a growing number of public sector and private sector clients are referencing ISO 20121 in their tender documents as a means of ensuring that their own sustainable policies are being implemented in the events they hold. In time, it is likely that demonstrating compliance to ISO 20121 will become a minimum requirement for anyone wishing to operate in the events industry, as event clients, sponsors, local authorities and other key stakeholders choose to work with organisations that have implemented the standard (ISO 20121, n.d.).

More recently, business events organisations wishing to demonstrate their commitment to sustainability have been supported by a range of performance-based standards developed specifically for this industry, with the aim of specifying precisely what is required to plan a conference, exhibition or incentive trip, for instance, that qualifies as being a sustainable event. The Events Industry Council's APEX initiative, in partnership with the international standards organisation ASTM (American Society for Testing and Materials) International, has created the industry's first comprehensive standards for environmentally sustainable meetings. The standards, composed of nine individual sectors encompassing the scope of the entire meeting and event planning process, provide meeting and event organisers with a comprehensive roadmap for improving and measuring event sustainability on an ongoing basis. These formal, voluntary standards are focused around prescriptive actions, specific measurable targets for producing events in a more sustainable manner. They were created by over 300 professionals from all areas of the business events industry, in collaboration with the ASTM and the Events Industry Council.

Table 12.1 indexes each of the APEX/ASTM Environmentally Sustainable Meeting Standards.

Within each sector, the same eight categories capture the environmental and social areas to be measured under the standard. They are: Staff Management and Environmental Policy; Communication; Waste Management; Energy; Air Quality; Water; Procurement; and Community Partners.

Since their launch, a growing number of business events organisations have striven to achieve certification. For example, among the first large-scale venues to achieve certification of the Meeting Venue standards were the Hong Kong Convention and Exhibition Centre, the Vancouver Convention Centre and the San Diego Convention Centre; and the convention bureau, Visit Denver, was the first destination marketing organisation to be certified in the destinations sustainability standard.

Table 12.1 APEX/ASTM Environmentally Sustainable Meeting Standards

Accommodations
Standard Specification for the Evaluation and Selection of Accommodations for Environmentally Sustainable Meetings, Events, Trade Shows and Conferences
E2772

Audio/Visual and Production
Standard Specification for Evaluation and Selection of Audio Visual (AV) and Production for Environmentally Sustainable Meetings, Events, Trade Shows, and Conferences
E2745

Communications & Marketing
Standard Specification for Evaluation and Selection of Communication and Marketing Materials for Environmentally Sustainable Meetings, Events, Trade Shows, and Conferences
E2746

Destinations
Standard Specification for Evaluation and Selection of Destinations for Environmentally Sustainable Meetings, Events, Trade Shows, and Conferences
E2741

Exhibits
Standard Specification for Evaluation and Selection of Exhibits for Environmentally Sustainable Meetings, Events, Trade Shows, and Conferences
E2742

Food & Beverage
Standard Specification for Evaluation and Selection of Food and Beverage for Environmentally Sustainable Meetings, Events, Trade Shows, and Conferences
E2773

Meeting Venue
Standard Specification for Evaluation and Selection of Venues for Environmentally Sustainable Meetings, Events, Trade Shows, and Conferences
E2774

On-Site Offices
Standard Specification for Evaluation and Selection of On-site Offices for Environmentally Sustainable Meetings, Events, Trade Shows, and Conferences
E2747

Transportation
Standard Specification for Evaluation and Selection of Transportation for Environmentally Sustainable Meetings, Events, Trade Shows, and Conferences
E2743

Source: Events Industry Council (n.d.).

How do the APEX/ASTM Environmentally Sustainable Meeting Standards compare with the ISO 20121 system in supporting business events professionals seeking to integrate sustainability considerations into the planning and execution of their events? The issue was investigated in detail by Walker (2012), who concluded that both of these standards ask users to think about sustainability in highly different ways: ISO 20121 assumes that in such a diverse and fragmented industry, a 'one-size-fits-all' solution is not possible; therefore it has chosen instead to embrace the management system model that ISO is renowned for while building on the relative success of BS 8901 specification for a sustainability management system for events. Instead of prescribing what specific sustainability issues should be addressed, it puts the decision solely in the hands of the user. This built-in flexibility can help promote the widespread use of a given standard but may also attract criticism for the potential lack of stringency. The APEX/ASTM standards, on the other hand, are far more prescriptive and specifically centred on environmental sustainability. The rationale here is that the business events industry needs a shared understanding of what the minimum level of performance required is in order to reduce the negative environmental impact of meetings, while increasing their social and economic benefits. The 'one-size-fits-all' philosophy is more apparent as the scope is limited to business events. Walker admits that both sets of standards have their inherent strengths and weaknesses but concludes that while each standard is robust and designed to stand alone, the resulting benefits can be optimised significantly by using them together: 'In fact, without this combined approach, each of the standards (at least within the meetings industry) may be at risk of not achieving the level of uptake required to ensure their viability' (Walker, 2012:54).

The role of the professional associations

Further support for business events practitioners seeking to observe sustainable principles has come from the industry's professional associations, through their responsibility for advising and educating their members and facilitating an exchange of information. But while Merrilees and Marles (2011) noted that the events industry associations were striving to increase their environmental policy position, Dickson and Arcodia's exploratory study found that they were only partially fulfilling their role, regarding sustainability (Dickson and Arcodia, 2010). Of the 50 identified associations surveyed by the authors, 54 per cent were business event associations. 18 per cent of the 50 websites in the sample had a page on their website dedicated solely to sustainable event information. The information contained on these pages in most cases included:

- Checklists and lists of suggestions on how to become more sustainable (for instance, 'Top 10 things you can do to go green'; AUMA's 1994 publication, 'The ecological way to appear at a trade fair')
- Reports (research- and opinion-based) on sustainability or climate change
- Reports on how many event managers are going green
- Information on carbon-offsetting or carbon-neutral events.

Furthermore, only 10 per cent of the websites analysed included a sustainability statement (a declaration of the association's position on sustainable events); and none of the websites included a mission statement or presidential statement making reference to sustainability. No websites contained information about accreditation for practitioners who used sustainable event practices, either their own or others'.

More positively, Merrilees and Marles's (2011) case study analysis of a major Australian business event, the Sanctuary Cove International Boat Show, found that various industry associations, including the Marina Industries Association, Meetings and Events Australia and Business Events Australia had collectively provided guidance and inspiration to the Boat Show to enable the organisers to assess their green credentials.

It is only to be expected that since the publication of these two studies, as sustainability has become a growing concern for organisations and for consumers in general, the professional associations serving the business events industry have expanded their roles in advising and guiding their members towards practices that mean their events have less negative impact on the natural environment and a more positive impact on communities.

Chapter summary

This chapter explored how the business events industry has endeavoured to incorporate sustainability practices into its management and operations with the aim of minimising its negative impact on the environment and maximising the positive effect it can have on the host communities. It began with a history of sustainability as a concept, followed by a review of the academic literature on green issues as applied to business events and an analysis of the sustainability measures taken by business events stakeholder groups: destinations, venues and planners. There followed a discussion of the social legacy of business events in terms of how such events can make a contribution to help the disadvantaged members of the communities living in the host destinations. The advantages of – and challenges involved in – making a meaningful impact were discussed. The various forms of support for business events sustainability initiatives were reviewed, including the development of voluntary standards and the contributions of the professional associations in this regard.

CASE STUDY 12.1: GLASGOW CONVENTION BUREAU'S SUSTAINABILITY INITIATIVES

Glasgow's green convention team

Glasgow

Scotland's largest city, Glasgow is one of the world's leading conference destinations, and business events contribute significantly to the city's economy. In the 2016/17 financial year alone, Glasgow won over 500 new international and UK conferences through to 2022, worth £142 million – the city's best-ever annual return.

The Glasgow Convention Bureau

As the official destination marketing organisation for metropolitan Glasgow, the Glasgow Convention Bureau (GCB) (www.glasgowconventionbureau.com) is the city's primary point of contact for conference organisers, working with its partners on more than 100 bids for major UK and international conferences each year.

The staff of 16 are engaged in a range of national and international research and sales activities, including bidding for, attracting and managing a range of association and corporate conferences, along with city partners at the Scottish Event Campus, universities, hotels and other venues. The GCB also manages the city's Conference Ambassador Programme and handles conference and event accommodation bookings.

The GCB operates under the auspices of Glasgow Life (www.glasgowlife.org.uk), the arm's length charity that delivers services on behalf of Glasgow City Council. It is funded predominantly by Glasgow City Council, with additional income generation through accommodation booking and membership fees from over 280 members. In 2017, the GCB was named 'Best UK Convention Bureau' for a record 11th consecutive year in a UK-wide poll conducted by the influential trade magazine *Meetings & Incentive Travel.*

Glasgow as a sustainable destination

The name 'Glasgow' comes from the Gaelic phrase for 'dear green place', and the city lives up to that title. It has over 90 parks and gardens, eight of which have won the UK's coveted Green Flag award, and the second largest proportion of green space for its residents of any European city: 32 per cent of its surface area.

Glasgow has aspirations to become one of Europe's most sustainable cities by 2020 – with a focus on improving quality of life in the city, protecting the environment and developing a green economy with sustainability at the top of the agenda. A major step towards this goal came in 2016, when Glasgow became the first city in the UK to be included in the sustainability ranking of international conference destinations – the Global Destination Sustainability Index (http://gds-index.com/). The Index ranked Glasgow as the seventh most sustainable conference destination in the world.

That elevated position in the Global Destination Sustainability Index served to consolidate Glasgow's already established reputation as an attractive destination for energy, sustainability and low carbon industry-related conferences. That reputation was founded on Glasgow's position at the forefront of developments in the energy, sustainability and low-carbon industries, as well as the city's acknowledged business and academic excellence in these areas.

For example, Glasgow is at the heart of Scotland's renewable energy industry, with companies such as Scottish Power and Star Renewable Energy being based in Glasgow, and their operations extending across the UK, Europe and the world.

By the end of 2018, Glasgow had hosted 20 major conferences in the energy and sustainability sectors over a 24-month period, delivering approximately 60,000 delegate days and boosting the city's economy by over £23 million. One such conference was the 38th Euroheat & Power Congress, attended by nearly 500 overseas delegates, which was held at the Scottish Event Campus (SEC) in Glasgow from 14–17 May 2017. Explaining why Glasgow was chosen as the destination for this event, Silke Schlinnertz, Head of Operations and Events for the congress, said:

> Glasgow's bid to host our congress marked the city out as a strong exemplar of the pattern of development that is likely to typify future UK district heating expansion – Glasgow is aiming to cut 30% of its CO_2 emissions by 2020, with district heating expected to play a major role. There is a genuine commitment in Glasgow to environmental sustainability and the values and principles that make it possible. Being the first UK city to join the GDS-Index underpins that and gives event planners one more reason to choose the city as their next meeting destination.

The Glasgow Convention Bureau's 'People Make Glasgow Greener' campaign

In May 2017, a collaborative project to champion Glasgow's credentials as a world leader in sustainable business events was launched by the GCB as part of its initiative to attract more business events while striving to reduce their impact on the environment. To drive the campaign forward, a 'green conventions team' was formed, comprising 20 representatives from across the city's tourism and hospitality sectors, academic and business communities, and local government.

The members of the team included: the Glasgow Chamber of Commerce; the Scottish Event Campus (SEC); Glasgow Restaurant Association (GRA); Greater Glasgow Hoteliers Association (GGHA); VisitScotland; ScotRail; Strathclyde Partnership for Transport (SPT); the Woodlands Community Development Trust; Locavore Farm; and Glasgow, Strathclyde and Glasgow Caledonian Universities.

An example of the type of initiatives that the campaign offers are the bespoke 'horticultural therapy' packages for conference organisers who are interested in offering sustainable team-building activities to their delegates. Working with Glasgow City Council's Land and Environmental Services department and local seed-planting business Kabloom, these activities take place across the city's parks and gardens, including the Woodlands Community Garden near the SEC, and include workshops on enhancing biodiversity, maintaining green spaces and replanting Scottish wildflowers. Delegates who take time out of their conferences to volunteer in this way benefit from the opportunity to give something back to the destination by enhancing the city's green spaces while at the same time enjoying a unique and immersive experience of Glasgow.

Another element of the campaign is the production of a toolkit identifying some of the city's leading sustainable businesses – from hotels and restaurants to conference venues and corporate entertainment providers – which simplifies the process of organising a sustainable conference in Glasgow. The toolkit is designed to make it easier for conference organisers to find the services they require from suppliers who share their own green objectives.

In August 2017, building on the People Make Glasgow Greener campaign, the GCB became the first destination marketing organisation in the UK to achieve a Green Tourism award, at Silver status, acknowledging the positive contribution the team had made to sustainability in their city.

CASE STUDY 12.2: MONTREAL CONVENTION CENTRE'S URBAN AGRICULTURE LAB

(Reproduced with the kind permission of the Palais des congrès de Montréal and the International Association of Convention Centres)

Urban Agriculture Lab

The Executive Chef of Montreal's convention centre, the Palais des congrès de Montréal, does not need to go far to find kale, lettuce or strawberries. He can find these on the rooftop of the venue, in the Urban Agriculture Lab. This state-of-the-art farming project is a story of community partnership that earned the Palais des congrès de Montréal (http://congresmtl. com/en/) the prestigious Innovation Award of the International Association of Convention Centres (http://www.aipc.org/) in 2017.

It began two decades previously with the convention centre's management adopting a vision and a strong commitment to sustainable development. Over the years, action plans and policies were drafted meticulously to preserve and perpetuate this commitment. Creating projects that align with the convention centre's vision, and more importantly, that employees take pride in, was a priority. Green events, employee training, energy-saving measures, recycled waste management, certifications, urban agriculture, social and community involvement are some of the areas the Palais des congrès de Montréal employees have been involved in.

Today the Urban Agriculture Lab appears at the top of the list of achievements.

The Palais des congrès de Montréal has become a showcase for experimentation in and promotion of Quebec urban farming technologies and techniques, allowing partners to use the spaces available on its rooftops to develop different greening projects.

Raymond Larivée, President and CEO of the Palais des congrès de Montréal explains

> We are proud of the sustainability leadership role we play within the industry through our tangible actions. By opening the Urban Agriculture Lab in tandem with university and community partners, the Palais is fostering experimentation with new rooftop urban farming technologies and practices, and in the process is also reducing heat islands in the city's downtown core.

The Lab is comprised of four components:

- Culti-VERT (5,770 square feet of extensive green rooftops and container gardening)
- Pollinating beehives (sheltering up to 150,000 bees)
- The VERTical initiative ('edible wall' tarpaulins on scaffolds, a first in North America spanning 6,000 square feet of floor space and 5,000 square feet of vertical space)
- Canada's first urban rooftop vineyard (2,000 square feet of Urban Vines).

While contributing to reducing heat island effects by 12–20 per cent, the Lab produces each summer about 60 to 80 kg of honey as well as 650 kg to one metric ton of pesticide-free and transportation-free fruit, vegetables and fine herbs. These fresh ingredients are used in dishes prepared by the convention centre's exclusive caterer Capital Catering and served to meeting delegates. They are also donated to homeless shelter La Maison du Père, a long-time partner of the Palais' sustainable development efforts.

In 2017 the Lab became a provincial research centre funded by the Quebec Department of Agriculture, Fisheries and Food. The various projects housed in the Lab certainly helped Montreal and the Palais to receive ASTM certification as a sustainable destination and meeting venue.

Chrystine Loriaux, the Palais des congrès Director of Marketing and Communications, provides further details:

> We have an immense rooftop surface right in the heart of the city, and we knew that by working with environmental experts we could make a positive contribution by repurposing this vast space. Scientists, engineers, crop farmers, bee farmers, managers and a host of other specialists worked together with the Palais' building management team to make this project happen, which we believe will inspire other property owners to do the same.

Visibility generated by the project has inspired various stakeholders in the city to follow the Palais' lead and develop similar projects adapted to their own needs and objectives. A nearby hotel, restaurant and business also decided to site gardens on their rooftops, joining the fight against urban heat islands.

The Palais' Urban Agriculture Lab is a living demonstration that a collaborative approach – uniting leaders from the meetings industry, university research, community organisations and local businesses – can lead to a flagship sustainability project.

IT'S MY JOB
JENNY YU-MATTSON, EXECUTIVE
DIRECTOR OF GLOBAL SUSTAINABILITY AT
LAS VEGAS SANDS CORPORATION

My key responsibility as the Executive Director of Global Sustainability at Las Vegas Sands Corporation (www.sands.com) is to develop and implement strategic corporate environmental responsibility programmes for the business operations of our company. Las Vegas Sands is the leading global developer of integrated resorts that feature luxury hotels, world-class gaming and entertainment, convention and exhibition facilities, celebrity chef restaurants and many other amenities. The company is credited with pioneering the concept of a MICE-driven integrated resort, a unique and highly successful product that serves both the business and leisure tourism markets. Starting with a single property in 1990, the footprint of Las Vegas Sands now extends worldwide, from Las Vegas to Macao, and from Pennsylvania to Singapore.

My interest in sustainability partly originates from the love of nature that I developed in my home town of Hangzhou, China, a city with beautiful lakes and mountains, and many ancient historical sites. Hangzhou is known as one of the most beautiful cities in

China, even though now, at times, the pure blue sky that I remember from my childhood is somewhat obscured due to air pollution.

Chinese families value education very highly, and my parents did everything they could to help me pursue the highest degree I could obtain. Thanks to them, I have had so many amazing opportunities they could never have imagined. My first step away from home was studying as an exchange student at Hong Kong Polytechnic University's Hotel and Tourism Management College, where I first learned the concept of the MICE industry. Hong Kong opened my eyes to the Western world and convinced me that I needed to study abroad for my master's degree, to gain more advanced experiences of the hospitality industry. So, in 2004, I moved to the US to begin my graduate studies in hotel administration at the University of Nevada Las Vegas (UNLV). Living and studying in a foreign country thousands of miles away from home proved to be quite challenging for me. It was the first time I had to take all of my courses completely in English. I also had to learn how to cook, drive and most challenging of all, how to appreciate American humour. With limited resources, I rode my bike to school every day, didn't waste any food and always adjusted the thermostats to minimise my energy bill. Looking back, I see that I had a very 'sustainable' lifestyle and was extremely healthy! At UNLV, I quickly understood that in order for me to succeed in the hospitality industry, gaining hands-on experience was just as important as academic achievements, so I took every opportunity I could find to volunteer at trade shows to get more experience of the MICE industry.

After completing my master's degree in 2006, I joined Las Vegas Sands as a Leadership Development Programme Associate. In the next two years, I rotated through most of the corporate and property departments and had the opportunity to work with a wide variety of people, from senior executives to entry-level team members. It was one of the most rewarding periods of my career as I learned all about the operations of a leading hospitality company from so many different perspectives. At the end of the programme, the Corporate Development Department offered me a job as a Project Manager. In that role, I first became involved in sustainability through our efforts to earn LEED (Leadership in Energy and Environmental Design) certification for the construction of The Palazzo hotel in Las Vegas. LEED (https://new.usgbc.org/leed) is one of the most popular green building certification programmes used worldwide, and in order to master its complexities, my boss told me that I needed to pass the LEED exam for New Construction. Without any engineering and design background, the LEED book was almost a foreign language to me. Many of the concepts were completely new, from commissioning and energy modelling to air quality testing. But by studying extra hard, I eventually managed to pass the exam with the second highest score in the test centre's history. Nevertheless, I soon learned that my high score didn't mean that I already knew everything about sustainable development. Understanding the theory was just the beginning, and I had to learn how to apply my learning to the real world by collaborating with operation teams who played a crucial role in implementing actual green initiatives for our company.

In 2008, the recession hit the US economy and our company's development projects were put on hold. That difficult time became a turning point in my career. Given the very challenging economic conditions of those years, efficiency projects were well received within the company, as we tried to reduce our overheads. The Corporate Development Department gradually switched from development to sustainability and that transition effectively helped my colleagues and me to hold on to our jobs. The first major project for me was managing the LEED Existing Buildings (EB) Certification process, which resulted in The Venetian Las Vegas becoming the largest hotel in the world to receive the LEED EB Gold Certification (in 2010). At the same time, we officially launched the Sands ECO 360 Global Sustainability programme, which focuses on continually improving Las Vegas Sands's environmental stewardship.

Meetings and conventions are integral to the Las Vegas Sands business model, and we were well aware that the events industry as a whole has a very large environmental footprint due to its sheer size and the volume of waste it generates. But the idea of sustainable meetings was still a relatively new concept at that time. However, a global green meetings community was beginning to develop and we were very fortunate to be involved in it from the very beginning, learning from the industry experts and developing our awareness of green practices alongside that of our clients. In 2011, I launched the Sands ECO 360 Meetings programme (https://www.sands.com/sands-eco-360/our-strategy/green-meetings.html) to support our forward-thinking clients in making their events more sustainable. Since then, the programme has become the globally adopted standard for Sands properties. We have now hosted many high-profile sustainable events internationally, and earned various much-coveted certifications and awards. A key feature of our approach to the greening of meetings is that instead of simply 'serving' our meetings clients, we partner with them to deliver sustainable events. We begin by spending time understanding the event organisers' sustainability goals, and then one of our designated Green Meeting Concierges customises each sustainable event experience to meet those goals. Together with the event planners, we challenge ourselves to achieve better results and drive innovation every year, by implementing initiatives that reduce the events' environmental footprint and encourage attendees to give back to the local community. Our customers can take advantage of the practices we have implemented, such as energy and water conservation, waste recycling, using sustainable products and materials, Sands ECO 360 environmentally friendly meeting room settings, a donation programme, sustainable food options and a wellness programme. We have many success stories to share, from attendees building hygiene kits from our recycled amenities on the trade show floor and meals featured with less water-intensive ingredients at IMEX America in Las Vegas, and Asia's first-ever zero waste to landfill event Responsible Business Forum in Singapore, to the International Environmental Co-operation Forum and Exhibition hosted at The Venetian Macao. With the dedication of our dedicated team, green meeting practices have been integrated into our standard operations and we have been recognised as a leader in this field.

We have now set our sights on new challenges as we align our strategy with the United Nations Sustainable Development Goals. We have also set ourselves ambitious greenhouse gas reduction targets, and are the first integrated resort company to have them approved by the Science Based Targets initiative.

As is often said, sustainability is a journey, and this is a field that requires constant learning and innovation, to keep pace with green developments. About half of the projects and initiatives we implement every year are new to us, so we constantly have to educate ourselves through various channels to make sound decisions later on. As climate change doesn't have borders, we are obliged to collaborate with other partners around the world in order to address this extremely serious global issue. For me, the most rewarding part of my job is working with like-minded people to help solve these problems, and coming up with innovative ideas that truly make a difference in building the foundation of a new world that my 17-month-old daughter's grandchildren will not only survive in, but thrive in. In this sense, sustainability for me has become more of an essential responsibility and passion, rather than a job.

You can read more about our work at: https://www.sands.com/sands-eco-360/our-vision.html.

IT'S MY JOB
GUY BIGWOOD,
GROUP SUSTAINABILITY DIRECTOR, MCI

After graduating with a degree in Computer Systems (IT) from the University of Westminster in London, I spent the first ten years of my professional life working in the IT industry in the UK, France and the US. In 1999, I moved to Spain to launch a new IT company, and two years later I decided to take a career change and landed my first job in the events industry, as Operations Director with the Yeti Group, one of Spain's leading events and communications companies.

My next career move introduced me to MCI (http://www.mci-group.com), an independently owned event agency with its headquarters in Geneva, Switzerland. Now, MCI's 2,200 experts in 63 cities and 31 countries serve clients across Europe, the

Americas, Asia-Pacific, India, the Middle East and Africa. But back in 2004, I was tasked with the job of starting up MCI's office in Spain and later in Portugal. It is now one of the leading event agencies, with operations in Lisbon, Barcelona and Madrid and a staff of 50.

As part of my role as the Spanish office's General Manager, in 2005 I had to organise a leadership event for Europe's top 500 entrepreneurs. The keynote speaker at this event was a US politician called Al Gore. Still relatively unknown for his environmental work, ex-Vice-President Gore shared his view of an 'Inconvenient Truth', the title of his soon to be released film about the state of the planet and climate change. His session touched a part of my soul and immediately inspired me to do something to tackle environmental change.

At the same time, my wife was diagnosed with ovarian cancer, and I was forced into a journey to understand why people get cancer, and what we can do to survive. It quickly became apparent that our lifestyles and environment significantly affect our health, and that we are contaminating our bodies by surrounding ourselves with toxic paints, carpets, foods and innumerable pollutants.

With Al Gore and cancer as my motivators I approached the MCI board of directors and complained that MCI did not have a group environmental strategy or programme. Their response was immediate and I was given responsibility for developing the MCI Corporate Social Responsibility (CSR) programme. (At that point I learned that you should never complain unless you are prepared to do something to fix the problem.)

At that time, I knew nothing about CSR and could not even spell 'sustainability'. So I made a few phone calls and found some brilliant people, who came to my rescue and helped me develop the first MCI CSR strategy around the concept of building a business with a balanced triple bottom line: people, planet and profit.

We launched our programme in 2007, with a focus on building, engaging and training a small team of CSR Champions to take our initial ideas to the MCI offices. Then we became the first events company to sign the UN Global Compact (the world's largest corporate sustainability programme), and I started attending their events and networking with experienced sustainability professionals. I quickly realised that to integrate sustainable development principles into the DNA of MCI, we needed to win and deliver events focused on sustainability. Ten years later, MCI has become the world's leading organiser of events about environmental and social sustainability issues, delivering over 1,000 projects in the past decade.

In 2007, I had no idea how far my idea for integrating sustainability into business events would develop. But it has gone from strength to strength, and in 2008 I launched MCI Sustainability Services, a global consulting practice within MCI, focused on helping cities, companies and associations to define, launch and accelerate their sustainability-related platforms, initiatives and events. We have delivered over 200 projects, and our clients include the United Nations, Singapore Tourism Board, Thailand Convention and Exhibition Bureau, Las Vegas Sands Corporation, SAP, the Dubai government and the Copenhagen Bella Center congress venue.

As MCI's Group Sustainability Director, much of the work undertaken by myself and my team has been in cooperation with other organisations that are equally passionate about sustainability issues in the context of meetings and events. For example, we partnered with the ICCA Scandinavia Chapter to develop the business events industry's first destination sustainability benchmarking programme. Originally entitled the Scandinavian Destination Sustainability Index, it was, in 2016, rebranded and extended into the Global Destination Sustainability Index (http://gds-index.com/). The GDS Index is a collaborative platform to help destinations, convention bureaus, event planners and suppliers promote and accelerate the adoption of sustainable practices in their city and in the business events industry as a whole. Now used in over 40 cities on five continents, the Index engages and inspires corporate, association and government clients to request and prize events destinations that have robust event sustainability initiatives. This is the world's first methodology for achieving MICE destination sustainability and benchmarking performance to reach that goal.

In 2008, I joined the board of the Green Meeting Industry Council (http://www.gmic-global.org/), where I served as President from 2010 to 2011. I have also been directly involved in creating a number of other sustainability standards for the business events industry, including the APEX/ASTM Environmentally Sustainable Meeting Standards, ISO 20121, the Copenhagen Sustainable Meetings Protocol, the GRI Event Reporting Sustainability Standards, the United Nations Sustainable Event Guidelines and national sustainability standards for Singapore, Korea and Thailand, among others.

I thoroughly enjoy inspiring people to get into action. My motto comes from the song by Elvis Presley: 'A little less conversation and a little more action please', and to that end my team and I have trained over 34,000 people and delivered hundreds of sessions and keynote presentations for global organisations such as the UN, Sustainable Brands, MPI, ICCA, SITE, UFI, BestCities, IMEX and for associations and governments around the world. Some of my favourite work has been helping IMEX to deliver the Future Leaders Forum in partnership with MCI and MPI.

What is especially gratifying for me are the many ways in which the work of the MCI Sustainability Department has been recognised, and I am incredibly humbled by the fact that we have received 21 awards for our work with MCI and our clients. This began with the IMEX-GMIC Meetings Award in 2010, for the work we did with the COP15 UN Climate Change Conference in Copenhagen. Most recently, I was personally honoured to be one of the recipients of the Events Industry Council's 2017 Pacesetter Awards, which celebrate the achievements of events industry professionals who exhibit individual excellence based on innovation, impact, vision, leadership, influence, collaboration, courage and perseverance.

I consider myself incredibly fortunate to have a job that I enjoy so much. My work is driven by a passion and purpose to accelerate the transition to a more sustainable events industry. The positive future of our businesses and the health of our families, friends and ourselves depends on this. It's fantastic work but with the travelling and tight time schedules it can be emotionally tiring at times. To recharge I escape into nature: hiking, rock climbing or mountain biking in the Pyrenees; or I relax by tending my organic garden at my home in Barcelona.

You can read more about our work at: www.lessconversationmoreaction.com; and www.mcisustainability.com.

References

AUMA (1994) The ecological way to appear at a trade fair. Confederation of German Trade Fair and Exhibition Industries.

Beauchamp, S. (2017) Vancouver makes giving back a part of the meeting experience. *Convene*, PCMA, 1 August.

Bossdorf, O., Parepa, M. and Fischer, M. (2010) Climate-neutral ecology conferences: Just do it! *Trends in Ecology & Evolution* 25(2): 61.

Chalip, L. (2006) Towards social leverage of sport events. *Journal of Sport & Tourism* 11(2): 109–127.

Chalip, L. (2014) From legacy to leverage, in *Leveraging Legacies from Sports Mega-Events: Concepts and cases*, London: Palgrave Macmillan, pp. 2–12.

Cornelissen, S., Bob, U. and Swart, K. (2011). Towards redefining the concept of legacy in relation to sport mega-events: Insights from the 2010 FIFA World Cup. *Development Southern Africa* 28(3): 307–318.

Davidson, R. (2009). Business tourism: Providing a social legacy. *Tourism Insights*, September.

Davidson, R. (2010) What Does Generation Y want from conferences and incentive programmes? Implications for the tourism industry, in Yeoman, I. et al. (eds) *Tourism and Demography*, Oxford: Goodfellow Publishers, pp. 115–129.

Dickson, C. and Arcodia, C. (2010) Promoting sustainable event practice: The role of professional associations. *International Journal of Hospitality Management* 29(2): 236–244.

Draper, J., Dawson, M. and Casey, E. (2011) An exploratory study of the importance of sustainable practices in the meeting and convention site selection process. *Journal of Convention & Event Tourism* 12(3): 153–178.

Elkington, J. (1994) Towards the sustainable corporation: Win-win-win business strategies for sustainable development. *California Management Review* 36(2): 90–100.

Emdén, F. (2008) Meeting with meaning. *Meetings International* 1: 73–75.

Events Industry Council (n.d.) APEX/ASTM environmentally sustainable meeting standards. Available at: http://www.eventscouncil.org/APEX/APEXASTM.aspx.

Four Seasons (n.d.) Meetings and events. Available at: https://www.fourseasons.com/meetings_and_events/greening-meetings/.

Getter, K. L. and Rowe, D. B. (2006) The role of extensive green roofs in sustainable development. *HortScience* 41(5): 1276–1285.

Getz, D (2009) Event Studies: Theory, research and policy for planned events, Oxford: Butterworth Heinemann.

Glasgow Convention Bureau (n.d.) Leave a lasting legacy. Available at: https:// glasgowconventionbureau.com/plan-your-meeting/leave-a-lasting-legacy/.

Gracan, D., Sander, I. and Rudancic-Lugaric, A. (2010) Green strategy of business tourism. *Tourism and Hospitality Management* (Supplement): 337–349.

Greenview (2017) Green Venue Report. The state of convention & exhibition centre sustainability. Available at: www.greenviewportal.com/trends/green-venue-report.

Guillot, C. (2013) Convention centres of the future, designed today. *Collaborate Meetings*, February/March.

Guizzardi, A., Mariani, M. and Prayag, G. (2017) Environmental impacts and certification: Evidence from the Milan World Expo 2015. *International Journal of Contemporary Hospitality Management* 29(3): 1052–1071.

Han, H. and Hwang, J. (2017) What motivates delegates' conservation behaviours while attending a convention? *Journal of Travel & Tourism Marketing* 34(1): 82–98.

Han, H. S. and Verma, R. (2014) Why attend tradeshows? A comparison of exhibitor and attendees' preferences. *Cornell Hospitality Quarterly* 55(3): 239–251.

Henderson, S. (2011). The development of competitive advantage through sustainable event management. *Worldwide Hospitality and Tourism Themes* 3(3): 245–257.

ISO 20121 (n.d.) Event Sustainability Management System. Available at: http://www. iso20121.org/.

Kang, K. H., Stein, L., Heo, C. Y. and Lee, S. (2012) Consumers' willingness to pay for green initiatives of the hotel industry. *International Journal of Hospitality Management* 31: 564–572.

Koelnmesse (n.d.) Environment. Available at: http://www.koelnmesse.com/Koelnmesse/ The-Company/Responsibility/Enviroment/index.php.

Laing, J. and Frost, W. (2010) How green was my festival: Exploring challenges and opportunities associated with staging green events. *International Journal of Hospitality Management* 29(2): 261–267.

Lee, W., Barber, T. and Tyrell, T. (2013) Green attendees' evaluation of green attributes at the convention centre: Using importance–performance analysis. *Anatolia – An International Journal of Tourism and Hospitality Research* 24: 221–240.

Liu, X. and Feng, X. (2014) Green development path in exhibition construction: Empirical research. Proceedings of the International Conference on Global Economy, Commerce and Service Science, pp. 152–154.

Mair, J. (2011) Can there be a sustainable future for conferences and conventions? Proceedings from 5th Global Event Congress, Norway, 13–15 June.

Mair, J. and Jago, L. (2010) The development of a conceptual model of greening in the business events tourism sector. *Journal of Sustainable Tourism* 18(1): 77–94.

Maritz (2012) The future of meeting venues. White Paper. Maritz Research.

Merrilees, B. and Marles, K. (2011) Green business events: Profiling through a case study. *Event Management* 15(4): 361–372.

Misener, L. and Mason, D. (2006) Creating community networks. Can sporting events offer meaningful sources of social capital? *Managing Leisure* 11(1): 39–56.

Park, E. and Boo, S. (2010) An assessment of convention tourism's potential contribution to environmentally sustainable growth. *Journal of Sustainable Tourism* 18(1): 95–113.

Pinchera, M. (2008) Beyond 'Green': The future viability of business demands a focus on people as much as planet. *MPI One+ Magazine*, August.

Rogers, T. (2008) *Conferences and Conventions: A global industry*, 2nd edn, Oxford: Butterworth Heinemann.

Rogers, T. and Davidson, R. (2016) *Marketing Destinations and Venues for Conferences, Conventions and Business Events*, Oxford: Routledge.

Russell, M. (2013) How to ensure your meeting's CSR activities actually make an impact. *Convene*, PCMA, 1 August.

Smith, A. (2009) Theorising the relationship between major sport events and social sustainability. *Journal of Sport & Tourism* 14(2–3): 109–120.

Smith, A. and Fox, T. (2007) From 'event-led' to 'event-themed' regeneration: The 2002 Commonwealth Games legacy scheme. *Urban Studies* 44(5/6): 1125–1143.

Sox, C. B., Benjamin, S., Carpenter, J. and Strick, S. (2013) An exploratory study of meeting planners and conference attendees' perceptions of sustainable issues in convention centres. *Journal of Convention & Event Tourism* 14(2): 144–161.

UNDP (2018) Practitioner's guide to sustainable procurement. United Nations Development Programme.

UNEP (1972) Stockholm 1972: Report of the United Nations Conference on the Human Environment. United Nations Environment Programme.

UNEP (2009) Green Meeting Guide. United Nations Environment Programme.

Walker, A. S. (2012) Process vs. performance standards for sustainable meeting and event management. Comparative Research in Law & Political Economy. Research Paper No. 17/2012.

WCED (1987) *Our Common Future*, Oxford: Oxford University Press.

Whitfield, J., Dioko, L. A. N. and Webber, D. E. (2014) Scoring environmental credentials: A review of UK conference and meetings venues using the GREENER VENUE framework. *Journal of Sustainable Tourism* 22: 299–318.

Business events ethics

Chapter objectives

On completion of this chapter the reader should be able to:

- Understand the parts played by personal ethics and professional ethics and the differences between these two systems.
- Appreciate the roles of corporate and association codes of conduct: their uses and limitations.
- Recognise the various ethical dilemmas that can be faced by business events professionals.
- Understand the contribution made by codes of conduct created for business events professionals.

Personal ethics and professional ethics

Although personal ethics and professional ethics both matter in the workplace, there are some key differences between them. Personal ethics refer to an individual's personal codes of conduct, of which honesty, integrity, fairness, openness, commitment and a sense of responsibility are a few typical examples. While such principles and values are generally cultivated within individuals from childhood, with a large part being played by their parents, friends and family, they remain with people all through their lives, constantly manifested through their everyday actions and words.

But ethics play just as important a role in people's professional lives. In the workplace, professional ethics refer to the code of conduct that a person must adhere to in respect of all aspects of their interactions and business dealings. Such codes of conduct, as devised by individual companies or entire professions, are compulsory and are imposed on all employees or professionals. It is this compulsory nature of business ethics that most differentiates them from personal codes of conduct, which the individual can choose whether or not to follow. At the level of the individual company, the consistently ethical conduct of employees plays a vital role in enhancing the reputation of the organisation. But most professions have developed their own ethical codes to ensure consistency of conduct across all members of each profession with respect to values such as confidentiality, proficiency, fairness and transparency, which are some of the most widespread professional ethics. At the level of the profession as a whole, ethical codes also serve as an indication to people outside the profession – who might interact with its members or be affected by its actions – as to what standards they can reasonably expect from members of that profession.

Codes of ethics therefore impose a great sense of responsibility upon individual employees and members of a profession; and, while they are not, generally speaking, laws, they are certainly authoritative enough to ensure that a person who violates their organisation's or profession's code of ethics risks losing their job or being removed from their profession.

Codes of ethics

By developing a code of ethics, an employer or the governing body of a profession attempts to make it clear that employees or members cannot claim ignorance as a defence for any unethical conduct.

Corporate codes

Recent revelations of corporate unethical behaviour, involving automobile pollution testing, toxic waste disposal and sexual harassment, for example, have further heightened public concern and scepticism about some companies' lack of honour, honesty and integrity. In response to public disquiet, a growing number of organisations are refining their codes of ethical conduct or developing and implementing such codes for the first time, to guide their employees' conduct. Schwartz (2001:248) defines a corporate code as a 'written, distinct and formal document which consists of moral standards used to guide employee or corporate behaviour'. The extent of their use in business circles is indicated by Kaptein (2017), who estimates that of the 200 largest organisations in the world, more than 80 per cent have already introduced such codes, and an ever-larger number of smaller organisations also have a code or are in the process of developing one. The content of such codes varies significantly from company to company, but in general they attempt to outline clear guidelines for managerial policy and employee decision-making in particular, as these apply to customer and public safety and welfare.

But many challenges face those charged with devising and implementing their company's ethical codes. Kaptein (2017) highlights some of the most common of these, including:

1 Translating a code into strategic decisions and concrete policy – how to apply the code in daily decision-making
2 Convincing those who are fervently opposed to the code of its value – how to deal with resistance or even outright rebellion against the code
3 Communicating the content of a code and motivating employees to observe it – how to ensure compliance with the code
4 Reminding employees to pay attention to the code – how to keep employees focused on the code
5 Communicating to those outside the company that the organisation takes the code seriously – how to convince outsiders that the company takes the code to heart
6 Determining how and when to bring the content of the code up to date – how to improve the content of the code?

The last point is often overlooked, but enlightened managers understand that codes of conduct should evolve in line with development within their companies and changes in the market environment within which they operate. Remaining ethical is not a static issue. Companies need to periodically review and evaluate their priorities and make necessary adjustments to avoid their ethical standards and training becoming outdated.

Henderson and McIlwraith (2013:21) provide a number of guidelines for the implementation of an effective corporate code of ethics:

1 Align human resources practices, from hiring to performance evaluation, with the company's ethics policy.
2 Incorporate ethics training into new employee orientation and ongoing professional development for team members.
3 Reference the policy in staff meetings and use it as a reference for addressing business issues.
4 Convene an ethics committee to regularly review and update the ethics policy.
5 Apply the policy at all levels of the organisation, including senior leadership and front-line staff.

The important role played by senior leadership has been emphasised by several other commentators, including Tucker et al. (1999) who note that a common theme in the literature on this topic is that the implementation and institutionalisation of effective ethical codes requires senior management's commitment, organisational changes, and human and financial resources. The point is echoed by the observation of Avey et al. (2012) that ethical leadership research asserts that the character of an individual leader (exemplified through traits such as honesty and concern for others) is important for fostering positive outcomes in organisations, particularly outcomes associated with their employees, such as trust and job satisfaction. According to the authors, leaders of any organisation must act as the primary influential models of ethical guidance for every member of the organisation, because if senior management do not act ethically and support others who do, an organisation's ethical code will have little meaning. It is therefore critical for managers and executives to:

- act in ways that are consistent with the company's ethical standards;
- systematically apply those standards in their dealing with employees.

Sadly, there are still far too many instances of high-profile companies that have ethical codes stipulating lofty standards conduct that are routinely and flagrantly contravened by all levels of management. It is a sobering thought that even as the American energy group Enron was heading for bankruptcy in 2001 due to its gross violation of all forms of honesty, morality and compliance, it was still giving all new employees its four-page ethical code to sign on their first day in the company (Hemingway and Maclagan, 2004).

Professional codes

Almost all professions have developed codes of ethics which govern the behaviour of their members and represent the applied morality of the profession. They serve as guidelines for the behaviour of their members and as an indication of the public's expectations of the profession. According to Gilman (2005), codes of ethics can specify acceptable and unacceptable behaviours in a profession. If accompanied by effective implementation that regularly identifies typical ethical issues confronted by practitioners, such codes can ground ethics in the challenges of practising a profession. Beyond identifying aspects of unacceptable behaviour and providing a framework for enforcing code violations, ethical codes can express the expectations of positive ethical behaviour by people exercising a particular profession. Finally, as previously mentioned, codes inform people outside the profession what they can and should expect as clients of those practising it. A professional code of ethics therefore is a promise to act in a manner that protects the public's well-being, indicating, for example, that a lawyer or doctor will maintain client–patient confidentiality; or that an accountant will not use client information for personal gain.

For as long as professionals adhere to these standards, the public usually accepts that professional associations can independently create and enforce their ethical codes. But in cases where these codes are repeatedly and grossly violated, the public's likely response is to lose trust in associations and demand protective legislation. For example, in the US, the Sarbanes–Oxley Act of 2002 was enacted by the government in response to the public outcry at early 21st-century corporate frauds. As the relevant associations had failed to prevent the public from being harmed by these abuses, the government intervened to introduce legislation to considerably tighten the rules on corporate governance and accountability.

However, it is evident that most professions would prefer to police themselves, rather than have an externally imposed set of regulations, and for most of them that is a major motivation to introduce codes of ethics, generally created by and enforced through the relevant professional associations – one of their key roles as discussed in Chapter 3. It is a role that, when carried out effectively, can also improve the public's perception of professional associations, as noted by Tucker et al. (1999:297):

> The view of many individuals is that associations are primarily self-serving, inwardly-focused entities. Communicating more extensively to all stakeholders about codes of ethics and their administration could potentially enhance the credibility of associations. The ultimate winner is society, which experiences a higher level of customer/client satisfaction accomplished through more self-regulation as opposed to greater government involvement.

But the main challenge, as in the case of corporate ethical codes, is to devise codes of conduct that are clear and precise. Unfortunately, there are too many examples of codes that are vague and open to interpretation. For instance, instead of providing specific examples of actions that are unacceptable under the code, they may simply state, for example, that members should 'maintain exemplary standards of professional conduct at all times'.

Towards the end of this chapter, the code of ethics of one of the key business events associations is reviewed. First, however, we analyse some examples of ethical issues encountered in business events.

Ethical issues in business events

Most business events professionals face ethical dilemmas at some points in their careers that can be difficult to navigate. And consequently, as in most professions, there are instances of unscrupulous practices and lapses in the moral judgement of a small minority of practitioners. A review of some of the most common situations in which these are regularly encountered now follows.

Familiarisation trips

In Chapter 10, the use of familiarisation (or 'fam') trips as a destination marketing tool was discussed. Convention bureaus use such trips to invite groups of events planners to their destination for periods lasting between two and four days to showcase their cities' or regions' attractions and assets as places to hold business events. However, the fact that such trips are generally free to the participants means that they are often the focus of a form of unethical behaviour known as 'fam scamming'. The term is based upon the word 'scam' in colloquial English, meaning to defraud, swindle or cheat. Doyle (2005:1) defines a fam scammer as a 'freeloader': 'someone who deliberately misrepresents himself or herself in order to qualify for a free fam trip, often to a faraway destination that includes not just air travel and accommodation, but exquisite meals and first-rate activities'. In its more invidious manifestation, fam scamming takes the form of someone pretending to be a conference organiser or incentive trip planner in order to secure an invitation to participate on a fam trip. These bogus planners may be people who have no connection whatsoever with the business events industry, but who understand the fam trips system and somehow manage to trick or charm convention bureau staff into believing that they are genuine planners. But more often, fam scamming takes the form of a bona fide planner accepting an invitation to participate in a fam trip when they are fully aware that they will never use that city or region as a destination, for example because it is geographically unsuitable or financially inaccessible for the planner's company or association. Doyle suggests that a third, subtler, form of fam scamming is when an executive-level planner passes an invitation addressed to himself/herself to a junior staff member who has no buying or influencing power whatsoever, usually as some form of 'perk'. While the junior member of staff may enjoy the free trip, there is no probability of any benefit for the host convention bureau, as that participant has no authority to recommend their destination to clients or colleagues. In an interview on this topic, Jamal Aaron Hageb, senior meetings manager for the American Bar Association, severely criticised planners who participate in fam trips to places that they are not truly considering for an event, or who take family and friends along with them, or request 'extras' such as limousine rides or tickets to a sporting event:

> I find it repulsive when people take advantage of the system and go on every fam that's possible. If you know your organisation is never going to do an event there, you're doing your organisation a disservice as well as the destination ... and taking an opportunity away from another planner who has a legitimate reason for going.
>
> (Davis, 2014)

He adds that at the American Bar Association, all employees must provide justification for going on any fam trips (ibid.).

The scale of the problem is suggested by one commentator with extensive experience of organising fam trips who, in an interview with the trade magazine *Smart Meetings*, estimated that 5–8 per cent of fam trip participants have no meeting or incentive business to place whatsoever and that their participation in fam trips costs convention bureaus, airlines and hoteliers millions of dollars every year. She has encountered a diverse range of these scammers and notes that a large percentage of them do it on a fairly regular basis, becoming more convincing with each trip. The same commentator adds that not all of these scammers are the 'unemployed, young or reckless types we might imagine them to be'. Quite often they are employed at real companies, or even are the owners of companies. They have business cards, work email addresses, and dress and act professionally. However, the scammer might be the company secretary posing as someone who makes buying or planning decisions, or the legitimate head of a company who is misrepresenting his or her company as one that holds off-site meetings (Smart Meetings, 2008).

In order to minimise their chances of becoming victims of unethical fam scamming, most convention bureaus carry out background checks on those they are considering inviting on such trips – research to verify that potential fam trip participants are qualified, and that they are who they say they are. This often includes requiring applicants to produce proof of events that they have booked in the past. For example, the destination marketing organisation Meet Puerto Rico rigorously screens planners and organisations it is considering hosting, making sure that Puerto Rico is on their shortlist for an upcoming event and that the event would bring a certain level of business to the destination. If a potential meeting is small, Meet Puerto Rico may finance the accommodation element of the planner's trip but not their airfare (Davis, 2014).

But however rigorous the screening of potential fam scammers, no system is infallible, and most convention bureaus have experience of such people succeeding in securing a place on their fam trips. Once at the destination, fam scammers can betray themselves by, for example, not participating in the site visits or showing little interest if they do so. However, it is generally agreed that by the time the scammer has been welcomed at the destination, along with the genuine members of the group, there is little point in going to the trouble of exposing them and sending them home. There are occasional rumours within the business events industry that a 'blacklist', a central database of 'fam scammers', is in circulation among destination marketing organisations. But for obvious issues of data protection, such lists, if they exist, remain private.

In any case, for every single instance of a 'fam scammer', there are most probably many examples of behaviour by fam trip guests which, while not unethical, contravenes the normal rules of etiquette and decent behaviour. Opting out of elements of a fam trip programme for no good reason is a common discourtesy to the organisers, as this deprives some of the destination's suppliers of the opportunity to meet the participants. An example of such egregious behaviour is provided by a representative of the Scottsdale Convention and Visitors Bureau in Arizona, who recalls fam trip participants slipping away from a carefully arranged group meal between planners and suppliers to drink and watch a sporting event in the hotel bar (Johnson, 2013).

It is worthy of note that similar discourteous behaviour is occasionally displayed by hosted buyers, events planners invited – at no cost to themselves or their companies – to attend business events trade shows. Hosted buyers who miss appointments with exhibitors at such events have attracted the censure of Joan Eisenstodt, of Eisenstodt Associates, a Washington, DC-based meeting consulting, facilitation and training company, who has often been called 'the conscience of the meetings industry'. In an interview with *Convene* magazine, she highlighted this abusive practice of some hosted buyers, adding that, in her view, 'nobody wants to address the ethical issues of it. I think the hosted buyer [model] is damaging in so many ways, but I think it's going to continue because people think it's the greatest solution to the buyer–seller relationship.' (Russell, 2016)

There is no doubt that the fam trip system (as well as the hosted buyer system) suffers from various degrees of unethical behaviour. Nevertheless, there are those in the business events industry who believe that certain convention bureaus and suppliers should shoulder at least part of the responsibility for this. Herrick (2013) cites one planner who expresses the view that '[convention bureaus] push meeting planners to attend when they are not a properly qualified lead for the fam. And [they continue] to invite meeting planners who are known to take advantage of fam trips over and over again.'

Gifts

Free purses, spa treatments and iPads; thousands of complimentary hotel nights and airline miles; countless five-star dinners; all-expenses-paid vacations for friends and family to beautiful destinations: these are all examples of items offered to planners as incentives to book their events with particular suppliers, according to some of the events industry professionals interviewed for an article in PCMA's *Convene* magazine (Davis, 2014). The author notes that although the giving and receiving of such benefits can and does present ethical problems for the events industry, it is sometimes more of a problem of perception: 'In fact, many "freebies" that people outside the [events] business might view as perks are actually part of the work of determining the best location for an event'. When a member of a company's events planning team is absent from work for two days, being hosted in a luxury hotel in another city, it may look like a perk to colleagues in other departments of the company; but for the planner wishing to evaluate possible new venues for the firm's events, it is an essential assignment.

In the business events industry as a whole, custom dictates that planners should be allowed to accept minor gifts from suppliers, such as a bottle of wine in their hotel room, and common courtesies such as free airport pickup, free food and drinks, and complimentary rooms during site inspections. But there are also times where people on both sides of the table – planners and suppliers – cross the line into unethical behaviour that could signal a lapse of integrity or an attempt to improperly influence the process of choosing a venue or service provider. In that respect, the suspicion of bribes being offered and received is never entirely absent when planners are given any type of gift or perk by hotels and other venues.

A lack of universally adopted professional guidelines or enforceable restrictions often leaves people to make their own personal rules. That can mean grey areas, especially for newcomers to the industry who may see their more experienced peers happily taking advantage of gifts or other special offers from suppliers.

How are meeting professionals supposed to navigate this world of free gifts? It begins in part with the avoidance of *conflicts of interest* or any activities that would reflect poorly on the individual, their organisation or the industry as a whole, such as accepting inappropriately extravagant gifts, incentives and/or services in any business dealings that could be perceived as a personal gain. A frequently offered piece of advice in this context is for planners to ask themselves – *before* accepting any gift from suppliers – 'would I be comfortable with my boss knowing that I had accepted this?'

Some companies simplify their employees' decisions of whether or not to accept gifts by issuing guidelines that specify the maximum cash value of gifts that employees are permitted to accept. In the PCMA/*Convene* 2016 ethics survey (Russell, 2016), planners were asked about any limits on the 'dollar amount' that their employers allowed them to accept from suppliers in terms of gifts and entertainment: 7 per cent of respondents reported that no gifts were allowed; 8 per cent US$25 per item per vendor; 9 per cent US$26–50 per item per vendor; 8 per cent US$51–100 US$ per item per vendor; and 59 per cent reported that their employers set no limits on what they could accept (10 per cent were categorised as 'other').

Loyalty points

Davis (2014) highlights another grey area: loyalty programme points and their potential to be seen to distort planners' choice of suppliers. Hotel points and airline miles are frequently awarded to organisations in return for the business they generate with these suppliers; but the points typically need to be awarded to an individual, not to a company. That recipient is often the planner who books the airline seats or the hotel rooms on behalf of business events participants. Interviewed by Davis, one senior manager in an events agency reacts to this situation:

> That's fine if an organisation knows about it and permits it, which many do. But planners who don't disclose the points they were awarded may not make their organisation or client aware of the impact it could have on the decision-making process.

In other words, planners leave themselves open to the accusation that – regardless of their actual intentions – their reason for choosing a particular hotel or airline for their event was due to the points they accumulated in their personal loyalty programme accounts, rather than it being the most appropriate hotel or airline for the planned event. This raises the ethical issue of a possible conflict of interest on the part of the meeting planner. Davis's interviewee emphasised that, as an independent planner, his policy was always to allow the clients he works for to take any reward points he generates on their behalf, to help them underwrite travel for their own employees – and he includes wording to that effect in his contracts with clients.

Commissions

A further source of temptation for unprincipled events planners is the system of hotels and other venues paying varying amounts of cash commissions to intermediaries, such as third-party meeting planners or PCOs who bring them business. This raises two questions: is the venue selection process distorted by planners who opt for the venues paying the highest rate of commission? And who should receive such commissions – the intermediary or the client who is paying the bill to hold their events in those venues?

In a rare survey on this topic, Toh et al. (2005) reported that 43 per cent of meeting planners polled by the trade magazine *Meeting News* admitted that levels of commission affect their venue selection, while 37 per cent said that they did not. Almost one-quarter of the respondents said that they keep the commissions as a 'bonus for a job well done' and only 14 per cent consider doing so to be unethical. In the survey, some independent meeting planners reported that they have refused to accept commissions or hotel points for themselves, preferring to pass such payments through to their clients. Toh et al. (2005) highlighted two specific issues related to the payment of commissions of this type.

Negotiations

Percentage commissions on rooms booked make it unattractive for independent meeting planners to negotiate for reduced room rates on behalf of their clients because that would reduce their own revenues.

Hidden commissions

The most egregious aspect of commissions is when they are hidden, so that clients are unaware that independent planners have asked for and received commissions, even when they, the planners, are being directly compensated by their clients. This not only affects site selection but also may raise room rates. Half of industry suppliers such as hotels said that they have paid out secret commissions, and 28 per cent of independent meeting planners admitted to accepting them.

The authors suggest solutions to each of these issues as follows: clients should remunerate meeting planners directly and fairly, making them less dependent on venue commissions as a source of revenue; full transparency – that all commissions be revealed up front, and there should be a three-way agreement among the venue, the client and the independent planner as to who is to receive the commissions and points, in order to avoid misunderstandings.

It is evident that navigating an ethical path through the grey areas of gifts and other potential benefits such as loyalty points and commissions can be extremely difficult for experienced planners, and even more so for new recruits in the events industry. One of Davis's (2014) interviewees suggests that young planners should cultivate mentors they respect who can provide advice in unclear situations: 'This is a business where there is so much that is offered, it can get confusing. A mentor or a supervisor who can answer questions on ethics is so important.'

Theft of intellectual property

The abuse of the system of RFPs – requests for proposals sent by clients to events agencies or third-party planners – is periodically discussed in the business events trade press. The unethical practice in this case takes place when the issuer of the RFP (an in-house corporate meeting planner or procurement manager, for example) takes the best creative ideas included in the proposals they receive and then either manages the event themselves or approaches another third-party planner to manage it at a lower fee than that quoted in the proposal they have plagiarised. Responding to RFPs is a time-consuming task involving providing much detail on costs, suppliers, etc., so it is doubly galling for the agency or third-party planner to find that as well as not being awarded the project, all or some of their creative ideas have been put to use in the design and delivery of the event that was the object of the RFP.

In an interview with Herrick (2013), the events ethics specialist Mariela McIlwraith expressed the view that 'if the planner then takes the idea as his or her own, bypassing the third-party planner who submitted the idea to them, that is breach of ethics'. But she admits that this type of problem is difficult to solve, as the challenge with intellectual property issues is that ideas cannot be copyrighted; only the expression of the idea can. McIlwraith adds that the scenario of intellectual property theft from a proposal may not always be one where the planner is intentionally unscrupulous, as it can be difficult at times to remember where any particular idea came from, when research for an event can include trade publications, websites, industry seminars as well as reviewing new and old RFPs. Her proposed solution is: 'planners have to ask themselves if they would have been able to construct the event plan without that proposal. If the answer is no, they have crossed a line.' Finally, she notes that while proving intellectual property theft can be one of the most difficult forms of litigation, there can be negative career consequences for planners who steal other planners' creative ideas: 'planners are a small community, and it will ruin your reputation, and make getting other jobs harder', she warns.

Various methods that planners can use to protect themselves against this form of unethical behaviour have been suggested. For example, Toh et al. (2005) advise charging the potential client for the agency's/planner's proposal, with the amount to be deducted from the project fee if it is accepted. But they acknowledge that this system carries the risk that those issuing RFPs may avoid sending them to agencies and planners who charge fees for their proposals. Another suggestion is for agencies and planners to establish the copyright of every proposal they send out, by adding the phrase 'all rights reserved' on the document's title page, as an indication that the ideas in the proposal are covered by some form of legal protection.

Incentive travel

Two issues of direct relevance to business events ethics were discussed by event professionals at the Incentives Retreat managed by the UK trade publication *Conference & Incentive Travel* (Flach, 2017). A panel of leading event planners and agency directors debated the moral concerns around where to book and hold incentive trips and the ethical issues that can arise during such trips.

One of the key concerns identified by planners for them and their delegates was the question of how to deal with destinations that are hostile towards minority communities. Russia was cited as an example because of its anti-homosexuality laws, which, in the participants' view, presented moral concerns in addition to delegate safety. However, one of the agency directors expressed the opinion that, depending on the context, people might choose to ignore these issues: 'If people love the World Cup, they will overcome their aversion to Russia and I think the location will still see business from groups'. Another member of the panel reported that she had had the experience of an incentive winner refusing to take part in a Malaysia incentive as he didn't feel that the country represented his lifestyle.

Another theme of the discussion was the occasional undesirable behaviour of some incentive travel participants, and the panel agreed that poor personal conduct or an ignorance of local customs or codes of behaviour can prove problematic when managing a group of delegates abroad. One member summed up the situation: 'Delegates tend to live in a bubble where they think there are no repercussions for any of their actions and you'll be able to get them out of any bad situation'. But another planner reminded the panel that 'Ultimately they are still on work time, so any issues such as sexual harassment or bullying are an HR issue and need to be dealt with in the appropriate way'.

Ethical codes for business events professionals

Within the business events industry, there exist various resources to help professionals navigate some of the ethical dilemmas explored in this chapter, principally organisation-specific (corporate) codes of conduct and association codes of conduct.

Organisation-specific codes of conduct

Organisation-specific codes can specify, for example, the criteria that planners should use in deciding whether or not to go on a hosted buyer trip or fam trips, as well as the maximum cash value of the gifts that employees can accept. According to Henderson and McIlwraith (2013:20):

> these should be the first point of reference for event professionals when seeking clarity of issues such as gift-giving and acceptance policies, personal use of company resources including hotel or mileage points earned on company business and human resources policies.

But in an interview with Herrick (2013), the ethics expert Joan Eisenstodt observed that 'surprisingly, many companies and organisations do not have ethics policies, and if they do, do not have specifics for different departments who might face ethical dilemmas'. Specifically, she noted that often a corporation's code of conduct insufficiently addresses realities faced by planners, who may face ethical issues that colleagues in other departments of the company do not: 'employees are made aware of ethics at an orientation or in the employee handbook, but that is usually the end of it, until a problem occurs – and it occurs often for planners'.

Nevertheless, it would appear that, in the US at least, more companies are introducing ethics policies and codes of conduct. Table 13.1, taken from the results of the PCMA/ *Convene* 2016 ethics survey of US business events professionals, planners and suppliers indicates the growth of such instruments over a six-year period.

Business events associations' codes of conduct

All of the leading business events associations have ethics policies – codes of conduct that outline the behaviour expected of their members and explain what constitutes professionalism. For example, applicants to the Certified Meeting Professional (CMP) programme must sign a code of ethics that stipulates, among other things, that they must 'actively encourage the integration of ethics into all aspects of the performance of [their] duties ... and never use [their] position for undue personal gain and to promptly disclose to appropriate parties all potential and actual conflicts of interest'.

The importance of this issue for business events associations generally is shown by the fact that any organisation applying for membership of the Events Industry Council must have, and submit, a code of ethics. An example of a code of ethics of a national business events association is given in Figure 13.1, which reproduces the ethical code of Meetings & Events Australia, the peak body representing the events industry in Australia.

In concluding this chapter, it is relevant to ask whether, taking into account the various moral dilemmas discussed in these pages, business events professionals are of the opinion that this industry is becoming more ethical or less ethical in its operations. One useful insight into this issue comes from the PCMA/*Convene* 2016 ethics survey in which professionals were asked whether, on balance, they thought that the meetings industry was operating in an ethical manner. It is useful to compare their responses to those given to the same question six years previously, as shown in Table 13.2.

Table 13.1 The growth of corporate codes of conduct

Does your organisation have a written ethics policy or other code of conduct that specifically addresses the meeting-planner role?

	2010	2016
Yes	28%	33%
No	72%	46%
Not applicable	–	21%

Source: PCMA/*Convene* 2016 ethics survey, in Russell (2016).

Table 13.2 Ethical or not?

On balance, do you think the meetings industry operates in an ethical manner, or is there room for reform?

	2010	2016
The meetings industry operates ethically on balance, but there is still room for reform	61%	80%
Ethics in the meeting industry are fine	34%	11%
The meetings industry needs serious reform	5%	9%

Source: PCMA/*Convene* 2016 ethics survey, in Russell (2016).

Meetings & Events Australia

CODE OF ETHICS

Each member of the Association shall conduct their business with integrity and in an ethical manner to earn and maintain the confidence of clients, colleagues, employers, employees and the public, and to maintain the reputation of the business events industry.

Article 1

Members shall pursue and maintain high standards of personal and professional conduct, and:

(a) Comply with the laws of Australia or of the country in which work is being performed and operate within the spirit of those laws.

(b) Ensure that all contracts and/or terms of business are clear, concise and are honoured in full unless terminated or modified by mutual agreement.

(c) Maintain skills through commitment to continued professional development and encourage colleagues to do the same.

(d) Uphold at all times the standing of the Association, our Industry and its Code of Ethics and actively encourage colleagues to do the same.

(e) Act honestly and fairly in all business dealings.

(f) Uphold high standards of corporate governance, and adopt terms of trade that would enhance the reputation of the industry as a sound, financially well-managed industry.

(g) Adopt risk management strategies, including the maintenance of appropriate insurance coverage so that all parties are not unreasonably exposed to risk.

(h) Shall not represent by use of the MEA logo or otherwise that their product or service is endorsed by MEA unless such endorsement agreement exists.

(i) Cooperate with any inquiry conducted by MEA to resolve any dispute involving consumers or another member.

Article 2

In their relationships with clients or customers, members shall:

(a) Where a principal/agent relationship exists, act as faithful agents in both professional and business matters.

(b) Advise them of any conflict of interest situation as it may occur or as it is perceived.

(c) Give professional opinion as objectively as possible when asked to do so and accept responsibility for advice given, actions taken and omissions.

(d) Declare any commissions, remuneration or additional benefit received from a third party that directly arises out of work performed for the client.

(e) Promptly respond to any client complaint about the service provided.

Article 3

In their relationships with employees and others, members shall:

(a) Protect the safety, health and welfare of employees and the public.

(b) Not disclose any confidential information without the specific consent of the provider of that information unless compelled by law.

(c) Not harm or attempt to harm, maliciously or recklessly, directly or indirectly, the professional reputation of others.

(d) Respect the privacy of others by distributing personal details only in circumstances that would be reasonably expected by the person, and by communicating with the person only when it is relevant to the circumstance that gave rise to the giving of the personal detail, or otherwise when permission is granted.

(e) Respect the intellectual property of others in the industry, particularly when ideas, creativity, and advice has been provided in good faith, but no agreement is in place to use such intellectual property.

(f) Make every effort to resolve complaints and grievances in good faith through reasonable direct communication and negotiation.

Breach of Ethics:

Any MEA member, client or third party (called the complainant) can bring to the attention of MEA a potential breach of the Code of Ethics. The following process applies for dealing with the allegation:'

1. In the first instance, the complainant shall raise the allegation of a breach of the code of ethics in writing to the MEA Chief Executive Officer. The complainant needs to:
   i. Outline the circumstances of the breach(s), providing as much information and evidence as possible to substantiate the complaint.
   ii. State whether they wish their identity to remain confidential. In opting for confidentiality, it should be understood by the complainant that in some circumstances, such confidentiality might form a barrier to proper investigation.

2. The MEA CEO shall respond to the complainant explaining the process and seeking any further information, including whether other complainants may be involved.

3. The MEA CEO shall write in confidence to the member being the subject of the complaint, notifying them of the complaint and seeking an explanation for the alleged breach.

4. On recommendation of the CEO that the matter requires further investigation, the Board of Directors shall appoint a minimum of three and a maximum of five members of the National Council to act as the Disciplinary Tribunal to deal with any breach of ethics cases, and shall from that group appoint a Chair. The appointees to the Disciplinary Tribunal shall have no conflict of interest as a result of a business or other relationship with either the complainant or the member, nor shall they be in direct competition with either party.

5. Should the CEO recommend against further action, the complainant may write to the President to seek that the Board of Directors take the complaint further. If the Board of Directors decides to not take the complaint further, such decision is final.

6. The Disciplinary Tribunal shall deal with the issue on a confidential basis. In their investigations, if appropriate to the circumstances, they can:
   i. Seek further evidence from complainant, the member or other relevant parties.
   ii. Decide that no further action is necessary.
   iii. Call a meeting between the complainant and the member to seek to resolve the matter.
   iv. Call a formal meeting with the member where the member has the opportunity to put their case.
   v. Take advice on customary industry practice.
   vi. Make recommendations to the Board of Directors on appropriate changes to the Industry's Code of Ethics, or if certain information and education strategies to the general membership are appropriate.
   vii. Rule that there has been a breach (s) of the Code of Ethics and instigate an appropriate disciplinary response.

7. Options for the Disciplinary Tribunal if a breach is found are:
   i. That the member be notified in writing that there has been a breach, and either giving a warning that should such a breach occur again, further action would be taken and/or stipulating that the member has been formally censured.
   ii. That all MEA members be notified of the breach.
   iii. Cancellation of membership.

8. Should the member disagree with the finding of the Disciplinary Tribunal, they may appeal to the full National Council for further consideration, and in so doing, state the grounds upon which the decision of the Tribunal shall be reconsidered.

9. The National Council shall act in accordance with Clause 19 of the MEA Constitution. Any decision of the National Council shall be final.

(By-Law of MEA adopted 20/04/04 by Board of Directors.)

Figure 13.1
Meetings & Events Australia code of ethics
Source: Meetings & Events Australia (n.d.).

What stands out is that around 20 per cent more respondents in 2015 than in 2010 believed that while the meetings industry operates ethically on balance, there is room for reform. While the results would appear to demonstrate that professionals in this industry aspire to operate even more ethically, it is also clear that further ongoing dialogue between all stakeholders is needed, in order to help raise ethical standards for the industry as a whole.

In the meantime, for individual planners facing any ethical dilemma in their professional lives, it is difficult to improve on the guidelines for planners proposed at an MPI chapter conference on this topic:

When you are trying to make a difficult ethical decision, consider these factors:

- Would my boss, co-workers, and family be proud of me?
- Will someone be hurt by this?
- Do I think it's fair?
- Would I want this done to me?
- Would I want this on the front page of my local newspaper?

(Pelletier, 2007)

Chapter summary

This chapter began by highlighting the differences between personal ethics and professional ethics. Focusing on ethics in the workplace, the uses and challenges of corporate and professional codes of conduct were discussed, including the role of professional codes of conduct in indicating to the general public what standards of behaviour can be expected from members of any profession. There followed a review of the most common ethical dilemmas faced by business events professionals: fam trips, gifts, airline and hotel loyalty points, hotel commissions, theft of intellectual property through the Request for Proposal system, the use or non-use of destinations that are openly hostile to minority communities, and the poor personal conduct of participants. The chapter ended with an analysis of the ethical codes of businesses and associations active in the business events industry.

References

Avey, J. B., Wernsing, T. S. and Palanski, M. E. (2012) Exploring the process of ethical leadership: The mediating role of employee voice and psychological ownership. *Journal of Business Ethics* 107(1): 21–34.

Carter, J. (2014) Dorchester Collection meetings and events hit by boycott. *Conference & Incentive Travel*, 9 May.

Cross, B. (2017) The dark side of the events industry. Available at: https://www.eventmanagerblog.com/dark-side-of-the-events-industry.

Davis, M. R. (2014) Ethics for meeting planners. *Convene*, 1 August.

Doyle, M. (2005) Catch me if you can – screening for fam abusers. *Corporate & Incentive Travel*, January.

Flach, C. (2017) The ethics of incentive travel. *Conference & Incentive Travel*, 13 December.

Gilman, S. (2005) Ethics codes and codes of conduct as tools for promoting an ethical and professional public service: Comparative success and lessons. World Bank.

Hemingway, C. A. and Maclagan, P. W. (2004) Managers' personal values as drivers for corporate social responsibility. *Journal of Business Ethics* 50(1): 33–44.

Henderson, E. and McIlwraith, M. (2013) *Ethics and Corporate Social Responsibility in the Meetings and Events Industry*, New Jersey: John Wiley & Sons.

Herrick, T. (2013) Ethics: Freebies, perks and points, oh my! *Corporate & Incentive Travel*, 1 June.

Johnson, D. (2013) Ethics: Are you behaving yourself? *SmartMeetings*, 24 July.

Kaptein, M. (2017) *The Living Code: Embedding ethics into the corporate DNA*, Oxford: Routledge.

Meetings & Events Australia (n.d.) Code of ethics. Available at: https://secure.meetingsevents.com.au/membershipbenefits/code-of-ethics.

Pelletier, S. (2007) Got ethics? *Meetingsnet.com*, 1 April.

Russell, M. (2016) What defines 'good work' in the meetings industry? *Convene*, 31 March.

Schwartz, M. S. (2001) The nature of the relationship between corporate codes of ethics and behaviour. *Journal of Business Ethics* 32(3): 247–262.

Smart Meetings (2008) Fam-scamming. Available at: https://www.smartmeetings.com/magazine_article/fam-scamming.

Toh, R. S., Dekay, C. F. and Yates, B. (2005) Independent meeting planners: Roles, compensation, and potential conflicts. *Cornell Hotel and Restaurant Administration Quarterly* 46(4): 431–443.

Tucker, L. R., Stathakopolous, V. and Patti, C. H. (1999) A multidimensional assessment of ethical codes: The professional business association perspective. *Journal of Business Ethics* 19: 287–300.

14 Business events technology

Chapter objectives

On completion of this chapter the reader should be able to:

- Understand the use of social media and apps in business events.
- Recognise the relative strengths and weaknesses of virtual and hybrid events.
- Appreciate the potential contributions to business events of face recognition technology, artificial intelligence and gamification.
- Understand the specific technology-based tools used by the exhibitions sector.
- Appreciate the challenges involved in bandwidth provision for business events.

Technological innovation

Since even before the Industrial Revolution, technology has played a pivotal role in the business world. Nowadays, keeping pace with technological developments and innovations and putting technology successfully to use still play a decisive role for businesses of all kinds. In the 21st century, the invention, diffusion and adoption of new technologies continues to transform our world, contributing to several significant changes in society and in people's behaviour, in particular how we communicate and interact with each other, as well as in the way we seek products, services and information. Businesses are being driven in particular by the dynamic, global transformation set in motion by the adoption of the Internet on a worldwide scale and the penetration of smartphones and tablets that enable their users to stay connected to the Internet even when away from their homes or workplaces.

In demographic terms, the proliferation of digital channels, platforms and devices has been accompanied by the coming of age of a generation for whom any memories of the time before the widespread deployment of the World Wide Web are vague, early-childhood recollections. This 'Generation Y' already plays a major role in accelerating the emergence of a new digital world, and their influence in all spheres – political, cultural and business – is set to expand as they become the majority in the workplace. Generation Y's expectations are being formed by the technologies they surround themselves with. They adapt their lifestyles to each new technological invention and they expect the brands they interact with and the employers they work for to do the same (Ernst & Young, 2011). But while members of Generation Y may constitute the cohort of consumers, citizens and employees who are the most digitally, globally and constantly connected, networked, collaborative and highly social, the use of digital communication technologies in private life and in professional life now crosses practically all generations.

Technology usage by the business events industry

Innovation in technology is one of the principal external forces that have a direct impact on the business events industry. The planning, marketing and execution of such events have all been significantly transformed in particular by the advent of computer technology. Few meeting planners who first joined the business events industry in the present century will recall the days of participants registering for conferences with faxes and bank drafts, carrying around heavy binders of printed information during the event itself, and speakers using flip charts and overhead projector acetate sheets for their presentations. As remarked by Krug et al. (1994):

> with a personal computer, it is now possible for convention managers, convention bureaus and meeting planners to accomplish their job tasks in a very short time, and with less effort, quickly completing meeting-related jobs that once took hours and required much paper handling.

The expanding role of technology and the new tools it provides continue to have a profound impact on the business events industry and the role of those employed in it, most of whom are now heavily reliant on technology to perform their job functions most effectively. Planners are continuously striving to integrate the most up-to-date technological methods within their events in order to enhance them and enrich the experience for the attendees, beginning with the creation of an attractive website that provides information, generates interest and offers online registration. And on the supplier side of the industry, convention bureaus and venues, for instance, have wholeheartedly embraced the marketing tools offered by advances in technology by, for example, offering virtual site visits and 360° panoramic tours of meeting spaces on their websites.

But some of the greatest impacts of technology have been on the behaviour of the actual participants in business events, who are no longer simply the passive end-consumers of conferences, exhibitions, incentive trips, etc. They are now content creators, marketers and advertisers in their own right. Using mobile digital technologies, they blog and chat with their friends, colleagues and followers, about the events they will be attending, are attending or have attended, thereby spreading word of mouth online. Participants' power to, for example, use social media to instantly commend conference speakers/ experiences that they enjoy or denigrate others that do not live up to their expectations has fundamentally altered the relationship between those who plan business events and those who attend them.

What are the technological tools that are having the greatest impact on the roles of all business events stakeholders? Figure 14.1 shows the principal meetings technologies introduced by meetings planners between 2012 and 2017, as identified by a survey undertaken by the International Association of Conference Centres. This chapter begins with an analysis of the foremost among these more established technologies, and this is followed by a review of how emerging technologies are being applied to business events.

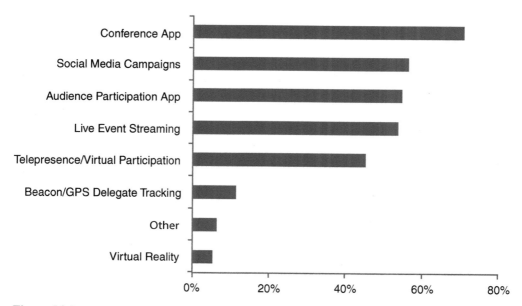

Figure 14.1
New meetings technologies introduced from 2012–2017
Source: IACC (2017).

Using the established technologies in business events

Social media

Today, most companies are pressing ahead with digital communication and marketing strategies, harnessing the power of digital channels such as social media, email and their websites to connect with their current and prospective customers. Business events professionals have therefore come to understand the value of using digital channels to engage with their key stakeholders, and their growing use of social media is one indication of that trend. Stakeholder engagement is key to effective use of social media marketing in particular, as while traditional forms of marketing (print, TV, radio) focus on broadcasting, with information flowing in just one direction, social media marketing offers the opportunity to move beyond broadcasting to engagement. When organisations can engage their audiences, they also get to leverage their audiences' networks, and consequently their marketing reach can grow exponentially.

In the business events industry, social media are not only used as marketing tools, but also as a means of enhancing the experience of those attending such events. Here, the use of social media by two stakeholders, convention bureaus and meeting planners, will be investigated.

The use of the social media by convention bureaus

Evidence suggests that convention bureaus were initially slow to adopt the opportunities offered by social media marketing. In their 2010 analysis of European national DMOs' use of social media as a marketing tool, Hamill et al. (2012) concluded that few of these were really engaged in effective social media marketing and that the majority of such organisations had yet to develop sophisticated and comprehensive social media strategies. Two years later, and focusing mainly on North American DMOs, the DMO Marketing Activity Study by Destination Marketing Association International (now Destinations International) showed that social and digital media were playing an increasingly large role in DMO marketing, noting that 'although traditional marketing (print/broadcast advertising, consumer shows/events) still commands a large share of DMO leisure marketing dollars, there is a noticeable commitment toward digital marketing' (DMAI 2012:10). The study demonstrated how DMOs were incorporating a wide variety of online activities into their overall destination marketing efforts, including social media, with almost all responding DMOs being present on Facebook, Twitter and YouTube platforms.

In their survey of European convention bureaus, Davidson and Keup (2014) found that YouTube, followed by Facebook, LinkedIn and Twitter were the applications most commonly used by convention bureaus in their digital marketing strategies, with blogs, Flickr and Slideshare also in use, but to a lesser extent. However, one issue highlighted in this survey was the fact that a significant proportion of convention bureaus were found to have no system in place for measuring the return on investment from their use of social media and other Web 2.0 applications. The most common explanation provided for this was lack of experience with such tools: convention bureaus reported using these too little or too recently to have considered measuring their performance. Respondents in the survey also emphasised the need for convention bureaus to have a strategy and resources in place for the use of these tools, as well as the need to have useful content.

This latter point serves as a reminder that digital marketing and content marketing – the process of developing and sharing relevant, valuable and engaging content with target audiences – are inextricably linked. Yet Rogers and Davidson (2016) cite an extract from the report 'The Business of Storytelling' by Marketing Challenges International (www.mcintl.com), suggesting that some convention bureaus may not be using this marketing tool effectively, as they continue to use digital only as a broadcasting and sales tool rather than as an engagement tool. The same report emphasises that all social networks revolve around content – whether in the form of pictures, videos, audio or words such as blog posts, white papers, case studies or client testimonials – and that it is the usefulness of such content that determines the success of any social media marketing programme. The extent to which convention bureaus add value through content determines the success of their digital marketing efforts.

In a related report by Marketing Challenges International (MCI, 2013), the author advises that when implementing social media marketing, convention bureaus should consider three key strategies: first, using social media as a simple and cost-effective way to promote the destination's brand; second, building professional networks of meeting planners and other decision makers by making connections on platforms such as LinkedIn, Facebook and Twitter; and lastly, using social media to provide value-added services for meeting planners to help with delegate boosting, including building special content guides or offering 'social concierge' services for meeting attendees. As an illustration of how convention bureaus can use social media as a means of providing value-added services for meeting planners and those attending their events, the author cites the example of the Phoenix and Seattle convention bureaus, both of which provide a 'social concierge' during conventions. Using a specially created hashtag for the conference, employees of these convention bureaus can tweet directly to attendees to answer questions about the destination and notify them of local events, deals, restaurants and entertainment. A different approach to providing useful social media-related services to planners is that taken by Visit Orlando. That convention bureau offers its potential clients the services of its own convention marketing executive, which works directly with planners on developing social media campaigns for their events, to assist in attendance-building. Finally, MCI (2013) demonstrates how social media marketing as part of convention services has also given some destinations an edge over others in winning events: in its bid presentation for the World Congress on Disaster and Emergency Medicine, the Toronto Convention and Visitors Association included the use of Twitter as a way of exchanging information before, during and after the meeting. Since one of the objectives of the World Association for Disaster and Emergency Medicine was to increase their student delegation, Toronto's proposed use of social media in the bid stood out, and the destination ultimately won the bid.

The use of social media by events planners

Events planners have also positively embraced social media as powerful new communication and marketing tools, and the use of social media before, during and after the event is now widespread.

Before the event

A survey of corporate event marketers undertaken by the Event Marketing Institute on behalf of the brand experience agency Freeman XP (Freeman XP/EMI, 2015) revealed that for these respondents, social media are mainly used before events to increase awareness, drive attendance, provide general information (such as schedules and news) and build engagement within their audience's community.

Planners' principal motives for using social media for these purposes were revealed in the Maritz (2012) study of meeting planners' use of social media. Respondents to that survey most frequently mentioned the affordability and the reach of social media as reasons for using them in their marketing strategies. The power of social media to generate word-of-mouth publicity was specifically highlighted by the survey respondents, with promoting by tweeting, pushing Facebook page mentions and encouraging bloggers to comment on meetings being considered as significant marketing trends. However, echoing the cautionary note struck by Marketing Challenges International above, the Maritz report emphasises the importance of meeting planners not only creating a 'buzz' through their use of social media, but also actively seeking to offer real benefits by creating remarkable content.

During the event

According to the findings of the Freeman XP/EMI (2015) survey, during events social media are mainly used to promote specific event elements or features as well as to share photos and content. This form of sharing content during the event is in itself a powerful marketing tool, as exemplified by one commentator (Zhu, 2017), who highlights the technique of livestreaming on social media of speakers' presentations as an effective means of sharing relevant content with people not present at an event, but who represent a potential audience for future editions of the conference or exhibition. In this way, she contends, the current edition of the event becomes the best advertisement for future editions.

But social media can also be used in ways that transform events by introducing more interactive elements. Lee's (2011) study showed that business events professionals perceived social media in the form of Twitter and Facebook as valuable tools that can enhance events by making them much more interactive. In the Freeman XP/EMI (2015) survey, almost a quarter of those surveyed were also using social media on a more interactive basis, directly involving participants in discussions and Q&A sessions. This form of participant engagement through the use of social media and mobile devices is increasingly being recognised as the lifeblood of most successful events. Participants come to business events to connect, converse and engage, and social media are being used to foster more engagement during events, by means of tools such as gamification, live polls and Q&As.

After the event

Post-event, according to the Freeman XP/EMI (2015) survey, almost half of event marketers use social channels to re-live or summarise highlights of the event and leverage their influencers. But almost a quarter of respondents reported using social media for polling/ surveys. In a different survey published the same year, 58 per cent of the respondents reported using social media for feedback (EMBlog, 2015), although the difference may be explained by the fact that in the case of the higher percentage, some of the feedback may have been solicited *during* the events, not necessarily afterwards. In any case, it is clear that as well as being widely used as a marketing tool for business events, social media have also revolutionised the feedback collection process of events. In addition to the formal feedback gleaned through polls, for example, more informal feedback is made available to event planners on social networks, as participants voluntarily post their opinions and impressions online. Through the use of dedicated hashtags, planners are able to tap into those conversations to understand anything that went wrong as well as what was effective in their events.

Event apps

In the pre-digital age, conference and exhibition participants had to carry around printed programmes that were sometimes as thick and as heavy as telephone books and were able to communicate with the other participants only when encountering them during breaks. The advent of mobile apps ('software applications') – computer programs designed to run on mobile devices such as smartphones or tablet computers – changed all that. The extraordinary rise in the number of apps in general and their frequency of use is attributed in part by Friedman (2014) to the continuing rapid increase in smartphone capabilities and their penetration within the global population, to the extent that the smartphone is expected to become the universal personal tool in an increasingly connected world.

Mobile apps have become a standard component of almost any large-scale business event. The most basic among them simply replace printed guides with more convenient digital versions, but the more sophisticated event apps offer a much wider range of features, including personalised session scheduling, session content and speaker information, social media, an activity feed and feedback forum, and an in-app email system allowing participants to communicate with each other. Parry (2014) believes that this is where apps can have the biggest impact, as they offer innovative ways for all parties involved to engage with each other, keeping their conversations alive well beyond the day or days of the face-to-face event. In this way, the use of apps is one example of how the physical and digital experiences at an event can complement each other to offer unique value.

Sennik (2018) suggests six reasons for creating an app for use at a business event.

Paperless, saving on costs

Event apps can be built in less time than it takes to arrange the printing of a paper programme, at less cost and wastefulness of expensive paper.

Attendee convenience and instant updates

With events, there are always last-minute changes – sessions are rescheduled, speakers switch, etc., so it is important to keep participants informed 'on the go'. Instant content updates that can be sent as push notifications to participants via the app can alert them of any changes.

Private social network and year-round engagement

By using an app, participants can network together and share their event experiences directly on the activity stream. A list of participant profiles can be included in the event app, and each profile can be saved as a vCard on the user's phone. Participants can share photos, make posts with comments and 'likes', and send private messages to each other.

Feedback, ratings and quick polls

Surveys are important for improving event experiences, and event apps allow organisers to manage survey data systematically and efficiently. After attending a session, participants can rate their impressions on the app. This information can be used to refine the conference programme and better tailor marketing campaigns on the whole.

Monetisation, promoting sponsors and exhibitors

In-app sponsor platforms allow organisers to monetise their app and drive leads for sponsors by hosting sponsor advertisements. Certain apps offer real-time analytics including a list of trending sponsors, most successful ads, and a full rundown of leads generated by each ad.

Analytics and reporting

Sophisticated event apps allow the organisers to measure, in real time, rates of app adoption, the level of engagement with social content, and other metrics, such as the number of downloads, profiles created, posts and likes, quick poll results, and session and speaker ratings. This enables them to create more impactful, engaging content and identify areas for improvement.

Kwok (2013) gives examples of additional functionalities offered by event apps, including one that suggests to participants other people they might like to contact at the event, based on bringing together attendees with similar interests; another app logs the sessions that users have chosen to attend and, based on that information, suggests other sessions that they might also like.

The polling functionality mentioned in the above list is only one of the features offered by the growing number of event apps designed to boost and improve audience participation.

Most event organisers understand that actively engaging participants in the proceedings is integral to holding their attention and increasing their satisfaction levels – if a participant has been actively involved in the proceedings, they are more likely to feel that the event was worthwhile.

In addition to live polling and surveys of participants during sessions, apps can also encourage interaction in real time during speaker presentations by enabling participants to submit questions to speakers, anonymously or not, by text, via their app. Some apps also enable participants' mobile devices to be used as microphones. These functionalities help avoid some of the obstacles generally encountered during Q&A sessions, such as the awkward pause each time an assistant takes a microphone to a participant with a question; or the fact that some members of the audience may lack the confidence to ask their questions in front of a large group of participants. Questions sent by text and displayed live on digital screens on the stage can also make it more convenient for speakers to handle and respond to live questions from participants, whether they are physically present in the audience or following the proceedings remotely.

While the advantages of event apps are numerous, in particular their power to increase participants' engagement and interaction with each other and with speakers, they are not without their challenges. The website of the London venue, 20 Bedford Way (20Bedfordway.com, n.d.) lists the following challenges:

- *Low delegate adoption:* one of the main issues with apps is the low take-up. This can happen for a number of reasons. Some delegates will not be familiar with the technology and will struggle with usability, potentially finding the app too complicated. There are also concerns around third-party messaging.
- *Security:* data security can be a major issue for delegates and is consequently one that app developers are now focusing on.
- *Development time:* some bespoke apps can take time to develop, which can be an issue for those events with a short lead-time.
- *Cost and return on investment:* some apps can be expensive, so organisers need to consider the return on investment carefully before committing.
- *Functionality:* some apps may not be able to do everything the organisers want or need them to do, or they may not be compatible with other technologies.

Kwok (2013) suggests that a further disadvantage of event apps is that users might be distracted during real-life conversations by the constant stream of tweets and notifications displayed on their mobile phone screens.

Virtual and hybrid meetings

Virtual meetings

By the beginning of the 21st century, advances in information and communications technology (ICT) had already provided organisations with an important choice regarding the formats in which they held their business events. That choice was between face-to-face (or 'co-located') events and virtual (or 'distributed') events. A virtual event may be defined as 'a synchronous communication mediated by ICT, making it possible for two or more geographically-remote people to interact' (Arnfalk, 2002). The topic of virtual trade shows is explored later in this chapter, as this section focuses specifically on virtual and hybrid meetings. Such meetings have attracted considerable interest among academic researchers, as demonstrated in the literature review of Sox et al. (2017). In this section some of the key practical considerations associated with both forms of event will be explored.

Virtual meetings do not involve a physical gathering of the participants. Rather, they denote the situation whereby meeting participants based in different locations and organisational units meet in a 'virtual' meeting place, employing audio-visual technologies, such as videoconferencing studios, and some form of computer-mediated communication such as Web conferencing. They are often considered as a subset of, and a driver for, virtual collaboration such as virtual teams, in which the team members are dispersed geographically, operating remotely from each other and from managers.

Virtual meetings are frequently promoted by arguments of cost savings, time savings and increased work efficiency, as participants lose no time in business travel and time away from their habitual place of work in order to attend such meetings. They have also been advanced as efficient solutions for dealing with urgent issues requiring discussion at very short notice, as there is no venue, transport or accommodation to be organised before the meeting can take place. The additional bonus of organisations' improved environmental performance, due to reductions in their employees' business travel, has also been proposed as an advantage of virtual meetings – although Lindeblad et al. (2016) have questioned the potential for virtual events to effectively reduce business travel. On the other hand, the challenge of keeping participants fully engaged throughout virtual meetings has been widely acknowledged, as multitasking (such as looking at emails) during computer-mediated events is widespread, particularly when no video communication is involved (Wasson, 2004; Brubaker et al., 2012). Other disadvantages of virtual meetings include the need for all participants to have the requisite equipment, and the challenge of scheduling a virtual meeting at a time convenient for all participants when dealing with a group of people across many different time zones. Moreover, virtual meetings are not considered to be an effective solution for extremely large groups.

Hybrid meetings

More recently, a type of meeting that combines face-to-face events with a virtual presence element has rapidly grown in acceptance as a means of business communication: hybrid events. A hybrid event may be defined as a seminar, conference or other meeting that simultaneously combines a 'live' in-person event at a physical location with a 'virtual' online streaming component for remote participants. In this way, they enable business event professionals to extend the reach of their live events to include those who cannot physically attend, thereby boosting the events' exposure. At hybrid events, the face-to-face networking and other benefits of an in-person event are preserved for those physically present in the venue, but they also involve people who were unable to travel to the meeting's destination or who were unwilling to do so because only part of the meeting's content is relevant to them.

A further advantage of hybrid meetings is their potential to create a legacy after the event, when organisers record the streamed content for later on-demand access. In this way, the information shared and exchanged at the face-to-face event may be accessed after the event by those who were unable to attend either physically or virtually. When a fee is charged for access to such content, it can become an additional revenue stream for the event.

In recent years, the widespread availability of high-bandwidth Internet in venues, in offices and for people 'on the go', has accelerated the adoption rates of hybrid meetings, but many organisers of such events are still in the process of learning how they can be designed in order to make them achieve their fullest potential. Many practitioners underline that careful and detailed planning is required, so that the physical and virtual components of hybrid events are fully integrated. A key challenge is that of keeping the remote participants engaged, as they are not a captive audience, and can be easily distracted. If they are not engaged in the proceedings, it is all too easy for them to opt out of the event with just a click of a mouse. As with all audiences, whether physical or remote, compelling content and delivery is vital in keeping their attention. But Carey (2015) suggests a number of additional tactics for use in stimulating the engagement of remote participants:

- Shorter sessions – changing the topic or format every 20 minutes to keep the event fresh
- Opting for a talk-show-host format rather than a typical presentation by a lone speaker, who may bore the virtual audience
- At the end of each session, when the in-person audience goes to break, asking the session's moderator to spend that time focusing exclusively on the remote audience, giving them the opportunity to ask questions and share their opinions.

Another observation by business events professionals is that speakers at hybrid events often need to be trained to make this format work well. For example, they must acknowledge remote attendees by looking at the camera. In this way, speakers can develop new skills to engage with remote audiences, to compensate for the loss of physical connection with them.

Despite the clear advantages of hybrid meetings, as indicated by Fryatt et al. (2012), many business events professionals still oppose the format, due partly to concerns over the potential cannibalisation of their face-to-face events – potential participants switching from attending physically to following the proceedings remotely. The authors cite research undertaken by Meeting Professionals International showing that anxieties surrounding the possible erosion of the numbers attending events in person are largely unsubstantiated, with data suggesting that face-to-face attendance either increases or remains the same when purely face-to-face meetings are offered in hybrid form. Indeed, Carey (2015) notes that when executed correctly, hybrid meetings can convert attendees to subsequently attend the event in person. According to the same source, some association hybrid events have converted about 40 per cent of virtual attendees into in-person attendees the following year (Carey, 2015).

Adoption rates for both virtual and hybrid meetings vary slightly across world regions, with their use being highest in the Asia-Pacific region, where according to American Express research (Amex, 2017), 35 per cent of respondents reported that over 10 per cent of their meetings in the year ahead would be held using one of those formats. In North America and in Europe, the proportions of respondents reporting that over 10 per cent of their meetings would be virtual/hybrid in 2018 were 28 per cent and 27 per cent, respectively.

While some business events professionals are predicting that in the future face-to-face events will be increasingly enhanced by virtual elements and hybrid events will become prevalent (GCB, 2013), it is equally clear that very few in-person meetings are vulnerable to being entirely replaced by virtual events.

Using the emerging technologies in business events

While the use of social media, apps and virtual/hybrid technology is already established in business events, a number of emerging technologies are at an earlier stage of being adopted by this industry. Their application to the planning, design and execution of business events nevertheless holds considerable promise as a means of making such events more efficient, effective and enjoyable. Mullen (2017) identified the following technology applications, noting that their adoption in the business events industry is moving at a rapid pace.

Face recognition

As event organisers adopt a range of automated check-in systems to speed up registration, companies are already experimenting with the potential role of face recognition technology in such systems. Mullen (2017) quotes James Morgan, founder of the Event Tech Lab, who anticipates that 'using facial recognition to speed up [registration] queue times as well as to add an extra layer to the security at events will provide both peace of mind and a better experience for attendees'.

As one of the first examples of this use of face recognition technology, Mullen describes how at the HRTechWorld conference in Amsterdam, the start-up Zenus-Biometrics experimented with a cloud-based face recognition live-streaming registration pilot. The check-in system identified attendees as they walked towards the device, calling up their information (attendees who opted into the system uploaded their photos before the event) and completing the check-in process digitally. According to the president of

Zenus-Biometrics, assuming the system specifications are met, the algorithms can sort the list of attendees and return the correct match 99 per cent of the time. He adds that the technology has potential to check in 500 people an hour, reducing registration costs to only a few cents per person. For security purposes, Zenus receives only anonymised images from the registration company, which are processed and instantly deleted.

The managing of data privacy is clearly something that is potentially of considerable concern to participants, some of whom may feel that having their facial images captured at an event, or having their movements tracked, infringes on their personal right to privacy. In fact, as with all applications of technology based on participants' data, it will be a challenge for event organisers to clearly communicate what data they are capturing, what they are going to do with it, and what will happen to the data after the event. It can be expected that if participants' data is used responsibly and that fact is communicated well to them, most will understand the advantages.

Artificial intelligence (AI)

Friedman (2016) defines artificial intelligence (AI) as a special class of software that is used to model human behaviour and human decision-making processes, so that computers and machines can reproduce those behaviours and processes. AI technology and sophistication have increased dramatically over the past few years as technology professionals have gained more experience in this field and the power of the computers being used for AI have dramatically increased in power and processing speeds.

It is widely expected that advancements in AI have the potential for creating efficiencies across all types of business events. As an example of this, Mullen (2017) reported the prediction of the Head of MICE & Groups at Expedia that instead of venues relying on static daily delegate rates, AI will be used to improve predictive pricing, resulting in better revenue management. Another illustration of the possible use of AI in a conference setting emerged from the 2018 Convening Leaders event of the Professional Convention Management Association, where AI was a featured trend, and where after collecting information on participants' interests and professional goals, a simple AI system was used to automatically 'pair up' conference attendees for networking purposes.

However, it is perhaps through the use of chatbots that AI will make its greatest initial impact upon business events. Chatbots – or simply 'bots' – consist of an automated program using AI which conducts conversations via text or by mimicking the spoken human voice. Many people are already familiar with bots from their use of Amazon Echo and Apple's Siri or from phoning the customer service numbers of banks, airlines, etc., and having a bot answer the phone and direct their calls. In the context of business events, smart bots can be used to provide instantaneous responses, through an event app, or through platforms such as Facebook Messenger, to participants' FAQs about the venue, agenda, speakers, etc. – 'What's the Wifi password'? 'Where is the exhibition stand of company X'? 'What time does the X session start'? and so on. They can also be used by planners to send out messages to event audiences in real time.

Several bots have already been created specifically for events, including Concierge EventBot by Sciensio, Eva by Event2Mobile, and ConfBot. The Concierge EventBot answers participants' questions by texts written in a conversational tone which can be personalised to individual participants. Typically, users simply text a question to get an answer, but they can also request human assistance via the bot. The founding partner of Sciensio claims that most of the bots have 93–95 per cent of such questions answered by the bot, with the remaining questions handled by humans (Mullen, 2017). The system of connecting participants with the Sciensio bot is integrated into an event's registration process, where they have the option to include their phone numbers and preferred social channels. Once participants complete their registration, they automatically receive a chat message introducing the bot, which provides a menu of options.

The future of event bots depends upon on how quickly AI evolves. Depending on user preferences, some commentators believe that eventually event organisers will move away from having dedicated event apps to delivering content through messaging platforms via event bots.

Gamification

'Gamification' as a term originated in the digital media industry. Originally coined by a British computer programmer and inventor Nick Pelling in 2002, the term only began to be widely used in 2010 and referred to the reward aspect of software games (Kamasheve et al., 2015). It has been defined as 'the application of lessons from the gaming domain to change behaviours in non-game situations' (Robson et al., 2015:412). Gamification applies the elements of games that make them engaging – such as interaction, competition and a sense of achievement – to non-game domains such as learning, and health and fitness. 'Gamified experiences' have also been introduced into work-related environments, as a means of improving business processes and outcomes, such as boosting employees' sales volumes through the use of leaderboards and trophies. The authors suggest that the recent heightened interest in gamification is the result of three developments: (1) new knowledge about how the design and management of gaming experiences makes them engaging and successful; (2) the way in which the pervasiveness of social media and mobile and Web-based technologies has changed how individuals and organisations participate in, share and co-create any type of experience; and (3) companies' heightened interest in finding new and impactful ways to better connect with, learn from and influence the behaviours of their employees and customers (ibid.: 412).

Learning contexts represent a natural application of gamification, as motivation and engagement are pivotal for positive learning outcomes. Therefore, the growing use of gamification in learning and instruction environments has brought this concept directly into the sphere of business events such as training seminars. But one of the most inventive uses of gamification in a business events context was explored by Wu (2015). In his analysis of how it could be employed to drive participants' engagement in their companies' incentive programmes and while taking part in incentive trips. For example, the implementing of gamification strategies as a means of encouraging relationship-building among incentive trip participants could take the form of awarding participants points every time they record meeting someone new or introducing a colleague to someone new; or taking part in one of the incentive trip activities with a colleague; or sharing an idea on how to achieve better results in the workplace. In order to qualify for points, participants would log their behaviour, once completed, into a tracking system that is linked to the reward scheme.

Wu emphasises the importance of creating a gamification *community*, to provide the 'players' with a meaningful setting in which to show off their achievement. This inflates the value of the status achieved (for example, 'top networker' on the incentive trip), making it a stronger motivator of behaviour. For incentive trip participants, creating a community of qualifiers several weeks before the trip could be leveraged to generate excitement for the event. Introducing gamification elements to that community (for example, awarding points for postings on Twitter, uploading images on social media, etc.) can help drive pre-participation in the event. Similarly, the same technique can be used to prolong the impact of the trip and to drive interest for future events, when there are also rewards for post-trip activities such as posting photographs of the event.

The potential for gamification to increase participant engagement and motivation makes it an attractive feature for use in all types of business events. However, when interviewed on the subject of their use of gamification in business events (PCMA, 2018), two representatives from events agencies struck a cautionary note on this topic:

> As with any engagement tool used to help deliver messages, gamification has to add value and be linked to the overall theme and messaging of the event. Gamification can work well when combined with the right content and audience. That's a fine line, however, and if the concept starts to feel like a gimmick, it can fall flat. It's important to understand the underlying goal. For example, our gamified learning programmes are designed to engage and increase learning retention. We then create fun, interactive, and immersive challenges to meet these objectives.

> When it's planned well and fits the objectives of your event, gamification can work as a very useful tech tool – it can boost engagement, drive conversation, embed key messages, and create an experience which people recall and share with others.

Technology for exhibitions

The particular characteristics of the exhibitions sector in terms of scale and formats mean that it is useful to separately highlight the impacts of technology on this form of business events. While in general most exhibitions have retained their traditional format, they have also taken advantage of the advances in technology to open additional channels for marketing and communicating with participants. As in the case of other types of events, the use of social media has grown rapidly. According to Dignam at al. (2014), there was a 90 per cent increase in the number of exhibitors using social media as a component of their trade show strategy in the two years prior to that study, citing benefits such as increased stand traffic, greater brand awareness, improved relationships with clients, additional press coverage and increased sales as a direct result of their social media campaigns.

Many other technologies, such as touchscreen displays, computer simulations and software solutions for scheduling meetings, are increasingly being used to improve the exhibition experience for participants. And to add to the convenience of online registration via exhibition websites, some events have initiated 'e-badging', enabling participants to print out their name tag on their own computers in advance of the actual event (Han and Verma, 2014).

A number of more recent uses of technology at exhibitions will now be analysed.

Virtual reality

Advances in technology do not always represent an unequivocal benefit for the business events industry, and the capacity for technology to function as a double-edged sword in this context is very well illustrated in the arrival of virtual exhibitions as a direct competitor for face-to-face events.

Removing the need for buyers to visit a physical location to interact with sellers, a virtual exhibition is an online version of an event at which goods and services for a specific industry are exhibited and demonstrated. The format can be as simple as a basic online directory or as complex as a virtual 3D world. Virtual exhibitions function in ways similar to a traditional offline exhibition, translating exhibit halls, educational seminars and networking events into a virtual environment. They allow visitors to visit stands, chat with exhibitors, attend seminars and keynote speeches, and even chat, network or talk live to other visitors. While doing so, visitors can swap electronic business cards with a keystroke and save that data instantly in their databases. The advantages of virtual exhibitions are numerous: exhibitors and visitors can save money on travel, accommodation and other costly expenses typically associated with exhibition attendance. The reduced cost of virtual exhibiting allows many more exhibitors to participate, which increases the value of the trade show on the whole. There is also increased attendance, as virtual events are easier for participants to join because there is no travel involved. They also offer exhibitors increased exposure in terms of time: whereas a physical trade show lasts for only one or two days, the duration of a virtual exhibition can be limitless, with visitors able to access stands, presentations, documents, videos, etc. at any time.

But despite these considerable advantages, it would appear that the threat of any widespread substitution of face-to-face exhibitions by virtual events of this kind has abated, at least for the time being, while at the same time the use of virtual reality (VR) within physical exhibitions is growing rapidly. As stated by Fenich (2014:214):

> The promise of virtual trade shows from their inception a few years ago has not been met … While some people fear that these virtual events will replace face-to-face ones, it is clear that for the foreseeable future, these services work best as an adjunct to actual events.

Han and Verma (2014) concur, noting the prospect that while some exhibitions may become completely virtual, others will offer a combination of physical and virtual components.

Among the first manifestations of virtual components at exhibitions are the VR headsets that deliver high-quality, 3D, highly engaging 'virtual' experiences in a digital environment via immersive images and sound, while blocking out the physical world around the user. Developed by companies including Oculus and Samsung, these headsets are a feature of the video game industry that has been a key pioneer in creating realistic user experiences. These VR technologies now have advanced in quality to the extent that they have entered the broader consumer and professional market, and VR headsets and similar devices are increasingly being used in the context of exhibitions to demonstrate products and engage visitors with experiences that are original and that evoke genuine emotions.

From the perspective of exhibitors, the use of this tool means that instead of them spending ten minutes or more trying to explain a complex product to a visitor to their stands, the product's features can be demonstrated in an immersive three- or four-minute video shown on a VR headset. This kind of technology is exceptionally useful for companies who cannot easily fit their products on to the exhibition floor, such as suppliers of theme park rides or construction companies. For manufacturers, VR headsets can be used to show not only the product itself but also the process through which it is made. For vehicle producers, they can let users experience their product in action. Or for holiday/conference destinations, the potential tourist/events planner can be transported into the city or resort for a few minutes. An early example of the use of this technology for destination marketing purposes was seen at Meeting Professionals International's World Education Congress in Atlantic City in 2016, when the Los Angeles Convention and Visitors Bureau offered event planners a VR site tour of their city.

By way of comparison with this B2B example, at the 2016 South by Southwest event, Anheuser-Busch, the brewers of Budweiser beer, used a VR experience to give visitors to their stand a deeper understanding of the product and brand. Using Oculus VR headsets, participants were given a full tour of the brewing plant, engaging all five of their senses. When entering the plant's refrigerator, cold air was blown into the room for a realistic effect. When the virtual tour took them to the hops room, Budweiser employees held a jar of hops under the participant's nose so they could experience what the room actually smells like. This entire experience was designed to help participants become more aware of the Budweiser brew process and to appreciate the product.

It is clear that the application of VR offers considerable advantages to both exhibitors and visitors, and that the potential of this tool has only begun to be realised. However, at least one commentator has expressed concerns that advances in VR technology of this kind have the potential to represent a long-term threat to the exhibitions sector. Friedman (2016) envisages a time when companies will be able to use these tools to offer their potential clients customised VR sales presentations on a 'direct-to-customer basis', in effect bypassing the need for a physical exhibition.

Augmented reality

While augmented reality (AR) and VR are often grouped into one category, their respective technologies are quite different. While VR completely transports the user into a virtual world, AR projects digital images and information on to the real, physical world, as viewed through smartphones, tablets or using QR codes or smart glasses that superimpose additional information onto the items being viewed. In the exhibitions environment, AR is being utilised by exhibitors as a tool to allow visitors to use their mobile devices to see beyond what is visible to the naked eye by adding layers of AR content to the products on display, such as technical specifications or the internal workings of machinery. An example of AR being used for this purpose was seen at the international Aircraft Interiors Expo 2018 in Hamburg, on the stand of Lufthansa Technik, one of the leading suppliers of connectivity solutions and installations for aircraft. The company created an AR application to show visitors to their stand – generally, airline representatives – the technical details of their products. Instead of transporting heavy and cost-intensive demonstration equipment to the exhibition, Lufthansa Technik used AR technology to enable customers to view, on mobile devices, a virtual 3D model of an antenna installation process. The model was split into four different layers to enable users to 'dive' deeper into the structure to see more details of the technology systems it contains.

On-site data capture

Some of the most insightful information on how technology is being employed at exhibitions can be found in the research reports commissioned by the International Association of Exhibitions and Events – Future trends: Impacting the exhibitions and events industry. A key theme of the 2014 edition of the report is on-site data capture.

The author describes how on-site data capture by exhibition organisers is becoming an important component of on-site and post-show analysis, helping them understand the on-site visiting patterns of those attending:

> The premise of on-site data capture is that the more data the show organiser has relative to attendee patterns the better the organiser is able to lay out the show floor, assess various activities on the show floor, and identify areas of the exhibition with high levels of interest for the attendee – or conversely those with low levels of attendee interest.
>
> (Friedman, 2014:4)

The technologies being used for tracking the movements of exhibition visitors include NFC (near field communications) and iBeacon (a form of low-power Bluetooth wireless communications). In addition, some exhibitions also are using RFID (radio frequency identification) technology in the form of bracelets and pendants. For example, the Reed Exhibitions public Comic-Con events use RFID bracelets to track traffic into and out of their exhibition halls. These wireless technologies work through the presence of readers or antennae placed strategically throughout the venue, and visitors' smartphones must be turned on to send and receive the NFC or RFID signals.

The same tracking technology can also be used by individual exhibitors. For example, when they place readers or antennae on their stands at different product stations, they can gauge levels of visitor interest by the length of time they spend at each station. They can also use readers as a lead-retrieval system, collecting visitors' details via the information contained in their RFID-enabled badges or bracelets, for instance.

The two-way capabilities of these systems (sending and receiving) mean that these same technologies can also be used by the exhibition organisers and exhibitors to distribute show information and exhibitor information to visitors' smartphones. But as Friedman emphasises, a key question for the exhibition industry is how to successfully implement the technology in such a way that it is acceptable to visitors to receive notifications from organisers and individual exhibitors, while also enabling the organisers to collect data that can then be analysed and turned into plans and activities to enhance the value of their exhibition or event. For example, if a trade show has 1,000 exhibitors, will each exhibitor be allowed to download a message to each visitor's smartphone – or only those who pay some form of premium for the right to do so? The effective use of technology at exhibitions depends upon all stakeholders agreeing on answers to questions such as these, and many others concerning data privacy and security (ibid.).

Venue bandwidth

It is evident from the preceding pages of this chapter that participants' mobile devices play a significant role in giving them access to the technology tools in use at business events. Moreover, participants are increasingly bringing multiple devices to events, not only to engage with the proceedings but also to stay in touch with their colleagues and clients and to be able to work while 'on the go'. They can only do so with a fast, strong and reliable Internet connection for their mobile devices, and this can create serious challenges for venues. The magnitude of increase in the use of mobile devices and apps has generated a new level of event organisers' and participants' expectations and demands with regard to Internet connectivity, defined as the capacity for data transfer on an electronic communication system. Consequently, the availability of an efficient Internet connection in the business event venue has become a vital indicator of a successful experience for participants. In an International Association of Conference Centres study of trends in venue design, the availability of high quality broadband was identified as the most important physical aspect required at a meeting venue (IACC, 2017). Similarly, the authors of the EIC/HSMAI (2013) white paper, Getting up to speed: Event bandwidth, emphasise that the correct bandwidth configuration has become just as important to achieving an event's objectives as compelling content, well-presented and appetising food and beverage, and adequate meeting space.

But the scale of the task facing venues is highlighted in Sever's report, commissioned by the Incentive Travel Foundation (ITF), where she notes that many hotel venues are struggling to meet this demand and the number of dissatisfied participants in business events has increased dramatically:

> When there is not enough bandwidth, hotel guests face the frustration of being unable to connect to check email, download presentations, stream video, etc. Often times when they are able to connect, the speed is much slower and can result in internet connections being dropped.
>
> (Sever, 2014:3)

In the same ITF survey of US convention hotels and resorts servicing business meetings and incentive travel groups, the most common challenge highlighted was that there was at certain times insufficient bandwidth, creating slow speeds, dropped Internet connections, and a lack of connectivity in meeting spaces and common areas within the hotels. One of the reasons cited for this situation was the fact that bandwidth demand can change dramatically for group meetings: 'if there are multiple groups in the property and the hotel does not know their bandwidth needs beforehand the groups may be competing for the available bandwidth (ibid.:7).

The lack of effective communication between event planners and venues appears to be a major factor. The EIC/HSMAI report suggests that part of the challenge is the lack of fluency in bandwidth terminology to match the more familiar vocabulary used to discuss, for example, room set-ups: 'Everyone understands what is meant by cabaret, theatre, and classroom style, for example. But familiarity with technology terminology is more limited.' (EIC/HSMAI, 2013:1) Sever's research revealed that none of the hotels interviewed asked group meeting planners about their bandwidth needs, and only one of them said they have seen bandwidth requirements in a Request for Proposal. Significantly, only one of the respondents actually knew the available bandwidth at their property.

It is clear that if advances in technology are to be fully harnessed to enhance efficiency and engagement at business events, there will need to be significant and ongoing investments in venues' bandwidth to keep pace with the growing demand. The uses to which bandwidth will increasingly be put are shown in Figure 14.2.

However, meaningful communication between event planners and venues is also essential. Meeting planners need to learn how to communicate their bandwidth needs to venues and venue representatives need to take steps to ask planners more searching questions about their bandwidth requirements, and also need to acquire more detailed knowledge of their venues' bandwidth capacities (EIC/HSMAI, 2013).

To coincide with the launch of the EIC/HSMAI white paper, the authors – members of the Events Industry Council's APEX Event Bandwidth Workgroup – developed a bandwidth estimator tool to assist planners in calculating how much broadband their meetings require (http://www.eventscouncil.org/APEX/bwidthestimator.aspx). The estimator requires planners to input the number of users, the type of usages (low: email and simple Web surfing; medium: Web applications and streaming video; high: instructor-led Web training, large file transfers and SD video stream), and whether there will be multiple

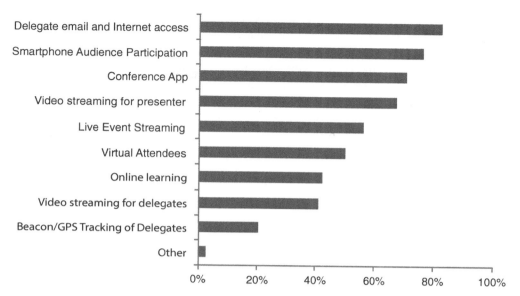

Figure 14.2
Predicted uses of bandwidth 2017–2022
Source: IACC (2017).

devices used. Once the planner inputs this information, the estimated bandwidth is calculated. Initiatives such as this, combined with the technological education and training of all stakeholders, are effective means of smoothing the paths towards ensuring that event planners and participants are able to fully enjoy the benefits of technology, including the use of the tools discussed in this chapter.

Looking ahead

It is evident that as the online and digital world continues its rapid expansion into practically every domain in our lives, the power to bring people together for the purposes of negotiating, debating, training and trading is no longer the exclusive preserve of the business events industry. Wholly virtual events such as group teleconferencing calls and virtual exhibitions are already a reality, offering particular advantages to participants that face-to-face events cannot match. Moreover, it seems more than likely that the harnessing of technology for communications of all kinds will continue to increase exponentially as future tech-savvy generations expand their presence in the worldwide workforce. The crucial question is: how will business events co-exist with the expanding digital world?

A director of the events agency Rapiergroup (Denny, 2017) has offered a number of insightful suggestions for how technology will shape business events by the middle of this century. He predicts that while at present the use of technologies such as VR, AR and AI is still at an early stage in this industry, by 2050 these will be well-established tools. For example, AI will no longer be discussed in excited tones as a novel concept, add-on feature or 'hot' topic. It will be a pervasive technology, underpinning almost every aspect of the event experience, from the logistical – ticket sales, venue and transport booking, and attendee management – to the experiential. At trade shows, intelligent facial recognition software – using deep learning algorithms – will completely transform exhibitor/visitor encounters, with exhibitors immediately knowing who a visitor to their stand is, their professional profiles and whether they are just dropping by to say hello or there for serious business. AI has the potential to make those interpersonal experiences seamless and constructive for all parties.

Regarding the emerging 'Internet of things' – smart, Internet-connected devices – Denny predicts that by 2050 almost every object encountered at an event will be intelligent, connected, and designed to anticipate and respond to participants' needs: from signposts that offer personalised directions to invisible touch points that remind participants when their next session is and how long it will take to get there. This trend will extend to smart buildings that can adapt to participants' changing needs throughout the day – such as intelligent atmosphere controls adjusted by occupancy levels and intelligent systems making minute adjustments in lighting, background music – and even scent – through connected sensors that respond to an audience's changing mood.

The power of VR to transport delegates outside the conference or exhibition venue will continue to alter the dynamics of product demonstrations at trade shows. For example, an aerospace manufacturer wishing to impress an international delegation with a tour of their latest model will no longer have to rely on 360° videos displayed on a screen. Instead, they will be able to offer visitors the opportunity to walk around the aircraft, touch its engine (because, by 2050, haptic technology will be widespread too) and take a VR test flight, all from the exhibition floor, thousands of kilometres from the factory. By the time VR users no longer need to wear headsets to access such experiences, there will be no more barriers to full immersion.

These future applications of technology to business events – and other applications as yet to be imagined – will continue to transform meetings into forms that would appear no less than miraculous to the Greek and Roman patricians who gathered together in ancient times to discuss the business of state. But one constant is unlikely to change: for as long as this industry continues to demonstrate its relevance to the various markets it serves and offers genuine value to participants in return for their investment in time and money, its future will be assured, and people will continue to seek connections with each other in real-time, face-to-face, physical spaces.

Chapter summary

This chapter examined the use of technology in the business events industry by destinations, venues, planners, and exhibitors as well as by the participants themselves. It began by reviewing the use of established technologies in the context of business events and considering their advantages and challenges: social media (with links to content marketing), event apps, and virtual and hybrid meetings. Participant engagement was highlighted as an issue. Next, the use, by business events professionals, of emerging technologies was explored: face recognition, artificial intelligence and bots, and gamification. The specific uses of technology in the context of exhibitions was analysed, with emphasis on the use of virtual reality and augmented reality by exhibitors and the harnessing of technology by exhibition organisers for the purpose of on-site data capture through the use of technology to track visitors' movements. The general issue of venue bandwidth was considered and scope for improvement in this regard was identified. Finally, predictions for how technology will continue to transform events in the near future were made.

CASE STUDY 14.1: THE ATTENDIFY MOBILE EVENT APP AT NEXTCON

NextCon

Attendify

Attendify (https://attendify.com/), formerly known as KitApps, was founded in Ukraine in March 2012, and is now based in Palo Alto, California. The company's mission statement centres around the principal aim of helping people build deeper relationships at in-person events. Paradoxically, for Attendify, that means using technology to create more face-to-face interactions, not replace them.

Attendify is a mobile event app platform that helps conference, meeting and event planners create and manage apps that boost attendee engagement, deliver more value to attendees and foster communities that last well beyond the event itself. It is the added social networking element that distinguishes Attendify's apps from traditional event apps, by providing attendees with useful features such as photo sharing, messaging, a private social timeline and tools for attendee networking, as well as a comprehensive guide to the event that they are attending.

The company's clients include Google, Bloomberg, Philips, AstraZeneca, AOL and American Express, all of whom have used Attendify's apps to provide attendees with an enhanced networking experience at their conferences, meetings and customer-facing events.

According to Attendify, for events using their products, engagement typically starts several days before the event and continues well beyond, with photos, messages and social interactions that create the context for successfully building new connections at events.

In order to manage their custom-built mobile event app, through Attendify, event planners have access to a full suite of social management tools that enable instant content updates, social moderation, live polling, push notifications and more. Traditional event guide features such as a customisable schedule, speaker profiles, sponsor lists and exhibition maps are also included and can be updated instantly through Attendify's app management tools. The full list of app features is shown in Table 14.1.

Nextiva and the NextCon event

Based in Scottsdale, Arizona, Nextiva (www.nextiva.com) launched and signed up its first customer in 2008. It is now a leading business communications company with over 750 employees, developing and selling cloud-based telephone services to more than 150,000 clients in the US.

Table 14.1 Attendify app features

Activity stream – a private social network for your event	Interactive event maps
	Favourites, creating reminders and notes
Dynamic event analytics updated and accessible in real-time	Push notifications
Gamification options	Schedules, personalised agenda
Attendee profiles (can be created by users or uploaded in advance)	Speakers
	Sponsors and exhibitors
Private messaging between attendees	Document hosting (PDF, Excel, PPT, Word)
Social ads for monetising your app	Multi-language support
Quick polls	Integrations with Eventbrite, CVENT, Salesforce and RegOnline
Ratings and reviews for speakers/sessions/presentations	Turnkey-solution websites and widgets
WebView feature to include your website/survey/social network page	Multi-user app management

Source: Riazanova (2018).

The company's inaugural NextCon conference was held in 2016 at Talking Stick Resort in Scottsdale, Arizona. Described as 'a conference for entrepreneurs, small business owners, tech professionals, and everyone in between', its objective was not only to help attendees build their businesses, but also to manage, grow and profit from them. Throughout the three-day event, there were breakout sessions, networking opportunities and an accompanying exhibition, as well as the star attraction – a line-up of keynote speakers that included Gopi Kallayil, Chief Evangelist and Brand Marketing for Google, Guy Kawasaki, former Chief Evangelist with Apple, Pat Wadors, Chief HR Officer for LinkedIn and Steve Wozniak, Co-Founder of Apple. Nextiva CEO Tomas Gorny launched his company's new operating system, NextOS, during his opening keynote speech.

With an event this complex, Nextiva, in its quest to create an unforgettable experience for attendees, quickly recognised the need for an interactive event app. Lindsay Berman, Nextiva's Creative Director, together with the Nextiva team, chose Attendify to be the official app of NextCon. Once the decision was made, they immediately started building and launched the app a few weeks before the beginning of the event. According to Lindsay Berman:

'Thanks to the user-friendly interface, it was very easy to enter content and add pages and photos. The app had everything we wanted – the interactive map, schedule, and speaker page. The activity stream was a bonus. We weren't sure if people would adopt it or not, but it was a huge success. We used push notifications a lot and they were a huge perk because we drafted them all ahead of time and scheduled them, so that we wouldn't have to worry about it during the show. Push notifications were very useful for unexpected changes or last-minute adjustments to both the venue and event schedule. During the event, I'd get on my walkie-talkie to ask our team to send out a push notification probably two or three times a day. The notifications went out instantly and since we had such a high app adoption rate, it was an effective way to communicate with attendees.'

Corporate social responsibility

Nextiva found that the Attendify app was also of significant value to its philanthropic efforts which it conducts through Nextiva Cares, a community outreach initiative in which Nextiva supports 12 Phoenix-based non-profit organisations. According to the company, NextCon was a useful opportunity to spread the word about Nextiva Cares and get not only attendees involved, but also speakers and sponsors. Nextiva turned their hashtag #NextCon16 into a campaign to benefit Nextiva Cares. Each time the #NextCon16 hashtag was used, Nextiva donated US$5 to Nextiva Cares. With Attendify's ability to cross-post social messages from the app's activity stream to various social platforms, engagement was extremely high and the hashtag was used 4,100 times, giving a total donation of $20,500.

Conclusion

According to Tony Calvis, Nextiva's Video Producer, the Attendify app directly contributed to the success of the inaugural NextCon event. Armed with valuable data gathered from the company's first use of the app, he was convinced that the following year's NextCon would be even more successful:

'The amount of data collected that could be visualised and acted upon was wonderful to have. We promoted the app as often as possible, but its adoption among attendees was truly satisfying to see and beyond what we expected. When we launched the app, we were really surprised at how much activity we were getting early on, even before the event began. It confirmed we were giving them a unique and fulfilling experience.'

CASE STUDY 14.2: FOUNDRY 45 AT HANNOVER MESSE

Foundry 45

The Atlanta-based company Foundry 45 (https://foundry45.com/) provides its clients with a range of virtual reality (VR) services for the purposes of training, recruiting, sales and marketing – including the use of VR at business events such as trade shows and conferences. In this case study, Foundry 45 describes how it helped AT&T, the world's largest telecommunications company, make a success of their exhibiting at the world's leading trade show for industrial technology.

In order to maintain their status as an industry leader, AT&T has always pursued ventures involving cutting-edge technology, and groundbreaking communication techniques. In this instance, the company's progressive mindset drew them to Foundry 45 to create an engaging virtual reality experience for their presentation at the biggest annual industrial technology trade show on the globe: Hannover Messe. Rather than having their booth operators recite a conventional pitch about AT&T's digital security capabilities, they transported their visitors to the Global Network Operations Center (GNOC) to experience first-hand what it's like to combat a Distributed Denial of Service (DDoS) attack. This VR application had a resounding impact on those who donned the headset and proved to cement AT&T's message into the heads of those who visited the booth.

Foundry 45 knew they would be among elite company at this trade show, but by sticking to the tried-and-true techniques they have established within their VR development, they ended up with an application that attracted hordes of visitors. Foundry 45 aimed to utilise the GNOC as a futuristic backdrop to narrativise how an AT&T engineer assists customers by notifying them of and eliminating a DDoS attack on their network. To allow the experience to feel more interactive, Foundry 45 included several moments which require user input by aiming the cursor and following the action to a different focal point. Inside the experience, Foundry 45 uses infographics to deliver background points; several flashy, calculating graphs; and floating, number-filled windows to establish a futuristic theme for the entire project. To accompany all the impressive visuals, Foundry 45 also features quality sound effects to complete the feeling of a digitised, high-tech atmosphere.

At the start of the experience, the user stands overlooking the GNOC's computer terminals while the narrator describes the content that will be present in the VR experience. The user then descends down to the nerve centre of operations as the narrator begins briefing him or her on the modern state of digital security and data transmission. During this section, the user absorbs information vital to AT&T's message in an interesting and engaging format. After the booth visitor understands the nature and frequency of DDoS attacks, he or she jumps into the process of detecting an attack on a customer. The viewer undergoes threat detection, customer notification and communication, as well as neutralisation of the digital threat. The need for one to glance about along with the plentiful artistic effects in the experience convinces the senses of the authenticity of the virtual space.

The presence of Foundry 45's virtual reality application at AT&T's booth made a significantly positive impact on the overall trade show experience. The appeal of new technology drew a plethora of visitors which blew AT&T's initial target number out of the water. Several testimonials assert that the efficacy of VR in terms of communication is unparalleled. While having a conversation and handing out merchandise are common trade show practices, the level of engagement permitted by VR attracts much more attention than any previously established routine. Visitors remembered AT&T's message because of this experience which occupied their senses for around two minutes!

IT'S MY JOB
PETER KOMORNIK,
CO-FOUNDER AND CEO OF SLIDO

I am the co-founder and CEO of Slido (www.sli.do/), an audience interaction platform that aims to transform the world of meetings and conferences by engaging audiences more fully in live events.

After finishing my bachelor's studies in Management at Comenius University in Bratislava, Slovakia, I decided to continue my studies abroad, as I had very much enjoyed the semester on an Erasmus programme that I spent in Norway during my undergraduate years of study. As a result, I now hold an MBA degree from a joint programme of studies at the SKK Graduate School of Business and Massachusetts Institute of Technology (MIT) during which I spent a semester studying Marketing at the Kellogg School of Management. After completing my studies, I worked for Samsung Electronics Slovakia for four years as Controlling Team Lead and then gained extensive experience at Google Slovakia as Industry Analyst.

While working for Google in 2012, I was also teaching an undergraduate course on online marketing at Comenius University. This is when the initial idea of Slido was born. My ambition was to improve classes and teaching methods by providing instant feedback to lecturers. I came up with a simple tech tool to instantly collect feedback from students via their smartphones, so that they didn't have to fill in printed surveys after each and every lecture.

With this idea, I attended a Start-up Weekend in Bratislava without any real intention of starting up a company yet. But there I met a talented developer Peter Slivka who joined forces with me to elaborate on the idea behind the Slido tool. Moving the project forward, Peter and I entered – and won – two start-up competitions in Bratislava and Vienna, which helped us to develop the initial Slido prototype. At first, the sole purpose of the product was to get instant feedback from the audience. But for our initial customers that wasn't enough. After using Slido for their conferences, our first clients suggested that we add features that would enable the participants to interact with the speakers throughout the whole conference, not only for feedback at the end of the event – because, on the practical level, the main struggle they were facing was a lack of questions during the Q&A sessions and panel discussions.

To solve this problem, the team built live questions and real-time polling into the Web app, which later became Slido's core features. This was the moment when Slido evolved into an audience interaction platform that has enabled tens of thousands of meetings planners to prompt questions from their audiences and engage their participants with live polls ever since.

But, for the company, the beginning was tough and the initial traction slow. In the first six months, only ten conferences used Slido, some more successfully than others, and as a result, the team was close to giving up. But, luckily, things changed for the better. We won our first corporate client and got the first financial injection from our angel investors. Nevertheless, with only 60 events using Slido in the following three months, slow growth was still an issue for our company. So I hired our first business developer – another Slovakian and another Peter – Peter Krajnak, who moved to the UK and set up a base in London. Our new strategy was to offer Slido for free on the foreign market to demonstrate the concept while also generating product awareness. Despite a slow start, the strategy worked, and London became Slido's main conference market and a stepping stone to the rest of the world.

Our first successes helped the team discover new possibilities of how to bring value to our customers, and this helped us to boost our own confidence in our product. As I recently said in an interview, 'You really need to believe in the value the product brings to be able to convince customers to buy it'.

My philosophy for Slido since the early days has always been that simplicity is the ultimate sophistication. As I am fond of saying, 'If we want to build a successful product, it needs to be so simple that it becomes almost invisible'. Organising a conference is a stressful activity and planners need a solution that is simple and effective. This approach worked, and Slido experienced a boom, spreading to more than 100 countries. Over 20,000 events in 2016 and 60,000 events in 2017 used Slido to create more engaging experience for their attendees.

In 2015, there was another lucky break for the company's growth. That summer, Google shut its Google moderator project and companies started looking for an alternative solution for collecting questions and ideas from their employees. This helped to open a number of doors to some of the most innovative companies and Slido entered the corporate sphere.

Since its foundation in 2012, Slido has been used at over 100,000 events, and our customers include well-known names such as SXSW, Money20/20, Web Summit, the BBC, Spotify and Adobe. We now have a team of 100 people, assisting customers all around the world. More than half of our team is working in our Customer Success service, ensuring that our clients have the best possible experience.

We keep on walking. This is a journey for us, and we are really humbled to be accompanied by some amazing companies and people on our way. We're grateful to every single one of them.

IT'S MY JOB
JOHNNY MARTINEZ, HEAD OF
MARKETING AND BUSINESS
DEVELOPMENT, SHOCKLOGIC

I was born in Venezuela and attended school in Caracas, my home city. As a teenager, I moved to the UK to join my father, who had already been living in Europe for several years. I did a foundation course at University College London (UCL) which earned me the qualifications to study at Warwick University, where I graduated in 2011 with a BA in Politics, International Studies and Business.

I have a long-standing interest in technology. My childhood friends used to nickname my father 'Inspector Gadget', because he always used to bring me the latest technological devices from Europe when he visited me in Caracas. So I was heavily exposed to technology from a very early age. For example, ever since I was very young I have always been very skilled at understanding mobile phones, their settings and how to use them to make my everyday life easier. From a young age, I used my phone calendar and reminders to keep me organised and on my toes, and my instant messaging and social media apps to keep me connected.

My other passion is for events. Throughout my school and university years, I was constantly involved in organising events. This was something that just developed naturally in me, and I was always certain that working in the events industry was going to be my future. For example, while I was at university, I was involved in planning a variety of events including the largest student-run festival in the world (One World Week) as well as various inter-university dance competitions and fashion shows. In 2010, I worked for the Global Poverty Project, delivering events and mobilising ambassadors to raise awareness about extreme global poverty.

My first experience of employment in the events sector was an internship in 2007 with Congrex, an events management company with offices all over the world. There, I learned how to process registrations and conference paper abstracts and became very acquainted with the work of the associations segment, PCOs and the MICE sector in general. After university, I secured a part-time job as a researcher at the BBC while also working as a club promoter in Soho (London). This was an interesting period of my life since I had to work throughout the afternoon and evening and then sleep during the day.

But my ambition was still very much to find work that combined events and technology, so I was delighted when, in 2011, my father offered me a job at his event technology company. Shocklogic (http://www.shocklogic.com/) was founded by my father and his business partners in 1997 as a response to the need to streamline and automate event management processes. The Shocklogic team is a mixture of meeting specialists and technical experts (or as our CEO puts it 'half meeting planners, half geeks'). This distinguishes us from the typical technology and software company and we believe that it is our unique selling point. Our products range from online registration management systems through on-site registration and barcoded badge systems to mobile event apps and trade show management software. Our diverse client base includes associations, educational organisations, PCOs, agencies, convention bureaus and corporates.

I currently manage our global sales and look after all our different marketing activities and partnerships. This means that I identify and oversee all commercial and potential client opportunities in Europe, Asia and the Americas. To do this job, I need a good understanding of the technical specifications and performance of our software and hardware. But my experience of events and of working with different projects has given me the ability to answers clients' questions from a technical point of view. For example, I can now advise organisers on the optimum Wi-Fi bandwidth or equipment they will need to create a flawless registration area at an event. I'm proficient in HTML, which allows me to edit email templates more efficiently and resolve any formatting issues from the source. I have also mastered the ability to juggle multi-communication channels between email, Skype, Trello, Zoom, Whatsapp, Twitter and others. This means that I have trained my head to quickly jump from one of these communication platforms to the other, as well as constantly switching between Spanish and English. Being fluent in both languages means that I can support our clients not only from Europe but also from the Spanish-speaking Americas.

At Shocklogic, no two days are the same. One day I can be working in the office, coordinating dozens of client projects, and another day I can be flying off somewhere to exhibit on behalf of Shocklogic at an international tradeshow such as IMEX, Confex, the Meetings Show and IBTM World. I enjoy working with associations that are making a difference such as the European Society of Organ Transplantation (ESOT) as well as supporting exciting clients such as Bloomberg, ASOS and the British Fashion Council.

I travel a lot for work-related purposes. In the past year alone, I have visited five different continents. I am also active in the life of some of the meetings industry associations. For example, I recently became an ambassador for the Professional Convention Management Association (PCMA) and I will soon be travelling to New York to attend the PCMA Education Conference.

For the future, I have identified four key career goals that I hope to achieve in the next ten years:

- I will lead a technology company like Shocklogic and inspire thousands of people in providing hardware and software solutions to meet the challenging needs of the whole event life cycle of any global meeting, convention or business event. My idea is to create an integrator company that collaborates with other technology companies to meet every event need in the industry.
- I will become a world-renowned speaker for meetings industry events organised by key international players such as IMEX, IBTM, ICCA, PCMA, MPI and IAPCO.
- I will revolutionise attendee engagement through innovative meeting design practices.
- I will become a top lobbyist and spokesperson on behalf of sustainability in the events industry. I firmly believe that in order for our industry to survive we must make sure that it reduces the negative impact that it can have on our planet. I want to have a key role in leading the industry in implementing environmentally friendly strategies for business events.

Regarding the advice that I would pass on to anyone considering a career in this industry, I always tell candidates and new recruits that if they're looking for a nine-to-five job then the meetings industry is not the right industry for them. I advise potential employees to gain as much experience of working in events as they can and to show the passion needed to work under pressure and regularly deal with last-minute changes. My CEO and father always taught me since I was a child to 'be kinder than necessary because everyone that you come across is fighting some kind of battle'. I still live by this principle.

References

20Bedfordway.com (n.d.) Event apps: The complete guide. Available at: https://20bedfordway.com/news/event-apps-guide/.

Amex (2017) 2018 global meetings and events forecast. American Express Global Business Travel.

Arnfalk, P. (2002) Virtual mobility and pollution prevention: The emerging role of ICT based communication in organisations and its impact on travel (Doctoral dissertation). International Institute for Industrial Environmental Economics (IIIEE), Lund University.

Brubaker, J. R., Venolia, G. and Tang, J. C. (2012) Focusing on shared experiences: Moving beyond the camera in video communication. Proceedings of the Designing Interactive Systems Conference, ACM, pp. 96–105.

Carey, R. (2015) Hybrid meetings: Big effort, big reward. *SmartMeetings*, 1 October.

Davidson, R. (2011) Web 2.0 as a marketing tool for conference centres. *International Journal of Event and Festival Management* 2(2): 117–138.

Davidson, R. and Keup, M. (2014) The use of Web 2.0 as a marketing tool by European convention bureaux. *Scandinavian Journal of Hospitality and Tourism* 14(3): 234–254.

Denny, P. (2017) Events 2050: The future of events and exhibitions. *Rapiergroup Insight*, 5 May. Available at: https://www.rapiergroup.com/news/events-2050-future-events-exhibitions/.

Dignam, M., Verma, R. and Han, H. (2014) Current and emerging trends of tradeshows: An assessment of stakeholders' preferences. ASAE Foundation, Washington, DC.

DMAI (2012) DMO marketing activities study. Destination Marketing Association International.

EIC/HSMAI (2013) Getting up to speed: Event bandwidth. Events Industry Council/Hospitality Sales and Marketing Association.

EMBlog (2015) Social media for events. Event Manager Blog. Available at: https://www.eventmanagerblog.com/.

Ernst & Young (2011) The Digitalisation of everything: How organisations must adapt to changing consumer behaviour. Ernst & Young.

Fenich, G. G. (2014) *Planning and Management of Meetings, Expositions, Events and Conventions*, Boston: Pearson Higher Education.

Freeman XP/EMI (2015) The viral impact of events. Extending & amplifying event reach via social media. Freeman XP/Event Marketing Institute.

Friedman, J. F. (2014) Future trends: Impacting the exhibitions and events industry. International Association of Exhibitions and Events.

Friedman, J. F. (2016) Future trends: Impacting the exhibitions and events industry. International Association of Exhibitions and Events.

Fryatt, J., Garriga Mora, R., Janssen, R., John, R. and Smith, S. (2012) Hybrid meetings and events. The Meeting Professional. Meeting Professionals International, September.

GCB (2013) Meetings and conventions 2030: A study of megatrends shaping our industry. German Convention Bureau.

Hamill, J., Attard, D. and Stevenson, A. (2012) National DMOs and Web 2.0, in Sigala, M., Christou, E. and Gretzel, U. (eds) *Social Media in Travel, Tourism and Hospitality*, Burlington, VT: Ashgate, pp. 99–120.

Han, H. and Verma, R. (2014) Why attend tradeshows? A comparison of exhibitor and attendee's preferences. *Cornell Hospitality Quarterly* 55(3): 239–251.

IACC (2017) Predicting the meeting rooms and spaces of the future and improving meeting dynamics. International Association of Conference Centres.

Kamasheve, A., Valeev, E., Yagudin, R. and Makismova, K. (2015) Usage of gamification theory to increase the motivation of employees. *Mediterranean Journal of Social Sciences* 6(1S3): 77.

Krug, S., Chatfield-Taylor, C. and Collins, M. (1994) *The Convention Industry Council Manual*, 7th edn, McLean, VA: The Convention Industry Council.

Kwok, R. (2013) Mobile apps: A conference in your pocket. *Nature* 498(7454): 395–397.

Lee, S. (2011) To tweet or not to tweet: An exploratory study of meeting professionals' attitudes toward applying social media for meeting sessions. *Journal of Convention & Event Tourism* 12(4): 271–289.

Lindeblad, P. A., Voytenko, Y., Mont, O. and Arnfalk, P. (2016) Organisational effects of virtual meetings. *Journal of Cleaner Production* 123: 113–123.

Maritz (2012) The future of social media for meetings. Research White Paper. Maritz Research.

MCI (2013) Social Media marketing for global destinations in the meetings and conventions industry. Marketing Challenges International.

Mullen, R. (2017) Five tech developments driving meetings and events forward. Available at: https://www.tnooz.com/article/five-tech-developments-driving-meetings-and-events/.

Parry, A. (2014) Event apps have the power to create year-round communities. Available at: https://www.eventindustrynews.com/event-apps-power-create-year-round-communities-says-attendify-ceo/.

PCMA (2018) Game on: How to get gamification right. Available at: https://www.pcma.org/game-on-how-to-get-gamification-right/.

Riazanova, D. (2018) What features do I get in my event app? Available at: http://help.attendify.com/getting-started-with-event-apps/what-features-do-i-get-in-my-event-app.

Robson, K., Plangger, K., Kietzmann, J. H., McCarthy, I. and Pitt, L. (2015) Is it all a game? Understanding the principles of gamification. *Business Horizons* 58(4): 411–420.

Rogers, T. and Davidson, R. (2016) Marketing Destinations and Venues for Conferences, Conventions and Business Events, Oxford: Routledge.

Sennik, A. (2018) 6 reasons to use an event app. Available at: http://help.attendify.com/getting-started/about-event-apps/6-reasons-to-use-an-event-app.

Sever, K. (2014) The use of technology in off-site business meetings and incentive travel: Challenges facing hotels from the hotels' perspective. Available at: http://theirf.org/research/the-use-of-technology-in-off-site-business-meetings-and-incentive-travel-challenges-facing-hotels-from-the-hotels-perspective/997/.

Sox, C. B., Kline, S. F., Crews, T. B., Strick, S. K. and Campbell, J. M. (2017) Virtual and hybrid meetings: A mixed research synthesis of 2002–2012 research. *Journal of Hospitality & Tourism Research* 41(8): 945–984.

Wasson, C. (2004) Multitasking during virtual meetings. *People and Strategy* 27(4): 47.

Wu, M. (2015) Gamification done right – the do's and don'ts. Available at: http://theirf. org/research/gamification-done-right—the-dos-and-donts/132/.

Zhu, J. (2017) Case study: How can planners use social media to leverage events? *Convene*, 8 August.

Index

Note: page numbers in *italic* indicate figures; those in **bold** indicate tables.